Major Problems in American Indian History

MAJOR PROBLEMS IN AMERICAN HISTORY SERIES

GENERAL EDITOR
THOMAS G. PATERSON

Major Problems in American Indian History

DOCUMENTS AND ESSAYS

EDITED BY
ALBERT L. HURTADO AND PETER IVERSON
ARIZONA STATE UNIVERSITY

D. C. HEATH AND COMPANY
Lexington, Massachusetts   Toronto

Address editorial correspondence to:

D. C. Heath and Company
125 Spring Street
Lexington, MA 02173

Acquisitions Editor: James Miller
Developmental Editor: Sylvia Mallory
Production Editor: Anne Starr
Designer: Jan Shapiro
Production Coordinator: Charles Dutton
Permissions Editor: Margaret Roll

Published simultaneously in Canada.

Printed in the United States of America.

International Standard Book Number: 0–669–27049–0

Library of Congress Catalog Number: 93–71043

10 9 8 7 6 5 4 3 2 1

For Our Teachers and Friends,
Allan G. Bogue
and
Wilbur R. Jacobs

About the Cover

The painting on the cover of this book, *Summer Rain Dance of 1960*, celebrates a traditional Pueblo Indian dance that occurs in early to mid-July to bring a bountiful summer harvest. It is the work of Phil Hughte (Zuni), a self-taught Indian artist from New Mexico. Hughte graduated with a Bachelor of Fine Arts degree from Northern Arizona University in 1977 and currently teaches art in Zuni, New Mexico.

As many of the older buildings in the pueblo of Zuni are torn down or modernized, Hughte enjoys painting scenes that he remembers from his childhood. Consulting with the elderly, he accurately reflects the strong cultural ties and beautiful surroundings of the pueblo.

Preface

Should Native American peoples be permitted to operate casinos on their reservations, even if doing so conflicts with state law? Should non-Indian merchants be allowed to sell replicas of such sacred Indian objects as Hopi kachina figures, originally fashioned exclusively for rituals, when this commercial activity sometimes leads to the theft of real sacred items?

Current controversies such as these point to both the immediacy of American Indians' problems and the complicated ways in which Native peoples' and non-Indians' legal rights intersect. Thus in many states, Native governments argue that treaties and federal Indian law give them the right to sponsor gaming, which provides jobs for their chronically unemployed people and brings in money for economic development. States respond that slot machines, roulette, and craps conflict with the public interest. And if there is a commercial demand for Indian art and artifacts, how effectively can non-Indian authorities prevent the theft of genuine sacred objects that may be hundreds of years old and have a deep spiritual meaning for Indian peoples?

These present-day issues underscore that to study American Indian history is not to immerse oneself in a dead past—rather, it is to explore a vibrant present that is the child of many pasts. North America's Indian peoples have differing ideas about the present and the future, and they have had many different histories. At the same time, they share a common resolve to exercise self-determination and to meet the future on their own terms. We hope that this book will help readers to understand the Indian past, present, and future and to see how they remain linked. We hope, too, that it will illuminate Indians' central place in the American past, present, and future.

American Indian history is one of the most interesting and exciting fields of study today. Indians have a rich and diverse heritage that has intertwined significantly with the history of the United States. But Indian history is a complicated history. The tribe—which we sometimes call a nation—is the basic political and social unit for Indian peoples, and there are hundreds of tribes. Most tribes consist of people with a common language, culture, and ancestors and with a history predating European conquest. In some cases, however, comparatively recent historical forces have created new tribes from the remnants of others. Some tribes act as a united political unit with a common leader; others are loose confederations with common cultural traditions, customs, and values but no political unity. So to many non-Indians, American Indian history is at first bewildering, whereas to

Indians, differences among tribes are no more mysterious than the differences among European nations.

Uncertainty about the Indian history before Columbus further complicates efforts to understand the Indian past. Some scholars argue that before Europeans came, there were more than 100 million American Indians, with as many as 15 million living north of the valley of Mexico. Others believe that only a fraction of those estimated numbers inhabited America before Europeans arrived. Whatever the precise number, nearly all serious students of Indian history agree that infectious diseases swept away many Indians, who lacked immunity to the new illnesses that Europeans brought with them. Whole tribes disappeared; others were severely weakened; some survivors joined tribes that had not been so badly ravaged, or they formed new groups. Profound demographic changes helped to shape American Indian history after 1492.

With all this complexity and uncertainty, how do we study American Indian history? Most contemporary scholars believe that it is necessary to combine sources and methods from anthropology and history to unravel the Indian past. We call this method ethnohistory. The basic ethnohistorical principle that applies is that only by understanding Indian culture can we appreciate Indian motivations and actions; only then can we see an Indian-centered past in which Native peoples made their own history. Many ethnohistorians have written tribal histories; others have examined prominent Indian leaders. Some scholars have explored the history of Indian economies, families, or women, or of ordinary Indian people. Others have been preoccupied with government policy, its administration, and the Indian response. The point is that while there are many ways in which to study the Indian past, most contemporary historians have abandoned the notion that Indian history is concerned merely with a series of wars. Today we understand that Indian accommodation to change is as important as Indian conflict and that Indian persistence, creativity, and adaptability in the twentieth century are as important as resistance to white expansion in the nineteenth. In short, over the past twenty years, the field has steadily evolved away from the history of Indian-white warfare and frontier violence, toward a deeper understanding of Indians as human beings caught up in dramatic historical events that continue to shape their lives in the twentieth century.

In 1492 Columbus initiated a troubling encounter between peoples of different worlds. For Europeans, the very existence of Indians raised unsettling new questions about race, religion, morality, and law. Who were the Native peoples of the Americas? What rights should they be accorded under European law and religious principles? Should they be brought into the new Euro-American societies that were emerging? Should they be segregated? Or should they be eliminated altogether? Indians asked a different set of questions. What valuable ideas and material goods did Europeans bring, and how could these be incorporated into Indian life? Should the newcomers themselves be welcomed or resisted? How could Indians adjust to their changing status as a minority group in Euro-American society? Would accommodation mean the loss of tribal identity? Could Indian*ness* somehow continue, but in an altered form? Would new identities emerge as Indians wrestled with changed circumstances, adapted new traditions, and held fast to old ones? These open questions have echoed for five hundred years. We consider them anew in this volume in the Major Problems in American History series.

Our intention is to introduce students to the multisided history of American Indians. Although we have included some older, classic essays in the field, most of the essays represent the best of the new scholarship published in the past decade. Wherever possible, we have included Indian voices in the documents and essays. We have designed this volume to give due emphasis to Indian history from 1492 to the present, with considerable attention to Indians in the twentieth century. This decision not only reflects the substantial body of new work on the recent Indian past but also underscores that Indian history is a continuing story. Far from being the "vanishing Americans" of myth, Indians are a rapidly growing population whose voices are heard throughout the land.

This book follows the same general format of other volumes in the series. Each chapter begins with a brief introduction to its topic, followed first by documentary readings and then by essays that illuminate the central theme. Headnotes that place the readings in historical and interpretive perspective introduce each chapter's primary sources and essays. A "Further Reading" section, suggesting important books and articles for those who wish to explore the subject in more depth, closes each chapter.

We have been fortunate to receive help and advice from many editors, students, and colleagues. Professor Thomas G. Paterson, general editor of the Major Problems in American History series, provided valuable insights. Sylvia Mallory and James Miller, our Heath history editors, brought the project to a successful conclusion. Production editor Anne Starr and permissions editor Margaret Roll also contributed their professional skills. Four Arizona State University graduate assistants, Richard Adkins, Myla Carpio, Paivi Hoikkala, and Karen Pierson, provided invaluable help. Many graduate students shared their ideas and challenged our notions about this book; we thank Jay Antle, Rebecca Bales, AnCita Benally, Melissa Dyea, and Kathy Evans. Professor Hurtado assigned these readings in a graduate seminar that sharpened our focus on the central questions of Indian history. Sometimes intense, but always civil, discussion with Donna Allen, Michael Anderson, Michelle Benavides, Gerald Betty, Timothy Braatz, William Carter, Gilbert Gonzales, John Daniel Honey, Michael Lawson, Charles Levine, José Maldonado, Erika Reed, and Tina Weil materially helped us to improve the book.

We also are indebted to the many scholars who generously provided comments and suggestions on the project in its various stages: James Axtell, Colin Calloway, Carter Blue Clark, R. David Edmunds, Gretchen Harvey, Laurence M. Hauptman, Frederick E. Hoxie, Karen Ordahl Kupperman, David Lewis, William McLoughlin, Valerie Sherer Mathes, James H. Merrell, Melissa L. Meyer, Clyde Milner II, Fred Nicklason, Kenneth N. Owens, Francis Paul Prucha, James Ronda, Neal Salisbury, Sherry L. Smith, William R. Swagerty, Margaret Connell Szasz, Robert A. Trennert, Richard White, and John Wunder. In addition, the following readers formally reviewed the draft tables of contents for D. C. Heath and offered us detailed, constructive criticism: Frederick E. Hoxie, Newberry Library; J. Donald Hughes, University of Denver; Karen Ordahl Kupperman, University of Connecticut; Gary Moulton, University of Nebraska, Lincoln; Neal Salisbury, Smith College; James Ronda, University of Tulsa; William R. Swagerty, University of Idaho; Michael Tate, University of Nebraska, Omaha; and Richard White, University of Washington. Finally, we dedicate this volume to our mentors, Allan G. Bogue and Wilbur R. Jacobs, master scholars and teachers who have forged a generation of historians of the frontier, the West, and American Indians.

A. L. H.
P. I.

Contents

PHOTOGRAPH ESSAY
American Indians: Encounter, Continuity, and Change
Page 273

CHAPTER 8
Indians in the Far West
Page 285

CHAPTER 9
War and Peace, 1851–1886
Page 325

CHAPTER 12
The Indian New Deal
Page 442

CHAPTER 13
Inclusion and Assimilation: World War II to Relocation
Page 483

CHAPTER 14
Indian Self-Determination and Sovereignty in Contemporary America
Page 519

Tribal Locations, c. 1492

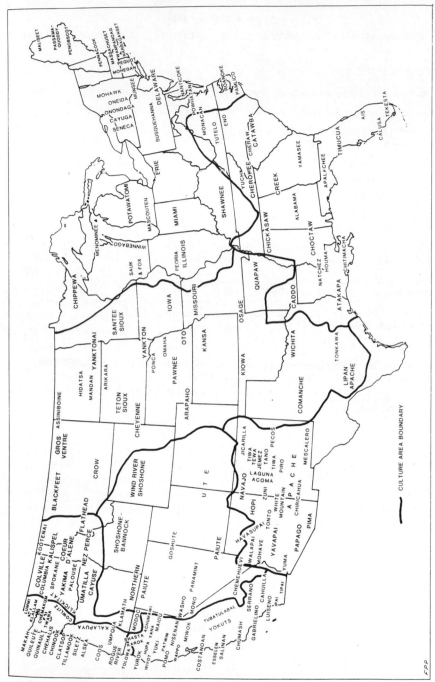

Reprinted from *Atlas of American Indian Affairs*, by Francis Paul Prucha, p. 5, by permission of the University of Nebraska Press. Copyright © 1990 by the University of Nebraska Press.

Interpreting the Indian Past

The ancestors of the American Indians had lived in the Americas for tens of thousands of years before Columbus and other Europeans arrived in the Western Hemisphere; yet only the barest outlines of their past are known, and much of it is in dispute. Although some Indian tribes recorded important events with pictures—for example, rock paintings (pictographs) and rock carvings (petroglyphs)—they did not have a written language based on an alphabet. Nevertheless, all tribespeople had an interest in their past and recounted the important events of their history in stories that were handed down from generation to generation. These oral accounts do not amount to a complete record of the pre-Columbian past, but they do convey a sense of Indian history before 1492. Indian oral history also confirms that there was not one unified Indian history but many individual tribal histories—a reflection of the Indian social, linguistic, and cultural diversity that survives to the present day.

To Indian oral accounts we may add the archaeological record. Archaeologists disagree over the date of the first human arrival in the Western Hemisphere; some argue that people may have been in North America as early as fifty thousand years ago. Most contemporary archaeologists believe that the ancestors of today's Indians came to America from Asia, by way of a land bridge that connected the continents, from fifteen thousand to thirty-five thousand years ago when glaciers locked up enough of the world's water to lower the sea level.

The first Indians hunted big game—woolly mammoths, giant bison, camels, and the like—that died out when the climate became drier and warmer about eight thousand years ago. These new conditions obliged Indians to embrace a way of life based on wild plant foods and small game. More than two thousand years ago, Indians in the Southwest—the ancestors of today's Pueblo Indians—cultivated maize, beans, and squash. These people built impressive stone and adobe towns that still exist. Likewise, Indians along the Mississippi River took up farming and built huge earthen mounds that continue to inspire wonder in the Midwest. Elsewhere many Indians came to rely on agriculture, as well as wild plants, game, and fish. Along with these adaptations to local environmental conditions grew a rich cultural diversity. Hundreds of different languages and tribes, as well as scores of cultures, covered the human landscape of North America when Columbus sailed into view.

Recent estimates of the pre-Columbian Indian population range from 7 million to 18 million people north of Mexico, though some scholars argue for much smaller *numbers. Although much is still in doubt, it is certain that millions of Indians lived in today's United States and Canada in 1492 and that they had an American history stretching back for more than ten thousand years. Truly, the American continent is the native land of the American Indians.*

◈ D O C U M E N T S

The first selection, by writer William MacLeish, is not a primary document but a fanciful flight across the continent at the time of Columbus's arrival. MacLeish briefly surveys several representative Indian tribes and captures the great cultural diversity among the native peoples of North America. In the second selection, the Pueblo Indians express their love of and attachment to the land in their beautiful "Song of the Sky Loom." The third document is a Maidu account of the creation of the world and its inhabitants. These California people believe that Earth-maker created dry land from soil that he scraped from underneath the nails of Turtle, who dived deep beneath the sea to find this vital substance. The fourth document presents the Skagit Indians' version of world creation. Here we see that the earth is a transitory place where periodic changes are to be expected. In the fifth document, animals help Mother-Corn to dig the ancestors of the Arikaras out of the ground. Accordingly, the Arikaras regard themselves as part of the earth. We see in the sixth document that the Cayugas of the great Iroquois Confederacy thought that animals helped to create the world. The Cayugas' sense of cooperation and complementarity between humans and animals is pervasive in Indian thought.

As a group, these documents provide a window through which to view the Indians' world as they conceived of it before the arrival of Europeans. Native peoples did not see with one pair of eyes or come equipped with a single set of ideas about their origins, their history, or their connection with the earth. The tribes of America comprised many nations, each with its own homeland, each with a particular world view that sometimes conflicted with those of its neighbors. How, one wonders, did diversity affect the Indians' ability to contend with European newcomers?

A Whimsical View of the Indian World in 1492, 1991

WILLIAM MACLEISH

There they go, three specks of sail far ahead of us, bearing off to the southwest. The Admiral has decided to follow flocks of migrating birds. He has heard that the Portuguese have found new lands for themselves in this manner.

We won't follow him down into the Bahamas. Our landfall lies full on the bow, the eastern edge of a country Christopher Columbus never saw.

It won't do, though, to close on this coast too quickly. We must pause in our flight of fancy to adjust our imaginations. To the west, beyond that vague line of scrub coast, lies an America separated from us by a lot more than the blue roils of the Gulf Stream. The place is five centuries removed. To close that distance, we must mentally clear away our handiwork—5,338 dams, 2.2 million miles of

"From Sea to Shining Sea: 1492," by William MacLeish, *Smithsonian,* November 1991, pp. 34–48. Reprinted by permission of the author.

paved highway, 87,377 square miles of urban development, 1.5 million square miles of farmland.

Subtracting the Loans, Clones and Drones

We must subtract some grasses and all honeybees from the landscape, along with starlings, wheat, rye, brown rats and house mice, and all domesticated animals except dogs and turkeys. (No, there are no horses; the North American native horse went extinct thousands of years ago.) There goes the eucalyptus and the apple tree, the wine grape and the chickpea. And lastly, there go our newly arrived fellow Americans, along with the 20 generations of human beings who will live on this land from this moment in 1492 until the end of the 20th century.

There are scores of places we should visit, but there is time for just five, and a brief flyover of the Great Plains. The resident cultures in all of these places share some traits, but each carries a clear identity. Three are still vibrant and populated, and of these, two, though acculturated and much diminished, will remain so in 1992. The others have peaked and dissolved over the past couple of centuries, but in 1492 we may see in their ruins signs of the sophistication that made them among the most advanced indigenous societies ever to develop in North America.

The people we are about to see in a brief wheeling over of what is now known as the United States of America claim lineages most of which stretch back 500 generations or more. Early on, they lived through and adjusted to climatic and environmental changes whose extremes were possibly far more severe than the ones global warming may produce in our own time. They are still adjusting, substituting one subsistence strategy for another, and moving on if it makes better sense to try to survive somewhere else. They and their fellow inhabitants number at most a few million in all, but their power and propensities in many instances have been sufficient to have changed the face of the land.

The habitats we'll experience aren't all that different from our own. Abundances are more noticeable, particularly among species like the bison and the wapiti [elk], and prairies, forests and wetlands are far more extensive. Oh, you'll recognize the place, all right, though you may feel a little lonely with all those landmarks gone.

Well, if everybody's ready . . .

The beach down there is where Daytona Beach, Florida, will be. Just 21 years from now, an irascible Spaniard named Juan Ponce de León will land somewhere around here, the first European to report being in this country. His expedition will eventually encounter, and be attacked by, the Calusa, the people we're heading for, also known as the "Fierce People."

Across the Wide Okeechobee

Southward, now. That great sheen ahead is Lake Okeechobee, untrammeled by modern drainage works, feeding one of the most productive environments on the continent. We swing west here to follow the Caloosahatchee River to its mouth at what is now Fort Myers, on the west coast of Florida. Have you seen prettier estuaries? Fresh water from the Caloosahatchee, and two other streams, mixes with the salt over miles of shallow flats—to the contentment of multitudes of shellfish—and brings in enough nutrients to supply carpets of sea grass. Under those shimmies on the surface are schools of pinfish, grunt and silver perch being attacked by bluefish and jack. Look, the commotion is drawing a shark. It and its kind come in from the Gulf, running the passes between the barrier islands to the west that serve, most of the time, to keep the sea in its place.

We have overflown the Calusa's front yard. Let's turn now and come back to them, low across the water. There is a canoe, a dugout, fishing close to the mangroves over by that island shaped like a comma. Many canoes, now. Another island, another village, hazed by the smoke of buttonwood and mangrove burning in hearths, and the smudge fires that keep down the mosquitoes. Black mangrove is the best kind of fuel. The more you chop it, the better it grows.

The clatter you hear comes from a dozen hammers at work. Stone is scarce here: the material of choice is shell. The dense and heavy central column of a whelk makes a fine hammer or chisel, and a big clam a serviceable anvil. The Calusa are a populous people—at least 4,000 live around these estuaries—and their fondness for shellfish as food or tool has created quite a trash problem over the centuries. Some of their dumps look to be 20 or 30 feet high, wouldn't you say? But that big mound of sand is no midden. It's probably a cemetery. Yes, that's it. See the moat around it? Everybody knows that the spirits of the dead can't cross water.

Ditching is a Calusa specialty. You may think we're coming to a creek mouth in the mangroves, but it's the beginning of a canal. Thirty feet wide, up to eight feet deep, it runs for more than seven miles to connect with a creek that flows into the Caloosahatchee. A large canoe—and some of these craft, fashioned by fire and adze out of huge pine trees, can carry 40 people or their weight in cargo—could start its run out in the flats and end up in the Okeechobee basin, out of the wind most of the way. There is supposed to be a canal bisecting the island we're heading for next, down south of the Caloosahatchee, close to the mainland. Even from this distance you can see the mounds and that imposing building on one of them. It must cover a couple of thousand square feet. I gather that the walls inside are covered with wooden masks and effigies carved with art of great power. During ceremonies held there, hundreds of men and women dance and sing.

This may be Calos, the central place of the Calusa people. If so, a regal man lives here. He has at his call a force of men known across the whole Florida peninsula, and down through its chain of keys, for their skill with the bow and the spear-thrower. He receives tributes of food and feathers and items of prestige. His influence pervades scores of communities. His [town] may not be a state, as the Aztec complex in the Valley of Mexico is a state, but it is on the verge. And, unlike the Aztec or most other prehistoric high cultures, it is building its sophistication on an economic base that does not include agriculture. Seafood, yes, and some deer and raccoons and alligators and snakes, and wild plants like seagrape and heart of palm and wild potato. But no significant reliance on crops.

Hunter-gatherers usually don't go in much for kings and nobles. For much of the first 2,000 years of their occupancy here, the Calusa didn't either. Their environment was rich enough to give them more than a satisfactory return on their investment of time and effort. By sticking to their estuaries and spending some time inland taking game and collecting plants, they provided themselves with the means for settling down.

There are few certainties to sustain us on this flight, just the inferences that skilled prehistorians can build out of bits of bone, stone, pottery and charcoal, and the strands of stories about "the time before the whites" that still remain in native memory. It's a fair surmise, though, that the Calusa eventually increased their numbers enough to cause some competition and stress. It may have become necessary to make sure that when one source of food ran thin, even for a season or two, other sources, often at increasing distances from the center, could be tapped. They may simply have found hierarchy the most efficient way of handling the problem.

Our time is short. And so, on a larger scale, is that of the Calusa. They will know about Columbus, probably soon after his arrival. Some of their canoes roam far out to sea, and they may be in intermittent touch with Cuba and the islands on the far side of the Gulf Stream. They'll know. And in another generation they'll have firsthand knowledge of the strangers. After that will come measles and smallpox and the other devastating diseases of Contact. Their culture will collapse before the economic exuberance of another. They will weaken and, eventually, fade before the raids of Europeans and of people from the north, who will come to be called Creek and, later, Seminole.

It's not the mounds that are startling. We've been seeing mounds all the way from Florida across the Southeast. It's the concentration, and the sheer size of some of them. There must be a hundred down there at the edge of this soggy floodplain on the eastern Illinois shore of the Mississippi. And that one with the terraces, by what looks like a grassed-over plaza: it must be a hundred feet high!

This is supposed to have been the largest center to develop in the country before Contact, and we don't even know its true name. It is called Cahokia, but that is a word derived from a group that will be living around here when whites start filtering in, somewhere around the middle of the 18th century. All there is below us now in 1492 is nature rejuvenant and a few hunters and farmers. Things have been that way for at least 150 years. If only we could strip away the vegetation and see the place as it was centuries before Contact, in the days of its greatness.

Move back in time those 750 years and you can see the change human occupation has already worked upon the landscape. There are small clearings all over the floodplain. People are growing wild plants they have tamed to one degree or another—goosefoot, knotweed and maygrass for their greens or starchy seeds, and sunflower and marsh elder for their oily ones. Some farmers are experimenting with a new crop, *Zea mays*. Ultimately it will become famous, grown around the world as "maize" or "corn." Its origins are in a Mexico of about seven millennia ago. It reached the Southwest centuries before the birth of Christ.

The communities that will become Cahokia are sited, deliberately, along bottoms where the Mississippi jumps its banks almost every year, laying down new sediments on the floodplains, leaving lakes and fish in the low spots. If the flooding is too severe, there are always bulges of higher and drier land on adjoining bluffs to farm. Add acorns and hickory nuts and wild berries and fruits. Add deer and waterfowl and fish, and you have something similar to what the Calusa have—a solid subsistence base that can produce storable and exchangeable surplus.

Watch the great mound now as we move forward in time. It rises in fits and starts over a period of three centuries. People wait at the borrow pits to fill their baskets with 60 pounds or so of earth, walk up this hill of their own making, dump their loads at designated spots, return. Fifteen million round trips will be required. Prodigious? Not necessarily. Assuming the project is in operation only half the time, 300 loads a day would suffice. A platoon of men—they do look well disciplined—could do the job and still take most of the afternoon off. I don't know what motivates them. We are all monument builders. Perhaps they wish to place their priests as close as they can to the sun, the great power for so much of humanity.

Getting a Fix on All-Important Maize

Other mounds are in the making, along with a circle of telephone-pole-size posts the elite use to determine equinoxes and solstices, the better to plan the cycles of religious ritual and growing. Maize is a staple now, a necessity as population and prosperity and consumer demand increase. Exchange along the trails and river systems brings chert [a type of rock] from distant quarries, some of it already [shaped] into efficient hoes; from the Great Lakes, copper for ornaments and points; from other Midwestern sites, hematite and lead for paint; whelks from the Gulf shores—perhaps even from a Calusa diver—for the pendants and other ornaments so prized by those in control. Exchange has been a part of life in this country for thousands of years, but the leaders of these people are giving it new dimensions. A man of rank dies and is laid to rest in a mound on a bed of more than 20,000 "imported" shell disks, and a dozen or two of his relatives and retainers are sacrificed to mark his passing. Coming forward through time, we have just passed A.D. 1100, the peak of Cahokian prosperity. Round about the countryside now there are smaller mound-towns, each with its elites. No one knows how far Cahokian ideas and influences extended, where they joined or clashed with other building centers in this pervasive "Mississippian" culture that now thrives in the heartland and the Southeast. For that matter, it is hard even to guess the size of the home population. The figure often used is about 10,000 souls. The place must be crowded on days of ceremony, when the leader, the embodiment of the sun, conducts his rituals on the great mound. What his purpose is remains with him. My guess is that with sacrifice and incantation he tries to attract the sun's attention, to focus its energy on him and on his people watching below.

In the next centuries before Contact, the moment of Cahokia's populous prosperity will pass away. Even now, the society itself seems in trouble. Chiefdoms often don't remain very stable over time. The competition for power can be intense. As in Renaissance Italy, no doubt alliances constantly form and fade. It may be fear of dissension from within that explains the presence of that stockade ringing the very center of Cahokia. It runs right through communities without regard to boundaries. Perhaps a job done in desperate haste.

The environment pretty clearly is becoming less bountiful, less resilient.

Climate change may have something to do with that. More rainfall, possibly. Swollen rivers, in any case, appear to be reshaping the floodplain, eating away at the best farmland. And the nearest bluffs have been worked over so heavily for limbs and logs that they're starting to gully. Nature's not to blame there. I'd say for the Cahokians, for many reasons, it is time to travel. Some may head southeast to lands in which the historic Natchez will live. Whatever their destination, they will leave behind stunning accomplishment—and a city that has no people, no name.

Early Developments in the Sunbelt

One look below at those dry washes abraded into the plateaus of northwestern New Mexico, and you know we're dealing with the dry life. That broad one ahead with the sandstone cliffs, on the northeast side, and the talus slopes on the southwest mark our destination—Chaco Canyon. These days, in 1492, it gets perhaps ten inches of precipitation in a good year. That doesn't make it in the least unusual around here. What does are the ruins. I count at least half a dozen huge edifices on the valley floor, poking through a couple of centuries' worth of wind drift and scrub, and several more up on the mesas. There must be hundreds of rooms in some of them. And on the south side of the wash, I can see the remains of dozens of small buildings. But no people.

What's that, you say? You can't run a community of this size on ten inches a year? That's right. You can't—and they didn't, and so they're gone.

But follow me along the cliff base, please. Those designs pecked into the rock above us—mountain goats, spirals, dancers, a woman with triplets—are petroglyphs done by the people who built these astounding condos. Across the way, on a rock overhang, are pictographs of a spectacular comet or exploding supernova, a moon, a hand. The Navajo, whose ancestors came down from Canada only centuries ago, call the artists Anasazi, meaning "alien ancient ones." We will never know their word for themselves. I'll bet it was something like "People Who Lead Water." Let's head out to the flats here. We seem to be walking on the bank of a large ditch, don't we? Good. Now let's imagine ourselves back in time again. To early August, four centuries before Spain's Admiral of the Ocean Sea landed on an island off the other side of the continent.

We're about to get drenched. Look out for the hail. This is really a ringtailed roarer of a storm! Look at the water sheeting off the cliff top. Those side canyons will be flumes in a minute. And here they come—around 50 men, wouldn't you say? They're well drilled, each running for his assigned spot in the system. And now the side canyon nearest us is dumping water into our ditch, which is diverting it up the valley a ways to slow it down and then delivering it to distribution boxes—big cisternlike pits lined with stone slabs. The men are working frantically now, keeping passages clear, lifting gates that divert the water and its rich muds from the boxes into small ditches leading to grids of small garden plots farther out on the flats.

In half an hour, the storm will be muttering off toward the Rio Grande valley a hundred miles to the east. The people in Chaco had enough water from snowmelt this past spring to get good germination for their maize and other crops.

Now, with this intricate catch-as-catchment-can irrigation system, they stand a good chance of getting enough late-summer storm runoff to their fields to insure good tasseling and full ears.

These people delight in stonework. They build these large houses with care and forethought, laying out most of them in D-shaped floor plans, but they are not above scrapping a whole wing and starting again with another design. They go to the trouble of facing the houses with exquisite stone veneers and then hide this beautiful work behind mud plaster.

A Nation of Ingenious Architects

Everywhere, they make architectural statements. They build walls across windy mesas; roads—more than 400 miles of them—laid out on the land as if with a ruler; huge round rooms in the earth for storage, social doings. They build shrines and leave offerings of bowls filled with turquoise. They build or influence others in the building of outlying settlements, scores of them, over at least 57,000 square miles of desert. Seeps and shallow wells, small reservoirs carved in cliff rocks, even the semi-saline Chaco River, give them water for cooking and for their own daily needs, four liters apiece on average, or to mix the mud for construction. Nature and the engineers do the rest.

Over time, these Chaco "great houses" have offered safety and storage, shelter and social congress, efficiencies of scale in maintaining systems of exchange reaching as far as the California coast. They have kept out the unknown, the enemy, and—in high-country winters, when the temperature sinks far below zero—some of the cold.

We can see the costs. Quite a few of the children playing in that large central plaza have the swollen bellies that indicate parasites, unbalanced diets, perhaps gastroenteritis—a disease that, along with tuberculosis, does well in crowds. Some of the adults look anemic. Archaeological analysis will indicate that many suffer from dental cavities caused by the sugars in the maize they eat and by the shortage of rougher food. Others are bent with arthritis aggravated by heavy labor. Those young men coming along the road from the south are carrying logs that will be used as beams for the new great house just down the way. That's Ponderosa pine, cut on mountain slopes more than 50 miles away. Each matched stick weighs more than 600 pounds.

Moving back up through time toward the moment of Contact, we're getting on well past A.D. 1100, the pinnacle for the Chaco stoneworkers. They have been at work for more than two centuries now, and there are visible signs of exhaustion in the landscape. Piñon and juniper are far less plentiful than before. And as we climb the thermals over Chaco, see if you can spot a single antelope near the canyon.

People are leaving the canyon now, calmly, purposefully. Abandonment, it appears, is ordinary and ongoing. It may be one of the costs of living in much of the pre-Columbian world, especially where resources are so chancy. Societies build communities to a certain density, leave them when they no longer function properly, live more simply for a time, start over. Some will migrate to the Rio Grande valley, where there is more water, and it takes less ingenuity to get it. Big pueblos will go up there shortly, and shortly fade. But the people will abide. The blood of those who live in native communities around Santa Fe in our time will be mixed with some that is "ancient and alien."

I count six canoes down there, seagoing craft with sleeker bows than the Calusa dugouts. Each is around 40 feet long and carries eight men. They're beautifully built, with high stems and sterns and plenty of freeboard to handle the big Pacific swells. Do you hear the crews chanting, keeping the beat for the stroke? Now they are still. They have been racing one another, but now one craft takes the lead and the others swing in behind. Not a sound. They keep their paddles in the water. Even when one lifts out, the dagger point of the blade keeps the drip small and silent.

See what the Makah are after? There's the spout. A gray whale, just under the surface. A big one, maybe 50 feet long, lazing along on its way to the Arctic. The lead canoe lunges foward, six paddlers digging water. The steersman aft guides them in and almost over the black shadow. The hunter in the bow stands, balances 18 foot of heavy harpoon and drives it down with a deep thrust of arms and shoulders. The head and its barbs are well in the animal. The hunter retrieves his shaft. Others make sure the line is paying out well, that the big floats of sealskin are ready to go overboard, that the boat is veering off properly. The whale is deep enough so its tail can't reach the boats, but the creature will tear up the ocean when it surfaces.

The Gray Is No Match for the Makah

Other canoes dart in, strike, fall back. There must be a dozen floats for the whale to fight against. It's weakening fast. One of the harpoons must have struck a lung or an artery. Within minutes, it is over. Men are stabbing small harpoons into the head. Their barbs are attached by short tethers to the sealskin floats that will buoy up the catch. One paddler dives overboard and rigs a line to close the whale's mouth so it won't take on water.

The whalers have been lucky. They were 20 miles or more from home when they struck the gray. It could have taken them farther out. Still, they'll be at it for at least a day. We'd better go on ahead, eastward toward the mouth of the strait that will be named Juan de Fuca and separates the state of Washington from the province of British Columbia. A rich sea, this. A northbound branch of the Japan Current, the Gulf Stream of the Pacific, brings warm water to these coasts, gentling the extremes of climate. Winds and Earth's rotation force surface waters away from the coast, replacing them with cold water, high in nutrients, that wells up from the depths and over the lip of the continental shelf.

We're coming in about 15 miles down from the high cape at the entrance to the strait. It seems an unforgiving place, rocky and brutal in foul weather. But offshore islands provide some protection, and a headland looms before us. You can see the village now, a couple of rows of houses paralleling the shore for a half-mile or more. This is the whalers' place. It is one of five main villages settled by those calling themselves "People of the Cape," an association with place that you find in groups across the country. The word for this whaling settlement, as it sounds in the mouth, is "Ozette."

Behind the houses, the land rises steeply and then rolls away in thicket and forest. Wet air from the sea rises to clear mountains to the east, and rain falls in feet—eight a year or more. Vegetation erupts: Sitka spruce on the coast, a few of them already a millennium old and more than 250 feet high. Giant hemlock and western red cedar stand a little inland. Ferns and mosses fight for space. The ground, where you can see it, is shot with clay lenses and tends to break loose on a slope. A couple of hundred years from now, something, quite possibly a big earthquake, will send a mudslide thundering into Ozette, burying houses intact as ash buried Pompeii in A.D. 79.

The Calusa spend some time at sea, as we've seen. But theirs is essentially an estuarine life. The people of the cape—and their relatives across the strait on Vancouver Island—are truly marine. If the men mending fishing gear down there on the cobble beach could give us the dimensions of their land, three-quarters of what they were talking about would be open water: the whaling grounds; the sealing grounds; the shoals where they take the halibut in summer; the choice spots where they troll for salmon in summer and early fall, a line tied to the paddle hand so that the stroke will give appealing action to bait or lure.

These mariners are expert woodsmen. They know what each tree will do for them. A hemlock leaning against another tree in the forest will produce a kind of compressed wood that is ideal for wedges. Yew has the strength and resiliency for bows and paddles. Cherry bark is best for wrapping harpoon heads, and red cedar bark makes good woven rain gear. Cedar lends itself to the carving of masks that rival those of the Calusa. It splits beautifully and lasts long in the wet, so houses, multifamily dwellings up to 60 feet long, are built of cedar. They are designed so that planks on roofs and walls can be removed and transferred to another frame in another camp, saving time and labor as the households move through their seasonal rounds of sea and river fishing, hunting, gathering.

South of us, along parts of the California shore, where acorn and marine resources support very high population densities that are possibly higher than anywhere else in the country, the mean size of some favored shellfish has been decreasing, signaling overexploitation. No such signals are evident here. One reason why may be that, at Ozette, control of access to food resources rests with individual households. This is a ranked society—as, by chance, are all those we have visited so far, though many in the country are fairly egalitarian—and that means that the elite get to eat higher on the halibut. But the system, which includes household control of access to many resources, keeps the entire community from descending on the nearest beach and putting more pressure on the local steamer clams than they can handle.

Yew for whaling, and sealing harpoons. Red cedar, adzed and smoothed and oiled, for canoes. Hemlock for the ingeniously steamed and shaped halibut hooks. The forest gives these people the sea. It has been doing so, with only insignificant changes in technology and subsistence strategies, for 2,000 or 3,000 years, perhaps more. Even in our day, these people, who will call themselves Makah, after the name of their language, do what they can to keep the covenant. They will send their boats after salmon. But, to maintain themselves in the 20th century, they will, with great sadness, open their forests to the clear-cutters.

We move on. No forests below us here. No trees for miles except for the green lines of them marking the watercourses that head to the Missouri River. It seems that human settlements—collections of circular, low dwellings—are mostly concentrated on the terraces above the floodplains of the larger rivers. There is some farming there, some fields of maize and probably other domesticates, like sunflowers. These prairie people also do a lot of plant, seed and nut collecting, fishing and hunting—including bison. They take the big animals with the bow, by ambush or the occasional drive. But notice how that little band there is prepared to hunt. On foot, using their stalking skills and, here and there, an animal skin to aid in deception.

These are plains people, but there are no horses down there. The last horses to live in this misnamed "New World" (which is just as old as any other) died out about 10,000 years ago, probably the victims of climate change and perhaps hunting pressure (horses were prey for humans in the Old World). There was no evidence that an attempt had been made here to domesticate the animals.

These people of the plains will have to await the coming of the Spanish before they can reacquaint themselves with the animal their ancestors saw, an animal that within the next century or two will give them new life and culture as chevaliers of the Big Sky.

We've seen enough now to know that people have a penchant for living on the edge. They like estuaries and floodplains, canyon floors and marine shelf breaks. With good reason. Food and other good things often abound where one ecosystem abuts another.

That is so, as well, along this limestone escarpment that heads east-west ahead of us across central New York. To the north lie marshy plains and to the south, highlands traversed longitudinally by valleys broadened by glacial ice. The climate of the flatlands is mild, tempered by winds off the big waters we will call the Great Lakes. The hills have harsher weather. You can see the difference too in the forests, as we drift over the escarpment. Stretching to Lake Ontario 30 miles away is a confusion of oak, hickory, chestnut—even trees you'd expect to find farther south, like dogwood and sassafras. Up on the higher ground, it's mostly maple and beech and hemlock.

We're just south of where the city of Syracuse will be, over a ridge higher than the others. The people living around this part of the escarpment take their name from it. They call themselves Onondaga, "People of the Great Hill." Their fields are down in that magnificent valley a couple of ridges east of the Great Hill. Yes, the cleared land does look strange to our eyes, trees like immense jackstraws. They are lying every whichway on the ground. Stone axes have stretched them out. The larger trees have been girdled, left to die standing, with the bark sliced right around the trunk. But look at the maize planted in hills. And the beans and squashes and sunflowers. The system works.

There is little forest primeval here, except on inaccessible ground. In the year of 1492 people have been using these woods for thousands of years, for firewood, for construction. They've been clearing land ever since agriculture took strong hold five or six centuries ago. Every 15 or 20 years, when the soils get tired and the pests too plentiful and it takes too long to find firewood in decent quantities, they've been moving a few miles and starting over. The woods are full of their old fields, and marks of the fires they have set to clear the way for more brushy forage for deer—as well as to open lanes in which to shoot them—and more blueberries and blackberries for themselves. These trees now are second growth, many less than a foot through, and that is the way these people like them—eminently choppable, about the right size for posts to support their longhouses.

The term is apt. The Onondaga may hold the record for the longest longhouse—400 feet, enough to shelter at least 100 people. The lodges here are a bit longer than 200 feet. But at 20 feet in both height and width, they are imposing. They are sheathed with elm bark, tight enough to keep out the winter, tough enough to last until 10 or 20 years have passed and it's moving time again.

There appears to be enough of everything for everyone. Population densities are fairly low. Fish are here for the seasonal taking. So are game, nuts and berries and, of course, the crops.

So why is this village palisaded?

That small group of men clustered at the edge of the clearing around this Onondaga village may provide a clue. They have captives with them. The captives are destined for adoption or for torture and death. This sort of violence has been growing for decades, here and in the settlements of other Iroquois enclaves spread across New York and, in Canada, around the Great Lakes and up the St. Lawrence valley.

A Wintry Tale Takes Hold

Climatologists gather, from evidence such as pollen and seed counts and vegetation, that the Little Ice Age, the general cooling that will last into the 19th century, first made its effects felt here in the early 15th century, 80 years before Columbus' arrival. It's possible that growing seasons have shortened so that people have started to switch from one principal food resource to another. Even with plenty of open land left, such switching may be sufficient to cause friction.

Gender roles may also play a hand, if they are anything like what they'll be at Contact. When corn came in, women—always the gardeners—tended it. As a result, they are now the prime producers. Besides, villages are large enough so that the hunting, constructing and general providing that men once did as individuals are now group efforts. How do males do what males seem endlessly condemned to do—prove themselves? Possibly by hunting the most dangerous game, another male.

Whatever the reasons, blood feuds and vendettas have reached a level not often seen in a country where violence is usually intermittent. Men may be spending more time in the summers trying to manipulate other settlements for the best deals in exchange or alliance—and attacking the same settlements when that seems feasible—than they spend in the fishing camps. The stories ethnographers of our time will collect in Iroquois villages tell of times past when dragons of discord were about, when serpents lay across well-traveled trails, when fear and horror visited the settlements.

Every once in a while, when people have had enough, they reshape their own culture. That large village near the Great Hill is a testament to such a process. It is a recent amalgam of two groups of people who were willing to give up brutal competition for the sake of cooperation. Another small settlement has sprung up close by, and it, too will coalesce with the village. Later the process beginning here will take hold strongly among the Seneca to the west.

Some focal point, some leader, is usually associated with such a drastic social change. Looking back, the Iroquois of the future will talk of the Peacemaker and his lieutenant, Hiawatha; of how they convinced warring groups to come together in consensus and work out ways to obtain and maintain peace. Right around us, right now, a confederacy is in the making, one that will influence American affairs straight through the Revolution. Its symbol is the longhouse. The Mohawk will be at the eastern door, and next to them the Oneida. The Seneca will be at the western door, and next to them the Cayuga. In the center will sit the keepers of the council fires, the keepers of the wampum belts that commemorate the alliance— the Onondaga, People of the Great Hill, pioneers of the peace.

Well, that's about it. Don't forget your personal belongings. Say, sometime why don't we take another spin like this one? We could look at *our* subsistence strategies, *our* lifeways, how *we* live in our landscapes.

No?

Just an idea.

A Pueblo Song of the Sky Loom, n. d.

Oh our Mother the Earth oh our Father the Sky
Your children are we
   with tired backs we bring you the gifts you love

So weave for us a garment of brightness

May the warp be the white light of morning
May the weft be the red light of evening
May the fringes be the falling rain
May the border be the standing rainbow

Weave for us this bright garment
that we may walk where birds sing
   where grass is green

Oh our Mother the Earth oh our Father the Sky

"Song of the Sky Loom," in William Brandon, *The Magic World: American Indian Songs and Poems,* 1971, p. 49. Reprinted with the permission of The Ohio University Press.

Maidu Account of the Beginning of the World, n. d.

All the earth was covered with water, and everything was dark in the beginning. There was no sun, no moon, no stars. Then one day a raft appeared, floating on the water. In it was Turtle. Down from the sky a rope of feathers came and dangled near the bow of the raft, and then a being, who shone like the sun, descended. He was Earth Initiate. When he reached the end of the rope he tied it to the bow of the raft, and stepped in. His face was covered, so that Turtle was not able to see it. In fact, no one has ever seen his face uncovered. Earth Initiate sat down and for a long time said nothing.

"Where do you come from?" Turtle asked at last.

"I come from above," Earth Initiate said.

Then Turtle asked: "Brother, can you not make for me some good dry land, so that I may sometimes come up out of the water?"

Earth Initiate did not answer at once, and Turtle asked, "Are there going to be any people in the world?"

After thinking for a while, Earth Initiate said, "Yes."

"How long before you are going to make people?" Turtle asked.

"I don't know," Earth Initiate answered. "You want to have some dry land: well, how am I going to get any earth to make it of?"

"If you will tie a stone about my left arm I will dive for some," Turtle answered.

So Earth Initiate did as Turtle asked. Reaching around he took the end of a rope from somewhere and tied it to Turtle.

"If the rope is not long enough I will jerk it once, and then you must haul me up; if it is long enough I will give two jerks and then you must pull me quickly, as I shall have all the earth that I can carry."

Turtle was gone for six years, and when he came up he was covered with green slime, he had been down so long. He returned with only a very little earth under his nails. The rest had all washed away.

Earth Initiate scraped the earth out from under Turtle's nails, and put it in the palm of his hand and rolled it about until it was round and about the size of a small pebble. This he laid on the stern of the raft, and went away and left it. Three times he returned to look at it, and the third time found that it had grown very large. The fourth time he looked at it it was as big as the world, the raft was on ground, and all around were mountains.

When Turtle knew the raft was on ground, he said: "I cannot stay in the dark all the time. Can't you make a light so that I can see?"

"Let's get out of the raft, and then we will see what we can do," Earth Initiate replied.

As they got out Earth Initiate said: "Look that way, to the east! I am going to tell my sister to come up."

Then it began to grow light, and day began to break, and the sun came up.

"Which way is the sun going to travel?" Turtle asked.

Reprinted from *Californian Indian Nights,* compiled by Edward W. Gifford and Gwendoline Harris Block, pp. 85–88, by permission of the University of Nebraska Press. Copyright 1930 by the Arthur H. Clark Company. Renewal copyright © 1958 by the Arthur H. Clark Company.

"I will tell her to go this way, and go down there," Earth Initiate answered.
After the sun went down it grew very dark.
"I will tell my brother to come up," said Earth Initiate.
Then the moon rose.
"How do you like it?" Earth Initiate asked Turtle.
"It is very good," Turtle answered. "Is that all you are going to do for us?"
"No, I am going to do more yet."
Then he called the stars each by name and they came out.

Then he made a tree, which had twelve different kinds of acorns growing on it. . . . For two days they sat under this tree, and then both set off to see the world which Earth Initiate had made. Turtle was not able to keep up with Earth Initiate. All he could see of him was a ball of fire flashing about under the ground and the water. When they returned from going around the world Earth Initiate called the birds from the air, and made the trees, and then the animals.

Some time after this he said: "I am going to make people."

So he took dark red earth and mixed it with water, and made two figures, one a man and one a woman. He lay down and placed the man on his right side and the woman on his left. Thus he lay all afternoon and night. Early in the morning the woman began to tickle him in the side. Earth Initiate kept very, very still and did not laugh. Soon after he got up, he put a piece of wood into the ground, and fire burst out.

The two people Earth Initiate made were very white. Their eyes were pink, their hair was black, their teeth shone brightly, and they were very handsome. He named the man Kuksu, and the woman Morning Star Woman. . . .

A Skagit Belief About the Origins of the World, n. d.

In the beginning, Raven and Mink and Coyote helped the Creator plan the world. They were in on all the arguments. They helped the Creator decide to have all the rivers flow only one way; they first thought that the water should flow up one side of the river and down on the other. They decided that there should be bends in the rivers, so that there would be eddies where the fish could stop and rest. They decided that beasts should be placed in the forests. Human beings would have to keep out of their way.

Human beings will not live on this earth forever, agreed Raven and Mink, Coyote, and Old Creator. They will stay only for a short time. Then the body will go back to the earth and the spirit back to the spirit world. All living things, they said, will be male and female—animals and plants, fish and birds. And everything will get its food from the earth, the soil.

The Creator gave four names for the earth. He said that only a few people should know the names; those few should have special preparation for that knowledge, to receive that special spirit power. If many people should know the names, the world would change too soon and too suddenly. One of the names is for the sun, which rises in the east and brings warmth and light. Another is for the

Ella Clark, *Indian Legends of the Pacific Northwest,* excerpts from pages 138–141. Copyright © 1953 The Regents of the University of California; © renewed 1981 Ella E. Clark. Reprinted by permission.

rivers, streams, and salt water. The third is for the soil; our bodies go back to it. The fourth is for the forest; the forest is older than human beings, and is for everyone on the earth.

After the world had been created for a while, everyone learned the four names for the earth. Everyone and everything spoke the Skagit language. When the people began to talk to the trees, then the change came. The change was a flood. Water covered everything but two high mountains—Kobah and Takobah. Those two mountains—Mount Baker and Mount Rainier—did not go under.

When the people saw the flood coming, they made a great big canoe. They loaded it with two of everything living on earth, with the male and female of every animal and plant. When the flood was over, the canoe landed on the prairie in the Skagit country. Five people were in the canoe. After the flood, when the land was dry again, they made their way back here.

A child was born to the man and his wife who had been in the canoe. He became Doquebuth, the new Creator. He created after the flood, after the world changed.

When he was old enough, Doquebuth was told to go to the lake—Lake Campbell it is called now—to swim and fast and get his spirit power. But the boy played around and did not obey orders. Coyote fed him, and the boy did not try to get his spirit power. So his family deserted him. When he came home, no one was there. His family had gone and had taken everything with them except what belonged to the boy. They left his dog behind and the hides of the chipmunks and squirrels the boy had shot when hunting. His grandmother left fire for him in a clamshell. From the skins which he had dried, the boy made a blanket.

When he found that his family had deserted him, he realized that he had done wrong. So be began to swim and to fast. For many, many days he swam and fasted. No one can get spirit power unless he is clean and unless his stomach is empty.

One day the boy dreamed that Old Creator came.

"Take my blanket," said Old Creator. "It is the blanket of the whole earth. Wave it over the waters, and name the four names of the earth. Then there will be food for everyone."

That is how the boy got his spirit power from Old Creator. He waved the blanket over the water and over the forest. Then there was food for everyone. But there were no people yet. The boy swam some more and kept on fasting.

Old Creator came to him again in a dream.

"Gather together all the bones of the people who lived here before the flood. Gather the bones and pile them into a big pile. Then wave my blanket over them, and name the four names of the earth."

The young man did as he was told in his dream, and people were created from the bones. But they could not talk. They moved about but were not quite completed.

The young Creator swam some more. A third time Old Creator came to him in a dream. This time he told the young man that he should make brains for the new people. So he waved the blanket over the earth and named the four names of the earth. That is how brains were made—from the soil of the earth.

Then the people could talk. They spoke many different languages. But where they should live the young Creator did not know. So he swam some more. In his dream, Old Creator told him to step over the big island, from ocean to ocean, and blow the people back where they belonged. So Doquebuth blew the people back to the place where they had lived before the flood. Some he placed in the buffalo country, some by the salt water, some by fresh water, some in the forests. That is why the people in the different places speak different languages.

The people created after the flood prophesied that a new language would be introduced into our country. It will be the only language spoken, when the next change comes. When we can understand animals, we will know that the change is halfway. When we can talk to the forest, we will know that the change has come.

The flood was one change. Another is yet to come. The world will change again. When it will change, we do not know.

The Arikaras Describe Their Origins, n. d.

A long time ago, the Arikara lived under the ground. There were four animals who looked with pity upon the people, and these animals agreed to take the people up on top of the earth. These animals were the long-nosed Mouse, the Mole, the Badger, and the Fox. The Fox was the messenger to the people to tell them of what the animals were doing. The Mole was the first to dig. He ran back, for he was blinded by the brightness of the sun. The animals went out. The people came out of the earth, the Fox being in the lead. As the people were coming out there was an earthquake. The Arikara came out. The other people were again held fast by the earth.

These people who came out from the ground then journeyed west. They came to a place where the earth shook, so that there was a chasm or a steep bank. The people waited and cried. The Badger stepped forward and began digging, so that it made a pathway for the people. . . . After all the people had passed the first obstacles they sat down and gave thanks and made offerings to the gods.

Again they went upon their journey, and it stormed. In front of them was a river. They could not cross it, for it was very deep; but a Loon was sent by the gods. The Loon came to the people, and said: "Your mother is traveling in the heavens to help you. I was sent by the gods to open up this river, so you could cross and go on your journey." The Loon flew across the river, flew back, then dived and came out on the other side of the river. The river was opened; it banked up on each side; the people crossed over and the waters came together again. Some people were left on the other side.

Again they journeyed, and they came to a place where Mother-Corn stopped and said: "The big Black-Wind is angry, for we did not ask it to come with us, neither did we make it one of the gods to receive smoke. But," said Mother-Corn, "the Black-Meteoric-Star understands this storm; it will help us." Mother-Corn went on, and said: "Here we are. We must hurry for the big Black-Wind is coming, taking everything it meets. There is a cedar tree. Get under that cedar tree. Get under that cedar tree," said Mother-Corn. "The Black-Meteoric-Star placed it there. The Star stands solid, for its right leg is cedar; its left leg is stone. It can not be blown away. Get under its branches." So the people crawled under its branches. The Black-Wind came and took many people, notwithstanding.

The people came out, and they went on. They came to another difficulty—a steep mountain bank, and they stopped. The Bear came forth, and said, "I will go through this place first." So the Bear went to digging steps for the people. Steps were made on both sides and the people went across.

After they had been gone for some time, a Dog came up, and said: "Why did you people leave me behind? I shall be the one that you shall kill, and my meat shall be offered to the gods. I shall also fix it so that all animals shall make great medicine-men of you. My father is the Sun. He has given me all this power. I will give my power to all animals, then I will stay with the people, so they will not forget my promise to them." The people were thankful to the Dog.

The Iroquois Depict the World on the Turtle's Back, n. d.

In the beginning there was no world, no land, no creatures of the kind that are around us now, and there were no men. But there was a great ocean which occupied space as far as anyone could see. Above the ocean was a great void of air. And in the air there lived the birds of the sea; in the ocean lived the fish and the creatures of the deep. Far above this unpeopled world, there was a Sky-World. Here lived gods who were like people—like Iroquois.

In the Sky-World there was a man who had a wife, and the wife was expecting a child. The woman became hungry for all kinds of strange delicacies, as women do when they are with child. She kept her husband busy almost to distraction finding delicious things for her to eat.

In the middle of the Sky-World there grew a Great Tree which was not like any of the trees that we know. It was tremendous; it had grown there forever. It had enormous roots that spread out from the floor of the Sky-World. And on its branches there were many different kinds of leaves and different kinds of fruits and flowers. The tree was not supposed to be marked or mutilated by any of the beings who dwelt in the Sky-World. It was a sacred tree that stood at the center of the universe.

The woman decided that she wanted some bark from one of the roots of the Great Tree—perhaps as a food or as a medicine, we don't know. She told her husband this. He didn't like the idea. He knew it was wrong. But she insisted, and he gave in. So he dug a hole among the roots of this great sky tree, and he bared some of its roots. But the floor of the Sky-World wasn't very thick, and he broke a hole through it. He was terrified, for he had never expected to find empty space underneath the world.

But his wife was filled with curiosity. He wouldn't get any of the roots for her, so she set out to do it herself. She bent over and she looked down, and she saw the ocean far below. She leaned down and stuck her head through the hole and looked all around. No one knows just what happened next. Some say she slipped. Some say that her husband, fed up with all the demands she had made on him, pushed her.

So she fell through the hole. As she fell, she frantically grabbed at its edges, but her hands slipped. However, between her fingers there clung bits of things that were growing on the floor of the Sky-World and bits of the root tips of the Great Tree. And so she began to fall toward the great ocean far below.

The birds of the sea saw the woman falling, and they immediately consulted with each other as to what they could do to help her. Flying wingtip to wingtip they made a great feathery raft in the sky to support her, and thus they broke her fall. But of course it was not possible for them to carry the woman very long. Some of the other birds of the sky flew down to the surface of the ocean and called up the ocean creatures to see what they could do to help. The great sea turtle came and agreed to receive her on his back. The birds placed her gently on the shell of the turtle, and now the turtle floated about on the huge ocean with the woman safely on his back.

The beings up in the Sky-World paid no attention to this. They knew what was happening, but they chose to ignore it.

When the woman recovered from her shock and terror, she looked around her. All that she could see were the birds and the sea creatures and the sky and the ocean.

And the woman said to herself that she would die. But the creatures of the sea came to her and said that they would try to help her and asked her what they could do. She told them that if they could some soil, she could plant the roots stuck between her fingers, and from them plants would grow. The sea animals said perhaps there was dirt at the bottom of the ocean, but no one had ever been down there so they could not be sure.

If there was dirt at the bottom of the ocean, it was far, far below the surface in the cold deeps. But the animals said they would try to get some. One by one the diving birds and animals tried and failed. They went to the limits of their endurance, but they could not get to the bottom of the ocean. Finally, the muskrat said he would try. He dived and disappeared. All the creatures waited, holding their breath, but he did not return. After a long time, this little body floated up to the surface of the ocean, a tiny crumb of earth clutched in his paw. He seemed to be dead. They pulled him up on the turtle's back and they sang and prayed over him and breathed air into his mouth, and finally, he stirred. Thus it was the muskrat, the Earth-Diver, who brought from the bottom of the ocean the soil from which the earth was to grow.

The woman took the tiny clod of dirt and placed it on the middle of the great sea turtle's back. Then the woman began to walk in a circle around it, moving in the direction that the sun goes. The earth began to grow. When the earth was big enough, she planted the roots she had clutched between her fingers when she fell from the Sky-World. Thus the plants grew on the earth.

To keep the earth growing, the woman walked as the sun goes, moving in the direction that the people still move in the dance rituals. She gathered roots and plants to eat and built herself a little hut. After a while, the woman's time came, and she was delivered of a daughter. The woman and her daughter kept walking in a circle around the earth, so that the earth and plants would continue to grow. They lived on the plants and roots they gathered. The girl grew up with her mother, cut off forever from the Sky-World above, knowing only the birds and the creatures of the sea, seeing no other beings like herself.

One day, when the girl had grown to womanhood, a man appeared. No one knows for sure who this man was. He had something to do with the gods above. Perhaps he was the West Wind. As the girl looked at him, she was filled with terror, and amazement, and warmth, and she fainted dead away. As she lay on the ground, the man reached into his quiver, and he took out two arrows, one sharp and one blunt, and he laid them across the body of the girl, and quietly went away.

When the girl awoke from her faint, she and her mother continued to walk around the earth. After a while, they knew that the girl was to bear a child. They did not know it, but the girl was to bear twins.

Within the girl's body, the twins began to argue and quarrel with one another. There could be no peace between them. As the time approached for them to be born, the twins fought about their birth. The right-handed twin wanted to be born in the normal way, as all children are born. But the left-handed twin said no. He said he saw light in another direction, and said he would be born that way. The right-handed twin beseeched him not to, saying that he would kill their mother. But the left-handed twin was stubborn. He went in the direction where he saw light. But he could not be born through his mother's mouth or her nose. He was born through her left armpit, and killed her. And meanwhile, the right-handed twin was born in the normal way, as all children are born.

The twins met in the world outside, and the right-handed twin accused his brother of murdering their mother. But the grandmother told them to stop their quarreling. They buried their mother. And from her grave grew the plants which the people still use. From her head grew the corn, the beans, and the squash—"our supporters, the three sisters." And from her heart grew the sacred tobacco, which the people still use in the ceremonies and by whose upward-floating smoke they send thanks. The women call her "our mother," and they dance and sing in the rituals so that the corn, the beans, and the squash may grow to feed the people.

But the conflict of the twins did not end at the grave of their mother. And, strangely enough, the grandmother favored the left-handed twin.

The right-handed twin was angry, and he grew more angry as he thought how his brother had killed their mother. The right-handed twin was the one who did everything just as he should. He said what he meant, and he meant what he said. He always told the truth, and he always tried to accomplish what seemed to be right and reasonable. The left-handed twin never said what he meant or meant what he said. He always lied, and he always did things backward. You could never tell what he was trying to do because he always made it look as if he were doing the opposite. He was the devious one.

These two brothers, as they grew up, represented two ways of the world which are in all people. The Indians did not call these the right and the wrong. They called them the straight mind and the crooked mind, the upright man and the devious man, the right and the left.

The twins had creative powers. They took clay and modeled it into animals, and they gave these animals life. And in this they contended with one another.

The right-handed twin made the deer, and the left-handed twin made the mountain lion which kills the deer. But the right-handed twin knew there would always be more deer than mountain lions. And he made another animal. He made the ground squirrel. The left-handed twin saw that the mountain lion could not get to the ground squirrel, who digs a hole, so he made the weasel. And although the weasel can go into the ground squirrel's hole and kill him, there are lots of ground squirrels and not so many weasels. Next the right-handed twin decided he would make an animal that the weasel could not kill, so he made the porcupine. But the left-handed twin made the bear, who flips the porcupine over on his back and tears out his belly.

And the right-handed twin made berries and fruits of other kinds for his creatures to live on. The left-handed twin made briars and poison ivy, and the poisonous plants like the baneberry and the dogberry, and the suicide root with which people kill themselves when they go out of their minds. And the left-handed twin made medicines, for good and for evil, for doctoring and for witchcraft.

And finally, the right-handed twin made man. The people do not know just how much the left-handed twin had to do with making man. Man was made of clay, like pottery, and baked in the fire.

The world the twins made was a balanced and orderly world, and this was good. The plant-eating animals created by the right-handed twin would eat up all the vegetation if their number was not kept down by the meat-eating animals which the left-handed twin created. But if these carnivorous animals ate too many other animals, then they would starve, for they would run out of meat. So the right- and the left-handed twins built balance into the world.

As the twins became men full grown, they still contested with one another. No one had won, and no one had lost. And they knew that the conflict was becoming sharper and sharper and one of them would have to vanquish the other.

And so they came to the duel. They started with gambling. They took a wooden bowl, and in it they put wild plum pits. One side of the pits was burned black, and by tossing the pits in the bowl, and betting on how these would fall, they gambled against one another, as the people still do in the New Year's rites. All through the morning they gambled at this game, and all through the afternoon, and the sun went down. And when the sun went down, the game was done, and neither one had won.

So they went on to battle one another at the lacrosse game. And they contested all day, and the sun went down, and the game was done. And neither had won.

And now they battled with clubs, and they fought all day, and the sun went down, and the fight was done. But neither had won.

And they went from one duel to another to see which one would succumb. Each one knew in his deepest mind that there was something, somewhere, that would vanquish the other. But what was it? Where to find it?

Each knew somewhere in his mind what it was that was his own weak point. They talked about this as they contested in these duels, day after day, and somehow the deep mind of each entered into the other. And the deep mind of the right-handed twin lied to his brother, and the deep mind of the left-handed twin told the truth.

On the last day of the duel, as they stood, they at last knew how the right-handed twin was to kill his brother. Each selected his weapon. The left-handed twin chose a mere stick that would do him no good. But the right-handed twin picked out the deer antler, and with one touch he destroyed his brother. And the left-handed twin died, but he died and he didn't die. The right-handed twin picked up the body and cast it off the edge of the earth. And some place below the world, the left-handed twin still lives and reigns.

When the sun rises from the east and travels in a huge arc along the sky dome, which rests like a great upside-down cup on the saucer of the earth, the people are in the daylight realm of the right-handed twin. But when the sun slips down in the west at nightfall and the dome lifts to let it escape at the western rim, the people are again in the domain of the left-handed twin—the fearful realm of night.

Having killed his brother, the right-handed twin returned home to his grand-mother. And she met him in anger. She threw the food out of the cabin onto the ground, and said that he was a murderer, for he had killed his brother. He grew angry and told her she had always helped his brother, who had killed their mother. In his anger, he grabbed her by the throat and cut her head off. Her body he threw into the ocean, and her head, into the sky. There "Our Grandmother, the Moon," still keeps watch at night over the realm of her favorite grandson.

The right-handed twin has many names. One of them is Sapling. It means smooth, young, green and fresh and innocent, straightforward, straight-growing, soft and pliable, teachable and trainable. These are the old ways of describing him. But since he has gone away, he has other names. He is called "He Holds Up the Skies," "Master of Life," and "Great Creator."

The left-handed twin also has many names. One of them is Flint. He is called the devious one, the one covered with boils, Old Warty. He is stubborn. He is thought of as being dark in color.

These two beings rule the world and keep an eye on the affairs of men. The right-handed twin, the Master of Life, lives in the Sky-World. He is content with the world he helped to create and with his favorite creatures, the humans. The scent of sacred tobacco rising from the earth comes gloriously to his nostrils.

In the world below lives the left-handed twin. He knows the world of men, and he finds contentment in it. He hears the sounds of warfare and torture, and he finds them good.

In the daytime, the people have rituals which honor the right-handed twin. Through the daytime rituals they thank the Master of Life. In the nighttime, the people dance and sing for the left-handed twin.

◈ *E S S A Y S*

Most historians of the United States have ignored Indians entirely or relegated them to bit parts in the sweeping drama of the conquest of the American continent. Indians, it seems, somehow exist outside the usual conceptual frameworks that historians employ. Only recently have historians and anthropologists developed the intellectual tools and attitudes needed to explore Indian history more fully. In the two essays that follow,

Calvin Martin and Frederick Hoxie, both acclaimed historians of the American Indian, explain some of the problems that historians face when they address Indian history. Martin, a professor of history at Rutgers University, describes the basic ideas of ethno-history—the use of anthropological ideas and historical documents to investigate the Indian past. He argues that we must understand the Indians' relationship with the environment in order to comprehend their history. Martin also believes that we must develop a deeper understanding of Indian intellectual and spiritual life, or we will fail to comprehend native peoples' motivations. Hoxie, the director of the D'Arcy McNickle Center at the Newberry Library in Chicago, laments the failure of historians to integrate the Indian story into American history as more than a sideshow. He also argues for new methodological and conceptual approaches, but he distinguishes his position from Martin's more radical idea that historians must change their sense of time when studying Indians (which is argued in an article not reprinted here). Hoxie suggests that the use of census data and the methods of social history might reveal much about Indian life.

    These essays raise important questions about how one studies Indian history. Indeed, if Indian culture was so radically different from European norms, how can we use European ideas and sources to understand Indian history at all?

Ethnohistory: A Better Way to Write Indian History

CALVIN MARTIN

It is a curious circumstance that for decades ethnologists and historians wrote about the North American Indian in virtual isolation of one another. Both were writing histories of the Indian from two very different theoretical and methodological orientations, with the predictable result that the Indian emerged as two different individuals. "There are two Indians of history," recently mused an eminent anthropologist: "one is the Indian of ethnology; the other, the Indian of recent history. The first is the Indian of cultural elements: the snowshoe, puberty ceremonies, kinship organization, and the potlatch. The second is the Indian of the mines, the *encomiendas,** the missions, and the fur trade."

    For the anthropologist—the ethnologist and his intellectual kinsman, the archaeologist—American Indian history begins some forty thousand years ago when the Paleolithic ancestors of the modern Indian wandered across the Bering land bridge (Beringia) into Alaska and filtered down into the rest of the continent, Mesoamerica, and South America. In the ensuing millennia their heirs fashioned cultures and societies uniquely adapted to a range of ecological possibilities coupled with varying degrees of outside influence. It is these internal and external social-cultural arrangements and adjustments that the anthropologist makes the object of his investigation. Moreover, the anthropologist brings to the study of American Indians a staggering time depth against which the past four hundred years seems but a drop in the bucket, albeit a momentous one.

    The historian, on the other hand, began writing about the Indian with only the barest understanding of who his subject was in his own cultural and social sphere;

"Ethnohistory: A Better Way to Write Indian History, *Western Historical Quarterly* 9 (January 1978), pp. 41–56. Reprinted by permission of Western Historical Quarterly and the author.
*A Spanish colonial institution that compelled Indians to give labor and tribute to Spaniards.

for him, the Indian was an incompletely developed Western European or American, as the case may be, and on this faulty premise he built a seriously flawed literature. His ignorance of the ethnographic literature and general ethnological theory left him at the mercy of his sources, most of them European-American, to be sure, but more importantly, most of them unaware of the subtle and unique features of Indian life. So, for many years the Indian was depicted as an "obstacle" to westward expansion and a "consolidating influence" upon frontier communities. Historians, observes Jack Forbes, had created a one-sided frontier, an Anglo-American frontier that did not adequately conceptualize the Indian frontier against which it abutted. Those few brave souls who ventured across the frontier into the Indian world of guardian spirits, cross-cousin marriages, swidden [slash and burn] farming, and all the rest of that exotic list of native institutions, were seemingly in another realm and disconcertingly in another discipline—anthropology.

The specimen under the glass did not change—an important point. Only the perspective on him changed when the historian scrutinized him through another lens. Blending the vision of the ethnologist with that of the historian has produced a stereoscopic image of the Indian—a three-dimensional, or ethnohistorial, view of him that all students of Indian-white relations should employ where possible.

There is of course nothing new about this advice, nor is there anything new about ethnohistory. As long ago as 1961 Nancy Lurie was writing that "ethnohistory is an old technique," that it "has become an intensified type of endeavor rather than a newly discovered or even revived field." The intensification she referred to began roughly a decade earlier as a result of Indian Claims Commission cases, when ethnologists were grilled by attorneys on the chronological dimensions of their testimony. They quickly discovered that their ethnographic sources were deficient in a legal context such as this; prodded by unsympathetic lawyers, they were forced to appeal to historical sources to add more cogency to their testimony. The outcome was a hybrid individual who in many cases developed an abiding commitment to his new identity, that of the ethnohistorian. The label is meant to denote an approach rather than a discipline; or, in the thinking of Wilcomb Washburn, "I see it [ethnohistory] as *process* and a *method,* not as a rigid discipline with fixed borders and strict entrance requirements." Washburn finds the ethnohistorical approach most advantageous in resolving the problems and unfolding the variegated elements of culture contact situations. Here and elsewhere in ethnohistorical studies, history provides an acute sense of chronology and change, while ethnology furnishes a vital, static interpretation of the cultures involved, especially the subordinate culture, which is probably as satisfactory and inclusive a definition as any of this still somewhat inchoate field.

In the pages that follow we might consider four subareas of ethnology—political, ecological, economic, and psychological anthropology—which seem to hold great promise of productive research for the historian of Indian and white relations. Let it be clear from the outset that the purpose of this discourse is no more and no less than to stimulate discussion and ideas by surveying the kinds of things that have been done in certain cases and by suggesting very generally what might be done in others.

Ethnohistorians of Indian-white relations have probably made their most impressive contribution in the area of political anthropology, or, more precisely, in delineating the intratribal and intertribal politics and alliances of native societies. To be blunt, in the words of Richard Metcalf, . . . "the roots of many apparently white-oriented political cleavages were indigenous." Metcalf has singled out the early seventeenth-century Pequot (Uncas versus Sassacus) and the early nineteenth-century Sauk (Blackhawk versus Keokuk) and Choctaw (in the career of Pushmataha) as giving evidence of internal cleavage predicated on issues running deeper than those generated by the white presence. He contends that the internal political rivalries we may have thought of as originating with white causes were in reality adapted to a white menace or opportunity, depending on the faction in question. His point is well taken, although possibly overstated in its disavowal of white perturbations as being a major, if not the major, catalyst of contention. Nonetheless, Metcalf, along with Nancy Lurie, Gary Nash, and Robert Berkhofer, has clearly enhanced our understanding of internal and external native alliances in emphasizing that there were often other issues involved in addition to white generated ones and that indeed whites were on occasion manipulated as a convenient ally in struggles as much internal as they were external.

The Smithsonian ethnologist, John C. Ewers, has made an analogous case for the late nineteenth-century northern Plains Indians who took sides in the celebrated Plains Indian wars according to well-established patterns of hostility. The Sioux, who had bullied the surrounding tribes during the first half of the century, reaped a bitter harvest when they discovered that their traditional enemies, the Crow and Arikara, members of the old Mandan-Hidatsa alliance, were now fighting alongside the United States Army. All of which sounds very much like Alden Vaughan's assessment of the seventeenth-century Puritan-Indian wars, that "war did not pit race against race but cause against cause." That appears to have been the case in at least these two series of campaigns.

There remains a good deal more to be done in the area of political anthropology as it relates to American Indian societies, yet it is evident that ethnohistorians have made valuable and substantial contributions to the field already. They have been less successful, it would appear, in clarifying the Indian's peculiar relationship with the land, a subject perhaps best approached through the medium of ecological anthropology. Formerly known as "cultural ecology," ecological anthropology seeks to explain the dialogue between man—his culture and social relationships—and nature. This becomes an especially rewarding and productive approach when applied to preindustrial societies like those of the American Indian, where nature (i.e., climate, topography, fauna, and flora) is more of a kinsman than a bondsman in cultural development. Among hunter-gatherer peoples and horticulturalists, nature is not muted, but is rather a powerful force (often conceived of as a living, personified entity) shaping man's way of life while bearing, in turn, the stamp of his cultural activities. Living close to nature, as it were, man in this economic condition tends to become responsive to nature's subtle inflections and reacts according to his received wisdom and otherwise culturally determined explanations. The result is a man-land dialogue quite foreign and in some ways jarring to our Western sensibilities.

Subsumed within the broad field of ecological anthropology is the "ecosystem" approach, involving a discrete envelope of land, climate, man, and other plant and animal life forms (biota). In some cases it is instructive to view European contact as an intrusion within an aboriginal ecosystem—as a "trigger" factor which set off a series of disruptions in the native way of life culminating in a renovated ecosystem. We know that as European influence penetrated aboriginal ecosystems, the former man-land relationships were often drastically modified: communication with the spirit realm typically became attenuated; the means and focus of resource exploitation frequently shifted, aligning themselves with a European-induced economy; traditional settlement patterns were often disrupted. In short, the Indian changed his physical and spiritual posture relative to his ecological setting. Ecological anthropology can be put to further uses, in addition to "ecosystem" studies.

For many years the dominant opinion among American historians was that the Indian—all Indians—lived according to a Stone Age economy of hunting and gathering with some casual farming here and there; the common assumption was that Indians lived cheek-by-jowl in a hostile environment whose plant and animal resources more often than not successfully eluded man's primitive technology. In part, this conviction grew out of an infatuation with the so-called Neolithic Revolution—the domestication of plants and animals which occurred several millennia before Christ in various parts of the Old World and Mesoamerica, culminating in higher degrees of social-cultural integration. It was once commonly thought, for instance, that the "state" level of social organization was everywhere predicated on a farming economy. As a corollary to this, old-fashioned social evolutionists were fond of arguing that all human societies, if given the opportunity, would elect to domesticate plants and animals on the assumption that life, under Neolithic circumstances, is inherently more secure and more leisurely. With increased leisure time, mankind, so the logic went, was more prone to "build" culture.

Detailed studies of hunter-gatherer, pastoral, and farming societies have confirmed in recent years the fallacy of this way of thinking. It is worth reminding ourselves that for most of his fifty-thousand-year existence modern man has managed quite well with hunting, gathering, and fishing. True, population densities in these nonagricultural societies were undoubtedly lower in many cases than they would have been under an agricultural regime, an academic point of concern to modern demographers but hardly of interest to functioning hunter-gatherers obliged to live within their means and think of their way as the best life. When plant and animal domestication did occur, evidently in the arid interiors of continents when local food sources may have been strained beyond the limit by a population bloated with recently arrived immigrants, it was probably not hailed as the panacea we have made it out to be. The reasons are several: "First in importance is the fact that, far from being pressed to the wall by want and unavailing exertion, hunter-gatherers (1) have a food base that is with minor exceptions adequate and reliable, (2) expend minimal labor to provide for their physical needs, and (3) live often to a ripe old age with few signs of anxiety or insecurity."

Indeed, there are times when hunting and gathering has definite advantages over either pastoralism or farming, something that becomes less surprising when one realizes that "hunting-and-gathering" is a misleading term; first of all, it is meant to include fishing and, secondly and most importantly, it gives undue emphasis to hunting. Most hunter-gatherers in temperate and tropical regions are and have been primarily "gatherers" of wild plants, fruits, nuts, seeds, and roots, secondarily fishermen and shellfishermen (depending on the season), and, least significantly, hunters. Subarctic and arctic hunters reverse this order, with hunting dominating other food-gathering strategies the closer one gets to the poles. Where drought, insects, birds, warfare, or other natural or human calamities might destroy the standing crop or the livestock of agriculturalists or pastoralists, hunter-gatherers are often able to survive with a broad margin of security derived from an incredible diversity of food sources.

On the matter of agriculture in prehistoric North America, it seems apparent that the sunflower and marsh elder plus various amaranths and chenopods were being cultivated in the Eastern Woodlands sometime before maize-beans-squash agriculture arrived from Mexico via the Southwest. Most authorities place the advent of the maize complex in early Woodland times, a thousand or so years before the time of Christ, although this inauguration date is disputed by some who prefer to move it up several hundred years A.D. What is significant for our purposes is not the date of arrival but the importance of the new horticultural methods relative to the hunting and gathering and fishing economies that preceded them. Rather than replacing these former techniques, maize-beans-squash agriculture was added as a supplement to an already highly diversified diet consisting of game, fish, mollusks, nuts, seeds, fruits, and berries, depending on the locality. Not all scholars agree on this point, although the trend does seem to be in the direction of soft-pedaling the dietary significance of plant domesticants in the prehistoric East.

Farther west, among the aboriginal Californians, Lowell John Bean and Harry Lawton have suggested that agriculture was indeed purposely rejected because it offered no improvement over the status quo, which included, in addition to acorn gathering, for instance, a culturally extensive burning program designed to improve browse forage, eliminate pests, encourage sprouting, and select for large-seed grasses. When Europeans arrived, the California Indian was seemingly contentedly fixed at a semiagricultural stage of economy—if not a dropout from agriculture, at least a nonbeliever in it.

All of this has interesting implications for the civilization program applied toward the Indian by eighteenth- and nineteenth-century Anglo-American use, something the Jeffersonians no doubt appreciated. . . . Perhaps no other individual embodied this assimilationist goal more completely than Thomas Jefferson, whose dabbling in natural sciences convinced him that the Indian—both his tribal society and equally degraded culture—was a product of crude environmental pressures. Thus, Jefferson and other prominent and concerned individuals argued that the best way to incorporate the Indian within white American society would be through upgrading his environment. For the Jeffersonian, education was the key: The native languages were to be replaced with English, which would be taught along with other rudimentary liberal arts skills; compulsive warfare and hunting would be discarded for a peaceful, pastoral life on the American yeoman model; tribalism would be dismantled for something more individualistic and republican; and so forth. Such was the so-called Jeffersonian assimilationist blueprint for the backward, yet salvageable, native.

And yet, writes Bernard Sheehan, despite all the sanguine hopes and enthusiastic forecasts, the Indian proved intractable. He remained, alas, a drunkard, a murderer, a pauper, a pagan, and the rest of it. The Indian's inherent degeneracy, so contemporaries thought, coupled with the powerful vices of the frontier environment nullified the goodwill of the Jeffersonian incorporationist plan. The only alternative, for Thomas L. McKenney, Lewis Cass, John C. Calhoun, Andrew Jackson, and others, was to ship the tribesmen west, beyond the Mississippi, out of harm's way. The ethnohistorian who is possessed of an ecological anthropological bent detects several problems inherent in the "farming" clause of the assimilationist program. One of them—shifting agriculture (i.e., slash-and-burn or swidden agriculture) of the sort widely although not exclusively practiced by contemporary Woodland and Prairie Indians—was undoubtedly more labor efficient than the intensive variety being proposed by white philanthropists and statesmen. "Intensive agriculture conserves the scarce resource of land, creating surplus land for Anglo-only at the expense of a higher labor input for every unit produced." Robert Netting has gone on to delineate exactly what is required in order to farm intensively—the fencing, terracing, frequent weeding, construction and maintenance of irrigation works (in certain cases), the maintenance of animals for their manure and draft purposes, and so forth—and concluded that "the heavy initial labor investments and the necessity for continuous supportive agricultural activities may make intensive agriculture more expensive than shifting cultivation in terms of time. . . . When plentiful high-quality land becomes available—land that will grow crops without fertilizing, elaborate ridging, and capital improvements—shifting methods are recognized as more practical."

There is thus a distinct possibility that the turn-of-the-century Woodland and Prairie Indians, excluding the Five Civilized Tribes in the Southeast who were already farming intensively or raising stock or both, had ecologically and economically sound reasons, among others, for resisting the pressure to farm the way their white neighbors did. There appears to be more involved here than simple intransigence in the face of progress; perhaps intensive farming was in reality not progress for these people after all.

Before continuing on, it would be helpful to clarity the status of farming among the native tribes of the East. When Europeans first landed, Eastern Woodland and Prairie tribesmen were well acquainted with farming, as they had been engaged in it for hundreds of years. Clearly, it was a major part of their subsistence economy. Over the course of the following decades, however, native subsistence strategies were compromised to conform to the new dispensation: warfare with whites and other native groups, which often meant displacement, crop destruction, and population loss; population decline owing to the effects of epidemic diseases and alcohol consumption; and participation in the fur trade, which put an unprecedented premium on the hunting and processing of furs and skins, perhaps to the neglect of the fields. In the process, many of these native groups became dangerously dependent upon European trade goods and gifts for their survival; the food staples, clothing, and powder and shot given them by traders and colonial agents became absolute essentials to survival, as the Pontiac Rebellion made painfully clear.

It was this bond of dependency that white philanthropists and legislators were endeavoring to break when they argued for the agricultural imperative. The broken-down tribal economies they were witnessing were casually agricultural, casually hunting and gathering, and clearly impoverished. Compromised by white influence, the *traditional* economies, which had worked perfectly well in a virgin context, had given way to *transitional* economies, which in many cases east of the Mississippi were barely able to keep body and soul together. Intensive farming, it was hoped, would raise the Indian's standard of living to the place where he could get out from underneath his debts to the government-licensed traders and present himself as a respectable individual. This was the official line, anyway. Unfortunately, there were individuals, among them Thomas Jefferson, who were not above manipulating the credit-debt system at the government factories to relieve the Indian of the "excess" land he had put up as collateral.

Among the Five Civilized Tribes, as was noted above, farming and stock raising were flourishing at the turn of the nineteenth century. Unlike their native brethren elsewhere in the East, several of the more prominent southeastern tribes (the Cherokee, Creek, Choctaw, and Chickasaw) were well on the road to assimilation within the dominant society. Yet for reasons which cannot be reviewed here, they were taken from their prosperous farms and rangelands and marched west of the Mississippi to an arid land where they had to start all over again and, after allotment (i.e., the Curtis Act), in many cases were obliged to start all over again on a now much-reduced acreage.

Returning to the subject of aboriginal, or traditional, subsistence methods, the impression one gets is that the North American Indian, whether hunter-gatherer or horticulturalist, geared his food collecting and producing activities toward efficiency and the economizing of time. Leisure time was so abundant that many European-American commentators were scandalized; nearly every description of the Indian character contained a standard reference to their (especially male) perverse laziness. French Jesuits found their Indian lambs "extremely lazy, gluttonous, profane, treacherous, cruel in their revenge, and given up to all kinds of lewdness, men and women alike"; while Samuel Hearne was informed by an Indian guide that the Chipewyan (Athapaskan) had " 'nothing to do but consult their own interests, inclinations, and passions; and to pass through this world with as much ease and contentment as possible.' " On the strength of this sort of incriminating evidence, a good many of us have surmised, along with the fur trade historian, Lewis Saum, that the Indian was "a rank hedonist and materialist"—or, simply, a lazy bum.

Part of the reason for this unflattering assessment arises from the fact that an efficient subsistence economy left these people with great quantities of time free from the food quest, time they devoted to various ceremonial and ritual activities, household chores, warfare, games, sleeping or lounging about, socializing, and politics. And among those tribes, such as the Six Nations, for whom chronic warfare became an accepted way of life, rest and relaxation when off duty must have been common and essential. However mitigating the circumstances, white observers regarded this whole behavioral complex as a dissipation of one's time.

Another more serious source for the myth of the "lazy" Indian has to do with two fundamentally different theories of economic motivation: the formalist and the substantivist. According to the former interpretation, human "wants are insatiable and . . . [the] means to satisfy these wants are invariably in short supply." Working from this premise, economic anthropologists of the formalist persuasion are accused by their substantivist critics of applying Western, industrial, market-oriented, price-governed theories of economy to non-Western, preindustrial, non-market-oriented, and non-price-governed societies, with grossly distorted and misleading results.

Substantivists argue, a priori, that there is no such thing as "economics" in a non-Western, preindustrial society—only "provisioning"; what Westerners call "economics" is in reality "socio-economic institutions and processes." That is, the economic process is "embedded in political, religious, social and kinship [i.e., noneconomic] institutions."

Judged according to the prevailing canons of thrift, which were in themselves value judgments based on the market-oriented, price-governed economy of seventeenth-, eighteenth-, and nineteenth-century Europe and America, the contemporary Indian did not make out very well. By this index, he invariably seemed lazy, because Western narrators failed to discern the "embedded" nature of aboriginal provisioning just as they failed to detect the aboriginal premium on "leisure time."

Besides fostering invidious character associations, the formalist economic frame of reference and its precursor, the marketplace mentality of pre-twentieth-century Europeans and Americans, have skewed our view of Indian participation in such transactions as the fur trade. The usual explanation for Indian motivation, in this case, derives from what Marshall Sahlins disparagingly refers to as the "Business Outlook": "The traders economically seduced the Indians by displaying their wares and in many other ways fostered capitalistic drives." Peter Farb justifiably got that impression from reading such people as Harold Innis, who until recently was the final word on the Canadian fur trade. "In the language of the economists," and the fur trade has rarely been interpreted using any other conceptual "language," "the heavy fixed capital of the beaver became a serious handicap with the improved technique of Indian hunting methods, incidental to the borrowing of iron from Europeans. Depreciation through obsolescence of the beaver's defence equipment was so rapid as to involve the immediate and complete destruction of the animal."

Alternatively, ethnohistorical evidence seems to show that hunter-gatherers, such as the Micmac, Montagnais-Naskapi, Cree, Ojibwa, and others in Canada, would normally have refrained from this mass slaughter of furbearers and other wildlife through fear of retaliation from offended game spirits. Exposure to diseases—diseases which originated with the earliest European visitors to the continent and which these Indians, at least, appear to have ascribed to malevolent wildlife—served to remove the traditional sanctions against overkilling game and seemingly motivated these vengeful northern hunters to obliterate certain species, including the commercially valuable beaver. This is not to say that these natives werc blasé about European trade goods and that there was no acquisitive impulse on their part to engage in their trade. Not at all. What it docs show, rather, is that there was more to the Indian's rationale for trading than economics as we conceive of it. There was clearly a spiritual dimension to the Canadian fur trade, as least, which corresponds very nicely with the substantivist interpretation of economic activity.

Spiritual explanations like this seem farfetched to a Western audience because our cosmology is devoid of a spiritual dimension comparable to that perceived by the American Indian. There is nothing inherently wrong with this, of course, except that historians writing about native Americans have sedulously avoided giving serious attention to this spiritual realm. In a word, the historical fraternity has stripped the Indian of his spiritual powers and perceptions and made him just as "secular" as the rest of us. This is an enormous conceit on our part, imagining as we do that these "barbarous superstitions" can be eliminated from the Indian equation without serious loss. What we lose by doing so is the essence of the Indians's intellect—a spiritual vision that is vital to comprehending Indian behavior.

The anthropologist Lucien Lévy-Bruhl was very much aware of the scholarly tendency to disengage the spiritual element from the secular element when probing the non-Western, preindustrial mind. The two are fused in such an individual; they are impossible to disentangle. "To them the things which are unseen cannot be distinguished from the things which are seen," he wrote in 1923. "The beings of the unseen world are no less directly present than those of the other; they are more active and more formidable. Consequently, that world occupies their minds more entirely than this one, and it diverts their minds from reflecting, even to a slight extent, upon the data which we call objective."

Lévy-Bruhl may have overstated his case in his insistence that empirical evidence is completely irrelevant, but basically his argument is sound. It is also corroborated by countless studies probing American Indian belief systems. Witness, for example, Indian agent Henry R. Schoolcraft's delineation of the Ojibwa world view:

> To give some idea of the Indian mythology, it is necessary to conceive every department of the universe to be filled with invisible spirits. These spirits hold, in their belief, nearly the same relation to matter, that the soul does to the body. They believe not only that every man, but also, *that every animal has a soul.* And, as might be expected, under this belief, *they make no distinction between instinct and reason.* Every animal is supposed to be endowed with a reasoning faculty. The movements of birds, and other animals, are deemed to be the result, not of mere instinctive animal powers . . . but of a process of ratiocination. They go a step further, and believe that animals, particularly birds, can look into, and are familiar with the vast operation of the world of spiritual life.

Schoolcraft's account is fairly typical of early white, literate descriptions of the Ojibwa cosmology—muddy while at once provocative. For clarification one turns to modern ethnographic sources, such as the work of Irving Hallowell, to learn that the Ojibwa have traditionally equated the activity of natural phenomena with that of *persons;* the sun, moon, thunder, and so forth, including, aboriginally at least, probably all significant animal species, were classified as "other-than-human" persons with whom one interacted in a great "cosmic" society according to a uniform social code. Even myths were regarded as "living personal entities" and treated with the same sort of respect one accorded other persons, human or otherwise. Most importantly, a dialogue between human and other-than-human persons was initiated by the vision quest, at puberty, and maintained over the remaining adult years by dream communication, singing, drumming, taking sweat baths, and appealing to shamans for intercession.

For reasons both obvious and mysterious, this sort of spiritual perception and exchange became blunted or subverted following white contact. Christianity naturally had a lot to do with it, as did white ridicule of these so-called superstitions. "'It is a strange thing,'" a heathen Algonkin reproached the Jesuit Paul Le Jeune ". . . 'that since prayer has come into our cabins, our former customs are no longer of any service; and yet we shall all die because we give them up.' 'I have seen the time,' said one of them, 'when my dreams were true; when I had seen Moose or Beavers in sleep, I would take some. When our Soothsayers felt the enemy coming, that came true; there was preparation to receive him. Now, our dreams and our prophecies are no longer true,—prayer has spoiled everything for us.'" In the words of a more recent native informant: "'With the coming of the whites and Christianity the demons of the bush have been pushed back to the north where there is no Christianity. And the conjuror does not exist any more with us, for there is no need of one. Nor is there need for the drum.'"

Despite their attenuation, many of these beliefs have persisted well into modern times. Even more to the point, they were commonly held in one form or another by virtually all the Indian societies we write about. In failing to take cognizance of that fact, we have missed many of the subtleties of Indian behavior. Actions which at first appear inscrutable are sometimes resolved by resourse to this spiritual-psychological dimension. A good example is the odd habit of certain subarctic Indians artificially creating a festival atmosphere in the face of starvation. "I returned to the Indian village where at this time much scarcity of food prevailed," recalled the trader Alexander Henry the elder, concerning an experience he had with a family of Ojibwa. "We were often for twenty-four hours without eating; and when in the morning we had no victuals for the day before us the custom was to black our faces with grease and charcoal, and exhibit through resignation a temper as cheerful as if in the midst of plenty." Strange behavior, indeed, when one is starving. Yet not so strange when we consider the spiritual context of hunting for these people. "If nothing was taken in the hunt, it was a sign of death. Informants said the animals saw the Indian's spirit in mourning and fled away." So much for the Indian's "merry and jocose" air during periods of famine. But why the use of charcoal? Diamond Jenness was told that famished Indians would darken "'their faces with charcoal to disguise their shadows [the third part of man's being, in addition to body and soul] and throw the animals off their guard.'"

In a world such as this, where magic was obviously very real and often employed as sorcery, one scrupulously avoided giving offense. Irving Hallowell felt that "the latent mistrust engendered by a belief in sorcery has the widest ramifications in Saulteaux [Ojibwa] society. I think it explains the suppression of criticism in face-to-face relations, also mentioned in the older sources, the hesitancy to command others, and the ready assent to requests even though the individual may not carry them out. Hospitality, lending, sharing, likewise may be motivated by anxiety, since a guest, a borrower or a neighbor may become piqued and seek retaliation by covert means." Hallowell probably exaggerated the function of sorcery over that of public opinion, including censure, in encouraging conformity to normative behavior among the early contact Ojibwa. Still, his observation is edifying. "Since the data assembled point very clearly to the fact that the emotional structure of the [northeastern] Indian was such that a great deal of emotional expression familiar to whites was inhibited," he went on to reason, "naturally it would appear to white observers that it was a matter of artful disguise rather than an integral part of the personality of the Indians. Their 'persona' did seem to offer evidence of concealment, dissimulation, lack of candor, and deceit. In psychological terms, this inhibitory pattern suggests the characteristics of a defense mechanism against anxieties. And the inference would be that, since the manifestations of this psychic mechanism are typified in the behavior of groups of individuals, the determining factors must lie in the culturally constituted world in which these individuals live."

The obvious lesson for those historians who are inclined to write about Indian character and personality traits is that they should reevaluate the credibility of their sources according to the principles and insights of psychological anthropology. Yet few of us have done this, being content to perpetuate the warped judgments of earlier commentators while perhaps softening their harsher tones. What is needed here is more than a little humane editing—many of us need to overhaul completely our thinking on Indian behavior. Clearly the Indian of our history books was an individual who responded to a different universe than ours. And it is our responsibility to discover just who he was, using the best means at our disposal—in this case, the techniques of the psychological anthropologist.

The Indian who emerges from these various ethnohistorical investigations appears "in the round," as Washburn so aptly phrased it. Or, to put it another way, ethnohistory offers a belated means of resolving the dilemma of the bifurcated Indian—the Indian of anthropology and the Indian of history. In reconciling the two we are presented with an individual who makes sense in his own social and cultural context, operating on a different epistemological and phenomenological track from that of the white man. Ethnohistorians have crossed the frontier, theoretically and figuratively, to confront the Indian who confronted us—this time on *his* terms.

The Problems of Indian History

FREDERICK HOXIE

The work of two influential American historians provides a vivid illustration of the problems of contemporary American Indian history. While their careers are separated by a century, Francis Parkman and Bernard Bailyn share an interest in

"The Problems of Indian History," by Frederick Hoxie, from *The Social Science Journal* 25, no. 4 (1988), pp. 389–399. Reprinted with permission from JAI Press Inc.

defining central themes in our national past and have adopted a common approach to Native Americans. Francis Parkman wrote in the late nineteenth century, and was one of the architects of modern scholarship; Bernard Bailyn, a Pulitzer Prize–winning author and a former president of the American Historical Association, exemplifies contemporary methods. Both men explored the origins of the American nation, and both balanced a concern for precise narrative against a broad vision of American exceptionalism. In each man's work, America is a special place whose distinctiveness unfolded in the seventeenth and eighteenth centuries. And for each man, Indians are a part of that distinctiveness. Brief quotations from each scholar not only illustrate this point, but also convey a sense of where Native American history has been in the past 100 years and where it is today.

In his introduction to the first volume of *France and England in North America,* Francis Parkman made the case for the significance of what historians now call early contact history, the story of initial encounters between Indians and Europeans:

> The springs of American civilization, unlike those of the elder world, lie revealed in the clear light of History. In appearance they are feeble; in reality, copious and full of force. Acting at the sources of life, instruments otherwise weak become mighty for good and evil, and men, lost elsewhere in the crowd, stand forth as agents of Destiny. . . . On the obscure strife where men died by tens or by scores hung questions of as deep import for posterity as on those mighty contests of national adolescence where carnage is reckoned by thousands.

Parkman saw the springs of American civilization in the struggle between the liberty, progress, the godliness of New England and the absolutism, reaction, and savagery of New France. Indians played a central role in this struggle because they largely sided with the French; their defeat heralded the dawn of a new civilization on the American continent. For Parkman, warfare that might seem "obscure" when viewed from Europe (in America men died only "by tens" or "by scores") was actually as important as the "mighty contests" of the continent ("where carnage is reckoned by thousands"). Even though Parkman's view of Indian people was both racist and chauvinistic, he recognized that the "clear light of history" would place the "obscure strife" of the frontier at center stage in the story of American national development.

Bernard Bailyn returned to some of Parkman's themes in his two prizewinning new books. *The People of British North America* and *Voyagers to the West.* Like Parkman, Bailyn set out to plumb "the heart and soul" of history. He asserts at the outset of the first of these volumes that the "peopling of the North American continent . . . transformed" the globe "more fundamentally than any development except the Industrial Revolution." The event was, in Bailyn's words, "one of the greatest events in recorded history"; and it is "the foundation of American history." Parkman's obsession with progress and reaction is not prominent in Bailyn's writing, but this modern scholar's focus on the "transformation" of North America parallels Parkman's interest in the victory of Anglo-Saxon ways. Nevertheless, there are differences in the way these two men view the process of European migration and settlement. Parkman, writing at the end of the American

Civil War, was steeped in the nationalism and patriotic fervor of his age, and saw European settlement in military terms; he was attracted by the "struggles" of leaders and the courage of pioneer woodsmen—all of which was reflected in his writing. Bailyn writes in the present era of social scientific analysis and technological sophistication. His metaphors are drawn from space travel and astronomy (events draw near like the rings of Saturn, human migrations are viewed as if from space), whereas Parkman's are drawn from Victorian morality and politics. Most striking, however, is the fact that even though Bailyn claims to be describing social processes, the "people" in his history do not include Indians and blacks. He notes at the outset of his work that the text that is to follow "does not involve in any significant extent the movement of either of the two non-Caucasian peoples. . . ." Why?

Perhaps Bailyn leaves out Indians because his concern is not military campaigns but social "process." Parkman's native warriors would have no obvious place in Bailyn's story. But that is not the reason this modern scholar gives. He asserts that non-Caucasians must be left out simply because Caucasians do not know enough about their history to include it in the narrative. Here is his statement:

> Despite the mass of writing, much of it polemical, that is available on both of these groups [Indians and blacks] we know as yet relatively little about their histories; we have nothing like the density of information about them that is available for other groups. [He continues in the attendant footnote.] A narrative history of the coastal North American Indian population is still almost impossible to assemble. Even the approximate size of the native population is in question.

The consequences of Bailyn's assertion for Afro-American history will be left for others to discuss. As for Native American history, it is remarkable that in the span of a century, Indians have gone from the forest primeval to a footnote, and Indian history has devolved from high adventure to demographic speculation. Parkman knew all he needed to know about Indian people: they were backward, recalcitrant, and violent. Bailyn acknowledges the vitality of Indians and blacks, but protests that he knows nothing about them. Even more remarkable, he asserts that it is impossible to know more. It is difficult to take seriously the claim that a century and a half after Henry Schoolcraft's ambitious amateur scholarship, a century after John Wesley Powell made Indians central to American anthropology, and 50 years after Frank Speck and Franz Boas demonstrated the significance of Indian cultures for a broad range of social science disciplines, a scholar of Bailyn's stature could claim it "impossible" to learn enough about Indians to include them in a narrative history of the United States. Why? How is it that 150 years of American ethnology and nearly a century of American frontier history have replaced Parkman's bloodthirsty savages with a querulous footnote?

A longer answer will follow, but the first response to Bailyn's despair is the observation that historians of the American Indian have thus far been much more successful at bashing Parkman's stereotypes than in erecting a replacement for his lurid vision of the frontier. Francis Jennings and others have demonstrated that Parkman "cooked" some of his sources and maintained an unrelenting dislike for Indians. Similarly, other scholars (including this author) have focused an inordinate amount of attention in the past two decades on the motives of white explorers, the immorality of government intentions and actions, and the conduct of frontier wars and border conflicts. The result is a critical view of Euro-American thought and behavior, a view that contrasts sharply with Parkman's rhetoric of civilization and progress, but has little close engagement with the history of individual native communities or the role (if any) of native people in the shaping of American civilization.

A few examples from the recent publishers' catalogs can illustrate this point. The University of Oklahoma and University of Nebraska presses have been pre-eminent in the field of Indian history for many years, and their new books provide a reasonable measure of current trends. The Spring 1988 catalog from Nebraska lists three new books with Indians as their principal subject. The first is a previously unpublished novel by Lakota anthropologist Ella Deloria, the second a history of Southern California Indian land tenure, and the third (published by the University of Alberta Press, but distributed by Nebraska) a history of sovereignty in North America. Similarly, the University of Oklahoma Press catalog for Fall and Winter 1987 lists five new books on Indians, but none of them treats a topic in social history or community structure or engages broad themes in American culture.

Because most contemporary scholarship does not explore the detailed history of Indian societies, and because historians working the field have been reluctant to engage central interpretive themes, the duality that Parkman outlines—between Euro-American "civilization" and Native American "savagery"—lives on in the minds of people like Bernard Bailyn who are his intellectual heirs. Historians today may not assign the same moral labels to the actors that they did a century ago, but they still see the process of early settlement in terms of a "clash of cultures," an inevitable and usually violent confrontation between "history" (which arrives from the East on boats), and the static precontact world of the Indians.

Bailyn's recent work provides an illustration of the persistence of this Parkmanian frame of reference. In Bailyn's view, colonial society was divided between settled coastal areas and primitive backwoods communities where social chaos, racial miscegenation, and frontier violence posed a constant threat to good order. In the Carolinas, for example, the relatively small number of whites meant that "miscegenation was commonplace; mulatto and 'mustee' [mixed Negro and Indian] children were everywhere; and manumission [freeing of slaves] was frequent. . . . These were no tender, affectionate relationships. This was a brutal, half-primitive world of bushwhacking frontiersmen. . . ." Bailyn asserts that this negative view of the frontier should reverse the conventional romantic stereotype. The borders of the European settlements were not arenas for heroism, but "the exotic far western periphery . . . of the metropolitan European culture system." He believes that rather than representing the prow of civilization, cutting boldly into the unknown, the backwoods was "a ragged outer margin of a central world, a regressive backward-looking diminishment of metropolitan accomplishment. . . . [The] mingling of primitivism and civilization [Bailyn concludes,] was an essential part of early American culture. . . ."

From these excerpts it should be clear why Bailyn believes that a history of

Indians in eastern North America is impossible to assemble. Modern historians like Bailyn, while rejecting the racism of Parkman, still fall back on the view that American history is essentially a story of civilization overcoming primitivism. From this point of view, Indian history is significant only when it intersects with the history of European settlement. And Indians themselves are significant primarily as "obstacles to progress."

So long as scholars define the American past in this way, Indian history has no significance on its own terms. If they focus only on "intersections" of Europeans and native "obstacles," Indians are merely symbols; they stand as the "other" rather than as representatives of a distinct cultural tradition with its own set of values, expectations, and objectives. If scholars imagine our history to be exclusively European, then ethnologies and ethnohistories of native groups are interesting only as background to the "real" story. Clearly, then, until historians devise a way of conceiving Indian history as important to the cultural formation of the United States, there will be no choice but to accept Bailyn's disclaimer that a narrative history of Indians is "impossible to assemble." Impossible because—when viewed from his perspective—it does not exist.

What are the problems within the historical profession that cause it to equate history with European expansion and to define an Indian narrative as impossible? The many problems fall into three categories: structural, methodological, and conceptual. The structural problems are familiar to many. First, research and scholarship in Indian history today is tied to personalities rather than to institutional commitments. There is great agreement on the need for more research and writing in the field. Bailyn's maligned footnote says it plainly, and most scholars would agree that they simply need to know more. But as one reviews the ranks of U.S. institutions producing scholars of American Indian history, one thinks of individuals rather than of programs. R. David Edmunds at Texas Christian University, Floyd O'Neill at the University of Utah, James Axtell at the College of William and Mary, and Donald Berthrong at Purdue are all senior scholars who have graduated a number of Ph.D. students in Indian history. Nevertheless, their students have not experienced a common curriculum or even a common methodological approach. Moreover, these instructors' colleagues consider them Colonial, Western, or Early National historians, not Indian historians. While one might argue in response that this is good—they are not ghettoized and segregated as "Indianists"—newcomers to the field find it difficult to speak a common historiographic language, and the scholars' departments have no formal commitment to Indian subjects. As a result these departments have no reason to reconceive either their curriculum or their own research. And, of course, as long as jobs are classified as "Western," "Colonial," or "Early National," there is precious little incentive to train graduate students in a new area.

A related structural problem is that the Indian studies programs set up over the past decade and a half have failed to produce scholarship that historians can point to as contributing to a new vision of the American past. This is not for want of trying or for lack of publication. The UCLA American Indian Studies center has published a number of reference works and literary collections. That center sponsors a journal, *The American Indian Culture and Research Journal;* the program at Berkeley sponsors *The American Indian Quarterly;* and the University of

California at Santa Barbara supports the publication of *New Scholar*. But the impact of these journals is still relatively slight and their concerns are more parochial than historiographic.

One of the most promising features of contemporary Indian intellectual life is the emergence of two dozen or so tribally controlled community colleges. The most active of these are building a core of largely Native American educators who are committed to developing their own vision of both the national and the tribal past. But these colleges are continually bedeviled by budgetary restraints, large teaching loads, and growing demands from their constituents. When administrators must worry about keeping their buildings heated and their instructors housed, curricular innovation cannot be a priority. And these young colleges, like larger universities, are always engaged in what one Indian friend calls "the carrot game," where administrators rush about in pursuit of grants for programs that fit foundation guidelines rather than local needs.

The final structural problem involves training people to alter or overturn the present reality. There is not yet a critical mass of American Indians with doctorates in history and anthropology who might form the nucleus of an organization or intellectual movement to accomplish this task, and the number of American Indian graduate students is not growing. While non-Indian interest is certainly significant, it must be joined by native scholarship and perspectives so that it can be linked to contemporary Indian communities and to modern versions of tribal traditions.

The methodological problems of Indian history can be summarized briefly: most of the methodological approaches employed today in American Indian history are indigenous to the historical tradition that has thus far failed to understand native cultures. Historians are using tools designed in Europe for an historical enterprise that has arisen in the New World. It is the intellectual equivalent of setting the foxes to conduct fieldwork among the chickens. Without adopting new methodologies, scholars are unlikely to develop new perspectives on the native past. Studies of federal Indian policy, for example, examine why and how a particular policy was adopted; they usually do not explore the relationship between political action and broader themes in American social and cultural development. Studies of tribal groups are similarly inadequate, as they plumb the intricacies of native life without engaging the complex interaction of traditional behavior and externally stimulated social change. Too many books on the Indians of a particular region or moment embrace the so-called ethnographic present, that timeless description of native life that assumes stasis and immunity from outside influence prior to European contact. These studies inevitably emphasize degeneration and decline following that contact, and thus fit themselves neatly in the Parkman-Bailyn typology. Their view of native history defines the tribal past as unrelated to a chronology of larger societies.

This call for new methodologies should be understood separately from Calvin Martin's recent assertion that Indian history cannot be understood in traditional historical categories. In a recent collection of essays titled *The American Indian and the Problem of History,* Martin argues that the "problem" of Indian history is a consequence of the fundamental differences between European and Native American cultures. According to Martin, Indian people are rooted in place rather than time, in nature rather than human society. He argues in response that scholars must devise a new language of history, "another category by which to render ourselves and our habitat, one that does not disfranchise and disarticulate the latter. The problem [he continues,] lies in our enslaving philosophy of time, enslaving us and Nature in separate spheres."

Martin is correct when he cautions scholars not to assume that Indian behavior is understandable in Western European terms; scholars need to acknowledge—even celebrate—the distinctiveness and complexity of tribal traditions. On the other hand, it is fatuous to think historians can or should cast off "time" and turn their back on the notion of rational inquiry. A great deal can be accomplished with a more modest approach; historians of Indian life should invent approaches that utilize all the sources, illuminate the meaning of events, and prod their colleagues into unfamiliar perspectives.

The principal conceptual problem in Indian history has already been described. It is the persistence of Eurocratic notions of where history originates and what aspects of native experience are significant in the national past. To be more precise, it is only recently that scholars have begun to treat early-American history as a coherent period that does not begin with the first European explorers. Neal Salisbury's *Manitou and Providence,* for example, a book on the making of New England, begins with a discussion of the sixteenth century. The *Mayflower* does not sail into view until midway in the book. Similarly, Richard White's *The Roots of Dependency* stands nearly alone in its effort to place a broad theme of Indian history in the equally broad context of American economic and social development. His study traces the theme of dependency in the economic relations of native people to Euro-Americans and demonstrates the persistence of that relationship over two and a half centuries.

Unlike these studies, most current work in Indian history focuses on government policy or tribal history without engaging issues of regional or cultural development. How does the Indian experience add to understanding the history of, for example, New England, the South, the Great Lakes, the Southwest, or the Plains? In what sense is a region's history continuous through the pre- and post-contact period? How does the environment of a region override cultural traditions as a force in its history? These are questions we have not yet explored.

Culturally, scholars have not examined the significance of the Indian experience in the development of American society's racial, religious, or political ideas. *The Roots of Dependency* gives us a new picture of the American economy—an economy that individualizes and marginalizes politically powerless groups. How accurate is that view? Is there a cultural parallel to White's story of economic dependency? A religious parallel? A social or family history parallel? There are many questions such as these that would cause scholars to rethink both American Indian historiography and U.S. historiography, but for the most part they have not yet tackled them.

A subset of the tendency not to examine broad cultural issues is a reluctance—or inability—to examine Indian history in relation to the history of other American minority groups or in comparison with the experience of colonized native people in other countries. How were the experiences of Creek refugees in Florida in the late-eighteenth century similar to those of the runaway slaves who became their kinsmen? In what way are tribal religious revivals similar to the resurgence of institutionalized religion among European ethnic groups? How is Indian Christianity different from black, Hispanic, or Korean Christianity? How does the urban experience of Native Americans compare to that of blacks, Appalachians, or Puerto Ricans? The questions, like the ethnic groups (and their stories), are endless.

If the problems of Indian history are structural, methodological, and conceptual, what are the solutions? First, scholars should understand the linkage between the problems listed above. Structural solutions must be pursued even as one casts about for new methodologies and new ideas. Scholars need to encourage the development of Indian history as a visible piece of the history and anthropology professions. It is unfortunate that many historians view Indian subjects as marginal ("after all, they are less than 1% of the population"), and anthropologists dismiss Native American culture as insufficiently exotic. Advocates of Indian history should also define available teaching positions prescriptively rather than descriptively; departments (and deans) need to think about what they would *like* rather than what they believe they can get.

Independent research efforts like the new American Indian Studies Center at Indiana University or the newly revived American Indian Programs at Wisconsin and Cornell universities deserve encouragement and support. At the same time it must be recognized that these are primarily academic programs that can be most effective within the academic world. There are constant and important social needs in Indian communities throughout the country, but university Indian studies faculty cannot be expected to play a social service role if they are also going to make significant contributions to scholarship.

Second, historians should seek to apply "new methods" to the study of Indian history, which can involve using new sources such as oral testimony, native language manuscripts, archaeological data, and underutilized archival collections (such as the French and Spanish colonial records). But more important is the adoption of new approaches to those sources, particularly ones that social historians have adopted in their studies of peasants, women, and industrial workers. The major method or approach that Indian historians have ignored is the quantitative analysis of manuscript census data. Census material began to appear with first contact, but formal tribal censuses did not appear until the early nineteenth century. By 1880 there were annual Bureau of Indian Affairs enumerations available for every federally recognized group. Special federal censuses supplemented these. Together they provide a rich resource for the study of population composition, family life, and cultural change. While certainly flawed and incomplete in many cases, these records describe isolated communities whose members did not migrate like the residents of Chicago's West Side or Boston's South End. Without the problem of geographic mobility, the censuses can provide a stunningly complete picture of modern tribal life as well as a supplement to data gathered from archival or archaeological sources.

Methods drawn from other disciplines are always fair game, and today the historical interests of many anthropologists appear particularly promising. These interests range from Marshall Sahlins' and Clifford Geertz's analyses of symbolic meaning in cultural "performances" and cross-cultural encounters to Eric

Wolf's materialistic concern with the evolution of world systems of trade and interaction. While the ideological positions of these scholars might cause them to affiliate with different tribes of anthropologists, historians can draw on their common insight: that culture is "historically ordered," the product of events which are, in Sahlins' phrase, "externally induced but indigenously orchestrated." Thus it is possible to look for the events, people, or forces that shape the "order" of both native and non-native societies, and to trace the interaction of these groups as encounters between cultural systems that are changed in the process of meeting. Sahlins puts forth a language of analysis that nudges students away from a "cook-book" version of ethnohistory where scholars simply plug the ethnographic literature into a traditional narrative of events. The historical interests of anthropologists also encourage others to view "frontier" areas as zones of mutual interaction and cultural adjustment, arenas of performance where people representing different cultural systems encounter, explain, and attempt to manipulate one another. Such a view is far more accurate—and far more interesting—than the two-dimensional scenarios of Francis Parkman and Bernard Bailyn.

There is a third method historians should adopt, but which thus far has no name. Presentations of American Indian history need not follow the standard forms of the discipline. It is not necessarily true that traditional monographs best fit Native American sources. The *Atlas of Great Lakes Indian History,* which the University of Oklahoma recently published, for example, is not really an atlas. It is not a compendium of maps, but a narrative Indian history of the Great Lakes region in map form. The text provides both a context and an explanation for the maps—they are at the center of the book—but it cannot stand without them. The format provides an ideal way of cataloging and presenting a mass of tiny pieces of information about tribal locations and migrations. By seeing the location of Indian villages in 1763 or the distribution of Indian population throughout the region at the time of the Black Hawk War, students and scholars can quickly grasp the meaning and complexity of the Indian presence. Other new forms of presentation might juxtapose sources. There is no easy prescription here, only the suggestion that scholars consider their sources and objectives before settling on the most effective form of exposition.

Conceptually, historians of native communities would benefit from thinking of Indian history as an aspect of American social history. As such, Indian history can be understood as the study of a particular group's institutions and ideas about itself, as well as its relationships with other groups within the larger society. If this theme were pursued, Indian historians could address both the distinctiveness of the native experience and the relationship between native history and the development of national and regional cultures.

In national terms, this approach would encourage historians to think comparatively as well as thematically. How were—or when were—Indian communities behaving like other social entities and how (and when) were they unique? The thematic questions are many: How did—and when did—tribal societies affect the development of distinctive American styles of racial thought, economic behavior, or social organization? How were they outside of this development process?

At the regional level, the social history approach would lead to an examination of the relationship between Indian histories and the histories of other social groups in the area. The proliferation of studies of so-called remnant groups along the eastern seaboard has opened up a new dimension to both New England and Southeastern history, as has twentieth-century Plains Indian history, and the current revival in the scholarship on California Indians. In all of these cases—and in others in different parts of the country—historians can see first the exposure of a history that had previously been ignored, and then see an effort to understand that new history in a broader regional context.

These new ways of understanding native history should also produce a series of hypotheses that might bridge the differences between tribal experiences and clarify the relationship, if any, between local and national histories. Just as traditional American historians are immersed in the work of synthesizing individual studies of labor strife in nineteenth-century cities, or the diverse experience of women at different stations on the social ladder, so historians of Native American life will be looking for interpretive themes and categories with which to examine the "Indian experience." Further, as Indian historians enter more fully into the field of social history, they will find new questions emerging. Historians of American women, for example, have explored the impact of industrialization on gender roles, but few of them have explored the Indian version of this phenomenon; the same could be said for studies of changes in household structure, religious practice, and economic activity. Finally, historians need to understand the purpose of the enterprise. Recently, the Newberry Library's D'Arcy McNickle Center [in Chicago] for the History of the American Indian sponsored a series of conferences titled "The Impact of Indian History on the Teaching of U.S. History." The meetings were designed to bring recent scholarship on Native Americans to a cross-section of undergraduate instructors. One of the most depressing aspects of the project—which otherwise was quite successful—was the reaction of department chairmen when invited: "Oh, yes," several replied, "We have someone who does Indians"; or the alternative "Sorry, no one here does Indians." The problems of Indian history are not someone else's problems. Certainly Indian people in tribal and urban communities throughout the country will proceed with their efforts to record and compile their own histories regardless of the actions of professional scholars and teachers. And those who are committed to the field will of course continue with their work. But if American scholars and the American public are going to escape the dualities of Parkman and Bailyn and rise above the deeply held preconceptions that underlie them, then both scholars and their readers will need to understand Indian history as a part of human history and to claim it as part of our national legacy. Authors often remember to quote from Robert Frost's "The Gift Outright" that "The land was ours before we were the land's," but they are not so apt to remember the poet's observation about how to break down the barriers between Americans and their native continent. His words contain one more way of describing problems, and the solutions, in Indian history:

> Something we were withholding made us weak
> Until we found that it was ourselves
> We were withholding from our land of living,
> And forthwith found salvation in surrender.

◈ *FURTHER READING*

Harold E. Driver, *Indians of North America,* 2d ed. (1969)

Don E. Dumond, "A Reexamination of Eskimo-Aleut Prehistory," *American Anthropologist* 89 (1987), 32–56

Brian M. Fagan, *The Great Journey: The Peopling of Ancient America* (1987)

Peter Farb, *Man's Rise to Civilization: The Cultural Ascent of the Indians of North America,* 2d ed. (1978)

Robert F. Heizer and Albert A. Elsasser, *The Natural World of the California Indians* (1980)

Frederick Webb Hodge, ed., *Handbook of the American Indian North of Mexico,* 2 vols. (1907–1910)

William Hodge, *The First Americans: Then and Now* (1981)

Jesse D. Jennings, ed., *Ancient North Americans* (1983)

Alice B. Kehoe, *North American Indians: A Comprehensive Account* (1981)

Alfred L. Kroeber, *Cultural and Natural Areas of Native North America* (1939)

Harriet Kupferer, *Ancient Drums, Other Moccasins: Native North American Cultural Adaptation* (1988)

Calvin Martin, ed., *The American Indian and the Problem of History* (1987)

——— , *In the Spirit of the Earth: Rethinking History and Time* (1992)

Jerald T. Milanich, *The Early Prehistoric Southeast: A Sourcebook* (1985)

Wendell H. Oswalt, *This Land Was Theirs: A Study of North American Indians,* 4th ed. (1988)

Donald L. Parman, and Catherine Price, "A 'Work in Progress': The Emergence of Indian History as a Professional Field," *Western Historical Quarterly* 20 (1989), 185–196.

Roy Harvey Pearce, "From the History of Ideas to Ethnohistory," *Journal of Ethnic Studies* 2 (1974), 86–92

George Irving Quimby, *Indian Life in the Upper Great Lakes, 11,000 B.C. to A.D. 1800* (1960)

Thomas E. Sheridan, "How to Tell the Story of a 'People Without History,'" *Journal of the Southwest* 30 (1988), 168–189

William C. Sturtevant, ed., *Handbook of North American Indians,* 20 vols. (1978–)

Helen Hornbeck Tanner, ed., *Atlas of Great Lakes Indian History* (1987)

David Hurst Thomas, ed., *Columbian Consequences* 3 vols. (1989–1991)

Russell Thornton, *American Indian Holocaust and Survival: A Population History Since 1492* (1987)

Waldo R. Wedel, ed., *The Plains Archaeology Source Book: Selected Papers of the Nebraska State Historical Society* (1985)

Indians and Europeans Meet

Five hundred years ago, residents of the Caribbean islands saw on the horizon ships unlike any they had ever before seen or imagined. These vessels carried Christopher Columbus and his men, who soon claimed the islands for Spain and who called the inhabitants "indios" because they thought that they had reached the East Indies off the coast of Asia. Columbus died believing devoutly in his immense geographical error, but his name for the native inhabitants of the Western Hemisphere remains as an ironic monument to Columbus's unrealized search for a shortcut to the riches of Asia.

Scholars debate the meaning of the European conquest that Columbus inaugurated. And in 1992—the five-hundredth anniversary of Columbus's first voyage—some Native Americans argued that genocide of native peoples was the principal legacy of the Columbian encounter and its aftermath. Certainly, the European conquest of America set off among the indigenous peoples of America a vicious cycle of population decline that may have amounted to as much as a 90 percent reduction. Most of the population losses came from the impact of epidemic diseases that Indians had not been exposed to before 1492. Smallpox, measles, bubonic plague, and other Old World maladies swept off large numbers of Indians at a single stroke and left native communities weakened and vulnerable. Yet Indians did not merely fade away when Europeans arrived. They adjusted to new conditions of life and, when conditions were favorable, asserted a measure of control in the new world that Indians and Europeans together created.

◈ D O C U M E N T S

When Columbus arrived in America, he expected to find Asia and its riches. Instead, he encountered the Carib people on San Salvador island. In the first document, a letter to the Spanish monarchs, Columbus describes the Caribs, discusses their ignorance of European weapons, and observes that they would make good servants. By 1519 Spanish explorers were expanding their grip to the American mainland. Hernán Cortés, who led the Spanish conquest of Mexico, found a formidable foe in the Aztec Empire that held sway over central Mexico. In the second document, Aztec emperor Moctezuma (also spelled *Mutezuma* or *Montezuma*) tells Cortés that he believes that the Spanish have come to reclaim Mexico, in accordance with Aztec history and prophecy. Aztec compliance proved a great convenience for Cortés, who, in order to master the Aztecs, was more than willing to accept the part that Moctezuma assigned him. The third document records in song the Aztec perspective on the sad outcome of Cortés's conquest. The account of Jacques Cartier in the fourth document contrasts sharply with those of Cortés and Columbus. Here we see Micmac Indians in the Gulf of St. Lawrence region clamoring to trade furs for French metalware in 1534. The fifth document is Arthur Barlowe's description of his hospitable reception by the Powhatan Indians of Virginia. Friendship and trade seemed to mark this early encounter with the English. The final document is the Pilgrim governor William Bradford's account of the first treaty of peace with the Wampanoags of Massachusetts Bay.

At first contact, European and Indian needs and expectations varied widely, but ultimately Europeans prevailed throughout the hemisphere. Could these early encounters have resulted in mutually beneficial relationships, or were Indians destined to be defeated from the start?

Columbus on the Indians' "Discovery" of the Spanish, 1492

"I [Columbus wrote], in order that they might feel great amity towards us, because I knew that they were a people to be delivered and converted to our holy faith rather by love than by force, gave to some among them some red caps and some glass beads, which they hung round their necks, and many other things of little value. At this they were greatly pleased and became so entirely our friends that it was a wonder to see. Afterwards they came swimming to the ships' boats, where we were, and brought us parrots and cotton thread in balls, and spears and many other things, and we exchanged for them other things, such as small glass beads and hawks' bells, which we gave to them. In fact, they took all and gave all, such as they had, with good will, but it seemed to me that they were a people very deficient in everything. They all go naked as their mothers bore them, and the women also, although I saw only one very young girl. And all those whom I did see were youths, so that I did not see one who was over thirty years of age; they were very well built, with very handsome bodies and very good faces. Their hair is coarse almost like the hairs of a horse's tail and short; they wear their hair down over their eyebrows, except for a few strands behind, which they wear long and never cut. Some of them are painted black, and they are the colour of the people of the Canaries, neither black nor white, and some of them are painted white and some red and some in any colour that they find. Some of them paint their faces, some their whole bodies, some only the eyes, and some only the nose. They do not bear arms or know them, for I showed to them swords and they took them by the blade and cut themselves through ignorance. They have no iron. Their spears are certain reeds, without iron, and some of these have a fish tooth at the end, while others are pointed in various ways. They are all generally fairly tall, good looking and well proportioned. I saw some who bore marks of wounds on their bodies, and I made signs to them to ask how this came about, and they indicated to me that people came from other islands, which are near, and wished to capture them, and they defended themselves. And I believed and still believe that they come here from the mainland to take them for slaves. They should be good servants and of quick intelligence, since I see that they very soon say all that is said to them, and I believe that they would easily be made Christians, for it appeared to me that they had no creed. Our Lord willing, at the time of my departure I will bring back six of them to Your Highnesses, that they may learn to talk. I saw no beast of any kind in this island, except parrots." . . .

The Emperor Moctezuma Links the Spanish
to the Fulfillment of the Aztecs' Destiny, 1519

[Moctezuma explains Aztec origins to Cortes] "For a long time we have known from the writings of our ancestors that neither I, nor any of those who dwell in this land, are natives of it, but foreigners who came from very distant parts; and likewise we know that a chieftain, of whom they were all vassals, brought our people to this region. And he returned to his native land and after many years came again, by which time all those who had remained were married to native women and had built villages and raised children. And when he wished to lead them away again they would not go nor even admit him as their chief; and so he departed. And we have always held that those who descended from him would come and conquer this land and take us as their vassals. So because of the place from which you claim to come, namely, from where the sun rises, and the things you tell us of the great lord or king who sent you here, we believe and are certain that he is our natural lord, especially as you say that he has known of us for some time. So be assured that we shall obey you and hold you as our lord in place of that great sovereign of whom you speak; and in this there shall be no offense or betrayal whatsoever. And in all the land that lies in my domain, you may command as you will, for you shall be obeyed; and all that we own is for you to dispose of as you choose. Thus, as you are in your own country and your own house, rest now from the hardships of your journey and the battles which you have fought, for I know full well of all that has happened to you from Puntunchan to here, and I also know how those of Cempoal and Tascalteca have told you much evil of me; believe only what you see with your eyes, for those are my enemies, and some were my vassals, and have rebelled against me at your coming and said those things to gain favor with you. I also know that they have told you the walls of my houses are made of gold, and that the floor mats in my rooms and other things in my household are likewise of gold, and that I was, and claimed to be, a god; and many other things besides. The houses as you see are of stone and lime and clay."

Then he raised his clothes and showed [Cortés] his body, saying, as he grasped his arms and trunk with his hands, "See that I am of flesh and blood like you and all other men, and I am mortal and substantial. See how they have lied to you? It is true that I have some pieces of gold left to me by my ancestors; anything I might have shall be given to you whenever you ask. Now I shall go to other houses where I live, but here you shall be provided with all that you and your people require, and you shall receive no hurt, for you are in your own land and your own house." . . .

Aztec Songs of Sorrow for the Fall of Mexico, c. 1521

Nothing but flowers and songs of sorrow
are left in Mexico and Tlatelolco,
where once we saw warriors and wise men.

We know it is true
that we must perish,
for we are mortal men.
You, the Giver of Life,
you have ordained it.

We wander here and there
in our desolate poverty.
We are mortal men.
We have seen bloodshed and pain
where once we saw beauty and valor.

We are crushed to the ground;
we lie in ruins.
There is nothing but grief and suffering
in Mexico and Tlatelolco,
where once we saw beauty and valor.

Have you grown weary of your servants?
Are you angry with your servants,
O Giver of Life?

Jacques Cartier on the Micmacs' Meeting the French, 1534

. . . The Cape of the said South land was called The Cape of Hope, through the hope that there we had to finde some passage. The fourth of July we went along the coast of the said land on the Northerly side to finde some harborough, where wee entred into a creeke altogether open toward the South, where there is no succour against the wind: we thought good to name it S. Martines Creeke. There we stayed from the fourth of July until the twelfth: while we were there, on Munday being the sixth of the moneth, Service being done, wee with one of our boates went to discover a Cape and point of land that on the Westerne side was about seven or eight leagues from us, to see which way it did bend, and being within halfe a league of it, wee sawe two companies of boates of wilde men going from one land to the other: their boates were in number about fourtie or fiftie. One part of the which came to the said point, and a great number of the men went on shore making a great noise, beckening unto us that wee should come on land, shewing us certaine skinnes upon pieces of wood, but because we had but one onely boat, wee would not goe to them, but went to the other side lying in the Sea: they seeing

Song from Miguel Leon Portilla, ed., *The Broken Spears: The Aztec Account of the Conquest of Mexico,* 1962, p. 149. Reprinted by permission of Beacon Press.

us flee, prepared two of their boats to follow us, with which came also five more of them that were comming from the Sea side, all which approched neere unto our boate, dancing, and making many signes of joy and mirth, as it were desiring our friendship, saying in their tongue Napeu tondamen assurtah, with many other words that we understood not. But because (as we have said) we had but one boat, wee would not stand to their courtesie, but made signes unto them that they should turne back, which they would not do, but with great furie came toward us: and suddenly with their boates compassed us about: and because they would not away from us by any signes that we could make, we shot off two pieces among them, which did so terrifie them, that they put themselves to flight toward the sayde point, making a great noise: and having staid a while, they began anew, even as at the first to come to us againe, and being come neere out wee strucke at them with two lances, which thing was so great a terrour unto them, that with great hast they beganne to flee, and would no more follow us.

The next day part of the saide wilde men with nine of their boates came to the point and entrance of the Creeke, where we with our ships were at road. We being advertised of their comming, went to the point where they were with our boates: but so soone as they saw us, they began to flee, making signes that they came to trafique with us, shewing us, such skinnes as they cloth themselves withall, which are of small value. We likewise made signes unto them, that we wished them no evill: and in signe thereof two of our men ventured to go on land to them, and cary them knives with other Iron wares, and a red hat to give unto their Captaine. Which when they saw, they also came on land, and brought some of their skinnes, and so began to deale with us, seeming to be very glad to have our iron wares and other things, stil dancing with many other ceremonies, as with their hands to cast Sea water on their heads. They gave us whatsoever they had, not keeping any thing, so that they were constrained to goe backe againe naked, and made us signes that the next day they would come againe, and bring more skinnes with them. . . .

Arthur Barlowe Describes His Hospitable Reception by Virginia Indians, 1584

. . . After [the Indians] had bene divers times aboord our shippes, my selfe, with seven more, went twentie mile into the River, that runneth toward the Citie of Skicoake, which River they call Occam: and the evening following, we came to an Island, which they call Roanoak, distant from the harbour by which we entred, seven leagues: and at the North ende thereof, was a village of nine houses, built of Cedar, and fortified round about with sharpe trees, to keepe out their enemies, and the entrance into it made it like a turne pike very artificially: when we came towards it, standing neere unto the waters side, the wife of Grangyno, the Kings brother, came running out to meete us very cheerefully, and friendly, her husband was not then in the village: some of her people she commanded to drawe our boate on the shoare, for the beating of the billoe: others shee appointed to carry us on their backes to the dry ground, and others to bring our oares into the house, for feare of stealing. When we were come into the utter roome, having five roomes in her house, she caused us to sitte downe by a great fire, and after tooke off our clothes, and washed them, and dried them againe: some of the women pulled off our stockings, and washed them, some washed our feete in warme water, and shee her selfe tooke great paines to see all thinges ordered in the best manner shee coulde, making great haste to dresse some meate for us to eate.

After we had thus dried our selves, shee brought us into the inner roome, where shee set on the boord standing along the house, some wheate like furmentie, sodden [boiled] Venison, and roasted, fishe sodden, boyled, and roasted, Melons rawe, and sodden, rootes of divers kindes, and divers fruites: their drinke is commonly water, but while the grape lasteth, they drinke wine, and for want of caskes to keepe it all the yeere after, they drinke water, but it is sodden with Ginger in it, and blacke Sinamon, and sometimes Sassaphras, and divers other wholesome, and medicinable hearbes and trees. We were entertained with all love, and kindnes, and with as much bountie, after their manner, as they could possibly devise. Wee found the people most gentle, loving, and faithfull, void of all guile, and treason, and such as lived after the manner of the golden age. The earth bringeth foorth all things in aboundance, as in the first creation, without toile or labour. The people onely care to defend them selves from the cold, in their short winter, and to feede themselves with such meate as the soile affoordeth: their meate is very well sodden, and they make broth very sweete, and savorie: their vessels are earthen pots, very large, white, and sweete: their dishes are woodden platters of sweete timber: within the place where they feede, was their lodging, and within that their Idoll, which they worship, of which they speake uncredible things. While we were at meate, there came in at the gates, two or three men with their bowes, and arrowes, from hunting, whome when we espied, we beganne to looke one towardes another, and offered to reach our weapons: but assoone as she espied our mistrust, she was very much mooved, and caused some of her men to runne out, and take away their bowes, and arrowes, and breake them, and withall beate the poore fellowes out of the gate againe. When we departed in the evening, and would not tarry all night, she was very sorie, and gave us into our boate our supper halfe dressed, pots, and all, and brought us to our boates side, in which wee laye all night, remooving the same a pretie distance from the shoare: shee perceiving our jealousie, was much grieved, and sent divers men, and thirtie women, to sitte all night on the bankes side by us, and sent us into our boates five mattes to cover us from the rayne, using very many wordes to intreate us to rest in their houses: but because wee were fewe men, and if wee had miscarried, the voyage had beene in very great daunger, wee durst not adventure any thing, although there was no cause of doubt: for a more kinde, and loving people, there can not be found in the world, as farre as we have hitherto had triall. . . .

William Bradford on Samoset, Squanto, Massasoit, and the Pilgrims, 1620

. . . All this while the Indians came skulking about them, and would sometimes show them selves aloofe of, but when any aproached near them, they would rune away. And once they stoale away their tools wher they had been at worke, & were gone to diner. But about the 16. *of March* a certaine Indian came bouldly amongst them, and spoke to them in broken English, which they could well understand, but marvelled at it. At length they understood by discourse with him, that he was not of these parts, but belonged to the eastrene parts, wher some English-ships came to fhish, with whom he was aquainted, & could name sundrie of them by their names, amongst whom he had gott his language. He became profitable to them in aquainting them with many things concerning the state of the cuntry in the east-parts wher he lived, which was afterwards profitable unto them; as also of the people hear, of their names, number, & strength; of their situation & distance from this place, and who was cheefe amongst them. His name was *Samaset;* he tould them also of another Indian whos name was *Squanto,* a native of this place, who had been in England & could speake better English then him selfe. Being, after some time of entertainmente & gifts, dismist, a while after he came againe, & 5. more with him, & they brought againe all the tooles that were stolen away before, and made way for the coming of their great Sachem, called *Massosoyt;* who, about 4. or 5. *days after,* came with the cheefe of his friends & other attendance, with the aforesaid *Squanto.* With whom, after frendly entertainment, & some gifts given him, they made a peace with him (which hath now continued this 24. years) in these terms.

1. That neither he nor any of his, should injurie or doe hurte to any of their peopl.
2. That if any of his did any hurte to any of theirs, he should send the offender, that they might punish him.
3. That if any thing were taken away from any of theirs, he should cause it to be restored; and they should doe the like to his.
4. If any did unjustly warr against him, they would aide him; if any did warr against them, he should aide them.
5. He should send to his neighbours confederats, to certifie them of this, that they might not wrong them, but might be likewise comprised in the conditions of peace.
6. That when ther men came to them, they should leave their bows & arrows behind them.

After these things he returned to his place caled *Sowams,* some 40. mile from this place, but *Squanto* continued with them, and was their interpreter, and was a spetiall instrument sent of God for their good beyond their expectation. He directed them how to set their corne, wher to take fish, and to procure other comodities, and was also their pilott to bring them to unknowne places for their profitt, and never left them till he dyed. He was a *native of this place,* & scarce any left alive besids him self. He was caried away with diverce others by one *Hunt,* a Mr. of a ship, who thought to sell them for slaves in Spaine; but he got away for England, and was entertained by a marchante in London, & imployed to New-found-land & other parts, & lastly brought hither into these parts by one Mr. *Dermer,* a gentle-man imployed by Sr. Ferdinando Gorges & others, for discovery, & other designes in these parts. . . .

◈ *E S S A Y S*

It is difficult—some would argue impossible—to reconstruct the motivations of American Indians in the era of their first contact with Europeans. Native people and Europeans seldom spoke each other's languages; and even after this problem was rectified, they still understood the world in different ways. How, then, can we begin to understand these crucial early decades of mutual discovery? In the first essay, McGill University anthropologist Bruce G. Trigger examines two different views of Indian behavior— "romantic" and "rationalist." Using historical evidence from early-contact events, Trigger argues that Indians acted rationally, often out of economic interest. But are these the only ways that the evidence can be interpreted? And are Indian motives so easily divided into romantic and rationalist categories? In the second essay, historian James H. Merrell of Vassar College takes a longer look at the Catawbas' encounter with the English and Africans in Virginia. Merrell traces the Catawbas' profound and subtle adaptations in a rapidly changing new world. How does the Catawba experience square with the ideas that Trigger elucidates?

Early Native North American Responses to European Contact

BRUCE G. TRIGGER

> No treatment of primitive economics could be complete without some consideration of the religious factor, however brief it may be. . . . It will serve our purpose here if we bear in mind the fact that the efficacy of an implement, for example, was determined by factors which operated from beyond the material world.

The approaching quincentenary of Christopher Columbus's arrival in the Caribbean is stimulating much discussion about how the native peoples of the New World perceived and reacted to European intruders during the sixteenth century. This occurs as both history and anthropology are being strongly influenced by the resurgence of cultural relativism, which accords to the beliefs transmitted within specific cultures a preeminent role as determinants of human behavior. This view has challenged and largely eclipsed the rationalist claim that human behavior is shaped mainly by calculations of individual self-interest that are uniform from one culture to another. Studies of how native peoples perceived the first Europeans they encountered will probably be strongly influenced by this shift in emphasis. I wish to investigate in this paper whether it is sound to assign cultural relativism a dominant role in the discussion of this issue. To answer that question, I will examine the conflicting claims of cultural relativists and rationalists and the utility of each position for interpreting the historical evidence. I will seek to demonstrate that, while cultural beliefs may have significantly influenced Indian reactions in the early stages of their encounters with Europeans, in the long run rationalist calculations came to play a preponderant role, and I will document how this cognitive reorganization occurred.

"Early Native North American Responses to European Contact: Romantic Versus Rationalistic Interpretations," by Bruce Trigger, *Journal of American History* 77 (March 1991), pp. 1195–1215. Reprinted by permission of the publisher.

Great caution is required in discussing this issue, since only a small corpus of documents furnishes eyewitness accounts of contacts between native North Americans and Europeans during the sixteenth century. Whole classes of encounters that must have been very frequent, such as those involving European fishermen and whalers along the east coast of Canada, went almost unrecorded. Even the most detailed accounts of North American exploration and settlement provide few data from which native perceptions and motives can reliably be inferred. There is nothing comparable to the detailed accounts of the conquests of Mexico and Peru that were written not only by Spanish participants but also by native witnesses and their mestizo descendants. Even in these cases, however, one cannot help suspecting that the native American evidence was strongly colored by a desire to please Europeans. Moreover, all of these historical records are stereotyped in various ways that must be understood before they can be used reliably as historical documents. The archaeological record for the sixteenth century in North America also remains poorly understood. While future findings will prove highly informative about changes in population, settlement patterns, and material culture, archaeology alone is unlikely to reveal much about native American perceptions and feelings. This lack of precise information about so many topics has long invited scholars to impose their own preconceptions on the data, a situation that is likely to continue.

Alternative Approaches

The most persistent manifestation of these preconceptions has been the conflict between romantic and rationalist explanations of human behavior. For over two centuries the romantic approach has emphasized contingently variable cultural patterns as the principal determinants of human behavior, while rationalism has assigned the major role to practical, or universal, human reason. On first inspection, these two views would appear to be complementary rather than antithetical. Although the varied behavior of different groups often appears to reflect idiosyncratic cultural premises, few scholars would deny that rational calculation plays a significant role in human behavior.

Yet the dichotomy between these two positions is intensified by the alignment of romanticism with an idealist epistemology while rationalism is identified with a materialistic one. Even Karl Marx's seemingly accommodating observation, "Human beings make their history . . . not under circumstances chosen by themselves . . . but broadly encountered, given, and transmitted from the past," is ultimately committed to a materialistic epistemology and hence primarily to a rationalistic rather than a romantic view of human behavior.

The long-term alliances between idealism and romanticism and between materialism and rationalism are not historical accidents. Reason always serves some end. It may be used to promote goals that are wholly determined by the idiosyncrasies of a specific cultural system. Alternatively, it may allow the pursuit of more practical goals that sustain or alter a society's relationship to the physical world and that create new patterns for the production, distribution, and control of matter, energy, and information. While no process of reasoning occurs independently of culture, practical reason has the capacity to transcend culture. By mutual agreement the universalistic processes are termed rationalistic, and the privileg-ing of them constitutes the basis of a materialistic view of human behavior. Some societies clearly are more consciously oriented toward such a privileging of prac-tical reason than are others.

Anthropologists agree that individuals are born into cultural traditions that have been shaped by centuries of development, and each of which is unique in many respects. They also acknowledge that cultural traditions are "sense-making systems," systems that shape people's perceptions and values and hence influ-ence their reactions to new experiences in important ways. More extreme ver-sions of cultural relativism maintain that cultural patterns determine human be-havior and view individuals as conceptually trapped within specific cultural traditions. These ideas have their roots within the German tradition of romanti-cism, which began in the eighteenth century; they were transmitted to American anthropology by Franz Boas. Through the advocacy of Victor Turner, Clifford Geertz, and Marshall D. Sahlins, the romantic approach has acquired enormous influence among American anthropologists in the last two decades. The study of behavior has been directed toward the investigation of beliefs and values, and there has been a growing fascination with structuralism, semiotics, hermeneutics, deconstructionism, and radical forms of relativism that deny the possibility of any objective understanding of human behavior. Each of these has played a signifi-cant role in making ideas, rather than behavior, appear to be the starting point for understanding human beings. Sahlins has also played a leading role in the appli-cation of a romantic approach to the study of early contact between Europeans and non-Europeans.

The major alternative to this romantic view is the rationalistic philosophy that anthropology borrowed from the French Enlightenment. It stresses the uni-versality of human nature and maintains that through the exercise of reason human groups at the same general level of development will respond in a similar way to the same kinds of challenges. Rationalists recognize that many of the problems that confront large hierarchical societies are radically different from those that must be resolved by small-scale ones. While this evolutionary perspec-tive implies that the problems that must be solved change as societies become more complex, it does not posit that the basic methods for doing this change. Instead a rationalist approach sees the ability to calculate that is common to all human beings as playing a major role in shaping the behavior of all human groups and posits that on the basis of such calculations the most important cultural vari-ations and changes can be explained.

The most widely applied of these concepts is the "principle of least effort," which underlies many explanations of economic, ecological, and locational be-havior. Game theory provides principles for exploring the management of risk and uncertainty. On the other hand, more specific formulations, such as that of "economic man," although widely applied, have proved much more controver-sial. In the late nineteenth and early twentieth centuries, racists believed that "primitive" groups were biologically less capable of rational thought and behav-ior than were "civilized" ones; but anthropologists, both before and since, have stressed the equal intelligence and rational capacity of all human groups. Ratio-nalism underlies all modern cultural evolutionary approaches, which emphasize the uniformity of cultures at the same level of development regardless of the cultural traditions to which they belong. It is also congenial to a materialistic interpretation of human behavior, which assumes that human beings are likely to be most calculating, and hence least culture-bound, with respect to those matters that relate most directly to their material well-being. Although this approach exerted great influence on American anthropology after World War II through the neoevolutionism of Leslie White, Julian Steward, Morton H. Fried, Elman R. Service, and Marvin Harris, its influence has waned in recent years as romanticism has grown increasingly popular.

This debate, while central to anthropology, creates many problems for the majority of anthropologists who are not directly engaged in it. Most of them seek to avoid becoming partisans in a simplistic confrontation between rationalism and cultural relativism. They acknowledge persuasive arguments on both sides but suggest that little is to be gained by drawing too hard and fast a distinction between the "traditional" and the "rational" or that the relative significance of these factors may vary from case to case and hence may be difficult and not very productive to generalize about. Many argue that, especially in spheres of human activity relating to ecology, technology, and the economy, rational calculations involving universal considerations of efficiency and practicality play a more important role than do culturally constrained perceptions of reality, while cultural traditions may play a more important role in determining the content of religious beliefs. While there is much to be said in favor of these observations, they remain at too general a level to constitute an effective alternative position.

There is also considerable uncertainty about what kinds of evidence offer support for a rationalist or a relativist position. This can best be illustrated with an example from the literature on the fur trade, where it is widely assumed that the historical demonstration that native people continued to perceive their trade relations with Europeans much as they had understood exchanges of goods or sharing of resources among themselves prior to European contact supports a relativist rather than a rationalist position. Yet it can be demonstrated that in at least some instances this was not so. Eighteenth-century Hudson's Bay Company officials, who were used to optimizing market strategies, were puzzled that the native people of subarctic Canada traded fewer furs when they were offered higher prices for them. In modern times historians and economists have concluded that in traditional Indian cultures economic behavior was so embedded in social and political activities that it precluded "economic rationality" after contact with Europeans.

More recently, however, it has been recognized that, because there was a limit to the amount of goods that nomadic hunters could carry about with them, it made sense for native traders to collect fewer furs when those were sufficient to satisfy their needs. Under these circumstances, minimizing effort made more sense than maximizing profits. While cultural considerations no doubt played a significant role in influencing the manner in which native Americans and Europeans perceived the fur trade, these rational calculations conform to a logic that is universal rather than culturally specific. This argument is especially persuasive when native cultures that initially had similar subsistence economies but different trading practices are found to have adopted the same fur-trading patterns.

The problem that confronts historians and anthropologists is not simply to agree that relativistic and rational factors both play roles in human behavior but to determine what roles and how those factors fit together in the larger totality of behavior. Romantics tend to believe that early contact between Europeans and native Americans can best be explained as an interaction between cultures, or more specifically between mentalities. In the words of Tzvetan Todorov, contact was primarily "the discovery *self* makes of the *other*." For rationalists such relations can be accounted for more effectively in terms of economic and political considerations. All of these factors were at work in concrete situations; what is disputed is which, if either, of them more effectively determined what happened. This is not a matter of analytical preference; it addresses fundamental issues concerning the nature of human behavior and how cultural change comes about.

In the rest of this paper, I will attempt to assess the relative value of romantic and rationalist approaches for explaining the behavior of native North Americans in their earliest encounters with Europeans. In encountering Europeans after 1492, native Americans experienced novel challenges of both a practical and a cognitive sort. They clearly had well-established traditions of intertribal diplomacy, which guided their relations with neighboring groups. These traditions combined rationalistic calculations with culturally influenced objectives. At the same time, each culture possessed beliefs about the creation and nature of the universe that, while having adaptive significance, were far more independently determined by cultural traditions than were aspects of culture that were subjected to practical application on a regular basis. With the exception of sporadic contacts with the Norse in Newfoundland and the eastern Arctic, none of the native Americans had ever previously had to deal with anything like the bearded, white-skinned beings who began haunting their seacoasts. The latter's huge ships, abundant metal goods, brightly colored clothes, and thundering guns and cannons placed them in a different category from any known or imaginable native group. So too did the extreme self-confidence and arrogance with which the Europeans frequently conducted themselves. How were native peoples to interpret such strangers as they appeared with increasing frequency along their coasts, giving away trinkets, carrying off native people, and leaving behind unknown diseases, before coming into closer contact as shipwrecked sailors, traders, would-be conquerors, and finally settlers?

First Perceptions

Indian folk traditions, often recorded generations after the events occurred, suggest that native North Americans believed the first European ships they saw to be floating islands inhabited by supernatural spirits and sometimes covered by white clouds (sails) from which lightning and thunder (cannons) were discharged, or else the mobile dwelling places of powerful spirits whom they prepared to welcome with sacrifices, food, and entertainment. These stories indicate that there was much about Europeans that offered itself to supernatural interpretation in terms of native religious concepts.

European records of early contacts with native Americans appear to corroborate the claim that in numerous instances native people interpreted the newcomers as supernatural. The Spanish who explored the settled the Caribbean islands in the late fifteenth century were convinced that native beliefs in their divinity were a source of power that they could use to control these people. In 1492 Christopher Columbus concluded that the inhabitants of the Bahamas believed that he had come from the sky. The Spanish recounted natives holding prisoners under water to determine whether Europeans were immortal. Accounts derived from Spanish and Aztec sources provide detailed descriptions of how native religious beliefs played a major role in the subjugation of one of the most populous and complex societies in the New World by a handful of European intruders. The Aztec ruler Moctezuma Xocoyotzin's fears that Hernán Cortés might be the god Quetzalcoatl returning to rule Mexico caused him not to resist the Spanish invasion directly. This in turn facilitated the collapse of the Aztec tributary system and the eventual conquest of their city-state and all of Mexico. It is also clear that Cortés surmised the general nature of Moctezuma's fears and exploited them to his own advantage.

The accounts of the explorations of Jacques Cartier, Álvar Núñez Cabeza de Vaca, and Hernando de Soto described isolated instances when the Indians brought the sick of their communities to them and requested that they heal them. This suggests that these leaders were regarded as powerful shamans, if not as divinities, by native peoples in widely separated parts of North America. Native people are also reported to have worshiped and brought offerings to crosses erected by Francisco Vázquez de Coronado in what was to be the southwestern United States and to a large stone column put up by Jean Ribault in Florida, although it is possible that at least in the Southwest such behavior was motivated more by political than by religious considerations. The account of Francis Drake's voyage to California in 1579 describes the Coast Miwoks as offering sacrifices and lacerating their faces in the presence of the English visitors, despite the latter's efforts to make them stop. In 1587 English colonists in Virginia reported that because Indians had died of illness in each town they had passed through while they themselves had not become sick, they were viewed as the spirits of the dead returning to human society.

Similar incidents continued to be reported on the frontiers of European exploration in North America. Kenneth Morrison believes that early in their encounters the Abenakis (of what is now northern New England) inferred from European behavioral patterns that the Europeans might be the cannibal giants of their mythology. Jean Nicollet was said to have struck terror into the Winnebagos (or some other tribe of the upper Great Lakes region), who believed him to be a thunder spirit when he visited them in 1634. In 1670 Father Claude Allouez was treated as a *manitou* (spirit) when he visited the Mascoutens and Miamis on the shores of the Wolf River in Wisconsin. They made an offering of tobacco and appealed to him for relief from famine and disease. It is recorded that the Ojibwas of Red Lake, Minnesota, thought the first airplane they saw to be a thunderbird, or storm spirit, and rushed to the shore of the lake when it landed in order to throw tobacco offerings on the water.

Europeans were prepared to exploit North American Indian beliefs in their supernatural powers. Sometimes the deaths of early European explorers and settlers were concealed in the hope that Indians might continue to believe that they were immortal. In the course of their *entrada* into what is now the southeastern United States, de Soto and his followers, drawing upon their experiences in Mexico and Peru, claimed that he was the Child of the Sun and in that capacity had a claim upon the obedience of local chiefs.

Many cultural relativists assume that these scattered pieces of evidence provide insights into how native North Americans generally perceived Europeans in the early stages of their encounter. They take it for granted that similar culturally conditioned beliefs determined native responses in many other instances of early contact, but that such beliefs either were less obvious or failed to be recorded by less sensitive or less interested European observers. This is a highly suppositious conclusion. Moreover, most of the native accounts of what happened were recorded long after the event, and many are clearly influenced by European values and religious concepts. While detailed ethnographic analysis has revealed undeniably traditional elements in some of these tales, it is dangerous to overgeneralize from them about how native peoples first perceived Europeans, especially when we consider the great variability in specific beliefs from one culture to another.

The total corpus of documentary evidence that religious beliefs played an important and widespread role in influencing native behavior is in fact very limited. For the most part, native American relations with Europeans are portrayed as having been governed by relatively straightforward concerns with exchange and defense. While some of the survivors of the Pánfilo de Narváez expedition found roles for themselves as shamans and traders among the hunter-gatherers of Texas, perhaps because they were not equipped to play an effective part in subsistence activities, hundreds of shipwrecked Spanish sailors were enslaved by chiefs in Florida. Did this plethora of prosaic accounts result from many European recorders failing to understand Indian behavior? The written historical evidence is inadequate to supply a definitive answer. In those cases where religious behavior is specifically ascribed to native people in sixteenth-century accounts, there is the equally difficult problem of the extent to which European observers uncritically ascribed their own ethnocentric views about non-Christian religious beliefs to native people, thereby either misinterpreting their actions or ascribing religious motives to them in situations where those did not apply.

Fortunately, evidence concerning those native beliefs is not limited to historical records. In recent years George Hamell has carried out an extensive analysis of the basic concepts underlying the traditional religious beliefs of the Algonquian-, Iroquoian-, and Siouan-speaking peoples of northeastern North America, using ethnographic data recorded from earliest European contact to the present day. He concludes that the cosmologies of these peoples equated certain natural materials with physical, spiritual, and social well-being, both during this life and after death. These substances included marine shell, white and red metals (native silver and copper), and white, green, and red crystals and other kinds of stones. Such substances, which came from beneath the earth and water, were associated with such supernatural beings as the horned serpent, panther, and dragon, who were the guardian spirits and patrons of animal medicine societies.

These concepts appear to explain the inclusion of objects made from marine shell, native copper, and rock crystal in native burials of the Eastern Woodlands in prehistoric times. Archaeological evidence of the continuity of these burial practices from the Archaic period to the historical era suggests a persistence of these beliefs for over six thousand years, although intertribal exchanges of shell, copper, and other materials had been at one of their periodic low ebbs in the centuries preceding European contact. Hamell further suggests that the Indians equated European copper, brass, and tin with native copper and silver and equated glass beads with crystals and colored rocks. Because the Europeans possessed such extraordinarily large amounts of metalware and glass beads and came from across the ocean, where in Indian cosmology mythical time and space converged, they were regarded as supernatural beings or the returning spirits of the dead.

Hamell's ideas may account for the historically attested interest of native groups in European copper, brass, and tin objects and in glass beads. They would also explain why copper and brass kettles were cut into tiny fragments and dispersed by exchange among the tribes of the Northern Woodlands during the sixteenth century and why most of these goods are found in burials rather than in abandoned living sites during this period. The renewed emphasis on securing objects made of ritually important substances and burying them with the dead would also account for the increasing intertribal exchange of marine shell during this period. Although marine shell was a North American product, it was as important as copper or crystals in native religious beliefs, and Europeans never provided a satisfactory substitute for it.

In the course of the sixteenth century, the increasing availability of European goods led to greater emphasis in much of eastern North America on east-west exchange patterns, which in some areas superseded the predominantly north-south ones of earlier periods. European goods may also have brought about major changes in native life. The final expansion of the Huron confederacy and the coming together of all the Huron tribes in a small area at the southeastern corner of Georgian Bay (of Lake Huron) by the end of the sixteenth century seems to have been motivated primarily by a desire to have access to the secure trade routes leading by way of Lake Nipissing and the Ottawa River to the St. Lawrence Valley, rather than simply by a need to place more distance between themselves and hostile Iroquoian groups to the south and east. Before Hamell began his research, I had observed that "in the Indian history of [the northeastern Woodlands], trading in exotic goods has often played a role that was out of all proportion to its utilitarian significance" and that "what appears in the archaeological record as a few scraps of metal seems in fact to have been a sufficient catalyst to realize certain potentials for development that were inherent in prehistoric Huron society, but which otherwise might never have come to fruition."

Hamell's research, while neither finished nor free from controversy, suggests that a combination of ethnographic and archaeological data may provide significant insights into how native people perceived Europeans and European goods in the early stages of their interaction. This in turn may assist in interpreting the limited historical texts that are available concerning contact in the sixteenth century. While there may have been considerable variability in the manner in which different native groups interpreted the first Europeans they encountered, the archaeological and ethnographic evidence that Hamell has assembled also suggests that throughout eastern North America there were numerous culturally shared religious beliefs that encouraged native peoples to attribute various supernatural powers to the Europeans.

Seventeenth-Century Pragmatism

In any discussion of how native peoples perceived Europeans, the far more abundant data from the seventeenth century are of vital importance. If native beliefs continued to play a preponderant role in determining native reactions to Europeans so long after first contact, it would reinforce the assumption that they had done so during the previous century. Recent historical and ethnographic research has challenged established rationalistic interpretations of native dealings with Europeans during the seventeenth century. In particular, a growing commitment to romantic and cultural relativist explanations of human behavior has led an increasing number of historians and anthropologists to reject the proposition that European goods had more than symbolic value to native peoples so long as their societies maintained any semblance of independence from European control. Hamell states that he looks to "Northeastern Woodland Indian myth for an explanation of . . . their history during the two centuries following European contact." Calvin Martin has attracted a wide audience with his thinly documented claim that the fur trade developed, not as a result of native peoples' needing or especially desiring European goods, but as a by-product of their declaring war on fur-bearing animals and seeking to exterminate them because they held animal spirits to be responsible for the epidemics of European diseases that had begun in the sixteenth century. William Eccles portrays native cultures as economically independent, resilient, and able to determine their own destinies at least until the British conquest of New France in 1760. Conrad Heidenreich argues more specifically that "it is doubtful . . . that the Huron maintained their relations with the French because they had become economically dependent on European goods." He claims that they had instead become militarily dependent on the French for protection against the Iroquois.

These arguments ignore a solid body of evidence that by the beginning of the seventeenth century the bulk of trade between Europeans and Indians was not in glass beads, other ornaments, and liquor. The first Indians who traded with Europeans may have hung metal axes and hoes on their chests as ornaments and used stockings as tobacco pouches. Yet, by the 1620s, the Montagnais at Tadoussac, near the mouth of the St. Lawrence River, were using large quantities of clothing, hatchets, iron arrowheads, needles, sword blades, ice picks, knives, kettles, and preserved foods that they purchased from the French. For some purposes, especially in wet weather, woolen clothing proved superior to their traditional skin garments. They had also ceased to manufacture birchbark baskets and stone axes. In the 1630s, the Mohawks, who lived close to the Dutch traders at Fort Orange (now Albany), continued to produce their own food but were purchasing a wide range of clothing and metalware from Europeans. By the early 1640s, they owned more than three hundred guns, which had been paid for partly with skins they had seized from neighboring tribes. The Hurons, who lived much farther inland and had considerable transportation problems, were more selective in their purchases of European goods. They were primarily interested in obtaining metal cutting tools. In particular they wanted knives of all sizes, axes, and iron arrowheads. They also purchased guns, when the French were willing to sell them, and copper and brass kettles. The latter were easier to transport than their heavy and fragile clay cooking pots, and when they were worn out, they could be cut up and used as raw material to manufacture metal arrowheads and cutting tools as well as ornaments. In addition, Huron traders carried home glass beads and metal brace-lets, which weighed relatively little. They do not appear to have purchased much cloth or many items of clothing, and unlike the coastal tribes, they did not seek alcoholic beverages when they came to trade. In selecting European goods, the Hurons showed a marked preference for tools with cutting edges that were supe-rior to their own and that replaced native implements such as stone axes that took a long time to manufacture.

Among the Huron, Iroquois, and other Iroquoian-speaking peoples, a stone-and bone-based technology did not completely disappear until the late seven-teenth century, which is later than G. T. Hunt and some archaeologists have be-lieved. They also continued to manufacture pottery vessels until then, and the arrival of metal cutting tools seems to have resulted in a florescence of bone working. Yet, well before 1650, there was a marked decline in the frequency of stone tools among these groups. This suggests that by 1636 the Hurons were suf-ficiently dependent on the French for metal cutting tools that one of their chiefs, Aenons, was not exaggerating when he said that if his people "should remain two years without going down to Quebec to trade, they would find themselves re-duced to such extremities that they might consider themselves fortunate to join with the Algonquins and to embark in their canoes." It is clear from the context of this report that Aenons was referring to the necessity of securing European goods, not to maintaining a military alliance against the Iroquois.

From the first arrival of the Jesuit missionaries in the 1620s, the Hurons and their neighbors regarded them as shamans. Beginning in the late 1630s, many Indians concluded that these priests were sorcerers or malevolent spirits, who were responsible for the great epidemics of European diseases that afflicted the native people of the region at that time. The Indians probably also continued to believe that the French, who were able to manufacture such large quantities of metal goods, must possess great supernatural power. Yet in their eyes this did not make Europeans intrinsically different from the Indians, who were also able to practice witchcraft and whose amulets and relations with appropriate spirits en-abled them to hunt, fish, and move about on snowshoes and in canoes more effec-tively than Europeans did. Ordinary Frenchmen who traded, traveled, lived with Indian families, and even intermarried with them were viewed as regular human beings. They had been observed to become ill and die, and a few of them had even been killed by the Indians. The slowness of most Europeans to master native lan-guages and skills led by many Indians to conclude that on the whole Europeans were slow-witted, which accorded with the traditional Iroquoian belief that hairy people were unintelligent.

The Indians were also appalled by what they saw as the greed, violence, and bad manners of the French, which all were recognizable, if negatively valued, patterns of human behavior. Huron chiefs felt confident of their ability to outwit and manipulate French traders and officials, even when they were becoming politically and economically reliant on them. All of this suggests that by the seventeenth century the fur-trading peoples of the northern Woodlands regarded most, if not all, Europeans as human beings who were different from themselves and in some respects more powerful, but with whom they could interact on a normal basis.

Cognitive Reorganization

It is thus evident that at some point those native groups that initially reacted to Europeans primarily on the basis of their traditional religious beliefs came to regard Europeans as human beings with whom, while continuing to take account of their special customs and sensibilities, they could do business as they did with any other foreign group. The Indians' increasing familiarity with Europeans led to a "cognitive reorganization" in which the rational component inherent in the mental processes of every human being began to play the dominant role in guiding native relations with Europeans, while religious beliefs ceased to play the important part that in many cases they had done in the early stages of the encounter. The key factor in bringing about this transformation was the Indians' observation and rational evaluation of European behavior. This development accords with the general principle that whenever culturally transmitted beliefs are employed to guide human behavior, they are subject to rational scrutiny on the basis of the resulting performance; where those beliefs encourage counterproductive behavior, the evaluation may result in their being rejected, revised, or judged inapplicable. In the case of early encounters between Indians and Europeans, the question remains: Under what circumstances did this cognitive reorganization occur?

Some answers are provided by historical data from the early sixteenth century. When Giovanni da Verrazzano visited the relatively sheltered Narragansetts of southern New England in 1524, he found them anxious to obtain blue beads as well as bells and other trinkets made of copper. They were not interested in steel or iron objects, mirrors, or cloth. This suggests that these Indians were interested only in objects that had precise counterparts in their traditional system of belief and exchange. By contrast, Indians living farther north along the coast of Maine, who presumably had more contact with European fishermen and their goods (they were wearing European copper beads in their ears), were far less trustful of Verrazzano and his crew and would take in exchange for their goods only "knives, fish-hooks, and sharp metal." Likewise, the Micmacs that Jacques Cartier encountered in Chaleur Bay in 1534 not only indicated very clearly that they wished to barter their furs with the French but also sought hatchets, knives, and other ironware, as well as beads, in exchange. The following year the Iroquoians of Hochelaga, on Montreal Island, seemed pleased with any European goods that Cartier gave them, while those who lived at Stadacona, within the limits of modern Quebec City, and who appear already to have had limited access to European goods being traded by Breton fishermen at the Strait of Belle Isle, sought hatchets, knives, and awls from the French, as well as beads and other trinkets.

While the more isolated Hochelagans brought their sick to Cartier for him to heal, the Stadaconans, on being informed by two of their boys (whom Cartier had kidnapped and taken to France the previous year) that the goods he was trading were of little value in his own country, demanded more of those goods in exchange from the French. At the same time it was the Stadaconans who cured Cartier's crew of the scurvy that was afflicting them. Cartier had attempted to conceal their sickness and deaths among his men, not because he believed the Stadaconans thought the French to be immortal, but because he feared they might attack if they realized how defenseless these intruders were. Soon after Cartier's visit, a large quantity of ironware was reported being taken to the Strait of Belle Isle to trade for furs.

These data indicate that while groups such as the Narragansetts of Rhode Island and the Hochelagans of the upper St. Lawrence (who were remote from European fishermen at Cape Breton and the Strait of Belle Isle) were pleased to secure glass beads and copper and tin trinkets, bands that lived closer to these trading areas were anxious to obtain metal cutting tools as early as the 1520s and 1530s. The latter groups also appear to have already adopted a naturalistic view of Europeans. This suggests that if many Indian groups initially viewed Europeans as supernatural beings, upon closer contact this interpretation was replaced by the conclusion that Europeans were human beings like themselves. At the same time, European metal cutting tools came to be universally valued for their utilitarian advantages. While iron knives may have performed no more efficiently than did stone hide scrapers, they cut better and were more durable and easier to keep sharp than were stone tools. Metal tools also performed better as perforators, needles, and projectile points than did the stone and bone tools the Indians had used theretofore. It was for practical reasons that coastal peoples soon were putting iron tools at the top of their shopping lists. Glass beads and scraps of copper continued to dominate the indirect trade with the interior, but by the beginning of the seventeenth century native groups living as far inland as the lower Great Lakes were seeking metal cutting tools in preference to all other European goods. . . .

These observations may help to interpret the records of other major encounters between Europeans and native North Americans in the early sixteenth century. The native rulers who lived in the path of de Soto's pillaging expedition through what is now the southeastern United States adopted various strategies to placate, deflect, defeat, or speed him on his way. Yet overwhelmingly they conducted their relations with him in terms of what must have been the normal idiom of intergroup diplomacy in that region of hierarchical societies. De Soto was treated as a powerful chief with whom an alliance might be desirable or submission inevitable, but only rarely was he recorded as having been approached as a shaman and asked to cure the sick. Moreover, on at least two occasions rulers pointedly rejected claims that he possessed supernatural powers, including the panic-stricken assertion by his successor Luis de Moscoso that de Soto had not died but gone to the sky for a few days to visit the gods. The Indian ruler of Guachoya, mocking the latter tale, promised to offer two human sacrifices in honor of de Soto—a tradition in that area at the burial of neighboring chiefs. It would appear that previous contacts with shipwrecked Spanish sailors, would-be conquerors such as Juan Ponce de León and Pánfilo de Narváez, and colonists such as Lucas Vázquez de Ayllón had provided the native people living on the periphery of this densely settled region with an opportunity to assess Europeans and that the results of their observations were transmitted inland through the diplomatic networks linking adjacent tribes and chiefdoms. Despite the devastating effects of the Spanish plundering and burning of their settlements, the Indians of what is now the southeastern United States quickly took advantage of new resources that were presented to them; hogs, for example, were soon being eaten.

The accounts of Coronado's *entrada* into the Southwest also describe a naturalistic evaluation of Europeans by native people, who at first ineffectually opposed the Spanish invaders and then resorted to accommodative responses until Spanish exactions provoked them to renewed overt and clandestine resistance. Trading contacts with the Indians of northern Mexico possibly provided them with the information necessary to understand in advance what kind of beings the Spanish and their horses were and how they were likely to behave. Echoes of perceptions surrounding the original encounter between the Spanish and Aztecs in central Mexico may have been heard in an allegedly fifty-year-old prophecy of the Pueblo Indians that strangers would come from the south and conquer them, although this prophecy did not stifle resistance as more deeply rooted cultural traditions had done with Moctezuma.

The available evidence for the sixteenth century suggests that, whatever the initial Indian understanding of Europeans, a relatively short period of direct contact between the two groups resulted in a naturalistic interpretation of the newcomers. It also led to a growing demand for some European tools, which were seen as allowing tasks to be performed more effectively than did traditional stone and bone tools. These shifts involved the Indians' rationally assessing the performance of persons and goods and a desire to adopt a technology that would reduce their expenditure of energy on some routine tasks and improve the quality of their products. This technology was adopted as soon as it became available on a regular basis, even though it rendered native groups reliant on European suppliers.

The first impressions that native peoples had of Europeans and the initial strategies that these peoples devised for dealing with them seem to have been strongly influenced by their traditional beliefs. In some situations these strategies crucially shaped relations between the two groups. Where contact remained limited or indirect, initial interpretations persisted without significant modification for long periods. As relations became more direct and intense, it appears that these interpretations were rapidly modified by rational assessments of what Europeans were like and what they had to offer. In at least some areas, these assessments spread inland ahead of European exploration. This appears to have happened more quickly in densely settled regions than in more thinly populated ones.

This utilitarian assessment of European technology does not mean that native people did not continue to assign their own social meanings to European goods or that native belief systems did not play a major role in determining how native people viewed Europeans or how European goods were used in religious contexts such as burials. On the contrary, there is evidence that basic native belief systems remained intact for long periods. This does not, however, rule out the importance of a rationalist perspective for understanding major aspects of native behavior, contrary to what more extreme relativists seek to maintain.

Conclusion

It is impossible to understand native American responses to their contact with Europeans in the early sixteenth century without a detailed knowledge of native cultures. Amerindian world views appear to have played an important role in structuring their initial understanding of these encounters, and this in turn influenced how native people behaved in these situations. The little that we know about these world views suggests that they varied from one region or ethnic group to another and that even adjacent, highly similar world views could, depending on historically contingent situations, structure native interpretations of contact in different ways. From the beginning some interpretations of Europeans were probably more "rational" than others.

Nevertheless, in areas where contact became frequent, it does not appear to have been long before all native perceptions and behavior were significantly influenced by rational appraisals of Europeans and what they had to offer. The long-term evidence indicates that economic determinists were not mistaken when they claimed that native people appreciated the material benefits to be derived from many items of European technology and that they sought to utilize this technology even at the cost of growing dependence upon their European trading partners. Native leaders also learned from observation to understand the motivations of the different European groups with whom they interacted and to devise strategies for coping with their demands. Native people were not constrained by their traditional beliefs to the extent that a rational assessment of the dangers and opportunities of the novel situations in which they found themselves was precluded. In general these assessments appear to have been strong enough to survive the psychological disruptions that must have accompanied the unprecedented epidemics of European diseases that afflicted native North Americans in the course of the sixteenth and seventeenth centuries.

If, in the long run, native people failed to devise strategies that could halt European aggression, it was not because they were unable to understand European behavior from a rational point of view. They failed because they were overwhelmed by European technological superiority, by growing numbers of European settlers as their own populations declined because of European diseases, and by increasing dependence upon European technology. They also failed because they were unable to modify their social organizations and values quickly enough to compete with the more disciplined European societies that were seeking to dominate and exploit North America. In North American Indian societies, decision making depended upon a slow process of achieving consensus, while European ones had evolved complex hierarchies of authority and command. Native groups therefore had less political maneuverability and less potential for concerted action when competing with Europeans. The creation of such structures, involving as it did the formation of new institutions and new patterns of behavior, was a slow process, even when the need for change was clearly perceived. Native societies became increasingly dependent upon European ones and were dominated by them because they lacked time to develop the human and material resources required to compete with them, not because of their incapacity to understand in rational terms what was happening to them.

Although the examples in this paper have been drawn from North America, these conclusions should apply equally to relations between European colonists and native groups elsewhere in the Americas and around the world. Giving due importance to a rationalist approach explains why in the course of the expansion of the European world system there has not been more variation in the basic patterns of relations between Europeans and native peoples, and why world systems formulations . . . are possible. Had relations between Europeans and native peoples been determined mainly by their respective ideologies, much more variation could be expected.

While cultural relativists have expanded our understanding of how in the beginning native reactions to Europeans were conditioned by their cultural beliefs, this approach must not undermine our appreciation of the ability of native people to monitor new situations and to devise strategies that allowed them to respond in a rational fashion to the opportunities as well as the disruptive challenges of a European presence. While the importance of native beliefs should never be underestimated, in the long run a rationalist and materialist analysis of cultural interaction seems to explain far more about what happened to native people following European contact than does an analysis that assigns primary explanatory power to their traditional beliefs.

The Indians' New World: The Catawba Experience

JAMES H. MERRELL

In August 1608 John Smith and his band of explorers captured an Indian named Amoroleck during a skirmish along the Rappahannock River. Asked why his men—a hunting party from towns upstream—had attacked the English, Amoroleck replied that they had heard the strangers "were a people come from under the world, to take their world from them." Smith's prisoner grasped a simple yet important truth that students of colonial America have overlooked: after 1492 native Americans lived in a world every bit as new as that confronting transplanted Africans or Europeans.

The failure to explore the Indians' new world helps explain why, despite many excellent studies of the native American past, colonial history often remains "a history of those men and women—English, European, and African—who transformed America from a geographical expression into a new nation." One reason Indians generally are left out may be the apparent inability to fit them into the new world theme, a theme that exerts a powerful hold on our historical imagination and runs throughout our efforts to interpret American development. From Frederick Jackson Turner to David Grayson Allen, from Melville J. Herskovits to Daniel C. Littlefield, scholars have analyzed encounters between peoples from the Old World and conditions in the New, studying the complex interplay between European or African cultural patterns and the American environment. Indians crossed no ocean, peopled no faraway land. It might seem logical to exclude them.

"The Indians' New World: The Catawba Experience," by James H. Merrell, *William and Mary Quarterly* 41 (1984), pp. 537–565. Reprinted with permission of the author.

The natives' segregation persists, in no small degree, because historians still tend to think only of the new world as the New World, a geographic entity bounded by the Atlantic Ocean on the one side and the Pacific on the other. Recent research suggests that process was as important as place. Many settlers in New England re-created familiar forms with such success that they did not really face an alien environment until long after their arrival. Africans, on the other hand, were struck by the shock of the new at the moment of their enslavement, well before they stepped on board ship or set foot on American soil. If the Atlantic was not a barrier between one world and another, if what happened to people was more a matter of subtle cultural processes than mere physical displacements, perhaps we should set aside the maps and think instead of a "world" as the physical and cultural milieu within which people live and a "new world" as a dramatically different milieu demanding basic changes in ways of life. Considered in these terms, the experience of natives was more closely akin to that of immigrants and slaves, and the idea of an encounter between worlds can—indeed, must—include the aboriginal inhabitants of America.

For American Indians a new order arrived in three distinct yet overlapping stages. First, alien microbes killed vast numbers of natives, sometimes before the victims had seen a white or black face. Next came traders who exchanged European technology for Indian products and brought natives into the developing world market. In time traders gave way to settlers eager to develop the land according to their own lights. These three intrusions combined to transform native existence, disrupting established cultural habits and requiring creative responses to drastically altered conditions. Like their new neighbors, then, Indians were forced to blend old and new in ways that would permit them to survive in the present without forsaking their past. By the close of the colonial era, native Americans as well as whites and blacks had created new societies, each similar to, yet very different from, its parent culture.

The range of native societies produced by this mingling of ingredients probably exceeded the variety of social forms Europeans and Africans developed. Rather than survey the broad spectrum of Indian adaptations, this article considers in some depth the response of natives in one area, the southern piedmont. Avoiding extinction and eschewing retreat, the Indians of the piedmont have been in continuous contact with the invaders from across the sea almost since the beginning of the colonial period, thus permitting a thorough analysis of cultural intercourse. Moreover, a regional approach embracing groups from South Carolina to Virginia can transcend narrow (and still poorly understood) ethnic or "tribal" boundaries without sacrificing the richness of detail a focused study provides.

Indeed, piedmont peoples had so much in common that a regional perspective is almost imperative. No formal political ties bound them at the onset of European contact, but a similar environment shaped their lives, and their adjustment to this environment fostered cultural uniformity. Perhaps even more important, these groups shared a single history once Europeans and Africans arrived on the scene. Drawn together by their cultural affinities and their common plight, after 1700 they migrated to the Catawba Nation, a cluster of villages along the border between the Carolinas that became the focus of native life in the region. Tracing the experience of these upland communities both before and after they joined the Catawbas can illustrate the consequences of contact and illuminate the process by which natives learned to survive in their own new world.

For centuries, ancestors of the Catawbas had lived astride important aboriginal trade routes and straddled the boundary between two cultural traditions, a position that involved them in a far-flung network of contacts and affected everything from potting techniques to burial practices. Nonetheless, Africans and Europeans were utterly unlike any earlier foreign visitors to the piedmont. Their arrival meant more than merely another encounter with outsiders; it marked an important turning point in Indian history. Once these newcomers disembarked and began to feel their way across the continent, they forever altered the course and pace of native development.

Bacteria brought the most profound disturbances to upcountry villages. When Hernando de Soto led the first Europeans into the area in 1540, he found large towns already "grown up in grass" because "there had been a pest in the land" two years before, a malady probably brought inland by natives who had visited distant Spanish posts. The sources are silent about other "pests" over the next century, but soon after the English began colonizing Carolina in 1670 the disease pattern became all too clear. Major epidemics struck the region at least once every generation—in 1698, 1718, 1738, and 1759—and a variety of less virulent illnesses almost never left native settlements.

Indians were not the only inhabitants of colonial America living—and dying—in a new disease environment. The swamps and lowlands of the Chesapeake were a deathtrap for Europeans, and sickness obliged colonists to discard or rearrange many of the social forms brought from England. Among native peoples long isolated from the rest of the world and therefore lacking immunity to pathogens introduced by the intruders, the devastation was even more severe. John Lawson, who visited the Carolina upcountry in 1701, when perhaps ten thousand Indians were still there, estimated that "there is not the sixth Savage living within two hundred Miles of all our Settlements, as there were fifty Years ago." The recent smallpox epidemic "destroy'd whole Towns," he remarked, "without leaving one *Indian* alive in the Village." Resistance to disease developed with painful slowness; colonists reported that the outbreak of smallpox in 1759 wiped out 60 percent of the natives, and, according to one source, "the woods were offensive with the dead bodies of the Indians; and dogs, wolves, and vultures were . . . busy for months in banqueting on them."

Survivors of these horrors were thrust into a situation no less alien than what European immigrants and African slaves found. The collected wisdom of generations could vanish in a matter of days if sickness struck older members of a community who kept sacred traditions and taught special skills. When many of the elders succumbed at once, the deep pools of collective memory grew shallow, and some dried up altogether. In 1710, Indians near Charleston told a settler that "they have forgot most of their traditions since the Establishment of this Colony, they keep their Festivals and can tell but little of the reasons: their Old Men are dead." Impoverishment of a rich cultural heritage followed the spread of disease.

Nearly a century later, a South Carolinian exaggerated but captured the general trend when he noted that Catawbas "have forgotten their antient rites, ceremonies, and manufactures."

The same diseases that robbed a piedmont town of some of its most precious resources also stripped it of the population necessary to maintain an independent existence, In order to survive, groups were compelled to construct new societies from the splintered remnants of the old. The result was a kaleidoscopic array of migrations from ancient territories and mergers with nearby peoples. While such behavior was not unheard of in aboriginal times, population levels fell so precipitously after contact that survivors endured disruptions unlike anything previously known.

The dislocations of the Saponi Indians illustrate the common course of events. In 1670 they lived on the Staunton River in Virginia and were closely affiliated with a group called Nahyssans. A decade later Saponis moved toward the coast and built a town near the Occaneechees. When John Lawson came upon them along the Yadkin River in 1701, they were on the verge of banding together in a single village with Tutelos and Keyauwees. Soon thereafter Saponis applied to Virginia officials for permission to move to the Meherrin River, where Occaneechees, Tutelos, and others joined them. In 1714, at the urging of Virginia's Lt. Gov. Alexander Spotswood, these groups settled at Fort Christanna farther up the Meherrin. Their friendship with Virginia soured during the 1720s, and most of the "Christanna Indians" moved to the Catawba Nation. For some reason this arrangement did not satisfy them, and many returned to Virginia in 1732, remaining there for a decade before choosing to migrate north and accept the protection of the Iroquois.

Saponis were unusual only in their decision to leave the Catawbas. Enos, Occaneechees, Waterees, Keyauwees, Cheraws, and others have their own stories to tell, similar in outline if not in detail. With the exception of the towns near the confluence of Sugar Creek and the Catawba River that composed the heart of the Catawba Nation, piedmont communities decimated by disease lived through a common round of catastrophes, shifting from place to place and group to group in search of a safe haven. Most eventually ended up in the Nation, and during the opening decades of the eighteenth century the villages scattered across the southern upcountry were abandoned as people drifted into the Catawba orbit.

No mere catalog of migrations and mergers can begin to convey how profoundly unsettling this experience was for those swept up in it. While upcountry Indians did not sail away to some distant land, they, too, were among the uprooted, leaving their ancestral homes to try to make a new life elsewhere. The peripatetic existence of Saponis and others proved deeply disruptive. A village and its surrounding territory were important elements of personal and collective identity, physical links in a chain binding a group to its past and making a locality sacred. Colonists, convinced that Indians were by nature "a shifting, wandring People," were oblivious to this, but Lawson offered a glimpse of the reasons for native attachment to a particular locale. "In our way," he wrote on leaving an Eno-Shakori town in 1701, "there stood a great Stone about the Size of a large Oven, and hollow; this the *Indians* took great Notice of, putting some Tobacco into the Concavity, and spitting after it. I ask'd them the Reason of their so doing, but they made me no Answer." Natives throughout the interior honored similar places—graves of ancestors, monuments of stones commemorating important events—that could not be left behind without some cost.

The toll could be physical as well as spiritual, for even the most uneventful of moves interrupted the established cycle of subsistence. Belongings had to be packed and unpacked, dwellings constructed, palisades raised. Once migrants had completed the business of settling in, the still more arduous task of exploiting new terrain awaited them. Living in one place year after year endowed a people with intimate knowledge of the area. The richest soils, the best hunting grounds, the choicest sites for gathering nuts or berries—none could be learned without years of experience, tested by time and passed down from one generation to the next. Small wonder that Carolina Indians worried about being "driven to some unknown Country, to live, hunt, and get our Bread in."

Some displaced groups tried to leave "unknown Country" behind and make their way back home. In 1716 Enos asked Virginia's permission to settle at "Enoe Town" on the North Carolina frontier, their location in Lawson's day. Seventeen years later William Byrd II came upon an abandoned Cheraw village on a tributary of the upper Roanoke River and remarked how "it must have been a great misfortunate to them to be obliged to abandon so beautiful a dwelling." The Indians apparently agreed: in 1717 the Virginia Council received "Divers applications" from the Cheraws (now living along the Pee Dee River) "for Liberty to Seat themselves on the head of Roanoke River." Few natives managed to return permanently to their homelands. But their efforts to retrace their steps hint at a profound sense of loss and testify to the powerful hold of ancient sites.

Compounding the trauma of leaving familiar territories was the necessity of abandoning customary relationships. Casting their lot with others traditionally considered foreign compelled Indians to rearrange basic ways of ordering their existence. Despite frequent contacts among peoples, native life had always centered in kin and town. The consequences of this deep-seated localism were evident even to a newcomer like John Lawson, who in 1701 found striking differences in language, dress, and physical appearance among Carolina Indians living only a few miles apart. Rules governing behavior also drew sharp distinctions between outsiders and one's own "Country-Folks." Indians were "very kind, and charitable to one another," Lawson reported, "but more especially to those of their own Nation." A visitor desiring a liaison with a local woman was required to approach her relatives and the village headman. On the other hand, "if it be an *Indian* of their own Town or Neighbourhood, that wants a Mistress, he comes to none but the Girl." Lawson seemed unperturbed by this barrier until he discovered that a "Thief [is] held in Disgrace, that steals from any of his Country-Folks," "but to steal from the *English* [or any other foreigners] they reckon no Harm."

Communities unable to continue on their own had to revise these rules and reweave the social fabric into new designs. What language would be spoken? How would fields be laid out, hunting territories divided, houses built? How would decisions be reached, offenders punished, ceremonies performed? When Lawson remarked that "now adays" the Indians must seek mates "amongst Strangers," he unwittingly characterized life in native Carolina. Those who managed to withstand the ravages of disease had to redefine the meaning of the term *stranger* and transform outsiders into insiders.

The need to harmonize discordant peoples, an unpleasant fact of life for all native Americans, was no less common among black and white inhabitants of America during these years. Africans from a host of different groups were thrown into slavery together and forced to seek some common cultural ground, to blend or set aside clashing habits and beliefs. Europeans who came to America also met unexpected and unwelcome ethnic, religious, and linguistic diversity. The roots of the problem were quite different; the problem itself was much the same. In each case people from different backgrounds had to forge a common culture and a common future.

Indians in the southern uplands customarily combined with others like themselves in an attempt to solve the dilemma. Following the "principle of least effort," shattered communities cushioned the blows inficted by disease and depopulation by joining a kindred society known through generations of trade and alliances. Thus Saponis coalesced with Occaneechees and Tutelos—nearby groups "speaking much the same language"—and Catawbas became a sanctuary for culturally related refugees from throughout the region. Even after moving in with friends and neighbors, however, natives tended to cling to ethnic boundaries in order to ease the transition. In 1715 Spotswood noticed that the Saponis and others gathered at Fort Christanna were "confederated together, tho' still preserving their different Rules." Indians entering the Catawba Nation were equally conservative. As late as 1743 a visitor could hear more than twenty different dialects spoken by peoples living there, and some bands continued to reside in separate towns under their own leaders.

Time inevitably sapped the strength of ethnic feeling, allowing a more unified Nation to emerge from the collection of Indian communities that occupied the valleys of the Catawba River and its tributaries. By the mid-eighteenth century, the authority of village headmen was waning and leaders from the host population had begun to take responsibility for the actions of constituent groups. The babel of different tongues fell silent as *"Kàtahba,"* the Nation's "standard, or court-dialect," slowly drowned out all others. Eventually, entire peoples followed their languages and their leaders into oblivion, leaving only personal names like Santee Jemmy, Cheraw George, Congaree Jamie, Saponey Johnny, and Eno Jemmy as reminders of the Nation's diverse heritage.

No European observer recorded the means by which nations became mere names and a [collection] of groups forged itself into one people. No doubt the colonists' habit of ignoring ethnic distinctions and lumping confederated entities together under the Catawba rubric encouraged amalgamation. But Anglo-American efforts to create a society by proclamation were invariably unsuccessful; consolidation had to come from within. In the absence of evidence, it seems reasonable to conclude that years of contacts paved the way for a closer relationship. Once a group moved to the Nation, intermarriages blurred ancient kinship networks, joint war parties or hunting expeditions brought young men together, and elders met in a council that gave everyone some say by including "all the Indian Chiefs of Head Men of that [Catawba] Nation and the several Tribes amongst them together." The concentration of settlements within a day's walk of one another facilitated contact and communication. From their close proximity, common experience, and shared concerns, people developed ceremonies and myths that compensated for those lost to disease and gave the Nation a stronger collective consciousness. Associations evolved that balanced traditional narrow ethnic allegiance with a new, broader, "national" identity, a balance that tilted steadily toward the latter. Ethnic differences died hard, but the peoples of the Catawba Nation learned to speak with a single voice.

Muskets and kettles came to the piedmont more slowly than smallpox and measles. Spanish explorers distributed a few gifts to local headmen, but inhabitants of the interior did not enjoy their first real taste of the fruits of European technology until Englishmen began venturing inland after 1650. Indians these traders met in upcountry towns were glad to barter for the more efficient tools, more lethal weapons, and more durable clothing that colonists offered. Spurred on by eager natives, men from Virginia and Carolina quickly flooded the region with the material trappings of European culture. In 1701 John Lawson considered the Wateree Chickanees "very poor in *English* Effects" because a few of them lacked muskets.

Slower to arrive, trade goods were also less obvious agents of change. The Indians' ability to absorb foreign artifacts into established modes of existence hid the revolutionary consequences of trade for some time. Natives leaped the technological gulf with ease in part because they were discriminating shoppers. If hoes were too small, beads too large, or cloth the wrong color, Indian traders refused them. Items they did select fit smoothly into existing ways. Waxhaws tied horse bells around their ankles at ceremonial dances, and some of the traditional stone pipes passed among the spectators at these dances had been shaped by metal files. Those who could not afford a European weapon fashioned arrows from broken glass. Those who could went to great lengths to "set [a new musket] streight, sometimes shooting away above 100 Loads of Ammunition, before they bring the Gun to shoot according to their Mind."

Not every piece of merchandise hauled into the upcountry on a trader's packhorse could be "set streight" so easily, Liquor, for example, proved both impossible to resist and extraordinarily destructive. Indians "have no Power to refrain this Enemy," Lawson observed, "though sensible how many of them (are by it) hurry'd into the other World before their Time." And yet even here, natives aware of the risks sought to control alcohol by incorporating it into their ceremonial life as a device for achieving a different level of consciousness. Consumption was usually restricted to men, who "go as solemnly about it, as if it were part of their Religion," preferring to drink only at night and only in quantities sufficient to stupefy them. When ritual could not confine liquor to safe channels, Indians went still further and excused the excesses of overindulgence by refusing to hold an intoxicated person responsible for his actions. "They never call any Man to account for what he did, when he was drunk," wrote Lawson, "but say, it was the Drink that caused his Misbehaviour, therefore he ought to be forgiven."

Working to absorb even the most dangerous commodities acquired from their new neighbors, aboriginal inhabitants of the uplands, like African slaves in the lowlands, made themselves at home in a different technological environment.

Indians became convinced that "Guns, and Ammunition, besides a great many other Necessaries, . . . are helpful to Man" and eagerly searched for the key that would unlock the secret of their production. At first many were confident that the "*Quera,* or good Spirit," would teach them to make these commodities "when that good Spirit sees fit." Later they decided to help their deity along by approaching the colonists. In 1757, Catawbas asked Gov. Arthur Dobbs of North Carolina "to send us Smiths and other Tradesmen to teach our Children."

It was not the new products themselves but the Indians' failure to learn the mysteries of manufacture from either Dobbs or the *Quera* that marked the real revolution wrought by trade. During the seventeenth and eighteenth centuries, everyone in eastern North America—masters and slaves, farmers near the coast and Indians near the mountains—became producers of raw materials for foreign markets and found themselves caught up in an international economic network. Piedmont natives were part of this larger process, but their adjustment was more difficult because the contrast with previous ways was so pronounced. Before European contact, the localism characteristic of life in the uplands had been sustained by a remarkable degree of self-sufficiency. Trade among peoples, while common, was conducted primarily in commodities such as copper, mica, and shells, items that, exchanged with the appropriate ceremony, initiated or confirmed friendships among groups. Few, if any, villages relied on outsiders for goods essential to daily life.

Intercultural exchange eroded this traditional independence and entangled natives in a web of commercial relations few of them understood and none controlled. In 1670 the explorer John Lederer observed a striking disparity in the trading habits of Indians living near Virginia and those deep in the interior. The "remoter Indians," still operating within a precontact framework, were content with ornamental items such as mirrors, beads, "and all manner of gaudy toys and knacks for children." "Neighborour-Indians," on the other hand, habitually traded with colonists for cloth, metal tools, and weapons. Before long, towns near and far were demanding the entire range of European wares and were growing accustomed—even addicted—to them. "They say we English are fools for . . . not always going with a gun," one Virginia colonist familiar with piedmont Indians wrote in the early 1690s, "for they think themselves undrest and not fit to walk abroad, unless they have their gun on their shoulder, and their shot-bag by their side." Such an enthusiastic conversion to the new technology eroded ancient craft skills and hastened complete dependence on substitutes only colonists could supply.

By forcing Indians to look beyond their own territories for certain indispensable products, Anglo-American traders inserted new variables into the aboriginal equation of exchange. Colonists sought two commodities from Indians—human beings and deerskins—and both undermined established relationships among native groups. While the demand for slaves encouraged piedmont peoples to expand their traditional warfare, the demand for peltry may have fostered conflicts over hunting territories. Those who did not fight each other for slaves or deerskins fought each other for the European products these could bring. As firearms, cloth, and other items became increasingly important to native existence, competition replaced comity at the foundation of trade encounters as villages scrambled for the cargoes of merchandise. Some were in a better position to profit than others. In the early 1670s Occaneechees living on an island in the Roanoke River enjoyed power out of all proportion to their numbers because they controlled an important ford on the trading path from Virginia to the interior, and they resorted to threats, and even to force, to retain their advantage. In Lawson's day Tuscaroras did the same, "hating that any of these Westward *Indians* should have any Commerce with the *English,* which would prove a Hinderance to their Gains."

Competition among native groups was only the beginning of the transformation brought about by new forms of exchange. Inhabitants of the piedmont might bypass the native middleman, but they could not break free from a perilous dependence on colonial sources of supply. The danger may not have been immediately apparent to Indians caught up in the excitement of acquiring new and wonderful things. For years they managed to dictate the terms of trade, compelling visitors from Carolina and Virginia to abide by aboriginal codes of conduct and playing one colony's traders against the other to ensure an abundance of goods at favorable rates. But the natives' influence over the protocol of exchange combined with their skill at incorporating alien products to mask a loss of control over their own destiny. The mask came off when, in 1715, the traders—and the trade goods—suddenly disappeared during the Yamassee War.

The conflict's origins lay in a growing colonial awareness of the Indians' need for regular supplies of European merchandise. In 1701 Lawson pronounced the Santees "very tractable" because of their close connections with South Carolina. Eight years later he was convinced that the colonial officials in Charleston "are absolute Masters over the *Indians* . . . within the Circle of their Trade." Carolina traders who shared this conviction quite naturally felt less and less constrained to obey native rules governing proper behavior. Abuses against Indians mounted until some men were literally getting away with murder. When repeated appeals to colonial officials failed, natives throughout Carolina began to consider war. Persuaded by Yamassee ambassadors that the conspiracy was widespread and convinced by years of ruthless commercial competition between Virginia and Carolina that an attack on one colony would not affect relations with the other, in the spring of 1715 Catawbas and their neighbors joined the invasion of South Carolina.

The decision to fight was disastrous. Colonists everywhere shut off the flow of goods to the interior, and after some initial successes Carolina's native enemies soon plumbed the depths of their dependence. In a matter of months, refugees holed up in Charleston noticed that "the Indians want ammunition and are not able to mend their Arms." The peace negotiations that ensued revealed a desperate thirst for fresh supplies of European wares. Ambassadors from piedmont towns invariably spoke in a single breath of restoring "a Peace and a free Trade," and one delegation even admitted that its people "cannot live without the assistance of the English."

Natives unable to live without the English henceforth tried to live with them. No upcountry group mounted a direct challenge to Anglo-America after 1715. Trade quickly resumed, and the piedmont Indians, now concentrated almost exclusively in the Catawba valley, briefly enjoyed a regular supply of necessary products sold by men willing once again to deal according to the old rules. By mid-century, however, deer were scarce and fresh sources of slaves almost impossible to find. Anglo-American traders took their business elsewhere, leaving inhabitants of the Nation with another material crisis of different but equally dangerous dimensions.

Indians casting about for an alternative means of procuring the commodities they craved looked to imperial officials. During the 1740s and 1750s native dependence shifted from colonial traders to colonial authorities as Catawba leaders repeatedly visited provincial capitals to request goods. These delegations came not to beg but to bargain. Catawbas were still of enormous value to the English as allies and frontier guards, especially at a time when Anglo-America felt threatened by the French and their Indian auxiliaries. The Nation's position within reach of Virginia and both Carolinas enhanced its value by enabling headmen to approach all three colonies and offer their people's services to the highest bidder.

The strategy yielded Indians an arsenal of ammunition and a variety of other merchandise that helped offset the declining trade. Crown officials were especially generous when the Nation managed to play one colony off against another. In 1746 a rumor that the Catawbas were about to move to Virginia was enough to garner them a large shipment of powder and lead from officials in Charleston concerned about losing this "valuable people." A decade later, while the two Carolinas fought for the honor of constructing a fort in the Nation, the Indians encouraged (and received) gifts symbolizing good will from both colonies without reaching an agreement with either. Surveying the tangled thicket of promises and presents, the Crown's superintendent of Indian affairs, Edmond Atkin, ruefully admitted that "the People of both Provinces . . . have I believe [*sic*] tampered too much on both sides with those Indians, who seem to understand well how to make their Advantage of it."

By the end of the colonial period delicate negotiations across cultural boundaries were as familiar to Catawbas as the strouds [coarse woolen goods] they wore and the muskets they carried. But no matter how shrewdly the headmen loosened provincial purse strings to extract vital merchandise, they could not escape the simple fact that they no longer held the purse containing everything needed for their daily existence. In the space of a century the Indians had become thoroughly embedded in an alien economy, denizens of a new material world. The ancient self-sufficiency was only a dim memory in the minds of the Nation's elders.

The Catawba peoples were veterans of countless campaigns against disease and masters of the arts of trade long before the third major element of their new world, white planters, became an integral part of their life. Settlement of the Carolina uplands did not begin until the 1730s, but once underway it spread with frightening speed. In November 1752, concerned Catawbas reminded South Carolina governor James Glen how they had "complained already . . . that the white People were settled too near us." Two years later five hundred families lived within thirty miles of the Nation and surveyors were running their lines into the middle of native towns. "[T]hose Indians are now in a fair way to be surrounded by White People," one observer concluded.

Settlers' attitudes were as alarming as their numbers. Unlike traders who profited from them or colonial officials who deployed them as allies, ordinary colonists had little use for Indians. Natives made poor servants and worse slaves; they obstructed settlement; they attracted enemy warriors to the area. Even men who respected Indians and earned a living by trading with them admitted that they made unpleasant neighbors. "We may observe of them as of the fire," wrote the South Carolina trader James Adair after considering the Catawbas' situation on the eve of the American Revolution, "'it is safe and useful, cherished at proper distance; but if too near us, it becomes dangerous, and will scorch if not consume us.'"

A common fondness for alcohol increased the likelihood of intercultural hostilities. Catawba leaders acknowledged that the Indians "get very Drunk with [liquor] this is the Very Cause that they oftentimes Commit those Crimes that is offensive to You and us." Colonists were equally prone to bouts of drunkenness. In the 1760s the itinerant Anglican minister, Charles Woodmason, was shocked to find the citizens of one South Carolina upcountry community "continually drunk." More appalling still, after attending church services "one half of them got drunk before they went home." Indians sometimes suffered at the hands of intoxicated farmers. In 1760 a Catawba woman was murdered when she happened by a tavern shortly after four of its patrons "swore they would kill the first Indian they should meet with."

Even when sober, natives and newcomers found many reasons to quarrel. Catawbas were outraged if colonists built farms on the Indians' doorstep or tramped across ancient burial grounds. Planters, ignorant of (or indifferent to) native rules of hospitality, considered Indians who requested food nothing more than beggars and angrily drove them away. Other disputes arose when the Nation's young men went looking for trouble. As hunting, warfare, and other traditional avenues for achieving status narrowed, Catawba youths transferred older patterns of behavior into a new arena by raiding nearby farms and hunting cattle or horses.

Contrasting images of the piedmont landscape quite unintentionally generated still more friction. Colonists determined to tame what they considered a wilderness were in fact erasing a native signature on the land and scrawling their own. Bridges, buildings, fences, roads, crops, and other "improvements" made the area comfortable and familiar to colonists but uncomfortable and unfamiliar to Indians. "The Country side wear[s] a New face," proclaimed Woodmason proudly; to the original inhabitants, it was a grim face indeed. "His Land was spoiled," one Catawba headman told British officials in 1763. "They have spoiled him 100 Miles every way." Under these circumstances, even a settler with no wish to fight Indians met opposition to his fences, his outbuildings, his very presence. Similarly, a Catawba on a routine foray into traditional hunting territories had his weapon destroyed, his goods confiscated, his life threatened by men with different notions of the proper use of the land.

To make matters worse, the importance both cultures attached to personal independence hampered efforts by authorities on either side to resolve conflicts. Piedmont settlers along the border between the Carolinas were "people of desperate fortune," a frightened North Carolina official reported after visiting the area.

"[N]o officer of Justice from either Province dare meddle with them." Woodmason, who spent even more time in the region, came to the same conclusion. "We are without any Law, or Order," he complained; the inhabitants' "Impudence is so very high, as to be past bearing." Catawba leaders could have sympathized. Headmen informed colonists that the Nation's people "are oftentimes Cautioned from . . . ill Doings altho' to no purpose for we Cannot be present at all times to Look after them." "What they have done I could not prevent," one chief explained.

Unruly, angry, intoxicated—Catawbas and Carolinians were constantly at odds during the middle decades of the eighteenth century. Planters who considered Indians "proud and deveilish" were themselves accused by natives of being "very bad and quarrelsome." Warriors made a habit of "going into the Settlements, robbing and stealing where ever they get an Oppertunity." Complaints generally brought no satisfaction—"they laugh and makes their Game of it, and says it is what they will"—leading some settlers to "whip [Indians] about the head, beat and abuse them." "The white People . . . and the Cuttahbaws, are Continually at variance," a visitor to the Nation fretted in June 1759, "and Dayly New Animositys Doth a rise Between them which In my Humble oppion will be of Bad Consequence In a Short time, Both Partys Being obstinate."

The litany of intercultural crimes committed by each side disguised a fundamental shift in the balance of physical and cultural power. In the early years of colonization of the interior the least disturbance by Indians sent scattered planters into a panic. Soon, however, Catawbas were few, colonists many, and it was the natives who now lived in fear. "[T]he white men [who] Lives Near the Neation is Contenuely asembleing and goes In the [Indian] towns In Bodys . . . ," worried another observer during the tense summer of 1759. "[T]he[y] tretton the[y] will Kill all the Cattabues."

The Indians would have to find some way to get along with these unpleasant neighbors if the Nation was to survive. As Catawba population fell below five hundred after the smallpox epidemic of 1759 and the number of colonists continued to climb, natives gradually came to recognize the futility of violent resistance. During the last decades of the eighteenth century they drew on years of experience in dealing with Europeans at a distance and sought to overturn the common conviction that Indian neighbors were frightening and useless.

This process was not the result of some clever plan; Catawbas had no strategy for survival. A headman could warn them that "the White people were now seated all round them and by that means had them entirely in their power." He could not command them to submit peacefully to the invasion of their homeland. The Nation's continued existence required countless individual decisions, made in a host of diverse circumstances, to complain rather than retaliate, to accept a subordinate place in a land that once was theirs. Few of the choices made survive in the record. But it is clear that, like the response to disease and to technology, the adaptation to white settlement was both painful and prolonged.

Catawbas took one of the first steps along the road to accommodation in the early 1760s, when they used their influence with colonial officials to acquire a reservation encompassing the heart of their ancient territories. This grant gave the Indians a land base, grounded in Anglo-American law, that prevented farmers from shouldering them aside. Equally important, Catawbas now had a commodity to exchange with nearby settlers. These men wanted land, the natives had plenty, and shortly before the Revolution the Nation was renting tracts to planters for cash, livestock, and manufactured goods.

Important as it was, land was not the only item Catawbas began trading to their neighbors. Some Indians put their skills as hunters and woodsmen to a different use, picking up stray horses and escaped slaves for a reward. Others bartered their pottery, baskets, and table mats. Still others traveled through the up-country, demonstrating their prowess with the bow and arrow before appreciative audiences. The exchange of these goods and services for European merchandise marked an important adjustment to the settlers' arrival. In the past, natives had acquired essential items by trading peltry and slaves or requesting gifts from representatives of the Crown. But piedmont planters frowned on hunting and warfare, while provincial authorities—finding Catawbas less useful as the Nation's population declined and the French threat disappeared—discouraged formal visits and handed out fewer presents. Hence the Indians had to develop new avenues of exchange that would enable them to obtain goods in ways less objectionable to their neighbors. Pots, baskets, and acres proved harmless substitutes for earlier methods of earning an income.

Quite apart from its economic benefits, trade had a profound impact on the character of Catawba-settler relations. Through countless repetitions of the same simple procedure at homesteads scattered across the Carolinas, a new form of intercourse arose, based not on suspicion and an expectation of conflict but on trust and a measure of friendship. When a farmer looked out his window and saw Indians approaching, his reaction more commonly became to pick up money or a jug of whiskey rather than a musket or an axe. The natives now appeared, the settler knew, not to plunder or kill but to peddle their wares or collect their rents.

The development of new trade forms could not bury all of the differences between Catawba and colonist overnight. But in the latter half of the eighteenth century the beleaguered Indians learned to rely on peaceful means of resolving intercultural conflicts that did arise. Drawing a sharp distinction between "the good men that have rented Lands from us" and "the bad People [who] has frequently imposed upon us," Catawbas called on the former to protect the Nation from the latter. In 1771 they met with the prominent Camden storekeeper, Joseph Kershaw, to request that he "represent us when [we are] a grieved." After the Revolution the position became more formal. Catawbas informed the South Carolina government that, being "destitute of a man to take care of, and assist us in our affairs," they had chosen one Robert Patten "to take charge of our affairs, and to act and do for us."

Neither Patten nor any other intermediary could have protected the Nation had it not joined the patriot side during the Revolutionary War. Though one scholar has termed the Indians' contribution to the cause "rather negligible," they fought in battles throughout the southeast and supplied rebel forces with food from time to time. These actions made the Catawbas heroes and laid a foundation for their popular renown as staunch patriots. In 1781 their old friend Kershaw told Catawba leaders how he welcomed the end of "this Long and Bloody War, in which You have taken so Noble a part and have fought and Bled with your white

Brothers of America." Grateful Carolinians would not soon forget the Nation's service. Shortly after the Civil War an elderly settler whose father had served with the Indians in the Revolution echoed Kershaw's sentiments, recalling that "his father never communicated much to him [about the Catawbas], except that all the tribe . . . served the entire war . . . and fought most heroically."

Catawbas rose even higher in their neighbors' esteem when they began calling their chiefs "General" instead of "King" and stressed that these men were elected by the people. The change reflected little if any real shift in the Nation's political forms, but it delighted the victorious Revolutionaries. In 1794 the Charleston *City Gazette* reported that during the war "King" Frow had abdicated and the Indians chose "General" New River in his stead. "What a pity," the paper concluded, "certain people on a certain island have not as good optics as the Catawbas!" In the same year the citizens of Camden celebrated the anniversary of the fall of the Bastille by raising their glasses to toast "King Prow [*sic*]—may all kings who will not follow his example follow that of Louis XVI." Like tales of Indian patriots, the story proved durable. Nearly a century after the Revolution one nearby planter wrote that "the Catawbas, emulating the examples of their white brethren, threw off regal government."

The Indians' new image as republicans and patriots, added to their trade with whites and their willingness to resolve conflicts peacefully, brought settlers to view Catawbas in a different light. By 1800 the natives were no longer violent and dangerous strangers but what one visitor termed an "inoffensive" people and one group of planters called "harmless and friendly" neighbors. They had become traders of pottery but not deerskins, experts with a bow and arrow but not hunters, ferocious warriors against runaway slaves or tories but not against settlers. In these ways Catawbas could be distinctively Indian yet reassuringly harmless at the same time.

The Nation's separate identity rested on such obvious aboriginal traits. But its survival ultimately depended on a more general conformity with the surrounding society. During the nineteenth century both settlers and Indians owned or rented land. Both spoke proudly of their Revolutionary heritage and their republican forms of government. Both drank to excess. Even the fact that Catawbas were not Christians failed to differentiate them sharply from nearby white settlements, where, one visitor noted in 1822, "little attention is paid to the sabbath, or religeon."

In retrospect it is clear that these similarities were as superficial as they were essential. For all the changes generated by contacts with vital Euro-American and Afro-American cultures, the Nation was never torn loose from its cultural moorings. Well after the Revolution, Indians maintained a distinctive way of life rich in tradition and meaningful to those it embraced. Ceremonies conducted by headmen and folk tales told by relatives continued to transmit traditional values and skills from one generation to the next. Catawba children grew up speaking the native language, making bows and arrows or pottery, and otherwise following patterns of belief and behavior derived from the past. The Indians' physical appearance and the meandering paths that set Catawba settlements off from neighboring communities served to reinforce this cultural isolation.

The natives' utter indifference to missionary efforts after 1800 testified to the enduring power of established ways. Several clergymen stopped at the reservation in the first years of the nineteenth century; some stayed a year or two; none enjoyed any success. As one white South Carolinian noted in 1826, Catawbas were "Indians still." Outward conformity made it easier for them to blend into the changed landscape. Beneath the surface lay a more complex story.

Those few outsiders who tried to piece together that story generally found it difficult to learn much from the Indians. A people shrewd enough to discard the title of "King" was shrewd enough to understand that some things were better left unsaid and unseen. Catawbas kept their Indian names, and sometimes their language, a secret from prying visitors. They echoed the racist attitudes of their white neighbors and even owned a few slaves, all the time trading with blacks and hiring them to work in the Nation, where the laborers "enjoyed considerable freedom" among the natives. Like Afro-Americans on the plantation who adopted a happy, childlike demeanor to placate suspicious whites, Indians on the reservation learned that a "harmless and friendly" posture revealing little of life in the Nation was best suited to conditions in post-Revolutionary South Carolina.

Success in clinging to their cultural identity and at least a fraction of their ancient lands cannot obscure the cost Catawba peoples paid. From the time the first European arrived, the deck was stacked against them. They played the hand dealt them well enough to survive, but they could never win. An incident that took place at the end of the eighteenth century helps shed light on the consequences of compromise. When the Catawba headman, General New River, accidentally injured the horse he had borrowed from a nearby planter named Thomas Spratt, Spratt responded by "banging old New River with a pole all over the yard." This episode provided the settler with a colorful tale for his grandchildren; its effect on New River and his descendants can only be imagined. Catawbas did succeed in the sense that they adjusted to a hostile and different world, becoming trusted friends instead of feared enemies. Had they been any less successful they would not have survived the eighteenth century. But poverty and oppression have plagued the Nation from New River's day to our own. For a people who had once been proprietors of the piedmont, the pain of learning new rules was very great, the price of success very high.

On that August day in 1608 when Amoroleck feared the loss of his world, John Smith assured him that the English "came to them in peace, and to seeke their loves." Events soon proved Amoroleck right and his captor wrong. Over the course of the next three centuries not only Amoroleck and other piedmont Indians but natives throughout North America had their world stolen and another put in its place. Though this occurred at different times and in different ways, no Indians escaped the explosive mixture of deadly bacteria, material riches, and alien peoples that was the invasion of America. Those in the southern piedmont who survived the onslaught were ensconced in their new world by the end of the eighteenth century. Population levels stabilized as the Catawba peoples developed immunities to once-lethal diseases. Rents, sales of pottery, and other economic activities proved adequate to support the Nation at a stable (if low) level of material life. Finally, the Indians' image as "inoffensive" neighbors gave them a place in South Carolina society and continues to sustain them today.

Vast differences separated Catawbas and other natives from their colonial contemporaries. Europeans were the colonizers, Africans the enslaved, Indians the dispossessed: from these distinct positions came distinct histories. Yet once we acknowledge the differences, instructive similarities remain that help to integrate natives more thoroughly into the story of early America. By carving a niche for themselves in response to drastically different conditions, the peoples who composed the Catawba Nation shared in the most fundamental of American experiences. Like Afro-Americans, these Indians were compelled to accept a subordinate position in American life yet did not altogether lose their cultural integrity. Like settlers of the Chesapeake, aboriginal inhabitants of the uplands adjusted to appalling mortality rates and wrestled with the difficult task of "living with death." Like inhabitants of the Middle Colonies, piedmont groups learned to cope with unprecedented ethnic diversity by balancing the pull of traditional loyalties with the demands of a new social order. Like Puritans in New England, Catawbas found that a new world did not arrive all at once and that localism, self-sufficiency, and the power of old ways were only gradually eroded by conditions in colonial America. More hints of a comparable heritage could be added to this list, but by now it should be clear that Indians belong on the colonial stage as important actors in the unfolding American drama rather than bit players, props, or spectators. For they, too, lived in a new world.

◈ *F U R T H E R   R E A D I N G*

Woodrow W. Borah and Sherburne F. Cook, *Essays in Population History* 3 vols. (1971–1979)

William Cronon, *Changes in the Land: Indians, Colonists, and the Ecology of New England* (1983)

Alfred Crosby, *The Columbian Exchange: Biological and Cultural Consequences of 1492* (1972)

——, *Ecological Imperialism: The Biological Expansion of Europe, 900–1900* (1986)

——, "Virgin Soil Epidemics as a Factor in Aboriginal Depopulation in America," *William and Mary Quarterly* 33 (1976), 289–299

William M. Denevan, *The Native Population of the Americas in 1492* (1976)

Henry F. Dobyns, "Estimating Aboriginal Population: An Appraisal of Techniques with a New Hemispheric Estimate," *Current Anthropology* 7 (1966), 395–416, and "Reply," 440–444

——, *Their Number Become Thinned: Native American Population Dynamics in Eastern North America* (1983)

Wilbur R. Jacobs, "The Indian and the Frontier in American History: A Need for Revision," *Western Historical Quarterly* 4 (1973), 43–56

——, "The Tip of the Iceberg: Pre-Columbian Indian Demography and Some Implications for Revisionism," *William and Mary Quarterly* 31 (1974), 123–132

William H. McNeill, *Plagues and People* (1976)

James Merrell, *The Indians' New World: Catawbas and Their Neighbors from European Contact Through the Era of Removal* (1989)

Anthony Pagden, *The Fall Of Natural Man: The American Indian and the Origins of Comparative Ethnology* (1982)

George Irving Quimby, *Indian Culture and European Trade Goods: The Archaeology of the Historic Period in the Western Great Lakes Region* (1966)

Ann F. Ramenofsky, *Vectors of Death: The Archeology of European Contact* (1987)

Kirkpatrick Sale, *The Conquest of Paradise: Christopher Columbus and the Columbian Legacy* (1990)

Carl O. Sauer, *The Early Spanish Main* (1966)

———, *Sixteenth Century North America* (1971)

Edward H. Spicer, *Cycles of Conquest: The Impact of Spain, Mexico, and the United States on the Indians of the Southwest, 1533–1960* (1962)

Bruce G. Trigger, *The Children of Aataentsic: A History of the Huron People to 1660* (1972)

Richard White, *The Middle Ground: Indians, Empires, and Republics in the Great Lakes Region, 1650–1815* (1991)

———, *The Roots of Dependency: Subsistence, Environment, and Social Change Among the Choctaws, Pawnees, and Navajos* (1983)

CHAPTER
3

Indians, Religion, and

Empire in Colonial Times

Before the arrival of Europeans, Indians followed many religious traditions. The Pueblo Indians had different beliefs and rituals than did the Ojibwa; Chumash and Iroquois Indians likewise led distinctive religious lives. While there was great religious variety among them, Indians' spiritual life on the whole differed considerably from the Christian beliefs of Europeans. Indians were not monotheists. Rather, a pantheon of culture heroes, earth creators, magical animals, and spirits populated the Indians' religious world. These beings could bring power, sickness, health, disaster, and knowledge to humans. In addition, all ordinary living creatures, and many inanimate things as well, possessed spiritual power. The Indians also had places that they associated with magical forces, where they fasted, prayed, and dreamed of sacred revelations and the power that came with them. Each tribe had its own priests, shamans (healers with special powers), and other spiritual leaders, but even ordinary people could possess power and communicate with the spirit world. In general, Indians' sense of religious well-being was strongly linked to place; each rock, stream, tree, valley, and mountain range had special power and meaning for the human inhabitants.

These beliefs and practices served Indians well for many centuries. Through their observations of prescribed rites, their prayer, and their respect for tradition, Indians enjoyed fertility, abundant crops, and health and well-being most of the time. When rain failed or game was scarce and people suffered, continued faith in time-worn beliefs ordinarily brought a return of storm clouds and animals. Thus the cycle of the seasons, ritual, food, healing ceremonies, and the land itself made religious belief palpable to Indians.

Europeans introduced new religious traditions into America. All European nations supported Christianity, although they did not all promote the same denomination. For example, Spain and France were Catholic, whereas the English church was Protestant. But despite their doctrinal and national disagreements, Protestant and Catholic settlers in America alike believed that Indian religions should be eradicated. At best, they thought that Indian spirituality was merely a manifestation of ignorance. At worst, clergymen concluded that Indians worshiped the devil. In the opinion of these Christians, Native American religions were not only wrong but also evil and had to be wiped out. Consequently, many Europeans wished to convert Indians to the Christian faith as they appropriated America for themselves. During the first centuries of the colonial era, the conquest of America was a contest for spiritual as well as political supremacy. What impact did these missionary efforts have on Indian history?

◈ D O C U M E N T S

The Indians' religious conversion was not an altogether voluntary experience, as the first document shows. The Spaniards called this document the *Requerimiento* (or "requirement"). Spanish law required conquistadors to read this statement to the Indians whom they encountered. This remarkable text not only required Indians to give up their religion if they did not submit to Spanish authority, but also made them responsible for any death or damage to themselves if they refused. In 1573, the Spanish king, Philip II, abolished the *Requerimiento* and condemned the use of force against Indians, but Spanish military and religious conquest continued to go forward together. Indians, however, did not always submit meekly to Spain's demands, as the second document, the interrogation of Pueblo Indian Pedro Naranjo, shows. After eighty-four years of Spanish rule, in 1680 the Pueblo Indians rebelled, expelled the intruders, and kept them out of New Mexico for a dozen years. Naranjo reveals that Pueblo religious beliefs played a central part in the rebellion. The third document, however, indicates that some Indians fully accepted Catholic religious teachings. Pablo Tac, a Luiseño Indian reared in a California mission, studied for the priesthood in Rome, where he recorded these recollections of mission life. And some Indians claimed that magic brought the Europeans to America. In document four Norval Morriseau, an Ojibway, explains that an Ojibway medicine man used magic to bring the first French people to Ojibway country. Thus Indian spiritual practices actually initiated the Ojibway encounter with Europeans, the Indians believed.

The remaining documents present observations on Native American religion and society by two non-Indians and finally by an Indian sachem, or chief. The fifth selection is from a letter of Pierre Charlevoix, a French traveler, who describes to the Duchess of Lesdiguières various Indian religious beliefs that he encountered in North America. Like most other Europeans, Charlevoix had ethnocentric biases that drove him to ridicule Indian spiritual beliefs. The sixth document gives the views of a New England missionary, Joseph Fish, who was convinced that Indian souls could be saved but was scandalized at the "lewdness" of his native parishioners. In the seventh document Red Jacket, a famous Seneca sachem, lectures a missionary who desires to work among the Senecas.

Spain Requires the Indians to Submit to Spanish Authority, 1513

On the part of the King, don Fernando [Ferdinand], and of doña Juana, his daughter, Queen of Castile and Léon, subduers of the barbarous nations, we their servants notify and make known to you, as best we can, that the Lord our God, Living and Eternal, created the Heaven and the Earth, and one man and one woman, of whom you and I, and all the men of the world, were and are descendants, and all those who come after us. But, on account of the multitude which has sprung from this man and woman in the five thousand years since the world was created, it was necessary that some men should go one way and some another, and that they should be divided into many kingdoms and provinces, for in one alone they could not be sustained.

Of all these nations God our Lord gave charge to one man, called St. Peter, that he should be Lord and Superior of all the men in the world, that all should obey him, and that he should be head of the whole human race, wherever men should live, and under whatever law, sect, or belief they should be; and he gave him the world for his kingdom and jurisdiction.

And he commanded him to place his seat in Rome, as the spot most fitting to rule the world from; but also he permitted him to have his seat in any other part of the world, and to judge and govern all Christians, Moors, Jews, Gentiles, and all other sects. This man was called Pope, as if to say, Admirable Great Father and Governor of men. The men who lived in that time obeyed that St. Peter, and took him for Lord, King, and Superior of the universe; so also have they regarded the others who after him have been elected to the Pontificate, and so it has been continued even until now, and will continue until the end of the world.

One of these Pontiffs, who succeeded that St. Peter as Lord of the world, in the dignity and seat which I have before mentioned, made donation of these isles and *terra firme* [mainland] to the aforesaid King and Queen and to their successors, our lords, with all that there are in these territories, as is contained in certain writings which passed upon the subject as aforesaid, which you can see if you wish.

So their Highnesses are kings and lords of these islands and land of *terra firme* by virtue of this donation; and some islands, and indeed almost all those to whom this has been notified, have received and served their Highnesses, as lords and kings, in the way that subjects ought to do, with good will, without any resistance, immediately, without delay, when they were informed of the aforesaid facts. And also they received and obeyed the priests whom their Highnesses sent to preach to them and to teach them our Holy Faith; and all these, of their own free will, without any reward or condition, have become Christians, and are so, and their Highnesses have joyfully and benignantly received them, and also have commanded them to be treated as their subjects and vassals; and you too are held and obliged to do the same. Wherefore as best we can, we ask and require you that you consider what we have said to you, and that you take the time that shall be necessary to understand and deliberate upon it, and that you acknowledge the Church as the Ruler and Superior of the whole world and the high priest called Pope, and in his name the King and Queen doña Juana our lords, in his place, as superiors and lords and kings of these islands and this *terra firme* by virtue of the said donation, and that you consent and give place that these religious fathers should declare and preach to you the aforesaid.

If you do so, you will do well . . . and we . . . shall receive you in all love and charity, and shall leave you your wives, and your children, and your lands, free without servitude, that you may do with them and with yourselves freely that which you like and think best, and they shall not compel you to turn Christians, unless you yourselves, when informed of the truth, should wish to be converted to our Holy Catholic Faith, as almost all the inhabitants of the rest of the islands have done. And besides this, their Highnesses award you many privileges and exceptions and will grant you many benefits.

But if you do not do this, and wickedly and intentionally delay to do so, I certify to you that, with the help of God, we shall forcibly enter into your country and shall make war against you in all ways and manners that we can, and shall subject you to the yoke and obedience of the Church and of their Highnesses; we shall take you and your wives and your children, and shall make slaves of them, and as such shall sell and dispose of them as their Highnesses may command; and we shall take away your goods, and shall do all the harm and damage that we can, as to vassals who do not obey, and refuse to receive their lord, and resist and contradict him; and we protest that the deaths and losses which shall accrue from this are your fault, and not that of their Highnesses, or ours, nor of these gentlemen who come with us. And that we have said this to you and made this Requirement, we request the notary here present to give us his testimony in writing, and we ask the rest who are present that they should be witnesses of this Requirement.

Pedro Naranjo's (Keresan Pueblo) Explanation of the 1680 Pueblo Revolt, 1681

In the . . . plaza de armas on [December 19, 1681], for the prosecution of the judicial proceedings of this case his lordship caused to appear before him an Indian prisoner named Pedro Naranjo, a native of the pueblo of San Felipe, . . . who was captured in the advance and attack upon the pueblo of La Isleta. He makes himself understood very well in the Castilian language and speaks his mother tongue and the Tegua. He took the oath in due legal form in the name of God, our Lord, and a sign of the cross, under charge of which he promised to tell the truth concerning what he knows. . . .

Asked whether he knows the reason or motives which the Indians of this kingdom had for rebelling, forsaking the law of God and obedience to his Majesty, and committing such grave and atrocious crimes, and who were the leaders and principal movers, and by whom and how it was ordered; and why they burned the images, temples, crosses, rosaries, and things of divine worship, committing such atrocities as killing priests, Spaniards, women, and children, and the rest that he might know touching the question, he said that since the government of Señor General Hernando Ugarte y la Concha they have planned to rebel on various occasions through conspiracies of the Indian sorcerers, and that although in some pueblos the messages were accepted, in other parts they would not agree to it; and that it is true that during the government of the said señor general seven or eight Indians were hanged for this same cause, whereupon the unrest subsided. Some time thereafter they [the conspirators] sent from the pueblo of Los Taos . . . two deerskins with some pictures on them signifying conspiracy after their manner, in order to convoke the people to a new rebellion, and the said deerskins passed to the province of Moqui [the Hopi pueblos], where they refused to accept them. The pact which they had been forming ceased for the time being, but they always kept in their hearts the desire to carry it out, so as to live as they are living to-day. Finally, in the past years, at the summons of an Indian named Popé who is said to have communication with the devil, it happened that in an estufa [kiva] of the pueblo of Los Taos there appeared to the said Popé three figures of Indians who never came out of the estufa. They gave the said Popé to understand that they were going underground to the lake of Copala. He saw these figures emit fire from all the extremities of their bodies, and that one of them was called Caudi, another Tilini, and the other Tleume; and these three beings spoke to the said Popé, who was in hiding from the secretary, Francisco Xavier, who wished to punish him as a sorcerer. They told him to make a cord of maguey fiber and tie some knots in it which would signify the number of days that they must wait before the rebellion. He said that the cord was passed through all the pueblos of the kingdom so that the ones which agreed to it [the rebellion] might untie one knot in sign of obedience, and by the other knots they would know the days which were lacking; and this was to be done on pain of death to those who refused to agree to it. As a sign of agreement and notice of having concurred in the treason and perfidy they were to send up smoke signals to that effect in each one of the pueblos singly. The said cord was taken from pueblo to pueblo by the swiftest youths under the penalty of death if they revealed the secret. Everything being thus arranged, two days before the time set for its execution, because his lordship had learned of it and had imprisoned two Indian accomplices from the pueblo of Tesuque, it was carried out prematurely that night, because it seemed to them that they were now discovered; and they killed religious, Spaniards, women, and children. This being done, it was proclaimed in all the pueblos that everyone in common should obey the commands of their father whom they did not know, which would be given through El Caydi or El Popé. This was heard by Alonso Catití, who came to the pueblo of this declarant to say that everyone must unite to go to the villa to kill the governor and the Spaniards who had remained with him, and that he who did not obey would, on their return, be beheaded; and in fear of this they agreed to it. Finally the señor governor and those who were with him escaped from the siege, and later this declarant saw that as soon as the Spaniards had left the kingdom an order came from the said Indian, Popé, in which he commanded all the Indians to break the lands and enlarge their cultivated fields, saying that now they were as they had been in ancient times, free from the labor they had performed for the religious and the Spaniards, who could not now be alive. He said that this is the legitimate cause and the reason they had for rebelling, because they had always desired to live as they had when they came out of the lake of Copala. Thus he replies to the question.

Asked for what reason they so blindly burned the images, temples, crosses, and other things of divine worship, he stated that the said Indian, Popé, came down in person, and with him El Saca and El Chato from the pueblo of Los Taos, and other captains and leaders and many people who were in his train, and he ordered in all the pueblos through which he passed that they instantly break up and burn the images of the holy Christ, the Virgin Mary and the other saints, the crosses, and everything pertaining to Christianity, and that they burn the temples, break up the bells, and separate from the wives whom God had given them in marriage and take those whom they desired. In order to take away their baptismal names, the water, and the holy oils, they were to plunge into the rivers and wash themselves with amole, which is a root native to the country, washing even their clothing, with the understanding that there would thus be taken from them the character of the holy sacraments. They did this, and also many other things which he does not recall, given to understand that this mandate had come from the Caydi and the other two who emitted fire from their extremities in the said estufa of Taos, and that they thereby returned to the state of their antiquity, as when they came from the lake of Copala; that this was the better life and the one they desired, because the God of the Spaniards was worth nothing and theirs was very strong, the Spaniards' God being rotten wood. These things were observed and obeyed by all except some who, moved by the zeal of Christians, opposed it, and such persons the said Popé caused to be killed immediately. He saw to it that they at once erected and rebuilt their houses of idolatry which they call estufas, and made very ugly masks in imitation of the devil in order to dance the dance of the cacina [kachina, or spirit]; and he said likewise that the devil had given them to understand that living thus in accordance with the law of their ancestors, they would harvest a great deal of maize, many beans, a great abundance of cotton, calabashes, and very large watermelons and cantaloupes; and that they could erect their houses and enjoy abundant health and leisure. As he has said, the people were very much pleased, living at their ease in this life of their antiquity, which was the chief cause of their falling into such laxity. Following what has already been stated, in order to terrorize them further and cause them to observe the diabolical commands, there came to them a pronouncement from the three demons already described, and from El Popé, to the effect that he who might still keep in his heart a regard for the priests, the governor, and the Spaniards would be known from his unclean face and clothes, and would be punished. And he stated that the said four persons stopped at nothing to have their commands obeyed. Thus he replies to the question. . . .

A Luiseño Recollection of Mission Life, 1835

. . . The Fernandino Father, as he was alone and very accustomed to the usages of the Spanish soldiers, seeing that it would be very difficult for him alone to give orders to that people, and, moreover, people that had left the woods just a few years before, therefore appointed alcaldes from the people themselves that knew how to speak Spanish more than the others and were better than the others in their customs. There were seven of these alcaldes, with rods as a symbol that they could judge the others. The captain dressed like the Spanish, always remaining captain, but not ordering his people about as of old, when they were still gentiles. The chief of the alcaldes was called the general. He knew the name of each one. . . . In the afternoon, the alcaldes gather at the house of the missionary. They

From Pablo Tac, *Indian Life and Customs at the Mission San Luis Rey: A Record of California Mission Life by Pablo Tac, An Indian Neophyte,* edited by Minna Hewes and Gordon Hewes (San Luis Rey, CA, 1958), pp. 12–13, 19–21.

bring the news of that day, and if the missionary tells them something that all the people of the country ought to know, they return to the villages shouting, "To-morrow morning. . . ."

Returning to the villages, each one of the alcaldes wherever he goes cries out what the missionary has told them, in his language, and all the country hears it. "Tomorrow the sowing begins and so the laborers go to the chicken yard and assemble there." And again he goes saying these same words until he reaches his own village to eat something and then to sleep. In the morning you will see the laborers appear in the chicken yard and assemble there according to what they heard last night.

With the laborers goes a Spanish majordomo and others, neophyte alcaldes, to see how the work is done, to hurry them if they are lazy, so that they will soon finish what was ordered, and to punish the guilty or lazy one who leaves his plow and quits the field keeping on with his laziness. They work all day, but not always. At noon they leave work, and then they bring them *posole.* (*Posole* is what the Spaniards of California call maize in hot water.) They eat it with gusto, and they remain sated until afternoon when they return to their villages. The shoe-makers work making chairs, leather knapsacks, reins and shoes for the cowboys, neophytes, majordomos and Spanish soldiers, and when they have finished, they bring and deliver them to the missionary to give to the cowboys. The black-smiths make bridle bits, keys, bosses for bridles, nails for the church and all work for all. . . .

In the Mission of San Luis Rey de Francia the Fernandino Father is like a king. He has his pages, alcaldes, majordomos, musicians, soldiers, gardens, ranchos, livestock, horses by the thousand, cows, bulls by the thousand, oxen, mules, asses, 12,000 lambs, 200 goats, etc. The pages are for him and for the Spanish and Mexican, English and Anglo-American travelers. The alcaldes to help him govern all the people of the Mission of San Luis Rey de Francia. The majordomos are in the distant districts, almost all Spaniards. The musicians of the Mission for the holy days and all the Sundays and holidays of the year, with them the singers, all Indian neophytes. Soldiers so that nobody does injury to Spaniard or to Indian; there are ten of them and they go on horseback. There are five gardens that are for all, very large. The Fernandino Father drinks little, and as almost all the gardens produce wine, he who knows the customs of the neophytes well does not wish to give any wine to any of them, but sells it to the English or Anglo-Americans, not for money, but for clothing for the neophytes, linen for the church, hats, muskets, plates, coffee, tea, sugar and other things. The products of the Mission are butter, tallow, hides, chamois leather, bear skins, wine, white wine, brandy, oil, maize, wheat, beans and also bull horns which the English take by the thousand to Boston.

[Daily life in a mission Indian household begins] when the sun rises and the stars and the moon go down, then the old man of the house wakens everyone and be-gins with breakfast which is to eat *juinis* heated and meat and tortillas, for we do not have bread. This done, he takes his bow and arrows and leaves the house with vigorous and quick step. (This is if he is going to hunt.) He goes off to the distant woods which are full of bears and hares, deer and thousands of birds. He is here all day, killing as many as he can, following them, hiding himself behind trees, climbing them, and then loaded with hares he returns home happy. But when he needs wood, then he leaves the house in the morning with his tumpline [carrying strap] on his shoulders and his ax, with companions who can help him when the load is very heavy, and in the afternoon he returns home. His old woman staying at home makes the meal. The son, if he is man, works with the men. His daughter stays with the women making shirts, and if these also have sons and daughters, they stay in the mission, the sons at school to learn the alphabet, and if they already know it, to learn the catechism, and if this also, to the choir of singers, and if he was a singer, to work, because all the musical singers work the day of work and Sunday to the choir to sing, but without a book, because the teacher teaches them by memory, holding the book. The daughter joins with the single girls who all spin for blankets for the San Luiseños and for the robe of the Fernandino Father. At twelve o'clock they eat together and leave the old man his share, their cups of clay, their vessels of well-woven fiber which water cannot leak out of, except when it is held before the face of the sun, their frying pans of clay, their grills of wood made for that day, and their pitchers for water also of clay. Seated around the fire they are talking and eating. Too bad for them if at that time they close the door. Then the smoke rising, being much, and the opening which serves as a window being small, it turns below, trying to go out by the door, remains in the middle of the house, and they eat, then speaking, laughing and weeping without wishing to. The meal finished they return to their work. The father leaves his son, the son leaves his sister, the sister the brother, the brother the mother, the mother her husband with cheer, until the afternoon. Before going to bed again they eat what the old woman and old man have made in that time, and then they sleep. . . .

An Ojibwa Recounts the Arrival of "Heavenly Visitors" to His People, n. d.

This story was told to my grandfather many years ago. One time, about two hundred years ago, in a place called Fort Hope, Ontario, there was a settlement of Ojibway Indians where there was a medicine-man who brought visitors from heaven to a huge wigwam shaped like a beaver house. Each spring the medicine-man would make this great wigwam and place holes in the top and sides, so that the great wind, if it blew on the top, would also blow out the sides.

After everyone was seated in a big circle about ten feet from the tent, the medicine-man inside would speak to the people outside and would say, "Now we shall have visitors again," and begin to pound his medicine drum. The great skies were clear and there was no wind.

All of a sudden a wind was heard to blow from the heavens and into the top of the wigwam, and from the holes on the sides came a refreshing breeze. In mid-air a rustle of people was heard but none were seen. Everyone was now looking and listening and from inside the wigwam people, men and women, were heard talking. The medicine-man inside spoke to the Indians without, saying, "Our visitors are here. Listen."

In those days the Indian people had never seen silk or satin, for everyone wore buckskin clothing. From the side of the opening on the wigwam appeared the finest silk in colours of red and blue and white. These the Ojibwa Indians believed were the dresses of the visitors. The material came from the sides of the wigwam because the wind was blowing from heaven into the open top, forcing some of the clothing worn by the visitors to appear on the sides. After about an hour the drum was beaten again and the visitors were heard to leave. Everyone looked at the top, but nothing was to be seen and everything became quiet. Then the medicine-man appeared at the door of the wigwam and spoke to his people, "My people, you have again seen and heard our visitors from heaven. Next spring we shall invite them again."

The old lady who told this to my grandfather about fifty years ago was very old, she was ninety-nine. She said, "We were all surprised, not at the great magic but at the material we saw at that time. For everyone then wore buckskin clothing and no silk or satin was known to the Indians. Afterwards, when the Hudson's Bay Company came to us they brought with them the material we had previously seen and touched, that had blown out of the great medicine lodge."

A French Traveler Observes Indian Religious Practices in Canada, 1721

Fort at the River Saint Joseph, September 8, 1721

Madam,

This letter will in all likelihood be a very long one, unless some unforeseen hindrance should oblige me to put off to some other opportunity what I have been able to collect, relating to the belief, traditions and religion of our Indians.

Nothing is more certain than that the Indians of this continent, have an idea of a supreme Being, though nothing at the same time can be more obscure. They all in general agree in looking upon him as the first spirit, and the governor and creator of the world, but when you press them a little close on this article, in order to know what they understand by the sovereign spirit, you find no more than a tissue of absurd imaginations, of fables so ill contrived, of systems so ill digested and so wild, that it is impossible to give any regular or just account of them. It is pretended that the Sioux approach much nearer than the other Indians towards a just conception of this first principle, but the little commerce we have hitherto had with them, does not permit me to be sufficiently informed of their traditions, to enable me to speak of them with any degree of certainty.

Almost all of the nations of the Algonquin language, give this foreign Being the appellation of the great Hare; some again call him Michabou, and others Atahocan. Most of them hold the opinion that he was born upon the waters, together with his whole court, entirely composed of four footed animals like himself; that he formed the earth of a grain of sand, which he took from the bottom of the ocean, and that he created man of the bodies of the dead animals. There are likewise some who mention a god of the waters, who opposed the designs of the great Hare, or at least refused to be assisting to him. This god is according to some, the great Tyger, but it must be observed, that the true tyger is not to be found in Canada; thus this tradition is probably of foreign extraction. Lastly, they have a third god called Matcomek, whom they invoke in the winter season, and concerning whom, I have learned nothing particular. . . .

The gods of the Indians have bodies, and live much in the same manner with us, but without any of the inconveniences to which we are subject. The word *spirit* amongst them, signifies only a being of a more excellent nature than others. They have no words to express what passes the bounds of their own understanding, their conceptions being extremely limited, with respect to whatever is not the object of their senses, or to any thing besides the common occurrences of life. They however ascribe to those imaginary beings, a kind of immensity and omnipresence, for in whatever place they are, they invoke them, and act in consequence. To all the questions you put to these barbarians, in order to obtain a farther account of their belief, they answer that this is all they have been taught or know of the matter; nay, there are only a few old men who have been initiated in their mysteries who know so much. . . .

Besides the first being, or the great spirit, and the other gods who are often confounded with them, there is likewise an infinite number of genii or inferior spirits, both good and evil, who have each a peculiar form of worship.

The Iroquois place Atahentsic at the head of these latter, and make Jouskeka the chief of the former; they even sometimes confound him with the god, who drove his grandmother out of heaven, for suffering herself to be seduced by a mortal. They never address themselves to the evil genii, except to beg of them to do them no hurt, but they suppose that the others are placed as so many guardians of mankind, and that every person has his own tutelary. In the Huron language these are called Okkis, and in the Algonquin Manitous: it is to them that they recourse in all perils and undertakings, as also when they would obtain some extraordinary favour; there is nothing but what they may think they may beg of them, let it be ever so unreasonable or contrary to good morals. . . .

There is nothing in all nature, if we believe the Indians, which has not its genius, of which there are some of all ranks, but with different powers. When they are at a loss to conceive any thing, they attribute it to superior genius, and their manner of expressing themselves then is, "This is a Spirit." This is said of greater justice of them, who have any singular talent, or who have performed an extraordinary action, "These are Spirits," that is they have a tutelary genius of an order superior to the common. . . .

Joseph Fish Preaches to the Narragansett Indians, 1768

June 20. 1768 . . . Found the School kept us as Usual, and more Schollars, of late, attending: about 15 Children, pretty Steadily come to School. Nothing Materially differing in Indians Circumstances Since last there: but Mr. Deake's Situation very difficult and distressing, on Account of his Debts. Tells me he Owes about £20- £Money, and all of it, to divers persons, now due, by Notes of hand or Obligations on Demand. His Creditors Patience no longer to be expected. Two Notes already committed to hands of Authority, to be heard. He expects a *Writ* or Two, before this Week is out: And can't See Any Way to avoid being taken out of his Business; which must break up the School. The Consequence he Apprehends will be, That the Indians, From their great Regard to Mr. *Greaves* N. Londo., Will Make Application to *Him,* or to the *Church* of England for a Schoolmaster and *Support.* On Consulting his Case, I promised him to write the Commissioners in his Behalf.

A[t] about Two, Preachd at Indian Meeting house, to 20 Indians, (They having heard that I would not Come today, and Numbers of them, through Carelessness, having forgot the Lecture.) From Matth: 22–39. *Thou Shalt love thy Neighbour as Thy Self*—A grace and Duty much Wanting and greatly Neglected Among these Indians. In the Fore part of My Discourse, Indians Seemd Sleepy and Careless—Digressed and rousd them, by Awakening Touches. Towards the Close of my Discourse, A Molatto (Ammon,) a Lusty Man, having for Some time discovered Something Singular in his Countenance, fell into great distress, manifested by Crying out bitterly, which continued through the Remainder of Sermon. Finishd off with a fervent Prayer, trembling as he Spoke. Found upon Speaking to him after Sermon, that the Word reachd his Conscience, Wakd up a Sense of his Guilt, in late evil Conduct, having been long reputed a Christian, but of late Years or Months, walkd unbecoming his Profession. Several other Indians, manifested Some deep Impressions from the *Word.*

After Lecture, Visited Two Families. Wm. Sachem (of the Sachems Party and his Uncle,) who never heard me preach Save once. Found him Serious and Attentive, while I talkd to him on the Affairs of his Soul. Has got a hope of Grace, in Former times but for Years past lives poorly. I endeavourd to Awake him to a Sense of his Duty and Danger. Here found about a Dozen Indians, Men and Women, who had been *Hoeing* for Will. I gave *Them* an Exhortation, and proceeded to find *Toby.*

The Indians commonly Fence their Fields with thick *Hedges*—No *Barrs,* I was obligd to break through their Hedges, with my Horse, and repair them, Well as I could. After travelling through the Thickets, many times no path, and passing deep valleys and Steep Hills, over Which I could but just climb, with my Horse in hand, for near 3/4 hour, (Mr. Deake in company my Guide) I found Sqr. *Tobys* (as Calld,) living much retird and then Alone. He's the Oldest Indian Man, in the Tribe. In his 86th Year. Entirely (or Near it) *blind.* Reckoned (not without good reason,) a pious Man. Talkd familiarly of *Death* and *Heaven.* Said he longd to go

Reprinted from *Old Light on Separate Ways: The Narragansett Diary of Joseph Fish,* William S. Simmons and Cheryl L. Simmons, eds., pp. 42–45. © 1982 by the University Press of New England. By permission of University Press of New England.

Home to his Fathers house, which he hopd for, in a little time. Twas now Night. Took leave of the Old Man. . . .

Tuesday, June 21. Returnd to the Indian houses, in the Morning. Visitted Four Indian Families. Discoursed with a Christian Indian Woman, (*Henry Harrys* Wife,) Under Soul Trouble, declining Health and many Afflictions. Her Daughter (a Widow) A bed with a Bastard Child—I endeavourd to awake the poor thoughtless, unconcernd Creature to a Sense of her Guilt and Danger. Calld at [?*Sachs*] Daughters—Droppd a Word of encouragement to a poor Creature in Travail.

Visited old Robins. His Daughter an Impudent Secure, Lewd person—Two Bastard Children with her. I endeavourd to Alarm her Conscience, by Shewing the certain Destruction of *Fornicators* etc.

Visited John *Shattock,* And, among other things, Reprovd him for not reading the *Bible* (as he Says he Can read it Well,) in his Family daily. Owns he has not read it for a long time. I endeavourd to Convince him of his Sinfull neglect, and excite him to his Duty. Left the Indians between Ten and Eleven o'Clock, and returnd home by post Road

Monday July 18. 1768 . . . Very hot and I much unwell; but reachd the School house about *One.* The School kept up, and about the Number of Schollars as before (15, or more). Mr. Deake Somewhat relievd of the pressures mentiond in Journal of last Visit. He approved of my Proposal to Commissioners for advancing half a years pay—Said twould much relieve him.

Many people at the Indian Meeting, Yesterday (Lords day,) English and Indians. Numbers behavd very wickedly, in time of the Indians Worship. In the day time or Evening Some of Them got drunk and Two Squaws fell upon another Squaw, that was heavy with Child, and beat, kickd and abusd her, So that her Life was much doubted of.

Preachd at Indian Mccting house to 30 Indians, Chiefly Women and young persons, from Matth. 5.4. Nothing Special Appeard in the Audience.

After Lecture Visited Samel. *Niles,* (about 1½ Mile North East from Meeting house) intending, to have Spent the Remainder of the Day and Next Day Forenoon, in Visiting Indians: but Mr. Deake and Niles told me there was (likely,) Scarce An Indian to be found at home; As the Busy Season calld them Abroad. So thought it pity to Spend my time, in Visiting Empty Houses. Concluded to deferr my intended Visits to the Next Journey. . . .

Red Jacket (Seneca) Lectures a Missionary, 1828

"Friend and Brother! . . . It was the will of the Great Spirit that we should meet together this day. He orders all things, and he has given us a fine day for our council. He has taken his garment from before the sun, and caused it to shine with brightness upon us. Our eyes are opened that we see clearly. Our ears are unstopped that we have been able to hear distinctly the words you have spoken. For all these favors we thank the Great Spirit, and him only.

"Brother!—This council fire was kindled by you. It was at your request that we came together at this time. We have listened with attention to what you have said. You requested us to speak our minds freely. This gives us great joy, for we now consider that we stand upright before you, and can speak what we think. All have heard your voice, and all speak to you as one man. Our minds are agreed.

"Brother!—You say you want an answer to your talk before you leave this place. It is right you should have one, as you are a great distance from home, and we do not wish to detain you. But we will first look back a little, and tell you what our fathers have told us, and what we have heard from the white people.

"Brother!—Listen to what we say. There was a time when our forefathers owned this great island. Their seats extended from the rising to the setting sun. The Great Spirit had made it for the use of Indians. He had created the buffalo, the deer, and other animals for food. He made the bear and the beaver, and their skins served us for clothing. He had scattered them over the country, and taught us how to take them. He had caused the earth to produce corn for bread. All this he had done for his red children because he loved them. If we had any disputes about hunting-grounds, they were generally settled without the shedding of much blood. But an evil day came upon us. Your forefathers crossed the great waters, and landed on this island. Their numbers were small. They found friends and not enemies. They told us they had fled their own country for fear of wicked men, and come here to enjoy their religion. They asked for a small seat. We took pity on them, granted their request, and they sat down amongst us. We gave them corn and meat. They gave us poison [alcohol] in return. The white people had now found our country. Tidings were carried back, and more came amongst us. Yet we did not fear them. We took them to be friends. They called us brothers. We believed them, and gave them a larger seat. At length their numbers had greatly increased. They wanted more land. They wanted our country. Our eyes were opened, and our minds became uneasy. Wars took place. Indians were hired to fight against Indians, and many of our people were destroyed. They also brought strong liquors among us. It was strong and powerful, and has slain thousands.

"Brother!—Our seats were once large, and yours were very small. You have now become a great people, and we have scarcely a place left to spread our blankets. You have got our country, but are not satisfied. You want to force your religion upon us.

"Brother!—Continue to listen. You say that you are sent to instruct us how to worship the Great Spirit agreeably to his mind; and if we do not take hold of the religion which you white people teach, we shall be unhappy hereafter. You say that you are right and we are lost. How do we know this to be true? We understand that your religion is written in a book. If it was intended for us as well as for you, why has not the Great Spirit given it to us; and not only to us, but why did he not give to our forefathers the knowledge of that book, with the means of understanding it rightly? We only know what you tell us about it. How shall we know when to believe, being so often deceived by the white people.

"Brother!—You say there is but one way to worship and serve the Great Spirit. If there is but one religion, why do you white people differ so much about it? Why not all agree, as you can all read the book?

"Brother!—We do not understand these things. We are told that your religion was given to your forefathers, and has been handed down from father to son. We also have a religion which was given to our forefathers, and has been handed down to us their children. We worship that way. It teaches us to be thankful for all the favors we receive, to love each other, and to be united. We never quarrel about religion.

"Brother!—The Great Spirit has made us all. But he has made a great difference between his white and red children. He has given us a different complexion and different customs. To you he has given the arts; to these he has not opened our eyes. We know these things to be true. Since he has made so great a difference between us in other things, why may we not conclude that he has given us a different religion, according to our understanding? The Great Spirit does right. He knows what is best for his children. We are satisfied.

"Brother!—We do not wish to destroy your religion, or take it from you. We only want to enjoy our own.

"Brother!—You say you have not come to get our land or our money, but to enlighten our minds. I will now tell you that I have been at your meetings and saw you collecting money from the meeting. I cannot tell what this money was intended for, but suppose it was for your minister; and if we should conform to your way of thinking, perhaps you may want some from us.

"Brother!—We are told that you have been preaching to white people in this place. These people are our neighbors. We are acquainted with them. We will wait a little while, and see what effect your preaching has upon them. If we find it does them good and makes them honest and less disposed to cheat Indians, we will then consider again what you have said.

"Brother!—You have now heard our answer to your talk, and this is all we have to say at present. As we are going to part, we will come and take you by the hand, and hope the Great Spirit will protect you on your journey, and return you safe to your friends."

◈ *E S S A Y S*

Each European nation claimed to be colonizing America for religious reasons, but Spain proceeded in its national missionary program more systematically and consistently than any other European state. For centuries, Spanish missionaries labored to convert American Indians to the Roman Catholic faith. Spain promoted these endeavors partly out of Christian piety and partly for practical reasons. Priests taught Indians not only to pray and to confess their sins but also to speak Spanish, to work at Spanish trades, and to obey royal authority. The conversion of millions of Native Americans throughout the hemisphere, however, did not mean that older native religious traditions were erased. Indeed, Indian and Catholic beliefs often coexisted, much to the horror of missionaries. In the first essay, Henry Warner Bowden, a professor of religion at Rutgers University, explains how divergent Indian and Catholic religious views influenced the Pueblo revolt of 1680.

The French, like the Spanish, also sent Catholic missionaries to America; for example, French priests conducted energetic missionary work among the native peoples of Canada. Kenneth M. Morrison, an associate professor of religious studies at Arizona State University, shows in the second essay that even when Native Americans accepted Christianity, they did not abandon their traditional beliefs. In New England, the missionary efforts of the colonists were not so well organized or widespread as those of Spain or even France, but Protestants did attempt to make Christianity available to the Indians who wanted it. In the final essay, James Ronda, a professor of history at the University of Tulsa, describes the initiatives by native peoples of Martha's Vineyard to control the influence of Christian faith on their lives.

These essays raise challenging questions about the Indian encounter with Christianity. Was it right for Europeans to proselytize among Native Americans? Were Indians who adapted Christianity to their own cultural norms somehow less than Christian, or less than Indian? Was the Christianization of Indians merely a part of their conquest and defeat, or did new religious ideas provide native peoples with new tools that they could use for their own ends?

Spanish Missions, Cultural Conflict and the Pueblo Revolt of 1680

HENRY WARNER BOWDEN

Historians who try to understand encounters between red men and white men in the seventeenth century are immediately confronted with a problem: Indians were not literate, and they left no records of the sort we are accustomed to studying. For centuries the only information about aboriginal populations in the Americas was derived from European narratives, conditioned by viewpoints that harbored an outsider's values. Archaeology added some indigenous references, but the evidence has usually been too meager for adequate generalization. Historians have pursued the goal of avoiding white men's biases and viewing Indian cultures as having an integrity all their own, but that goal has remained an ideal, causing more despair than hope of eventual success. As far as the history of early New Mexico is concerned, the situation is worsened by the fact that most church and government archives were burned during the fighting of 1680–1696.

In the twentieth century contributions of anthropological field workers have provided a wealth of new learning about Indian life. This scientific information is less distorted by culturally conditioned biases, and its disclosures are not tied to European source materials. Our modern data afford independent perspectives, new sources of information and opportunities for revising historical knowledge. A discriminating use of anthropological materials can free us from the narrow vision of a single cultural viewpoint and allow us more adequately to interpret past events that involved separate cultural units. Students of history now have the opportunity to work with new tools and ask new questions in addition to applying familiar methods to fresh data.

From an anthropologist's perspective, we can utilize a more comprehensive definition of religion and study its functional qualities in a particular cultural setting. That kind of inquiry makes it possible to understand the content of any people's world view, the unifying and normative place which religion has in the society's ethos and, most important, those aspects posing fundamental contrasts to alien cultures. The selection of Spanish missionary efforts in seventeenth-century New Mexico may be especially fruitful for a new interpretation of certain

From Henry Warner Bowden, "Spanish Missions, Cultural Conflict, and the Pueblo Revolt of 1680," *Church History* 44 (1975), pp. 217–228. Reprinted by permission of the American Society of Church History and the author.

historical events because it provides a context in which the religious focus was apparent and significant for both cultures. The Rio Grande Pueblos organized most of their activities around a well-articulated system of religious symbols and practices; the Spaniards had long been conscious of religious motives behind many of their heroic efforts. An analysis of what was really at issue between Spanish and Pueblo cultures on the religious level can shed light on their similarities, antipathies and reasons for armed conflict between them.

Of course anthropological information is not a panacea to be used uncritically, and one must confront the difficulties involved in a study that proceeds from present observations back into the past. It may be that contemporary reports of Pueblo rituals, calendar cycles, social structure and so forth, represent patterns that did not exist in the same configurations during the 1600s. It is also possible that an analysis of conflicts between the religions of Indian and Spaniard could highlight tensions disproportionately. Points of conflict in a specific context will indicate what was cherished enough at that time to defend against external pressures for change. But such conflicts do not show us the relative value of those cultural elements in a setting where they were unchallenged and allowed to seek their own level. The best we can hope for in studying two cultures is to identify their salient features in the limited context of their confronting each other. One should not conclude from comparative study that the controverted issues were categories of major significance within a society, relative to their own hierarchies of values. Another pitfall to avoid is that of attributing awareness or deliberate motives to people when they may not have been conscious of the issues in the way we describe them. Historical events must be interpreted with ideas based on as much information as relevant sources provide, but we can never go on to say that those specific categories and definitions were in the minds of the protagonists at the time. Despite these difficulties, it is still fair to say that facts and insights from anthropologists provide new avenues in the historian's search for an adequate understanding of red-white contact and the role religions played in the process. What follows is an attempt to demonstrate the results of such a study conducted within a limited area.

In 1598 the upper Rio Grande valley was viewed as an outpost of Spanish civilization, an opportunity for colonizing, mining and missionary exploits. By that time it had been the home of Keresan- and Tanoan-speaking Indians for over three hundred years. Under the leadership of Juan de Oñate an initial force of 400 persons, including 10 Franciscan friars, made their way upriver to the territory where approximately 30 to 40 thousand Pueblos inhabited an estimated 75 to 80 permanent towns. The first decade was a time of mismanagement and unsteady beginnings for both churchmen and civilians, but in 1609 the crown stabilized the colony with strong financial and administrative support, largely for the sake of its missionary enterprise. With Santo Domingo and Santa Fe established as bases of operations for church and state respectively, the prospects for growth were bright.

Missionary work among the Indians seemed to go well from the outset. As village leaders of the six tribal groups became acquainted with the friars and their message, they are reported to have welcomed them, expressed polite interest in their ideas and asked to know more. The district was soon divided into mission stations, and though the manpower shortage spread them thinly, priests were assigned to cover each area. Congregations were formed; catechetical instruction was begun; slowly a number of churches and chapels were built adjacent to the major pueblos. Various statistical reports of this period are not very reliable, but a realistic estimation is that an average of less than thirty Franciscans labored among colonists and natives during the seventeenth century and ministered to a baptized population of approximately 20,000 Pueblos.

One cannot discern a pattern of constantly increasing growth. There was a great deal of internecine strife between ecclesiastical and governmental authorities, and missionary efforts seem to have been hampered as a result. By 1630 the missions had spread numerically and geographically as far as they could in view of their problems with secular opposition, replacement difficulties and delays in supply and communication. After that, their history is one of trying to maintain the level of achievement rather than pursuing larger and more ambitious objectives.

Converting more people to Christian practices was, nevertheless, the reason for New Mexico's existence, and the friars performed their tasks with singleness of purpose. That zeal led them to concentrate on restricting Indian religious activities, especially during the 1670s. There had been some conflict between native and Spanish priests from the start, and sporadic outbursts of hostility had occurred at intervals, but in 1675 the clash of cultures became more pronounced on each side with resentment and bitterness increasing proportionately. Native ceremonies and liturgical articles had long been outlawed by Spanish officials, but those injunctions were suddenly enforced with renewed vigor. Essential ceremonial chambers (*kivas*) and many altars were seized, dances were strictly forbidden, masks and prayer sticks were destroyed, priests and medicinemen were imprisoned, flogged or hanged. Throughout the decade there was a determined action by both arms of Spanish culture to eradicate every vestige of Indian life, world view as well as ethos.

In August 1680 a general uprising of native peoples put a stop to those repressive measures. Every pueblo from Acoma to Pecos, from Taos to Isleta rose to destroy the Spanish presence north of El Paso. Of the 2,500 colonists approximately 380 were killed, including 21 of the 33 resident friars. All survivors were forced to retreat south, taking what few possessions they could carry while fleeing for safety. The successful Indians methodically rid themselves of every reminder of Spanish intrusion. They destroyed a great deal of property, including churches with their records, images and ceremonial paraphernalia. Renouncing the alien faith, Pueblos bathed to cleanse themselves from the effects of baptism. They abandoned foreign dress, stopped using Spanish names and left their Christian wives. Their rejection of Hispanic cultural patterns and the restoration of revitalized native ways was as thorough as the united efforts of chiefs and people could make them.

Why did the revolt occur? What were the primary factors leading to bloodshed at that particular time, and what can account for its deliberately anti-ecclesiastical character? Ranches and government buildings were also hit, but almost every church in the territory was demolished. Colonists of all types were killed when unfortunate enough to be caught in vulnerable positions, but the clergy were usually the first to die in every pueblo. Why did the spokesmen and symbols of Christianity receive the concentrated fury of Pueblo vengeance? The answer to these questions can be sought in a study of religions, their nature and place in the two cultures whose conflict rose to such an overt level. Religion was a factor at the core of each way of life, and if we can understand what contrasted at the center, we will be in a better position to interpret conflicts in the wider circles of cultural interaction, even to the point of seeing reasons for war.

During the initial stages of red-white contact there were enough similarities between their religions to allow for a degree of mutual understanding. On the tangible level, each side used altars, religious calendars, aids for prayer (feathered sticks or rosary beads), luxurious costumes for a distinct priesthood which presided over regularly appointed ceremonies, ritual chants in languages somewhat removed from everyday usage. Christian baptism corresponded easily to the Pueblo practice of head washing and the giving of a new name when one was initiated into special organizations. Catholic saints elevated from the ranks of men and women formed a parallel with Pueblo heros who once lived among the people in human shape, now petitioned as powerful spirits. Spaniards were wont to experience visions, demonic as well as beatific, and this too provided a link with a people who saw horned snakes, cloud people (*shiwanna*) and witches. The use of incense and holy water was close to Pueblo priests who made "clouds" with yucca suds for rain or sprayed consecrated water on an ailing patient. Kissing the hand of a friar was likened to the practice of "drawing in the breath" of a native priest or a loved one.

More intangibly, each religious system was based on beliefs that the world was ordered according to divine sanctions. The wills and wisdom of dominions beyond human making were thought by adherents of both cultures to be actively engaged in directing the weather, fortunes of war, personal fate and national destiny. Conversely both interpreted disease, drought and famine as either the result of malevolent spirits or the displeasure of gods who would not overlook human frailty. Within these positive and negative emphases it would be difficult to say whether the love of good or fear of evil predominated in the day-to-day actions of either people. But each religion in its own way emphasized divine power as that which gave order and meaning to their adherents' identity and mode of life.

These similarities were not appreciated by the Franciscans in New Mexico as an avenue for introducing their mission program. Unlike the Jesuits in Arizona and northwestern Mexico, they did not begin by utilizing aspects of existing religion and move from them to Christian formulations. Instead they were convinced either that the Indians possessed no religion at all or that they had been lured by the Devil into a repugnant congeries of idol worship and superstition. These spiritual conquerors matched their military counterparts in holding that the natives were barbarians who lacked any civilized notion of law or legitimate authority. Indian settlements were not viewed as properly organized communities; their forms of body covering were not considered true clothing; their sexual practices were judged to be disgracefully unregulated. So from the outset the friars set themselves the goal of stamping out every particle of native religion and substituting Catholic doctrines and practices, using force if necessary.

In keeping with these attitudes the Franciscans' behavior toward the Pueblos' religion conflicted sharply with tangible aspects of local custom. Almost without exception they did not try to master native languages or translate Christian ideas into them. They insisted that Indians learn Spanish. To supplant misguided native beliefs and ceremonial patterns, the missionaries operated on a policy of compulsory attendance at mass—for all baptized Indians but not all Spaniards. They made native officials (*fiscals*) punish their own people for failure to conform to this rule. With the aid of governors and soldiers they raided ancient ceremonial chambers and tried to prevent their future use. Masks and ritual paraphernalia of all kinds were periodically confiscated and burned. Traditional leaders who persisted in continuing the old rituals were arrested, and the gentle sons of St. Francis directed that they be whipped or executed as a menace to this life and an obstacle to the next.

These areas of tension in physical confrontations were symptoms of more fundamental conflicts that lay beneath the surface. No one at that time seemed to realize how different their cultural orientations were, but modern anthropology has helped us see that there were serious contradictions between Pueblo and Spaniard in the categories of world view, personal identity and moral obligation.

Pueblo views of the world were diametrically opposed to western European ones. The underworld rather than heaven or the sky was their locus for sources of life. There was no reference to a primal god, an *ex nihilo* [from nothing] creation of matter, or any transcendental direction over the affairs of the natural world. Gods, men, animals and plants emerged through an opening in the underworld's roof (seen as a naval or *shipapu* from earth, the middle stratum of the cosmos), and all of them came from below to dwell on the surface of this world. In the time of beginnings many gods or *katsina* had lived with the people and taught them how to cope with their new environment. Patterns and procedures thought to stem from that time and from those sources carried the sanction of ultimate authority:

> Thus the Indians got their culture—their houses, weapons, tools, and cultivated plants, their clans, priests and societies, their songs, prayers, ceremonies and paraphernalia. That is why they live, work and worship . . . as they do: because their ways of life were established by the gods long ago. . . . To ignore or violate, to lose the customs of the old days . . . [would be] to bring misfortune . . . even extinction, upon themselves.

Compared with the Spanish notion of a heavenly creator who guided his people from above, the Pueblo view derived strength from the opposite direction, and it was much more explicit about divinely instituted patterns of activity.

Instead of beginning with a belief that the natural world was the Lord's footstool and man's economic resource, Indians of the Rio Grande gave the earth a sacred status of its own. In comparison with Europeans who felt free to use natural materials for any secular purpose they fancied, Pueblos had a more profound respect for the basically sacred constitution of natural objects. Their place in this world was what really mattered to them, and sacred space radiated in concentric circles from the center, which was either the local village or a nearby place of emergence. Everything in the cosmos had its place by reference to this center. Everything from points on the compass to changing seasons was bounded and controllable because the earth was an orderly environment that circumscribed the harmony of all good things. Instead of wishing to escape this world or destroy it through exploitation, Pueblos affirmed their existence in it and husbanded their lives along with nature as parts of a single sanctified life system. It was a complete, substantial and satisfying world, and one could know enough about life, death and proper conduct to feel gratified by living in it according to established ways.

Another point at which the two cultures stood in striking contrast to each other had to do with personal identity; that is, their worlds were different, and they thought of the people in them differently too. The European view enhanced the role of the individual, his free choice and opportunities to distinguish himself from others. Whether by valor or charity, by deeds of might or sacrifice, personal merit was a virtue to be prized and cultivated. For Pueblos, however, personal identity was always defined by reference to the community, not at its expense. The self as any Spaniard would have defined it was submerged, and all of Indian society's values emphasized the well-being of the collectivity rather than that of the individual. Personal distinction was shunned, not sought; innovation was discouraged. Anyone who strove constantly to distinguish himself from his fellows was more likely to be ostracized and charged with witchcraft than to receive admiration from his townspeople.

The antithetical nature of this cultural trait is fairly easy to see when measured against Christian doctrines of salvation and the church. From its beginnings Christianity has almost always conveyed the assumption that its adherents were a separate people, sheep separated from the goats, wheat from the chaff, a faithful remnant saved from destruction by a merciful God. This salvation of separate individuals has usually included some degree of voluntary belief and personal morality, a combination of faith and works in which the responsibility of the believer played an important role in securing the final result. In Pueblo life there were no such thoughts. Everyone belonged to the group, and everyone was certain to reach the afterworld (enter *shipapu*), regardless of his merits or demerits. The only qualification on this cultural universalism was the idea that those failing to lead a good life would have a more difficult time reaching the place of emergence/reentry. There was no place of reward for the good and another of retribution for those less virtuous. As one valuable description put it, "to die in a pueblo is not to become dead but to return to the only real life there is; one 'changes houses' and rejoins the ancestors. . . ." Just as there was no community-separating heaven and hell, there was no concept of atonement, no vicarious sacrifice, no redemption—none of these because there was no need.

Christianity came to the Pueblos preaching doctrine that required a psychological sense of separation from the aboriginal group. The missionaries saw the church as an institution composed of believers gathered in anticipation of ultimate rescue out of this life. The church thus embodied a community-dividing thrust. Not all members of society would be saved, only the baptized. Not all Indians or Spaniards were expected at mass (and incidently punished for failure to attend), only those gathered into the communion of saints. The church cut through families and clans, through moities and secret societies. Its contrast with native religious forms was stark enough when it stood simply as a competitive institution; but its major threat to native life stemmed from a disruptive capacity to offer salvation only to individuals.

Differing ideas of moral obligation comprised a third general category of conflict. For Spanish preachers ethical guidelines were thought to derive from biblical and theological traditions, sources transcending any particular cultural group. Pueblos derived their sense of duty and propriety within an understanding of the community and its needs. The missionaries defined good and bad actions on a standard possessed by the church, seen as a divine institution that did not, in ideal terms at least, coincide with the totality of any cultural unit or their various civil offices. Natives based their model of ethical judgment on a standard that comprehended all facets of their society and did not see any reason for going beyond them. Europeans thought that sanctions against improper conduct would apply in the afterlife, usually in addition to, not in place of, temporal effects. Indians expected ultimate sanctions, like death for witchcraft, to apply in this life with no rewards or punishments reserved for the future.

The more important differences between Indian and European emerged in actually trying to live by these divergent views of right conduct while attempting to convert one's opposite number. The friars stressed attendance at mass, morning and evening prayer, monogamy with no divorce and obedience to Spanish magistrates as fundamental elements of moral life. Pueblo activities were aligned with the order of nature and had been organized into an elaborate system of societies which presided over a cycle of ritual ceremonies. The Indians' central obligation was to participate in and to perpetuate those rites which insured a well-ordered life for the pueblo and its circle of physical needs. Most village adults belonged to at least one of many societies, usually from eight to twenty in a pueblo, that presided over vital functions like planting, irrigation or rain making, hunting, harvesting, rules enforcement and curing physical ailments. Existence itself, the very elements that gave meaning and structure to Indian life as a cultural unit, depended on cycles of corporate activity grouped rationally around an agrarian calendar year. Social structures conformed to the works necessary for cooperating with natural rhythms. Ritual activities were orchestrated to facilitate these works; food, shelter and health followed as a result of attention to ceremonial obligations. If this combination of activities and moral obligations were ever suppressed to a serious degree, the threat to Pueblo existence would be quite serious indeed.

None of the standard interpretations of Spanish activity and Pueblo resistance in the seventeenth century have noticed the important role religion played in the tensions between the two cultures. They have usually stressed disputes over land and water rights, abuses in the *ecomienda* labor system or the obtrusive presence of a military *entrada* in another nation's territory. The major theme in historical writing for well over a century now has been to interpret Indian rebellion as an expression of economic and political self-determination. Discussions of the Pueblo Revolt of 1680 thus parallel other patriotic revolutions in the western hemisphere against a familiar archetype of tyranny and oppression.

But is this an adequate explanation? It does not account for why the uprising occurred when it did, that is, why the various nations were desperate enough at that particular time to combine their strength and cooperate as never before. It does not explain why a war ostensibly over land, labor and personal freedom should have taken such an overtly anti-Christian turn. It implies that Spanish civil and ecclesiastical authorities would have been successful if their means had been less harsh. It fails to realize how antithetical the two cultures really were in the seventeenth century and how deeply the Pueblos were committed to maintaining the integrity of their cultural system, one that grounded their existence in realities they knew always to have pertained. Interpretations of the conflict offered thus far have overemphasized the political and economic factors, leaving several important questions unanswered and omitting consideration of relevant information about the values and motivations of people actually confronting a rival culture.

Suggestions for a more adequate historical interpretation would build on the physical and non-material cultural differences already discussed and then concentrate on events beginning in 1667. From that year to 1672 there was an extended drought and crop failure. Most of the population, Indian and colonist alike, was reduced to eating "hides that they had and the straps of the carts, preparing them for food by soaking . . . and roasting them in the fire with maize, and boiling them with herbs and roots." In 1671 a great pestilence carried off many people and livestock. By 1672 the nomadic Apaches and Navajos, also pinched by dwindling food supplies, increased their raids on the settled areas and brought more ruin. One of the Spaniards' feudal promises had always been to protect their charges from such raids; now that promise was seen for what it was worth. By 1675 at least six pueblos had been wiped out, and most others were in desperate straits.

In the light of such conditions it is not surprising to see that the Pueblos began to abandon Spanish habits and return to their folkways. In the past they had been willing to accept the advantages of Spanish technology and even the externals of the new religion, as long as imported items served material and social ends. When missionaries insisted that acceptance of Christianity forbade any retention of aboriginal beliefs and required denial of native rituals, there were probably some opportunists willing to go even that far. But when all of them realized that the new ways were no better than the old ones in bringing rain, curing disease or preventing invasions—indeed, when they seemed to be the cause of so much suffering—then a massive return to the more trusted patterns of ancient teaching was in the offing.

Ironically enough, at the same time Indian practices were being revitalized, the Spanish mounted an energetic campaign to extinguish them altogether. Relations between church and state had been stormy throughout most of the century, but in the person of Juan Francisco de Treviño, arriving as governor sometime after 1670, the missionaries finally found a civil magistrate willing to enforce their suppression of native religion with wholehearted cooperation. As the Indians were moving in one direction, Spanish forces tried with increasing brutality to move them toward the opposite pole. In 1675 forty-seven ceremonial leaders were arrested. Three were hanged, another committed suicide, and the others were released after being whipped only because the Indians made a show of force. Plans for a wider and more effective revolt were not long in forthcoming, and most of the central figures, including el Popé, came from among those leaders publicly humiliated.

The fighting of 1680 caught the Spanish by surprise, and their evacuation left the Indians free to follow pre-contact standards of conduct as they wished. There was an abortive attempt to reconquer the land in 1682, but for the better part of fifteen years the Pueblos had little molestation from soldiers or friars. New Mexico was conquered again by 1696, and Indian resistance took two new forms. Thousands moved west to live with a similar but more remote culture, the Hopi; those who stayed in the river valleys compartmentalized their lives into outward conformity to the dominant culture and inner loyalty to their own.

In piecing together the best possible historical interpretation of these events it is important to notice that political, economic and personal factors did play a role, but they do not tell the whole story. The cultural antagonism between Spaniard and Pueblo had fundamentally religious roots, and an adequate understanding of the 1680 hostilities must give them priority. In the last analysis the Indian war was an attempt to preserve the kind of life which they thought the gods had ordained and which aliens were obviously destroying. The tribes united voluntarily to expel the Spanish because their coercive tactics were preventing a life based on true beliefs and conduct—an ethos seen not only as proper, but as the one way to stave off the disease and famine confronting them. The Pueblo Revolt was an act of people determined to reject Christian civilization because it posed a direct threat to their culture and religion, to their integrated structures which embodied indispensable elements for Pueblo survival.

This study of a particular cultural conflict may be useful in shedding more light on one set of concrete historical circumstances and in providing a more comprehensive interpretation of all the factors that were in operation there. But it stands as only one case study in a field that needs a great deal of attention. Historians are now in a position to capitalize on sophisticated treatments of religion in cultural contexts and blend them with more standard surveys of missionary activity. The day has come when we can adjust one-sided interpretations of red-white relations, correcting them with a wealth of new material and a more comprehensive understanding of Indian life. This new awareness is the key to better history of hundreds of cultures whose integrity and richness we are just beginning to appreciate. Once this is under way, the scope and quality of Christian missions can be more realistically viewed within specific contexts.

Montagnais Missionization in Early New France

KENNETH M. MORRISON

The Montagnais kin groups which entered the Canadian mission at Sillery [near Quebec] in 1639 throw significant light on the process of religious change. The *Jesuit Relations* richly document the Montagnais' culture, and describe in detail their struggle to comprehend Catholicism. As a result, it is possible to achieve an Indian history grounded in the reality assumptions of a particular Native American people. The Montagnais demonstrate that when religious change is described as conversion, both Native Americans' role in missionization and their syncretic intentions [that is, the Indians' desire to merge traditional and Christian beliefs]

From "Montagnais Missionization in Early New France: The Syncretic Imperative," by Kenneth Morrison, *American Indian Culture and Research Journal* 10, no. 3 (1986), pp. 1–23. Reprinted by permission of Kenneth Morrison.

are missed. The Montagnais resisted Jesuit teachings for the better part of ten years, but some of them settled at Sillery for their own reasons. The challenge remains to reconstruct the reasoning by which some Montagnais adopted what appears to be the radically alien lifestyle the missionaries offered.

To begin with, it is useful to ask how we can achieve the insiders' view of missionization. The answer consists in identifying the common theoretical ground which has emerged between religious studies and several social science and humanistic disciplines. A good place to start is Susanne K. Langer's *Philosophy in a New Key*. Langer heralded what might be thought of as a radical humanism focusing on meaning as an empirical, cross-disciplinary field of inquiry. Although Langer is seldom cited in social science literature or, for that matter, in the study of the humanities, the problem of meaning she highlighted has received concerted attention in the post-war era.

There are a number of examples of an emerging methodological focus on meaning. One can cite the interdisciplinary study of symbol, myth and ritual. Equally fruitful lines of investigation have emerged in the philosophy of language, sociolinguistics, cognitive anthropology, and the sociology of knowledge, as well as social and ethnic history. Taken together, these collaborations have brought home the need for an ethnohistorical investigation which assumes that history has alternative causal explanations in cross-cultural situations.

The Montagnais-Naskapi relationship with the French is a case in point. A quick review of the histories of seventeenth-century Canada suggests that the Montagnais story is so familiar that alternative explanations are not needed. The Montagnais were among the first northeastern Native Americans to experience regular contact with Europeans. They were pioneers in developing commercial, political and military alliances with the French. They were also among the first to regret the negative impact of European contact. After 1633, when the French re-established their base at Quebec, the Montagnais began to find themselves commercially displaced, subject to Iroquoian harassment, and politically subordinate to the French. To make matters worse, overtrapping led to a dramatic decrease in Montagnais food resources, and winter famines became commonplace. European diseases also took a heavy toll. Finally, in this situation of apparently massive cultural dissolution, the Montagnais capitulated in despair to the Jesuit missionaries who promised salvation.

Briefly put, it is the primary goal of this essay to establish the way in which these causal variables intersected with the Montagnais understanding of French Catholicism. What is particularly relevant here is what the priests and the Montagnais saw as salvation. Historians have rightly emphasized the practical concerns of both parties, but they have also taken European pragmatism as the Montagnais norm. It appears that the Montagnais had nothing to lose and everything to gain from a privileged relationship with the French. The alliance certainly made economic, political and military sense. That some Montagnais apparently accepted what we have come to think of as ideological colonization is more difficult to comprehend. The history of the Montagnais has revealed some of the factors governing their reaction to the Jesuits, but these do not tell the whole story. Post-contact crisis posed problems with which the Montagnais had to grapple, but their own religious, philosophical and social tradition channeled their conservative response.

Religion and Montagnais Existential Assumptions: Person, Power, Gift

Despite the fact that the Jesuits never really understood Montagnais motives, their annual *Relations* expose the reasoning of the Montagnais. The *Jesuit Relations* are extraordinary documents because they present accurate ethnological descriptions of Montagnais life. Moreover, the *Relations* are invaluable because they not only record what the Montagnais had to say, but also describe how they acted. In these ways, the missionaries have provided unparalleled documentary access to Native American experience. What remain misleading in the Jesuit texts, however, are the religious assumptions by which the Jesuits judged Montagnais culture. If the French priests eventually embraced something resembling cultural relativism, they still contended that the Montagnais lacked those qualities we call religious.

The Jesuits' religious anthropology merits attention because, try as they did, the priests could not relegate the Montagnais to irreligious savagery. At first, the priests held only that they were called to bring the Montagnais what they lacked. The Jesuits thought of the Montagnais as religiously deficient: they lacked knowledge of God and His written revelation, as well as the dogma and ritual which properly belong to institutionalized religion. Under the circumstances, the Jesuits faced a clear-cut, if difficult, task. After two years of work among the Montagnais, Father Paul Le Jeune described missionization pragmatically, although, as will be clear from the following discussion, he did not grasp the Montagnais' understanding of power: "The more imposing the power of our French people is made in these Countries," the priest declared, "the more easily they can make their belief received by these Barbarians, who are influenced even more through the senses than through reason."

The priests had concluded that the Montagnais were as satanically misguided as they were ignorant. The *Jesuit Relations* catalog a wide variety of Montagnais delusions: in common with other Native American peoples, the Montagnais were trammeled by strange stories, were led by shamanistic charlatans, and were perversely dependent on dreams. In time, the Jesuits felt that all of Montagnais culture evinced religious backwardness and degradation. But, at the same time, much of Montagnais life defied condemnation.

Jesuit relativism began in the recognition that the Montagnais lived by a pervasive value system that set the stage for their Christian enlightenment. The priests were forced to recognize that however superstitious the Montagnais seemed, they had intractable notions of right and wrong. The more closely the priests looked, the more they admired the social values that the Montagnais professed. In the end, and as clear evidence of the limitations of their anthropological thought, the Jesuits created the paradoxical image of the noble savage—people who were naturally good but religiously and civilly backward, people who were, in short, inexplicable in either rational or moral terms. Of course, the Jesuits were left with God's will as the bottom line.

The problem of cross-cultural anthropology remains. If the field of religious studies is fundamentally concerned with confronting and making sense of cultural otherness, we need to recognize at the outset the rational impediments to understanding that cultural differences have always imposed. In effect, a primary requirement for understanding the course of the Montagnais religious change is to confront the meaning "otherness" itself had in particular historical situations. We must begin with the recognition that what we gloss as religion may not describe Montagnais' reality. There is, for example, the commonplace notion that Native American religions are holistic, inseparable from what we think of as the linguistic, political, economic and social aspects of culture. Such a view may be useful in highlighting genuine differences in religious outlook, but it also creates a real problem which eludes our empirical concerns. If religion is so pervasive, the end effect is that religion as a category may disappear.

There is now considerable interdisciplinary agreement that religion is not simply another part of culture. One could cite Peter Berger as providing evidence of the religiously-grounded nature of socio-cultural reality systems. In a complementary interpretation, Clifford Geertz contends that religion has to do with world creation, maintenance and transformation. Geertz defines the major challenge: "The notion that religion tunes human actions to an envisaged cosmic order, and projects images of cosmic order onto the plane of human experience is hardly novel. But it is hardly investigated either, so that we have very little idea of how in empirical terms, this particular miracle is accomplished."

Sam D. Gill adds a major qualification which focuses our attention on the historical role of religion: religion is that activity by which people continually take responsibility for the meaning of the worlds they in fact create. As such, religion has no necessary feature, nor mandatory content. As Gill puts it:

> We will consider as religious those images, actions, and symbols that both express and define the extent and character of the world, especially those that provide the cosmic framework in which human life finds meaning and the terms of fulfillment. We will also consider as religious those actions, processes and symbols through which life is lived in order that it be meaningful and purposive.

Given this common emphasis on the relation between religion and cultural meaning, confusing religion with particular aspects of culture should no longer be troubling. Religion is nothing more, nor less, than that human activity through which people assign responsibility for meaning, worldly and otherwise.

There are other problems which an existential, activity-oriented view of religion avoids. Much of what we ordinarily consider integral to religion is inapplicable to Montagnais (and other Native American) reality. If A. Irving Hallowell was correct in rejecting the terms supernatural and spirit—contending as he did that they did not fit Algonkian experience—then Montagnais-Jesuit dialogue faced tremendous hurdles. Applied to the seventeenth century, Hallowell's point means that what the Jesuits thought of as the transcendental nature of religion was simply not relevant to the Algonkian peoples, who emphasized the immanent character of religion. As one shaman declared in 1637, the only life he cared for was the life of this world.

Another Montagnais shaman expressed this difference in orientation to Father Le Jeune during the winter of 1633–1634. "'Thy God,' he replied, 'has not come to our country, and that is why we do not believe in him; make me see him and I will believe in him.'" Such statements were commonplace; the Montagnais continually insisted that it was obvious that Christian revelation had been addressed to the French. In 1637 Makheabichtichiou tellingly made the point: "'The son of God did not love our country,' (said he) 'for he did not come here, and did not say anything to us about all that.'" Le Jeune protested in this instance that Jesus had not been born among the French either, but they had still come to accept him. Moreover, the priest urged Makheabichtichiou to give rational assent to Christian teachings. The Montagnais answered in typical terms: "'I have nothing to say against all this,' he answered, 'for I have not been taught anything to the contrary.'" Yet another man declared: "'I do not know him . . . , if I could see him, I would thank him.'" For their part, the Montagnais felt that they had religious knowledge sufficient to meet their needs and appropriate to their situation.

In effect, then, the idea of belief or faith in some sacred and transcendental otherness which we commonly associate with religion was not particularly relevant to Montagnais interests. From this point of view French religion at first seemed absurd. The Montagnais found it incomprehensible that the missionaries believed in a transcendent God. "'Thou hast no sense,'" the Montagnais accosted Paul Le Jeune in 1634, "'how canst thou believe in him, if thou hast not seen him.'" On another occasion a shaman declared flatly: "'When I see him, I will believe in him, and not until then. How believe in him who we do not see?'"

Nor were the Montagnais theistically oriented, which accounts for Le Jeune's shocked dismissal of their religious attitude as "ingratitude." As the priest put it: "although they believe that the [Culture Hero] Messou has restored the world, that Nipinoukhe and Pipounoukhe bring the seasons, that their Khichikouai teach them where to find Elks or Moose, and render them a thousand good offices,— yet up to the present I have not been able to learn that they render them the slightest honor." The priest did not comprehend that what mattered to the Montagnais was concrete experience, and he did not understand that rituals attached to hunting ensured proper relations with these mythological beings. The Montagnais' religious discrimination was everyday and practical.

Still, the religious outlook of the Montagnais people was systematic, and that system channeled their evaluation of the Jesuits' religious claims. While they did approach religious change pragmatically, they made largely unconscious and usually unarticulated assumptions about the character of reality. Three ideas are central to Montagnais reality assumptions, as they were to all Algonkian-speaking Native Americans. These are the concepts of Person, Power, and Gift, which dominated their perception, cognition and social behavior.

Hallowell cited as evidence for Algonkian interest in religious immanence the fact that for them the idea of person was not limited to human beings. Likewise, in the 1630s, Paul Le Jeune learned from his study of the language that European ways of thinking did not apply to the Montagnais. In particular, the idea that the world was constituted by persons, human and otherwise, rather than by nature or natural forces, was central to Montagnais thought. Le Jeune discussed this reality assumption in detail and, although his writings provide ample evidence, never truly understood that the idea of person had more than intellectual implications. The concept actually organized the Montagnais social world, a world which had as much to do with action as with thought. For them, the sun, moon, winds, thunder, plants, minerals and even man-made objects were all potential persons. As Le Jeune put it, "the Savages persuade themselves that not only men and other animals, but also other things are endowed with souls, and that all the souls are immortal."

Montagnais life concerned itself with maintaining positive relations with these other-than-human persons. The Jesuits discovered that all human abilities, and particularly the ability to hunt, to practice medicine, and to wage successful war, depended on right relations with these entities. For example, the shaman's power to cure and to kill derived from them. The Montagnais name for shaman— *Manitouisiouekhi*—means "those who are acquainted with the Manitou, with him who is superior to men." The shaman, accordingly, fasted in order to seek power from various classes of persons. Le Jeune reported that the Montagnais "gave the name Manitou to all Nature superior to man, good or bad."

In discussing this personalistic sense of causality that the Montagnais shared with other Algonkians, Hallowell was also emphatic that, as a necessary result, any idea of impersonal cause was foreign to their thinking. Thus, the idea of power was closely related to the Montagnais concept of person. In fact, the word for power—manitou—was also synonymous with the concept of person, human and otherwise, and whether used in a positive or a negative sense. There were persons of both kinds. Another way of thinking in these terms is to acknowledge that for the Montagnais history included the actions of both human and other-than-human persons. Moreover, their sense of causality, linked as it was to personal intent, was not at all concerned with the abstract causal forces—economic, political, military, and even medical—by which we impersonally explain their experience. Thus, the net effect of the ideas of Person and Power was to lead the Montagnais to ground their value judgments upon how people acted. Montagnais thinking, and the social values their rationality sustained, was behaviorally precise.

The idea of Gift was intimately related to the first two concepts because it defined the criteria by which the Montagnais assessed personal motives. Sharing, gift giving, and reciprocity identified the ideal characteristics of powerful people and so allowed the Montagnais to decide ethical issues of personal and social responsibility. For the Montagnais, kinship, or its absence, defined trust or distrust. The Jesuits identified what they saw as Montagnais vices, especially those that affected relations with dangerous and feared outsiders. These included ungratefulness, deceitfulness, treachery, and revenge. The priests also came to appreciate the normative values which derived from Montagnais religion and which shaped their internal social life. These social virtues consisted of good-naturedness, peacefulness, patience, compassion, hospitality, and generosity. In these negative and positive ways, the Montagnais emphasized the moral implications of a world composed of unrelated and related persons. For them, it was cosmologically given that power ought to be used to help other people.

A mythically grounded rule of responsible reciprocity regulated the relations between all classes of people. For example, as the Montagnais understood it, they prayed to the Master of the Game, asking for help in feeding their families. When the prayers were successful, the animals heard and answered the plea. The hunter in turn generously helped his kinfolk and paid respect to the bones of the animal. Mutuality, generosity, and cooperation were not only the basic values of Montagnais social life, but also the very means used to maintain proper relations with the persons of the larger world. The dominant role ritual played in all of their activity reflected this central concern for proper relationships.

Although these ideas are properly understood as the fundamental existential assumptions of the Montagnais world-view, they were not mere abstractions. Rooted as they were in the language, the concepts affected the Montagnais' perceptual and cognitive style and thereby shaped the pragmatism the Montagnais applied to Jesuit religious claims. It is significant that these criteria explain Montagnais estimations of the French as people. In the first place, the French continually violated the rule of reciprocity. Not only did they hold tenaciously to their private property, they sometimes even refused to share food. Sharing was an imperative for the Montagnais and group opinion carried considerable weight in maintaining contempt for the French. Given French notions of property, the Montagnais concluded that they were unlikely to be friends, thinking, Paul Le Jeune declared, "that we do not wish to ally ourselves with them as brothers, which they would very much desire."

This uncertainty about French political intentions (best understood in light of Montagnais skepticism about French social ethics) highlights the contrast between different modes of Montagnais and European pragmatism. In a provocative essay which examines Hallowell's characterization of Algonkian thought, anthropologist Mary Black raises issues which help explain Montagnais motives in the 1630s. Her findings can be summarized as follows: the Algonkian category of person was too general to fit all situations. Hallowell stressed that Algonkians were highly discriminating in their recognition of other-than-human persons; in particular, he noted that many persons had the ability to shift bodies. Also, in one situation a bear (for example) could be simply an animal; in another, the bear could turn out to be a shaman in disguise.

Black underlines Hallowell's conclusion that Algonkians acted cautiously toward all potential persons. Algonkian speakers could only judge the personal character (and power for good or ill) of entities linguistically classed as animate according to how they acted in particular situations. It follows that Algonkians had to assume that reality was not always as it seemed. Moreover, since power was unevenly distributed, it behooved Algonkians to act cautiously for fear of being disrespectful toward potentially dangerous persons. Black calls this phenomenon "percept ambiguity" and, as we shall see, it goes far to explain the kind of anxiety the Montagnais experienced in dealing with the post-contact crisis of the 1630s.

Religion and Crisis

Whether explained in Montagnais or European terms, the decade of the 1630s was a time of mounting crisis. When the French returned to Canada in 1633, the Montagnais felt little concern for the future. Between 1633 and 1635 they showed generalized contempt for French culture. The colonists were ineffectual in making a living off the land, and consistently demonstrated that they did not share Montagnais social values. Not surprisingly, the Montagnais concluded not only that French religion had little to offer, but also that it was probably dangerous. As a result, they resisted baptism. Nevertheless, events of those years began to undercut Montagnais confidence. Their hunting economy began to fail as the beaver became depleted, and disease attacked young and old alike.

In 1636–1637, the Montagnais began to hedge their bets religiously. While they had faced the fact of growing crisis, they had also decided that they could do something about the situation. The numbers of baptisms increased from 22 in 1635 to 115 in 1636. These numbers fail to convey the whole story, however, because more and more the Montagnais themselves sought baptism for their children, partly because they thought of the sacrament as a potentially powerful medicine. As significantly, dying adults also began to ask to be baptized.

The Montagnais had become increasingly despondent—an emotional state that they had always seen as a primary cause of disease. For this reason, the Montagnais had begun to react fearfully to the possibility that the Jesuits' hell truly existed. In 1637, for example, they asked what was causing so many deaths, saying that "since the coming of the French their nation was going to destruction . . ." They repeatedly lodged such complaints against the French but, in fact, a growing belief in hell paralleled serious disruptions in Montagnais social life. The Montagnais worried that they might have drawn trouble to themselves.

By all indications, the Montagnais were truly uncertain where to place the blame. Several cases of windigo [spirit possession] cannibalism indicate the way in which the Montagnais internalized their own responsibility for the crisis. The number of human windigoes threatening the Montagnais in this decade reflects the Indians' sense of ethical malaise. Windigoes were at once a mythological symbol of anti-social savagery and a human psychotic condition. In 1636, for instance, a powerful other-than-human person warned the Montagnais that a cannibal would attack and eat them if they attempted to settle near the French.

It is also significant that their war with the Iroquois made the Montagnais even more anxious and impelled them to seek a closer alliance with the French. The Montagnais annually fielded small war parties, but these were insignificant when compared with Iroquoian military strength. To make matters much worse, the French not only refused to side with the Montagnais, but also criticized traditional war itself. The Montagnais were perplexed when the Jesuits accused them of bloodlust, and decried their war feasts as rank savagery. The priests also criticized the dreams and visions in which other-than-human persons aided the Montagnais against the enemy. Throughout the 1630s, the situation deteriorated to a point where the Montagnais became militarily impotent. In 1637, for instance, Paul Le Jeune accosted one headman. The Jesuit warned him of defeat because the war party's shaman had blasphemed against the Christian God. Disaster did occur and Le Jeune later confronted the shaman publicly, declaring "that he had been the cause of their defeat."

By 1638, some Montagnais concluded that the priests had power on their side and sought baptism as a symbolically potent expression of solidarity with the French. Many of the Montagnais deliberately camped near French settlements, apparently hoping that an alliance would help solve their economic, political, military, and even social problems. Fear of baptism was still common, but the number of cures associated with the sacrament began to increase. As evidence that the French priests were seen as more powerful than traditional medicine men, one shaman, Pigarouich, destroyed his ritual paraphernalia and accepted baptism. The following year the Jesuits noted that calamities like a smallpox epidemic seemed to attract more and more of the Montagnais.

In the short term, the Montagnais took Christian claims seriously for three main reasons. First, given the ambiguous nature of power, they came to see the Jesuits as religious specialists comparable to, and more capable than, their own shamans. Second, although they remained distrustful of baptism, they came to see it positively. The sacrament not only healed in some cases, it also ensured continued contact between living and dead Montagnais. Third, the person(s) of Jesus and He-Who-Made-All reinvigorated the traditional hunting economy, based as it was on reciprocal relations between human and animal persons. In all of these ways, Catholicism made sense in traditional terms. Each of these factors deserves discussion.

Montagnais assessment of the Jesuits' personal character shaped their overall reaction to the new religious system. From the first, the Montagnais appreciated that the priests were religious specialists and responded with appropriate caution. Still, during the first years of contact, the Montagnais held to their contemptuous view of the French, not in the least because of their relations with the priests. The Jesuits were rude and discourteous. They were incompetent in the vital matter of making a living and, when visiting among the Montagnais, were utterly dependent on Indian willingness to care for them. As significantly, the priests acted in selfish ways. The Jesuits appeared to expect that the Montagnais ought to provide for them, while they showed themselves unwilling to share.

It took many years for the Jesuits and the Montagnais to reach mutual understanding, largely because the Montagnais distrusted their own religious practitioners. Though the shamans were essential to group survival, they often acted in ways that threatened well-being. The shamans could and did use religious means to inflict sickness and even to kill. As Le Jeune expressed it in 1637, "I hardly ever see any of them die who does not think he has been bewitched." In this regard, the Jesuits also seemed dangerous, even to the extent of being the cause of bad weather. In fact, the Montagnais claimed that old-time Indians had warned that the Jesuits would come and kill them. The Montagnais accused the priests on several occasions of using their power to murder them. As the Montagnais searched for the cause of epidemic illness, they frequently accused the French, and especially the Jesuits, of making them sick. Then too, the priests encouraged the Montagnais to understand that their God, He-Who-Made-All, was vengeful. They often observed that particular Montagnais individuals apparently fell sick, or died in brutal ways, because they had acted disrespectfully toward the Christian God.

In effect, the Jesuits' actions and teachings kept the Montagnais off balance. Much of the priests' behavior horrified them. Jesuit brashness seemed to violate the need for respect between humans and other powerful persons. On many occasions the priests ridiculed the powers of the Montagnais world, pitting themselves against other-than-human persons and the shamans as they did so. On one such occasion, Le Jeune noticed that the Montagnais had thrown eels into the fire and asked them why. "'Keep still,' they replied, 'we are giving the devil something to eat, so that he will not harm us.'"

Jesuit criticism also made the Montagnais uncertain about Christian power. For example, the priests often scoffed at the revelations the Montagnais received in dreams. Eventually, they made a crucial distinction between those dreams in which demons attacked would-be Christians and those that were mere superstitions. For the short term, the mixed message may have confused the Montagnais, but it is not surprising that they began to compare the priests to their shamans. The Jesuits took it upon themselves to interpret dreams for Montagnais, thereby displacing the shamans in one of their most important functions. In one conversation, Le Jeune confronted the shaman Pigarouich for refusing to give up his belief in dreams. Ironically, the Jesuit ended up affirming the reality of dreams, declaring to the shaman that "'the devil meddles with your imaginations in the night; and, if you obey him, he will make you the most wicked people in the world.'"

Most importantly, the priests acted with an impunity that effectively communicated their powerful confidence. So great was their self-assurance that they frequently urged the Montagnais to kill their shamans. The net effect of Jesuit behavior was to convince many Montagnais that the priests were not only equivalent to the shamans, but also more powerful. In 1637, Makeabichtichiou told his countrymen that "those who believe in God are protected against sorcerers."

Ultimately, the priests adapted their behavior toward the Montagnais in ways that communicated genuine concern, and this benevolence fit the traditional criterion of generosity. Since rational argument proved ineffective in convincing the Montagnais of Christian truths, and since the Indians were easily alarmed, the Jesuits cultivated more human methods. To prove their benevolent power, the Jesuits devoted themselves to Montagnais well-being. They provided food, took in orphans, nursed and cured the sick. The Montagnais could not understand charity, as Paul Le Jeune stressed more than once:

> To convert the Savages, not so much knowledge is necessary as goodness and sound virtue. The four Elements of an Apostolic man in New France are Affability, Humility, Patience and a generous Charity. Too ardent zeal scorches more than it warms, and ruins everything; great magnanimity and compliance are necessary to attract gradually these Savages. They do not comprehend our Theology well, but they comprehend perfectly our humility and our friendliness, and allow themselves to be won.

In effect, the priests began to operate within the kin values central to Montagnais life and, in so doing, defused Montagnais criticism. Moreover, they mediated between the Montagnais and the colonial government, thus showing that they aimed at creating an effective and genuine alliance between equals.

The tension between caution and trust regulated other aspects of the Montagnais' scrutiny of Catholicism. Baptism produced a terrified kind of uncertainty because it seemed to be the priests' preferred way of killing. The Jesuits never did eradicate entirely the Montagnais' fear of the sacrament, but Indian religious pragmatism gave them the means to abate it. Unwittingly, by baptizing only the dying, the Jesuits achieved an unexpected opening. The Montagnais were told that baptized persons went to heaven. Since the Jesuits insisted that heaven and the traditional land of the dead were different places, the living relatives of the dead found themselves confronting a dilemma. Traditionally, the

Montagnais stressed the maintenance of proper and reciprocal relations with dead kin. The result was that some Montagnais—particularly parents who had lost a loved child—sought baptism as a way to ensure continued contact.

Other Montagnais also hedged their bets. Some sought baptism as a means to deal with disease, since the Jesuits apparently cured many individuals. Still others, worried that Jesuit threats of eternal damnation might be real, sought to avoid hell even at the cost of present death. As one man put it: "Many of their nation had this idea, that baptism is injurious to life, but that it is a good thing with which to protect oneself from the fires with which we threaten them."

In perceiving the Jesuits as shamans, and in overcoming their fear of baptism, the Montagnais were not repudiating traditional religious practice. They took Jesuit criticism seriously because, while they were inclined to blame the French for their troubles, they also worried that they themselves might have been at fault. The traditional religious system provided no easy answers to everyday problems, but it did require that the Montagnais do everything in their power to identify and rectify error. Frank G. Speck identified this issue of responsibility, at least as it pertained to hunting: ". . . Failure on the chase, the disappearance of game from the hunter's districts, with ensuing famine, starvation, weakness, sickness, and death, are all attributed to the hunter's ignorance of some hidden principles of behavior toward the animals, or to his willful disregard of them." Since crisis was so pervasive in the 1630s, the Montagnais had to heed missionary criticism, at least to the extent of examining themselves for personal responsibility for the deepening crisis.

It is true that the Jesuits spent far more time condemning Montagnais life than approving it, but still much of what they had to offer made sense in traditional terms. Nowhere was this truer than in the intersection of Catholicism and hunting. Hunting stood at the very heart of Montagnais religious life, as the Jesuits realized, even though they called Montagnais prayers ridiculous. It seemed both naive and superstitious to call upon the animals to give their lives. In 1634, Paul Le Jeune noted that the Montagnais could not understand why the French prayed: "'Ask him,' they say to me, 'for Moose, Bears, and Beavers; tell him that thou wishest to eat. . . .'" To ask for food was the most common Montagnais prayer, and seemed to the missionaries nothing short of self-serving. Nevertheless, the priests realized that the Montagnais needed prayers in the 1630s. The Montagnais faced disaster in the collapse of their hunting economy. Time after time, the shamans proved incapable of improving hunting and the Jesuits saw a basic opportunity.

As early as the winter of 1633–1634, when Paul Le Jeune wintered with one family band, the Montagnais began to hear that the shamans were responsible for their troubles. Le Jeune lost no opportunity to urge the Montagnais to redirect their prayers' from the Master of Game to He-Who-Made-All. And praying to Jesus seemed to help. Jesus himself began to appear in dreams to promise a successful hunt. Le Jeune relates one instance when two Montagnais reported that Jesus offered to aid them: "'I have seen thy Manitou, and I thy Jesus.' . . . 'Oh what a good year he promised us! What Beavers, what Elks!'" The Jesuits were undoubtedly dismayed when the two men stipulated that Jesus expected tobacco in return for his assistance.

Here again we have persuasive evidence that the Montagnais did not need to repudiate basic reality assumptions in order to embrace Christianity. At first uncertain as to the value of the Jesuits' religious contentions, the Montagnais could experiment as needed. In this case, the result was gratifying: Jesus turned out to be a hitherto unknown, but extremely powerful, Master of the Animals.

The Syncretic Imperative

To acknowledge that the Montagnais had a distinctive way of thinking is to begin to appreciate the complex forces that governed their exploration of Catholicism. In the first place, we must note the cognitive heterogeneity of Montagnais life. The Jesuits were well aware of such differences: "It is, indeed," wrote Paul Le Jeune, "true that these people have not all the same idea in regard to their belief, which will some day make it appear that those who treat of their customs are contradicting each other." Although the ideas of Person, Power, and Gift structured the Montagnais' overall tradition, the tradition itself was possessed unevenly. The Montagnais did have an egalitarian society. Still, some knowledge was the special preserve of women, of men, of children, hunters and shamans. Age, experience and social role defined the way in which individuals had access to the tradition. Those factors also shaped the kinds of concerns groups of people had with Catholicism.

At the level of social life (which, given the consensual character of Montagnais society, was paramount), the Montagnais evaluated French claims, bringing to bear both existential assumptions and practical experience. In other words, missionization can be understood best as a discourse between Montagnais individuals and the priests. As a central feature of this dialogue, however, the Montagnais also had to evaluate collectively the Jesuits' often shocking statements. One necessary result frustrated the priests: try as they might, they found it extremely difficult to persuade individuals who feared family ridicule to listen to them.

Given this religious heterogeneity, the idea that the Montagnais converted to Catholicism is too simple to encompass the complex intellectual, ethical, and social decisions they had to make to bridge their own cultural differences and to find common ground with the French way of life. If, as the evidence suggests, conversion did not take place as we have thought, it may be that we mistakenly see religions as dogmatically incompatible and exclusive in their deistic orientation. Such was the Jesuit view. The priests expected that the Montagnais would scuttle and abandon their tradition. There is no evidence, however, that even those who entered the mission at Sillery ever understood—at least until it was too late—that Catholicism posed a radical threat. Rather, the Montagnais learned piecemeal what the Jesuits considered acceptable and what they considered evil and sinful.

In the end, as at the beginning, the missionaries and neophytes saw religious dialogue in opposed terms. The Jesuits thought of conversion as a goal, an end point, an object to be won. The Montagnais, on the other hand, could not see where the Jesuits were leading. In any case, the Montagnais were impelled both by continuing crisis and a failure of traditional religious techniques. It was no coincidence that Paul Le Jeune contended that "fear is the forerunner of faith in these Barbarous Minds." Terrified they were, and the Montagnais had to pay closer attention than the priests to the practical implications of religious change. The Jesuits demanded, but the Montagnais weighed their options and decided what did or did not make sense.

The Montagnais continued to understand themselves and the French in terms of the categories of Person, Power, and Gift. One might say, for example, that they came to think of Jesus and Mary as additional other-than-human persons, admittedly very powerful persons who offered daily assistance. In 1626, the Jesuits reported that the Montagnais had associated the person Jesus with the person of the Sun. In an analogous way, some Montagnais thought of the Christian Holy Spirit, who the Jesuits pictured as a dove, as the equivalent of the great person Thunder. The Montagnais continued to reach from the known to the unfamiliar. In 1637, the Jesuits noted that the Montagnais applied the term manitou to both God and the devil. In a similar fashion, the Christian idea of a personal creator had some impact. When asked who had created the world and human beings, one shaman expressed uncertainty. It seems that the Montagnais had some vague idea of a high god they began to associate with the Jesuit creator. Such a figure did not replace, however, the culture hero, Messou, the restorer.

It can be said even that this God—He-Who-Made-All—made functional sense. At least there is no evidence to suggest any conflict occurred between the Montagnais idea of a world organized by many plant, animal and other personal powers and the Jesuit concept of a creator God. As time went by, He-Who-Made-All served to unify and focus the Montagnais cosmology of powerful persons. In fact, the Jesuits blithely adjusted their theology to fit Montagnais presupposition:

> I told them that this great Captain [He-Who-Made-All] overwhelms us with blessings,—it is he who gives us light with the Sun, who maintains for us the fish with the waters, and the animals with the land; it is he who forms our bodies in our mothers' wombs, who creates our souls by his word.

Whatever the Jesuits claimed about the preeminence of the Christian God, nothing in Montagnais religious practice constituted a dogmatic creed. So the fundamental problem with the term "conversion" has to do with the assumption that to convert is to change traditions, to shift religious direction. Admittedly, such an assumption does seem warranted when it is applied to crosscultural situations. But conversion has another, related meaning which stresses the idea of *giving assent.*

This second meaning has considerable implications for understanding the syncretic direction of the mission process. Instead of thinking of conversion as radical ideological change from one religion to another, conversion can be seen as a process of rediscovery. As a result of their contact with Catholic religious powers, and from their ritual use of Catholic symbols, the Montagnais converted themselves. In other words, they came to reexperience and thereby revitalize the basic religious truths of their traditional life. The Montagnais world continued to be charged with personal presence and human and other-than-human persons remained bound by mutual obligation.

Whatever we may think of the colonial implications of missionization in other settings, the Montagnais controlled the process during the 1630s. Since the

Jesuits never really understood the Montagnais religious system, they could not eradicate it. The Jesuits, like the Protestant missionaries in New England, did demand religious change without understanding the cultural processes involved. For the Montagnais who attempted to live out the contradictions of Jesuit demands, mission life posed few choices, but some of these allowed them considerable freedom. They could leave the missions, and many did. They could submit and accept the view of some of the catechists that life had become loathsome. They might also attempt to make sense of Christian religiosity in order to end the considerable cognitive dissonance missionization produced. Ultimately, they could try to integrate old and new, as did the Montagnais who first lived at Sillery. As it turns out, these "Christians" failed to strike such a balance and paid the highest cost. This was the eventual tragic fate of Sillery.

Generations of Faith: The Christian Indians of Martha's Vineyard

JAMES P. RONDA

In New England there was an Indian king that said he saw that there were many of their people of the Indians turned to the New England professors. He said they were worse since than they were before they left their own religion. And an Indian said, before the English came, that a white people should come in a great thing of the sea, and their people should be loving to them and receive them; but if they did hurt or wrong the white people, they would be destroyed. And this hath been seen and fulfilled, that when they did wrong the English they never prospered and have been destroyed. So that Indian was a prophet and prophesied truly.

These lines from the 1672 travel journal of George Fox remain the standard gloss on the complex relationship between Indians and Christianity in colonial New England. As Fox's informants testified, those who accepted the Christian god and become "praying Indians" declined in numbers and lost their tribal identity. The cultural demise of the converts was paralleled by the physical extinction of those who openly resisted the Puritan gospel and were swept away by the servants of an angry English Jehovah. The Indians who spoke with Fox scarcely considered the possibility of self-sustaining communities where native people might live as both Christians and Indians.

Modern scholarship has generally concurred. Studies of New England missions have emphasized either the culturally destructive effects of conversion or native resistance to the gospel. While many Puritan missionaries demanded what amounted to cultural suicide from their converts, we must not overlook the possibility of genuine conversion on the part of Indians searching for spiritual meaning in an increasingly hostile world. So long as the mission did not demand immediate and radical cultural change, there was a fair chance that Indians would accept substantial portions of the Christian message. The vital, self-sufficient Christian

"Generations of Faith: The Christian Indians of Martha's Vineyard," by James P. Ronda, *William and Mary Quarterly* 38 (1980), pp.369–394. Reprinted with permission of the author.

Indian communities and churches of Martha's Vineyard testify to the actuality of becoming a faithful Christian while remaining no less an Indian.

In numbers of Indians and English, and in relations between the peoples, Martha's Vineyard was substantially different from the mainland. When Thomas Mayhew, Jr., began missionary work among Indian islanders in the 1640s, the Wampanoag population was at least fifteen hundred and may have been as high as three thousand. At the same time, the English numbered about sixty-five, all living at the east end of the island. Although reduced by disease, natives clearly outnumbered English folk throughout the seventeenth century. On the eve of King Philip's War there were only one hundred eighty English settlers while the Wampanoag population was well over one thousand. Fragmentary census records show that whites did not become the majority on the island until the 1720s. On the mainland, the mission was part of a wider attack on Indian land and leadership mounted by a large and well-armed English population, but Thomas Mayhew's preaching had no such resources or ambitions. His efforts had little success until 1645, when an epidemic swept the island and the failure of the powwows [shamans] to cure the sick touched off a rapid series of conversions. Most important, the mission did not insist upon sudden cultural change. Mayhew and the very small English population could not compel Indians to follow John Eliot's demand that natives must "have visible civility before they can rightly enjoy visible sanctities in ecclesiastical communion." No codes required Vineyard Indians to cut their hair, wear English clothing, give up customary mourning ceremonies, or attend church meetings. It was in this more permissive environment, as Indian congregations and praying towns rose and flourished, that political power and cultural leadership remained in Wampanoag hands. Study of the Martha's Vineyard faithful reveals Christianity Indianized as well as Indians Christianized. William Simmons has aptly characterized Indian Christianity on the island as "the most profound social conversion to occur anywhere in New England."

Only on Martha's Vineyard can the process by which Indian converts transformed Christianity to suit native cultural needs be traced through four generations. That tracing is possible because a substantial body of biographies of Martha's Vineyard converts exists for the period 1642–1722. This evidence is unlike any other compendium of convert stories in mission literature. The narratives in the *Jesuit Relations,* the confessions of faith in the Eliot tracts, and the testimonies of converts in the Moravian records all suffer from stereotyped language and missionary ghost-writing. Though some of those narratives contain such vivid phrases as "I am as a dead man in my soul, and desire to live," and "God broke my head," they only rarely and dimly exhibit Indians as active shapers of their own lives and thoughts. Only for Martha's Vineyard do we have multi-generational records that allow us to view the dynamics of conversion and community over a long period.

These records are contained in Experience Mayhew's *Indian Converts,* the product of a lifetime of direct contact with Martha's Vineyard Indian Christians. Grandson of Thomas Mayhew, Jr., Experience was born on the island in 1673, spoke Wampanoag, and knew most of the people whose stories he wrote. In the early 1720s he began to collect material for capsule biographies of Christian Indians. *Indian Converts* is a kind of oral history assembled by an informed observer with a sharp eye for detail and a keen ear for arresting tales. Mayhew composed 126 biographies, touching 208 Indians in at least sixteen family lineages. Although primarily concerned with the lives of the godly and the good, he did not fail to note their frailties. The struggles of Jacob Sockakonnit with alcoholism, the unruliness of the children of Deacon Abel Wauwompuhque, Jr., and the touchy temper of Abiah Paaonit were all faithfully set down. While it is possible to claim too much for this evidence, the greater danger is to claim too little. *Indian Converts* was written neither to raise funds for the mission nor to perpetuate the Mayhew family's reputation. Rather, Mayhew intended to demonstrate the validity of Indian Christianity by showing that not all the gospel seeds sown among the natives had fallen on stony ground. Supplemented by other mission records, the *Indian Converts* provides a rare look into the lives of New England's Indian Christians.

Conversion on Martha's Vineyard most often followed family lines. *Indian Converts* shows that as early as the 1650s Christian Indian families were perpetuating the faith within their lineages. Mayhew took pains to trace the gospel pedigree in many such families. To illustrate the generations of faith on the island, two Wampanoag lines are offered here for detailed discussion. The families reveal the generational conversion links, the emergence of Indian Christianity, and the persistence of native identity after conversion.

One of the most prominent lineages at Gay Head was the Mittark-Panu connection. In 1663, the sachem Mittark became embroiled with his people in a controversy over conversion, left for the east end of the island, and remained there among the English in semi-exile for three years. In 1666, he returned to Gay Head, where he founded the Indian Congregational Church. As Mittark made the transition from sachem to preacher, he worked to convert members of his family and to ensure the perpetuation of the gospel within his lineage. In his own generation, Mittark's most important convert was his brother, Abel Wauwompuhque, Sr. As a Gay Head magistrate, Wauwompuhque was in a unique position to influence both converts and those who had not accepted the new belief. Mayhew characterized him as "a zealous reprover of the sins of the times in which he lived." But for all his reproving, Wauwompuhque did not abandon the traditional Indian style of resolving disputes. Rejecting coercion and seeking consensus, he "earnestly endeavored to promote peace and unity." Mittark the sachem-turned-preacher and Wauwompuhque the magistrate were signs in the first generation that Christianity did not necessarily mean cultural and political disruption.

The test came in subsequent generations. Would Christianity grow to become an integral part of Indian life, or would it require constant infusions of English missionary support and direction? The second generation of the Mittark-Panu lineage demonstrated the vitality of Christian families on the island. When Akoochuk married one of Mittark's daughters, he soon felt family pressure to convert. Abandoning his habit of heavy drinking, he became a mainstay of the Gay Head Christian community and one of Mittark's *antoskouaog* or counsellors. He was called a magistrate by the English but functioned as a traditional counsellor, whose duties included giving advice to neighbors, meting out justice as "a terror to evil doers," and dispensing charity. It was for his charity, long a counsellor's responsibility, that Akoochuk was best known. Mayhew recorded that he ministered to the poor, "not only feeding them, . . . but also giving them what was convenient to carry home with them."

Mittark's nephew Annampanu was also an important second-generation convert. Annampanu did not accept the faith until late in life, having in his younger days a "loving and following after strong drink." The record does not show why he changed his ways to become a full member of the Gay Head congregation, but it is clear that he became very much a part of the Christian family tradition founded by Mittark. In old age, when he had no home of his own, Annampanu lived with other Christian Indian families. "He was," wrote Mayhew, "a blessing to them by his many good prayers in them, and good councils given to them. He then also used to go about doing good, as in visiting the sick and afflicted, and counselling and comforting of them."

The most important figure in the second generation of the Mittark-Panu lineage was Abel Wauwompuhque, Jr., a genuine product of Christian family nurture. Though raised in a household dominated by his convert father and uncle, he did not experience conversion as a child. A good deal of drinking and an inclination "to the same youthful vanities as unconverted young men generally are" marked his young manhood. After his marriage to a Christian Indian, Wauwompuhque abandoned his "youthful vanities," made a public profession of faith, and joined the Gay Head church. He soon found that the Christian example of his own family, like that of his father's, did not automatically produce faithful children. Some of his "were persons of no good character." Nevertheless, he was regarded as an exemplary magistrate and a possible future preacher for the Gay Head congregation. However, events in 1690 changed island history as well as the future of the Mittark-Panu line.

In 1690, parts of Martha's Vineyard were struck by a devastating epidemic. Abel Wauwompuhque Jr., was "very sorely visited by the disease and lost his hearing." As illness had caused Indian traditionalists to question ancient ways in the 1640s, so this sickness led Wauwompuhque to become a serious inquirer into matters of faith and doctrine, and a voracious reader of religious books in both English and Algonkian. He quickly learned lip reading and sign language. "He would also," reported Experience Mayhew, "ask many necessary questions and not be satisfied till either by writing, or some other means, he had obtained an answer to them." In 1712, when Gay Head Indian preacher Japheth Hannit died, Wauwompuhque became spiritual leader of the Indian faithful. Mayhew commended his sermons as a stout assault on "their drunkenness, whoredom, thieving, lying, sabbath-breaking, and letting them know, that those who do such things should not inherit the kingdom of God." Until his death in 1722, Abel Wauwompuhque, Jr., remained a potent force among Indian Christians. As deacon, magistrate, and preacher, he exemplified the maturity of Indian Christianity on Martha's Vineyard.

The third generation of the Mittark-Panu lineage continued to produce Christian leaders for the Gay Head Indian community. Joash Panu, son of Annampanu and one of Mittark's daughters, was taught his early lessons by his mother. Mayhew noted with approval that after Panu married, he established proper family worship with his wife Naomi and their children. Although Gay Head believers felt that he was worthy of full membership in the Indian church, he was reluctant to seek it. He confessed that he was waiting for a clear sign from God, a call to the ministry. That call evidently came in 1716, the year in which Panu was formally ordained as preacher at Gay Head. He soon gained a reputation for effective, forceful preaching. "The longer he continued in the work of the ministry, the more zealous and earnest his discourses appeared to be." Mayhew, who heard Panu preach, observed that his sermons were not "impertinent, unstudied discourses, but had many very good things in them, and these delivered in something of order and method."

Joash and Naomi Panu were earnest Christian parents. Yet they, like both Abel Wauwompuhques, discovered that piety and Christian commitment were not necessarily passed intact from one generation to the next. Their son Laban was hardly the perfect Christian child. Until age nine, he was "rude and disorderly, apt to profane the sabbath day, and could scarcely be restrained from playing at meeting." Mayhew lamented that "the many good instructions and exhortations given him by his parents" failed to change Laban's behavior. Accepting the more rigorous methods of English nurture, the Panus decided "to deal more sharply with him," and this discipline produced "a remarkable change in the carriage and behavior of their child." Unfortunately, however, the boy fell sick and soon died. During his illness young Laban spoke often of "his own frailty and mortality" and the mercy of God preparing him for joy in heaven. Those sentiments surely pleased his parents, but his death in 1715 robbed the Mittark-Panu connection and the Gay Head community of a future leader.

The Mittark-Panu lineage illustrates the continuity of political and cultural leadership on the Gay Head end of the island. From Mittark to Joash Panu, political power remained in native hands. The family successfully negotiated the conversion passage and made the Christian practices of prayer, Bible reading, family devotions, and public worship essential parts of their lives. If the Mittark-Panu line demonstrates the persistence of one family, the rise of the Coomes-Amos lineage suggests ways in which hitherto unimportant Wampanoags gained considerable influence as members of God's tribe.

One of the largest Christian Indian families on Martha's Vineyard, the Coomes-Amos lineage contributed twenty-seven persons to Mayhew's compilation, for sixteen of whom he was able to construct detailed biographies. The Christian line was founded by Hiacoomes of Great Harbor, Taphaus and Amos of Chappaquiddick, and Myoxeo, a minor sachem at Nunpang. This large connection showed considerable diversity in Christian commitment. At least eight lineage members never formally professed the faith, yet each of these held important positions of leadership on the island. Because the line was so large, it is neither possible nor desirable to discuss all individuals in every generation. The following analysis offers a representative sample from each generation to illustrate the growth of a powerful Christian Indian family.

Thomas Mayhew, Jr.'s first Indian convert on Martha's Vineyard was Hiacoomes, a Great Harbor Wampanoag. In 1642, when Mayhew was preaching to the handful of English settlers around Edgartown, Hiacoomes was attracted to the ways of his new neighbors. No sachem but a man of "mean descent," he also seems to have captured English attention. Edgartown Puritans were pleased when

Hiacoomes attended several Sunday meetings, something no other Indian had done. What began as social visits by pastor Mayhew and other English folk to Hiacoomes's wigwam became opportunities for the Puritan divine to undertake missionary teaching, which he improved by inviting Hiacoomes to come regularly to the Mayhew house. Under Mayhew's direction, the Indians exchanged the supernatural order and symbols of the powwows and traditional healing rites for equally supernatural Christian explanations. Those explanations stressed the wiles of Satan, the strength of sin, and the transforming power of Christian belief. Hiacoomes accepted this new set of symbols and became a Christian. He enjoyed increased standing in the eyes of the English, but his study of Christian doctrine and ties to the English earned him the derisive label, "the English man," from other Wampanoags. The new convert's influence increased in 1643 and 1644 when disease killed many Indian islanders but left Hiacoomes's family untouched. Hiacoomes became established as a powerful Christian preacher when, during the epidemic crisis of 1645–1646, he helped convert several prominent sachems and faced down a group of angry powwows. By the 1650s, he was a respected magistrate and spiritual leader. Ordination as a minister in 1670 capped a life in which faith brought rewards of power and esteem.

One of Hiacoomes's first converts was the sachem Myoxeo. When disease struck the island in 1643, many Wampanoags saw the illness as a sign of divine displeasure and responded with renewed zeal for the ancient rituals. But when epidemic illness returned in 1645 and again left Hiacoomes's family unscathed, the reaction was quite different. Clearly worried about the impotence of his powwows in the face of strange ailments, Myoxeo invited Hiacoomes to make what amounted to a pastoral call at the sachem's wigwam, where he gathered a considerable number of Indians, among them the influential east end sachem Tawanquatuck. The exchange between Hiacoomes and Myoxeo at first focused on Hiacoomes's declaration that his one god was far more powerful than Myoxeo's thirty-seven. When the sachem was brought to accept monotheism as a sovereign remedy, Hiacoomes went on to discourse on sin, punishment, and salvation. Revealing their expectation that Christianity would give them special power and protection from present dangers, Myoxeo and Tawanquatuck agreed "that true believers did live above the world, and did keep worldly things always under their feet." Myoxeo eventually assumed the post of magistrate at Edgartown.

The conversion experiences of the two Chappaquiddick founders of the Coomes-Amos line are less well documented. Experience Mayhew noted that he had "heard nothing remarkable" about Taphaus. Something more is known of Amos, one of the first Indian Christians at Chappaquiddick. Converted by Hiacoomes, he established a convert family, and his children married into the Coomes line.

Conversion efforts by Hiacoomes and Thomas Mayhew, Jr., bore fruit in the second generation. Once again, family and kinship meant more than any other factor in propagating the faith. Hiacoomes struggled to convert his several children, but only the story of one of his younger sons, Samuel, survived for Mayhew to record. The sometimes troubled life of Samuel Coomes suggests the tensions in many Christian Indian families and the special dilemma of a dutiful son living in the shadow of a newly important father. When Samuel was very young, Hiacoomes sent him to live with Thomas Mayhew, Sr. There the boy learned the essentials of the Christian faith as well as reading and writing. "Notwithstanding all these advantages," Experience Mayhew wrote, "he was in his youthful days a carnal man." Samuel's excessive drinking and his sexual adventures with an English woman must have given Hiacoomes cause to wonder if Christian nurture, even at the hands of a Mayhew, was effective.

After Samuel's marriage to an Indian Christian woman, his behavior began to change, but drinking remained a serious problem as long as his father lived in Samuel's household. When Hiacoomes died in 1690, his son's habits were transformed. Though Samuel never formally joined an Indian church, he became an active layman in the Chilmark congregation. "If a meeting house was to be repaired, or any thing else was to be done for the promoting of religion," Experience Mayhew recorded, "none would contribute more liberally to it than he. And when there was a day of public Thanksgiving, and provision to be made for it, which among our Indians is brought into common stock, (which the poor as well as the rich may come to and be filled) this our Samuel was one of the principal providers for that feast." Hiacoomes was "of mean descent," but his son Samuel's family and active faith made him a respected member of the Indian Christian community and a powerful magistrate.

One of Myoxeo's children, his daughter Rachel, also became prominent in Christian Indian society. Like Samuel Coomes, Rachel was sent as a child to live in the Mayhew household but proved resistant to Christianity. Her early years were punctuated by drinking and wild behavior. These ended with her marriage to Jonathan Amos. Soon after their wedding, the couple moved to Dartmouth in the Bay Colony, but, disturbed by the "low ebb" of religion on the mainland, eventually returned to Chilmark to "enjoy God in all His ordinances here, where they both thought church-discipline was better managed than there." Experience Mayhew portrayed Rachel Amos as the model Christian Indian woman. She carefully instructed each of her eight daughters in gospel fundamentals and conducted family worship when her husband was absent. As the wife of a deacon, she assisted Jonathan in his charitable duties. And, as a practicing Christian, she was "very constant and serious in her attendance on, and improvement of the privileges to which she was admitted."

Her husband was the son of Amos of Chappaquiddick. As with so many other second-generation Christian Indians, his family heritage propelled him into active public service in the convert community. Beyond the fact that he was raised in a Christian family and was literate, little is known of Jonathan Amos's early life. In the Chilmark Indian church he earned respect as a pious believer and a faithful supporter of the congregation. That respect became more evident in 1698 when David Wuttinomanomin, long-time Chilmark deacon, died. The office of deacon was especially important in Martha's Vineyard Indian churches because it perpetuated and gave Christian meaning to ancient patterns of charity, feasting, and care for the poor. Amos undertook those responsibilities and executed them with considerable skill. He often spoke fervently at meeting about charity as an essential Christian duty. When the Chappaquiddick Indian pulpit fell vacant in 1703, the congregation called Amos as their preacher. Much of the worship in

Indian churches consisted of lengthy prayers, bringing the needs and failings of the believers to the attention of both God and the community. Experience Mayhew heard Jonathan Amos deliver such petitions and declared, "I think I have scarcely ever heard any man in prayer plead with God with greater importunity than he used to do; and these his fervent prayers availed much." For all his spirited rhetoric, however, Amos experienced personal temptations, and "it pleased God to permit him to fall very shamefully." After one spectacular drinking bout, he made public confession of his sins, and Mayhew insisted that the preacher never fell again. Whatever Jonathan Amos's private failings, his role as deacon and minister suggests the ways Christianity permeated the lives of so many Martha's Vineyard Indians.

In its third and fourth generations, the Coomes-Amos family grew in size if not in influence. Yet the early deaths of several Coomes-Amos children from the infectious diseases that frequently swept the island weakened the family. An increasing number of family members "felt unworthy" of full church membership, a state common among mainland Puritans. Experience Mayhew seems to have sensed the dilemma of the children of pious parents when he wrote about later Coomes-Amos offspring. Typical of the third generation, Abigail Amos, a daughter of Rachel and Jonathan, was literate, well catechized, and "not . . . given to keep evil company." She was an obedient child who grew to be a diligent worker alongside her seven sisters. But she never married, died young, and at the end of her life was overwhelmed by a sense of all-pervasive sin and spiritual insufficiency.

On Martha's Vineyard, Christian Indian families faithfully propagated the gospel from generation to generation. Those Indians, like their Puritan counterparts, maintained that Christian family life was essential to prepare the heart for an infusion of grace. But the converts on the island were more than clusters of praying Indian families. They were members of genuine communities and churches with Wampanoag clerical and lay leadership. The presence of that native leadership over a long period illustrates the strength of Christian Indian culture, a culture secure and confident enough to sustain its own corporate life without depending on English sources. Cotton Mather and other preachers made occasional forays to the island, but the day-to-day spiritual lives of Indian Christians were fully in the hands of native pastors, ruling elders, home-devotion leaders, discoursers, catechists, and musicians.

As the influence of the powwows declined in the 1640s and 1650s, a leadership vacuum developed on the island, and Indian pastors, beginning with Hiacoomes and John Tackanash, began to fill that void. The formal ordination of these two men in 1670 by John Eliot and John Cotton, Jr., put the stamp of approval on an indigenous ministerial elite. The traditional shamanistic functions were now subsumed under the larger preacher-pastor role. Indian ministers became the new holy men, the special repositories of wisdom, healing, and power. Communicants looked to them for advice, support, encouragement, and ethical guidance, and they acted as intermediaries in English-Indian disputes. A close look at the ministers reveals the workings of Christian Indian life on the island and some of the reasons for its vitality.

John Tackanash has long stood in the shadow of his fellow preacher, Hiacoomes. The two were ordained at the same time, but because Hiacoomes was the first Mayhew convert he has captured the larger measure of historical attention. While Hiacoomes was an effective evangelist, Tackanash deserves to be recalled as a leader who steadily built Indian churches throughout the island and strengthened Indian Christian life at its beginnings. Nothing is known of his early life. Experience Mayhew observed that Tackanash and Hiacoomes were longtime friends; Hiacoomes may have been responsible for Tackanash's conversion. After his ordination, Tackanash promptly took up duties as pastor and teacher at several locations—in Chilmark at Talhano praying town and Nashnakemmuck Indian church; in Edgartown at Nashamoiess praying town and Sanchacantacket Indian church; and in West Tisbury at Takeme praying town. He evidently made a lasting impression on all who knew him and heard him preach. Experience Mayhew wrote that "he was reckoned to exceed the said Hiacoomes, both in his natural and acquired abilities; and being accounted a person of a very exemplary conversation."

Tackanash's conception of the ministerial role represented a synthesis of traditional powwow functions and English clerical practices. A bearer of the new wisdom and an interpreter of that knowledge to believers, Tackanash served not only as preacher and pastor but also as a healer who applied medical as well as spiritual remedies. Priding himself on his theological scholarship, he "followed his study and reading closely, allowing himself . . . but little time for such diversions as many ministers and other persons use." This Indian pastor's desire to fully understand Christian doctrine often led him to consult with English divines for information and direction. English islanders frequently attended his services, recognizing his ordination as valid for both peoples. When Tackanash died in January 1684, he left behind flourishing, well-disciplined Indian congregations.

Toward the end of the seventeenth century, the first generation of Indian convert leadership passed from the scene. If the Christian Indians of Martha's Vineyard were to remain a functioning community of worship, they would have to produce from among themselves a second generation of pastors. This need was even more acute by the end of the century as Experience Mayhew devoted an increasing share of his time to mainland preaching and no fulltime English missionary planned to live on the island. If Indian Christianity were to survive, it would have to do so by its own power. Wampanoag preachers such as Japheth Hannit, William Lay, Joash Panu, and Isaac Ompany exemplified the response to that challenge.

Indian Converts provides an exceptionally detailed account of the life and ministry of Japheth Hannit. Born at Chilmark in 1638, he was the son of a minor sachem. Both his parents were converts; they sent Japheth, at age thirteen, to the Indian school established by Thomas Mayhew, Jr. From schoolmaster Peter Folger, young Japheth learned to read and write both English and Algonkian. Though the pious son of believing parents, the young man did not promptly join any established Indian church. In fact, when John Tackanash formally organized the Chilmark congregation in 1670, Hannit found himself "in a most distressed condition." He "feared to offer himself to the society of God's people, lest he should be unqualified for the privileges to which they were admitted." He eventually made a public profession of faith but still declined for a time to take communion.

Although his Christian family background and education prepared him for an active role in the Indian church, Hannit at first accepted only civil and military posts. During King Philip's War he was "employed by the English to observe and report how things went among the Indians," and Mayhew thought him instrumental in keeping the island at peace "when the people on the Main were all in war and blood." Sometimes in 1680, and for reasons now unclear, Hannit resolved those questions that had kept him from full participation in the Indian church. He undertook a preaching apprenticeship with his uncle Janawanit and John Tackanash. When Tackanash died, Hannit assumed the Chilmark pulpit. Like Tackanash, he saw himself as both a Puritan preacher and a traditional powwow healer and holy man. "He was faithful and diligent in the work of God, unto which he was called, preaching the Word in season and out of season, with all long-suffering and doctrine, and used frequently to catechise the children of his flock in public." Although Hannit steadily worked at improving his preaching, Mayhew noted that his "sermons were not very accurate, . . . and he seemed to me to do his best when he did not try to oblige himself to any strict method in them." Hannit was more effective in maintaining church discipline and in resolving quarrels within his congregation. Always working to avoid open conflict that might weaken the church, "he would not side with any party of them, but would in such case make most winning and obliging speeches to them all, tending to accommodate the matter about which they were ready to fall out; and so wonderful an ability had he this way, that he seldom failed of the end he aimed at." He was equally diligent in such ministerial duties as regular visiting of the sick, a traditional Indian practice. In this and other ways, pastors like Hannit were the new powwows.

Japheth Hannit's fellow ministers functioned much as he did, engaging in regular preaching, catechizing, and family visitation. Clergymen like William Lay and Joash Panu of Chilmark, and Isaac Ompany of Christiantown developed ministerial styles that reflected their own abilities and temperaments as well as the need to keep believers strong in the faith. As both preacher and magistrate, Lay used pulpit and court to further the Christian cause by direct application of fear and punishment. If as preacher he could not convert an errant Indian, as magistrate he would order the maximum number of lashes allowed for a particular misdeed. When some English islanders complained of such harshness, Lay offered an arresting comment on English-Indian cultural differences and his recognition of them. "When an Englishman was whipped, the shame of it was commonly at least one half of the punishment, but the case being not so with the Indians, they ought to have the more in smart, for that they had no more shame in them."

Joash Panu and Isaac Ompany substituted sharp tongues for stinging whips. Panu was an ardent student of homiletics who carefully wrote out the heads of all his sermons and collected outlines from other clergymen. As Chilmark pastor between 1716 and 1720, he was known as "a most zealous preacher against the sins of his own countrymen, crying aloud and not sparing to show the people their transgressions." Mayhew often heard Panu's sermons and admired both their force and thoughtful order. Zealous reproving, so much a part of Puritan and Indian preaching styles, was bound to elicit some anger from even the most pious believers. Isaac Ompany, preacher at Christiantown, was the target of considerable verbal abuse from his congregation. "In his preaching," wrote Mayhew, "he was not very popular, and with many he was the less so, because he was a sharp and serious reprover of the sins to which he could not but see his countrymen were much addicted."

The pastoral care provided by Tackanash, Lay, Panu, Ompany, and the other Indian ministers was essential for the survival of Wampanoag Christian life on Martha's Vineyard. But in most ways the day-to-day leadership was in the hands of laymen. Within Indian churches there was a vigorous tradition of lay direction, a tradition that pervaded Indian Christian life both in worship and in the wider community. Indian men and women served as ruling elders, deacons, discoursers, catechists, festival managers, counselors, and musicians. These native initiatives reveal both the strength of Christianity on the island and the Indianization of the gospel.

For men like Joshua Momatchegin, ruling elder at Chappaquiddick, and Thomas Sockakonnit, deacon at Edgartown, Christianity was not an alien ideology. Rather, it gave shape and meaning to their lives. Momatchegin, who had been ordained by Eliot and Cotton in 1670, was especially concerned with the mounting problem of alcoholism at Chappaquiddick. Admitting that he lived in "dark and declining times," he struggled to bind the faithful together and witness against the "flood of strong drink." Every Indian church had at least one deacon, and Thomas Sockakonnit was typical of those who filled the office. Sockakonnit organized the charitable activities of the Edgartown church, and when no preacher was available he led the congregation in prayer, scripture reading, and psalm singing.

While Indian laymen filled the English offices of ruling elder and deacon, the special needs of converts for regular religious instruction required a new lay post, that of discourser. Discoursers were lay preachers who served in family worship and also filled pulpits when regular preachers were unavailable. Two of the most prominent were Noquittompany, discourser at Christiantown and father of the preacher Isaac Ompany, and Abiah Paaonit, wife of Chilmark pastor Elisha Paaonit. Noquittompany long resisted conversion, preferring to "lie at home, or go a fishing or hunting on the Lord's day, to the great grief of such as were better disposed." When his conversion finally came, he spoke of himself as "a praying man" and "a new creature." In old age he became a discourser. Mayhew's vivid portrait of "the character and carriage of this good man" accents "his ability and willingness to entertain with good discourses, all those with whom he conversed. His God and Savior, and those things which have a relation to another life after this is ended, were the subjects about which he continually delighted to confer; and he used earnestly to invite and excite his neighbors and friends to the great duties which ought to be attended by all such as fear God, and would be happy in the enjoyment of him." Abiah Paaonit was an especially effective discourser among Indian women. Women concerned about faith and practice often visited her, and she would "lay her work aside that she might sit and discourse with them." Assuring his readers that these were not occasions for idle gossip,

Mayhew insisted that Paaonit's talks "were not vain and frothy, but such as were good for the use of edifying, and might administer grace to the hearers."

The persistence of traditional religious practices in the corporate life of Martha's Vineyard Indian Christians was manifested in such activities as group singing and observance of a steady round of festival days. The island's Wampanoags filled the year with rituals celebrating planting and harvest. Those events, as well as powwow healing rites, featured group singing and chanting. Indian churches, in turn, held communal feasts for worship, charity, and fellowship, in the organization of which lay persons took the initiative. Thus on such occasions Yonohhumuh of Gay Head, a successful farmer and one of Mittark's counselors, purchased or donated much of the food, arranged for its preparation, invited poor families to attend, and secured a preacher to deliver a sermon and administer communion. The singing of metrical psalms was a central part of Indian Christian worship. Since the singing was done in antiphonal fashion, every congregation had at least one tune-setter, yet another lay office.

While men served as ruling elders and deacons, the lay tradition also provided important roles for women. Abiah Paaonit was by no means unique as an active lay leader. Margaret Osooit of Gay Head, for example, often met with Indian women troubled by personal wrong-doing or family difficulty, and "she would not willingly leave them till she brought them to a confession of their faults, sometimes with tears, and to engage to endeavor to reform what was amiss in them." Momchquannum of Edgartown was one of many literate converts who regularly catechized young Indians. She sought out boys and girls and "frequently admonished [them] for their faults, and excited [them] to their duty."

The activities of Sarah Cowkeeper are worthy of special note because this woman made a substantial contribution to the life of the Indian Christian community. She was a long-time member of the Edgartown Indian church and was known for her industry and piety. Because she lived on a main road into Edgartown, travelers often spent the night in her home. Taking her Christianity seriously, Cowkeeper regularly visited and fed the sick, though she herself was poor. The rituals of charity were very much a part of her faith, despite the fact that she had to clothe and feed her own large family. In addition, Mayhew made special mention of "the care she took of poor fatherless and motherless children; when she heard of any such under suffering circumstances, she used to fetch them to her own house, and . . . keep them till they could in some other way be provided for." When her family complained, she replied that God would provide food and care for all. Sarah Cowkeeper's Christian commitment gave added dimension to her Indian name, Assannooshque, "woman that is a giver of victuals."

Assannooshque and her spiritual sisters were part of a sizable group of Indian Christian women on Martha's Vineyard. Indeed, so many Wampanoag women were active Christians that Experience Mayhew found "a greater number of women appearing pious than of the men among them." In *Indian Converts* he offered the biographies of thirty-seven "good women," most of whom were second- or third-generation Christians. Mayhew was able to glean information about the ages at conversion of thirty-three women, finding that fourteen waited until they were adults to join churches, while nineteen had a childhood conversion experience of some kind. Mayhew reported that seventeen of the thirty-seven women were literate. Most important for the future of the Christian Indian communities, twenty-four of these "good women" were instrumental in converting their children. Though Mayhew was either unwilling or unable to suggest reasons why so many Indian women were attracted to the gospel, that attraction appears to have had four main sources.

The Christianity preached by Thomas Mayhew, Jr., and his Indian successors tended to elevate and honor the roles and tasks of Indian women. The wife-mother-housekeeper functions were given special value in a public way unknown in pre-contact Wampanoag life. Experience Mayhew's glowing description of Hepzibah Assaquanhut expresses an ideal that emphasized the self-worth and importance of women in families. Assaquanhut "was a good wife . . . , being a discreet and chaste keeper at home, and one that loved her husband and children, being also very obedient to him; and was one that labored diligently with her hands, to provide necessaries for the family." This description of the ideal Christian Indian woman is more complex than it appears. The gospel, as preached to and by Indian women, held that what women did in their lives was an act of virtue and worship as well as duty. Thus Abigail Ahhunnut, who outlived three husbands, found favor with the body of Indian believers because "she was such a wife to them all, as whoso finds, finds a good thing, and obtains favor of the Lord." Like Ahhunnut, Mary Coshomon's patient relationship with her husband won esteem among Indian Christians. "She was remarkable," reported Mayhew, "for her dutiful carriage towards her husband, even showing him great reverence and respect; and when he was guilty of any miscarriage, she would bring no railing accusations against him, but would in a very submissive manner advise and entreat him."

An Indian Christian woman's faithful performance of household tasks was also noted and praised. Industry in the wigwam became not simply a domestic duty but a service to God. Clean and orderly homes were pointed to as marks of a godly and sober woman. Mayhew's catalogue of the interior of Sarah Hannit's wigwam has more than passing ethnographic interest. "The fair and large *wigwam* wherein she with her husband lived, was a great part of it her own work; the mats, or platted straw, flags and rushes with which it was covered, being wrought by her own hands; and those of them that appeared within side the house, were neatly embroidered with the inner barks of walnut trees artificially softened, and dyed several colors for that end."

If Christianity had attracted Indian women by valuing their traditional roles, it had even stronger appeal for women with special abilities. Articulate and literate women like Abiah Paaonit and Margaret Osooit found the Indian church and community a supportive arena for their ready minds and quick wits. When male powwows were discredited during the epidemics of the 1640s, the way was opened for Christian women healers. Most prominent of these was Hannah Nohnosoo, a herb doctor with a large practice among both Indian and English islanders. Like her powwow predecessors, Nohnosoo believed that the efficacy of her medicine depended on a proper relationship with supernatural forces. When asked if she could cure a certain disease, she replied, "I do not know but I may, if it please God to bless means for that end." Her patients included both

Wampanoag and English women who were "divers years after marriage without the blessing of children, having barren wombs and dry breasts, which persons in a married state are scarce ever pleased with." Mayhew claimed that after Hannah Nohnosoo's ministrations, these women became "joyful mothers of children, for which comfort, under God, they have been obliged to her."

Nohnosoo's Chilmark neighbor Hannah Ahhunnut also possessed abilities that combined Christian faith and medical skill. Ahhunnut regularly visited the sick, bringing them food and herbal medications. Like Hannah Nohnosoo, she believed that prayer was an essential to healing; her sickroom visits combined applications medicinal and spiritual. One of Hannah Ahhunnut's most valued skills was her experience as a midwife. She was sent for whenever a birth was expected to be especially dangerous. By methods as much religious as medical, she brought Christian comfort and encouragement while aiding in the delivery.

From the time of Thomas Mayhew, Jr., Christianity on the island was closely linked to formal schooling for converts. Educational opportunities extended to Indian women proved a powerful incentive for both conversion and continued Christian affiliation. The Indian churches promoted literacy among women and gave educated women a place to use their learning. Of the thirty-seven women in *Indian Converts,* seventeen were literate. Indian women clearly prized learning. Rebecca Sissetom, who was taught to read as a child, "appeared to delight in her book." Sarah Hannit struggled to read her favorite book, an Algonkian translation of William Perkins's *Six Principles of Religion.* Women who knew how to read wanted to pass on the skill to their children. Abigail Kesoehtaut "loved to read in good books and after she was married, and had some children, (not being nigh any school) she did herself teach them to read, and did otherwise carefully instruct them." Few could match the zeal for learning displayed by Jerusha Ompan. An unmarried daughter in a large family, she labored under a heavy burden of household duties. Denied time to read during the day, "she would not ordinarily fail of reading in the night, and for that end always used to be provided with something to make a light withal."

Christianity attracted Indian women by honoring their traditional tasks, rewarding their special abilities, and offering them educational opportunities. Indian churches also provided certain women with special support and solace in the face of a steadily worsening social problem. By the 1680s, alcoholism and the violence bred of excessive drinking had become epidemic among island Indian males. Native preachers lashed out at the abuse of alcohol, describing alcoholics as members of "the drinking tribe." Mayhew called heavy drinking "the National Sin of our Indians." Alcoholism was a serious problem even among Christian Indian men. Some eleven of the thirty-seven males in Mayhew's section on "good men" either had had or were continuing to have difficulties with alcohol. Immoderate drinking caused tension and violence within many Indian families.

The experiences of two women, Hannah Tiler and Hannah Sissetom, suggest ways by which Indian Christianity prepared women to deal with alcoholic and often abusive husbands. Hannah Tiler of Edgartown was the child of Christian parents. But in her case such nurture did not produce the desired results; Experience Mayhew found that young Hannah "was as bad by nature as any other." Her marriage to a vicious drunkard further threatened her wavering faith. According to Mayhew, her husband "would frequently have his drunken fits, and was often very contentious in them." Husband and wife became caught in a ceaseless round of drinking sprees and fierce arguments. Finally convinced that the cycle had to be broken, Hannah Tiler turned to Christian friends in the Edgartown Indian congregation for support and advice. At first she sharply criticized her husband for his drinking but soon discovered that "this was an occasion of sore contentions betwixt them." Counseled by fellow Christians to use gentler means, she tried "mild entreaties and a good carriage." Although this approach proved equally ineffective, "she found peace in it, and God helped her, in this way of well-doing, to cast all her care on him."

Experience Mayhew recorded the tempestuous marriage of Hannah and Haukkings Sissetom with an almost clinical fascination. Hannah was raised by an English family on the island; Haukkings was part of the Christian Sissetom lineage. The placid first years of their marriage were marked by regular family worship and steady attendance at the Edgartown Indian church. However, Haukkings developed "such an excessive lust after strong drink that he was frequently overcome by it," spent his wages on hot liquors, and thus reduced his family to poverty. Confronted with his failings by both his wife and members of the congregation, "he sometimes appeared to be under great convictions" and seemed prepared to reform. But these resolutions were short-lived; "the temptation prevailed too much against him, and sometimes overcame him." Urged by her English neighbors to employ stiff words and strong measures, Hannah replied that she tried but found that such efforts only angered her husband. With children to feed and instruct, she turned to the Indian church and the Christian Sissetoms. The solution suggested by the Sissetom family and approved by the church was to have Haukkings's mother live with the family. Mayhew reported that the older Sissetom woman was "very kind and obliging" to Hannah, "endeavoring to comfort her under all her trials."

The least satisfying evidence presented by Experience Mayhew deals with convert children. Unlike his accounts of ministers and lay adults, Mayhew's descriptions of "pious children" are thin and often stereotyped. If some children displayed less than godly behavior before their conversion, Mayhew would have us believe that all became sober, obedient, faithful, and industrious after accepting the gospel. Despite the deficiencies in the evidence, the twenty-two narratives of boys and girls who died in the faith between the ages of four and twenty reveal several salient characteristics of Indian Christianity as it grew on Martha's Vineyard.

These biographies show how seriously Christian Indian parents took their educational and religious responsibilities. Nurture in the principles of the faith was an essential part of Christian Indian family life. Most parents began that teaching when their children were very young. Bethia Tuphaus's parents began to instruct her "in the things of God, as soon as she was in any measure capable of understanding them." Lydia and Jerusha Ohquanhut were taught at an equally early age. In only a handful of cases does the evidence show how children responded to this guidance. Mayhew insisted that early instruction produced "good impressions on the young heart" of many an Indian child. Only rarely, as when

Jane Pomit wept and was "much affected when spoken to about the things of God," is there any hint that children were bewildered and frightened by a heavy dose of Christian teaching. What is clear is that Indian parents fully incorporated Christian ideas about sin, salvation, punishment, and death into their family lives.

There is only meagre evidence to illustrate the ways in which children demonstrated their Christian faith. They were expected to be obedient to parents and energetic at their work, but did they display any special patterns of piety that might manifest the Indianization of Christianity? In the pre-contact Northeast it was common for young men to undertake solitary vision quests searching for personal identity, special powers, and a guardian spirit. By Mayhew's account, solitary prayer in isolated places was common among young Indians, and it is possible that this practice represented a kind of Christian vision quest. Since Christian Indian children were taught that the act of prayer put the believer into contact with God and his awesome power, boys and girls like Eleazar Ohhumuh, Jeremiah Wesachippau, and Elizabeth Pattompan may have been behaving in ways that originated deep in the traditional past of Martha's Vineyard.

Beginning slowly in the 1640s and gathering momentum by the 1670s, Christianity became an integral part of the lives of many Martha's Vineyard Wampanoags. Indians worshipping at native churches and living in praying towns were no less Indian for their Christian beliefs. Tobit Potter, Martha Coomes, and James Nashcompait all claimed Christianity as their faith and Wampanoag as their tribe. What needs to be thoughtfully analyzed are the attractions of the new gospel and the reasons why it flourished from generation to generation.

Pre-contact religion of the island offered a set of explanations, interpreted through the powwows, of the world and the supernatural forces alive in it. Those explanations and the rituals of healing, thanksgiving, and charity satisfied Indian spiritual needs and gave a sense of order and meaning to the routines of daily life. In the 1640s, those explanations and the powwow interpreters encountered diseases that resisted traditional cures. Since healing rites were at the heart of Wampanoag religion, the failure of the ceremonies appeared more than a simple lapse of medical skill. That the rites had lost their power seemed a sign of deep disorder in the traditional relationship between the human and spirit worlds. At the same time, the Mayhew mission introduced a rival set of explanations, explainers, and ritual techniques. That Hiacoomes, the first convert, was not stricken in the wave of epidemics had a powerful impact on Indian islanders. The Christianity propounded first by Mayhew and later by native preachers claimed to be more than a reliable cure-all for new diseases. It offered a cluster of credal statements about God, man, and the world that proved believable to a people who had always lived in a spirit-filled world. Thus the sachem Tawanquatuck spoke in 1646 about the decline of the old wisdom and the rise of the new: "A long time ago the *Indians* had wise men among them, that did in a grave manner teach the people knowledge; but they . . . are dead, and their wisdom is buried with them and now men live a giddy life in ignorance till they are white-headed, and tho ripe in years, yet they go without wisdom to their graves." The sachem left no doubt that he wanted the gospel—a gospel that would explain a confused world and help set it in order.

An essential part of the Christian gospel for Indian islanders was a new identity, one that did not deny all aspects of native culture but offered membership in God's tribe. Worship in Indian churches and life among believing neighbors powerfully strengthened the sense of Christian commitment and solidarity. The fragments of sermons included in Mayhew's collection show native preachers struggling to encourage God's Indians by zealous reproving of sin. Such preaching served to remind Wampanoag believers of their Christian identity by holding up unregenerate Indians as examples of faithlessness, violence, and wrong-doing. John Shohkow, ruling elder at Christiantown, offered this direction for native pilgrims. Indian Christians were to "follow hard after God, . . . that they should not be weary or faint in their minds, but go on sincerely and diligently to seek the Lord, and then they might expect to receive all needful good from him." What emerged from preaching, worship, and corporate rituals was an image of the ideal Christian Indian. Shaped as much by Indian cultural needs as by English Puritan requirements, the ideal called for charity, prudence, industry, temperance, family worship, and attendance at public meeting, as well as belief in the gospel message. This Christian identity did not represent a radical break with the traditional past. Communal ceremonies for healing and charity were rooted in Wampanoag culture. Being part of God's tribe at once preserved and extended those ancient values, while giving them a fresh rationale.

The rise of Christian family lineages gave an added dimension to conversion and new identity. Some Indians in Eliot's mainland mission rejected Christianity because they did not want to renounce family and kinship ties. Such renunciations were not necessary on Martha's Vineyard. An Indian child or adult could convert or profess the faith within a supportive Christian family. The presence of many Christian lines offered Indian believers emotional shelter and a sense of belonging. Because identity had always been linked to kinship, it was possible to know who one was as a Christian Indian without stepping outside family relationships.

That sense of identity and community was strengthened by the names used by native Christians. Some mainland missionaries attempted to persuade Indians to abandon traditional names in favor of English ones as a sign of conversion. This was not the case on Martha's Vineyard. What did happen illustrates yet another blending of Indian and English ways. First- and second-generation native Christians generally assumed English names while still using and being known by their Indian ones. Paul, a deacon in the Edgartown church, was also known by his Wampanoag name, Mashquattuhkooit. John Shohkow, a Christiantown ruling elder, kept his traditional name, Assaquanhut. Sometime in the second generation, Indian Christian families began to make use of the dual European given name/patronym style. But this was done with an important and interesting difference. The surname was based on the last part of the traditional Indian name. Hence, Noquittompany's children used Ompany as a last name, and Hiacoomes's descendants used Coomes. Isaac Ompany's name showed both his Christian faith and his native heritage. Mayhew noted that this process was "a thing very common among our Indians."

Being an Indian Christian on Martha's Vineyard also meant some measure of acceptance by the English. This was especially so for convert sachems like Myoxeo and Tawanquatuck who became magistrates. Preachers Japheth Hannit and John Tackanash were addressed as Master. Experience Mayhew found that Indian Christians like Joseph Pompmahchohoo and Hannah Nohnosoo were persons of good report among their English neighbors. There was some tension, however, between Indian Christians and English settlers. Matthew Mayhew, writing in 1694, admitted that English islanders who were not church members resented Indian piety and thought "it no small disparagement to themselves that Indians should be accounted worthy of what themselves cannot be admitted to." English cultural arrogance was surely present, but Wampanoag Christians had family and church resources to buffer that prejudice. As hostility toward natives increased throughout New England in the years before King Philip's War, Christianity served Indian islanders as a lifeboat to whether the storm. That lifeboat might be more aptly termed a survival ideology—a set of beliefs and behaviors that allowed Indians to meet English expectations while maintaining native identity.

A fundamental part of that ideology and a potent attraction to the gospel was the offer of literacy. James Axtell has written that among Puritans "literacy was a universal prerequisite to spiritual preparedness." Eliot's early converts who could not read and had no access to Algonkian Bibles and catechisms made professions of faith correctly characterized by Neal Salisbury as owing "a great deal to the missionaries' suggestions." Martha's Vineyard Indians who wanted to partake of the gospel had to learn to read. Thomas Mayhew, Jr., recognized this when he obtained the services of Peter Folger as schoolmaster at Great Harbor. By the end of the first convert generation, several Indians were sufficiently literate to read both English and Indian books.

Often considerable effort was put forth to become literate. Janawannit and Akoochuk struggled as adults to read English. Indian parents who were poorly educated frequently made substantial sacrifices to ensure the schooling of their children. David Paul, believing that Christian learning would bless both the minds and the souls of his children, went to great lengths to secure a good education for them. Because his farm was far from the nearest school, Paul paid a Christian family to board his children. When the school closed, he hired a young Indian ministerial candidate to tutor them. Perhaps no two people portray better how much books and reading meant to Christian Indians than Job Somannan and Tobit Potter. Somannan was known throughout the island as the lame weaver of Christiantown. After a long day at the loom he would turn to his Algonkian and English books for comfort and strength. "He was," said Experience Mayhew, "a great lover of good books." So was the orphan Tobit Potter, illegitimate son of Elizabeth Uhquat. Potter lived and worked with an English family in Tisbury. When asked by Mayhew about his diligent reading after long hours of work, he replied that he would not take twenty shillings for any of his books.

Because so many were literate, the Martha's Vineyard Indian faithful displayed a genuine understanding of Christian fundamentals. The conversion experiences of Eliot's praying Indians have been criticized for "their lack of intellectual content," there being "no indication that the converts understood the Word, except as applied to themselves, or the most basic tenets of Puritan theology." Such was not the case among the Wampanoag converts. Exposed to sermons by Indian preachers, taught in Christian homes, and conversant with books in both

English and Algonkian, native Christians demonstrated a sure grasp of ideas such as sin, grace, redemption, and reward or punishment after death. They knew these ideas as realities in their own lives and as subjects for communal discussion. Concerned lest his English readers doubt the authenticity of Indian religious expressions, Experience Mayhew made a special point of closely questioning natives on matters of faith and doctrine. From the scores of interviews he conducted emerges a consistent picture of Indians clearly comprehending and using Christian theological language. Thus Mary Coshomon spoke about "the wisdom, goodness, and sovereignty of God"; Japheth Skuhwhannan "discoursed frequently of Jesus Christ, and the way of life and salvation"; and James Nashcompait witnessed to "the mercy of God in sending his Son to redeem mankind from sin and damnation." When Indian pastor Peter Ohquonhut questioned Yonohhmuh on his faith, the native believer talked knowingly about God, sin, and salvation through Christ.

To become embedded in the Indian universe, Christianity had to do more than serve as an intellectually acceptable set of spiritual explanations. Wampanoags did not divide life into separate sacred and secular categories. For them, the ritual and the explanation were part of a single experience. Christianity had to fill the void left by the decline of traditional communal rites. Ancient beliefs had their public celebrations, and Christianity had to provide equally public acts of faith, solidarity, and reassurance. A recent survey of North American Indian mission literature concludes that Catholic Christianity, with its ceremonies, images, processions, and symbols, was far more effective in this replacement process than was Protestantism. On Martha's Vineyard, Indians shaped Christian forms to serve native public and familial needs. The communal functions once undertaken at powwow ceremonies were now carried on in worship services, thanksgiving feasts, and home devotions. Each Sunday, Indian Christians gathered for a full day of preaching, worship, and fellowship. The typical order of worship consisted of an opening prayer, the singing of a metrical psalm, a sermon in Algonkian, and further prayers and psalms. This service was performed twice each Sunday. Communion was usually celebrated seven or eight times a year. It was customary for members of a congregation to meet on the Thursday or Friday before communion Sunday to examine persons who had been suspended from participation in the sacrament. Those found to have repented were then permitted to take the eucharist. Public worship and private family devotions, with sermons, exhortations, prayers, and sung psalms, filled the spiritual space left by the decay of traditional beliefs. Indian Christianity became its own tradition, nourishing the lives of native believers.

Lawrence W. Levine has written that "culture is not a fixed condition but a process: the product of interaction between the past and the present. Its toughness and resiliency are determined not by a culture's ability to withstand change, which indeed may be a sign of stagnation not life, but its ability to react creatively and responsively to the realities of a new situation." The Indian Christians of Martha's Vineyard demonstrated just that sort of toughness and resiliency. Many Indian islanders used Christianity to revitalize their lives in a world growing more and more unfriendly. That one could be a Christian and still live in a wigwam and bear a traditional name was not doubted by the Martha's Vineyard faithful. One of those faithful was Old Katherine, a basket maker at Edgartown. She exemplifies that blending of Indian tradition and Christian commitment. Old Katherine was devoted to public worship services, which "she attended with very great constancy and seriousness." She was equally devoted to charity. Whenever she heard that a neighbor needed extra money for food, she would spend long hours making additional baskets for sale to English villagers. Even when she grew old and "was but meanly clothed," she continued to travel long distances for sabbath observances. In the coldest storms of winter she made her way to meeting with a dedication that astounded her friends. Old Katherine, like many other Martha's Vineyard Indian Christians, found that the rituals of her faith gave shape and meaning to her life. She remains a witness to the vitality of a culture that was simultaneously Christian and Indian.

◈ *F U R T H E R   R E A D I N G*

James Axtell, *The European and the Indians: Essays in the Ethnohistory of Colonial North America* (1981)
———, "Invading America: Puritans and Jesuits," *Journal of Interdisciplinary History* 14 (1989), 635–646
———, *The Invasion Within: The Contest of Cultures in Colonial North America* (1985)
John Francis Bannon, *The Spanish Borderlands Frontier, 1513–1821* (1970)
Herbert Eugene Bolton, "The Mission as a Frontier Institution in the Spanish American Colonies," *American Historical Review* 22 (1917), 42–61
Nancy Bonvillain, "The Iroquois and the Jesuits: Strategies of Influence and Resistance," *American Indian Culture and Research Journal* 10:1 (1986), 29–42
Henry Warner Bowden, *American Indians and Christian Missions* (1981)
Sherburne F. Cook, *The Conflict Between the California Indian and White Civilization* (1976)
Rupert Costo and Jeannette Henry Costo, eds., *The Missions of California: A Legacy of Genocide* (1987)
Charles R. Cutter, *The Protector de Indios in Colonial New Mexico, 1659–1821* (1986)
Carol Devens, "Separate Confrontations: Gender as a Factor in Indian Adaptation to European Colonization in New France," *American Quarterly* 38 (1986), 461–480
Patricia Olive Dickason, "Amerindians Between French and English in Nova Scotia, 1713–1763," *American Indian Culture and Research Journal* 10:4 (1986), 31–56.
Francis F. Guest, "An Examination of the Thesis of S. F. Cook on the Forced Conversion of Indians in the California Missions," *Southern California Quarterly* 61 (1979), 1–77
Ramón Gutiérrez, *When Jesus Came the Corn Mothers Went Away: Marriage, Sexuality and Power in New Mexico, 1500–1846* (1991)
Thomas D. Hall, *Social Change in the Southwest, 1350–1880* (1989)
Robert F. Heizer, "Impact of Colonization on the Native California Societies," *Journal of San Diego History* 24 (1978), 121–139
Albert L. Hurtado, "Sexuality in California's Franciscan Missions: Cultural Perceptions and Sad Realities," *California History* 71 (1992), 371–385
Cornelius J. Jaenen, *Friend and Foe: Aspects of French-Amerindian Cultural Contact in the Sixteenth and Seventeenth Centuries* (1976)
Elizabeth A. H. John, *Storms Brewed in Other Men's Worlds: The Confrontation of Indians, Spanish, and French in the Southwest, 1540–1795* (1975)
John L. Kessell, *Friars, Soldiers, and Reformers: Hispanic Arizona and the Sonora Mission Frontier* (1976)
———, *Kiva, Cross and Crown: The Pecos Indians and New Mexico* (1979)
———, *Mission of Sorrows: Jesuit Guevavi and the Pimas, 1691–1767* (1970)

Eleanor Leacock, "Montagnais Women and the Jesuit Program for Colonization," in Mona Etienne and Eleanor Leacock, eds., *Women and Colonization: Anthropological Perspectives* (1980)

Kenneth M. Morrison, "Baptism and Alliance: The Symbolic Mediations of Religious Syncretism," *Ethnohistory* 37 (1990), 416–437

Gary B. Nash, "Perspectives on the History of Seventeenth-Century Missionary Activity in Colonial America," *Terrae Incognitae* 11 (1979), 17–27

George Harwood Phillips, "Indians and the Breakdown of the Spanish Mission System in California," *Ethnohistory* 21 (1974), 291–301

James P. Ronda, "The Sillery Experiment: A Jesuit-Indian Village in New France, 1637–1663," *American Indian Culture and Research Journal* 3 (1979), 1–18

———, " 'We Are Well as We Are': An Indian Critique of the Seventeenth Century Missions," *William and Mary Quarterly* 34 (1977), 66–82

Neal Salisbury, *Manitou and Providence: Indians, Europeans, and the Making of New England, 1500–1643* (1982)

David J. Weber, "Blood of Martyrs, Blood of Indians: Toward a More Balanced View of Spanish Missions in Seventeenth Century North America," in David Hurst Thomas, *Columbian Consequences,* 3 vols. (1989–1991), Vol. 2, 429–448

———, *The Spanish Frontier in North America* (1992)

Bobby Wright, " 'For the Children of the Infidels'?: American Indian Education in the Colonial Colleges," *American Indian Culture and Research Journal* 12:3 (1988), 1–14

CHAPTER
4

Fur Trade, Empire,

and Indians

Beginning in colonial times, the fur trade was an important aspect of European terri-
torial expansion in North America. Beaver, otter, and other animal pelts attracted
entrepreneurs because of the furs' beauty and warmth and their value in European
markets. Eventually, the beaver came to dominate the fur trade, since its unique coat
made a durable and handsome felt for hats. Deer hides, buffalo hides, and other ani-
mal skins also became articles of Indian-white commerce throughout America. Lively
trade in these items characterized Indian-white relations in much of what are now
the United States and Canada.

Often it was Indians who trapped fur-bearing animals and traded the pelts to
white merchants, but the richness of fur resources also drew enterprising indepen-
dent white trappers and traders, as well as large commercial trapping concerns such
as the Hudson's Bay and North West companies in Canada and John Jacob Astor's
American Fur Company in the United States. Independent trappers and representa-
tives of the commercial organizations often lived among Indians and married native
women, a practice that was known popularly as "the custom of the country" or à la
façon du pays. Such unions provided kinship relations that smoothed whites' trade
with Indians and gave the white husband protection of the tribe. However, the fur
trade was not an altogether peaceful enterprise. It brought conflict between Indians
and the whites who encroached on tribal territory, between national states vying for
colonial supremacy, and among tribes that sought to expand their hunting grounds.
The commercial demands of the fur trade, moreover, led to the rapid depletion of fur
resources as the trappers extinguished the most valuable species. Consequently, inter-
tribal warfare erupted when Indians looked for country that still had animals in
commercial quantities. For some tribes, the trade brought a period of prosperity; yet
it also cultivated a dependence on Europeans for guns, traps, and other manufac-
tured items that were necessary to the commerce. Further, it created a taste among In-
dians for various trade goods and for the adulterated but powerful alcoholic bever-
ages that gradually would pollute tribal society. Thus although the fur business
fostered commerce and paved the way for territorial expansion by Europe and, later,
by the United States, it generated a cycle of trade, violence, dependence, and poverty
for American Indians.

The eighteenth-century fur trade was an important factor in British-French imperial rivalry. In the first document, Cadwallader Colden, a colonial physician, scientist, and historian, complains that New York merchants do not diligently apply themselves to the trade, and he explains other aspects of British, French, and Indian relations. The second selection is an excerpt from a report by Edmond Atkin, the British southern superintendent of the Indians. It shows that the French more successfully adapted the trade to Indian needs and sensibilities than the English did. The third document is taken from a speech by an Ottawa chief, demanding goods on credit from a trader. In the fourth document, President Thomas Jefferson describes to General Henry Dearborn the kinds of goods that Indians of the upper Missouri River valued most, according to reports from the Lewis and Clark expedition. In the final selection, an account of a speech by the Hidatsa chief La Borgne to the Crow (Corbeau) Indians, the benefits of Indian trade with whites are made clear.

Together, these selections give Indian and white points of view on the fur trade. They also show how insidious the trade was—Europeans and Americans pressed for advantage in trading with Indians, and Indians cultivated new sources of manufactured goods. However, this involved too of made Indians more dependent on whites, whether they were British, French, or Anglo-American.

Cadwallader Colden Gives a Contemporary Historian's Account of the Fur Trade and Colonial New York, 1724

It has of late been generally believed, that the Inhabitants of the Province of New-York are so advantageously situated, with respect to the Indian Trade, and enjoy so many Advantages as to Trade in general, that it is in their Power not only to rival the French of Canada, who have almost entirely engrossed the Furr-Trade of America, but that it is impossible for the French to carry on that Trade in Competition with the People of this Province. The enquiring into the Truth of this Proposition, may not only be of some Consequence, as to the Riches and Honour of the British Nation (for it is well known how valuable the Furr-Trade of America is), but likewise as to the Safety of all the British Colonies in North-America. New-France (as the French now claim) extends from the Mouth of the River Misissippi, to the Mouth of the River St. Lawrence, by which the French plainly show their Intention of enclosing the British Settlements, and cutting us off from all Commerce with the numerous Nations of Indians, that are every where settled over the vast Continent of North-America. The English in America have too good Reason to apprehend such a Design, when they see the French King's Geographer publish a Map, by which he has set Bounds to the British Empire in America, and has taken in many of the English Settlements both in South-Carolina and New-York, within these Boundaries of New-France. And the good Services they intend us, with the Indians, but too plainly appears at this Day, by the Indian War now carried on against New-England. . . .

I shall begin [this discussion of the trade] with Canada, and consider what Advantages they have either by their Situation, or otherwise. Canada is situated upon the River of St. Lawrence, by which the five great Lakes (which may properly be called, The five Inland Seas of North-America) empty themselves into the

Ocean. The Mouth of this great River is in the Lat. of 50 Degrees, overagainst the Body of Newfoundland. . . . The five great Lakes which communicate with each other, and with this River, extend about one thousand Miles Westward, further into the Continent. So far the French have already discovered, and their Discoveries make it probable, that an Inland Passage may be found to the South-Sea [the Pacific Ocean], by the Rivers which run into these Lakes, and Rivers which run into the South-Sea.

The Method of carrying Goods upon the Rivers of North-America, into all the small Branches, and over Land, from the Branches of one River to the Branches of another, was learned from the Indians, and is the only Method practicable through such large Forests and Deserts as the Traders pass thro', in carrying from one Nation to another, it is this; the Indians make a long narrow Boat, made of the Bark of the Birch-tree, the Parts of which they join very neatly. One of these Canoes that can carry a Dozen Men, can itself be easily carried upon two Men's Shoulders; so that when they have gone as far by Water as they can (which is further than is easily to be imagined, because their loaded Canoes don't sink six Inches into the Water) they unload their Canoes, and carry both Goods and Canoes upon their Shoulders over Land, into the nearest Branch of the River they intend to follow. Thus, the French have an easy Communication with all the Countries bordering upon the River of St. Lawrence, and its Branches, with all the Countries bordering upon these In-land Seas, and the Rivers which empty themselves into these Seas, and can thereby carry their Burdens of Merchandize thro' all these large Countries, which could not by any other means than Water-carriage be carried thro' so vast a Tract of Land.

This, however, but half finishes the View the French have, as to their Commerce in North-America. Many of the Branches of the River Mississippi come so near to the Branches of several of the Rivers which empty themselves into the great Lakes, that in several Places there is but a short Land-Carriage from the one to the other. As soon as they have got into the River Mississippi, they open to themselves as large a Field for Traffick in the southern Parts of North-America, as was before mentioned with respect to the northern Parts. If one considers the Length of this River, and its numerous Branches, he must say, That by means of this River, and the Lakes, there is opened to his View such a Scene of inland Navigation as cannot be parallel'd in any other Part of the World.

The French have, with much Industry, settled small Colonies, and built stockaded Forts at all the considerable Passes between the Lakes, except between Cataracui Lake (called by the French Ontario) and Lake Erie, one of our Five Nations of Indians, whom we call Sennekas, (and the French Sonontouans) having hitherto refused them leave to erect any Buildings there.

The French have been indefatigable in making Discoveries, and carrying on their Commerce with Nations, of whom the English know nothing but what they see in the French Maps and Books. The Barrenness of the Soil, and the Coldness of the Climate of Canada, obliges the greatest number of the Inhabitants to seek their living by travelling among the Indians, or by trading with those that do travel. The Governor, and other Officers, have but a scanty Allowance from the King, and could not subsist were it not by the Perquisites they have from this Trade; neither could their Priests find any means to satisfy their Ambition and Luxury without it: So that all Heads and Hands are employ'd to advance it, and the Men of best Parts think it the surest way to advance themselves by travelling among the Indians, and learning their Languages; even the Bigotry and Enthusiasm of some hot Heads has not been a little useful in advancing this Commerce; for that Government having prudently turn'd the Edge of the Zeal of such hot Spirits upon converting the Indians, many of them have spent their Lives under the greatest Hardships, in endeavouring to gain the Indians to their Religion, and to love the French Nation, while, at the same time, they are no less industrious to represent the English as the Enemies of Mankind. So that the whole Policy of that Government, both civil and religious, is admirably turn'd to the general Advancement of this Trade. Indeed the Art and Industry of the French, especially that of their religious Missions, has so far prevail'd upon all the Indians in North-America, that they are every where directed by French Councils. Even our own Five Nations, (the Iroquois) who formerly were mortal Enemies of the French, and have always liv'd in the strictest Amity with the English, have, of late, (by the Practices of the French Priests) been so far gain'd, that several of the Mohawks, who live nearest the English, have left their Habitations, and are gone to settle near Montreal in Canada: and all the rest discover a Dread of the French Power. That much of this is truly owing to the Priests, appears from many of the Sachems of the Iroquois wearing Crucifixes when they come to Albany: And those Mohawk Indians that are gone to Canada, are now commonly known, both to the French and English, by the Name of The Praying Indians, it being customary for them to go through the Streets of Montreal with their Beads, praying and begging Alms. . . .

[Although the French had many advantages, they had to contend with a long, difficult, and dangerous route from France to the Indian country. The path included treacherous North Atlantic sea lanes and harbors that were poorly protected from the weather.]

Besides . . . Difficulties in the Transportation, the French labour under greater in the purchasing of the principal Goods proper for the Indian Market; for the most considerable and most valuable Part of their Cargo consists in Strouds [coarse woolen], Duffils [another coarse woolen], Blankets, and other Woolens, which are bought at a much cheaper Rate in England than in France. The Strouds (which the Indians value more than any other Cloathing) are only made in England, and must be transported into France before they can be carried to Canada. Rum is another considerable Branch of the Indian Trade, which the French have not, by reason they have no Commodities in Canada fit for the West India Market. This they supply with Brandy, at a much dearer Rate than Rum can be purchased at New-York, tho' of no more Value with the Indians. Generally, all the Goods used in the Indian Trade, except Gun-Powder, and a few Trinkets, are sold at Montreal for twice their Value at Albany. To this likewise must be added, the necessity they are under of laying the whole Charge of supporting their Government on the Indian Trade. I am not particularly informed of their Duties or Imposts, but I am well assured, that they commonly give six or seven hundred Livres [French pounds] for a Licence for one Canoe, in proportion to her Largeness, to go with her Loading into the Indian Country to trade.

I shall next consider the Advantages the Inhabitants of New-York have in carrying on this Trade. In the first place, the Ships that constantly use the Trade to England perform their Voyage to and from London twice every Year; and those that go to Bristol (the Port from whence the greatest part of the Goods for the Indian Trade are exported) frequently return in four Months. These Goods are bought much cheaper in England than in France: They are transported in less Time, with less Charge, and much less Risque, as appears by the Premio for Insurance between London and New-York, being only Two per Cent. Goods are easily carried from New-York to Albany, up Hudson's River, the Distance being only 140 Miles, the River very strait all the way, and bold, and very free from Sandbanks, as well as Rocks; so that the Vessels always sail as well by Night as by Day, and have the Advantage of the Tide upwards as well as downwards, the Flood flowing above Albany. It may therefore be safely concluded, that all sorts of Goods can be carried to Albany at a cheaper Rate than they can be to Quebeck, which is also three times further from the Indian Country than Albany is. To put the Truth of this out of all dispute, I need only observe what is well known both at New-York and Albany, viz. That almost all the Strouds carried by the French into the Indian Countries, as well as large Quantities of other Goods, for the Use of the French themselves, are carried from Albany to Montreal. . . .

Whoever then considers [the] Advantages New-York has of Canada, in the first buying of their Goods, and in the safe, speedy, and cheap Transportation of them from Britain to the Lakes, free of all manner of Duty or Imposts, will readily agree with me, that the Traders of New-York may sell their Goods in the Indian Countries at half the Price the People of Canada can, and reap twice the Profit they do. This will admit of no Dispute with those that know that Strouds (the Staple Indian Commodity) this Year are sold for Ten Pounds apiece at Albany, and at Montreal for Twenty-five Pounds, notwithstanding the great Quantity of Strouds said to be brought directly into Quebeck from France, and the Great Quantities that have been clandestinely carried from Albany. It cannot therefore be denied that it is only necessary for the Traders of New-York to apply themselves heartily to this Trade, in order to bring it wholly into their own Hands; for in every thing besides Diligence, Industry, and enduring Fatigues, the English have much the Advantage of the French. And all the Indians will certainly buy, where they can, at the cheapest Rate. . . .

Edmond Atkin Reveals the Reasons for French Success in the Indian Trade, 1755

. . . As it is commonly supposed, that the French have acquired their influence, and maintain their Power among the Indian Nations, intirely by their Forts;—it seems also to have been generally thought, that if they are not [to] be removed, yet our Building Forts in the same Places, and in such other places where the French still propose to do it, will be a Sufficient remedy to put an intire stop to the same, and to secure our own Interest. But this will be found on a more intimate

Reprinted from *The Appalachian Indian Frontier: The Edmond Atkin Report and Plan of 1775,* edited, with an introduction by Wilbur R. Jacobs, pp. 8–11, by permission of the University of Nebraska Press. Copyright © 1967 by Wilbur R. Jacobs.

acccquaintance with that subject, to be a very great Error. How usefull and necessary soever Forts really are, for establishing between the Crowns of Great Britain
and France marks of Possession, or for the mutual protection of their Traders and
Friends, and for fixing [securing the loyalty of] the doubtfull and wavering
among the Indians; yet it is truly a great absurdity to imagine, that either the
French or ourselves can maintain an Interest & Influence, more especially among
the Inland Nations, barely by the Possession of Forts, without being at the same
time possess'd of their *Affections;* Or that anything less than such a Wall as is
built between China and Tartary [Mongolia] can, when the Indians are our Enemies, secure our wide extended and exposed Colonies from their Incursions.
Most of the French inland Forts are small, and very weak, having but few Men.
And tho' the Indians are unskilled, and unprovided for the Attack of Forts, yet the
Garrisons of the largest may easily be starv'd by them into a Surrender whenever
they please. We must [look] therefore into the Conduct and Management of the
French in those Forts, in order to discover by the *Arts* practiced therein the true
causes from whence, under a Commerce clogged with a most hazardous Navigation & expensive Transportation of Goods, with the additional load of paying all
the Charges of their Government, and under a total inability at any rate of supplying all the wants of the Indians, they have still gain'd their Affections, and consequently that surprising Influence which we have felt. Those Arts will be found to
be the most Simple, the most easy and certain, and the least expensive imaginable. The two Principal ones are, the Provision of *Gunsmiths,* and not so much
valuable Presents as a judicious Application of them. We furnish the Indians with
Guns enough in exchange for their deer skins and Furrs; but the French mend
them and keep them in repair Gratis. We are sometimes almost lavish of presents
on particular Occasions, which in the way they are given produce but little good
Effect with those that receive them, and still less with their Nation. But the French
by a constant prudent Practice, make even Trifles productive of the most desirable National Consequences. When an Indian after undergoing the mortification
of having a Gun (perhaps from trial and use becomes a favourite one) suddenly
by some slight accident to the Lock, or Touch hole, render'd intirely useless to
him, I say when he sees it afterwards as suddenly restored to its former State, and
as usefull as before, it gladdens his Heart more than a present of a new Gun
would. He then looks on our Trader and the Frenchman with different Eyes. The
former only Sold him the Gun (perhaps at an extravagant price); the latter when
it is spoiled, hath as it were new made [it] for nothing. This endears the Frenchman to him. He is glad to have such a Friend near him. Their mutual Convenience
unites them. Gratitude inclines the Indian to oblige him by any means in his
Power. The presents to Indians are made at the expence of the Crown of France.
Besides those given by the Governors at periodical Meetings, some are left in the
occasional disposition of the Commanders of Forts the Year round. A present of
any Value is never given by them but to an Indian of Sway and Consequence
[among the Warriours], or as an Orator among the people. And then he comes by
it easy, and without any Trouble. Whereas when such do receive Presents of some
Value from us, they earn them much too dearly by tiresome tedious Journies of
some hundred Miles, and the loss of time from their Hunts, which they know
would have turn'd to better Account. Even trifles are put on the footing of things

of Value at the French Forts, by bestowing them chiefly on the old Head Men of Note, who being past the fatigue of War and constant Hunting for their Livelyhood, but on Account of their Age held in great Veneration for their Wisdom and Experience, spend the remainder of their days almost intirely in the Town Round Houses, where the Youth and others daily report; relating to them the History of their Nation, discoursing of Occurrences, and delivering precepts and Instructions for their Conduct and Welfare, Which is all the Indian Education. To these old men who are unable to purchase Necessaries, or to perform long Journeys, when they visit those Forts the French give from time to time a Load or two of Powder and Ball, a Flint, a Knife, a little Paint, a flap or shirt, and the like. The Old Men repay the French largely for those Trifles, in their Harrangues at the round Houses, by great Encomiums on their kindness, and recommendations of them to favour; which often inculcated, make impressions on the Youth, that grow up with them into a confirm'd prejudice. On the other hand those old men complain, that our Traders, who confine their kindness and Civility almost wholly to the Young Hunters for the sake of their deerskins, shew Slights to them which lessen them in the Eyes of their People. The vast Quantity of Ammunition with which the French furnish the Indians every where by their Water Carriage more Conveniently than we can, hath strengthened their influence, that Article being the only means the Indians have to get everything else they stand in need of. Ammunition, especially Bulletts, being heavy and a Horse Load but of small Value, our Traders who are oblig'd to carry on their Trade in the Southern Parts, where the most numerous Indians are, many hundred Miles wholly by Horse Carriage, naturally consulting their own greatest profitt, have carried but scanty supplies of that Article, and in a great measure left it to the French; who have thereby imperceptably accquir'd an Addition to their Interest, in a manner which hath hitherto pass'd almost unnotic'd; But is of so much consequence to them, that the Governour of new Orleans in a letter to the French Secretary of State, (which being intercepted in the late War [Seven Years' War] is now in my hands) gave it as his opinion, "That were it not for those great supplies of Ammunition, some Nations of Indians devoted to the English, would not suffer Frenchmen to remain among them. And therefore he propos'd even to restrain the Quantity, to make them more Submissive." The same reason should lead us by some means or other to encrease it. . . .

An Ottawa Chief Demands Trade Goods on Credit, 1761

. . . "Englishmen," he said, "we, the Ottawas were some time since informed of your arrival in this country, and of your having brought with you the goods of which we have need. At this news we were greatly pleased, believing that through your assistance our wives and children would be enabled to pass another winter; but what was our surprise, when a few days ago we were again informed that the goods which as we had expected were intended for us were on the eve of departure for distant countries, of which some are inhabited by our enemies! These accounts being spread, our wives and children came to us crying and desiring that we should go to the fort to learn with our own ears their truth or falsehood. We accordingly embarked almost naked as you see; and on our arrival here we have inquired into the accounts and found them true. We see your canoes ready to depart and find your men engaged for the Mississippi and other distant regions.

"Under these circumstances we have considered the affair; and you are now sent for that you may hear our determination, which is that you shall give to each of our men, young and old, merchandise and ammunition to the amount of fifty beaver skins on credit, and for which I have no doubt of their paying you in the summer, on their return from their wintering." . . .

President Thomas Jefferson's Inventory of Indian Trade Goods, 1807

14 February 1807

Th: Jefferson salutes Genl. Dearborne with friendship and communicates the following information from Capt. Lewis, which may be useful to Colo. Freeman and our future explorers, and indeed may enable us understandingly to do acceptable things to our Louisiana neighbors when we wish to gratify them. He says the following are the articles in highest value with them.

1. *Blue* beads. This is a coarse cheap bead imported from China, & costing in England 13d. the lb. in strands. It is far more valued by the Indians than the *white* beads of the same manufacture, & answers all the purposes of money, being counted by the fathom. He says that were his journey to be performed again, one half or ⅔ of his stores *in value,* should be of these.
2. Common brass buttons, more valued than any thing except beads.
3. Knives.
4. Battle axes & tomahawks.
5. Sadler's seat awls, which answer for mockasin awls.
6. Some glover's needles.
7. Some iron combs.
8. Some nests of camp kettles. Brass is much preferred to iron, tho both are very useful to the indians.

Feb. 14. 07.

Arrow points should have been added.

Le Borgne, a Crow Chief, Tells the Hidatsas to Protect and Trade with Whites, 1805

[In 1805, North West Company trader Charles McKenzie wrote down this statement by Le Borgne:] "My Son and my friends, rejoice—White men are to visit your Land and you will feel easy in their company—but we shall regret their absence. White men are curious—they came from far—they know much and wish to learn more. Three only form their party; Your party consist of a thousand and more—you see their skin, it is white—their hearts are as white as their skin— they are good and will do you no harm. Give them plenty to eat; let them have the best, and be the first served—let your women be kind to them—never ask any thing from them: they are generous, and they will pay you for your kindness—White men love Beaver and they are continually in search of Beaver for its Skin—What use they make of the Skin I know not:—but they give us good things in return—they exchange it for Guns, Ammunition &c. Our Fathers were not acquainted with White men—We live better than our Fathers lived. Do your Neighbours the Serpent nation enjoy the Security and happiness we enjoy? If the white men could furnish the Serpents as they furnish us with arms, we should not carry away so many of the Serpents' Scalps—the white men are powerful—they are like magic—I, therefore, once more entreat you to protect with indulgence those I recommend—You, my Son, must never let the Young white Chief out of your Sight—go with him wherever he goes—should any misfortune happen to him we shall be ashamed to meet white men. This Summer I intend to visit the Great White Chief at his Fort—I shall tell him that his Young friends are safe in charge of my Son who is a Great man—and the Great Chief of the white people will be Kind to you:—but I have heard some of the Women, as I was passing through the camp, call out 'Return, white men, go home, we are afraid'; Say, my friends, what means this?"

After a pause of some minutes, an elderly man raising his voice Said, "We were suspicious of these white men—we were afraid they might throw evil medicines among us and Soil our Lands; but you have removed our fears, and you can depend upon our goodness. The *Corbeaux* are in two Tribes—they have two Chiefs: the *Red Calf* who receives favours from the white men; and the *Red Fish* who receives none; It was the *Red Fish* that told us to be angry."

No sooner had the old man ceased Speaking than the *Red Calf* addressed Mr. La Roque [a North West Company trader]:—"Father," said he, "if you are willing to go with us, we are willing to receive you—but should an enemy stand in our way, or attack us in our Journey—You and Your Young men must assist us in beating him off."

Mr. La Roque said he would assist his friends on all occasions. [Then the Red Calf told his new Father how he was to conduct himself in order to keep friends with all and assure a Safe Journey.] Then *Le Borgne* made a harangue of great length . . . and concluded by observing, "that his heart was full, and that he would be in a state of anxiety until the return of the white men.—". . . .

◈ *E S S A Y S*

The fur trade endured in North America for centuries. As we have seen, it was the object of European colonial and American national policies as well as of private business ventures. The trade became a crucial part of many tribes' economy and culture. Once they grew reliant on trade goods, Indians had little choice but to continue down the commercial road to dependence. Nevertheless, Arthur J. Ray, professor of geography at York University in Ontario, argues that Indians shaped the trade in various ways. Ray criticizes studies of the fur trade for not paying sufficient attention to Indian motives and actions. Likewise, Professor Sylvia Van Kirk of the University of Toronto suggests in the second essay that scholars have given little attention to the role of Indian women in fur trade society. She examines the importance of interracial marriage *à la façon du pays,* "after the custom of the country."

These essays and the documents illustrate that peaceful relations were not necessarily benign. Given the presence of Europeans in America, what alternatives to trading with them did Indians have? Could Indians have continued to follow the same kind of life that existed before 1492? What do these readings tell us about the lives of Indian women? How was the Indian woman's historical experience different from the Indian man's?

The Fur Trade as an Aspect of Native American History

ARTHUR J. RAY

Howard Adams, among others, has made the point that the dominant white Euro-Canadian culture has projected racist images of the Indians that "are so distorted that they portray natives as little more than savages without intelligence or beauty." He argued further that the Indians "must endure a history that shames them, destroys their confidence, and causes them to reject their heritage." There is a great deal of truth in Adams's statements, and clearly a considerable amount of historical research needs to be done to correct these distorted images. One important aspect of any new meaningful Indian history necessarily will be concerned with the involvement of the Indian peoples in the fur trade and with the impact of that participation upon their traditional cultures as well as those of the European intruders. Work in this area will be important not only because it holds a potential for giving us new insights into Indian history, but also because it should serve to help establish Indian history in its rightful place in the mainstream of Canadian historiography. As some of Canada's most prominent historians have emphasized, the fur trade was a molding force in the economic, political, and social development of Canada, and the Indian peoples played a central role in this enterprise. For these reasons Indian history should not simply be devoted to recounting the manner in which the aboriginal peoples of Canada were subjugated and exploited, but it must also consider the positive contribution that the Indian peoples made to the fur trade and, hence, to the development of Canada. If this positive contribution is recognized, it should help destroy some of the distorted images that many Canadians have of Indians and their history.

Given that fur trade history and Indian history are inextricably bound together, several questions immediately arise. How much attention have historians devoted to the roles that the Indians played in the fur trade in the considerable body of fur trade literature that already exists? What images of the Indian peoples emerge from this literature? What aspects of Indian involvement have yet to be explored fully?

Until relatively recently the Indian peoples have not figured prominently in works dealing with the fur trade. Rather, they generally appear only as shadowy figures who are always present, but never central characters, in the unfolding events. In part, this neglect appears related to the fact that historians have been primarily concerned with studying the fur trade as an aspect of European imperial history or of Canadian business and economic history. And, reflecting these basic interests, the considerable biographical literature that fur trade research has generated deals almost exclusively with Euro-Canadian personalities. Relatively few Indian leaders have been studied to date.

Although the tendency to consider the fur trade primarily as an aspect of Euro-Canadian history has been partly responsible for the failure of scholars to focus on the Indians' role in the enterprise, other factors have been influential as well. One of the basic problems with most studies of Indian-white relations has been that ethno-historians and historians have taken a retrospective view. They see the subjugation of the Indian peoples and the destruction of their lifestyles as inevitable consequences of the technological gap that existed between European and Indian cultures at the time of contact. From this technological-determinist perspective, the Indian has been rendered as an essentially powerless figure who was swept along by the tide of European expansion without any real hope of channeling its direction or of influencing the character of the contact situation. The dominance of this outlook has meant that in most fur trade studies the Indian has been cast in a reflexive role. Reflecting this perspective, until recently most ethno-historical research has been approached from an acculturation-assimilation point of view. The questions asked are generally concerned with determining how Indian groups incorporated European technology as well as social, political, economic, and religious customs into their traditional cultures.

While also interested in these issues, historians have devoted a considerable amount of attention toward outlining the manner and extent to which Euro-Canadian groups, particularly missionaries and government officials, helped the Indians to adjust to the new socio-economic conditions that resulted from the expansion of Western cultures into the new world. Often historical research has taken a certain moralistic tone, assuming that members of the dominant white society had an obligation to help the Indians adopt agriculture and European socio-economic practices and moral codes, so that the Indian peoples could fit into the newly emerging social order. Thus, historians who undertake these types of studies are frequently seeking to determine whether or not the traders, missionaries, and government officials had fulfilled their obligations to help "civilize" the Indian.

Granting that much good work has been done in the above areas, it is my opinion that many new insights into Indian history can be obtained if we abandon the retrospective, technological-determinist outlook and devote more attention to an examination of Indian involvement in the fur trade in the context of contemporary conditions. Such an approach would necessarily recognize that the nature of the trading partnerships that existed between Indian groups and various European interests changed substantially over time and place, making it difficult, frequently misleading, and certainly premature, given the amount of research that still needs to be done, to make any sweeping statements at this time about the nature of Indian-white relations in the context of the Canadian fur trade.

In order to pursue this work effectively, two courses of action need to be followed—one is not currently popular, and the other is extremely tedious. First, students of Indian history need to abandon the assumption that the Indians were ruthlessly exploited and cheated in all areas and periods by white traders. At present this is a very popular theme for both Indian and liberal white historians. All of us have heard the story many times of how the Indians sold Manhattan Island for a few pounds of beads, and we have been informed of the many instances when Indians parted with valuable furs for trinkets and a drink. But, why are we never informed of what the Indians' perceptions of trade were? It may well be that they too thought they were taking advantage of the Europeans. For example, in 1634, when commenting on Montagnais beaver trapping in eastern Canada, Father Le Jeune [a Jesuit missionary] wrote:

> The Castor or Beaver is taken in several ways. The Savages say it is the animal well-beloved by the French, English and Basques,—in a word, by the Europeans. I heard my [Indian] host say one day, jokingly, *Missi picoutau amiscou,* "The Beaver does everything perfectly well, it makes kettles, hatchets, swords, knives, bread; and in short, it makes everything." He was making sport of us Europeans, who have such a fondness for the skin of this animal and who fight to see who will get it; they carry this to such an extent that my host said to me one day, showing me a beautiful knife, "The English have no sense; they give us twenty knives like this for one Beaver skin."

While there is no denying that European abuses of Indians were all too common, there are several things wrong with continually stressing this aspect of the fur trade and Indian history. As the previous quote suggests, it gives us only half the story. Of greater importance, by continually focusing only on this dimension of the trade, we run the serious risk of simply perpetuating one of the images of Indian historiography that Adams, among others, most strongly objects to, namely, the view that the Indians were little more than "savages without intelligence." It also glosses over a fundamental point that must be recognized if the Indian is to be cast in an active and creative role. We must not forget that the Indians became involved in the fur trade by their own choice. Bearing that in mind, an objective and thorough examination of the archival records of the leading trading companies, admittedly a wearisome task, gives considerable evidence that the Indians were sophisticated traders, who had their own clearly defined sets of objectives and conventions for carrying on exchange with the Europeans.

This can be demonstrated by following several lines of inquiry. One of these involves attempting to determine the kind of consumers the Indians were at the time of initial contact and how their buying habits changed over time. Probably one of the most striking pictures that emerges from an examination of the early correspondence books of the Hudson's Bay Company is that, contrary to the popular image, the Indians had a sharp eye for quality merchandise and a well-defined shopping list. In short, they were astute consumers and not people who were easily hoodwinked.

If this is doubted, the early letters that the traders on Hudson Bay sent to the governor and committee of the Hudson's Bay Company in London should be read carefully. A substantial portion of almost every letter deals with the subject of the quality of the company's trade goods and with the Indians' reactions to it. Not only do these letters reveal that the Indians could readily recognize superior merchandise, but they also indicate that the Indians knew how to take advantage of the prevailing economic situation to improve the quality of the goods being offered to them. The following quote, typical of those that were written in the period before 1763, demonstrates the point and at the same time indicates one of the problems that is associated with carrying on research of this type. On 8 August 1728, Thomas McCliesh sent a letter from York Factory to the governor and committee in London informing them:

> I have sent home . . . samples [of inappropriate merchandise]. I have likewise sent home 59 ivory combs that will not be traded, they having no great teeth, and 3900 large musket flints and small pistol flints, likewise one hatchet, finding at least 150 such in three casks that we opened this summer which causes great grumbling amongst the natives. We have likewise Sent home 18 barrels of powder that came over in 1727, for badness I never saw the like, for it will not kill fowl nor beast at thirty yards distance: and as for kettles in general they are not fit to put into a Indian's hand being all of them thin, and eared with tender old brass that will not bear their weight when full of liquid, and soldered in several places. Never was any man so upbraided with our powder, kettles and hatchets, than we have been this summer by all the natives, especially by those that border near the French. Our cloth likewise is so stretched with the tenter-hooks, so as the selvedge is almost tore from one end of the pieces to the other. I hope that such care will be taken so as will prevent the like for the future, for the natives are grown so politic in their way of trade, so as they are not to be dealt by as formerly . . . and I affirm that man is not fit to be entrusted with the Company's interest here or in any of their factories that does not make more profit to the Company in dealing in a good commodity than in a bad. For now is the time to oblidge [*sic*] the natives before the French draw them to their settlement.

From McCliesh's letter one gets the impression that few of the goods on hand were satisfactory as far as the Indians were concerned. Taken out of context, comments of this type, which are common in the correspondence from the posts, could be construed to indicate that the governor and committee of the Hudson's Bay Company hoped to enhance their profits by dealing in cheap, poor quality merchandise whenever possible. However, such a conclusion would distort the reality of the situation and overlook important developments that were underway in the eighteenth century. If one examines the letters that the governor and committee sent to the Bay during the same period, as well as the minutes of their meetings in London and correspondence with British manufacturers and purchasing agents, other important facts emerge.

These other documents reveal that from the outset the governor and committee were concerned with having an array of the types and quality of goods that would appeal to the Indians. From the minute books of the company we learn that in the earliest years of operations the London directors relied heavily upon the experience and judgment of Pierre-Esprit Radisson to provide them with guidance in developing an inventory of merchandise that would be suitable for their posts in Canada. Radisson helped choose the patterns for knives, hatchets, guns, and so forth that manufacturers were to use, and he was expected to evaluate the quality of items that were produced for the company. The governor and committee also sought the expertise of others in their efforts to maintain some quality control. For instance, in 1674 they attempted to enlist the services of the gunsmith who inspected and approved the trade guns of the East Indian Company. They wanted him to evaluate the firearms that the Hudson's Bay Company was purchasing.

In their annual letters to the post on the Bay, the governor and committee generally asked the traders to comment on the goods that they received and to indicate which, if any, manufacturer's merchandise was substandard. When new items were introduced, the directors wanted to know what the Indians' reactions to them were.

The question that no doubt arises is, if the governor and committee were as concerned with the quality of the products they sold, as suggested above, then why was there a steady stream of complaints back to London about their goods? Before a completely satisfactory answer to this question can be given, a great deal more research needs to be done in these records. However, several working hypotheses may be put forth at this time for the sake of discussion and research orientation. In developing its inventory of trade goods, the Hudson's Bay Company, as well as other European groups, had to deal with several problems. One of these was environmental in character. Goods that may have been satisfactory for trade in Europe, Africa, or Asia often proved to be unsuitable in the harsh, subarctic environment. This was especially true of any items that were manufactured of iron. For example, one of the problems with the early flintlocks was that the locks froze in the winter.

The extremely cold temperatures of the winter also meant that metal became brittle. Hence, if there were any flaws or cracks in the metal used to make mainsprings for guns, gun barrels, knives, hatchets, or kettles, these goods would break during the winter. In this way the severe environment of the subarctic necessitated very rigid standards of quality if the goods that were offered to the Indians were going to be satisfactory. These standards surely tested the skills of the company's suppliers and forced the company to monitor closely how the various manufacturers' goods held up under use.

Besides having to respond to environmental conditions, the traders also had to contend with a group of consumers who were becoming increasingly sophisticated and demanding. As the Indians substituted more and more European manufacturers for traditional items, their livelihood and well-being became more dependent upon the quality of the articles that they were acquiring at the trading posts. This growing reliance meant that the Indians could no longer afford to accept goods that experience taught them would fail under the stress of hard usage and the environment, since such failures could threaten their survival. It was partly for these reasons that the Indians developed a critical eye for quality and could readily perceive the most minute defects in trade merchandise.

Indian groups were also quick to take advantage of competitive conditions. They became good comparison shoppers and until 1821 used European trading rivalries to force the improvement of quality and range of goods that were made available to them. For example, during the first century of trade on Hudson Bay, the Indians frequently brought to Hudson's Bay Company posts French goods that they judged to be superior to those of English manufacture. The Indians then demanded that the Hudson's Bay Company traders match or exceed the quality of these items or risk the loss of their trade to the French. Similar tactics were used by the Indians in later years whenever competition was strong between Euro-Canadian groups. Clearly such actions were not those of "dumb savages," but rather were those of astute traders and consumers, who knew how to respond to changing economic conditions to further their own best interests. The impact that these actions had on the overall profitability of the trade for Euro-Canadian traders has yet to be determined.

The issue of profits raises another whole area of concern that is poorly understood and should be studied in depth. To date we know little about how the economic motivations of the Europeans and the Indians influenced the rates of exchange that were used at the posts. In fact, there is still a great deal of confusion about the complicated system of pricing goods and furs that was used in Canada. We know that the Hudson's Bay Company traders used two sets of standards. There was an official rate of exchange that was set by the governor and committee in London which differed from the actual rate that was used at the posts. Of importance, the traders advanced the prices of their merchandise above the stated tariff by resorting to the use of short measures. Contemporary critics of the Hudson's Bay Company and modern native historians have attacked the company for using such business practices, charging that the Indians were thereby being systematically cheated, or to use the modern expression, "ripped off." But was this the case? Could the company traders have duped the Indians over long periods of time without the latter having caught on? Again, common sense and the record suggest that this was not the case.

The traders have left accounts of what they claimed were typical speeches of Indian trading leaders. One central element of all of these addresses was the request by these leaders that the traders give the Indians "full measure and a little over." Also, the Indians usually asked to see the old measures or standards. Significantly, the Indians do not appear to have ever challenged the official standards, while at the same time they knew that they never received "full measure." What can we conclude from these facts?

In reality, the official standards of trade of the Hudson's Bay Company, and perhaps those of other companies as well, served only as a language of trade, or point of reference, that enabled the Indians and the traders to come to terms relatively quickly. The traders would not sell goods at prices below those set in the official standard. The Indian goal, on the other hand, was to try to obtain terms that approximated the official rate of exchange. An analysis of the Hudson's Bay Company post account books for the period before 1770 reveals that the company traders always managed to advance prices above the standard, but the margin of the advance diminished as the intensity of French opposition increased. And even under monopoly conditions such as existed in Western Canada before the 1730s, the Hudson's Bay Company traders were not able to achieve an across-the-board increase that exceeded 50 percent for any length of time. This suggests strongly that the Indians successfully used competitive situations to improve the terms of trade and that they had their limits. If prices were advanced beyond a certain level, the Indians must have perceived that their economic reward was no longer worth the effort expended, and they broke off trade even if there was no alternative European group to turn to.

These remarks about the *overplus* system apply to the period before 1770.

What we need to know is the extent to which the Indians were able to influence the rates of exchange during the time of bitter Hudson's Bay Company and North West Company rivalry. A preliminary sample of data from that period suggests their impact was much greater and that range of price variation was much more extreme than in the earlier years. Similarly, it would be helpful to have some idea what effect the re-establishment of the Hudson's Bay Company's monopoly after 1821 had on trade good prices and fur values in Western Canada. Being able to monitor prices under these contrasting conditions would enable us to obtain some idea of how the Indians were coping with the changing economic situation and how their responses influenced the material well-being of the different tribal groups.

Although this sample of the early accounting records shows that the Indians were economic men in the sense that they sought to maximize the return they obtained for their efforts, the same documents also indicate that, unlike their European counterparts, the Indians did not trade to accumulate wealth for status purposes. Rather, the Indians seem to have engaged in trade primarily to satisfy their own immediate requirement for goods. On a short-term basis their consumer demand was inelastic. In the early years this type of response was important in two respects. It was disconcerting to the European traders in that when they were offered better prices for their furs, the Indians typically responded by offering fewer pelts on a per capita basis. This type of a supply response was reinforced by gift-giving practices. Following the Indian custom, prior to trade tribal groups and the Europeans exchanged gifts. As rivalries for the allegiance of the Indians intensified, the lavishness of the gifts that the traders offered increased.

The ramifications that Indian supply responses to rising fur prices and to European gift-giving practices had for the overall conduct of the fur trade have yet to be fully explored. Clearly the costs that the Europeans would have had to absorb would have risen substantially during the periods when competition was strong, but to date no one has attempted to obtain even a rough idea of the magnitude by which these costs rose during the time of English-French or Hudson's Bay Company–North West Company rivalry. Nor has serious consideration been given to the manner in which such economic pressures may have favoured the use and abuse of certain trade articles such as alcohol and tobacco.

Concerning the use of alcohol, the excessive consumption of this drug was an inevitable consequence of the manner in which the economies of the Indian and European were linked together in the fur trade and of the contrasting economic motives of the two groups. As rivalries intensified, the European traders sought some means of retaining their contacts with the Indians, while at the same time keeping the per capita supply of furs that were obtained at as high a level as was possible. However, in attempting to accomplish the latter objective, the Europeans faced a number of problems. The mobile life of the Indians meant that their ability to accumulate material wealth was limited, especially in the early years when the trading posts were distant from the Indians' homelands. And, there were social sanctions against the accumulation of wealth by individual Indians. To combat these problems, the traders needed to find commodities that could be transported easily or, even better, consumed at the trading post.

Unfortunately, alcohol was ideal when viewed from this coldly economic perspective. It offered one of the best means of absorbing the excess purchasing power of the Indians during periods of intensive competition. Furthermore, alcohol could be obtained relatively cheaply and diluted with water prior to trade. Hence, it was a high profit trade item, an article that helped the traders hold down their gift-giving expenses, and it could be consumed at the forts. Given these characteristics, the only way that the abusive use of alcohol in trade could have been prevented in the absence of a strong European or native system of government was through monopoly control.

The traditional Indian consumer habits and responses to rising fur prices were important in another way. They were basically conservationist in nature, although not intentionally so. By trapping only enough furs to buy the goods they needed in the early years, the pressures that the Indians exerted on the environment by their trapping activities were far less than they would have been had the objective been one of accumulating wealth for status purposes. If the latter had been the primary goal, then the Indians would have been tempted to increase their per capita supply of peltry as fur prices rose, since their purchasing power was greater.

In light of the above, the period between 1763 and 1821 is particularly interesting and warrants close study. During that period Euro-Canadian trading rivalries reached a peak, and one of the consequences of the cutthroat competition that characterized the time was that large territories were over-hunted and trapped by the Indians to the point that the economies of the latter were threatened. The question is, had the basic economic behaviour of the Indians changed to such an extent that it facilitated their over-killing fur and game animals? Or, was the heavy use of addictive consumables such as alcohol and tobacco a major factor in the destruction of the environment?

Yet another aspect of the fur trade that has received too little attention is the connection that existed between the European and eastern North American markets and the Western Canadian operations of the trading companies. It needs to be determined how prices for trade goods and furs in these markets, as well as transportation costs, influenced rates of exchange at the posts. For instance, it has become popular to cite cases where European traders advanced the prices of certain articles by as much as 1,000 percent over what it cost the companies to buy them in Europe. Similarly, accounts of occasions when the Indians received a mere pittance for valuable furs are common. But it is rarely reported, and indeed it is generally not known, what percentage of the total gross revenues of a company were made by buying and selling such items. Nor is it known if losses were sustained on the sales of other commodities. Equally important, there is not even a rough idea of what the total overhead costs of the companies were at various times. Hence, their net profit margins remain a mystery, and what was considered to be a reasonable profit margin by European standards in the seventeenth, eighteenth, and early nineteenth centuries is not known. Answers to all of these questions must be found before any conclusions can be reached about whether or not the Indian or the European trader was being "ripped off."

And indeed, the Indian side must be considered when dealing with this question and when attempting to understand how the trading system responded to changing economic conditions. Even though Harold Innis pointed out that Indian trading specialists played a crucial role in the development and expansion of the fur trade, a common view of the Indians in the enterprise is still one that portrays them basically as simple trappers who hunted their own furs and accepted whatever prices for these commodities that the traders were willing to give them. The fact of the matter is that the records show that in the period before 1770, probably 80 percent of all of the furs the Europeans received in central Canada came from Indian middlemen who acquired their peltry through their own trading networks.

Furthermore, these middlemen charged the Europeans substantially more for these furs than they had paid to obtain them from the trapping bands with whom they dealt. In turn, the middlemen advanced the prices for their trade goods well above the levels they had been charged by the Europeans, sometimes by margins of almost 1,000 percent.

These practices of the Indian middlemen raise a difficult question. If the Indians were not engaged in the trade to accumulate wealth, as suggested earlier, then why did the middlemen advance their prices to the extent that they did? Did their price levels simply enable them to maintain a material standard that they had become accustomed to? Before this question can be answered, a great deal more needs to be known about the problems that the Indian middlemen had to cope with in their efforts to acquire and transport goods and furs. A clearer understanding of their motives for engaging in the trade is also required. For example, why did some Indian groups quickly assume the middleman role while others were apparently content to continue as trappers? How did middlemen groups fare, economically, in comparison with trapping groups?

The Indians played a variety of other roles in the fur trade. They served as provision suppliers, canoe builders, canoe and boat men, and farm labourers around the posts, to name only a few. The Indians quickly assumed these roles as economic conditions changed, rendering old positions obsolete and opening up new opportunities.

This brings to mind another broad research area that should be explored more fully than it has been to date. It deals with determining how the various Indian groups perceived and responded to changing economic situations. Work in this area would serve to destroy another distorted image that many Euro-Canadians have of Indian societies, namely, the view that these societies are rigid and incapable of responding to change. Historically there is little evidence to support such a notion for the period before 1870. While the fur trade was a going concern and the Indians were not tied to the reserves and shackled with bureaucratic red tape, they made many successful adaptations to new circumstances. More needs to be written about this aspect of Indian history. If this work is done, perhaps a picture will emerge that shows the Indians to be innovative, dynamic, and responsive people, whose creativity and initiative have been thwarted in the post-treaty period.

In conclusion, this paper has focused upon the early phases of the Western Canadian fur trade, and the discussion has been restricted primarily to the economic dimension of trade. However, this restriction is justified because many of the problems of Indian-white relations are rooted in the past. Also, many of the distorted images that Euro-Canadians currently hold regarding Indians, thereby causing problems in the relationships between the two groups, have been generated and perpetuated by the manner in which the fur trade history has been written. Correcting these images requires starting at the beginning, and it is not simply a matter of rewriting what has already been done. New research has to be conducted in the various archival collections across the country, and records that have received little attention to date, such as accounting records, need to be exhaustively explored. In conducting this research and presenting our results, the urge to overcompensate for past wrongs and inaccuracies by placing the Indian on a pedestal must be resisted. If the latter course of action is taken, a new mythology that will not stand the test of time will be created. Even more serious, it would probably serve only to perpetuate the warped images that such research set out to destroy, because it would fail to treat the Indians as equals with their own cultures and sets of values. Finally, if one of the objectives of studying the fur trade is to attempt to obtain a better understanding of Indian-white relations, it must be based on solid objective historical research.

The Role of Native American Women in Fur Trade Society

SYLVIA VAN KIRK

In essence the history of the early Canadian West is the history of the fur trade. For nearly 200 years, from the founding of the Hudson's Bay Company in 1670 until the transfer of Rupert's Land to the newly created dominion of Canada in 1870, the fur trade was the dominant force in shaping the history of what are today Canada's four western provinces.

This long and unified experience gave rise in western Canada to a frontier society that seems to me to be unique in the realm of interracial contact. Canada's western history has been characterized by relatively little violent conflict between Indian and white. I would like to suggest that there were two major reasons why this was so. First, by its very nature the Canadian fur trade was predicated on a mutual exchange and dependency between Indian and white. "The only good Indian" was certainly not "a dead Indian," for it was the Indian who provided both the fur pelts and the market for European goods. New research has revealed that not just Indian men but also Indian women played an active role in promoting the fur trade. Although the men were the hunters of beaver and large game animals, the women were responsible for trapping smaller fur-bearing animals, especially the marten whose pelt was highly prized. The notable cases of Indian women emerging as diplomats and peacemakers also indicate that they were anxious to maintain the flow of European goods, such as kettles, cloth, knives, needles and axes, that helped to alleviate their onerous work role.

The second factor in promoting harmonious relations was the remarkably wide extent of intermarriage between incoming traders and Indian women, especially among the Cree, the Ojibwa, and the Chipewyan. Indian wives proved indispensable helpmates to the officers and men of both the British-based Hudson's Bay Company and its Canadian rival, the North West Company. Such interracial

"The Role of Native Women in the Fur Trade Society of Western Canada, 1670–1830," by Sylvia Van Kirk, *Frontiers* 7, no. 3 (1984), pp. 9–13. Reprinted by permission of Frontiers: A Journal of Women's Studies.

unions were, in fact, the basis for a fur trade society and were sanctioned by an indigenous rite known as marriage *à la façon du pays.*

The development of marriage *à la façon du pays* underscores the complex and changing interaction between the traders and the host Indian societies. In the initial phase of contact, many Indian bands actively encouraged the formation of marital alliances between their women and the traders. The Indians viewed marriage in an integrated social and economic context: marital alliances created reciprocal social ties that served to consolidate their economic relationships with the incoming strangers. Thus, through marriage, many a trader was drawn into the Indian kinship circle. In return for giving the traders sexual and domestic rights to their women, the Indians expected reciprocal privileges such as free access to the posts and provisions.

The Indian attitude soon impressed upon the traders that marriage alliances were an important means of ensuring good will and cementing trade relations with new bands or tribes. The North West Company, a conglomerate of partnerships that began extensive trading into the West in the 1770s, had learned from its French predecessors of the benefits to be gained from intermarriage, and it officially sanctioned such unions for all ranks, from *bourgeois* (officer) down to *engagé* (laborer). The Hudson's Bay Company, on the other hand, was much slower to appreciate the realities of life in Rupert's Land (the name given to the chartered territory of the Hudson's Bay Company encompassing the vast drainage basin of Hudson Bay). Official policy formulated in faraway London forbade any intimacy with the Indians, but officers in the field early began to break the rules. They took the lead in forming unions with women related to prominent Indian leaders, although there was great variation in the extent to which their servants were allowed to form connections with native women.

Apart from the public social benefits, the traders' desire to form unions with Indian women was increased by the absence of white women. Although they did not come as settlers, many of the fur traders spent the better part of their lives in Rupert's Land, and it is a singular fact in the social development of the Canadian West that for well over a century there were no white women. The stability of many of the interracial unions formed in the Indian Country stemmed partly from the fact that an Indian woman provided the only opportunity for a trader to replicate a domestic life with wife and children. Furthermore, although Indian mores differed from those of whites, the traders learned that they trifled with Indian women at their peril. As one old *voyageur* (canoeman) explained, a man could not just dally with any native woman who struck his fancy. There was a great danger of getting his head broken if he attempted to take an Indian girl without her parents' consent.

It is significant that, just as in the trade ceremony, the rituals of marriage *à la façon du pays* conformed more to Indian custom than to European. There were two basic aspects to forming such a union. The first step was to secure the consent of the woman's relations; it also appears that the wishes of the woman herself were respected, for there is ample evidence that Indian women actively sought fur trade husbands. Once consent was secured, a bride price had then to be decided; though it varied considerably among the tribes, it could amount to several hundred dollars' worth of trade goods. After these transactions, the couple were usually ceremoniously conducted to the fort where they were duly recognized as man and wife. In the Canadian West marriage *à la façon du pays* became the norm for Indian-white unions, which were reinforced by mutual interest, tradition, and peer group pressure. Although ultimately "the custom of the country" was to be strongly denounced by the missionaries, it is significant that in 1867, when the legitimacy of the union between Chief Factor William Connolly and his Cree wife was tried before a Canadian court, the judge declared the marriage valid because the wife had been married according to the customs and usages of her own people and because the consent of both parties, the essential element of civilized marriage, had been proved by twenty-eight years of repute, public acknowledgment, and cohabitation as man and wife.

If intermarriage brought the trader commercial and personal benefit, it also provided him with a remarkable economic partner. The Indian wife was possessed of a range of skills and wilderness know-how that would have been quite foreign to a white wife. Although the burdensome work role of the nomadic Indian woman was somewhat alleviated by the move to the fur trade post, the extent to which the traders relied upon native technology kept the women busy.

Perhaps the most important domestic task performed by the women at the fur trade posts was to provide the men with a steady supply of "Indian shoes" or moccasins. The men of both companies generally did not dress in Indian style (the buckskinned mountain man was not part of the Canadian scene), but they universally adopted the moccasin as the most practical footwear for the wilderness. One wonders, for example, how the famed 1789 expedition of Alexander Mackenzie would have fared without the work of the wives of his two French-Canadian *voyageurs.* The women scarcely ever left the canoes, being "continually employ'd making shoes of moose skin as a pair does not last us above one Day." Closely related to her manufacture of moccasins was the Indian woman's role in making snowshoes, without which winter travel was impossible. Although the men usually made the frames, the women prepared the sinews and netted the intricate webbing that provided support.

Indian women also made a vital contribution in the preservation of food, especially in the manufacture of the all-important pemmican, the nutritious staple of the North West Company's canoe brigades. At the posts on the plains, buffalo hunting and pemmican making were an essential part of the yearly routine, each post being required to furnish an annual quota. In accordance with Indian custom, once the hunt was over, the women's work began. The women skinned the animals and cut the meat up into thin strips to be dried in the sun or over a slow fire. When the meat was dry, the women pounded it into a thick flaky mass, which was then mixed with melted buffalo fat. This pemmican would keep very well when packed into ninety-pound buffalo-hide sacks, which had been made by the women during the winter. But pemmican was too precious a commodity to form the basic food at the posts themselves. At the more northerly posts the people subsisted mainly on fish, vast quantities of which were split and dried by the women to provide food for the winter. Maintaining adequate food supplies for a post for the winter was a precarious business, and numerous instances can be cited of Indian wives keeping the fur traders alive by their ability to snare small game such as rabbits and partridges. In 1815, for example, the young Nor'Wester

George Nelson would probably have starved to death when provisions ran out at his small outpost north of Lake Superior had it not been for the resourcefulness of his Ojibwa wife who during the month of February brought in fifty-eight rabbits and thirty-four partridges. Indian women also added to the diets by collecting berries and wild rice and making maple sugar. The spring trip to the sugar bush provided a welcome release from the monotony of the winter routine, and the men with their families and Indian relatives all enjoyed this annual event.

As in other preindustrial societies, the Indian women's role also extended well beyond domestic maintenance as they assisted in specific fur trade operations. With the adoption of the birchbark canoe, especially by the North West Company, Indian women continued in their traditional role of helping in its manufacture. It was the women's job to collect annual quotas of spruce roots, which were split fine to sew the seams of the canoes, and also to collect the spruce gum that was used for caulking the seams. The inexperienced and understaffed Hudson's Bay Company also found itself calling upon the labor power of Indian women, who were adept at paddling and steering canoes. Indeed, although the inland explorations of various Hudson's Bay Company men such as Anthony Henday and Samuel Hearne have been glorified as individual exploits, they were, in fact, entirely dependent upon the Indians with whom they traveled, being especially aided by Indian women. "Women," marveled one inlander, "were as useful as men upon Journeys." Henday's journey to the plains in 1754, for example, owed much of its success to his Cree female companion, who not only provided him with a warm winter suit of furs, but also with much timely advice about the plans of the Indians. The Hudson's Bay Company men emphasized to their London superiors that the Indian women's skill at working with fur pelts was also very valuable. In short, they argued that Indian women performed such important economic services at the fur trade posts that they should be considered as "Your Honours Servants." Indian women were indeed an integral part of the fur trade labor force, although, like most women, because their labor was largely unpaid, their contribution has been ignored.

The reliance on native women's skills remained an important aspect of fur trade life, even though by the early nineteenth century there was a notable shift in the social dynamic of fur trade society. By this time, partly because of the destructive competition between rival companies that had flooded the Indian country with alcohol, relations between many Indian bands and the traders deteriorated. In some well-established areas, traders sometimes resorted to coercive measures, and there were cases where their abuse of Indian women became a source of conflict. In this context, except in new areas such as the Pacific Slope, marriage alliances ceased to play the important function they had once had. The decline of Indian-white marriages was also hastened by the fact that fur trade society itself was producing a new pool of marriageable young women—the mixed-blood "daughters of the country." With her dual heritage, the mixed-blood woman possessed the ideal qualifications for a fur trader's wife: acclimatized to life in the West and familiar with Indian ways, she could also make a successful adaptation to white culture.

From their Indian mothers, mixed-blood girls learned the native skills so necessary to the functioning of the trade. As Governor Simpson of the Hudson's Bay Company emphasized in the 1820s, "It is the duty of the Women at the different Posts to do all that is necessary in regard to Needle Work," and the mixed-blood women's beautiful bead work was highly prized. In addition to performing traditional Indian tasks, the women's range of domestic work increased in more European ways. They were responsible for the fort's washing and cleaning; "the Dames" at York Factory, for example, were kept "in Suds, Scrubbing and Scouring," according to one account. As subsistence agriculture was developed around many of the posts, the native women took an active role in planting and harvesting. Chief Factor John Rowand of Fort Edmonton succinctly summarized the economic role of native women in the fur trade when he wrote in the mid-nineteenth century, "The women here work very hard, if it was not so, I do not know how we would get on with the Company work." With her ties to the Indians and familiarity with native customs and language, the mixed-blood wife was also in a position to take over the role of intermediary or liaison previously played by the Indian wife. The daughters of the French-Canadian *voyageurs* were often excellent interpreters; some could speak several Indian languages. The timely intervention of more than one mixed-blood wife was known to have saved the life of a husband who had aroused Indian hostility. Indeed, in his account of fur trade life during the Hudson's Bay Company's monopoly after 1821, Isaac Cowie declared that many of the company's officers owed much of their success in overcoming difficulties and maintaining the Company's influence over the natives to "the wisdom and good counsel of their wives."

In spite of the importance of native connections, many fur trade fathers were most concerned to introduce their mixed-blood daughters to the rudiments of European culture. Since the place of work and home coincided, especially in the long winter months, the traders were able to take an active role in their children's upbringing, and they were encouraged to do so. When the beginnings of formal schooling were introduced at the posts on the Bay in the early 1800s, it was partly because it was felt to be essential that girls, who were very seldom sent overseas, should be given a basic education that would inculcate Christian virtue in them. Increasingly fathers also began to play an instrumental role in promoting the marriage of their daughters to incoming traders as the means to securing their place in fur trade society. In a significant change of policy in 1806, the North West Company acknowledged some responsibility for the fate of its "daughters" when it sanctioned marriage *à la façon du pays* with daughters of white men, but now prohibited it with full-blooded Indian women.

As mixed-blood wives became "the vogue" (to quote a contemporary), it is notable that "the custom of the country" began to evolve more toward European concepts of marriage. Most importantly, such unions were definitely coming to be regarded as unions for life. When Hudson's Bay Company officer J. E. Harriott espoused Elizabeth Pruden, for example, he promised her father, a senior officer, that he would "live with her and treat her as my wife as long as we both lived." It became customary for a couple to exchange brief vows before the officer in charge of the post, and the match was further celebrated by a dram to all hands and a wedding dance. The bride price was replaced by the opposite payment of a dowry, and many fur trade officers were able to dower their daughters quite handsomely. Marriage *à la façon du pays* was further regulated by the Hudson's Bay Company after 1821 with the introduction of marriage contracts, which emphasized the husband's financial obligations and the status of the woman as a legitimate wife.

The social role of the mixed-blood wife, unlike that of the Indian wife, served to cement ties within fur trade society itself. Significantly, in the North West Company there were many marriages that cut across class lines as numerous Scottish *bourgeois* chose their wives from the daughters of the French-Canadian *engagés* who had married extensively among the native people. Among the Hudson's Bay Company men, it was appreciated that a useful way to enhance one's career was to marry the daughter of a senior officer. Whatever a man's initial motivation, the substantial private fur trade correspondence that has survived from the nineteenth century reveals that many fur traders became devoted family men. Family could be a particular source of interest and consolation in a life that was often hard and monotonous. As Chief Factor James Douglas pointedly summed it up, "There is indeed no living with comfort in this country until a person has forgot the great world and has his tastes and character formed on the current standard of the stage . . . habit makes it familiar to us, softened as it is by the many tender ties which find a way to the heart."

However, the founding of the Selkirk Colony in 1811, the first agrarian settlement in western Canada, was to introduce new elements of white civilization that hastened the decline of an indigenous fur trade society. The chief agents of these changes were the missionaries and the white women. The missionaries, especially the Anglicans who arrived under the auspices of the Hudson's Bay Company in 1820, roundly denounced marriage *à la façon du pays* as immoral and debased. But while they exerted considerable pressure on long cohabiting couples to accept a church marriage, they were not in any way champions of miscegenation. In fact, this attack upon fur trade custom had a detrimental effect upon the position of native women. Incoming traders, now feeling free to ignore the marital obligations implicit in "the custom of the country," increasingly looked upon native women as objects for temporary sexual gratification. The women, on the other hand, found themselves being judged according to strict British standards of female propriety. It was they, not the white men, who were to be held responsible for the perpetuation of immorality because of their supposedly promiscuous Indian heritage. The double standard tinged with racism had arrived with a vengeance.

Both racial prejudice and class distinctions were augmented by the arrival of British women in Rupert's Land. The old fabric of fur trade society was severely rent in 1830 when Governor Simpson and another prominent Hudson's Bay Company officer returned from furlough, having wed genteel British ladies. The appearance of such "flowers of civilization" provoked unflattering comparisons with native women; as one officer observed, "This influx of white faces has cast a still deeper shade over the faces of our Brunettes in the eyes of many." In Red River especially, a white wife became a status symbol; witness the speed with which several retired Hudson's Bay Company factors married English schoolmistresses after the demise of their native wives. To their credit, many Company officers remained loyal to their native families, but they became painfully anxious to turn their daughters into young Victorian ladies, hoping that with accomplishments and connections the stigma of their mixed blood would not prevent them from remaining among the social elite. Thus, in the 1830s a boarding school was established in Red River for the children of Company officers; the girls' education was supervised by the missionary's wife, and more than one graduate was praised for being "quite English in her Manner." In numerous cases, these highly acculturated young women were able to secure advantageous matches with incoming white men, but to some extent only because white ladies did not in fact adapt successfully to fur trade life. It had been predicted that "the lovely, tender exotics" (as they were dubbed) would languish in the harsh fur trade environment, and indeed they did, partly because they had no useful social or economic role to play. As a result, mixed marriages continued to be a feature of western Canadian society until well into the mid-nineteenth century, but it was not an enduring legacy. Indian and mixed-blood women, like their male counterparts, were quickly shunted aside with the development of the agrarian frontier after 1870. The vital role native women had played in the opening of the Canadian West was either demeaned or forgotten.

◈ *F U R T H E R   R E A D I N G*

Jennifer S. H. Brown, *Strangers in Blood: Fur Trade Company Families in Indian Country* (1980)

W. J. Eccles, "The Fur Trade and Eighteenth-Century Imperialism," *William and Mary Quarterly* 40 (1983), 341–362

John C. Ewers, *Indian Life on the Upper Missouri* (1968)

——, "The Influence of the Fur Trade upon Indians of the Northern Plains," in Malvina Bolus, ed., *People and Pelts: Selected Papers of the Second North American Fur Trade Conference* (1972)

Preston Holder, "The Fur Trade as Seen from the Indian Point of View," in John Francis McDermott, ed., *The Frontier Re-examined* (1967)

Wilbur R. Jacobs, "Frontiersmen, Fur Traders, and Other Varmints: An Ecological Appraisal of the Frontier in American History," *American Historical Association Newsletter* 8 (November 1970), 5–11

——, "Unsavory Sidelights on the Colonial Fur Trade," *New York History* 34 (1953), 135–148

Ruth Landes, *Ojibwa Woman* (1971)

Calvin Martin, "The European Impact on the Culture of a Northwestern Algonquian Tribe: An Ecological Interpretation," *William and Mary Quarterly* 31 (1974), 3–26

——, *Keepers of the Game: Indian-Animal Relationships and the Fur Trade* (1978)

Montana, the Magazine of Western History 43 (Special fur trade issue, Winter 1993)

Roger L. Nichols, "The Arikara Indians and the Missouri River Trade: A Quest for Survival," *Great Plains Quarterly* 2 (1982), 77–93

——, "Backdrop for Disaster: Causes of the Arikara War of 1823," *South Dakota History* 14 (1984), 93–113

Jacqueline Peterson and John Alfinson, "The Indian and the Fur Trade," in W. R. Swagerty, ed., *Scholars and the Indian Experience: Critical Reviews of Recent Writing in the Social Sciences* (1984)

Jacqueline Peterson and Jennifer S. H. Brown, *The New Peoples: Being and Becoming Métis in North America* (1985)

Arthur J. Ray, *Indians in the Fur Trade: Their Role as Trappers, Hunters, and Middlemen in the Lands Southwest of Hudson's Bay, 1660–1870* (1974)

Arthur J. Ray and Donald Freeman, *"Give Us Good Measure": An Economic Analysis of Relations Between the Indians and the Hudson's Bay Company Before 1763* (1978)

James P. Ronda, *Astoria and Empire* (1990)

———, *Lewis and Clark Among the Indians* (1984)

Thomas F. Schilz, "The Gros Ventre and the Canadian Fur Trade, 1754–1831," *American Indian Quarterly* 12 (1988), 41–56

William R. Swagerty, "Marriage and Settlement Patterns of Rocky Mountain Trappers and Traders," *Western Historical Quarterly* 11 (1980), 159–180

Adrian Tanner, "The End of Fur Trade History," *Queens Quarterly* 90 (1983), 176–191

Robert A. Trennert, Jr., *Indian Traders on the Middle Border: The House of Ewing, 1827–1854* (1981)

Sylvia Van Kirk, "Women and the Fur Trade," *The Beaver* 303 (1972), 4–21

Richard White, *The Middle Ground: Indians, Empires, and Republics in the Great Lakes Region, 1650–1815* (1991)

———, *The Roots of Dependency: Subsistence, Environment, and Social Change Among the Choctaws, Pawnees, and Navajos* (1983)

W. Raymond Wood and Thomas D. Thiessen, eds., *Early Fur Trade on the Northern Plains: Canadian Traders Among the Mandan and Hidatsa Indians, 1738–1818* (1985)

New Nations, New Boundaries: Indians in the Revolutionary Era

The era of the American Revolution was a period of rapid change and adjustment for Indian tribes. In the 1760s, the British government in London attempted to limit the colonial expansion into Indian country. The royal officials who proposed this measure knew how expansion caused friction that all too often erupted into frontier warfare. Colonists expected the crown to assist them in their backcountry conflicts, but the British government preferred to avoid the trouble and expense of fighting in America. An Indian uprising in 1763, sometimes named Pontiac's War after the Ottawa leader Pontiac, gave plenty of evidence that British concerns were well founded. The Proclamation of 1763, which the British government issued in the hope of conciliating the Indians, provided for a boundary between white settlements and Indian country beyond the crest of the Appalachian Mountains. Colonists regarded the proclamation line as an unwarranted intrusion, and it became one of the many grievances that led to the Revolution against the British government.

After the Revolution, the new United States government assumed responsibility for Indian affairs. The United States faced essentially the same problem that British authorities had wrestled with in 1763: how to promote orderly westward expansion while minimizing Indian and white conflicts. As for the Indians themselves, once-powerful eastern tribes, like those of the Iroquois Confederacy, found that their power had been broken. Some Indian groups were surrounded by white settlements and had to adjust to these new circumstances. Still others tried to reestablish their independence in the Ohio River valley. It is one of the ironies of American history that a revolution fought in the name of independence limited the freedom of American Indians.

◈ *D O C U M E N T S*

During its first years of existence, the United States labored to establish a workable Indian policy. Treaties became a centerpiece of federal Indian policy. Treaties with Native
Americans had the same constitutional standing as treaties with foreign nations. In theory, Indian tribes freely agreed to treaties after negotiations with federal representatives.
In each case, the United States Senate then ratified the treaty just as if it were an international one. Thus the United States accorded Indian tribes standing as nations, even
though the federal government asserted its sovereignty over Indian peoples within its
borders. Federal Indian treaties served many purposes. They established peace, outlined
reciprocal obligations, and—very often—conveyed Indian land to the federal government. Although the United States negotiated with tribes as if they were independent nations, frequently they were nations that recently had been conquered by military force
or that had no power to resist federal demands.

Federal laws and presidential decrees augmented federal Indian policy. Typically,
these laws and directives promised to protect Indian interests. The realities of warfare,
conquest, and frontier expansion, however, made Indian rights tenuous.

In 1784 the new government dictated two treaties to Iroquois tribes, some of which
had sided with the British during the Revolution. One of these treaties, the Treaty of
Fort Stanwix, reprinted here as the first document, required Iroquois tribes to give up
land and to hand over hostages to the Americans until American prisoners were relin-
quished. The second document is taken from an act of Congress that regulated trade
with Indians and established the beginnings of a federal Indian bureaucracy. The third
selection, an excerpt from the Northwest Ordinance, provided for the creation of territorial government under federal aegis in the territory north of the Ohio River and included
a clause protecting Indian rights. The fourth document is Miami chief Little Turtle's
statement at the Treaty of Greenville negotiations in 1795. Little Turtle, who had just
lost a war with the United States, hoped that this treaty would provide lasting peace and
security. The documentary selections close with a statement by the famous Shawnee
leader Tecumseh, who argues here against the principle of giving up land by treaty, unless by unanimous consent of the tribe.

Treaty of Fort Stanwix, 1784

Articles

*Concluded at Fort Stanwix, on the twenty-second day of October, one thousand
seven hundred and eighty-four, between Oliver Wolcott, Richard Butler, and Arthur Lee, Commissioners Plenipotentiary from the United States, in Congress assembled, on the one Part, and the Sachems and Warriors of the Six Nations, on
the other.*

The United States of America give peace to the Senecas, Mohawks,
Onondagas and Cayugas, and receive them into their protection upon the following conditions:

Article I. Six hostages shall be immediately delivered to the commissioners by
the said nations, to remain in possession of the United States, till all the prisoners,

white and black, which were taken by the said Senecas, Mohawks, Onondagas and Cayugas, or by any of them, in the late war, from among the people of the United States, shall be delivered up.

Article II.   The Oneida and Tuscarora nations shall be secured in the possession of the lands on which they are settled.

Article III.   A line shall be drawn, beginning at the mouth of a creek about four miles east of Niagara, called Oyonwayea, or Johnston's Landing-Place, upon the lake named by the Indians Oswego, and by us Ontario; from thence southerly in a direction always four miles east of the carrying-path, between Lake Erie and Ontario, to the mouth of Tehoseroron or Buffaloe Creek on Lake Erie; thence south to the north boundary of the state of Pennsylvania; thence west to the end of the said north boundary; thence south along the west boundary of the said state, to the river Ohio; the said line from the mouth of the Oyonwayea to the Ohio, shall be the western boundary of the lands of the Six Nations, so that the Six Nations shall and do yield to the United States, all claims to the country west of the said boundary, and then they shall be secured in the peaceful possession of the lands they inhabit east and north of the same, reserving only six miles square round the fort of Oswego, to the United States, for the support of the same.

Article IV.   The Commissioners of the United States, in consideration of the present circumstances of the Six Nations, and in execution of the humane and liberal views of the United States upon the signing of the above articles, will order goods to be delivered to the said Six Nations for their use and comfort.

Oliver Wolcott	*Oneidas.*
Richard Butler,	Otyadonenghti,
Arthur Lee.	Dagaheari.
Mohawks.	*Cayuga.*
Onogwendahonji,	Oraghgoanendagen.
Towighnatogon.	
	Tuscarora.
Onondagas.	Ononghsawenghti,
Oheadarighton,	Tharondawagen.
Kendarindgon.	
	Seneca Abeal.
Senecas.	Kayenthoghke.
Tayagonendagighti,	
Tehonwaeaghriyagi.	

Witnesses: Sam. Jo. Atlee, Wm. Maclay, Fras. Johnston, Pennsylvania Commissioners. Aaron Hill, Alexander Campbell, Saml. Kirkland, Miss'y. James Dean, Saml. Montgomery, Derick Lane, Capt. John Mercer, Lieut. William Pennington, Lieut. Mahlon Ford, Ensign. Hugh Peebles.

Ordinance for the Regulation and Management of Indian Affairs, 1786

Whereas the safety and tranquillity of the frontiers of the United States do, in some measure, depend on maintaining a good correspondence between their citizens and the several nations of Indians, in amity with them: and whereas the United States in congress assembled, under the ninth of the articles of confederation and perpetual union, have the sole and exclusive right and power of regulating the trade, and managing all affairs with the Indians, not members of any of the states; provided, that the legislative right of any state, within its own limits, be not infringed or violated:

Be it ordained by the United States in Congress assembled, That from and after the passing of this ordinance, the Indian department be divided into two districts, viz: The southern, which shall comprehend within its limits all the nations in the territory of the United States, who reside southward of the river Ohio; and the northern, which shall comprehend all the other Indian nations within the said territory, and westward of Hudson river: provided, that all councils, treaties, communications, and official transactions, between the superintendent hereafter mentioned for the northern district, and the Indian nations, be held, transacted, and done, at the outpost occupied by the troops of the United States, in the said district. That a superintendent be appointed for each of the said districts, who shall continue in office for two years, unless sooner removed by congress, and shall reside within, or as near the district for which he shall be so appointed, as may be convenient for the management of its concerns. The said superintendents shall attend to the execution of such regulations as congress shall, from time to time, establish respecting Indian affairs. The superintendent for the northern district shall have authority to appoint two deputies, to reside in such places as shall best facilitate the regulations of the Indian trade, and to remove them for misbehaviour. There shall be communications of all matters relative to the business of the Indian department, kept up between the said superintendents, who shall regularly correspond with the secretary of war, through whom all communications respecting the Indian department shall be made to congress; and the superintendents are hereby directed to obey all instructions which they shall, from time to time, receive from the said secretary of war. And whenever they shall have reason to suspect any tribe or tribes of Indians of hostile intentions, they shall communicate the same to the executive of the state or states whose territories are subject to the effect of such hostilities. All stores, provisions or other property, which congress may think necessary for presents to the Indians, shall be in the custody and under the care of the said superintendents, who shall render an annual account of the expenditures of the same to the board of treasury.

And be it further ordained, That none but citizens of the United States shall be suffered to reside among the Indian nations, or be allowed to trade with any nation of Indians within the territory of the United States. That no person, citizen or other, under the penalty of five hundred dollars, shall reside among or trade with any Indian, or Indian nation, within the territory of the United States, without a license for that purpose first obtained from the superintendent of the district, or one of the deputies, who are hereby directed to give such license to every person who shall produce, from the supreme executive of any state, a certificate, under the seal of the state, that he is of good character, and suitably qualified and provided for that employment; for which license he shall pay the sum of fifty dollars to the said superintendent, for the use of the United States. That no license to trade with the Indians shall be in force for a longer term than one year, nor shall permits or passports be granted to any other persons than citizens of the United States, to travel through the Indian nations, without their having previously made their business known to the superintendent of the district, and received his special approbation. That previous to any person or persons obtaining a license to trade as aforesaid, he or they shall give bond, in three thousand dollars, to the superintendent of the district, for the use of the United States, for his or their strict adherence to, and observance of, such rules and regulations as congress may, from time to time, establish for the government of the Indian trade. All sums to be received by the said superintendents, either for licenses or fines, shall be annually accounted for by them, with the board of treasury.

And be it further ordained, That the said superintendents, and the deputies, shall not be engaged either directly or indirectly, in trade with the Indians, on pain of forfeiting their offices. . . . And the said superintendents, and deputy superintendents, shall each of them give bond with surety to the board of treasury, in trust for the United States; the superintendents, each, in the sum of six thousand dollars, and the deputy superintendents, each, in the sum of three thousand dollars, for the faithful discharge of the duties of their office.

And it is further ordained, That all fines and forfeitures, which may be incurred by contravening this ordinance, shall be sued for, and recovered before any court of record within the United States, the one moiety [share] thereof to the use of him or them who may prosecute therefor, and the other moiety to the use of the United States. And the said superintendents shall have power, and hereby are authorized, by force, to restrain therefrom all persons who shall attempt an intercourse with the said Indians, without a license therefor obtained as aforesaid.

And be it further ordained, That in all cases where transactions with any nation or tribe of Indians, shall become necessary to the purpose of this ordinance, which cannot be done without interfering with the legislative rights of a state, the superintendent in whose district the same shall happen, shall act in conjunction with the authority of such state.

Done by the United States in congress assembled, this seventh day of August, A.D. one thousand seven hundred and eight-six, &c.

Northwest Ordinance, 1787

Article III

Religion, morality, and knowledge, being necessary to good government and the happiness of mankind, schools and the means of education shall forever be encouraged. The utmost good faith shall always be observed toward the Indians; their lands and property shall never be taken from them without their consent; and, in their property, rights, and liberty, they never shall be invaded or disturbed, unless in just and lawful wars authorized by Congress; but laws founded in justice and humanity shall, from time to time, be made, for preventing wrongs being done to them and for preserving peace and friendship with them.

Little Turtle (Miami) on the Treaty of Greenville, 1795

Elder Brother [U.S. negotiator], and all you present: I am going to say a few words, in the name of the Pottawatamies, Weas and Kickapoos. It is well known to you all, that people are appointed on those occasions, to speak the sentiments of others; therefore am I appointed for those three nations.

Elder Brother: You told your younger brothers, when we first assembled, that peace was your object; you swore your interpreters before us, to the faithful discharge of their duty, and told them the Great Spirit would punish them, did they not perform it. You told us, that it was not you, but the President of the Fifteen Fires [states] of the United States, who spoke to us; that, whatever he should say, should be firm and lasting; that it was impossible he should say what was not true. Rest assured, that your younger brothers, the Miamis, Ottawas, Chippewas, Pottawatamies, Shawnees, Weas, Kickapoos, Piankeshaws, and Kaskaskias, are well pleased with your words, and are persuaded of their sincerity. You have told us to consider of the boundaries you showed us; your younger brothers have done so, and now proceed to give you their answer.

Elder Brother: Your younger brothers do not wish to hide their sentiments from you. I wish to be the same with those of the Wyandottes and Delawares; you have told us that most of the reservations you proposed to us belonged to our fathers, the French and the British. Permit your younger brothers to make a few observations on this subject.

Elder Brother: We wish you to listen with attention to our words. You have told your younger brothers that the British imposed falsehoods on us when they said the United States wished to take our lands from us, and that the United States had no such designs. You pointed out to us the boundary line, which crossed a little below Loromie's Store and struck Fort Recovery and runs from thence to the Ohio, opposite the mouth of the Kentucky River.

Elder Brother: You have told us to speak our minds freely, and we now do it. This line takes in the greater and best part of your brothers' hunting ground. Therefore, your younger brothers are of the opinion you take too much of their lands away and confine the hunting of our young men within the limits too contracted. Your brothers, the Miamis, the proprietors of those lands, and all your younger brothers present, wish you to run the lines as you mentioned to Fort Recovery and to continue it along the road; from thence to Fort Hamilton, on the great Miami River. This is what your brothers request you to do, and you may rest assured of the free navigation of that river, from thence to its mouth, forever.

Brother: Here is the road we wish to be the boundary between us. What lies to the east we wish to be yours; that to the west, we would desire to be ours.

Elder Brother: In speaking of the reservations, you say they are designed for the same purpose as those for which our fathers, the French and English, occupied them. Your younger brothers now wish to make some observations on them.

From *Indian Oratory: Famous Speeches by Noted Indian Chieftains*, by W. C. Vanderwerth, pp. 56–59. Copyright © 1971 by the University of Oklahoma Press.

Elder Brother: Listen to me with attention. You told us you discovered on the Great Miami traces of an old fort. It was not a French fort, brother; it was a fort built by me. You perceived another at Loromies. 'Tis true a Frenchman once lived there for a year or two. The Miami villages were occupied as you remarked, but it was unknown to your younger brothers until you told them that we had sold the land there to the French or English. I was much surprised to hear you say that it was my forefathers had set the example to other Indians in selling their lands. I will inform you in what manner the French and English occupied those places.

Elder Brother: These people were seen by our forefathers first at Detroit. Afterwards we saw them at the Miami village—that glorious gate, which your younger brothers had the happiness to own, and through which all the good words of our chiefs had to pass, from the north to the south, and from the east to the west. Brothers, these people never told us they wished to purchase our lands from us.

Elder Brother: I now give you the true sentiment of your younger brothers the Miamis, with respect to the reservation at the Miami villages. We thank you for kindly contracting the limits you at first proposed. We wish you to take this six miles square on the side of the river where your fort now stands, as your younger brothers wish to inhabit that beloved spot again. You shall cut hay for your cattle wherever you please, and you shall never require in vain the assistance of your younger brothers at that place.

Elder Brother: The next place you pointed to was the Little River, and said you wanted two miles square at that place. This is a request that our fathers, the French or British, never made us. It was always ours. This carrying place [portage] has heretofore proved in a great degree the subsistence of your younger brothers. That place has brought us in the course of one day the amount of one hundred dollars. Let us both own this place and enjoy in common the advantages it affords. You told us at Chicago the French possessed a fort. We have never heard of it. We thank you for the trade you promised to open in our country, and permit us to remark that we wish our former traders may be continued and mixed with yours.

Elder Brother: On the subject of hostages, I have only to observe that I trust all my brothers present are of my opinion with regard to peace and our future happiness. I expect to be with you every day when you settle on your reservations, and it will be impossible for me or my people to withhold from you a single prisoner. Therefore, we don't know why any of us should remain here. These are the sentiments of your younger brothers present, on these particulars.

Tecumseh (Shawnee) Speaks Out Against Land Cessions, 1810

. . . It is true I am a Shawnee. My forefathers were warriors. Their son is a warrior. From them I only take my existence; from my tribe I take nothing. I am the maker of my own fortune; and oh! that I could make that of my red people, and of my country, as great as the conceptions of my mind, when I think of the Spirit that rules the universe. I would not then come to Governor Harrison, to ask him to tear the treaty, and to obliterate the landmark; but I would say to him, Sir, you have liberty to return to your own country. The being within, communing with past ages, tells me, that once, nor until lately, there was no white man on this continent. That it then all belonged to red men, children of the same parents, placed on it by the Great Spirit that made them, to keep it, to traverse it, to enjoy its productions, and to fill it with the same race. Once a happy race. Since made miserable by the white people, who are never contented, but always encroaching. The way, and the only way to check and stop this evil, is, for all the red men to unite in claiming a common and equal right in the land, as it was at first, and should be yet; for it never was divided, but belongs to all, for the use of each. That no part has a right to sell, even to each other, much less to strangers; those who want all, and will not do with less. The white people have no right to take the land from the Indians, because they had it first; it is theirs. They may sell, but all must join. Any sale not made by all is not valid. The late sale is bad. It was made by a part only. Part do not know how to sell. It requires all to make a bargain for all. All red men have equal rights to the unoccupied land. The right of occupancy is as good in one place as in another. There cannot be two occupations in the same place. The first excludes all others. It is not so in hunting or travelling; for there the same ground will serve many, as they may follow each other all day; but the camp is stationary, and that is occupancy. It belongs to the first who sits down on his blanket or skins, which he has thrown upon the ground, and till he leaves it no other has a right.

◈ E S S A Y S

For Indians, the outbreak of the Revolution posed troubling questions. Should they take part in the fighting, and if so, with whom should they side? Should they remain neutral so as to avoid offending the ultimate victors? In the first essay, historian Francis Jennings, former director of the Newberry Library Center for the History of the American Indian, outlines the dilemma that Indians faced during this crucial conflict.

Once the war was over, Indians had to adjust to new realities. Daniel H. Usner, Jr., associate professor of history at Cornell University, shows in the second essay that in the southern states, Choctaws, Creeks, and other tribes lived amid agricultural expansion, the spread of large cotton plantations, and the proliferation of slavery. The third essay, by R. David Edmunds, professor of history at Indiana University, Bloomington, describes the path chosen by the Shawnee leader Tecumseh, who attempted to resist American advances by creating a united Indian front based on a native religious revival.

Resistance, accommodation, flight—which of these strategies was best for Indians? And what might the fledgling United States have done to forestall frontier warfare and the suffering of whites and Indians alike?

The Indians' Revolution

FRANCIS JENNINGS

. . . There were more than two sides in the American Revolution. The British Crown and the Continental Congress formulated general strategies and policies that became distorted and sometimes negated when they were put into effect by

From Francis Jennings, "The Indians' Revolution," in Alfred Young, ed., *The American Revolution: Explorations in the History of American Radicalism* (Northern Illinois University Press: DeKalb, 1976). Used with permission of the publisher. For Jennings' further work on the Indians' revolution, see *Empire of Liberty: Crowns, Colonies and Tribes in the Seven Years War in America* (W. W. Norton & Co.: New York, 1988).

officers who served themselves as well as their governments. There were thirteen separate and individually sovereign states, which had bitter quarrels among themselves, which they sometimes settled by force of arms even while they jointly engaged in struggle against the Crown. There were colonies in the West Indies and Canada that did not rebel. Though the revolutionaries solicited Quebec to join them, and invaded that province to make persuasion stronger, the French-speaking Catholic inhabitants preferred the liberties and religious toleration guaranteed by the Crown to the more doubtful prospects of subordination to the English-speaking Protestants of the Continental Congress.

Still other affiliates of the Crown that did not rebel were the tribal governments that exerted jurisdiction over lands "reserved" for Indian use. Multiple ambiguities and semantic distortions have excluded tribal governments—as distinct from Indian "auxiliaries"—from recognition as political participants in the revolutionary struggle. The so-called international law created to serve the purposes of governments in the state form does not recognize a parity between bureaucratic states and kin-ordered tribes. A large literature purports to describe Indian communities as congregations of wild men—savages bereft of "real" government, existing in a condition of chronic anarchy. On such convenient assumptions, there had been agreement between Crown and colonist, until 1776, that the country west of the Appalachian Mountains was under British sovereignty. Disputes never challenged that basic agreement; disputes centered upon the competition of particular jurisdictions within the empire to administer the sovereignty. The Indians, however, did not agree that they lived in Crown lands that had merely been reserved for them. They conceived themselves as living in their own territories under their own free and independent governments, and they started fighting well before 1776 to maintain as much as circumstances would permit of political independence. . . .

This paper argues that the American revolutionaries fought for empire over the west as well as for their own freedom in the east. While the colony-states fought for independence from the Crown, the tribes had to fight for independence from the states. It makes a huge embarrassment to ideology that the Revolution wore one face looking eastward across the Atlantic and another looking westward into the continent, but Indians have always obtruded awkwardly from the smooth symmetry of historical rationalization.

Indian trade and Indian land had first brought Europeans to the shores of America. In one sense, the Indian struggle for independence had started with Jamestown, but natives and colonists had managed to accommodate erratically with each other in the symbiotic community of trade. In spite of occasional wars of particular tribes against particular colonies, there had never been a universal conflict of red against white. Some tribes—notably in Virginia and New England—had been subjected by force, but until 1750 most Indians continued to live in "free" tribes allied by treaty to one or more English colony. Crisis came then because of the accelerated growth of colonial population with a concomitant demand for expansion into the Indian territories west of the Appalachians.

Had Great Britain been the only European power colonizing North America, perhaps the pace of colonization might have been regulated and arrangements made to give the Indians alternatives other than desperate war; but France had planted colonies in Canada and Louisiana, and France was determined to halt British expansion beyond the Appalachians by establishing a long chain of Indian protectorates controlled from strategically placed French forts. The British Crown and colonies were equally determined to destroy the French barrier and to seize all the territory between the Atlantic and Pacific oceans. Competition accelerated the plans of both powers, and they raced to confront each other at the strategic junction of waters where the Ohio River begins. Here they set in motion the events that resulted in the first world war of modern times, the vast imperial conflict called the Seven Years War.

The Ohio region and its resident Indians will be constantly at or near the center of attention in this essay. Although southern tribes, especially the Cherokees, faced much the same problems as the Ohio Indians, they lay in a separate theater of action, with a distinct history.

The events to be discussed mark a period when many Indian tribes joined together in great confederations to fight for their territorial integrity. These struggles began with diplomatic maneuvers in 1750 and continued through tribal war on the largest scale ever known in this country, intermixed with the imperial and secessionist conflicts of Great Britain with France and the revolutionary United States. The era ended with the Treaty of Greenville that followed the Battle of Fallen Timbers, twelve years after the official conclusion of the American colonists' war for independence. . . . The tribes' independence, power, and possessions were central issues of what we see only as the American Revolution. Blended in with that familiar process was a tribal revolution conducted by governments effective enough to wage devastating war and to enforce recognition through formal diplomatic protocol by Crown, colonies, and the United States.

The tribes of the upper Ohio in 1750 were Delawares, Shawnees, and "Mingo" Iroquois, confederated in a complex multiple alliance called the Covenant Chain. (The name is specific: there were many alliance "chains" in colonial times, and many "covenants," but only one Covenant Chain.) In this confederation the Ohio Indians were not only "brothers" of the British, but also "nephews" of the Iroquois Six Nations, whose grand council met at Onondaga (where Syracuse, New York, now stands). That is to say, all the Indians were allied by treaty to certain British colonies that diplomatically recognized the Iroquois as responsible spokesmen for the other tribes, and because of this favored status the Iroquois had been able to assume a degree of authority, symbolized by the deferential "uncle" form of address, over the tributary tribes. It was an uneasy relationship in which the tributary Delawares and Shawnees often paid more heed to the ceremony than the substance of deference, but it held together as long as Iroquois diplomacy seemed to preserve the Ohio from European intrusion. Also consequential were guarantees of protection against attack by English colonial forces, and continuing participation in trade with English merchants for such necessities as cloth, tools, and guns. Englishmen gained reciprocally in the trade, and they valued the Covenant Chain also as a barrier against the French and as a stabilizing instrument of order in the "back country."

In 1751 the Covenant Chain was suddenly strained when an advance agent of the Ohio Company of Virginia appeared at the Ohio. This agent, Christopher

Gist, stirred suspicion immediately because he carried no stock of goods like the traders who traveled normally in Indian country. Gist's real purpose, of course, was to scout the land for his employing company in preparation for the planting of a new colony under Virginia's auspices, and his errand transformed the Ohio region into a cockpit of imperial and revolutionary wars.

An astonishing number of conflicting parties engaged very quickly. The traders then plying through the region were mostly based in Pennsylvania and antagonistic to new competition from Virginia. Pennsylvania's Proprietary, Thomas Penn, claimed the Ohio's headwaters as within his chartered bounds, disputed Virginia's right to assume jurisdiction there, and attempted to hamper the Ohio Company by influence in London and diplomacy among the tribes. The government of Canada, backed by the French crown, determined to forestall all English expansion west of the Appalachians by enforting and garrisoning the Ohio. Iroquois statesmen, accompanied by tributary chiefs, rushed from treaty to treaty in frantic vain attempts to stop the advance of all Europeans.

The Iroquois nuclear League of Six Nations was having its own troubles farther east. Shrewd New Yorkers had contrived swindling schemes for seizing vast tracts of Indian territory, the most notorious of which (called the Kayaderosseras patent) embraced 800,000 acres of land belonging to the Mohawk tribe of the Six Nations. Though the Mohawks had been New York's most faithful allies since the colony's foundation, their friendship departed with their territory. On 16 June 1753, Chief Hendrick stood up in conference with the provincial council of New York, faced Governor George Clinton squarely, and poured out his bitter anger:

> Brother when we came here to relate our Grievances about our Lands, we expected to have something done for us, and we have told you that the Covenant Chain of our Forefathers was like to be broken, and brother you tell us that we shall be redressed at Albany, but we know them so well, we will not trust to them, for they [the Albany merchants] are no people but Devils, so we rather desire that you'll say, Nothing shall be done for us; Brother By and By you'll expect to see the Nations [of Indians] down [here in New York City] which you shall not see, for as soon as we come home we will send up a Belt of Wampum to our Brothers the [other] 5 Nations to acquaint them the Covenant Chain is broken between you and us. So brother you are not to expect to hear of me any more, and Brother we desire to hear no more of you.

This was the Indians' declaration of independence, instantly recognized as such by the [New] Yorkers. . . .

. . . The experienced members of the Crown's Board of Trade in London immediately recognized the Mohawk declaration as a diplomatic event "of a very serious nature." The board saw that "the Indians . . . considered the alliance and friendship between them and the Province of New York to be dissolved," and this was most alarming because "the steady adherence of these Indians to the British interest" had been vital to the security of all the northern colonies "from the fatal effects of the encroachments of a foreign power"—that is, France. Without the Indians, "all our efforts to check and disappoint the present view of this power may prove ineffectual." It was curious language from a government that claimed, when treating with the French, to hold a protectorate over the Iroquois. . . .

With what was lightning speed for that sluggish body, the Board of Trade moved to remedy the situation. It instructed the colonial governors to assemble the most impressive joint treaty with the Indians of the Covenant Chain that had yct been held, and to treat in the king's own name rather than in behalf of the individual colonial governments that the Indians so distrusted. Thus was born the famous Albany Congress of 1754.

The gentlemen of Virginia had their own notions of how to deal with that foreign power at the Ohio, and they did not intend to let the Crown hinder their own encroachments. Virginia "excused" itself from attendance at Albany and the possible restrictions that attendance might have entailed; and Virginia continued its rash, calamitous adventuring. The colony fielded troops under young George Washington to attack the French forces on their march. The French were experienced, intelligent, and brave. Washington was self-confident and brave. The headstrong young Virginian disregarded the advice given by his experienced Iroquois ally and succeeded in getting himself completely surrounded, and surrendered. The French chased English traders and Iroquois chieftains out of the region and built Fort Duquesne at the strategic forks of the Ohio. Delaware and Shawnee tributaries of the Covenant Chain found themselves, alone and without resource, living in a country occupied by enemy troops. While the Mohawks had severed the Chain's links with New York, the French had smashed its links with the western tributaries.

At Albany the Indians were angry and suspicious. "Never were so few Indians seen at any public meeting," mourned one colonial observer. The colonial delegates made the Congress a vehicle for the very abuses that the Crown was trying to correct. Connecticut speculators of the Susquehannah Company poured rum down some Indians outside the council chamber to get signatures on a "deed" for an enormous tract of land that these Indians had no authority to convey. The clandestine methods of the Susquehannah Company were rendered more necessary because Pennsylvania claimed the same territory and was using much the same methods. The mood of its representatives was expressed by veteran interpreter Conrad Weiser, who had approached the Congress with the thought that "I may fall in with some greedy fellows for money." His wish was fulfilled. The fellows greedy for land found the fellows greedy for money, and Thomas Penn got another deed. It did not simplify the Crown's problems, nor assuage the Indians' grievances, that Penn's new deed for the region at the forks of the Ohio conflicted with the claims of Virginia.

In the midst of this welter of intrigue and conspiracy, the Albany conferees produced an edifice of dreams—the Plan of Union that the mythology of the frontier characterizes as a foreshadowing of the federal union of the United States. Such hindsight is willful illusion. No colony ratified the Albany Plan, and the Crown rejected it, and they all had good reasons. Albany, in 1754, was the last gasp of an old system rather than a precursor of the new. . . . The only intercolonial cooperation to be evidenced at Albany was an agreement to abdicate the separate regulation of Indian affairs previously exercised by the colonies.

In response, the Crown gradually created a Department of Indian Affairs. It started, without much thought to constitutional issues, as a function of the military. To eject the French from the Ohio, the Crown dispatched two regiments of regular troops under Major General Edward Braddock. On 15 April 1755, Braddock commissioned the New York merchant and public official William Johnson "to have the sole Management and direction of the Affairs of the Six Nations of Indians and their Allies, to the end that the said Indians may be heartily engaged in and attached to the British Interest." There was not even a name for the new office; Johnson acquired effective authority by supplementary commissions of command over provincial troops, and his primary responsibility was to lead an expedition against the French. His duties with the Indians were simply to round up as many as he could to join the expedition. In his supplementary instructions, however, were the seeds of his office's growth into a powerful institution. He was authorized to attract Indian recruits by making a large promise: "You are to acquaint the Indians of the Six Nations . . . with his Majesties design to Recover their Lands at Niagara, and upon the River Ohio, out of the hands of the French, and to protect them against future Incroachments, for the benefitt of their Tribes." It will be observed that His Majesty's expressed design was not to recover his own lands, but the Six Nations'. That sentence, with its ambiguities and seeming commitments, became the center of attention and hope for all the Indians. Though the Crown wavered, vacillated, and reneged, the tribes constantly forced the issue.

Certainly the sentence meant nothing to Johnson's superior officer, General Braddock. After commissioning Johnson, Braddock sent him off to the north, while he himself began his march westward toward Fort Duquesne. On his way he met with chiefs of the Ohio tribes who wished to negotiate terms for their help in evicting the French. Braddock not only failed to assure the Indians of protection against future encroachments, he guaranteed that the encroachment would take place. It was inconceivable to this powerful, haughty man that he should thereby pronounce his own death sentence.

Here is the conversation and its consequences as given in the only surviving report—a description narrated by Delaware chief Shingas to an English colonial prisoner of war.

> . . . Shingas asked General Braddock whether the Indians that were Friends to the English might not be Permitted to Live and Trade Among the English and have Hunting Ground sufficient to Support themselves and Familys as they had no where to Flee too But into the Hands of the French and their Indians who were their Enemies (that is, Shingas' Enemies). On which General Braddock said that No Savage Should Inherit the Land. . . . [The next day] Shingas and the other Chiefs answered That if they might not have Liberty To Live on the Land they would not Fight for it. To which General Braddock answered that he did not need their Help.

Shingas remarked that his tribesmen were "very much Enraged" by Braddock,

> and a Party of them went Immediately . . . and Join'd the French, But the Greater Part remained neuter till they saw How Things would go . . . And they made it their Business to draw nigh the Place where the Engagement Happened that they might see what Passed at it, and were still in hopes that the English would be Victorious, But after the French had ruined Braddock's Army they immediately compelled the Indians To join them and let them know that if they refused they would Immediately cut them off. On which the Indians Joined the French for their Own Safety. . . .

Braddock's beaten army, though it still greatly outnumbered the French force at Fort Duquesne, retreated all the way to the coast, leaving the backcountry wide open to the Indian raids. Colonists and Indians alike observed that a fully equipped army, as good as any in the empire, could be beaten by an opposing force less than half its number and made up mostly of poorly armed "savages." What the Indians had concluded from this observation was demonstrated in flames and blood. The entire system of management of Indian affairs lay in ruins. What the Albany Congress had suggested about provincial blundering was now plainly proved. Individual tribes in isolation could be mastered and directed by individual colonies, but tribes collected and supported by a hostile empire could only be resisted by the resources of the Crown. In 1756 the Board of Trade began salvage operations with a new commission to Sir William Johnson. It greatly increased his authority and proceeded directly from the Crown. Johnson had already been elevated to the status of baronet; now he was given large new titles: "Colonel of Our Faithfull Subjects, and Allies, the Six united Nations of Indians, and their Confederates, in the Northern Parts of North America" and "Our Sole Agent and Superintendant of the said Indians and their Affairs." . . .

Johnson's appointment signified more than an effort to manage Indian affairs with greater competence; it was the beginning of substantial change in the constitution of the empire. Previously the colonies had been under the Crown's protection and the Indians under the colonies' protection—or at their mercy. Johnson represented not only the Crown's assumption of administration over Indian affairs, but also the extension of the Crown's protection directly to the tribes. His instruction to redress the Indians' grievances was an exertion of the Crown's protection *against* the colonies, for the grievances in question had been created by colonial governments as well as private persons.

With his new authority, Johnson championed the Mohawks against the shareholders in the Kayaderosseras grant (in New York), and finally, after many years, achieved a settlement acceptable to the Indians. Meanwhile, as the Mohawks' friend, he found a way through the maze of Pennsylvania's incredibly complex political struggles. Though it would be a mistake to credit him with the achievement of peace in Pennsylvania—which was accomplished primarily by tribal diplomacy, with an assist from the Quakers—Johnson cooperated through his deputy in the crucial treaties at Easton, Pennsylvania, in 1757 and 1758, when Delawares and Iroquois negotiated to restore the Covenant Chain. In the murk of intrigue at Easton, Johnson's goal was clear: all the tribes must once more become tributary to the Iroquois, the Iroquois would be responsible solely to him, and he would be responsible solely to the Crown. To attain this great goal, Johnson proposed a policy to stand on three legs: (1) an alliance cemented by trade with the Indians on fair terms; (2) redress of Indian complaints about land transactions; and (3) "by a solemn public Treaty to agree upon clear and fixed Boundaries between our Settlements and their Hunting Grounds, so that each Party may know their own and be a mutual Protection to each other of their respective Possessions."

The complex and controverted history of the Easton Treaty of 1758 need not be recited here. Many clashing interests and personalities were involved. To whomever the credit may be due, the outcome of the treaty showed a distinct resemblance to Johnson's goal and Johnson's policy. The Covenant Chain was reestablished in the east, and an Iroquois delegation accompanied the Delaware emissary from the Ohio when he carried word of the treaty back to his people. The Iroquois immediately assumed their former position of superiority. They told the Ohio council, "We desire you would lay hold of the covenant we have made with our brethren the English. . . . We likewise take the tomahawk out of your hands . . . it is the white people's; let them use it among themselves." Delaware spokesman Beaver agreed, and expressed the renewal of his tribe's tributary status in conventional metaphor: "I have not made myself a king. My uncles [the Iroquois] have made me like a queen, that I always should mind what is good and right."

The Delawares abandoned the French, the French abandoned Fort Duquesne, and the Ohio opened up to the British army that had until then been halted in its approach. Late in 1758 the war turned around for Great Britain where it had begun, at the forks of the Ohio. A few months later, in 1759, the reinvigorated Iroquois under Johnson's command captured Fort Niagara, the key to the Canadian west.

But the western Indians discovered that it was harder to get rid of the British than the French. On 4 December 1758, shortly after the fall of Fort Duquesne, the Delawares were summoned to a treaty on the site. Two substantially discrepant reports of the treaty survive: one was recorded by a French officer as the description carried to him by the Delaware chief, Custaloga; the other was dutifully sent to Britain as the official minutes of the occasion. Custaloga noted that the Indians (Delawares and Iroquois alike) had asked the English to withdraw from the smoking ruins. No such disturbance of harmony found its way into the English minutes, though it seems apparent from Colonel Henry Bouquet's speech to the Indians that he was responding defensively to Indian suggestions. "I return you hearty Thanks for the Speech you made," he remarked; but he did not record that speech. He went on, "We are not come here to take Possession of your hunting Country in a hostile Manner, as the French did when they came amongst you, but to open a large and extensive Trade with you and all the other Nations of Indians to the Westward who chuse to live in friendship with us." In these official minutes, the Delawares have become happy that 200 soldiers are to be left by the British "to support and defend the Traders."

One of the Pittsburg traders told a different tale six months later. Quaker James Kenny confided to his journal, "how that I have observ'd that the Indians are very Jealous of the English comeing here with an Army. They seem Jealous of thire lands being settled . . . old [Delaware chief] Pisquitomen, the Beaver's Brother, and some others Came to our Houses and the Old Man put it Closely to me to tell what the English or the General Meant by Coming here with a Great Army."

Discontent grew stronger among the Indians as British troops marched west to seize and garrison Detroit, and as Virginia (ignoring all promises to Indians) sent officials and settlers to occupy western lands. The Iroquois Six Nations split amongst themselves; though the Mohawks held to their alliance with Sir William Johnson, the Senecas circulated a war belt among the western tribes to solicit a general uprising against the British garrisons. . . .

All came to crisis in 1763 when France ceded all of Canada's territorial claims to Great Britain in the treaty that ended the two empires' long war. The news that the the trans-Appalachian west had been ceded stunned the Indians. In their view, as reported by [George] Croghan [Johnson's deputy], "the French had no Right to give away their Country; as, they Say, they were never Conquered by any Nation." To make things worse, the British commander-in-chief General Jeffrey Amherst decided to discipline the tribes by withholding from them the trade in arms and ammunition which was still essential to their way of making a living.

The tribes rose in May 1763 in the liberation war for independence, miscalled Pontiac's Conspiracy. It acquired the name because Ottawa chief Pontiac launched the first attack, against Fort Detroit, but Pontiac was a minor figure in the tribal diplomacy that brought the war into being. The Senecas and Delawares had been circulating war belts among the tribes for about two years before combat began, and the French traders of the backcountry obviously played a conspiratorial role. When news of Pontiac's initiative reached the Delawares, they were ready to act upon the grievances they had been voicing for five years; they immediately laid siege to Fort Pitt.

The rising failed. Although the Indians won minor successes, both major forts held out until the sieges were lifted. Secret advance intelligence enabled Fort Detroit's commander to thwart Pontiac's intended surprise. At Fort Pitt, under orders from General Amherst, the fort commander parleyed with the besieging Indian chiefs and presented them with blankets from the smallpox hospital. The epidemic that subsequently raged among the warriors made easier the task of Colonel Henry Bouquet when he marched to the fort's relief.

Though the Indians had not won, they had not fully lost. They sued for peace because they could not overwhelm the British, and because they wanted to forestall punitive destruction of their villages. Under strong urging from Sir William Johnson, the British came to terms because they could not overwhelm the Indians. Though they could burn villages and inflict suffering, experience had long shown (and would again) that such measures were not necessarily sufficient to destroy the Indians' will to continue fighting guerrilla war. In short, the peace that followed the liberation war named for Pontiac reflected a military stalemate. Nevertheless, it left the British with the strategic advantage: their forts and garrisons remained to become a permanent occupation establishment. The price for that advantage was financially and politically extravagant. For an empire already burdened with the unprecedented debt acquired during the recently completed Seven Years War, the cost of the western garrisons was an intolerable extra load. Politically, the military establishment would ultimately aggrieve the empire's colonists as much as the Indians.

Naturally, the empire ministers could not foresee all the future consequences of the western occupation, but they understood budgets, and they recognized that the Indians, though subdued, were not submissive. Naturally, also, the ministers resorted to political action to reduce the necessity for maintaining military action; but the harder they worked to mollify the tribes, the more they exacerbated quarrels with their colonies. The Indians were wooed with the Royal Proclamation of 1763, with which the Crown offered them a bargain that advanced the Crown's interests by sacrificing what the colonists regarded as their own interests. A frontier line of separation was decreed, and the territory west of it was declared an Indian sanctuary in which no more colonial settlements would be permitted. Thus, if the Indians would accept a few widely scattered garrisons, the Crown would preserve them from the tide of civilians. The only civil jurisdictions allowed to operate validly beyond the Proclamation Line were those of British-appointed Indian superintendents. . . .

. . . Though the Proclamation Line and the superintendents' offices continued in force, it would seem that nobody but the Indians believed that the line could be anything but a temporary measure. Neither the great land speculators nor the penniless squatters got very excited about the line, partly perhaps because the super-intendents were so accommodating. The speculators made certain arrangements to the benefit of the superintendents, and the superintendents surveyed the line with gratifyingly large bulges at spots where the speculators had plans for immi-nent development. Lobbyists besieged ministers in London and made them part-ners in great schemes for new inland colonies that would, among other things, preclude the possibility of tribal territory evolving into native provinces. Squat-ters continued to squat beyond the line, and the protesting Indians were merely advised not to disturb the peace so that all could be made well eventually.

If the Indians had just agreed to roll over and play dead, no doubt the Crown and colonies would have worked out an arrangement convenient for all, but the tribes expressed their discontent in word and deed. Because of the Crown's vac-illating approach to a political solution of the problem of western stability, the military solution had to be maintained—and paid for. The payment was what finally tore the empire apart. It seemed reasonable to His Majesty's ministers that the colonists should bear some part of the charge for their own defense. It seemed reasonable to the colonists that, since the lands beyond the line had been pro-claimed to be outside colonial jurisdictions, the policing of such Crown lands should be wholly at the Crown's expense. Two such conflicting assumptions might have produced an eternal wrangle if submitted to the judgment of the courts, but the Crown's ministers submitted the issue to Parliament instead, and Parliament chose to command rather than negotiate. In 1765 Parliament enacted the Stamp Tax. The colonists challenged Parliament's right to tax them, on the grounds that their own legislatures held that right exclusively, and to underscore their point they rioted a bit. Parliament avoided immediate confrontation by re-scinding the Stamp Tax, but in 1767 it declared its own supremacy in principle over any and all legislatures subject to the Crown of England. The colonists cor-rectly perceived this declaration as a restructuring of sovereignty that threatened their liberties and interests, and rioted some more. In a comparatively short time, the Crown concluded that the violence of the eastern colonies was more danger-ous than the violence of the western tribes, and the troops whose cost had precip-itated the crisis were gradually moved east to restore authority where the need was greater. As the troops continued to require upkeep, Parliament enacted more taxes. Then, indeed, the colonists' grievances became indisputably genuine. Taxes that once had been levied ostensibly to protect them from the French and Indians had become quite plainly taxes levied to suppress their civil liberties.

Meantime, the land speculators had discovered that the Proclamation Line could be bent but not broken. The Virginians of the Ohio Company especially were frustrated. By virtue of its ancient sea-to-sea charter, Virginia claimed juris-diction over an immense western domain which included, to begin with, the Ohio country; but the Crown viewed Virginia as a royal province subject to the royal pleasure in such matters as boundaries. Ministers seriously considered establish-ing alternative new colonial jurisdictions where Virginia made its claims, and they disregarded the Ohio Company's grant as legally lapsed. Some of the richest and most important Virginians saw their future in the west, and they would not be denied it. Their anger and determination mounted simultaneously with the gen-eral colonial resentment against Parliament's taxes and the Crown's measures of repression.

Virginia's way out of the impasse was Lord Dunmore's War. After the evacuation of Fort Pitt by the royal garrison in 1772, a band of Virginia militia men occupied the fort and used it as a base from which to terrorize the Ohio Indians. In 1774 Virginia's Governor Dunmore climaxed the process by fomenting a war with the Shawnees to force them to cede land rights to Virginia, apparently hoping thereby to compel the Crown to recognize a *fait accompli*. Had he succeeded, Virginia would have acquired permanent possession of the whole Ohio region. Dunmore did not succeed in his ultimate objective, though by creating an either-them-or-us situation, he forced the cooperation of the Indian superintendents in his war. The quality of that war, and the effect it created among the Indians, is illustrated by what happened to Cayuga chief James Logan. Logan, like his father, the celebrated Shickellamy, had been a strong adherent of the British all his life; but without any provocation Virginia's frontier ruffians massacred his entire family. Logan stopped being an adherent of the British. He took thirty scalps in revenge, according to tradition, before he succumbed to depression and drink. His lament has become classic: "I appeal to any white man to say if ever he entered Logan's cabin hungry and he gave him not meat; if ever he came cold and naked, and he clothed him not. . . . [But now] there runs not a drop of my blood in the veins of any living creature. . . . Who is there to mourn for Logan?—Not one!"

The news of these doings aroused strong feeling in Iroquoia where angry Iroquois chiefs confronted Sir William Johnson to demand that the frontiersmen be brought under control. They attributed their own anger to their young men, in a diplomatic device to permit the continuation of speaking terms with Johnson, but their intent was clear. The young men, they said, were "much affected and exasperated at the cruel murders" committed by the "lawless people" of the British colonies. It was a strange complaint to come from a "savage" people, but it was not a slip of the tongue. The Iroquois questioned seriously whether the British were capable of making responsible contracts and living up to their terms. "Brother," they addressed Johnson,

> We are sorry to observe to you that your people are as ungovernable, or rather more so, than ours. You must remember that it was most solemnly, and publicly settled, and agreed at the General Congress held at Fort Stanwix in 1768 on behalf of the great King of England our Father, and the Governors, and Commissioners of the several Provinces then assembled there, that the Line then pointed out and fixed between the Whites and Indians should forever after be looked upon as a barrier between us, and that the White People were not to go beyond it. —It seems, Brother, that your People entirely disregard, and despise the settlement agreed upon by their Superiors and us; for we find that they, notwithstanding that settlement, are come in vast numbers to the Ohio, and gave our people to understand that they wou'd settle wherever they pleas'd. If this is the case we must look upon every engagement you made with us as void and of no effect.

Having made their point, the Iroquois pleaded for a peaceable solution.

> . . . but we hope it is not so, and that you will restrain your people over whom you say you have authority, and make them lay aside their ill designs, and encroachments, . . . and we must beg that if your people insist upon settling so near ours, they may be made subject to some authority that can keep them in order.

By a curious coincidence, the same thought was in the minds of the members of Parliament. To make the rebels of Massachusetts Bay subject to some authority, Parliament, in 1774, enacted four Coercive Acts. Then Parliament added an act for the government of Quebec which, by extending Quebec's boundaries to the Ohio River, nullified the land seizures made by Virginia in Lord Dunmore's War. For various reasons, the colonists promptly identified the Quebec Act with the Coercive Acts and called them all "Intolerable." Although the initial outcry against the Quebec Act stressed the horrors of "Papacy," because it permitted Canada's Catholics to worship without disturbance, something more than toleration made it intolerable. . . .

The issue was land. The territorial pretensions of the colonies with sea-to-sea charters extending through the Ohio country—Virginia, Connecticut, and Massachusetts—were now nullified by an act of Parliament which, unlike the merely administrative Royal Proclamation of 1763, could only be reversed by another, most improbable, act of Parliament. To obtain and develop a new tract of territory, a company speculating in land above the north bank of the Ohio River would have multiple barriers to hurdle—the Crown's, the superintendent's, the Indians', and that of the almost inaccessible governor of Quebec. Remote geographically, the governor ruled with the support of a permanent garrison under his direct command, and was unhampered by the pressures of a representative assembly. . . .

After the battles of Lexington and Concord, the Second Continental Congress made an address to "the oppressed inhabitants of Canada," in which the Congress "perceived the fate of the protestant and catholic colonies to be strongly linked together"—so much for the popish menace—and appealed to the Canadians to overthrow the yoke of their "present form of tyranny." A few months later, the Congress's armies invaded Quebec to confer the boon of liberty upon those poor, deserving Catholics. Had the enterprise succeeded, the Ohio country would certainly have been liberated back into the jurisdictions of the invaders; but Quebec held out, a British fleet arrived with thousands of reinforcements, and the invaders fell back to the enforced protection of their own liberties in their own lands. (There may be significance in the fact that not until then did Congress declare independence.)

In the war that followed, Indians were drawn in by active recruiting on both sides, in spite of their strongly expressed desires to stay neutral; and it should not be forgotten that their peaceful inclinations were overcome, in some part, by the machinations of Protestant missionaries. At first divided and vacillating, the bulk of the Indians were eventually driven by events to fight for their "ancient protector and friend" the king of England.

It is not necessary to follow the military history of the Indians in the American war for independence. Iroquois and Delaware warriors fought fiercely and with considerable success until Great Britain was defeated. Then came the diplomats and lawyers to the treaty tables, and Britain ceded sovereignty to the United States of all the territory west from the Atlantic Coast to the Mississippi River. The rationale was that Great Britain had acquired sovereignty from France, which had claimed it in the first instance because the French King was Christian and his subjects had "discovered" the place. Neither France nor Great Britain had discovered North America before the people who greeted the European "discoverers" at the Atlantic shores, and neither European power had ever succeeded in imposing rule on the native inhabitants of that vast area between the mountains and the Mississippi. Neither had been able to dissolve the tribes or to enact and enforce laws regulating the conduct of individual Indian persons in their own country. Neither had been able to do more than station tiny islands of garrisons in order to preserve a presence through trade and treaty. But the game called international law is played with legal fictions, and at Paris in 1783 Britain passed the card called sovereignty to the United States. The British ambassadors did not even try to get some consideration for the property of their Indian allies, as they did for property of loyalists of European descent. Except for refuge permitted in Canada, the tribes and all they possessed were abandoned.

The governments of the United States were not themselves very sure about what sovereignty meant for them, besides relief from Britain. Though confederated for mutual support, each state claimed sovereignty for itself, and Virginia maintained its claims to the west as part of itself. Virginia had offered Congress a conditional cession of its claims in 1781, but the conditions forestalled acceptance. After the peace with Great Britain in 1783, Congress failed to seek treaties with the Indian tribes, and the reason seems to have been indecision as to whether Congress or Virginia held jurisdiction. While the bargaining continued over the terms for Congress's acceptance of Virginia's cession offer, Pennsylvania forced the issue. Pennsylvania wanted no more trouble with Indians at Pittsburgh, and was equally intent on having no more trouble there with Virginians. The simplest means to acquire undisputed authority in the trouble spot was to follow the ancient practice of the Colony's founder, William Penn—to recognize the Indian property right and negotiate a purchase on terms satisfactory to the Indians; then, with possession of the Indian right backing up Pennsylvania's own charter right, Pennsylvania would be one up on Virginia. But, unless Congress first made formal peace with the Indians, Pennsylvania would have to make its own peace with tribes who would then remain in a state of enmity with the other states. What, then, would be left of Congress's supposed monopoly of the conduct of Indian affairs?

On 12 September 1783, Pennsylvania did Congress the courtesy of requesting approval of its intended Indian purchase. Congress stalled, being still enmeshed in its difficulties with Virginia; so Pennsylvania decided to proceed with its treaty and purchase the property regardless of Congress's approval. Congress faced the ridiculous possibility of losing any role in Indian affairs, for the other states would not have been slow in following Pennsylvania's precedent. At the point of crisis, Congress capitulated to Virginia's demands for concessions in order to avoid the total loss of its own authority in the west. On 23 February 1784, Pennsylvania appointed its commissioners to treat with the Indians. On 1 March 1784, Congress accepted Virginia's cession and the national domain came into being. On 4 March 1784, Congress appointed its own commissioners to treat with the Indians, and they assumed political control of the subsequent treaty conference. Speaking for the United States, they made the peace, allotting time to the Pennsylvanians only for the specific purpose of purchasing property within what were now Pennsylvania's unchallenged bounds.

The irony of this first American treaty with the tribes—the Treaty of Fort

Stanwix of 1784—was that Pennsylvania's subordinate land purchase was accepted by the Indians as valid, and it lasted, but the general peace with the United States was regarded as invalid, and did not last. The distinction is clear. The validity of the purchase resulted from a fair and acceptable bargain, while the invalidity of the peace was a direct function of its being the product of duress. The commissioners of the United States were accompanied by a body of troops. The commissioners dictated the treaty terms as an ultimatum, and seized hostages to enforce compliance. Looking down the gun barrels, the Indians signed where told; but a treaty made under duress was no more valid in Indian custom than a contract made under duress was valid in American law. The western Indians, far out of range of the guns at Fort Stanwix, simply ignored the treaty dictated there.

The theory of the United States commissioners was that the victory over Great Britain had been simultaneously a conquest of the Indians, and that it made the Indians' lands forfeit to their conquerors. The commissioners therefore *assigned* boundaries of lands reserved for the Indians at the pleasure of the United States government, instead of negotiating cessions of territory from the Indians on agreed terms of purchase. The trouble with this theory was that the Indians did not agree that they had been conquered, and they subsequently defeated two United States expeditionary forces to demonstrate their point—Harmar's Humiliation, 1790, and St. Clair's Shame, 1791.

Fighting continued until General Anthony Wayne defeated the Indians' western confederation at the Battle of Fallen Timbers in 1794. It is always called a "decisive" battle, but Wayne was too intelligent to regard it as conquest. In August 1795 he *negotiated* the Treaty of Greenville as an agreement between peers. In return for specific "cessions and relinquishments of lands" made by the Indian tribes, and "as the great means of rendering this peace strong and perpetual," Wayne agreed that the United States would relinquish claims "to all other Indian lands, northward of the river Ohio, eastward of the Mississippi, and westward and southward of the Great Lakes, and the waters uniting them, according to the boundary line agreed on by the United States and the King of Great Britain."

The meaning of the agreement was spelled out precisely and unambiguously: "The Indian tribes who have a right to those lands, are quietly to enjoy them, hunting, planting, and dwelling thereon, so long as they please, without any molestation from the United States; but when those tribes, or any of them, shall be disposed to sell their lands, or any part of them, they are to be sold only to the United States; and until such sale, the United States will protect all the said Indian tribes in the quiet enjoyment of their lands, against all citizens of the United States, and against all other white persons who intrude upon the same. And the said Indian tribes again acknowledge themselves to be under the protection of the said United States, and no other Power whatever."

The consequence of this treaty for the United States was peace in the Northwest Territory, a new flood of immigration into the territory, and the creation of the State of Ohio in 1803. The consequence for the Indians was the firm establishment of the practice by the United States of dealing with the Indian tribes as "nations," a practice continued until 1871. That the treaties so made were often fraudulent and always violated is another matter.

Current theories of history do not fit well on data such as have been recited above. Nationalist and racist doctrines suppress the facts of tribal government in myths about savagery. Theories of history based on class conflict, whether of socialist or capitalist orientation, do not provide for the hybrid relationships that occur when societies with different systems of social organization adjust to each other on terms other than quick assimilation of the one by the other. The romantic theory of revolution, in which all the lowly unite to rise against their oppressors, is embarrassed by the American Revolution's multiplicity of variously oppressed and exploited peoples who preyed upon each other; what most aggrieved the poor frontiersman was his sovereign's ban on robbing the even poorer native, and the first target of the Indian's hatchet was the frontierman's skull. But realism must also contemplate the disparity between upper class rhetoric and conduct. The gentry cried out passionately for liberty in general, but itemized it as rights for themselves to hold slaves and attack Indians.

Heedless of theories, Americans began the building of their empire with an inheritance of ethnocentric semantics that made logic valid to themselves out of the strange proposition that invasion, conquest, and dispossession of other peoples support the principle that all men are created equal.

American Indians on the Cotton Frontier

DANIEL H. USNER, JR.

... By 1793, when use of Whitney's patented gin began to spread across the southern hinterland, the region between the Chattahoochee and the Mississippi Rivers was still very much Indian country. The Indian population in that area numbered at least 30,000 individuals, most of whom lived in the more than one hundred villages that constituted the Creek, Choctaw, and Chickasaw nations. Within the same territory were only about 2,500 whites and 2,000 blacks, mostly concentrated in settlements along the lower Tombigbee River and around the Natchez banks of the Mississippi. In order to counteract the United States' claims to territory and its demands for navigating the Mississippi River, Spanish officials made serious efforts during the 1790s to attract American settlers to Louisiana. A generous land policy offered immigrants sizable grants of free land in proportion to the size of their families and the number of their laborers. Larger diplomatic considerations, however, compelled Spain in the Treaty of San Lorenzo, 1795, to cede to the United States all lands east of the Mississippi River and above the thirty-first parallel. In 1798 the United States Congress organized that cession into the Mississippi Territory, which was by the turn of the century occupied by nearly 5,000 whites, 3,500 black slaves, and 200 free blacks, in addition still to more than 30,000 Indians.

Daniel H. Usner, Jr., "American Indians on the Cotton Frontier," *Journal of American History,* 1985, pp. 297–317. Reprinted by permission of the Organization of American Historians

Indian nations not only comprised the majority of the new territory's population in 1798 but held title, guaranteed by treaties with both Spain and the United States, to most of its land. Indian policy, therefore, was an integral priority in the United States government's territorial organization of Mississippi. The United States entered the nineteenth century with four major goals in Indian affairs. The first goal of establishing and maintaining alliances with tribes required, in compliance with Indian customs, a well-regulated, steady trade relationship. In the Mississippi Territory the task was especially difficult because Spain, which had developed strong political and commercial ties with the tribes of the area, possessed adjacent territories—Louisiana until 1803 and Florida until 1819. To enforce a second policy goal, the maintenance of peace and order among Indian peoples and between them and American citizens, United States agents in the Mississippi Territory entered a highly volatile world shaped by two decades of Anglo-American encroachment into Indian country and of intertribal struggle over diminishing resources. As reported by [Governor] Winthrop Sargent in 1799, the Choctaws already felt "that their Country once affording abundance had become desolate by the hands of a People who knew them not but to increas their Wretchedness." Partially to diffuse resentment among Indians over such conditions and to make them more tractable, the government also pursued a third goal of reforming Indian societies by teaching "the Arts of husbandry, and domestic manufactures" and encouraging, as Secretary of War Henry Dearborn further suggested to Choctaw agent Silas Dinsmoor, "the growth of Cotton as well as Grain." Finally and most importantly, the goal of acquiring land cessions from Indian nations shaped policy in the Mississippi Territory. "[T]he time will come when a cession of land may be necessary to us and not injurious to them," Secretary of State Timothy Pickering informed Sargent. Suggesting how bribery might work as a means toward effecting that end, he mentioned that when the time came "the grant of an annuity should be the consideration."

An important instrument for implementing all of those goals was the establishment of government trading posts among the many tribes of the eastern woodlands and midwestern prairies. The first two having been legislated into existence by Congress in 1795, those stores or trade factories provided Indians with fixed exchange rates and ample supplies of merchandise and thereby facilitated regulation of Indian trade. . . .

. . . While the literature on United States trade houses has tended to emphasize losses incurred by the government, the impact of a deteriorating trade position upon Indian livelihood evidenced at the factories has remained poorly understood.

At a time when prices for deerskins were dropping in Europe and when supplies of game were diminishing in the southeastern woodlands, the economic position of Indians was further exacerbated by the fiscal tightening exerted by their private and public trading partners. Through most of the eighteenth century, colonial officials and merchants had followed Indian trade protocol, which included the practices of offering presents, smoking the calumet [peace pipe], and sharing food. By the end of the century, however, the United States began to discourage outright gift giving and, through its trade houses, to replace what had been political obligations with accountable debts. Influential leaders and intermediary traders still received extra merchandise for their peltry, but each advance was now carefully recorded in the debt column of the tribe's account book. In the Mississippi Territory the results of that practice materialized first among the Creeks in the Treaty of Fort Wilkinson, 1802. Of the $25,000 received by the tribe for a cession of land between the Oconee and the Ocmulgee rivers, $10,000 went "to satisfy certain debts due from Indians and white persons of the Creek country to the factory of the United States."

After sending the Creek treaty to Congress, President Thomas Jefferson turned his attention to that portion of Chickasaw territory "of first importance to us" and evaluated several means through which the United States "may advance towards our object." One means was to encourage plow agriculture, which would reduce the acreage of farmland needed by Indians; another was to nourish their allegiance "by every act of justice & of favor which we can possibly render them." But a third approach involved selectively extending credit to draw the Chickasaws into debt. Jefferson realized it would be beneficial "to establish among them a factory or factories for furnishing them with all the necessaries and comforts they may wish (spirituous liquors excepted), encouraging these and especially their leading men, to run in debt for these beyond their individual means of paying; and whenever in that situation, they will always cede lands to rid themselves of debt." . . .

. . . Choctaw, Creek, and Chickasaw treaties made during the first decade of the Mississippi Territory's existence reflected the entanglement of Indian villagers in the region within a chronic cycle of trade indebtedness and land cessions, a cycle that would steadily weaken their power and eventually culminate in removal. By 1822 the Choctaw nation, for example, ceded nearly thirteen million acres of land but still owed approximately thirteen thousand dollars to the United States trade house. The transfer of Indian land to the United States was, as the Choctaw and Chickasaw treaties of 1805 explicitly illustrate, further accelerated by cooperation between the federal government and merchant companies— a lesson that would not be lost on future administrators of Indian affairs.

Indian inhabitants of the Mississippi Territory responded to their deteriorating economic position in a variety of ways, evincing a resourceful adaptability among native Americans too often neglected by historians. Beginning in the late eighteenth century, numerous Choctaw families and even some Creek villagers migrated across the Mississippi River and settled in the still-plentiful hunting grounds of the Ouachita, Red, and Atchafalaya river basins. As government trade-house records reveal, those who remained in their homelands continued to produce, although at a diminishing rate, deerskins and other furs. Still hoping to perpetuate their traditional exchange economy through adaptation, Indian men and women provided an array of other goods and services to the trade stores. During the five years from 1809 through 1813, the Choctaw factory received $22,877 worth of raw deerskins (44,232 skins), $4,109 worth of dressed deerskins, raccoon, lynx, and other miscellaneous pelts, $1,749 worth of beeswax (7,958 pounds), $145 worth of tallow (1,161 pounds), $249 worth of corn (443 barrels), and $24 worth of snakeroot (96 pounds). Indians occasionally sold their labor to the trade house in exchange for merchandise, working as boat hands, messengers, and boatbuilders. In January 1809, for example, the Choctaw factor

"Bartered with an Indian" two yards of strouds valued at $3.50 for a "Canoe" (pirogue) that he gave to the trade house.

Many Indians became seasonal laborers or itinerant peddlers around the towns and plantations of the Mississippi Territory. As early as 1808 Choctaw women picked cotton during the harvest season for cloth, blankets, utensils, and even cash wages. John A. Watkins first became acquainted with the Choctaws in 1813–1814, "as they came into Jefferson Co. in the fall and winter in large numbers, the women to pick cotton, the men to hunt in the Louisiana swamps." From bark-covered huts that were always left open on the south side, hunters pursued deer and bear across the Mississippi while women worked in cotton fields east of the river. Those seasonally mobile camps of Choctaw families—the cotton economy's first migrant labor force—also sold dressed deerskins, bear oil, and venison at landings along the Mississippi or took those and other products to Natchez, where according to Watkins "they were usually exchanged for blankets, stroud & calico supplemented by a jug of whiskey."

To maintain an economic base within their diminishing tribal domains, the Indian peoples also changed their farming and settlement patterns. Many Creeks, Choctaws, and Chickasaws had been raising livestock for some time, but at the opening of the nineteenth century that activity became a more important means of livelihood. As more grazing land was needed and as immigrants and travelers created a demand for foodstuffs, Indian villages began to spread outward from their previously more compact centers. The process was most visible among the Upper Creeks, many of whom settled on the outskirts of their towns as they became more attentive to cattle, hogs, and horses. The inhabitants of Hoithlewalli, for example, formed new settlements with fenced-in fields along the small tributaries of the Oakfuskee Creek, once reserved by the town for bear hunting and now providing "delightful range for stock." Choctaw and Chickasaw farmers also homesteaded outward from their villages during the early territorial period. Traveling from Natchez to the Chicksaw nation in the summer of 1805, Dr. Rush Nutt observed some Choctaws "building log houses & cultivating the earth in corn, cotton, & other garden vegetables." Farther along the Natchez Trace—at Chukasalaya, Estockshish, and Bear Creek—he found Chicasaws establishing supply stations for travelers, raising "plenty of hogs & cattle," and farming grain crops. Chickasaw families were also settling westward in the Yazoo delta in order to use better range for their horses, cattle, and hogs.

The Indian trade economy that had grown around the exchange of deerskins for European manufactures was not impervious to accommodating the cotton economy, although the latter did threaten to displace the former entirely. During the eighteenth century Indians in the Lower Mississippi Valley had adopted European and African food crops, developed their own herds of livestock, and traded those and other items to colonists. In keeping with that pattern of adaptation, Indian villagers in the Mississippi Territory began to grow their own cotton for the export market. Traders Abram Mordecai and John and William Price established cotton gins at "Weathersford's racetrack" and "the Boat Yard," both along the Alabama River, where they purchased cotton produced by Creek farmers. Chickasaw chiefs inquired as early as 1803 whether the United States factor at Chickasaw Bluffs would accept their cotton for cash.

But even though the cotton economy began to replace the deerskin trade economy, Indian communities in the Mississippi Territory continued to create economic niches for some settlers and slaves. Before the region became a United States territory, many French and English traders had established their deerskin commerce in particular villages by marrying Indian women. Into the nineteenth century many of their offspring continued to play prominent roles in the regional economy and were joined by American newcomers licensed by the territorial government. As transportation on roads through Indian country increased, some of those traders even opened facilities that provided food and lodging to travelers. In addition to the actual traders who dealt directly with Indian villagers, Indian commerce employed black as well as white laborers at several different tasks: transporting products by packhorses or by boats, helping to preserve and to pack the deerskins, and doing construction work on the facilities. At both private trade firms and government factories, settlers worked for wages, and slaves were hired out by their owners. The experience among Indians gained by some black slaves, particularly those owned by whites and Indians engaged in trade, was evident to early territorial witnesses by the presence of blacks in settlements and villages who could interpret between the various Indian languages and English.

Obstacles to landownership and uncertainties of cotton production during the territorial years challenged settlers in Mississippi to find means of livelihood that resembled the Indian mixture of hunting, farming, and herding. That adaptation by whites to the cotton frontier, more than the production of cotton itself, brought them face to face with local Indians. Before the United States even began to survey land in the Mississippi Territory, an estimated two thousand settlers had already squatted on unused lands. . . .

. . . As the territory entered the second decade of the nineteenth century, mounting hostility from the Creek Indians and impending war against Great Britain deepened uncertainty and instability, pushed down the value of cotton . . . and slowed the sale of public lands. In one petition sent to Congress by inhabitants of the Mississippi Territory, the trap that cotton already set for the South—an economy highly sensitive to the price of a single commodity—was clearly defined: "Confiding as we have done on the measures of Government which were intended to restore foreign intercourse, and which held out the probability of success, we have continued to cultivate the article of cotton, to the growth of which our soil is so propitious, and omitted all or most other pursuits calculated to command money."

Under those circumstances, squatting on the periphery of private landholdings and Indian villages or on federal lands and then raising livestock to sell to planters, townspeople, and newcomers became a pervasive means to economic security. Already familiar with open grazing in the backwoods of Georgia and the Carolinas, many settlers in Mississippi's promising pine forests acquired cattle, horses, and hogs from Indians. Some bought the animals; others sequestered strays. In time, a family of squatters might earn enough from its own herding to purchase title to the land, or, if not, the mobility of livestock eased their relocation to another tract when threatened with eviction. Meanwhile, competition over grazing lands and ambiguity between trading and rustling heightened antagonism in their relations with Indians. Symbiotically, the success of some farmers in producing cotton and buying slaves—by creating a growing market for food—allowed those who were unable or unwilling to grow the staple a distinct avenue to economic security and social autonomy. From that process, among others, emerged the yeoman farmers of the nineteenth-century South, whose intermittent participation in the cotton economy through livestock trade buffered them from the risks of cotton agriculture and yet perpetuated their hopes of becoming slave-owning cotton farmers themselves.

By the second decade of the nineteenth century, the Mississippi Territory was fast becoming a cotton export region. Within a decade the non-Indian population had surpassed the number of Indians, increasing nearly fivefold to more than 23,000 settlers and 17,000 slaves. Although most white settlers still contended with obstacles to land acquisition and relied on multiple means of subsistence, planters who already possessed land or who could afford to purchase some in the private market committed more slaves to the production of more cotton. As one such individual described the process, "Here you will ask, what do they want with so many Negroes, the answer is, to make more Money—again, you will ask what do they want with so much Money, the answer is to buy more Negroes. . . . A Man's merit in this country, is estimated, according to the number of Negroes he works in the field."

The influx of Afro-American slaves into the territory affected the economic life of Indians as deeply and equivocally as did white migration. More vulnerable to territorial laws than were Indians, Afro-Americans also struggled to preserve some economic autonomy and resilience within the narrowing interstices of a slave-labor, cotton economy. By trading among themselves and with Indians and whites—in foodstuffs, home manufactures, and even forbidden horses—slaves tried to secure for themselves what has been lately called an "internal economy," distinct from but tied to the larger regional system of staple agriculture. But legislation and slave patrols discouraged forms of economic exchange and social interaction that had previously brought blacks and Indians together—for example, in weekend marketing on the streets of Natchez. Meanwhile, some individuals within the Indian nations—principally members of mixed-blood, trade families—were themselves becoming owners of black slaves and planters of cotton. Although those developments eventually generated greater racial separation and stratification between southern Indians and blacks, they were too nascent before 1820 to close all channels of interethnic communication.

Throughout the colonial period slaves had perceived Indian country as potential refuge from bondage, and the increasing presence there of blacks owned by tribal members during territorial years may have even encouraged some runaways to take advantage of the confusion accompanying the movement of slaves to and from Indian jurisdictions. Cases of slaves being arrested by United States Indian agents for "want of a passport" and disputes over ownership of slaves who "ran away or were stolen" suggest that the blacks involved were playing an active role in creating their uncertain status within Indian country. Whether as slaves or as runaways, blacks who interacted closely with Indians during the early nineteenth century contributed to the formation of multiracial families and even of scattered communities across the South. One such community, whose members became known as "Cajuns of Alabama," grew rapidly during the territorial period along the west bank of the Mobile River; another group known as "Freejacks" took shape on the Tchefuncte River in Louisiana, along the Natchez-to-New Orleans road.

Given the potential for increasing ties with blacks, Indians found their own activities and mobility being curtailed by the Mississippi territorial government's efforts to reinforce the institution of slavery. In addition to federal laws requiring licenses and prohibiting alcohol in Indian trade, which were enforced by all territorial governors, Governor Sargent issued an ordinance in May 1800 to strengthen control jointly over commerce with Indians and slaves in Mississippi. The mere sight of an Indian or slave carrying into a house or store "any article which may be supposed for sale, or any bottle, jug or other thing in which liquor may be conveyed" was sufficient evidence for convicting the storekeeper or housekeeper. An initial law requiring slaves who participated in the Natchez marketplace to carry permits issued by their owners was extended over the entire territory in 1805 to declare that "no person whatsoever shall buy, sell, or receive of, to or from a slave, any commodity whatsoever without the leave or consent of the master, owner or overseer of such slave, expressive of the article so permitted to be bought, sold or bartered." Guilty persons would pay to slave owners four times the value of the item exchanged, the slave would receive ten lashes, and owners who allowed a slave "to go at large and trade as a freeman" had to pay a fine of fifty dollars. A statute enacted in 1810 further increased the risk of independent marketing to slaves by making it lawful for any citizen to apprehend a slave suspected of carrying goods without written consent.

The exchange of two items in particular—cotton and horses— threatened the property of planters and received special attention from lawmakers. In the spring of 1800, slaves were prohibited from the "raising and Vending of Cotton" and from "holding property in horses." Although some owners apparently permitted those activities, both the need to prevent theft of those valuable products and the desire to limit avenues of financial independence activated a comprehensive prohibition against possession of cotton and horses by slaves. To reduce the chances of petty rustling by black and Indian herdsmen, an act of March 4, 1803, prescribed that "no person whosoever shall send or permit any slave or Indian to go into any of the woods or ranges in the territory, to brand or mark any horse, mare, colt, mule, ass, cattle, hog, sheep, under any pretence whatsoever; unless the slave be in company, and under the direction of some reputable white person."

In southern folklore and history, Natchez and the road linking it with Nashville became legendary for crime and violence during the early nineteenth century. As the oldest and largest town in the territory (until Mobile was annexed in 1813), Natchez resembled urban places in other frontier or colonial regions in its very real function as a nexus of underground exchange activity and of volatile ethnic contact. "Ebriety [drunkeness] of Indians and Negroes on Sundays," complained Sargent on arriving in Natchez, made it "a most Abominable place"—a message that signaled his and subsequent governors' commitment to reversing customary trends. The seasonal encampment of one hundred or so Choctaw families around Natchez, where they bartered for ammunition and other supplies for hunting trips, had become a familiar part of the cultural landscape before the end of the eighteenth century. Under United States territorial control, however, officials and propertied residents loathed what they saw as pilfering, loitering, and carousing; thus they discouraged Indians from visiting the area. In 1807 Gov. Robert Williams even tried, with little effect, to require that Indians leaving their tribal lands carry passports to be issued at the discretion of government agents.

Incidents of drunken affrays and robberies among Choctaws, blacks, and whites, of violent and often fatal assaults committed against Indians, and of Indian thefts of livestock and crops were too numerous and various to describe here, but they all involved a confrontation between two different systems of justice. Much of the aggravation and theft perpetrated by Indians represented a form of banditry committed to protest against and compensate for the abandonment of protocol and respect by the growing American population. Because Choctaws traveling to hunt or to trade, for example, encountered more and more settlers unwilling or unable to share some corn or meat with them, as had traditionally been the case, they would simply take what was available from a field or pasture. Whenever an Indian was killed by a white or black assailant, an acute clash between tribal and territorial laws ensued. Although officials often expressed concern over the Indians' "Spirit of Retaliation," territorial courts rarely convicted and punished white men who murdered Indians on the pretense that guilt was difficult to prove in such crimes. Meanwhile, Indians followed their own rules of retributive justice, which required the kin of a victim to avenge his death by killing either the guilty person or some surrogate. As those of other United States territories, the early government of Mississippi tried, with great difficulty, to replace tribal systems of law and order with its own codes of trial and punishment. But in some cases of homicide against Indians, officials compromised by paying merchandise to relatives in compensation for their loss. In January 1809, for example, the Choctaw agent gave two hundred dollars' worth of strouds, blankets, and ammunition to the uncle and brother of an Indian killed the previous summer by William Bates. Bates reimbursed the agency in August. A revealing case of territorial conflict with Indian jurisdiction occurred in 1810, when two young Choctaws who executed another Choctaw under blood law outside the tribal boundary were arrested and imprisoned at Fort Stoddert. Fearful of "unpleasant consequences," Gov. David Holmes pardoned them but urged Judge Harry Toulmin "that they should be made sensible that they have been guilty of an infraction of our laws and that in future such conduct will not be tolerated."

Behind all of the legislative and police action directed against slaves and Indians reigned a deep anxiety over black insurrection, Indian warfare, and even combined rebellion by the two groups. News of the Gabriel Prosser revolt that was barely averted in Virginia drove Sargent to address a circular letter of November 16, 1800, to slave owners in the Mississippi Territory, exhorting "the utmost Vigilance" toward all slaves. Recent assaults on two overseers were evidence enough that greater attention to the slave laws had to be given by "all good Citizens." Fear that the increasing in-migration of slaves would introduce experienced insurgents from other slave regions nearly produced in the territorial legislation a law that would have prohibited the importation of "Male Slaves, above the age of Sixteen."

The self-conscious endeavor by white Mississippians to establish slavery safely in the midst of a large Indian population elicited from their officials an obsessive concern with well organized and trained militias, adequate weaponry, and a responsive federal army—all overtly effective means of controlling subjugated ethnic groups. Although military officials repeatedly assured the government that the army and the militia were prepared to quell any outbreak of Indian or black hostility, the very prospect of having to mobilize against rebellion in one part of the territory heightened the fear of exposing another part to concurrent attack. In January 1811 hundreds of slaves in the adjacent territory of Louisiana turned their hoes and axes against planters outside New Orleans. Their march toward the city was quickly and violently stopped by troops of the United States Army's Southern Division, led by the cotton planter Gen. Wade Hampton. That revolt, which resulted in the brutal and speedy killing of nearly one hundred blacks in Louisiana, intensified apprehension in the Mississippi Territory over thinly stretched defenses against both external and internal enemies. The declaration of war against Great Britain in 1812 then brought the fear of racial war on different fronts to a climax. In a letter to General Wilkinson concerning possible withdrawal of troops from the territory for action elsewhere, Governor Holmes recited his faith in the friendship of the Choctaws but warned that "knowledge of our defenceless state . . . may tempt them to commit aggressions." Regarding blacks, Holmes continued, "Of the slaves, who compose so large a portion of our population I entertain much stronger apprehensions. Scarcely a day passes without my receiving some information relative to the designs of those people to insurrect."

The Creek War of 1813–1814, waged in the eastern valleys of the Mississippi Territory, has recently received skillful attention in regard to both its wide context of international affairs and its internal dimension of tribal politics. But the function of the military conflict in expanding the cotton economy and in enforcing concommitant racial control is not yet fully appreciated. As already indicated, the territorialization of Mississippi imposed multiple pressures upon Indian societies. In the Creek nation, those pressures provoked increasing rebelliousness from a large segment of its population. Persistent demands by the Forbes company and the United States government that trade debts be paid through cessions of land severely tested the patience of Creek villagers. Indian leaders contested debts that were accounted to the nation but that actually had been incurred by individuals whose tribal status they did not recognize. When the company tried to add interest to their account, the Creeks grew angrier, insisting that "there was no word for it in their language" and accusing their old trade partner of wanting "to tear the very flesh off their backs."

Further aggravating those issues, settlers were sprawling from the Tennessee and Tombigbee-Alabama valleys, and territorial militiamen were making frequent border patrols into Creek country. The government's program of reforming, or "civilizing," Indian societies, which was aggressively implemented among the Lower Creeks by agent Hawkins, undermined the ability of the Creek nation to respond effectively to such pressures by expediting the emergence of a new class of assimilated Creek citizens who were themselves becoming cotton planters and slave owners. The tour of the rising Shawnee leader, Tecumseh, among the southern tribes during the summer and fall of 1811 injected into the already fractionalized Creek nation a surge of religious nativism and political militance, which took hold most strongly among the angry young men of the Upper Creek towns. In the summer of 1812, the tribal council ordered the execution of a group of Red Sticks, as the rebels were called, who were accused of killing settlers in Tennessee on their return from the town in Indiana where Tecumseh and his brother, the "Shawnee Prophet," resided. And in November it agreed to pay some $22,000 of debts owed the Forbes company by turning over to the firm each year the tribe's annuities from the United States. Those two explosive developments helped bring civil war to the Creek people by 1813.

United States intervention against the rebellious Creeks came swiftly and forcefully, making the Mississippi Territory the theater of one of the nation's bloodiest and most costly Indian wars. In July 1813 a party of Red Sticks, carrying ammunition and other supplies from Pensacola, was attacked by a joint force of territorial militiamen and Lower Creek adversaries. In retaliation Creek rebels attacked Fort Mims at the confluence of the Alabama and the Tombigbee rivers. On August 30, 1813, approximately 250 of the men, women, and children who had sought refuge inside the fort were killed during a siege that lasted five hours. News of the "massacre," which included reports that black slaves had joined the Red Sticks, threw the Mississippi Territory and adjacent states into an alarm that speedily mobilized soldiers and citizens into action.

The invasion of Upper Creek country by four separate armies of militiamen and federal troops proved to be a painful experience for Indians and non-Indians. Red Stick fighters and their families managed to evade United States soldiers and their Indian allies, who in turn resorted to burning abandoned villages to the ground. After suffering ten months of sickness, hunger, desertion, and severe discipline, the invasionary armies backed the Creek rebels into a bend of the Tallapoosa River. On March 27, 1814, approximately 1,000 Red Sticks stood up against a combined force of 1,400 whites, 500 Cherokees, and 100 Lower Creeks in the Battle of Horseshoe Bend, losing by the end of the day approximately 800 tribesmen killed. Having led personally the western Tennessee volunteers and provided much of the strategy in the Creek War, Andrew Jackson—a merchant, planter, and land speculator long interested in the Mississippi Territory— received command of the United States Army's Seventh Military District and proceeded to impose a peace treaty on the Creek nation. The beleaguered Creek leaders who signed the Treaty of Fort Jackson on August 9, 1814, agreed to cede fourteen million acres of land—more than one-half of present-day Alabama— even though most of them were Lower Creeks who had not rebelled against the United States.

The military subjugation of the Creek Indians greatly accelerated the transformation of ethnic relations already underway in the Mississippi Territory. Indian trade in deerskins and other frontier commodities would never recover in the Deep South, forcing most Indian villagers to become marginal participants in the emerging cotton economy while allowing some to accumulate their own property in cotton lands and Negro slaves. Although banditry and violence would continue to serve many Indians in Mississippi and Alabama as means of resistance, the Creek War demonstrated the futility and danger of military confrontation and drove surviving militants out of the territory and into Florida. The Creek land cession that resulted from their defeat drastically contracted the area of Indian country and intensified the physical isolation of Indian villages from other inhabitants. Furthermore, the sudden availability of so much land to settlers, coinciding with the post-Napoleonic expansion of the demand for cotton in Europe, set in motion the great wave of public land sales and immigration that guaranteed the dominance of cotton agriculture over the territory's political offspring—the states of Mississippi and Alabama.

The "Alabama Fever," as the postwar boom in land sales and cotton production was called, revived the conflict between immigrant settlers and land speculators. As the average price of public land in the Creek cession rose above five dollars per acre by 1818, crowds of angry squatters assembled at land auctions to push for registration of their claims at the minimum price. Hostility toward large purchasers was tempered, however, by the heady climb of cotton prices above thirty cents per pound. Eager to produce for such an export market, small farmers and wealthy planters alike borrowed more and more money in order to purchase both land and labor. In 1817, the year in which Alabama became a separate territory and Mississippi acquired statehood, cotton annually exported from the region exceeded seventeen million pounds. The fragile financial basis of the expansion, though, soon reached its breaking point. Just as Alabama was becoming a state, cotton prices plummeted in the panic of 1819 well below twenty cents per pound and stranded Alabamians with a land debt of eleven million dollars. But the cotton-export economy had already taken hold of land and labor across the South. Following a short period of contraction and adjustment, white Mississippians and Alabamians proceeded to import more slaves from eastern states and to expand cotton production across more land, of course borrowing more money to finance both.

Development of a cotton economy drastically altered the economic relations of Indian peoples with citizens and slaves in the Mississippi Territory. The United States government, through its own trade houses and with cooperation from private companies, pressured Indian tribes into making repeated cessions of land. In the concomitant transfer of public land into the private market, the federal government allowed speculation by land companies and made ownership difficult for early nineteenth-century migrants. Settlers coped with that obstacle and with the uncertainty of cotton production through means of livelihood similar to those of neighboring Indians. Territorial laws meanwhile restricted the economic activities of slaves and limited their interaction with free individuals, confining them more to the production of cotton for their owners. The Creek War, more than any other action, accelerated the physical confinement of Indians into ethnic enclaves. By 1820 an American Indian population of more than 30,000 persons was surrounded by 42,000 whites and 33,000 blacks in the state of Mississippi and by another 85,000 whites and 42,000 blacks in Alabama.

While a new socioeconomic order originated from those processes, the strategies used to mitigate or to avert them created undercurrents of resistance that have been only slowly and inadequately uncovered by historians. The different economic adaptations selected variantly by Indian inhabitants of the Mississippi Territory greatly influenced impending struggles over removal, with some committed to commercial agriculture becoming the most staunch defenders of tribal homelands. Slaves in Mississippi and Alabama, meanwhile, continued to take economic initiatives in defiance of their owners' economic interests, maintaining a market in self-produced and pilfered goods reminiscent of earlier exchange with Indians and settlers. Although they had greater freedom of choice, nonslavehold-ing whites also struggled to secure a safe, albeit uneasy, relationship with the cotton export market. Becoming endemic to life in the nineteenth-century South, those widespread attempts to minimize dependence on the expanding cotton economy made the conquest of peoples and places by King Cotton more tenuous and complex than perhaps the participants themselves believed it to be. Old Car-others McCaslin bought the land, as portended by William Faulkner, "with white man's money from the wild men whose grandfathers without guns hunted it, and tamed and ordered or believed he had tamed and ordered it for the reason that the human beings he held in bondage and in the power of life and death had removed the forest from it and in their sweat scratched the surface of it to a depth of per-haps fourteen inches in order to grow something out of it which had not been there before and which could be translated back into the money he who believed he had bought it had had to pay to get it and hold it."

American History, Tecumseh, and the Shawnee Prophet

R. DAVID EDMUNDS (Cherokee)

High upon a granite pedestal overlooking "the Yard" at the United States Naval Academy at Annapolis stands a bronze statue of an Indian warrior. Midshipmen passing in and out of Bancroft Hall traditionally salute the statue before taking examinations in the hope that the renowned warrior's medicine will assist them during their tests. Most midshipmen, if asked whom the statue represents, will reply that it is a replica of Tecumseh, the famous war chief of the Shawnees. In reality, however, the statue was never intended to be Tecumseh. It represents Tamenend, a chief among the Delawares.

The midshipmen's incorrect identification of the bronze figure is not surpris-ing, for Americans have long regarded Tecumseh as one of their foremost Indian heroes. . . . His biographers have presented an Indian of superhuman qualities; and Alvin M. Josephy, in his volume *The Patriot Chiefs,* entitles his chapter on the Shawnee as "Tecumseh: The Greatest Indian."

If the white observers and historians have been laudatory in their description of Tecumseh, they have been universal in their condemnation of his brother, Tenskwatawa, the Shawnee Prophet. Both British and American leaders de-nounced the holy man as a "pretender" and a "coward," and historians have en-larged upon such qualities to present an image of a charlatan who manipulated the tribesmen for his own purposes. While Tecumseh's political and miliary move-ment is pictured as logical and praiseworthy, the Prophet represents the darker side of Indian life. A religious fanatic, Tenskwatawa is presented as riding his brother's coattails to a position of minor prominence.

Unquestionably, the Shawnee brothers emerged to positions of leadership

"Tecumseh, the Shawnee Prophet, and American History: A Reassessment," by R. David Edmunds, *Western Historical Quarterly* 14 (July 1983), pp. 261–276.

during a period of great stress for native Americans. Although the Treaty of Greenville supposedly had drawn a line between Indian and American lands in Ohio, the treaty was ignored. Frontier settlement continued to advance north from the Ohio valley, threatening the remaining Indian land base in the region. Meanwhile, white hunters repeatedly trespassed onto Indian lands to hunt game needed by the tribesmen, and by the first decade of the nineteenth century game was becoming scarce. The fur trade declined in a similar manner, and after 1800 many warriors were hard pressed to provide for their families. Not surprisingly, the Indians retaliated by stealing settlers' livestock, and the resulting clashes produced casualties on both sides. Obviously, both Indians and whites suffered, but losses were much larger among the natives. Governor William Henry Harrison of Indiana admitted that "a great many of the Inhabitants of the Fronteers [*sic*] consider the murdering of the Indians in the highest degree meritorious," while Governor Arthur St. Clair of the Northwest Territory reported that "the number of those unhappy people (the Indians) who have been killed since the peace at Greenville . . . is great enough to give serious alarm for the consequences."

Much of the Indian-white conflict was triggered by alcohol. Frustrated over their declining political and economic status, beleaguered tribesmen drowned their sorrows in frontier whiskey. Although illegal, alcohol was in plentiful supply, and brawls resulting from the Bacchanalia spread social chaos throughout the Indian villages. Once-proud warriors quarreled among themselves or abused their kinsmen, while others retreated into drunken stupors. Some Shawnees, weakened by their dissipation, fell victims to influenza, smallpox, and other diseases. Others sat passively in their lodges, bewildered by the changes swirling around them. Meanwhile, the clans—traditional kinship systems designed to regulate and provide cohesiveness among the separate Shawnee villages—were unable to cope with the multitude of problems besetting the tribe.

Overwhelmed by the chaos within their villages, the Shawnees pondered the causes. Although many tribesmen realized that the majority of their problems emanated from outside sources such as loss of lands, economic deterioration, injustice, and alcohol, others suspected darker elements and probed inward, examining the fabric of tribal society. Predictably, traditional Shawnees concluded that much of their trouble resulted from witchcraft, for the fear of witches and their evil power permeated Shawnee culture, and neighboring tribes believed the Shawnees to have a particular affinity for sorcery and the supernatural.

The basis for such fear lay deep in tribal tradition. The Shawnees believed that in the dim past, when they first crossed the Great Water in search of their homeland, they had been opposed by a huge water serpent who represented the evil powers in the universe. Although their warriors had killed the serpent, witches had saved part of its body, which still held a potent and malevolent power. Contained in medicine bundles, this evil had been passed down through the ages and was used by witches to spread disorder throughout the tribe. . . .

Not surprisingly, many associated the Americans with these forces of evil. The Shawnees believed that the sea was the home of the Great Serpent—the embodiment of disorder. Their forefathers had always warned that pale-skinned invaders might emerge from the water to disrupt the harmony of the Shawnee homeland. Since the Americans had first appeared on the eastern seashore, many tribesmen were certain the invaders were the children of the Serpent, intent upon the Indians' downfall. . . . And even Black Hoof, a government chief committed to the American cause, admitted, "The white people has spoiled us. They have been our ruin."

Yet the same chaos that threatened the tribesmen also produced a man who promised them deliverance. Known as Lalawethika ("The Noisemaker" or "Loud Mouth"), the man had been born in 1775 on the Mad River in eastern Ohio. Prior to Lalawethika's birth, his father had been killed by the Americans and his mother had abandoned him when he was only four years old. Raised by a sister, his childhood had been overshadowed by two older brothers, Chiksika and Tecumseh. Lalawethika never excelled as a hunter or a warrior, and during his adolescence he became an alcoholic. Following the Treaty of Greenville he lived in a small village headed by Tecumseh, where he unsuccessfully aspired to the status of shaman. But in April 1805 this alcoholic ne'er-do-well experienced a vision that changed his life and propelled him to the forefront of Indian leadership.

While lighting his pipe from the fire in his lodge, Lalawethika collapsed, falling into a coma so deep his wife and neighbors believed him to be dead. As his wife began her mourning song he astonished his family by first stirring, then regaining consciousness. Visibly shaken, he informed the gathered onlookers that indeed he had died and had visited heaven, where the Master of Life had shown him both an Indian paradise and a hell where eternal fires lay in wait for sinful tribesmen. Alcoholics like himself suffered the most, for molten lead was poured down their throats until flames shot out their nostrils. Amidst much trembling, Lalawethika vowed to renounce his former ways and never again drink the white man's whiskey. No longer would he be known as Lalawethika. Henceforward he would be called Tenskwatawa—"The Open Door"—a name symbolizing his new role as a holy man destined to lead his people down the narrow road to paradise.

In the following months Tenskwatawa experienced other visions and enlarged upon his doctrine of Indian deliverance. Much of his teachings addressed the decline of traditional moral values among the Shawnees and other tribes. Tenskwatawa claimed he "was particularly appointed to that office by the Great Spirit" and that his "sole object was to reclaim the Indians from bad habits and to cause them to live in peace with all mankind." While he continued to denounce whiskey as "poison and accursed," he also condemned the violence that permeated tribal society. He urged warriors to treat each other as brothers, to stop their quarreling, and to refrain from striking their wives and children. Husbands and wives should remain faithful to each other, and marriages should be monogamous. Shawnee warriors currently married to more than one women "might keep them," but such marriages displeased the Master of Life.

Convinced that his forefathers had enjoyed a happier existence, the new Shawnee Prophet attempted to revitalize some facets of traditional tribal culture. Indeed, much of Tenskwatawa's teaching was nativistic in both tone and content. He asked his followers to return to the communal life of the past and to renounce all desire to accumulate property as individuals. Those tribesmen who hoarded their possessions were doomed, but others who shared with their kinsmen, "when they die are happy; and when they arrive in the land of the dead, will find their wigwams furnished with everything they had on earth." He also instructed them to use only the food, implements, and dress of their fathers. Pork, beef, and mutton were unclean, and the tribesmen were instructed to eat only the game they killed in the forests. Neither were the Indians to eat bread, but only corn, beans, and other crops raised by their ancestors. Stone or wood implements should replace metal tools, and although guns could be used for self-defense, the warriors were to hunt with bows and arrows. With the exception of weapons, all items of American manufacture were to be discarded. In a similar manner, the Indians were to dress in skin or leather clothing and were ordered to shave their heads, leaving only the scalp lock of their forefathers. False gods should be forgotten, but the tribesmen should pray to the Master of Life, asking that he return fish to the streams and game to the forest. To assist his disciples, Tenskwatawa provided them with sacred "prayer sticks." The sticks were inscribed with pictographs illustrating certain spirits who would help the tribesmen in their supplications. If the Shawnees were faithful and their hearts pure, the Master of Life would restore order, the earth would be fruitful, and they would prosper.

While Tenskwatawa attempted to revitalize some part of Shawnee culture, he condemned others. He warned that many of the traditional dances and ceremonies no longer had any meaning and offered new ones in their place. He also instructed his followers to throw away their personal medicine bundles, which he claimed had been powerful in the past, but no longer possessed the potency needed to protect the Shawnees from the new dangers that threatened them. Tenskwatawa alone spoke for the Master of Life, and only those tribesmen who subscribed to the new faith would ever know happiness. But his disciples would be rewarded above all men, for they alone would eventually "find your children or your friends that have long been dead restored to life."

If the Prophet condemned some of the old religious practices, he was particularly suspicious of those tribesmen who held religious beliefs differing from his own. At best those shamans or medicine men who opposed his doctrine were misguided fools. At worst they were witches, in league with the Great Serpent to spread disorder among the tribes. And the Prophet did not limit his accusations to religious leaders. For the holy man, religion and politics were the same. He had been chosen by the Master of Life to end the chaos in the Shawnee world. All those who opposed him also opposed the Master of Life. Therefore, he was particularly suspicious of tribesmen who were becoming acculturated or who had been converted to Christianity. Such men also were suspect of witchcraft. Unless they repented, they too should be destroyed.

Tenskwatawa's distrust of those Indians who adhered to American values reflected his general condemnation of the Long Knives [Europeans]. He informed his followers that the Master of Life had made the British, French, and Spanish, but the Americans were the children of the Great Serpent. In his visions Tenskwatawa had seen the Americans take the form of a great crab that crawled from the sea, and the Master of Life had told him, "They grew from the scum of the great water when it was troubled by the Evil Spirit. And the froth was driven into the woods by a strong east wind. They are numerous, but I hate them. They are unjust. They have taken away your lands, which were not made for them." Only if the Indians rejected the Americans would order ever be restored to the Shawnee world. The Prophet instructed his people to cease all contact with the Long

Knives. If they met an American in the forest, they might speak to him from a distance, but they should avoid touching him or shaking his hand. They were also forbidden to trade Indian foods to their white neighbors, for these provisions were the special gifts of the Master of Life, to be used by his children, not the spawn of the Serpent. Tenskwatawa instructed his disciples to cut their ties with frontier merchants, and "because they (the Americans) have cheated you," the Indians were to pay "no more than half their credits." Moreover, Indian women married to American men should return to their tribes, and the children of such unions were to be left with their fathers.

The new faith soon spread to other tribes, who like the Shawnees were unable to adjust to the great changes sweeping around them. By the autumn of 1805 warriors from the Delawares and Wyandots were traveling to Greenville, Ohio, where the Prophet had established a new village. There Tenskwatawa converted the visitors, then sent them back to proselytize their home villages. The Delawares proved particularly susceptible to the new religion, and during the late winter of 1806 they accused about one dozen of their tribesmen of witchcraft. In March 1806 the Prophet journeyed to the Delaware villages, where he examined the captives, exonerating some, but condemning others. The Delawares eventually burned four of their kinsmen before the witch-hunt terminated. Predictably, all those burned were converted Christians whose acculturation made them more suspicious.

The witch-hunt among the Delawares frightened Moravian missionaries associated with the tribe and brought a storm of protest from government officials. During the spring of 1806 Harrison wrote to the Delawares denouncing the Prophet and asking, "If he is really a prophet, ask him to cause the sun to stand still—the moon to alter its course—the rivers to cease to flow—or the dead to rise from their graves. If he does these things, you may believe that he has been sent from God."

Ironically, Harrison's challenge played into Tenskwatawa's hands. In the spring of 1806 several astronomers had traveled through Indiana and Illinois locating observation stations to study an eclipse of the sun scheduled to occur on June 16. Although Harrison either ignored or forgot about the event, the Prophet remembered. Among the Shawnees such an eclipse was known as a "Black Sun," an event surrounded with dread and portending future warfare. Accepting Harrison's challenge, in early June Tenskwatawa surprised even his closest followers by promising to darken the sun. On June 16, while his disciples and skeptics both assembled in his village, the Prophet remained secluded in his lodge throughout most of the morning, but as the noon sun faded into an eerie twilight he stepped forth exclaiming, "Did I not speak the truth? See, the sun is dark!" He then assured his audience that he would restore the sun's former radiance, and as the eclipse ended even those tribesmen who still remembered him as Lalawethika, the drunken loudmouth, now were convinced of his medicine. . . .

. . . In the following months so many tribesmen were enroute to the Prophet's village that white traders found most of the Chippewa towns along the southern shores of Lake Michigan deserted. The Menominees, Sacs, and Winnebagos also were swept up in the religious frenzy, and during the summer of 1807 they trekked to Greenville in large numbers.

Unable to comprehend the religious nature of the movement, American offi-cials at first believed that Tenskwatawa was only a figurehead controlled by more traditional chiefs among the Shawnees. During 1807 several groups of American agents arrived at the Prophet's village to investigate the character of the new movement. After meeting with Tenskwatawa, most of the envoys agreed that the holy man was the dominant Indian leader in the village. Moreover, the Prophet was able to persuade them that his religion posed no threat to the government. But Harrison and other officials refused to admit that the movement was an indige-nous uprising, resulting from desperate conditions among the Indians. Instead, they charged that the Prophet was actually a British agent, intent upon raising the tribes against the United States. . . .

The large numbers of Indians who journeyed to Tenskwatawa's village en-hanced his prestige, but they also alarmed white settlers in Ohio. Moreover, the influx of tribesmen exhausted Tenskwatawa's food supply, and he was hard pressed to feed his followers. In November 1807 the Potawatomis suggested that he withdraw from Greenville and establish a new village on the Tippecanoe River in Indiana. The new site would be much less exposed to white influence and was located in a region where game was more plentiful. Therefore, in April 1808 the Prophet and his followers abandoned Ohio and moved to Prophetstown.

The withdrawal to Indiana temporarily removed Tenskwatawa from white scrutiny, but his logistical problems continued. Since Prophetstown was located further west, it was more accessible to potential converts, and during 1808 and 1809 Indians flocked to the new village in numbers surpassing those who had visited him at Greenville. Although the villagers planted fields of corn and scoured the surrounding countryside for game, they could not feed the multitude. To obtain additional food, the Prophet brazenly turned to the Americans. In June 1808 he sent a delegation of warriors to Harrison assuring the governor of his peaceful intentions and asking for provisions. The Indians were so persuasive that Harrison sent food to Prophetstown and invited Tenskwatawa to meet with him in Vincennes. Two months later, in August 1808, the Prophet and his retinue arrived at Vincennes and spent two weeks conferring with Harrison. The governor was astonished at "the considerable talent of art and address" with which Ten-skwatawa mesmerized his followers. Moreover, the holy man's pleas of friend-ship toward the United States were so convincing that Harrison provided him with additional stores of food and gunpowder and reported to his superiors that his earlier assessments of the Shawnee were in error, for "the influence which the Prophet has acquired will prove advantageous rather than otherwise to the United States." . . .

But the facade of friendship was too fragile to last. Although the Prophet feigned goodwill toward the government, he could not control his followers, many of whom were less devious in their relations with the United States. As Indian depredations spread along the Wabash Valley, Harrison became con-vinced of the Shawnee's duplicity. During the summer of 1809 Tenskwatawa again visited with the governor in Vincennes, but this time Harrison was less hospitable. Tenskwatawa's protestations of friendship had little impact, and Har-rison informed the War Department that his suspicions of the Prophet "have been strengthened rather than diminished in every interview I have had with him since his arrival." Moreover, by the summer of 1809 Harrison was making preparations for the Treaty of Fort Wayne, and he assumed that such a transaction would terminate any pretense of amity between the government and the holy man.

Harrison was correct. The Treaty of Fort Wayne, signed in September 1809, ceded over three million acres in Indiana and Illinois to the United States. Negotiated by friendly chiefs among the Miamis, Delawares, and Potawatomis, the treaty was adamantly opposed by Tenskwatawa. In response, he redoubled his efforts to win new disciples. Messengers were sent to the Ottawas and Potawatomis, and many Wyandots who earlier had shunned the new faith now were converted to the Prophet's teachings. Once again Harrison received reports that the Indians were burning witches, and friendly chiefs among the Miamis and Piankashaws complained that warriors long faithful to the government now were flocking to Prophetstown.

Concerned over the new upsurge in the Prophet's influence, Harrison sent informers to the Tippecanoe and invited Tenskwatawa to again meet with him in Vincennes, but the holy man refused. He also ignored an invitation by the governor to travel to Washington and meet with the president. Instead, he informed Harrison that the recent treaty was illegal ánd threatened to kill all those chiefs who had signed it. He also vowed that the lands would never be settled by white men and warned Harrison to keep American settlement south of the mouth of the Vermillion River.

The Treaty of Fort Wayne ended any pretense of cooperation between Tenskwatawa and the government. By 1810 the lines were drawn. Tenskwatawa and his movement were unequivocally opposed to American expansion, and in the years following the treaty the anti-American sentiment was both transformed and intensified.

Tecumseh's role in the formation of this movement was entirely a secondary one. He subscribed to the new faith and lived with the Prophet at Greenville, where he assisted his brother in meeting the delegations of both Indian and white visitors. Tecumseh sometimes spoke in council upon such occasions, but no more so than Blue Jacket, Roundhead, or other Indians prominent in the village. In 1807 he accompanied a group of tribesmen who met with Governor Thomas Kirker of Ohio, but in this instance he spoke in defense of his brother, convincing the governor that the Prophet and his movement were no threat to peace. Although primary materials from this period are full of references to the Prophet, almost none mention Tecumseh. Most accounts of Tecumseh's activities during these years are from the "reminiscences" of American observers recorded decades later.

Indeed, Tecumseh did not challenge the Prophet's position of leadership until 1810, two years after the move to Prophetstown and five years after the religious movement's beginnings. During 1808 Indians continued to flock to Prophetstown to see the holy man, not his brother; and in that year it was the Prophet, not Tecumseh, who met with Harrison at Vincennes. In the summer of 1808 Tecumseh did visit Malden seeking supplies for the Indians at Prophetstown, but he made no claims to leadership; and British accounts of the visit, which are quite specific in listing other Indians' names, refer to him only as "the Prophet's brother," not as Tecumseh, a chief among the Shawnees.

The springboard to Tecumseh's emergence was the Treaty of Fort Wayne. From Tecumseh's perspective it was obvious that the religious emphasis of his brother could no longer protect the remaining Indian land base. During the summer of 1809 he visited a few Indian villages in Illinois, but after the treaty Tecumseh took a new initiative and began to travel widely, emphasizing a political and military solution to the Indians' problems. The tribesmen should still adhere to the new religion, but they should abandon their old chiefs who remained friendly to the Americans. Instead, all warriors should politically unite under Tecumseh, for in his own words, "I am the head of them all. . . . I am alone the acknowledged chief of all the Indians."

Therefore, for two years—in 1810 and 1811—Tecumseh traveled extensively among the Indians of the West. During these years he met twice with Harrison, who reported to his superiors that Tecumseh now had emerged as "really the efficient man—the Moses of the family." In this period Tecumseh slowly eclipsed the Prophet's position of leadership, but ironically as the character of the Indian movement changed, its appeal to the tribesmen declined. In 1810 and 1811 parties of warriors recruited by Tecumseh temporarily joined the village at Prophetstown, but their numbers never approached the multitude of Indians who earlier had flocked to the Prophet. And although the Prophet no longer dominated the movement, he continued to exercise considerable influence. For example, his ability to convince his followers that they could easily obtain a victory over the Americans contributed to their ill-fated attack upon Harrison's forces at the Battle of the Tippecanoe in 1811. Obviously, after the battle the Prophet's influence was broken, and Tecumseh remained the dominant leader of the battered movement. But Tecumseh's preeminence was of short duration, for he was killed less than two years later, on October 5, 1813, at the Battle of the Thames.

It is evident, therefore, that the Prophet, not Tecumseh, was the most important figure in the emergence of the Indian movement prior to the War of 1812. Tecumseh used the widespread religious base earlier established by his brother as the foundation for his unsuccessful attempt to unite the tribes politically and militarily. Although the Prophet has been pictured as either a charlatan or a religious fanatic whose teachings seem quite bizarre, such an appraisal reflects an ethnocentric bias. He certainly seemed logical to the Indians, and for several years he exercised a widespread influence throughout the Old Northwest. In retrospect, such a phenomenon is not surprising. In times of oppression native American peoples have often turned to a religious deliverance. The Shawnee Prophet fits into a historical pattern exemplified by the Delaware Prophet, Handsome Lake, Wovoka and the Ghost Dance, and many others. Indeed, Tecumseh's emphasis upon political and military unification was much less typical than the Prophet's messianic nativism.

Why then has Tecumseh emerged as "the Greatest Indian"? The answer is obvious. If white Americans could design an "ideal Indian," they would have designed Tecumseh. His concepts of political and military unification under a centralized leadership appealed to whites because it was what *they* would have done. His solution had much less appeal to native Americans who had little tradition of either centralized leadership or of pan-Indian confederacies in response to American expansion. White Americans also praised Tecumseh's intervention in behalf of prisoners, but such intervention reflected European concepts of warfare more than those practiced by native Americans. Much of traditional Indian warfare was based upon vendetta, and prisoners expected the worst. Indeed, captured warriors took pride in their ability to withstand torture and laugh in the faces of their captors.

White Americans have championed Tecumseh because he, more than any other Indian, exemplifies the American or European concept of the "noble savage": brave, honest, a true "prince of the forest"—natural man at his best. Since his death, his American and British contemporaries and later historians have continued to embellish his memory with qualities and exploits that have added to his image. Many of the attributes and incidents were apocryphal (for example, his reputed love affair with the white woman Rebecca Galloway, or the assertion that his skin was of a lighter hue than other Indians'), but they only strengthened what Americans wanted to believe and have been incorporated into his biographies. Even his death added to the romantic appeal of the man. He fell, fighting to the last, in the Battle of the Thames—the red Armageddon. And his body was not among the dead on the field, but buried mysteriously by his followers in the forest. In contrast, the poor Prophet survived the war, was exiled in Canada, returned to the United States, was removed to the West, and in 1836 died an inglorious death in Kansas.

This reassessment does not mean that Tecumseh was not a remarkable man. Indeed, he was a brave and farsighted leader who sacrificed his life for his people. But the real Tecumseh stands on his own merits. He does not need the romantic embellishments of ethnocentric historians. Tragically, the Tecumseh who has emerged from the pages of history is, in many respects, a "white man's Indian."

◈ *FURTHER   READING*

Gary Anderson, "American Agents vs. British Traders: Prelude to the War of 1812 in the Far West," in Ronald Lora, ed., *The American West: Essays in Honor of W. Eugene Hollon* (1980)

Russel Lawrence Barsh, "The Nature and Spirit of North American Political Systems," *American Indian Quarterly* 10 (1986), 181–198

Michelle Daniel, "From Blood Feud to Jury System: The Metamorphosis of Cherokee Law from 1750 to 1840," *American Indian Quarterly* 11 (1987), 97–125

Richard Drinnon, "The Metaphysics of Empire-Building: American Imperialism in the Age of Jefferson and Monroe," *Massachusetts Review* 16 (1975), 666–688

R. David Edmunds, " 'Nothing Has Been Effected': The Vincennes Treaty of 1792," *Indiana Magazine of History* 74 (1978), 23–25

———, *The Shawnee Prophet* (1983)

———, *Tecumseh and the Quest for Indian Leadership* (1984)

Barbara Graymont, *The Iroquois in the American Revolution* (1972)

Michael D. Green, " 'We Dance in Opposite Directions: Mesquakie (Fox) Separatism from the Sac and Fox Tribe," *Ethnohistory* 30 (1983), 129–140

William T. Hagan, *Longhouse Diplomacy and Frontier Warfare: The Iroquois Confederacy in the American Revolution* (n. d.)

Joseph B. Herring, "Kenekuk, the Kickapoo Prophet: Acculturation Without Assimilation," *American Indian Quarterly* 9 (1985), 295–307

Reginald Horsman, *Expansion and American Indian Policy, 1783–1812* (1967)

Paul A. Hutton, "William Wells: Frontier Scout and Indian Agent," *Indiana Magazine of History* 74 (1978), 183–222

Bruce E. Johansen, *Forgotten Founders: How the American Indian Helped Shape Democracy* (1982)

Alvin M. Josephy, Jr., *The Patriot Chiefs* (1969)

Clara Sue Kidwell, "Choctaws and Missionaries in Mississippi Before 1830," *American Indian Culture and Research Journal* 11 (1987), 51–72

William G. McLoughlin, *Cherokees and Missionaries, 1789–1839* (1984)

———, "Thomas Jefferson and the Beginning of Cherokee Nationalism, 1806–1809," *William and Mary Quarterly* 32 (1975), 547–580

Edwin C. McReynolds, *The Seminoles* (1957)

Peter C. Mancall, "The Revolutionary War and the Indians of the Upper Susquehanna Valley," *American Indian Culture and Research Journal* 12 (1988), 39–57

James H. O'Donnell III, *Southern Indians in the American Revolution* (1973)

Frank L. Owsley, Jr., "Prophet of War: Josiah Francis and the Creek War," *American Indian Quarterly* 9 (1985), 273–293

———, *Struggle for the Gulf Borderlands: The Creek War and the Battle of New Orleans, 1812–1815* (1981)

Francis Paul Prucha, *American Indian Policy in the Formative Years: The Indian Trade and Intercourse Acts, 1790–1834* (1962)

Bernard W. Sheehan, *Seeds of Extinction: Jeffersonian Philanthropy and the American Indian* (1973)

Jack M. Sosin, *The Revolutionary Frontier, 1763–1783* (1967)

Craig Symonds, "The Failure of America's Indian Policy on the Southwestern Frontier, 1785–1793," *Tennessee Historical Quarterly* 35 (1976), 29–45

Anthony F. C. Wallace, *The Death and Rebirth of the Seneca* (1970)

———, "Prelude to Disaster: The Course of Indian-White Relations Which Led to the Black Hawk War of 1832," in Ruth M. Whitney, comp. and ed., *The Black Hawk War, 1831–1832* (1970)

Richard White, *The Middle Ground: Indians, Empires, and Republics in the Great Lakes Region, 1650–1815* (1991)

J. Leitch Wright, Jr., *Britain and the American Frontier, 1783–1815* (1975)

———, *The Only Land They Knew: The Tragic Story of the American Indians in the Old South* (1981)

Mary C. Wright, "Economic Development and Native American Women in the Early Nineteenth Century," *American Quarterly* 33 (1981), 525–535

CHAPTER

6

Indian Removal:

The Dilemma of Indian Policy

in the Early Republic

In the early nineteenth century, white Americans advanced rapidly westward beyond the Appalachian Mountains. Expansion put new pressure on western tribes
and in the East created islands of Indian territory within states. In some instances, as
with the Cherokees in Georgia, the Indians made every effort to accommodate to
white society. In the Cherokees' case, the Indian initiatives did not satisfy white Georgians, who demanded that the federal government remove the tribe. In response, the
Cherokees and their white supporters argued that the national government should
support the Indians in the peaceful possession of their homeland.

The debate came to a head during the presidency of Andrew Jackson, who sided
with the state of Georgia. The federal government responded by moving the Cherokees west to the Indian Territory (present-day Oklahoma). Several thousand Cherokees died on the way to their new homes; the Cherokees fittingly commemorate this
tragedy as their "Trail of Tears." The Cherokee experience foreshadowed the fate of
many other Indians who would be leaving ancestral lands for a new home in the
West. Federal officials hoped that removal could be accomplished peacefully, but
sometimes bloody conflicts erupted. In the Illinois country, the brief Black Hawk
War (1832) pitted disgruntled Sac and Fox tribes against the U.S. Army and Illinois
militia-men, who were determined to push the Indians across the Mississippi River.
In Florida, the Seminole War dragged on from 1835 to 1842, causing embarrassment to the Jackson administration and the U.S. Army, but this war failed to completely subdue or remove the Seminoles. Historians have argued about the merits of
Indian removal ever since.

◈ *D O C U M E N T S*

Indian removal was an issue hotly debated among both Indians and whites. Land-
hungry whites, of course, made no bones about their desire for Indian lands and paid little attention to legal and moral niceties. Other whites held reasoned and principled posi-

206

tions on both sides of the argument. Indians were not unanimous in their opinions about removal. Many staunchly opposed relocation; others concluded that they would not be secure until they moved away from white influence.

In the first document, Commissioner of Indian Affairs Thomas L. McKenney briefly summarizes the problem in 1828. In the second selection, dating from 1829, President Jackson sets forth a rationale and a basic plan for Indian removal. In the third document, Speckled Snake, a Cherokee, ridicules Jackson's declarations of sympathy for the Indians. The fourth document presents the opinion of Cherokee newspaperman Elias Boudinot, editor of the Cherokee *Phoenix*. Boudinot, educated in New England schools and married to a white woman, criticized removal at first but finally came to believe that removal was necessary to save the Cherokee nation. Nevertheless, many Cherokees remained firmly opposed. After the Cherokees had moved to their new home, foes of removal killed Boudinot and other Indians who had signed the removal treaty.

Indian Commissioner, Thomas L. McKenney Explains Removal, 1828

. . . I forbear also to remark, except briefly, upon measures of general policy in regard to our Indians. The subject is growing in interest every day, and is surpassed only by the extreme delicacy of their situation, and of our relations with them. I refer especially to those whose territory is embraced by the limits of States. Every feeling of sympathy for their lot should be kept alive, and fostered; and no measures taken that could compromit [compromise] the humanity and justice of the nation; and none, I am sure, will be. But the question occurs—*What are humanity and justice in reference to this unfortunate race?* Are these found to lie in a policy that would leave them to linger out a wretched and degraded existence, within districts of country already surrounded and pressed upon by a population whose anxiety and efforts to get rid of them are not less restless and persevering, than is that law of nature immutable, which has decreed, that, under such circumstances, if continued in, *they must perish?* Or does it not rather consist in withdrawing them from this certain destruction, and placing them, though even at this late hour, in a situation where, by the adoption of a suitable system for their security, preservation, and improvement, and at no matter what cost, they may be saved and blest? What *the means* are which are best fitted to realize such a triumph of humanity, I leave to be determined upon by those who are more competent than I am to decide. But that something must be done, and done soon, to save these people, if saved at all, it requires no very deep research into the history of the past, or knowledge of their present condition, embracing especially their relation to the States, to see.

President Andrew Jackson Favors Removal, 1829

. . . The condition and ulterior destiny of the Indian tribes within the limits of some of our States have become objects of much interest and importance. It has long been the policy of Government to introduce among them the arts of civilization, in the hope of gradually reclaiming them from a wandering life. This policy has, however, been coupled with another wholly incompatible with its success. Professing a desire to civilize and settle them, we have at the same time lost no opportunity to purchase their lands and thrust them farther into the wilderness. By this means they have not only been kept in a wandering state, but been led to look upon us as unjust and indifferent to their fate. Thus, though lavish in its expenditures upon the subject, Government has constantly defeated its own policy, and the Indians in general, receding farther and farther to the west, have retained their savage habits. A portion, however, of the Southern tribes, having mingled much with the whites and made some progress in the arts of civilized life, have lately attempted to erect an independent government within the limits of Georgia and Alabama. These States, claiming to be the only sovereigns within their territories, extended their laws over the Indians, which induced the latter to call upon the United States for protection.

Under these circumstances the question presented was whether the General Government had a right to sustain those people in their pretensions. The Constitution declares that "no new State shall be formed or erected within the jurisdiction of any other State" without the consent of its legislature. If the General Government is not permitted to tolerate the erection of a confederate State within the territory of one of the members of this Union against her consent, much less could it allow a foreign and independent government to establish itself there. Georgia became a member of the Confederacy which eventuated in our Federal Union as a sovereign State, always asserting her claim to certain limits, which, having been originally defined in her colonial charter and subsequently recognized in the treaty of peace, she has ever since continued to enjoy, except as they have been circumscribed by her own voluntary transfer of a portion of her territory to the United States in the articles of cession of 1802. Alabama was admitted into the Union on the same footing with the original States, with boundaries which were prescribed by Congress. There is no constitutional, conventional, or legal provision which allows them less power over the Indians within their borders than is possessed by Maine or New York. Would the people of Maine permit the Penobscot tribe to erect an independent government within their State? And unless they did would it not be the duty of the General Government to support them in resisting such a measure? Would the people of New York permit each remnant of the Six Nations within her borders to declare itself an independent people under the protection of the United States? Could the Indians establish a separate republic on each of their reservations in Ohio? And if they were so disposed would it be the duty of this Government to protect them in the attempt? If the principle involved in the obvious answer to these questions be abandoned, it will follow that the objects of this Government are reversed, and that it has become a part of its duty to aid in destroying the States which it was established to protect.

Actuated by this view of the subject, I informed the Indians inhabiting parts of Georgia and Alabama that their attempt to establish an independent government would not be countenanced by the Executive of the United States, and advised them to emigrate beyond the Mississippi or submit to the laws of those States.

Our conduct toward these people is deeply interesting to our national character. Their present condition, contrasted with what they once were, makes a most powerful appeal to our sympathies. Our ancestors found them the uncontrolled possessors of these vast regions. By persuasion and force they have been made to retire from river to river and from mountain to mountain, until some of the tribes have become extinct and others have left but remnants to preserve for a while their once terrible names. Surrounded by the whites with their arts of civilization, which by destroying the resources of the savage doom him to weakness and decay, the fate of the Mohegan, the Narragansett, and the Delaware is fast overtaking the Choctaw, the Cherokee, and the Creek. That this fate surely awaits them if they remain within the limits of the States does not admit of a doubt. Humanity and national honor demand that every effort should be made to avert so great a calamity. It is too late to inquire whether it was just in the United States to include them and their territory within the bounds of new States, whose limits they could control. That step can not be retraced. A State can not be dismembered by Congress or restricted in the exercise of her constitutional power. But the people of those States and of every State, actuated by feelings of justice and a regard for our national honor, submit to you the interesting question whether something can not be done, consistently with the rights of the States, to preserve this much-injured race.

As a means of effecting this end I suggest for your consideration the propriety of setting apart an ample district west of the Mississippi, and without the limit of any State or Territory now formed, to be guaranteed to the Indian tribes as long as they shall occupy it, each tribe having a distinct control over the portion designated for its use. There they may be secured in the enjoyment of governments of their own choice, subject to no other control from the United States than such as may be necessary to preserve peace on the frontier and between the several tribes. There the benevolent may endeavor to teach them the arts of civilization, and, by promoting union and harmony among them, to raise up an interesting commonwealth, destined to perpetuate the race and to attest the humanity and justice of this Government.

This emigration should be voluntary, for it would be as cruel as unjust to compel the aborigines to abandon the graves of their fathers and seek a home in a distant land. But they should be distinctly informed that if they remain within the limits of the States they must be subject to their laws. In return for their obedience as individuals they will without doubt be protected in the enjoyment of those possessions which they have improved by their industry. But it seems to me visionary to suppose that in this state of things claims can be allowed on tracts of country on which they have neither dwelt nor made improvements, merely because they have seen them from the mountain or passed them in the chase. Submitting to the laws of the States, and receiving, like other citizens, protection in their persons and property, they will ere long become merged in the mass of our population. . . .

Speckled Snake's (Cherokee) Reply to President Jackson, 1830

Brothers! We have heard the talk of our great father; it is very kind. He says he loves his red children. *Brothers!* When the white man first came to these shores, the Muscogees gave him land, and kindled him a fire to make him comfortable; and when the pale faces of the south made war on him, their young men drew the tomahawk, and protected his head from the scalping knife. But when the white man had warmed himself before the Indian's fire, and filled himself with the Indian's hominy, he became very large; he stopped not for the mountain tops, and his feet covered the plains and the valleys. His hands grasped the eastern and the western sea. Then he became our great father. He loved his red children; but said, "You must move a little farther, lest I should, by accident, tread on you." With one foot he pushed the red man over the Oconee [River], and with the other he trampled down the graves of his fathers. But our great father still loved his red children, and he soon made them another talk. He said much; but it all meant nothing, but "move a little farther; you are too near me." I heard a great many talks from our great father, and they all begun and ended the same, *Brothers!* When he made us a talk on a former occasion, he said, "Get a little farther; go beyond the Oconee and the Oakmulgee [River]; there is a pleasant country." He also said, "It shall be yours forever." Now he says, "The land you live on is not yours; go beyond the Mississippi; there is game; there you may remain while the grass grows or the water runs." *Brothers!* Will not our great father come there also? He loves his red children, and his tongue is not forked.

Cherokee Editor Elias Boudinot Opposes Removal, 1828

. . . Our last Washington papers contain a debate which took place in the house of representatives, on the resolution, recommended by the Committee on Indian Affairs, published in the second Number of our paper. It appears that the advocates of this new system of civilizing the Indians are very strenuous in maintaining the novel opinion, that it is impossible to enlighten the Indians, surrounded as they are by the white population, and that they assuredly will become extinct, unless they are removed. It is a fact which we would not deny, that many tribes have perished away in consequence of white population, but we are yet to be convinced that this will always be the case, in spite of every measure taken to civilize them. We contend that suitable measures to a sufficient extent have never been employed. And how dare these men make an assertion without sufficient evidence? What proof have they that the system which they are now recommending, will succeed? Where have we an example in the whole history of man, of a Nation or tribe, removing in a body, from a land of civil and religious means, to a perfect wilderness, *in order to be civilized.* We are fearful these men are building castles in the air, whose fall will crush those poor Indians who may be so blinded as to make the experiment. We are sorry to see that some of the advocates of this system speak so disrespectfully, if not contemptuously, of the present measures of improvement, now in successful operation among most of the Indians in the United States—the only measures too, which have been crowned with success, and bid fair to meliorate the condition of the Aborigines. . . .

⟨◈⟩ *E S S A Y S*

The debate over Indian removal continues to this day. Some historians argue that removal was unnecessary, cruel, and immoral, whereas others believe that under the circumstances, it was the only realistic option. The historian Francis Paul Prucha, professor emeritus at Marquette University, argues that President Jackson had little choice but to remove Indians from eastern states. The chief executive's power to protect Indians was limited, and Indians would surely have suffered if they had been permitted to remain where they were. Historian Mary Young of the University of Rochester is less generous in her opinion of Jackson and the removal policy. She argues in the second essay that Cherokee history tells us much about the early republic, its values, and its shortcomings. Considering the political climate and the dominant racial attitudes of the early nineteenth century, could Jackson—or any other president, for that matter—have protected Indians who lived amid whites determined to have Indian lands? What choices did the Cherokees have?

Andrew Jackson's Indian Policy: A Reassessment

FRANCIS PAUL PRUCHA

A great many persons—not excluding some notable historians—have adopted a "devil theory" of American Indian policy. And in their demonic hierarchy Andrew Jackson has first place. He is depicted primarily, if not exclusively, as a western frontiersman and famous Indian fighter, who was a zealous advocate of dispossessing the Indians and at heart an "Indian-hater." When he became President, the story goes, he made use of his new power, ruthlessly and at the point of a bayonet, to force the Indians from their ancestral homes in the East into desert lands west of the Mississippi, which were considered forever useless to the white man.

This simplistic view of Jackson's Indian policy is unacceptable. It was not Jackson's aim to crush the Indians because, as an old Indian-fighter, he hated Indians. Although his years in the West had brought him into frequent contact with the Indians, he by no means developed a doctrinaire anti-Indian attitude. Rather, as a military man, his dominant goal in the decades before he became President was to preserve the security and well-being of the United States and its Indian and white inhabitants. His military experience, indeed, gave him an overriding concern for the safety of the nation from foreign rather than internal enemies, and to some extent the anti-Indian sentiment that has been charged against Jackson in his early career was instead basically anti-British. Jackson, as his first biographer pointed out, had "many private reasons for disliking" Great Britain. "In her, he could trace the efficient cause, why, in early life, he had been left forlorn and wretched, without a single relation in the world." His frontier experience, too, had convinced him that foreign agents were behind the raised tomahawks of the red men. In 1808, after a group of settlers had been killed by the Creeks, Jackson told his militia troops: "[T]his brings to our recollection the horrid barbarity committed on our frontier in 1777 under the influence of and by the orders of Great Britain, and it is presumeable that the same influence has excited those barbarians to the late and recent acts of butchery and murder. . . ." From that date on there is hardly a statement by Jackson about Indian dangers that does not aim sharp barbs at England. His reaction to the Battle of Tippecanoe was that the Indians had been "excited to war by the secrete agents of Great Britain."

Jackson's war with the Creeks in 1813–1814, which brought him his first

"Andrew Jackson's Indian Policy: A Reassessment," by Francis Paul Prucha, *Journal of American History* 56 (December 1969), pp. 527–539. Reprinted by permission of the publisher.

national military fame, and his subsequent demands for a large cession of Creek lands were part of his concern for security in the West. In 1815, when the Cherokees and Chickasaws gave up their overlapping claims to lands within the Creek cession, Jackson wrote with some exultation to Secretary of War James Monroe: "This Territory added to the creek cession, opens an avenue to the defence of the lower country, in a political point of view incalculable." A few months later he added: "The sooner these lands are brought into markett, [the sooner] a permanant security will be given to what, I deem, the most important, as well as the most vulnarable part of the union. This country once settled, our fortifications of defence in the lower country compleated, all [E]urope will cease to look at it with an eye to conquest. There is no other point of the union (america united) that combined [E]urope can expect to invade with success."

Jackson's plans with regard to the Indians in Florida were governed by similar principles of security. He wanted "to concentrate and locate the F[lorida] Indians at such a point as will promote their happiness and prosperity and at the same time, afford to that Territory a dense population between them and the ocean which will afford protection and peace to all." On later occasions the same views were evident. When negotiations were under way with the southern Indians for removal, Jackson wrote "[T]he chickasaw and choctaw country are of great importance to us in the defence of the lower country[;] a white population instead of the Indian, would strengthen our own defence much." And again: "This section of country is of great importance to the prosperity and strength of the lower Mississippi[;] a dense white population would add much to its safety in a state of war, and it ought to be obtained, if it can, on any thing like reasonable terms."

In his direct dealings with the Indians, Jackson insisted on justice toward both hostile and peaceful Indians. Those who committed outrages against the whites were to be summarily punished, but the rights of friendly Indians were to be protected. Too much of Jackson's reputation in Indian matters has been based on the first of these positions. Forthright and hard-hitting, he adopted a no-nonsense policy toward hostile Indians that endeared him to the frontiersmen. For example, when a white woman was taken captive by the Creeks, he declared: "With such arms and supplies as I can obtain I shall penetrate the creek Towns, untill the Captive, with her Captors are delivered up, and think myself Justifiable, in laying waste their villages, burning their houses, killing their warriors and leading into Captivity their wives and children, untill I do obtain a surrender of the Captive, and the Captors." In his general orders to the Tennessee militia after he received news of the Fort Mims massacre, he called for "retaliatory vengeance" against the "inhuman blood thirsty barbarians." He could speak of the "lex taliones," [law of compensation in kind; for example, revenge] and his aggressive campaign against the Creeks and his escapade in Florida in the First Seminole War are further indications of his mood.

But he matched this attitude with one of justice and fairness, and he was firm in upholding the rights of the Indians who lived peaceably in friendship with the Americans. One of his official acts as major general of the Tennessee militia was to insist on the punishment of a militia officer who instigated or at least permitted the murder of an Indian. On another occasion, when a group of Tennessee volunteers robbed a friendly Cherokee, Jackson's wrath burst forth: "that a sett of men should without any authority rob a man who is claimed as a member of the Cherokee nation, who is now friendly and engaged with us in a war against the hostile creeks, is such an outrage, to the rules of war, the laws of nations and of civil society, and well calculated to sower the minds of the whole nation against the united States, and is such as ought to meet with the frowns of every good citizen, and the agents by promptly prosecuted and punished as robers." It was, he said, as much theft as though the property had been stolen from a white citizen. He demanded an inquiry in order to determine whether any commissioned officers had been present or had had any knowledge of this "atrocious act," and he wanted the officers immediately arrested, tried by court-martial, and then turned over to the civil authority.

Again, during the Seminole War, when Georgia troops attacked a village of friendly Indians, Jackson excoriated the governor for "the base, cowardly and inhuman attack, on the old woman [women] and men of the chehaw village, whilst the Warriors of that *village* was with me, fighting the battles of our *country* against the common enemy." It was strange, he said, "that there could exist within the U. States, a cowardly monster in human shape, that could violate the sanctity of a flag, when borne by any person, but more particularly when in the hands of a superanuated Indian chief worn down with age. Such base cowardice and murderous conduct as this transaction affords, has not its paralel in history and should meet with its merited punishment." Jackson ordered the arrest of the officer who was responsible and declared: "This act will to the last ages fix a stain upon the character of Georgia."

Jackson's action as commander of the Division of the South in removing white squatters from Indian lands is another proof that he was not oblivious to Indian rights. When the Indian Agent Return J. Meigs in 1820 requested military assistance in removing intruders on Cherokee lands, Jackson ordered a detachment of twenty men under a lieutenant to aid in the removal. After learning that the officer detailed for the duty was "young and inexperienced," he sent his own aide-de-camp, Captain Richard K. Call, to assume command of the troops and execute the order of removal. "Captain Call informs me," he wrote in one report to Secretary of War John C. Calhoun, "that much noise of opposition was threatened, and men collected for the purpose who seperated on the approach of the regulars, but who threaten to destroy the cherokees in the Valley as soon as these Troops are gone. Capt. Call has addressed a letter to those infatuated people, with assurance of speedy and exemplary punishment if they should attempt to carry their threats into execution." Later he wrote that Call had performed his duties "with both judgement, and prudence and much to the interest of the Cherokee-Nation" and that the action would "have the effect in future of preventing the infraction of our Treaties with that Nation."

To call Jackson an Indian-hater or to declare that he believed that "the only good Indian is a dead Indian" is to speak in terms that had little meaning to Jackson. It is true, of course, that he did not consider the Indians to be noble savages. He had, for example, a generally uncomplimentary view of their motivation, and he argued that it was necessary to operate upon their fears, rather than on some higher motive. Thus, in 1812 he wrote: "I believe self interest and self preservation the most predominant passion. [F]ear is better than love with an indian."

Twenty-five years later, just after he left the presidency, the same theme recurred; and he wrote: "Long experience satisfies me that they are only to be well governed by their fears. If we feed their avarice we accelerate the causes of their destruction. By a prudent exertion of our military power we may yet do something to alleviate their condition at the same time that we certainly take from them the means of injury to our frontier."

Yet Jackson did not hold that Indians were inherently evil or inferior. He eagerly used Indian allies, personally liked and respected individual Indian chiefs, and, when (in the Creek campaign) an orphaned Indian boy was about to be killed by Indians upon whom his care would fall, generously took care of the child and sent him home to Mrs. Jackson to be raised with his son Andrew. Jackson was convinced that the barbaric state in which he encountered most Indians had to change, but he was also convinced that the change was possible and to an extent inevitable if the Indians were to survive.

Much of Jackson's opinion about the status of the Indians was governed by his firm conviction that they did not constitute sovereign nations, who could be dealt with in formal treaties as though they were foreign powers. That the United States in fact did so, Jackson argued, was a historical fact which resulted from the feeble position of the new American government when it first faced the Indians during and immediately after the Revolution. To continue to deal with the Indians in this fashion, when the power of the United States no longer made it necessary, was to Jackson's mind absurd. It was high time, he said in 1820, to do away with the "farce of treating with Indian tribes." Jackson wanted Congress to legislate for the Indians as it did for white Americans.

From this view of the limited political status of the Indians within the territorial United States, Jackson derived two important corollaries. One denied that the Indians had absolute title to all the lands that they claimed. The United States, in justice, should allow the Indians ample lands for their support, but Jackson did not believe that they were entitled to more. He denied any right of domain and ridiculed the Indian claims to "tracts of country on which they have neither dwelt nor made improvements, merely because they have seen them from the mountain or passed them in the chase."

A second corollary of equal import was Jackson's opinion that the Indians could not establish independent enclaves (exercising full political sovereignty) within the United States or within any of the individual states. If their proper status was as subjects of the United States, then they should be obliged to submit to American laws. Jackson had reached this conclusion early in his career, but his classic statement appeared in his first annual message to Congress, at a time when the conflict between the Cherokees and the State of Georgia had reached crisis proportions. "If the General Government is not permitted to tolerate the erection of a confederate State within the territory of one of the members of this Union against her consent," he said, "much less could it allow a foreign and independent government to establish itself there." He announced that he had told the Indians that "their attempt to establish an independent government would not be countenanced by the Executive of the United States, and advised them to emigrate beyond the Mississippi or submit to the laws of those States." "I have been unable to perceive any sufficient reason," Jackson affirmed, "why the Red man more than the white, may claim exemption from the municipal laws of the state within which they reside; and governed by that belief, I have so declared and so acted."

Jackson's own draft of this first annual message presents a more personal view than the final public version and gives some insight into his reasoning. He wrote:

> The policy of the government has been gradually to open to them the ways of civilisation; and from their wandering habits, to entice them to a course of life calculated to present fairer prospects of comfort and happiness. To effect this a system should be devised for their benefit, kind and liberal, and gradually to be enlarged as they may evince a capability to enjoy it. It will not answer to encourage them to the idea of exclusive self government. It is impracticable. No people were ever free, or capable of forming and carrying into execution a social compact for themselves until education and intelligence was first introduced. There are with those tribes, a few educated and well informed men, possessing mind and Judgment, and capable of conducting public affairs to advantage; but observation proves that the great body of the southern tribes of Indians, are erratic in their habits, and wanting in those endowments, which are suited to a people who would direct themselves, and under it be happy and prosperous.

Jackson was convinced from his observation of the political incompetence of the general run of Indians that the treaty system played into the hands of the chiefs and their white and half-breed advisers to the detriment of the common Indians. He said on one occasion that such leaders "are like some of our bawling politicians, who loudly exclaim we are the friends of the people, but who, when the[y] obtain their views care no more for the happiness or wellfare of the people than the Devil does—but each procure[s] influence through the same channell and for the same base purpose, *self-agrandisement.*"

Jackson was genuinely concerned for the well-being of the Indians and for their civilization. Although his critics would scoff at the idea of placing him on the roll of the humanitarians, his assertions—both public and private—add up to a consistent belief that the Indians were capable of accepting white civilization, the hope that they would eventually do so, and repeated efforts to take measures that would make the change possible and even speed it along.

His vision appears in the proclamation delivered to his victorious troops in April 1814, after the Battle of Horseshoe Bend on the Tallapoosa River. "The fiends of the Tallapoosa will no longer murder our Women and Children, or disturb the quiet of our borders," he declared. "Their midnight flambeaux will no more illumine their Council house, or shine upon the victim of their infernal orgies. They have disappeared from the face of the Earth. In their places a new generation will arise who will know their duties better. The weapons of warefare will be exchanged for the utensils of husbandry; and the wilderness which now withers in sterility and seems to mourn the disolation which overspreads it, will blossom as the rose, and become the nursery of the arts."

The removal policy, begun long before Jackson's presidency but wholeheartedly adopted by him, was the culmination of these views. Jackson looked upon removal as a means of protecting the process of civilization, as well as of providing land for white settlers, security from foreign invasion, and a quieting of the clamors of Georgia against the federal government. This view is too pervasive in Jackson's thought to be dismissed as polite rationalization for avaricious white aggrandizement. His outlook was essentially Jeffersonian. Jackson envisaged the transition from a hunting society to a settled agricultural society, a process that would make it possible for the Indians to exist with a higher scale of living on less land, and which would make it possible for those who adopted white ways to be quietly absorbed into the white society. Those who wished to preserve their identity in Indian nations could do it only by withdrawing from the economic and political pressures exerted upon their enclaves by the dominant white settlers. West of the Mississippi they might move at their own pace toward civilization.

Evaluation of Jackson's policy must be made in the light of the feasible alternatives available to men of this time. The removal program cannot be judged simply as a land grab to satisfy the President's western and southern constituents. The Indian problem that Jackson faced was complex, and various solutions were proposed. There were, in fact, four possibilities.

First, the Indians could simply have been destroyed. They could have been killed in war, mercilessly hounded out of their settlements, or pushed west off the land by brute force, until they were destroyed by disease or starvation. It is not too harsh a judgment to say that this was implicitly, if not explicitly, the policy of many of the aggressive frontiersmen. But it was not the policy, implicit or explicit, of Jackson and the responsible government officials in his administration or of those preceding or following his. It would be easy to compile an anthology of statements of horror on the part of government officials toward any such approach to the solution of the Indian problem.

Second, the Indians could have been rapidly assimilated into white society. It is now clear that this was not a feasible solution. Indian culture has a viability that continually impresses anthropologists, and to become white men was not the goal of the Indians. But many important and learned men of the day thought that this was a possibility. Some were so sanguine as to hope that within one generation the Indians could be taught the white man's ways and that, once they learned them, they would automatically desire to turn to that sort of life. Thomas Jefferson never tired of telling the Indians of the advantages of farming over hunting, and the chief purpose of schools was to train the Indian children in white ways, thereby making them immediately absorbable into the dominant culture. This solution was at first the hope of humanitarians who had the interest of the Indians at heart, but little by little many came to agree with Jackson that this dream was not going to be fulfilled.

Third, if the Indians were not to be destroyed and if they could not be immediately assimilated, they might be protected in their own culture on their ancestral lands in the East—or, at least, on reasonably large remnants of those lands. They would then be enclaves within the white society and would be protected by their treaty agreements and by military force. This was the alternative demanded by the opponents of Jackson's removal bill—for example, the missionaries of the American Board of Commissioners for Foreign Missions. But this, too, was infeasible, given the political and military conditions of the United States at the time. The federal government could not have provided a standing army of sufficient strength to protect the enclaves of Indian territory from the encroachments of the whites. Jackson could not withstand Georgia's demand for the end of the *imperium in imperio* [nation within a nation] represented by the Cherokee Nation and its new constitution, not because of some inherent immorality on his part but because the political situation of America would not permit it.

The jurisdictional dispute cannot be easily dismissed. Were the Indian tribes independent nations? The question received its legal answer in John Marshall's decision in *Cherokee Nation* v. *Georgia,* in which the chief justice defined the Indian tribes as "dependent domestic nations." But aside from the juridical decision, were the Indians, in fact, independent, and could they have maintained their independence without the support—political and military—of the federal government? The answer, clearly, is no, as writers at the time pointed out. The federal government could have stood firm in defense of the Indian nations against Georgia, but this would have brought it into head-on collision with a state, which insisted that its sovereignty was being impinged upon by the Cherokees.

This was not a conflict that anyone in the federal government wanted. President Monroe had been slow to give in to the demands of the Georgians. He had refused to be panicked into hasty action before he had considered all the possibilities. But eventually he became convinced that a stubborn resistance to the southern states would solve nothing, and from that point on he and his successors, John Quincy Adams and Jackson, sought to solve the problem by removing the cause. They wanted the Indians to be placed in some area where the problem of federal versus state jurisdiction would not arise, where the Indians could be granted land in fee simple [unencumbered ownership] by the federal government and not have to worry about what some state thought were its rights and prerogatives.

The fourth and final possibility, then, was removal. To Jackson this seemed the only answer. Since neither adequate protection nor quick assimilation of the Indians was possible, it seemed reasonable and necessary to move the Indians to some area where they would not be disturbed by federal-state jurisdictional disputes or by encroachments of white settlers, where they could develop on the road to civilization at their own pace, or, if they so desired, preserve their own culture.

To ease the removal process Jackson proposed what he repeatedly described as—and believed to be—*liberal* terms. He again and again urged the commissioners who made treaties to pay the Indians well for their lands, to make sure that the Indians understood that the government would pay the costs of removal and help them get established in their new homes, to make provision for the Indians to examine the lands in the West and to agree to accept them before they were allotted. When he read the treaty negotiated with the Chickasaws in 1832, he wrote to his old friend General John Coffee, one of the commissioners: "I think it is a good one, and surely the religious enthusiasts, or those who have been weeping over the oppression of the Indians will not find fault with it for want of liberality or justice to the Indians." Typical of his views was his letter to Captain James Gadsden in 1829:

> You may rest assured that I shall adhere to the just and humane policy towards the Indians which I have commenced. In this spirit I have recommended them to quit their possessions on this side of the Mississippi, and go to a country to the west where

there is every probability that they will always be free from the mercenary influence of White men, and undisturbed by the local authority of the states: Under such circumstances the General Government can exercise a parental control over their interests and possibly perpetuate their race.

The idea of parental or paternal care was pervasive. Jackson told Congress in a special message in February 1832: "Being more and more convinced that the destiny of the Indians within the settled portion of the United States depends upon their entire and speedy migration to the country west of the Mississippi set apart for their permanent residence, I am anxious that all the arrangements necessary to the complete execution of the plan of removal and to the ultimate security and improvement of the Indians should be made without further delay." Once removal was accomplished, "there would then be no question of jurisdiction to prevent the Government from exercising such a general control over their affairs as may be essential to their interest and safety."

Jackson, in fact, thought in terms of a confederacy of the southern Indians in the West, developing their own territorial government which should be on a par with the territories of the whites and eventually take its place in the Union. This aspect of the removal policy, because it was not fully implemented, has been largely forgotten.

In the bills reported in 1834 for the reorganization of Indian affairs there was, in addition to a new trade and intercourse act and an act for the reorganization of the Indian Office, a bill "for the establishment of the Western Territory, and for the security and protection of the emigrant and other Indian tribes therein." This was quashed, not by western interests who might be considered hostile to the Indians, but by men like John Quincy Adams, who did not like the technical details of the bill and who feared loss of eastern power and prestige by the admission of territories in the West.

Jackson continued to urge Congress to fulfill its obligations to the Indians who had removed. In his eighth annual message, in December 1836, he called attention "to the importance of providing a well-digested and comprehensive system for the protection, supervision, and improvement of the various tribes now planted in the Indian country." He strongly backed the suggestions of the commissioner of Indian affairs and the secretary of war for developing a confederated Indian government in the West and for establishing military posts in the Indian country to protect the tribes. "The best hopes of humanity in regard to the aboriginal race, the welfare of our rapidly extending settlements, and the honor of the United States," he said, "are all deeply involved in the relations existing between this Government and the emigrating tribes."

Jackson's Indian policy occasioned great debate and great opposition during his administration. This is not to be wondered at. The "Indian problem" was a complicated and emotion-filled subject, and it called forth tremendous efforts on behalf of the Indians by some missionary groups and other humanitarians, who spoke loudly about Indian rights. The issue also became a party one.

The hue and cry raised against removal in Jackson's administration should not be misinterpreted. At the urging of the American Board of Commissioners for Foreign Missions, hundreds of church groups deluged Congress with memorials condemning the removal policy as a violation of Indian rights; and Jeremiah Evarts, the secretary of the Board, wrote a notable series of essays under the name "William Penn," which asserted that the original treaties must be maintained. It is not without interest that such opposition was centered in areas that were politically hostile to Jackson. There were equally sincere and humanitarian voices speaking out in support of removal, and they were supported by men such as Thomas L. McKenney, head of the Indian Office; William Clark, superintendent of Indian affairs at St. Louis; Lewis Cass, who had served on the frontier for eighteen years as governor of Michigan Territory; and the Baptist missionary Isaac McCoy—all men with long experience in Indian relations and deep sympathy for the Indians.

Jackson himself had no doubt that his policy was in the best interests of the Indians. "Toward this race of people I entertain the kindest feelings," he told the Senate in 1831, "and am not sensible that the views which I have taken of their true interests are less favorable to them than those which oppose their emigration to the West." The policy of rescuing the Indians from the evil effects of too-close contact with white civilization, so that in the end they too might become civilized, received a final benediction in Jackson's last message to the American people—his "Farewell Address" of March 4, 1837. "The States which had so long been retarded in their improvement by the Indian tribes residing in the midst of them are at length relieved from the evil," he said, "and this unhappy race—the original dwellers in our land—are now placed in a situation where we may well hope that they will share in the blessings of civilization and be saved from that degradation and destruction to which they were rapidly hastening while they remained in the States; and while the safety and comfort of our own citizens have been greatly promoted by their removal, the philanthropist will rejoice that the remnant of that ill-fated race has been at length placed beyond the reach of injury or oppression, and that the paternal care of the General Government will hereafter watch over them and protect them."

In assessing Jackson's Indian policy, historians must not listen too eagerly to Jackson's political opponents or to less-than-disinterested missionaries. Jackson's contemporary critics and the historians who have accepted their arguments have certainly been too harsh, if not, indeed, quite wrong.

The Cherokee Nation: Mirror of the Republic

MARY YOUNG

In the early nineteenth century, the United States government through its own agents and through federally subsidized missionaries undertook an ambitious and comprehensive effort to change the economy, institutions, and culture of the Cherokee Indian Nation. By 1830, substantial change had occurred. The Cherokee had schools, churches, plantations, slaves, and a written language,

"The Cherokee Nation: Mirror of the Republic," by Mary Young, *American Quarterly* 33 (1981), pp. 502–524. Reprinted by permission of the Johns Hopkins University Press.

newspaper, and constitution. At precisely that point, President Andrew Jackson encouraged the state of Georgia to extend its jurisdiction over the most populous part of the Cherokee Nation. By both action and inaction, the federal executive abetted thousands of trespassers who violated both United States treaties guaranteeing protection of Cherokee borders and a Supreme Court decision upholding treaty guarantees against the sovereign pretensions of the state of Georgia. The president and his War Department fostered a small faction of the tribe who, in 1835, signed the Treaty of New Echota, ceding Cherokee holdings in Georgia, North Carolina, Tennessee, and Alabama, and promising to remove the Cherokee people to present-day Oklahoma. The vast majority of the tribe rejected the Treaty, whose signers possessed no authority under the Cherokee constitution. In 1838, volunteer militia under federal command expelled approximately 16,000 Cherokee from their lands. They rode, walked, sickened, and died along the Trail of Tears to the Cherokee Nation West. After those who survived had settled in the West, earlier migrants or "Old Settlers," those who had participated in the Treaty of New Echota, and the new arrivals from the Cherokee Nation East struggled violently over who should control the government of the still "civilized" but deeply divided Nation.

As often as their story has been told, the Cherokee experiment in building and defending a modern Nation still evokes varied and conflicting interpretations. How "civilized"—or acculturated—were the Cherokee of the 1830s? Did the transformation of their social and political institutions represent "progress" in the sense of more effective defense of traditional values or the discovery of more effective ways of coping with change, or did it represent primarily the exploitation of a tradition-oriented majority by a white-oriented, white-parented planter elite? Should one view the Treaty Party as traitors or as far-sighted patriots? Scholars do not agree. The character and the fate of Cherokee "civilization" were political questions in the 1820s and 1830s, and federal officials, Georgia governors, Protestant missionaries, and Cherokee chiefs did not agree, either.

To their own and later generations, the Cherokee of the 1820s and 1830s symbolized the "civilized" tribes. If the effort to remodel Native American culture after the collective self-image of Jackson's generation worked anywhere, it worked among the Cherokee. In the familial metaphor presidents so often employed, the Cherokee were the White Father's "red children of the forest." If among these precocious children the experiment of civilization failed, where might it succeed? If, as Jackson's opponents believed, Cherokee improvement demonstrated the improvability of all Native Americans, and if the president's policy of Indian removal fatally damaged that progressive Nation, then the Cherokee migrants' Trail of Tears symbolized the tragic destruction by the United States of its own cherished work.

The young Republic's experiment in self-reproduction succeeded, in retrospect, better than either its authors or its beneficiaries could comfortably acknowledge. Like "children" in one sense, the Cherokee mirrored their various parental models in images too accurate, in some particulars, for child or parent to perceive. At the same time, the Cherokee grew into themselves, not mere replications of their "parents." The American society that shaped and conditioned Cherokee efforts to remodel themselves was involved in its own processes of growth, change, differentiation, and conflict. In perceiving, manipulating, and distorting the Cherokee Nation, the *soi-disant* [so-called] parent society reproduced no ideal model, but multiple and refracted images of its own internal conflicts.

In the early nineteenth century, church and state collaborated to present the Cherokee with a unitary vision of republican, Christian, capitalist civilization. Their model American lived under written laws framed by chosen representatives and enforced by impartial public authority. Law protected property, and industrious males strove to increase their property by honest labor at the plow, the forge, or the mill, while industrious females kept the family clothed, and the home neatly groomed and governed. All worshiped a stern, transcendent, but benevolent God Whose Will was known through His written Word.

To achieve this model of civilization, presidents, federal agents, and federally subsidized missionaries ceaselessly recommended that the Cherokee abandon clan revenge for written law enforced by elected public authorities, paying particular attention to laws governing the descent of property. They recommended that the Cherokee allot their lands—held in common—to individual, male family heads; that men rather than women take major responsibility for farming; that these potential patriarchs use the plow and fence their fields. Women should abandon agriculture in favor of the wheel and the loom, so that their husbands need not hunt an ever-diminishing supply of game to trade for civilized clothing. Children, meanwhile, should be at school, learning to spin and weave, if female; or plow and reap, if male. Both sexes should discover how to count their money and read understandingly in the New Testament. Thus might sloth give way to industry; and magic, superstition, heathen dance, and conjuring, to reason, reflection, and revealed religion. Thus might American natives become model Americans.

As subjects, rather than objects, of cultural change, the Cherokee exercised a wider range of choice than any of their mentors intended to offer them. They perceived not only idealized self-images, but day-to-day habits and behavior; not only agents and missionaries but soldiers, planters, traders, and horse-thieves. According to position, disposition, and opportunity, various persons and parties in the tribe watched, listened, selected, and improved themselves in quite different ways.

Were the Cherokee "civilized" in 1808? in 1871? in 1830? This question carried heavy political import for all parties, since the extent of Cherokee "improvement" was widely regarded as a measure of their qualifications for keeping their lands. Overtly, the tribal leaders accepted the definitions of "civilization" their improvers gave them. They offered censuses of their wealth, descriptions of their dress, housing, furniture, tableware, and work habits; copies of their constitutions and laws; and enumerations of their Christian converts, to prove that if not equal—that is to say, identical—to white people, they tended rapidly toward equality. John Ridge and Elias Boudinot, among the brightest of their anglicized young men, traveled among pious audiences in the northeastern states advertising the similarities between good society in New Echota and good society in New Haven or Baltimore.

Since the practical disadvantages of civil amalgamation under conditions of legal inequality and racial prejudice proved abundantly obvious, tribal leaders adopted the familial metaphor and took care to explain that their Nation as a whole was still in its "infancy," unready for full integration with a white population under a white-controlled government. The same elite made no secret, however, that they thought *themselves* adults, and they identified their own grownup status with the sovereign respectability of their independent Nation. When the white "parents" found these Cherokee grownups unwilling to sell their land and remove, they assaulted the Nation.

Faced with brutal trespass aided and abetted by the government pledged to protect their rights, the Cherokee elite brought their own varieties of selective perception to bear on the "parents." If the United States was indeed a republic of laws, were not Cherokee treaties sacred? Could not the American legal system shield Cherokee rights? Principal Chief John Ross believed inflexibly that such was the case. If the United States exemplified a Christian commonwealth, would not the good people of the country rush to the aid of the beleaguered and the oppressed? So tribal officials like John Ross, John Ridge, and Elias Boudinot believed—even more naively and firmly than their Christian champions in politics, Edward Everett, Theodore Freylinghuysen, and Jeremiah Evarts.

Or, had the United States become, in truth, a nation of thieves and hypocrites—or squatters and rapists and drunkards specializing in felonious assault? When the Cherokee of the 1830s abandoned their hope of assistance from the Christian public—that is, when the Christian public abandoned them—John Ridge and Elias Boudinot finally rejected hope for equitable treatment and adopted this wilder image of Americans as their own, and signed a treaty agreeing to remove themselves beyond the reach of their wild white neighbors.

All these honorable men saw rightly, but partially. Both white and Cherokee society proved more complex and less predictable than most parties cared to allow. The process of change in Cherokee society created a Nation unique in its own ways, but in its very complexity more nearly like that of the United States than either red or white fully acknowledged.

Naturally enough, the Cherokee found numerous models among the planters who were their near neighbors. Most of the presidents who paternally recommended civilization to the southern Indians were themselves planter-aristocrats. George Washington, the "noblest Roman" among the Americans of his time, owned a plantation and slaves. So did John Ross, Richard Taylor, Major Ridge, John Ridge, and scores of others among the Cherokee upper class. The tribal elite themselves appreciated the fact that the habit some red planters developed of hiring white farm laborers provoked other farmers to intrude without invitation. How much of the extensive agricultural improvement attributed to Cherokee industry derived from the efforts of black and white laborers cannot be determined with cliometric exactitude. But from the mid-1820s, between five and ten percent of the eastern Cherokee Nation consisted of black slaves.

Andrew Jackson's portraits reflect his sometimes Roman, sometimes Napoleonic image. Many Cherokee respected the Old General as a fellow warrior. Jackson, a gentleman planter, had also owned a store, raced horses, and gambled. John Ross's brother Lewis, one of the wealthiest Scotsmen in the Nation, earned his money in trade. After their removal to the vicinity of Fort Gibson in the

Cherokee Nation West, the Cherokee joined the soldiers in gambling and horseracing. Frequently they got drunk with their fellow gamblers, and their delegation in Washington vainly petitioned for the removal of the fort as a temperance measure.

Apart from making their report on July 4, the framers of the Cherokee constitution of 1827 made much not only of their independence, but also of the similarity between their constitution and that of the United States. In truth, their constitution more nearly resembled those of some southern states than that of the federal union. The Cherokee constitution of 1827 gave their legislature the privilege of electing the executive, the Principal Chief; their later constitution of 1839 provided for the chief's popular election. In this evolutionary pattern, they followed Georgia.

The Cherokee constitution required officeholders to believe in a Supreme Being and a future state of rewards and punishments. Several states did so too, while not even the elastic clause placed that burden of belief on Thomas Jefferson or Andrew Jackson. Like most states, the Cherokee disfranchised those of African descent. Like all state constitutions of the period, theirs, departing from ancient Cherokee tradition, confined political privileges to males. The Cherokee legal code, like the codes of other slaveholder states, progressively reduced the right of slaves to own property, learn to read, move about, and assemble. The social disorganization incident on removal, and the roving gangs of black Seminole and Creek desperadoes in the Nation West, provoked the Nation to intensify the rigors of its slave code, though missionaries testified that the tribal government enforced restrictions on slaves even less reliably than it carried out other laws.

As in other southern states, notably Georgia, the planter-merchant class proved more active politically than other elements of the population and the law reflected their cultural and economic interests as well as the accommodation of those interests to the interests of other classes. Laws provided for the collection of debts, protected property and regulated its descent, handed out licenses and franchises, fixed fees for ferries and turnpikes, and enabled citizens to borrow from the national treasury. More Whiggish than his fellows, John Ross would have had his government establish a national bank.

Cherokee "aristocrats" democratized their government by progressively increasing the number of salaried offices available to the aspiring. Their anger in the face of losing office and valuable saline privileges at the government's disposal helps explain the tenacity with which, in the early 1840s, the Old Settlers Party of the Cherokee West resisted the takeover of their government by the more numerous migrants from the Cherokee Nation East.

Respectable state governments of the antebellum period concerned themselves with cultural improvement, especially education. In the range of their concern for culture, the Cherokee elite reflected the New England model more strongly than the Georgian, though a "progressive" Georgian like Wilson Lumpkin might have denied the difference. After the missionary school at Brainard got underway, the Cherokee National Council provided it with a Board of Visitors. In the 1840s, when their treasury permitted such expenditure, the Nation established a public school system. In this establishment they were ahead of their neighbors in Arkansas, who did not enjoy the luxury of federal annuity payments. Presbyterians, Baptists, and Methodists in the 1840s vied for control of the Nation's schools, while the pagan Cherokee poor, like the Irish and other minority voters of Massachusetts, complained that the expensive institutions mainly served the children of the Prostestant elite.

In subsidizing a national newspaper with avowedly educational and propagandistic objectives, the Cherokee State went beyond even New England's mandate. More than most contemporary governments, the Cherokee accepted cultural improvement as a public obligation. The leaders of the new Nation had obvious reasons for identifying their hegemony with cultural progress. Since their government, unlike others, depended on federal annuities and missionary subsidies rather than on taxation, they found less reason than the gentlemen planters of Georgia to identify respectability with economy in government. Cherokee criminal law, which relied on fines and physical punishments rather than penitential incarceration, resembled the codes of such less progressive states as Tennessee and North Carolina. Probably, however, the Cherokee modeled their penalties initially on the practice of federal army units stationed near them. Courts-martial at the garrison of Southwest Point in the early nineteenth century regularly handed out up to one hundred lashes for theft, as did the Cherokee. North Carolina's maximum was thirty-nine.

Since the Cherokee state represented a population quite different from Georgia's, North Carolina's, or the army's, its constitution and laws reflect both compromise among elements of the tribe and cultural differences between white and Cherokee. The United States viewed the introduction of written law enforced by public authority as a response to its "civilization" program. So, in part, it was. But the laws and constitutions of the Cherokee reflect as well the striving of mixed-bloods for political ascendency, their compromises with those whose tastes and ambitions were more traditional than their own, and the motive that unified nearly all Cherokee, especially the traditionalists—keeping their country.

The first written laws punished theft. Clearly they benefited those who had the most worth stealing, and reflected both growing national wealth and increasing differentiation between richer and poorer. Yet most families owned pigs, black cattle, horses, or sheep. Losing one's only horse could prove much more damaging than parting with the best seven out of ten. To treat horse theft, as William McLoughlin has done, as a kind of patriotic resistance movement may well be just, but one should not overlook the fact that what the laws sought to prevent was theft by Cherokee from Cherokee. Delinquency may, as McLoughlin points out, have provided a few of the poor with an alternative career, but one can hardly believe their Cherokee victims applauded it.

The law of oblivion for murders (1810) redefined murder to exclude accidental homicide and to include fratricide. The notion of agreeing upon mutual forgiveness, or "oblivion," putting an end to a cycle of revenge, was thoroughly traditional, though the law modified the traditional definitions of murder entailed in the system of clan revenge. Yet we must notice that not until the emigration crisis of 1828, when the federal government hired western Cherokee to go among their relatives in the East persuading them to sell their improvements to the

United States and emigrate West, did Cherokee law explicitly penalize the crime of murder. Until that time, no written command prevented clans from continuing to work revenge.

Cherokee property law remained notably more egalitarian than comparable legislation among whites. The tribe defined land as the common property of all. Improvements belonged to those who made them, purchased them, or inherited them. No one might settle within a quarter mile of another's improvement without his or her permission. Though the Council modified tradition by providing for the inheritance of a father's property by his children, mothers enjoyed entire control over improvements they made or personal property they acquired. Any white husband who mistreated his Cherokee wife might face a fine and forfeiture.

Cherokee creditors could satisfy themselves out of a delinquent debtor's property—provided, however, the debtor retained his home, farm, horse, saddle, some corn, a cow and a calf, and a pig or so. Otherwise, the tribal custom of hospitality might place too large a burden on the debtor's kin or neighbors.

Laws such as those prohibiting theft benefited all ranks. The poor had unimpeded access to the means of production. The wealthy could add to their estates as much land as their slaves could till. Cherokee observers emphasized how much this departure from bourgeois custom benefited the common citizen. Unfriendly white critics alleged that free land made the rich richer and the poor careless.

In deference to those who resented missionary influence, the constitution of 1827 disqualified ministers of the gospel from holding office in Council. In deference to ministers of the gospel, the constitution explained that such persons had better things to do. John Huss, "The Spirit," a preacher of uncommon talent who achieved Presbyterian ordination for a sermon that had to be interpreted from his Cherokee, did not serve on the Council. More appropriately, he became Chief Justice of the Supreme Court. The Council mandated in the 1827 constitution was an elective body created by enacted law. It nonetheless had evolved from less formal Councils that had been called on an *ad hoc* basis at least since the eighteenth century. Traditional full-blood leaders expected—and were expected—to exercise influence by winning election to council. They had no such expectation of the Supreme Court, an institution created *de novo* in the 1820s. The 1839 constitution, formed by emigrés in the Cherokee Nation West, contained no prohibition against ministerial councillors. Young Wolf, a Methodist licentiate, served on the National Council and credited himself with persuading that body not to prohibit intermarriage with whites. Young Wolf had a wife of German descent.

In deference to missionary opinion, the National Council prohibited polygamy—first for whites, then for everyone. Unlike other Cherokee laws, this one prescribed no penalty for violators.

Such legislation reflects a generation of political conflict and compromise. The mixed-blood elite's usefulness in doing public business with the United States gave it an advantage; the fortunate politicians improved their advantage tactfully and most of them proved loyal partisans of the Nation they strove to unify.

Charles Renatus Hicks, a literate Moravian convert, established his role as adviser to old Chief Pathkiller during the first decade of the nineteenth century. At the same time, Pathkiller himself emerged as principal spokesman for his people, while his competitors took their ambitions to Arkansas. Chief Doublehead's treachery in the treaty negotiations of 1806, the tradition of bribery as a method of negotiation, and conflicts over the leasing of ferries, sawmills, and the distribution of tribal annuities all contributed to the creation, in 1809, of a committee composed largely of mixed-bloods. The committee took charge of the annuity and asked for it in cash. Charles Renatus Hicks became national treasurer. Shortly after forming the committee, the mixed-bloods co-opted several more traditional leaders to membership.

Andrew Jackson's successful maneuvering of the 1816 treaty negotiations and the War Department's enthusiasm for general removal provoked the tribe to formulate its first written constitution. Several leading women, who had refrained from interfering directly in negotiations with the whites (since white gentlemen did not bring their women with them) presented the Council of fifty-four towns at Amohoee in April, 1817, with an address on the crisis. For the sake of their children and grandchildren, the Council must prevent further cessions. The land, the women explained, belonged to all "who worked at the mother's side." The Council responded with a document that conferred on the committee exclusive responsibility for conducting treaty negotiations and gave the National Council power to veto the committee's actions. By formally centralizing responsibility, the Towns defeated the United States' favorite tactic—ignoring chiefs who seemed stubborn and conferring sovereign power to sell on those who proved compliant.

The committee and Council functioned together as a legislative body as well. As their laws reflected increasing missionary influence, traditional leaders grew restive. Pathkiller and Charles Renatus Hicks both died in 1827, and thus raised the question of who might succeed them. White Path, who had recently suffered expulsion from the Council, tried to foment a rebellion against the establishment of a new constitution that would formalize methods of electing the Council and the Principal Chiefs. According to white observers, few influential men of any party joined White Path. In any case, the constitutional party met with the dissidents and all agreed to harmonize their differences. White Path again won election to the Council, which continued for many years to reflect strong full-blood representation.

As compromise and accommodation marked the tribe's political rearrangements, variety and relative tolerance distinguished their cultural and economic development. By 1830, the Presbyterians had converted, churched, and disciplined perhaps 200 of the approximately 18,000 eastern Cherokee—though [unconverted Indians] usually outnumbered church members. Moravians also established small congregations. The more permissive and egalitarian Methodists, in the Cherokee Nation as elsewhere, rapidly outdistanced the Presbyterians, acquiring a society membership of approximately 800. Baptists in the Nation East concentrated their efforts on the Cherokee of North Carolina, whom they supplied with preaching and literature in the native language, vocational instruction, exhortations to temperance, and such remarkably effective political leadership that General John Wool, charged with assembling migrants for removal, expelled Reverend Evan Jones from North Carolina. Afterward, the War Department tried, unsuccessfully, to keep Jones out of the Cherokee Nation West. In the 1850s,

Evan Jones and his son John provided active leadership for the traditionalist Keetowuh Party in Cherokee national politics.

The Baptist and Methodist emphasis on lay preaching, emotional piety, and song probably accounts as much for their long-run dominance of Cherokee Christendom as does their relative doctrinal elasticity. Presbyterians noted that the Baptist practice of baptism by total immersion corresponded to the curing ceremonies of native "conjurors," and that Methodists treated conjuring as a branch of medicine rather than as a species of idolatry. Not even all Presbyterians insisted on making conjuring a matter of church discipline.

Though the Presbyterian missionaries of the American Board clearly regarded themselves as upholding more rigorous doctrinal standards than did the Baptists or Methodists, even Presbyterianism could embrace the special spirit of the Cherokee community. When John Huss preached his ordination sermon, he took for a text Matthew 7: 13–14: "Enter ye at the strait gate: for wide *is* the gate, and broad the way, that leadeth to destruction, and many there be which go in thereat: Because strait *is* the gate, and narrow is the way, which leadeth unto life, and few there be that find it." The sentiment of his text, especially the concluding lines, expresses perfectly the Presbyterian experience among the Cherokee. But in expounding the text, Huss stressed the evils of drink, a matter on which Matthew keeps silent, and the importance of avoiding quarrels. Matthew does bless the peacemaker; he also reports another kind of statement: "I come not to bring peace, but the sword." Huss chose from Matthew a sermon on the harmony ethic, and he chose his sins, like his theme, from Cherokee experience rather than from the letter of the Gospel.

When any church attacked traditional practices—ballplaying, conjuring, or lively and prolonged ceremonial dancing—it succeeded in relocating some celebrations and in making them disreputable among some of the "respectable" class. A Presbyterian Female Society expelled members for attending ball-plays. Yet those who preferred the traditional ways continued to follow them, and politicians who sought votes patronized ball-plays and dances. Not until the 1850s did the tribe fracture into enduring political factions along cultural lines. Pagans and Christians of the 1820s and 1830s could still be neighbors, accommodating their inevitable contentions as they arose.

The westward migration of several thousand Cherokee between the 1790s and the general removal of 1838–1839 almost certainly contributed to the geographic segregation of the traditional from the progressive. Many of those who first went West voluntarily resented the accommodation tribal leaders were offering to federal diplomats; others took the trip to escape the land of the Bible and the Cherokee police, or Light Horse Cavalry. Opportunities for hunting both bison and Osages beckoned; and fur traders followed the hunters. By the 1820s, though, both missionaries and police had arrived in Arkansas. The fur trade of the western Cherokee attracted merchants; the broad acres along the river beckoned slaveholding planters. In the 1820s, Arkansas, like the Cherokee portion of North Carolina, had its full-blood villages and its towns where English predominated, as well as bilingual settlements. Missionaries and temperance societies met more active resistance in the West than in the eastern Nation. Laws there were fewer and the hunting better, but the virus of cultural change thrived in Arkansas as well as Georgia. After the 1838 migration, people tended to settle near neighbors they found culturally congenial, though no wholesale segregation of the churched from the unchurched came to prevail.

Most significantly, cultural variations among the Cherokee in the 1830s reflected the choices of those who varied, and while most mixed-bloods got richer than most full-bloods, cultural conservatism did not necessarily follow racial lines, nor did it entail poverty for those who continued in the old ways. Cherokee law established new and violent sanctions against theft and slave delinquency; however, in most other respects the experiment in "civilization" broadened, rather than constricted, the people's range of choice as to how they would live.

In 1830, some Cherokee [men] wore frock coats, pantaloons, stiff collars, and top hats. Other males wore pantaloons, a blanket, a turban, and ear-bobs. Old men still wore deerskin hunting shirts, leggings, and moccasins.

When the troops came to Georgia and North Carolina in 1838, Chief John Ross's traditionalist followers suffered extensive material loss. Many refused to register their claims with any agents but Ross's. The Principal Chief's agents recorded claims for an extensive array of goods, both real and personal. George Beamer, of Hanging Dog Creek, left behind him a fourteen-foot square log house, "skelped down inside," having a "cabbin" roof, a loft, and two doors: a nearly finished fourteen-foot square round log house, never occupied: a "Potatoe or hot house," also fourteen-feet square, well-finished; a new house, fifteen by thirteen, "skelped down inside and ready for covering"; a twelve-acre upland field; another eight acres of cleared land, three-quarters of it bottom land; eight acres fenced and not cleared; thirteen peach trees; and an apple tree. Tahlaltuskee of Chutoogatah Town, Georgia, left among his possessions a twelve-foot square sugar camp with a shed roof, and one hundred troughs. Standing Wolf, of Cheohee, North Carolina, left cabins much like George Beamer's and three ten-foot-square covered rail hog pens, a sheep pen, five well-fenced fields totaling twenty-two acres, twenty small peach trees, and ten small apple trees. He also took leave of a nine-by-fifteen fish trap and "1 Canoe, very strong 30 feet long and 2 feet wide." Will, Standing Wolf's more modest neighbor, left simply a board "camp," seven apple trees, and a one and one-half acre field. Buck, of Stekoa Town, North Carolina, left a fourteen-foot-square round-log loom house among his several cabins; his neighbor, Cullesawee, left a blacksmith shop.

Similar "savages" left behind them barrows, breeding sows, chickens, ducks, geese, guinea hens, wash pots, skillets, teacups and saucers, teaspoons, pewter dishes, plows, plow gears, chains, axes, augurs, chisels, planes, wheels and looms, tomahawks, cane sifters, ox yokes, currycombs, weeding hoes, mattocks, a man's plaid cloak, an umbrella, a large looking glass, scissors, andirons, door locks, featherbeds, counterpanes, deerskins, rifles, frying pans, churns, saddles, horse collars, "Delph ware [Delft china] valued $6," good fur hats, silver bands, bows and arrows, beaver traps, blow-guns, "2 callico frocks," log chains, fish hooks, and "4 empty barrels."

Such claims derived from the districts where federal appraisers generally recorded comparatively small improvements; where a few round-log cabins, with stick and clay chimneys, a hothouse, and a dozen acres of land with a few fruit trees put their owner in the middle class; where a few elderly men and women still owned claims to an acre or two in town fields; where the most impressively equipped "improvement" was Evan Jones's Baptist missionary establishment in the Valley.

To the south and west of the hillbilly Cherokee, the solid yeomanry built hewed-log cabins, with hinged doors and shutters, and stone chimneys, round-log kitchens, corncribs and stables; they cultivated more land and generally did without hothouses.

At the upper end of the social scale, twenty men in the Cherokee Nation registered claims for real property exceeding ten thousand dollars assessed valuation. The very wealthy included "Rich Joe Vann," who was worth just under thirty thousand dollars; Lewis Ross, Major Ridge, John Ridge, John Ross, John Martin, Michael Hildebrand, Alexander McCoy, Joseph Crutchfield, Edward Gunter, John Gunter, Jr., Joseph Lynch, and the heirs of John Walker, Jr. At one time or another, all the men listed played active roles in Cherokee politics. None earned his living exclusively from planting, though all but one had one or several large plantations. Stores, taverns, mills, and ferries accounted for their exceptional wealth. Their way of life nonetheless reflected the plantation culture of the upland South. Their hewed-log, frame, or brick houses, painted and "well-finished throughout," boasted multiple windows, piazzas, and an occasional portico. Their numerous outbuildings included large kitchens with multiple brick fireplaces, great stables and barns, fields ranging into the hundreds of acres, "Negro houses," orchards, and sometimes ornamental trees and gardens.

Full-blooded Major Ridge, whose hospitality the Treaty Party councils frequently enjoyed, was the only member of the elite who owned a hothouse. In a hothouse, one could keep warm in winter, store potatoes, or sweat oneself out in ritual purification. Major Ridge owned plenty of fireplaces and storehouses; in 1832 he received Presbyterian baptism. But the sometime Speaker of the National Council also hosted councils and Green Corn Festivals, and probably catered to the tastes of his guests.

The coincidence of political and economic elites that this list reflects appears hardly accidental. The National Council regulated ferries, traders, the sale of liquor, and the admission of millers and other artisans into the Nation. The way to wealth might be paved with legislation; certainly its protection repaid attention to politics. This aspect of the Cherokee elite's activity also resembles—perhaps in exaggerated form, since the community was comparatively small—the style to which the gentlemen planter of Georgia also aspired.

A simple skeptic might regard the patriotism of this elite, and their work of nation-building, as the outward sign of inward avarice. So Andrew Jackson believed. When the elite fractured into pro-Treaty and anti-Treaty factions, each attributed mere avarice to the other. The men and women who left behind their canoes, blow-guns, Delft, pewter, and fishtraps believed otherwise. Andrew Jackson thought the plain Indian merely deluded, but he may have been wrong.

Sovereign independence protected Cherokee control over roads, ferries, taverns, plantations, and artisans. National legislation tended increasingly to render that control exclusive; to restrict individual Cherokee rights to hire white agricultural labor, to award franchises for roads and ferries to mixed-blood politicians who required no white partners, rather than to old chiefs who did; and to place discriminatory taxes on traders who were not Cherokee citizens—though the United States nullified the discrimination. Such exclusiveness infuriated good citizens in Georgia. They complained that it was not white intruders the Cherokee minded, just white intruders without Indian bosses. When Georgia established counties in the Nation and set up the Guard, one of the Guard's first acts was to break down the Turnpike gates at John Martin's ferry.

The Cherokee Nation West, however, offered broad fields for slaves to work, opportunities in trade, roads, ferries, and even salines. And the United States from 1828 on offered ample compensation for eastern improvements that had to be abandoned. Many wealthy people took advantage of such opportunities between 1828 and 1838.

Contrary to the maxim that "dukes don't emigrate," in the period 1828–1838, it was mainly "dukes" who did. By 1828, the "poorer" Cherokee usually stayed behind. When they faced eviction, they migrated as far as the Carolina hills. John Ross's insistence on getting a fair price for the gold mines argues that he had as keen a sense for economic values as Governor Lumpkin of Georgia. But John Ross as a planter and merchant could find riches enough in the West—in the 1840s and 1850s he did. Perhaps he "merely" craved power, as his enemies cease-lessly supposed. But missionary Daniel S. Butrick, who "itinerated" more miles in the Cherokee Nation than almost any other white man living there, thought Ross more nearly a "captive" to his constituency than they to him. If he craved power, the only way he could satisfy the craving was to serve the deepest interest his people thought they had—keeping their country. Several hundred of these "deluded" people risked starvation or death from exposure to elude the troops who came to take them from their mountains. General John E. Wool, detailed to occupy the Cherokee Nation prior to removal, offered blankets and rations to the destitute. In February, 1837, he reported, " . . . those in the mountains of North Carolina during the summer past, preferred living upon the roots and sap of trees rather than receive provisions from the United States and thousands, I have been informed, had no other food for weeks. Many have said they will die before they leave the country."

In the summer of 1838, thousands left their homes literally at the point of bayonet, herded like swine into camps and onto steamboats from which hundreds still managed to escape. Probably, they revered John Ross and supported his gov-ernment not because he "deluded" them, but because he did everything in his power to keep their country.

If twenty-twenty hindsight defines John Ross as a patriot who did what he could to defend traditional Cherokee territory, were men such as John Ridge, Major Ridge, and Elias Boudinot, who drew up the Treaty of Echota, traitors? By Cherokee law, they had committed treason. The written law that defined selling the country without consent of the National Council as a capital crime specified that the criminal be convicted in court. If the accused failed to appear for trial, he became an outlaw—anyone's target. But in 1835 no Cherokee courts could oper-ate in Georgia, where the Treaty Party leaders lived. Georgia, which sought to supplant Cherokee jurisdiction with state law, made the exercise of office under the Cherokee constitution a penitentiary offense. State authorities prohibited the arrest of the signers in Georgia, and the Georgia Guard and federal troops occupied the Cherokee Nation. The signers could not be tried. Perhaps more important, John Ross, a stickler for legalisms, did not recognize the New Echota agreement as a treaty: no treaty, no crime.

Instead, the treason of the Treaty Party was handled in terms of an older tradition of clan revenge. If missionary testimony can be credited, members of the clans to which John Ridge, Major Ridge, and Elias Boudinot belonged agreed among themselves to kill these leading members of the Treaty Party, and carried out their intentions in the Cherokee Nation West in June, 1839. At that time, the party opposed to the Treaty, recent emigrants, did not recognize any official public authority as finally established in the Nation West. The anti-Treaty relatives of the signers apparently fell back on the "unwritten law," which the written law avowedly recorded, and on the older tradition of clan revenge. According to that older system, members of one's own clan might agree to kill a clansman so that no other person of his clan need suffer for his guilt. Had everyone accepted the older tradition, the murder of the Ridges and Boudinot by members of their own clan would have ended the conflict, since these men would not have been subject to revenge for killing their own. Since by 1839, traditional definitions of clan relations existed side by side with Anglo-American kinship and legal systems, to say nothing of different norms governing the treatment of murder and revenge, blood feuds could not be limited so simply. In the Cherokee Nation West, they increased and multiplied. The revenge motif persisted; the customs and assumptions that had limited its range did not.

Whatever the legal norms involved, the Ridge-Boudinot faction did sell their country in defiance of national authorities and several members of the faction profited personally from the transaction. Georgia authorities protected their property and federal agents appraised it generously. Did they sell out for profit?

Anyone who had wanted to sell out for profit without hazarding assassination could have done so at any time after August, 1831, by appealing to federal emigration agent Benjamin Franklin Currey for an appraisal, and enrolling for emigration at United States' expense. Currey's anxiety to enroll prominent emigrants profited many planters who foresook the hazards of politics in Georgia and pursued the opportunity to preempt plantation sites in Oklahoma.

The Ridges and Boudinot, who stayed until a treaty was signed and ratified, saw themselves as men who understood the real Cherokee condition as John Ross did not. They had many reasons for believing that they saw correctly. In late adolescence, John and Elias had studied at the missionary boarding school in Cornwall, Connecticut. They married the white daughters of school employees. The managers of the school disavowed their action, the women's relatives accused the young ladies of endangering the missionary cause out of mere lust, and pious citizens of Cornwall tolled the church bell as they burned pictures of Elias Boudinot and Harriet Gould, his wife, on the village green. Though both the Prudential Committee of the American Board of Commissioners for Foreign Missions and the missionaries to the Cherokee defended the two scholars, Ridge and Boudinot undoubtedly acquired an understanding of racism that light-skinned

Lewis Ross, who married a white relative of Cherokee agent Return J. Meigs, and light-skinned John Ross, who joined a Masonic Lodge in Jasper, Tennessee, never appreciated.

While John Ross sent his children to preparatory school in Lawrenceville, Pennsylvania, and spent his winters in Washington, the dark-skinned men of the treaty party and their mixed-blood children spent their days mainly among Georgians. Repeatedly, John Ridge tried to persuade John Ross that the Cherokee's condition had become intolerable. It is clear that by 1832, both John Ridge and Elias Boudinot had concluded that removal was inevitable and that delaying the inevitable might destroy both the wealth and, more important, the moral fiber of the nation. By November, 1834, their party concluded that with "all the unrelenting prejudices against our language and color in full force, we must believe that the scheme of *amalgamation* with our oppressors is too horrid for a serious contemplation. . . . Without law in the States, we are not more favored than the poor African. . . . "

They hoped to persuade John Ross to make a treaty; in 1833 and again in 1835 they expected him to do so. But John Ross retained control of the press and the Council, refused to permit discussion, appeared willing to accept even state citizenship rather than leave the gold mines, and treated Ridge and Boudinot as traitors long before they had in fact become so. In the winter of 1835, after John Ross agreed to act with the Treaty Party and then went off to Washington without dealing with the only man authorized to make a treaty on behalf of the United States, Elias Boudinot signed the treaty he hoped might save his people from being overrun by Georgians. His missionary mentors disapproved his action; yet they had taught its rationale. The virtuous and the enlightened have a duty to do what they can for the good of the people, even when the people fail to understand what is good for them.

After John Ross and his delegation in Washington refused to accept the New Echota Treaty and failed to negotiate an alternative to it, John Ridge signed that treaty too. Had no one signed a treaty, Georgians promised within the year to take possession with all necessary force of everything the Cherokee still owned in that state. John Ross was of course perfectly correct, in the long run, in his belief that if the Cherokee could not sustain their legal rights in Georgia, they would in the end sustain them nowhere. Yet if, as John Ridge had come to believe, the United States was "utterly corrupt," her practice belying her principles, one might as well buy time, and temporarily, asylum. This the Treaty Party did. They also made permanent a factional split that lasted longer than the Cherokee Nation West managed to persist as a territorial entity. John Ross seemed no better able than Andrew Jackson to entertain the notion of a loyal opposition. By sending the Nation down the Trail of Tears, Jackson, Ridge, and Boudinot made certain that no other Cherokee would develop such notions either.

In the 1850s, the slavery issue divided the Cherokee Nation, and the "full-bloods" identified themselves as a party, rather than a persuasion. But the factional division that originally rent the Nation, the division that persisted, the struggle whose bitterness destroyed the reputability of compromise, did not result from cultural change, or from the mundane malignity of self-interested Cherokee politicians. Political oppression—the sustained cooperative effort of the United

States and the sovereign state of Georgia to destroy first the unity and then the existence of the Cherokee Nation East—created that faction.

An alternate reading of antebellum Cherokee politics might, however, cast a different light on the impact of federal policy on tribal unity and national reintegration. The model of constitutional government so deliberately fostered by Meigs and his missionary allies offered not only an opportunity for the political ascendancy of a white-oriented elite, but also a means for reestablishing and maintaining at least some kind of political order in a society that was rapidly becoming more differentiated and stratified, more diverse in its social and spiritual values, than the "traditional society" pictured by the informants who spoke to John Howard Payne and James Mooney, or by twentieth-century scholars such as Fred Gearing and John Philip Reid.

Ironically, the omnipresence of common enemies—the Treaty commissioners, the emigration agents, Andrew Jackson, and the messengers from his War Department—probably did much to maintain such political unity and relative social harmony as the Cherokee enjoyed in the generation between 1810 and 1840. Whatever importance one may attach to outbreaks of antimissionary sentiment, or to White Path's abortive "rebellion" of 1827, it seems clear that the Cherokee could not devote themselves wholeheartedly to factional disputes over cultural alternatives until the late 1840s and 1850s, when they experienced a degree of relief from Washington's recurrent threat to take their land away from them.

The Cherokee Nation's reputation as a model Christian Indian republic proves well deserved. Cherokee men, women, and children learned well the lessons of literacy, the artisan skills, and the governmental techniques their agents and missionaries taught them. More gradually, many Cherokee became converted Christians—or perhaps they converted Christianity, as they converted other features of the model, to their own special needs. Yet the Cherokee Nation mirrored not only the ideal images their mentors sought to foster, but the competitive, contentious, and exploitive human relationships their masters so cunningly, if half-consciously, modeled for them as well.

◈ *F U R T H E R   R E A D I N G*

W. David Baird, *Peter Pitchlynn: Chief of the Choctaws* (1972)
——, "The Reduction of a People: The Quapaw Removal, 1824–1834," *Red River Historical Review* 1 (1974), 21–36
Robert F. Berkhofer, *Salvation and the Savage: An Analysis of Protestant Missions and American Indian Response, 1787–1862* (1965)
Black Hawk, *Black Hawk: An Autobiography,* Donald Jackson, ed., (1955)
Carter Blue Clark, "Chickasaw Colonization in Oklahoma," *Chronicles of Oklahoma* 54 (1976), 44–59
Michelle Daniel, "From Blood Feud to Jury System: The Metamorphosis of Cherokee Law from 1750 to 1840," *American Indian Quarterly* 11 (1987), 97–125.
Angie Debo, *The Rise and Fall of the Choctaw Republic,* 2d ed. (1961)
Arthur H. DeRosier, Jr., *The Removal of the Choctaw Indians* (1970)
Cecil D. Eby, *"That Disgraceful Affair," the Black Hawk War* (1973)
Clyde R. Ferguson, "Confrontation at Coleraine: Creeks, Georgians and Federalist Indian Policy," *South Atlantic Quarterly* (1979), 224–243

Grant Foreman, *Indian Removal: The Emigration of the Five Civilized Tribes of Indians* (1932)

Arrell Morgan Gibson, *The Chickasaws* (1971)

——, ed., *America's Exiles: Indian Colonization in Oklahoma* (1976)

Michael D. Green, *The Politics of Removal: Creek Government and Society in Crisis* (1982)

Allen Guttmann, *States' Rights and Indian Removal: The Cherokee Nation v. the State of Georgia* (1965)

Reginald Horsman, *The Origins of Indian Removal* (1970)

William G. McLoughlin, *Cherokee Renascence in the New Republic* (1986)

——, "Experiment in Cherokee Citizenship, 1817–1829," *American Quarterly* 33 (1981), 3–25

Kim McQuaid, "William Apes, Pequot: An Indian Reformer in the Jacksonian Era," *New England Quarterly* 50 (1977), 605–625

John K. Mahon, *History of the Second Seminole War, 1835–1842* (1967)

Virginia Bergman Peters, *The Florida Wars* (1979)

Robert Vincent Remini, *The Legacy of Andrew Jackson: Essays on Democracy, Indian Removal, and Slavery* (1988)

Michael Paul Rogin, *Fathers and Children: Andrew Jackson and the Subjugation of the American Indian* (1975)

Ronald N. Satz, *American Indian Policy in the Jacksonian Era* (1975)

——, *Tennessee's Indian Peoples: From White Contact to Removal, 1540–1840* (1979)

Robert A. Trennert, "The Business of Indian Removal: Deporting the Potawatomi from Wisconsin, 1851," *Wisconsin Magazine of History* 63 (1979), 36–50

Dale Van Every, *Disinherited: The Lost Birthright of the American Indian* (1966)

Herman J. Viola, *Thomas L. McKenney: Architect of America's Early Indian Policy, 1816–1830* (1974)

Anthony F. C. Wallace, *Prelude to Disaster: The Course of Indian-White Relations Which Led to the Black Hawk War of 1832* (1970)

Wilcolmb W. Washburn, "Indian Removal Policy: Administrative, Historical and Moral Criteria for Judging Its Success or Failure," *Ethnohistory* 12 (1965), 274–278

Ellen M. Whitney, ed., *The Black Hawk War, 1831–1832,* 3 vols. (1970–1975)

Thurman Wilkins, *Cherokee Tragedy: The Story of the Ridge Family and the Decimation of a People* 2d rev. ed. (1986)

Mary E. Young, "Indian Removal and the Attack on Tribal Autonomy: The Cherokee Case," in John K. Mahon, ed., *Indians of the Lower South: Past and Present* (1975)

——, "Indian Removal and Land Allotment: The Civilized Tribes and Jacksonian Justice," *American Historical Review* 64 (1958), 31–45

——, *Redskins, Ruffleshirts, and Rednecks: Indian Allotments in Alabama and Mississippi, 1830–1860* (1961)

CHAPTER
7

Indian Life on the Plains

Before 1860

When most people think about Indians, they picture the Plains warrior on his pony, hunting buffalo or galloping with flowing war bonnet and brandished lance. Indeed, the daily lives of Plains Indian peoples such as the Sioux, Cheyennes, and Arapahos depended on the vast bison herds that spread over the Great Plains. The Indians erected buffalo-skin tipis wherever the hunting was good, and moved on when the game retreated.

In the popular imagination, this roving existence came to be associated with all Indians, and the conception of the Indian as a fierce hunter-warrior-nomad was a stereotype that supposedly justified the dispossession of all native peoples. To anyone who hated Indians, this image explained why all Indians had to be eliminated from the American scene: Indians made poor use of the land, so the thinking went, and posed a violent threat to the extension of white settlement. And to reformers who wanted to remake Indian tribes in the likeness of Anglo-American society, the image seemed to prove the need for imposing a settled life on Indians so that they could take up farming and embrace peaceful ways.

Whatever the preconceptions of observers, the stereotyped image of horse-mounted, buffalo-hunting Indians obscured the realities of Plains Indian life and history. The selections in this chapter will show that Plains tribes were far more complex than the image suggests. The history of these peoples also provides a fresh insight into American westward expansion.

◈ *DOCUMENTS*

In the late eighteenth and early nineteenth centuries, the buffalo was the foundation of Plains Indian culture. The buffalo provided food, fuel, and shelter and occupied a central place in the religious ceremonies of Indians who lived on the Great Plains. Vast herds of bison, antelope, and other game amazed travelers who encountered them on the plains. Millions of animals grazed from Canada to Mexico; thousands could be seen at a glance.

In early November 1806, Lieutenant Zebulon Montgomery Pike led a U.S. Army exploring expedition across the Kansas territory. In the first document, Pike describes bison herds and wild horses near present-day Dodge City. He also mentions the wanton killing of some of these animals. Within a few years, the whites' demand for buffalo robes led some tribesmen to hunt bison just for their hides. In the second document, dating from 1822, the Pawnee chief Sharitarish explains this practice, and its consequences, to President James Monroe during a visit to Washington, D.C. The third selection is the Treaty of Fort Laramie (1851), an agreement between the United States and principal Plains Indian tribes. The treaty provides for the payment of annuities to each tribe and describes tribal boundaries, but it also permits Indians to hunt and fish on other lands.

By the mid-1850s, Indians found themselves in the midst of a dispute between pro-slavery and antislavery forces in Kansas. In the fourth document, Commissioner of Indian Affairs George Manypenny describes the Kansas situation in 1856. Old Lady Horse, a Kiowa, relates in the final excerpt the Kiowa conception of how the buffalo disappeared and ended the Plains way of life in the second half of the nineteenth century.

Lieutenant Zebulon Montgomery Pike Observes Buffalo in the Kansas Country, 1806

. . . Ist November, Saturday.   Marched early, just after commencing our line, heard a gun on our left; the doctor, Baroney and myself being in advance, and laying on the ground waiting for the party; a band of Cabrie [antelope] came up, amongst our horses, to satisfy their curiosity; we could not resist the temptation of killing two, although we had plenty of meat. At the report of the gun they appeared astonished, and stood still until we hallowed at them to drive them away. Encamped in the evening on an island, upon using my glass to observe the adjacent country, I observed on the prairie a herd of horses; doctor Robinson and Baroney, accompanied me to go and view them; when within a quarter of a mile, they discovered us, and came immediately up near us, making the earth tremble under them (this brought to my recollection a charge of cavalry). They stopt and gave us an opportunity to view them, among them there were some very beautiful bays, blacks and greys, and indeed of all colours. We fired at a black horse, with an idea of creasing him, but did not succeed; they flourished round and returned again to see us, when we returned to camp.

2d November, Sunday.   In the morning for the purpose of trying the experiment, we equipped six of our fleetest coursers with riders and ropes, to noose the wild horses if in our power, to come among the band. They stood until they came within forty yards of them, neighing and whinnowing, when the chase began, which we continued about two miles, without success. Two of our horses ran up with them; we could not take them. Returned to camp. I have since laughed at our folly, for taking the wild horses, in that manner, is scarcely ever attempted, even

From *The Journals of Zebulon Montgomery Pike, with Letters and Related Documents,* by Zebulon Montgomery Pike, edited by Donald Jackson, pp. 342–343. Copyright © 1966 by the University of Oklahoma Press.

with the fleetest horses, and most expert ropers (see my account of wild horses, and the manner of taking them in my dissertations on the province of Texas). Marched late. River turned to north by west. Hills change to the north side. Distance 13½ miles. Killed one buffalo.

3d November, Monday.   Marched at ten o'clock passed numerous herds of buffalo, elk, some horses &c. all travelling south. The river bottoms, full of salt ponds; grass similar to our salt meadows. Killed one buffalo. Distance 25½ miles.

4th November, Tuesday.   This day brought to our recollection, the fate of our countrymen at Recovery; when defeated by the indians, in the year '91. In the afternoon discovered the north side of the river to be covered with animals; which, when we came to them proved to be buffalo cows and calves. I do not think it an exaggeration to say there were 3,000 in one view. It is worthy of remark, that in all the extent of country yet crossed, we never saw one cow, and that now the face of the earth appeared to be covered with them. Killed one buffalo. Distance 24½ miles.

5th November, Wednesday.   Marched at our usual hour; at the end of two miles, shot a buffalo and two deer and halted, which detained us so long that we foolishly concluded to halt the day and kill some cows and calves, which lay on the opposite side of the river. I took post on a hill, and sent some horsemen over, when a scene took place which gave a lively representation of an engagement. The herd of buffalo being divided into separate bands covered with dust, and first charged on the one side then to the other, as the pursuit of the horsemen impelled them: the report and smoke from the guns, added to the pleasure of the scene, which in part compensated for our detention.

6th November, Thursday.   Marched early, but was detained two or three hours by the cows, which we killed. The cow buffalo, was equal to any meat I ever saw, and we feasted sumptuously on the choice morsels. I will not attempt to describe the droves of animals we now saw on our route; suffice it to say, that the face of the prairie was covered with them, on each side of the river; their numbers exceeded imagination. Distance 16 miles. . . .

Chief Sharitarish Foretells the End of the Pawnee Way of Life, 1822

My Great Father:—I have travelled a great distance to see you—I have seen you and my heart rejoices. I have heard your words—they have entered one ear and shall not escape the other, and I will carry them to my people as pure as they came from your mouth.

My Great Father— . . . If I am here now and have seen your people, your houses, your vessels on the big lake, and a great many wonderful things far beyond my comprehension, which appear to have been made by the Great Spirit and placed in your hands, I am indebted to my Father [Major Benjamin O'Fallon] here, who invited me from home, under whose wings I have been protected . . . but there is still another Great Father to whom I am much indebted—it is the Father of us all. . . . The Great Spirit made us all—he made my skin red, and yours white; he placed us on this earth, and intended that we should live differently from each other.

He made the whites to cultivate the earth, and feed on domestic animals; but he made us, red skins, to rove through the uncultivated woods and plains; to feed on wild animals; and to dress with their skins. He also intended that we should go to war—to take scalps—steal horses from and triumph over our enemies—cultivate peace at home, and promote the happiness of each other.

My Great Father:—Some of your good chiefs, as they are called [missionaries], have proposed to send some of their good people among us to change our habits, to make us work and live like the white people. . . . You love your country—you love your people—you love the manner in which they live, and you think your people brave. I am like you, my Great Father, I love my country—I love my people—I love the manner in which we live, and think myself and warriors brave. Spare me then, my Father; let me enjoy my country, and I will trade skins with your people. I have grown up, and lived thus long without work—I am in hopes you will suffer me to die without it. We have plenty of buffalo, beaver, deer, and other wild animals—we have an abundance of horses—we have everything we want—we have plenty of land, if you will keep your people off of it. . . .

There was a time when we did not know the whites—our wants were then fewer than they are now. They were always within our control—we had then seen nothing which we could not get. Before our intercourse with the whites, who have caused such a destruction in our game, we could lie down to sleep, and when we awoke we would find the buffalo feeding around our camp—but now we are killing them for their skins, and feeding the wolves with their flesh, to make our children cry over their bones.

Here, my Great Father, is a pipe which I present you, as I am accustomed to present pipes to all the red skins in peace with us. It is filled with such tobacco as we were accustomed to smoke before we knew the white people. It is pleasant, and the spontaneous growth of the most remote parts of our country. I know that the robes, leggings, moccasins, bear claws, etc., are of little value to you, but we wish you to have them deposited and preserved in some conspicuous part of your lodge, so that when we are gone and the sod turned over our bones, if our children should visit this place, as we do now, they may see and recognize with pleasure the deposits of their fathers; and reflect on the times that are past.

The Treaty of Fort Laramie, 1851

Articles of a treaty made and concluded at Fort Laramie, in the Indian territory, between D. D. Mitchell, superintendent of Indian affairs, and Thomas Fitzpatrick, Indian agent, commissioners specially appointed and authorized by the President of the United States, of the first part, and the chiefs, headmen, and braves of the following Indian nations, residing south of the Missouri River, east

of the Rocky Mountains, and north of the lines of Texas and New Mexico, viz, the
Sioux or Dahcotahs, Cheyennes, Arrapahoes, Crows, Assinaboines, Gros-Ventre
Mandans, and Arrickaras, parties of the second part, on the seventeenth day of
September, A.D. one thousand eight hundred and fifty-one.

Article 1.   The aforesaid nations, parties to this treaty, having assembled for the
purpose of establishing and confirming peaceful relations amongst themselves,
do hereby covenant and agree to abstain in future from all hostilities whatever
against each other, to maintain good faith and friendship in all their mutual intercourse, and to make an effective and lasting peace.

Article 2.   The aforesaid nations do hereby recognize the right of the United
States Government to establish roads, military and other posts, within their respective territories.

Article 3.   In consideration of the rights and privileges acknowledged in the preceding article, the United States bind themselves to protect the aforesaid Indian
nations against the commission of all depredations by the people of the said
United States, after the ratification of this treaty.

Article 4.   The aforesaid Indian nations do hereby agree and bind themselves to
make restitution or satisfaction for any wrongs committed, after the ratification of
this treaty, by any band or individual of their people, on the people of the United
States, whilst lawfully residing in or passing through their respective territories.

Article 5.   The aforesaid Indian nations do hereby recognize and acknowledge
the following tracts of country, included within the metes and boundaries hereinafter designated, as their respective territories, viz:
   The territory of the Sioux or Dahcotah Nation, commencing [at] the mouth of
the White Earth River, on the Missouri River; thence in a southwesterly direction
to the forks of the Platte River; thence up the north fork of the Platte River to a
point known as the Red Bute, or where the road leaves the river; thence along the
range of mountains known as the Black Hills, to the head-waters of Heart River;
thence down Heart River to its mouth; and thence down the Missouri River to the
place of beginning.
   The territory of the Gros Ventre, Mandans, and Arrickaras Nations, commencing at the mouth of Heart River; thence up the Missouri River to the mouth
of the Yellowstone River; thence up the Yellowstone River to the mouth of Powder River in a southeasterly direction, to the head-waters of the Little Missouri
River; thence along the Black Hills to the head of Heart River, and thence down
Heart River to the place of beginning.
   The territory of the Assinaboin Nation, commencing at the mouth of Yellowstone River; thence up the Missouri River to the mouth of the Muscle-shell River;
thence from the mouth of the Muscle-shell River in a southeasterly direction until
it strikes the head-waters of Big Dry Creek; thence down that creek to where it
empties into the Yellowstone River, nearly opposite the mouth of Powder River,
and thence down the Yellowstone River to the place of beginning.

The territory of the Blackfoot Nation, commencing at the mouth of Muscle-shell River; thence up the Missouri River to its source; thence along the main range of the Rocky Mountains, in a southerly direction, to the head-waters of the northern source of the Yellowstone River; thence down the Yellowstone River to the mouth of Twenty-five Yard Creek; thence across to the head-waters of the Muscle-shell River, and thence down the Muscle-shell River to the place of beginning.

The territory of the Crow Nation, commencing at the mouth of Powder River on the Yellowstone; thence up Powder River to its source; thence along the main range of the Black Hills and Wind River Mountains to the head-waters of the Yellowstone River; thence down the Yellowstone River to the mouth of Twenty-five Yard Creek; thence to the head waters of the Muscle-shell River; thence down the Muscle-shell River to its mouth; thence to the head-waters of Big Dry Creek, and thence to its mouth.

The territory of the Cheyennes and Arrapahoes, commencing at the Red Bute, or the place where the road leaves the north fork of the Platte River; thence up the north fork of the Platte River to its source; thence along the main range of the Rocky Mountains to the head-waters of the Arkansas River; thence down the Arkansas River to the crossing of the Santa Fé road; thence in a northwesterly direction to the forks of the Platte River, and thence up the Platte River to the place of beginning.

It is, however, understood that, in making this recognition and acknowledgement, the aforesaid Indian nations do not hereby abandon or prejudice any rights or claims they may have to other lands; and further, that they do not surrender the privilege of hunting, fishing, or passing over any of the tracts of country heretofore described.

Article 6. The parties to the second part of this treaty having selected principals or head-chiefs for their respective nations, through whom all national business will hereafter be conducted, do hereby bind themselves to sustain said chiefs and their successors during good behavior.

Article 7. In consideration of the treaty stipulations, and for the damages which have or may occur by reason thereof to the Indian nations, parties hereto, and for their maintenance and the improvement of their moral and social customs, the United States bind themselves to deliver to the said Indian nations the sum of fifty thousand dollars per annum for the term of ten years, with the right to continue the same at the discretion of the President of the United States for a period not exceeding five years thereafter, in provisions, merchandise, domestic animals, and agricultural implements, in such proportions as may be deemed best adapted to their condition by the President of the United States, to be distributed in proportion to the population of the aforesaid Indian nations.

Article 8. It is understood and agreed that should any of the Indian nations, parties to this treaty, violate any of the provisions thereof, the United States may withhold the whole or a portion of the annuities mentioned in the preceding article from the nation so offending, until, in the opinion of the President of the United States, proper satisfaction shall have been made.

In testimony whereof the said D. D. Mitchell and Thomas Fitzpatrick com-missioners as aforesaid, and the chiefs, headmen, and braves, parties hereto, have set their hands and affixed their marks, on the day and at the place first above written.

D. D. Mitchell
Thomas Fitzpatrick
Commissioners

Sioux:
Mah-toe-wha-you-whey, his x mark.
Mah-kah-toe-zah-zah, his x mark.
Bel-o-ton-kah-tan-ga, his x mark.
Nah-ka-pah-gi-gi, his x mark.
Mak-toe-sah-bi-chis, his x mark.
Meh-wha-tah-ni-hans-kah, his x mark.

Cheyennes:
Wah-ha-nis-satta, his x mark
Voist-ti-toe-vetz, his x mark.
Nahk-ko-me-ien, his x mark.
Koh-kay-y-wh-cum-est, his x mark.

Arrapahoes:
Bè-ah-té-a-qui-sah, his x mark.
Neb-ni-bah-seh-it, his x mark.
Beh-kah-jay-beth-sah-es, his x mark.

Crows:
Arra-tu-ri-sash, his x mark.
Doh-chepit-seh-chi-es, his x mark.

Assinaboines:
Mah-toe-wit-ko, his x mark.
Toe-tah-ki-eh-nan, his x mark.

Mandans and Gros Ventres:
Nochk-pit-shi-toe-pish, his x mark.
She-oh-mant-ho, his x mark.

Arickarees:
Koun-hei-ti-shan, his x mark.
Bi-atch-tah-wetch, his x mark.

In the presence of—

A. B. Chambers, secretary.
S. Cooper, colonel, U.S. Army.
R. H. Chilton, captain, First Drags.
Thomas Duncan, captain, Mounted
    Riflemen.
Thos. G. Rhett, brevet captain R. M. R.
W. L. Elliott, first lieutenant R. M. R.
C. Campbell, interpreter for Sioux.
John S. Smith, interpreter for
    Cheyennes.
Robert Meldrum, interpreter for the
    Crows.

H. Culbertson, interpreter for
    Assiniboines and Gros Ventres.
Francios L'Etalie, interpreter for
    Arickarees.
John Pizelle, interpreter for the
    Arrapahoes.
B. Gratz Brown.
Robert Campbell.
Edmond F. Chouteau.

Old Lady Horse (Kiowa) Tells How the Buffalo Disappeared, n. d.

Everything the Kiowas had came from the buffalo. Their tipis were made of buf-falo hides, so were their clothes and moccasins. They ate buffalo meat. Their containers were made of hide, or of bladders or stomachs. The buffalo were the life of the Kiowas.

Most of all, the buffalo was part of the Kiowa religion. A white buffalo calf must be sacrificed in the Sun Dance. The priests used parts of the buffalo to make their prayers when they healed people or when they sang to the powers above.

So, when the white men wanted to build railroads, or when they wanted to farm or raise cattle, the buffalo still protected the Kiowas. They tore up the railroad tracks and the gardens. They chased the cattle off the ranges. The buffalo loved their people as much as the Kiowas loved them.

There was war between the buffalo and the white men. The white men built forts in the Kiowa country, and the woolly-headed buffalo soldiers [the Tenth Cavalry, made up of black troops] shot the buffalo as fast as they could, but the buffalo kept coming on, coming on, even into the post cemetery at Fort Sill. Soldiers were not enough to hold them back.

Then the white men hired hunters to do nothing but kill the buffalo. Up and down the plains those men ranged, shooting sometimes as many as a hundred buffalo a day. Behind them came the skinners with their wagons. They piled the hides and bones into the wagons until they were full, and then took their loads to the new railroad stations that were being built, to be shipped east to the market. Sometimes there would be a pile of bones as high as a man, stretching a mile along the railroad track.

The buffalo saw that their day was over. They could protect their people no longer. Sadly, the last remnant of the great herd gathered in council, and decided what they would do.

The Kiowas were camped on the north side of Mount Scott, those of them who were still free to camp. One young woman got up very early in the morning. The dawn mist was still rising from Medicine Creek, and as she looked across the water, peering through the haze, she saw the last buffalo herd appear like a spirit dream.

Straight to Mount Scott the leader of the herd walked. Behind him came the cows and their calves, and the few young males who had survived. As the woman watched, the face of the mountain opened.

Inside Mount Scott the world was green and fresh, as it had been when she was a small girl. The rivers ran clear, not red. The wild plums were in blossom, chasing the red buds up the inside slopes. Into this world of beauty the buffalo walked, never to be seen again.

◈ *E S S A Y S*

In the seventeenth and eighteenth centuries, the spread of European colonization, along with that of trade, firearms, and the horse, had set in motion forces that gradually altered Plains Indian life. Tribes adopted the horse, increased their reliance on the buffalo, and contended with each other for the best hunting grounds. In the first essay, Richard White, a professor of history at the University of Washington, examines more than a century of Sioux territorial expansion in the West. Rather than seeing the Sioux as "naturally" violent and aggressive, White examines their motives for warfare and expansion. Dan Flores, a professor of history at the University of Montana, takes a detailed look in the second essay at the bison and the history of the southern Plains Indians. Flores's sophisticated analysis of the environmental relationship between humans and animals reveals the precariously balanced ecology that Indians helped to destroy by hunting bison for the buffalo robe market.

Were Plains Indians the agents of their own destruction? What role did white expansion and the growth of the market economy play? What do these articles tell us about Indians' motivations?

The Winning of the West:
The Expansion of the Western Sioux in the
Eighteenth and Nineteenth Centuries

RICHARD WHITE

The mounted warrior of the Great Plains has proved to be the most enduring stereotype of the American Indian, but like most stereotypes this one conceals more than it reveals. Both popularizers and scholars have been fascinated with the individual warrior to the neglect of plains warfare itself. Harry Turney-High, in his classic *Primitive Warfare,* provided the most cogent justification of this neglect. The plains tribes, he contended, were so loosely organized that they remained below the "military horizon"; there really was no warfare on the plains, only battles that were little more than "a mildly dangerous game" fought for largely individual reasons. In much of the literature, intertribal warfare has remained just this: an individual enterprise fought for individualistic reasons—glory, revenge, prestige, and booty. Robert Lowie's statement on warfare, in what is still the standard work on the Plains Indians, can be taken as typical of much anthropological thought: "The objective was never to acquire new lands. Revenge, horse lifting, and lust for glory were the chief motives. . . . "

There is, however, a second group of anthropologists, W. W. Newcomb, Oscar Lewis, Frank Secoy, and more recently Symmes Oliver, who have found this explanation of intertribal warfare unconvincing. These scholars, making much more thorough use of historical sources than is common among anthropologists, have examined warfare in light of economic and technological change. They have presented intertribal warfare as dynamic, changing over time; wars were not interminable contests with traditional enemies, but real struggles in which defeat was often catastrophic. Tribes fought largely for the potential economic and social benefits to be derived from furs, slaves, better hunting grounds, and horses. According to these scholars, plains tribes went to war because their survival as a people depended on securing and defending essential resources.

Historians have by and large neglected this social and economic interpretation of plains warfare and have been content to borrow uncritically from the individualistic school. Western historians usually present intertribal warfare as a chaotic series of raids and counter-raids; an almost irrelevant prelude to the real story: Indian resistance to white invasion. This exaggerated focus on the heroic resistance of certain plains tribes to white incursions has recently prompted John Ewers, an ethnologist, to stress that Indians on the plains had fought each other

From "The Winning of the West: The Expansion of the Western Sioux in the Eighteenth and Nineteenth Centuries," *Journal of American History* 65 (Sept. 1978), pp. 319–343. Reprinted by permission.

long before whites came and that intertribal warfare remained very significant into the late nineteenth century.

The neglect by historians of intertribal warfare and the reasons behind it has fundamentally distorted the historical position of the Plains Indians. As Ewers has noted, the heroic-resistance approach to plains history reduces these tribes who did not offer organized armed resistance to the white American invaders, and who indeed often aided them against other tribes, to the position of either foolish dupes of the whites or of traitors to their race. Why tribes such as the Pawnee, Mandan, Hidatsa, Oto, Missouri, Crow, and Omaha never took up arms against white Americans has never been subject to much historical scrutiny. The failure of Indians to unite has been much easier to deplore than to examine.

The history of the northern and central American Great Plains in the eighteenth and nineteenth centuries is far more complicated than the tragic retreat of the Indians in the face of an inexorable white advance. From the perspective of most northern and central plains tribes the crucial invasion of the plains during this period was not necessarily that of the whites at all. These tribes had few illusions about American whites and the danger they presented, but the Sioux remained their most feared enemy.

The Teton and Yanktonai Sioux appeared on the edges of the Great Plains early in the eighteenth century. Although unmounted, they were already culturally differentiated from their woodland brothers, the Santee Sioux. The western Sioux were never united under any central government and never developed any concerted policy of conquest. By the mid-nineteenth century the Plains Sioux comprised three broad divisions, the Tetons, Yanktons, and Yanktonais, with the Tetons subdivided into seven component tribes—the Oglala, Brulé, Hunkpapa, Miniconjou, Sans Arc, Two Kettles, and Sihaspas, the last five tribes having evolved from an earlier Sioux group—the Saones. Although linked by common language, culture, interest, and intermarriage, these tribes operated independently. At no time did all the western Sioux tribes unite against any enemy, but alliances of several tribes against a common foe were not unusual. Only rarely did any Teton tribe join an alien tribe in an attack on another group of Sioux.

Between approximately 1685 and 1876 the western Sioux conquered and controlled an area from the Minnesota River in Minnesota, west to the head of the Yellowstone, and south from the Yellowstone to the drainage of the upper Republican River. This advance westward took place in three identifiable stages: initially a movement during the late seventeenth and early eighteenth centuries onto the prairies east of the Missouri, then a conquest of the middle Missouri River region during the late eighteenth and nineteenth centuries, and, finally, a sweep west and south from the Missouri during the early and mid-nineteenth century. Each of these stages possessed its own impetus and rationale. Taken together they comprised a sustained movement by the Sioux that resulted in the dispossession or subjugation of numerous tribes and made the Sioux a major Indian power on the Great Plains during the nineteenth century.

The Teton tribes who first appeared on the prairies of Minnesota in the eighteenth century were well armed and formidable. They had acquired guns from the French, ending the Cree-Assiniboine monopoly of firearms that had enabled those tribes to push the Tetons and Yanktonais south from the headwaters of the

Mississippi. To the east of the Tetons, the Ojibwas were growing in power, but the brunt of their attacks would be borne by the Santee Sioux who acted as a buffer against powerful eastern tribes. Thus, neither the Ojibwas nor the Crees drove the Sioux out onto the prairies. Instead, the potential profits of the region's abundant beaver and the ready food supply provided by the buffalo herds lured them into the open lands.

Initially the profits of the beaver trade exerted a more powerful attraction than the subsistence gained from buffalo hunting. The fur trade brought to the Sioux European goods and the guns that not only enabled them to repulse the Crees and their Assiniboine allies, but also to dispossess the tribes who held the western hunting and trapping grounds they desired. During the late seventeenth and early and mid-eighteenth centuries, the Tetons and Yanktonais pushed the Omahas, Otos, Cheyennes, Missouris, and Iowas to the south and west and occupied their lands.

The western Sioux became the dominant trappers and traders of the prairies. Until the early years of the nineteenth century the Tetons, Yanktonais, and, later, the Yanktons, regularly gathered at the great trade fairs held with the Santee. First at the Blue Earth River and later at the Yanktonai villages on the Cheyenne and James Rivers, the western tribes traded their own catch of furs, plus those acquired from tribes further west, for European goods that the Santees had obtained. As late as 1796 Jean Baptiste Truteau described the Sioux as primarily trappers and traders who also hunted buffalo:

> The Sioux tribes are those who hunt most for the beaver and other good peltries of the Upper Missouri. They scour all the rivers and streams without fearing anyone. They carry away every springtime . . . a great number of them, which they exchange for merchandise with the other Sioux situated on the St. Peter's [Minnesota] and Des Moines Rivers. . . .

The Sioux pushed westward, however, involving them in a cultural and economic dilemma to which they responded unevenly. The fur trade provided them with guns and trade goods, but they depended on buffalo hunting for their food supply and most of their other necessities. According to the winter counts, pictographic records kept by the Sioux, western Dakotas were trading for horses by 1707 and had almost certainly acquired some animals even earlier. But, surprisingly, the Sioux assimilation of the horse into existing cultural patterns occurred only gradually. The winter counts do not record a mounted war party until 1757–1758, and it was unsuccessful. But with the acquisition of the horse, buffalo hunting undoubtedly became easier and more lucrative.

For years the two systems of hunting existed in an uneasy balance: during the summer the Sioux followed the buffalo; in the winters they trapped beaver; and with spring the bands traveled to the trade fairs. But by the late eighteenth century it had become obvious that the Teton bands to the west were devoting more and more time to the acquisition of horses and to the hunting of buffalo, while the Yanktons and Yanktonais still concentrated on beaver trapping. As late as 1803, the Yanktonais abandoned good buffalo hunting grounds along the Missouri to move to the headwaters of the Minnesota River where there were few buffalo but abundant beaver.

This cultural evolution took place east of the Missouri River. By 1770 the advantage the gun had given the Sioux over the tribes further west had largely disappeared and the balance of tribal power on the eastern Great Plains seemed stable. The Sioux dominated the Missouri River drainage below the Arikara villages on the Great Bend, but these villages, along with those of the Mandans and Hidatsas further up the Missouri, blocked further advance. These horticultural peoples with their large populations, numerous horses, and fortified towns easily resisted incursions by the less numerous and poorly mounted Sioux. Further to the south the Omahas, under their great Blackbird, had acquired guns and halted the Sioux advance down the Missouri. The Sioux, of course, were not totally confined. Some bands regularly raided the Arikaras for horses, and the Tetons, either independently or in alliance with the Arikaras, moved across the Missouri to hunt or raid the Mandans and Hidatsas. But the Sioux were only interlopers in this territory; their power was limited.

The deterioration of this balance of power and the beginning of the second stage of Sioux expansion resulted from a combination of internal and external developments. During the last quarter of the eighteenth century, Sioux hunters depleted the buffalo and beaver populations east of the Missouri. This, by itself, would have forced the Tetons and Yanktonais either to expand their hunting grounds or to alter their economy. The initial response of the Oglalas at least appears to have been not conquest, but rather imitation of the horticultural economy of the village tribes. The prosperity of these villagers—with their abundant supplies of corn, beans, squash, and their lucrative trade in hides, meat, and horses with the buffalo nomads to the west—seems to have exerted a real attraction for the Sioux. For a time the Oglalas actually settled with the Arikaras and adopted their horticultural and buffalo-hunting economy. But the arrival of European traders aborted this evolution of the Sioux into sedentary horticultural villagers.

In the late eighteenth century French and Spanish traders moved up the Missouri River creating a new source of European trade goods for the villagers and for the nomadic tribes beyond. These white traders not only seriously undercut the Sioux role as middlemen, but they also set out to capture the trade of the Sioux. In the eyes of the Missouri traders, the Sioux, through their trade fairs, drew off the fur trade of the plains and Rockies from its natural route down the Missouri and diverted it into English Canada. For the French and Spanish, therefore, successful commerce on the Missouri necessarily meant the destruction of old Sioux trading patterns. The commerce they eventually succeeded in capturing, however, was not the old trade in beaver pelts, but a new trade in buffalo robes and pemmican. As products of the buffalo hunts became convertible into European trade goods, the Tetons found less and less reason to devote time to beaver trapping. By 1804 the major Teton trade items were buffalo robes and hides, and the need for horses and hunting grounds had replaced trapping grounds as the major motives for war.

But far more significant in stimulating Sioux expansion than any deliberate action traders took was the accidental, if inevitable, result of their presence: the arrival of European epidemic diseases. The Sioux, because they lived in small wandering groups, were far less vulnerable to these epidemics than the populous agricultural villages. The Brulé winter counts record smallpox in 1779–1780, 1780–1781, and 1801–1802 (the epidemics are dated slightly differently in other winter counts), but their losses were slight when compared to those of the Arikaras, Hidatsas, and Mandans. In 1795 Truteau reported that the Arikaras had been reduced from "32 populous villages" to two and from 4,000 warriors to 500—a loss of population which, in turn, caused severe social and economic disruption. The smallpox reached the Mandan and Hidatsa villages in 1781, inflicting losses proportionate to those of the Arikaras. On the lower Missouri during the opening years of the nineteenth century, the smallpox reduced the Omahas from 700 to 300 warriors and killed Blackbird, their famous and powerful chief. These losses broke their power and their control of the Missouri below the Sioux.

The epidemics not only weakened the powerful tribes that had previously held the Sioux in check, but they also ended any attempts of the Oglalas to become horticultural villagers themselves. During the late eighteenth century the Sioux pushed the Arikaras steadily up the Missouri where they joined with their old enemies, the Mandans and Hidatsas, now also under great pressure from the Sioux. By the 1790s pre-epidemic horse raids had given way to war parties of up to 2,000 men that had succeeded in pushing the Mandans out of the Heart River country into the Knife River district of their Hidatsa allies. Although not always successful, Sioux attacks could be overwhelming, as when, in the early 1790s, the Sioux captured and destroyed an entire Mandan village near Deer Creek. The alliance of the Mandans and Hidatsas with the Arikaras was short-lived, however, and by 1800 the Arikaras had moved back downstream. According to white traders, their return made them little more than serfs of the Sioux who cut them off from the buffalo, cheated them, robbed them, and, as the Sioux said, made them fulfill the economic role of women.

This intertribal warfare was no game, no mere pattern of revenge killings against ancient enemies. Enemies of the Sioux, faced with disastrous losses, repeatedly sought peace. In 1803, for example, the Omahas and Poncas attempted to end their warfare with the Brulés. The largest Brulé band under BlackBull agreed, but simultaneously the Partisan, a leader of another Brulé band and supposedly envious of BlackBull's growing influence, led a horse raid against the Poncas. When the Poncas retaliated by stealing nine Sioux horses, they attacked the wrong Brulé village, BlackBull's, not the Partisan's, and the fragile peace was broken. In 1804 the Brulés, under BlackBull, fell upon a Ponca village, killing half of its inhabitants, and in September of that year they destroyed an Omaha village of forty lodges, killing seventy-five men. In desperation the Omahas and Poncas abandoned their permanent villages and crops, which made them vulnerable to both the smallpox and the nomadic Sioux. For a time they became horse nomads, not from desire, but from necessity. But even this strategy weakened them, diminishing their access to the guns the traders brought up the Missouri. By 1809 some white observers predicted that the once powerful Omahas would disappear entirely. Their difficulties vividly demonstrated the near impossibility of securing peace with the loosely organized Sioux.

Thus by 1803–1804, when the arrival of Merriwether Lewis and William Clark announced the new American presence on the Missouri, the Sioux had reduced the old borders and balance of power on the river to shambles. The

Mandans, Hidatsas, Arikaras, and Omahas possessed only the shadow of their former strength. The Sioux now dominated the upper Missouri nearly to the Yellowstone River. Furthermore, the Sioux had crossed the Missouri, fighting and hunting in the area bordering the Mandan-Hidatsa villages. An Oglala party under Standing Bull had reached the Black Hills in 1775–1776, and by the turn of the century the Oglalas were contesting the plains country between the Missouri and those mountains with the Kiowas, Arapahos, Crows, and Cheyennes.

Lewis and Clark immediately recognized the Sioux as the dominant power on the Missouri, the one tribe that could seriously threaten American commerce on that river. Because of their trade fairs (in decline, but still viable) the Sioux could disrupt white trade without fear of economic retaliation. They could always obtain needed European goods at the spring fairs further east. Lewis and Clark vilified the Sioux, but their very abuse revealed their high estimation of Sioux power.

> These are the vilest miscreants of the savage race, and must ever remain the pirates of the Missouri, until such measures are pursued by our government as will make them feel a dependence on its will for their supply of merchandise. Unless these people are reduced to order by coercive measures I am ready to pronounce that the citizens of the United States can never enjoy but partially the advantages which the Missouri presents.

American invective, however, was much stronger than American power in the area and was totally incapable of subjugating the Sioux. In 1807 the Sioux and their Arikara dependents first obtained tribute from a trading party under Manuel Lisa, and then drove a government party under Nathaniel Pryor, sent to escort the Mandan chief Shahaka to his village, back downstream. "I suppose a severe punishment of the Aricaras indispensible, taking for it our time and convenience," Thomas Jefferson wrote to Lewis the next year. And another year passed before Lewis decided to send a force of 250 soldiers, trappers, and traders with 300 Indian auxiliaries against the Arikaras. The party he actually dispatched in the summer of 1809, however, consisted of only 150 men, and when Pierre Chouteau, who commanded it, attempted to recruit his 300 auxiliaries among the Tetons, the very bands who had attacked Pryor, he found them more interested in looting the expedition than joining it. According to Chouteau, the Sioux warned him that "one tribe ought not countenance an attempt to destroy another, and if I still persisted in that resolution myself and my party might be destroyed before we reached the Ricaras." They advised Chouteau to pardon the Arikaras and distribute presents, and the supposedly punitive expedition eventually did exactly that.

White Americans obviously represented an important new element in the intertribal politics of the upper Missouri; but as the Chouteau and Pryor expeditions had demonstrated, they hardly dominated the region. And, despite their initial conflicts, the Sioux found the Americans to be useful, if dangerous, allies during their third period of expansion. For over three decades after the Chouteau expedition, the ambitions of the Sioux and the Americans proved generally complimentary, and as late as 1838 Joshua Pilcher, the American agent for the upper Missouri, would write that "no Indians ever manifested a greater degree of friendship for the whites in general, or more respect for our Government, than the Sioux."

The conquests of the western Sioux during the nineteenth century were politically united in only the loosest sense. The various Sioux tribes expanded for similar demographic, economic, and social reasons, however, and these underlying causes give a unity to the various wars of the Sioux.

Unlike every other tribe on the Great Plains during the nineteenth century, the Sioux appear to have increased in numbers. They were not immune to the epidemics that decimated the other tribes, but most of the Tetons and Yanktonais successfully avoided the disastrous results of the great epidemics, especially the epidemic of 1837 that probably halved the Indian population of the plains. Through historical accident the very conquests of the Sioux protected them from disease. This occurred in two opposite ways. The advance of Oglalas and Brulés to the southwest simply put them out of reach of the main epidemic corridor along the Missouri. Furthermore, Pilcher, the Indian agent on the Missouri, succeeded in giving them advance warning of the danger in 1837, and, unlike the Blackfeet and other nomadic tribes that suffered heavily from the epidemic, they did not come in to trade. The Tetons were infected, and individual tribes lost heavily, but the losses of the Sioux as a whole were comparatively slight. The Yanktons, Yanktonais, and portions of the Saone Tetons, however, dominated the Missouri trade route, but paradoxically this probably helped to save them. In 1832 the Office of Indian Affairs sent doctors up the river to vaccinate the Indians. Many of the Sioux refused to cooperate, but well over a thousand people, mostly Yanktonais, received vaccinations. Only enough money was appropriated to send the doctors as far upriver as the Sioux; so the Mandans and Hidatsas further upriver remained unvaccinated. As a result, when smallpox came, the Yanktonais were partially protected while their enemies in the villages once again died miserably in great numbers. The renewed American efforts at mass vaccination that followed the epidemic came too late for the Mandans, but in the 1840s thousands more Sioux were given immunity from smallpox.

The combination of freedom from disease, a high birth rate (in 1875 estimated as capable of doubling the population every twenty years), and continued migration from the Sioux tribes further east, produced a steadily growing population for the western Sioux. Although the various censuses taken by the whites were often little more than rough estimates, the western Sioux appear to have increased from a very low estimate of 5,000 people in 1804 to approximately 25,000 in the 1850s. This population increase, itself partly a result of the new abundance the Sioux derived from the buffalo herds, in turn, fueled an increased need for buffalo. The Sioux used the animals not only to feed their expanding population, but also to trade for necessary European goods. Since pemmican, buffalo robes, hides, and tongues had replaced beaver pelts as the main Indian trade item on the Missouri, the Sioux needed secure and profitable hunting grounds during a period when the buffalo were steadily moving west and north in response to hunting pressure on the Missouri.

Increased Indian hunting for trade contributed to the pressure on the buffalo herds, but the great bulk of the destruction was the direct work of white hunters and traders. The number of buffalo robes annually shipped down the Missouri increased from an average of 2,600 between 1815 and 1830 to 40,000 to 50,000 in 1833, a figure that did not include the numbers slaughtered by whites for pleasure. In 1848 Father Pierre-Jean De Smet reported the annual figure shipped downriver to St. Louis to be 25,000 tongues and 110,000 robes.

Despite what the most thorough student of the subject has seen as the Indians' own prudent use of the buffalo, the various tribes competed for an increasingly scarce resource. By the late 1820s the buffalo had disappeared from the Missouri below the Omaha villages, and the border tribes were already in desperate condition from lack of game. The Indians quickly realized the danger further up the Missouri, and upper Missouri tribes voiced complaints about white hunters as early as 1833. By the 1840s observations on the diminishing number of buffalo and increased Indian competition had become commonplace. Between 1833 and 1844 buffalo could be found in large numbers on the headwaters of the Little Cheyenne, but by the mid-1840s they were receding rapidly toward the mountains. The Sioux to a great extent simply had to follow, or move north and south, to find new hunting grounds. Their survival and prosperity depended on their success.

But buffalo hunting demanded more than territory; it also required horses, and in the 1820s, the Sioux were hardly noted for either the abundance or the quality of their herds. Raids and harsh winters on the plains frequently depleted Sioux horse herds, and the Sioux had to replenish them by raiding or trading farther to the south. In this sense the economy of the Sioux depended on warfare to secure the horses needed for the hunt. As Oscar Lewis has pointed out in connection with the Blackfeet, war and horse raiding became important economic activities for the Plains Indians.

The Yanktonais, Yanktons, and Saone Tetons had a third incentive for expansion. Power over the sedentary villagers secured them what Tabeau [a fur trader] had called their serfs. Under Sioux domination these villages could be raided or traded with as the occasion demanded, their corn and beans serving as sources of supplementary food supplies when the buffalo failed. A favorite tactic of the Sioux was to restrict, as far as possible, the access of these tribes to both European goods and the hunting grounds, thus forcing the village peoples to rely on the Sioux for trade goods, meat, and robes. To escape this exploitation, the villagers, in alliance with the nomadic tribes who traded with them, waged a nearly constant, if often desultory, war.

It is in this context of increasing population, increasing demand for buffalos and horses, the declining and retreating bison populations, and attempted domination of the sedentary villagers that the final phase of Sioux expansion during the nineteenth century took place. And, as the Omahas had found out, the loose structural organization of the western Sioux worked to make the impetus of their advance even more irresistible. Accommodation with one band or tribe often only served to increase inroads from others. There was no way for a tribe to deal with the whole Sioux nation.

On the Missouri the Sioux had long feared the logical alliance of all the village tribes against them, and they worked actively to prevent it. After 1810, the

Arikaras sporadically attempted to break away from Sioux domination by allying themselves with the Mandans and Hidatsas. In response, the Sioux blockaded the villages, cutting them off from the buffalo and stopping the white traders who came up the Missouri from supplying them. The Mandan-Arikara alliance, in turn, sent out war parties to keep the river open. But these alliances inevitably fell apart from internal strains, and the old pattern of oscillating periods of trade and warfare was renewed.

But if the Sioux feared an alliance of the sedentary village tribes, these tribes had an even greater fear of a Sioux-American partnership on the Missouri. The Arikaras, by attacking and defeating an American fur trading party under William Ashley in 1823, precipitated exactly the combination from which they had most to fear. When 1,500 Sioux warriors appeared before their village that year, they were accompanied by United States troops under Colonel Henry Leavenworth. This joint expedition took the Arikara village and sacked it, but the Sioux were disgusted with the performance of their American auxiliaries. They blamed American cautiousness for allowing the Arikaras to escape further upstream. Although they remained friendly to the United States, the whole affair gave them a low estimation of the ability of white soldiers that would last for years. They finished the removal of the Arikaras themselves, forcing them by 1832 to abandon both their sedentary villages and the Missouri River and to move south to live first with, and then just above, the Skidi Pawnees. The Yanktonais, 450 lodges strong, moved in from the Minnesota River to take over the old Arikara territory.

With the departure of the Arikaras, the Mandans and Hidatsas alone remained to contest Sioux domination of the Missouri. In 1836 the Yanktonais, nearly starving after a season of poor hunts, began petty raids on the Mandans and Hidatsas. In retaliation, a Mandan-Hidatsa war party destroyed a Yanktonai village of forty-five lodges, killing more than 150 people and taking fifty prisoners. The Sioux counterattacks cost the Mandans dearly. During the next year they lost over sixty warriors, but what was worse, when the smallpox hit in 1837, the villagers could not disperse for fear of the hostile Yanktonais who still occupied the plains around the villages. The Mandans were very nearly destroyed; the Hidatsas, who attempted a quarantine, lost over half their people, and even the luckless Arikaras returned in time to be ravaged by the epidemic. The villages that survived continued to suffer from Yanktonai attacks and could use the plains hunting grounds only on sufferance of the Sioux.

The Oglala-Brulé advance onto the buffalo plains southwest of the Missouri was contemporaneous with the push up the Missouri and much more significant. Here horse raids and occasional hunts by the Sioux gave way to a concerted attempt to wrest the plains between the Black Hills and the Missouri from the Arapahos, Crows, Kiowas, and Cheyennes. By 1825, the Oglalas, advancing up the drainage of the Teton River, and the Brulés, moving up the drainage of the White River, had dispossessed the Kiowas and driven them south, pushed the Crows west to Powder River, and formed with the Cheyennes and Arapahos an alliance which would dominate the north and central plains for the next half century.

Historians have attributed the movement of the Sioux beyond the Black Hills into the Platte drainage to manipulations of the Rocky Mountain Fur Company, which sought to capture the Sioux trade from the American Fur Company. But, in fact, traders followed the Sioux; the Sioux did not follow the traders. William Sublette of the Rocky Mountain Fur Company did not lure the Sioux to the Platte. He merely took advantage of their obvious advance toward it. He was the first to realize that by the 1830s Brulé and Oglala hunting grounds lay closer to the Platte than to the Missouri, and he took advantage of the situation to get their trade. The arrival of the Sioux on the Platte was not sudden; it had been preceded by the usual period of horse raids. Nor did it break some long accepted balance of power. Their push beyond the Black Hills was merely another phase in the long Sioux advance from the edge of the Great Plains.

What probably lured the Sioux toward the Platte was an ecological phenomenon that did not require the total depletion of game in the area they already held and that was not peculiar to the plains. Borders dividing contending tribes were never firm; between the established hunting territory of each people lay an indeterminate zone, variously described as war grounds or neutral grounds. In this area only war parties dared to venture; it was too dangerous for any band to travel into these regions to hunt. Because little pressure was put on the animal populations of these contested areas by hunters, they provided a refuge for the hard-pressed herds of adjacent tribal hunting grounds. Since buffalo migrations were unpredictable, a sudden loss of game in a large part of one tribe's territory could prompt an invasion of these neutral grounds. Thus, throughout the nineteenth century, there usually lay at the edges of the Sioux-controlled lands, a lucrative area that held an understandable attraction for them. In the contest for these rich disputed areas lay the key not only to many of the Sioux wars, but also to many other aboriginal wars on the continent.

These areas were, of course, never static. They shifted as tribes were able to wrest total control of them from other contending peoples, and so often created, in turn, a new disputed area beyond. Between 1830 and 1860, travelers on the plains described various neutral or war grounds ranging from the Sand Hills north of the Loup River in Nebraska down to the Pawnee Fork of the Arkansas. But for the Sioux four areas stand out: the region below Fort Laramie between the forks of the Platte in dispute during the 1830s; the Medicine Bow–Laramie plains country above Fort Laramie, fought over in the 1840s; the Yellowstone drainage of the Powder, Rosebud, and Big Horn rivers initially held by the Crows but reduced to a neutral ground in the 1840s and 1850s; and portions of the Republican River country contested from the 1840s to the 1870s. Two things stand out in travelers' accounts of these areas: they were disputed by two or more tribes and they were rich in game.

Francis Parkman vividly described and completely misinterpreted an episode in the Sioux conquest of one of these areas, the Medicine Bow Valley, in 1846. He attributed the mustering of the large expedition that went, according to his account, against the Shoshones, and according to others against the Crows, to a desire for revenge for the loss of a son of Whirlwind, an important Sioux chief, during a horse raid on the Shoshones. But in Parkman's account, Whirlwind, who supposedly organized the expedition, decided not to accompany it, and the Oglalas and Saones who went ended up fighting neither the Crows nor the Shoshones. What they did, however, is significant. They moved into disputed

Medicine Bow country west of Fort Laramie, land which all of these tribes contested.

The Sioux entered the area warily, took great precautions to avoid, not seek out, Crow and Shoshone war parties, and were much relieved to escape unscathed after a successful hunt. Parkman was disgusted, but the Sioux were immensely pleased with the whole affair. They had achieved the main goal of their warfare, the invasion and safe hunting of disputed buffalo grounds without any cost to themselves. White Shield, the slain man's brother, made another, apparently token, attempt to organize a war party to avenge his loss, but he never departed. The whole episode—from the whites' confusion over what tribe was the target of the expedition, to their misinterpretation of Indian motives, to Parkman's failure to see why the eventual outcome pleased the Sioux—reveals why, in so many accounts, the logic of Indian warfare is lost and wars are reduced to outbursts of random bloodletting. For the Sioux, the disputed area and its buffalo, more than the Shoshones or Crows, were the targets of the expedition; revenge was subordinate to the hunt. Their ability to hunt in safety, without striking a blow, comprised a strategic victory that more than satisfied them. To Parkman, intent on observing savage warriors lusting for blood revenge, all this was unfathomable.

Not all expeditions ended so peacefully, however. Bloodier probes preceded the summer expedition of 1846, and others followed it. When the Sioux arrived in strength on the Platte in the mid-1830s, their raiding parties were already familiar to peoples from the Pawnee south to the Arkansas and the Santa Fe Trail. As early as the 1820s, their allies, the Cheyennes and Arapahos, had unsuccessfully contested hunting grounds with the Skidi Pawnees. But by 1835, these tribes had agreed to make peace.

The arrival of the Oglalas and Brulés at the Laramie River presented both the Pawnees and the Crows with more powerful rivals. The Crows were by now old enemies of the Tetons. Initially as allies of the Mandans and Hidatsas, and later as contestants for the hunting grounds of the plains, they had fought the Sioux for at least fifty years. By the 1840s, however, the once formidable Crows were a much weakened people. As late as the 1830s they had possessed more horses than any other tribe on the upper Missouri and estimates of their armed strength had ranged from 1,000 to 2,500 mounted men, but the years that followed brought them little but disaster. Smallpox and cholera reduced their numbers from 800 to 460 lodges, and rival groups pressed into their remaining hunting grounds. The Blackfeet attacked them from the north while the Saones, Oglalas, and Brulés closed in on the east and south. Threatened and desperate, the Crows sought aid west of the Rockies and increasingly allied themselves with the Shoshones and Flatheads.

The Pawnees, the last powerful horticultural tribe left on the plains, did not have a long tradition of warfare with the Sioux. The four Pawnee tribes—the Republicans, Skidis, Tapages, and Grands—lived in permanent earth-lodge villages on the Platte and Loup rivers, but twice a year they went on extended hunts in an area that stretched from between the forks of the Platte in the north to the Republican, Kansas, and Arkansas rivers in the south. Sioux horse raids had originally worried them very little, but, after the wars with Arapahos and Cheyennes, the growing proximity of the Sioux and their advantage in firearms had begun to concern the Pawnees enough to ask Americans to act as intermediaries in establishing peace. In the 1830s they remained, in the words of their white agent, along with the Sioux, one of the "two master tribes in the Upper Indian Country . . . who govern nearly all the smaller ones."

Under BullBear the Oglalas spearheaded the conquest of the Platte River hunting grounds of the Skidi Pawnees. By 1838, the Pawnee agent reported that the Skidis, fearing the Sioux would soon dominate the entire buffalo country, were contesting "every inch of ground," and, he added, "they are right for the day is not far off when the Sioux will possess the whole buffalo region, unless they are checked." In 1838, smallpox struck both the Oglalas and the Pawnees, but, as happened further north, the populous horticultural villages of the Pawnees suffered far more than the nomadic Sioux bands. The next year the intertribal struggle culminated in a pitched battle that cost the Pawnees between eighty and one-hundred warriors and led to the *de facto* surrender of the Platte hunting grounds by the Skidis.

The murder of BullBear in 1841 during a factional quarrel prompted a split in the Oglalas. One band, the Kiyuskas, BullBear's old supporters, continued to push into the Pawnee lands along the Platte and Smoky Hill Rivers, while the other faction, the Bad Faces, moved west and north often joining with the Saone bands who were pushing out from the Missouri in attacks on the Crows. During these advances the Utes and Shoshones would be added to the ranks of Teton enemies, and further north the Yanktonais and Hunkpapas pushed into Canada, fighting the Metis, Plains Crees, and Assiniboines.

The Oregon, California, and Utah migrations of the 1840s made the Platte River Valley an American road across the plains. Like the traders on the Missouri before them, these migrants drove away game and created a new avenue for epidemic diseases, culminating in the cholera epidemic of 1849–1850. For the first time, the whites presented a significant threat to Sioux interests, and this conflict bore as fruit the first signs of overt Teton hostility since Chouteau's and Pryor's expeditions [in 1809 and 1807, respectively]. But on the whole whites suffered little from the initial Teton reaction to the Oregon trail. The Crows and Pawnees bore the consequences of the decline of the Platte hunting grounds.

The Brulés and Kiyuska Oglalas attacked the Pawnees on the South Platte and the Republican. The Tetons did not restrict their attacks to the buffalo grounds; along with the Yanktons and Yanktonais from the Missouri, they attacked the Pawnees in their villages and disrupted the whole Pawnee economy. While small war parties stole horses and killed women working in the fields, large expeditions with as many as 700 men attacked the villages themselves. This dual assault threatened to reduce the Pawnees to starvation, greatly weakening their ability to resist.

The Sioux struck one of their most devastating blows in 1843, destroying a new village the Pawnees had built on the Loup at the urging of the whites. They killed sixty-seven people and forced the Pawnees back to the Platte, where they were threatened with retribution by whites for their failure to remove as agreed. The Pawnees vainly cited American obligations under the treaty of 1833 to help defend them from attacks by other tribes; and they also repeatedly sought peace. Neither availed. Unlike the Otos, Omahas, and Poncas, who eventually gave up all attempts to hunt on the western plains, the Pawnees persisted in their semiannual expeditions. The tribal census taken in 1859 reveals the price the Pawnees paid. When Zebulon Pike had visited the Pawnees in 1806 he found a roughly equivalent number of men and women in each village. In his partial census, he gave a population of 1,973 men and 2,170 women, exclusive of children. In 1859, agent William Dennison listed 820 men and 1,505 women; largely because of war, women now outnumbered men by nearly two to one.

The final blow came in 1873, three years before the Battle of the Little Bighorn, when the Sioux surprised a Pawnee hunting party on the Republican River, killing about 100 people. The Pawnees, now virtually prisoners in their reservation villages, gave in. They abandoned their Nebraska homeland and, over the protests of their agents, moved to Indian Territory. White settlers may have rejoiced at their removal, but it was the Sioux who had driven the Pawnees from Nebraska.

The experience of the Crows was much the same. Attacked along a front that ran from the Yellowstone to the Laramie Plains, they were never routed, but their power declined steadily. The Sioux drove them from the Laramie Plains and then during the 1850s and 1860s pushed them farther and farther up the Yellowstone. In the mid-1850s, Edwin Denig, a trapper familiar with the plains, predicted their total destruction, and by 1862 they had apparently been driven from the plains and into the mountains. They, too, would join the Americans against the Sioux.

In a very real sense the Americans, because of their destruction of game along the Missouri and Platte, had stimulated this warfare for years, but their first significant intervention in intertribal politics since the Leavenworth expedition came with the celebrated Laramie Peace Conference of 1851. Although scholars have recognized the importance of both intertribal warfare and the decline of the buffalo in prompting this conference, they have, probably because they accepted without question the individualistic interpretation of Indian wars, neglected the Indian political situation at the time of the treaty. They have failed to appreciate the predominance of the Sioux-Cheyenne-Arapaho alliance on the northern and central plains.

By 1851, American Indian officials had recognized that white travel and trade on the Great Plains had reduced the number of buffalo and helped precipitate intertribal wars. They proposed to restore peace by compensating the Indians for the loss of game. Their motives for this were hardly selfless, since intertribal wars endangered American travelers and commerce. Once they had established peace and drawn firm boundaries between the tribes, they could hold a tribe responsible for any depredations committed within its allotted area. Furthermore, by granting compensation for the destruction of game, the government gave itself an entrée into tribal politics: by allowing or withholding payments, they could directly influence the conduct of the Indians.

Although American negotiators certainly did not seek tribal unity in 1851, it is ethnocentric history to contend that the Fort Laramie treaty allowed the Americans to "divide and conquer." Fundamentally divided at the time of the treaty, the plains tribes continued so afterward. The treaty itself was irrelevant; both the boundaries it created and its prohibition of intertribal warfare were ignored from the beginning by the only tribal participants who finally mattered, the Sioux.

Indeed the whole conference can be interpreted as a major triumph for the

Tetons. In a sense, the Fort Laramie Treaty marked the height of Sioux political power. Of the 10,000 Indians who attended the conference, the great majority of them were Sioux, Cheyennes, and Arapahos. Sioux threats kept the Pawnees and all but small groups of Crows, Arikaras, Hidatsas, and Assiniboines from coming to Fort Laramie. The Shoshones came, but the Cheyennes attacked their party and part turned back. With the Sioux and their allies so thoroughly dominating the conference, the treaty itself amounted to both a recognition of Sioux power and an attempt to curb it. But when American negotiators tried to restrict the Sioux to an area north of the Platte, Black Hawk, an Oglala, protested that they held the lands to the south by the same right the Americans held their lands, the right of conquest: "These lands once belonged to the Kiowas and the Crows, but we whipped those nations out of them, and in this we did what the white men do when they want the lands of the Indians." The Americans conceded, granting the Sioux hunting rights, which, in Indian eyes, confirmed title. The Sioux gladly accepted American presents and their tacit recognition of Sioux conquests, but, as their actions proved, they never saw the treaty as a prohibition of future gains. After an American war with the Sioux and another attempt to stop intertribal warfare in 1855, Bear's Rib, a Hunkpapa chief, explained to Lieutenant G. K. Warren that the Tetons found it difficult to take the American prohibition of warfare seriously when the Americans themselves left these conferences only to engage in wars with other Indians or with the Mormons.

After the treaty, the lines of conflict on the plains were clearly drawn. The two major powers in the area, the Sioux and the Americans, had both advanced steadily and with relatively little mutual conflict. Following the treaty they became avowed and recognized rivals. Within four years of the treaty, the first American war with the Tetons would break out; and by the mid-1850s, American officers frankly saw further war as inevitable. The Sioux, in turn, recognized the American threat to their interests, and the tribes, in a rare display of concerted action, agreed as a matter of policy to prohibit all land cessions and to close their remaining productive hunting grounds to American intrusions. These attempts consistently led to war with the Americans. After a century of conquest the Sioux had very definite conceptions of the boundaries of their tribal territory. Recent historians and some earlier anthropologists contended that Indians never fought for territory, but if this is so, it is hard to explain the documented outrage of the Saones, Oglalas, and Brulés at the cession of land along the Missouri by the Yanktons in 1858. The Tetons had moved from this land decades before and had been replaced by the Yanktons, but from the Teton point of view the whole western Sioux nation still held title to the territory and the Yanktons had no authority to sell it. Fearing that acceptance of annuities would connote recognition of the sale, the Saone tribes refused them, and the cession provoked a crisis on the western plains and hardened Teton ranks against the Americans.

The warfare between the northern plains tribes and the United States that followed the Fort Laramie Treaty of 1851 was not the armed resistance of a people driven to the wall by American expansion. In reality these wars arose from the clash of two expanding powers—the United States, and the Sioux and their allies. If, from a distance, it appears that the vast preponderance of strength rested with the whites, it should be remembered that the ability of the United States to bring this power to bear was limited. The series of defeats the Sioux inflicted on American troops during these years reveals how real the power of the Tetons was.

Even as they fought the Americans, the Sioux continued to expand their domination of plains hunting grounds, as they had to in order to survive. Logically enough, the tribes the Sioux threatened—the Crows, Pawnees, and Arikaras especially—sided with the Americans, providing them with soldiers and scouts. For white historians to cast these people as mere dupes or traitors is too simplistic. They fought for their tribal interests and loyalties as did the Sioux.

It is ironic that historians, far more than anthropologists, have been guilty of viewing intertribal history as essentially ahistoric and static, of refusing to examine critically the conditions that prompted Indian actions. In too much Indian history, tribes fight only "ancient" enemies, as if each group were doled out an allotted number of adversaries at creation with whom they battled mindlessly through eternity. Historians have been too easily mystified by intertribal warfare, too willing to see it as the result of some ingrained cultural pugnacity. This is not to argue that the plains tribes did not offer individual warriors incentives of wealth and prestige that encouraged warfare, but, as [anthropologist W.W.] Newcomb pointed out, the real question is why the tribe placed such a premium on encouraging warriors. This is essentially a historical question. Without an understanding of tribal and intertribal histories, and an appreciation that, like all history, they are dynamic, not static, the actions of Indians when they come into conflict with whites can be easily and fatally distorted.

Bison Ecology and Bison Diplomacy: The Southern Plains, 1800–1850

DAN FLORES

In bright spring light on the Great Plains of two centuries ago, governor Juan Bautista de Anza failed in the last of the three crucial tasks that his superiors had set him as part of their effort to reform New Mexico's Comanche policy. Over half a decade, Anza had followed one success with another. He had brilliantly defeated the formidable Comanche *nomnekaht* (war leader) Cuerno Verde in 1779, and as a consequence in 1786, he had personally fashioned the long-sought peace between New Mexico and the swelling Comanche population of the Southern Plains. His third task was to persuade the Comanches to settle in permanent villages and to farm.

But the New Mexico governor found the third undertaking impossible. Observers of Plains Indian life for 250 years and committed to encouraging agriculture over hunting, the Spaniards were certain that the culture of the horse Indians was ephemeral, that the bison on which they depended were an exhaustible resource. Thus Anza pleaded with the tribes to give up the chase. The Comanches thought him unconvincing. Recently liberated by horse culture and by the teeming wildlife of the High Plains, their bands found the Arkansas River pueblo the

Dan Flores, "Bison Ecology and Bison Diplomacy: The Southern Plains from 1800 to 1850," *Journal of American History* 78 (September 1991), pp. 465–485. Reprinted by permission.

governor built for them unendurable. They returned to the hunt with the evident
expectation that their life as buffalo hunters was an endless cycle. And yet Anza
proved to be a prophet. Within little more than half a century, the Comanches and
other tribes of the Southern Plains were routinely suffering from starvation and
complaining of shortages of bison. What had happened?

Environmental historians and ethnohistorians whose interests have been environmental topics have in the two past decades been responsible for many of our
most valuable recent insights into the history of native Americans since their contact with Euro-Americans. Thus far, however, modern scholarship has not reeval-
uated the most visible historic interaction, the set piece if you will, of native
American environmental history. On the Great Plains of the American West during the two centuries from 1680 to 1880, almost three-dozen native American
groups adopted horse-propelled, bison-hunting cultures that defined "Indianness"
for white Americans and most of the world. It is the end of this process that has
most captured the popular imagination: the military campaigns against and the
brutal incarceration of the horse Indians, accompanied by the astonishingly rapid
elimination of bison, and of an old ecology that dated back ten thousand years, at
the hands of commercial hide hunters. That dramatic end, which occurred in less
than fifteen years following the end of the Civil War, has by now entered American mythology. Yet our focus on the finale has obscured an examination of earlier phases that might shed new light on the historical and environmental interaction of the horse Indians and bison herds on the Plains.

In the nineteenth-century history of the Central and Southern Plains, there
have long been perplexing questions that environmental history seems well suited
to answer. Why were the Comanches able to replace the Apaches on the bison-
rich Southern Plains? Why did the Kiowas, Cheyennes, and Arapahoes gradually
shift southward into the Southern Plains between 1800 and 1825? And why, after
fighting each other for two decades, did these Southern Plains peoples effect a
rapprochement and alliance in the 1840s? What factors brought on such an esca-
lation of Indian raids into Mexico and Texas in the late 1840s that the subject
assumed critical importance in the Treaty of Guadalupe-Hidalgo? If the bison
herds were so vast in the years before the commercial hide hunters, why were
there so many reports of starving Indians on the Plains by 1850? And finally,
given our standard estimates of bison numbers, why is it that the hide hunters are
credited with bringing to market only some 10 million hides, including no more
than 3.5 million from the Southern Plains, in the 1870s?

Apposite to all of these questions is a central issue: How successful were the
horse Indians in creating a dynamic ecological equilibrium between themselves
and the vast bison herds that grazed the Plains? That is, had they developed sus-
tainable hunting practices that would maintain the herds and so permit future generations of hunters to follow the same way of life? This is not to pose the "anachronistic question" (the term is Richard White's) of whether Indians were
ecologists. But how a society or a group of peoples with a shared culture makes
adjustments to live within the carrying capacity of its habitat is not only a valid
historical question, it may be one of the most salient questions to ask about any
culture. Historians of the Plains have differed about the long-term ecological sus-
tainability of the Indians' use of bison, particularly after the Euro-American fur

trade reached the West and the tribes began hunting bison under the influence of the market economy. The standard work, Frank Roe's *The North American Buffalo,* has generally carried the debate with the argument that there is "not a shred of evidence" to indicate that the horse Indians were out of balance with the bison herds. Using the new insights and methods of environmental history, it now appears possible systematically to analyze and revise our understanding of nineteenth-century history on the Great Plains. Such an approach promises to resolve some of the major questions. It can advance our understanding of when bison declined in numbers and of the intertwining roles that Indian policies—migrations, diplomacy, trade, and use of natural resources—and the growing pressures of external stimuli played in that decline. The answers are complex and offer a revision of both Plains history and western Indian ecological history.

Working our way through to them requires some digression into the large historical forces that shaped the Southern Plains over the last hundred centuries. The perspective of the *longue durée* is essential to environmental history. What transpired on the Great Plains from 1800 to 1850 is not comprehensible without taking into account the effect of the Pleistocene extinctions of ten thousand years ago, or the cycle of droughts that determined the carrying capacity for animals on the grasslands. Shallower in time than these forces but just as important to the problem are factors that stemmed from the arrival of Europeans in the New World. Trade was an ancient part of the cultural landscape of America, but the Europeans altered the patterns, the goods, and the intensity of trade. And the introduction of horses and horse culture accomplished a technological revolution for the Great Plains. The horse was the chief catalyst of an ongoing remaking of the tribal map of western America, as native American groups moved onto the Plains and incessantly shifted their ranges and alliances in response to a world where accelerating change seemed almost the only constant.

At the beginning of the nineteenth century, the dominant groups on the Southern Plains were the two major divisions of the Comanches: the Texas Comanches, primarily Kotsotekas, and the great New Mexico division, spread across the country from the Llano Estacado Escarpment west to the foothills of the Sangre de Cristo Mountains, and composed of Yamparika and Jupe bands that only recently had replaced the Apaches on the High Plains. The Comanches' drive to the south from their original homelands in what is now southwestern Wyoming and northwestern Colorado was a part of the original tribal adjustments to the coming of horse technology to the Great Plains. There is reason to believe that the Eastern Shoshones, from whom the Comanches were derived before achieving a different identity on the Southern Plains, were one of the first intermountain tribes of historic times to push onto the Plains. Perhaps as early as 1500 the proto-Comanches were hunting bison and using dog power to haul their mountain-adapted four-pole tipis east of the Laramie Mountains. Evidently they moved in response to a wetter time on the Central Plains and the larger bison concentrations there.

These early Shoshonean hunters may not have spent more than three or four generations among the thronging Plains bison herds, for by the seventeenth century they had been pushed back into the mountains and the sagebrush deserts by tribes newly armed with European guns moving westward from the region around the Great Lakes. If so, they were among a complex of tribes southwest of the lakes that over the next two centuries would be displaced by a massive Siouan drive to the west, an imperial expansion for domination of the prize buffalo range of the Nothern Plains, and a wedge that sent ripples of tribal displacement across the Plains.

Among the historic tribes, the people who became Comanches thus may have shared with the Apaches and, if linguistic arguments are correct, probably with the Kiowas the longest familiarity with a bison-hunting life-style. Pressed back toward the mountains as Shoshones, they thus turned in a different direction and emerged from the passes through the Front Range as the same people but bearing a new name given them by the Utes: Komantcia. They still lacked guns but now began their intimate association with the one animal, aside from the bison, inextricably linked with Plains life. The Comanches began acquiring horses from the Utes within a decade or so after the Pueblo Revolt of 1680 sent horses and horse culture diffusing in all directions from New Mexico. Thus were born the "hyper-Indians," as William Brandon has called the Plains people.

The Comanches became, along with the Sioux, the most populous and widespread of all the peoples who now began to ride onto the vast sweep of grassland to participate in the hunter's life. They began to take possession of the Southern Plains by the early 1700s. By 1800 they were in full control of all the country east of the Southern Rocky Mountains and south of the Arkansas River clear to the Texas Hill Country. Their new culture, long regarded as an ethnographic anomaly on the Plains because of its western and archaic origins, may not be unique, as older scholars had supposed it to be—at least if we believe the new Comanche revisionists. Irrespective of their degree of tribal unity, however, when they began to move onto the Southern Plains with their new horse herds, their culture was adapting in interesting ways to the wealth of resources now available to them.

To the Comanches, the Southern Plains must have seemed an earthly paradise. The Pleistocene extinctions ten thousand years earlier had left dozens of grazing niches vacant on the American Great Plains. A dwarf species of bison with a higher reproductive capability than any of its ancestors evolved to flood most of those vacant niches with an enormous biomass of one grazer. In an ecological sense, bison were a weed species that had proliferated as a result of a major disturbance. That disturbance still reverberated, making it easy for Spanish horses, for example, to reoccupy their old niche and rapidly spread across the Plains. Those reverberations made the horse Indians thrive on an environmental situation that has had few parallels in world history.

The dimensions of the wild bison resource on the Southern Plains, and the Great Plains in general, have been much overstated in popular literature. For one thing, pollen analysis and archaeological data indicate that for the Southern Plains there were intervals, some spanning centuries, others decades, when bison must have been almost absent. Two major times of absence occurred between 5000 and 2500 B.C. and between A.D. 500 and 1300. The archaeological levels that lack bison bones correspond to pollen data indicating droughts. The severe southwestern drought that ended early in the fourteenth century was replaced by a five-hundred-year cycle of wetter and cooler conditions, and a return of bison in large numbers to the Southern Plains from their drought refugia to the east and west. This long-term pattern in the archaeological record seems to have prevailed on a smaller scale within historic times. During the nineteenth century, for example, droughts of more than five years' duration struck the Great Plains four times at roughly twenty-year intervals, in a long-term dendrochronological pattern that seems to show a drying cycle (shorter drought-free intervals) beginning in the 1850s.

More important, our popular perception of bison numbers—based on the estimates of awed nineteenth-century observers—probably sets them too high. There very likely were never 100 million or even 60 million bison on the Plains during the present climate regime because the carrying capacity of the grasslands was not so high. The best technique for determining bison carrying capacity on the Southern Plains is to extrapolate from United States census data for livestock, and the best census for the extrapolation is that of 1910, after the beef industry crashes of the 1880s had reduced animal numbers, but before the breakup of ranches and the Enlarged Homestead Act of 1909 resulted in considerable sections of the Southern Plains being broken out by farmers. Additionally, dendrochronological data seem to show that at the turn of the century rainfall on the Southern Plains was at median, between-droughts levels, rendering the census of 1910 particularly suitable as a base line for carrying capacity and animal populations.

The 1910 agricultural census indicates that in the 201 counties on the Southern Plains (which covered 240,000 square miles), the nineteenth-century carrying capacity during periods of median rainfall was about 7,000,000 cattle-equivalent grazers—specifically for 1910, about 5,150,000 cattle and 1,890,000 horses and mules. The bison population was almost certainly larger, since migratory grazing patterns and coevolution with the native grasses made bison as a wild species about 18 percent more efficient on the Great Plains than domestic cattle. And varying climate conditions during the nineteenth century, as I will demonstrate, noticeably affected grassland carrying capacity. The ecological reality was a dynamic cycle in which carrying capacity could swing considerably from decade to decade. But if the Great Plains bovine carrying capacity of 1910 expresses a median reality, then during prehorse times the Southern Plains might have supported an average of about 8.2 million bison, the entire Great Plains perhaps 28–30 million.

Although 8 million bison on the Southern Plains may not be so many as historians used to believe, to the Comanches the herds probably seemed limitless. Bison availability through horse culture caused a specialization that resulted in the loss of two-thirds of the Comanches' former plant lore and in a consequent loss of status for their women, an intriguing development that seems to have occurred to some extent among all the tribes that moved onto the Plains during the horse period. As full-time bison hunters the Comanches appear to have abandoned all the old Shoshonean mechanisms, such as infanticide and polyandry, that had kept their population in line with available resources. These were replaced with such cultural mechanisms as widespread adoption of captured children and polygyny, adaptations to the Plains that were designed to keep

Comanche numbers high and growing. That these changes seem to have been conscious and deliberate argues, perhaps, both Comanche environmental insight and some centralized leadership and planning.

Comanche success at seizing the Southern Plains from the native groups that had held it for several hundred years was likewise the result of a conscious choice: their decision to shape their lives around bison and horses. Unlike the Comanches, many of the Apache bands had heeded the Spaniards' advice and had begun to build streamside gardening villages that became deathtraps once the Comanches located them. The Apaches' vulnerability, then, ironically stemmed from their willingness to diversify their economy. Given the overwhelming dominance of grasslands as opposed to cultivable river lands on the Plains, the specialized horse and bison culture of the Comanches exploited a greater volume of the thermodynamic energy streaming from sunlight into plants than the economies of any of their competitors—until they encountered Cheyennes and Arapahoes with a similar culture. The horse-mounted Plains Indians, in other words, made very efficient use of the available energy on the Great Plains, something they seem instinctively to have recognized and exulted in. From the frequency with which the Comanches applied some version of the name "wolf" to their leaders, I suspect that they may have recognized their role as human predators and their ecological kinship with the wolf packs that like them lived off the bison herds.

The Comanches were not the only people on the Southern Plains during the horse period. The New Mexicans, both Pueblo and Hispanic, continued to hunt on the wide-open Llanos [plains], as did the praire Caddoans, although the numbers of the latter were dwindling rapidly by 1825. The New Mexican peoples and the Caddoans of the middle Red and Brazos rivers played major trade roles for hunters on the Southern Plains, and the Comanches in particular. Although the Comanches engaged in the archetypal Plains exchange of bison products for horticultural produce and European trade goods and traded horses and mules with Anglo-American traders from Missouri, Arkansas, and Louisiana, they were not a high-volume trading people until relatively late in their history. Early experiences with American traders and disease led them to distrust trade with Euro-Americans, and only once or twice did they allow short-lived posts to be established in their country. Instead, peace with the prairie Caddoans by the 1730s and with New Mexico in 1786 sent Comanche trade both east and west, but often through Indian middlemen.

In the classic, paradigmatic period between 1800 and 1850, the most interesting Southern Plains development was the cultural interaction between the Comanches and surrounding Plains Indians to the north. The Kiowas were the one of those groups most closely identified with the Comanches.

The Kiowas are and have long been an enigma. Scholars are interested in their origins because Kiowa oral tradition is at odds with the scientific evidence. The Kiowas believe that they started their journey to Rainy Mountain on the Oklahoma Plains from the north. And indeed, in the eighteenth century we find them on the Northern Plains, near the Black Hills, as one of the groups being displaced southwestward by the Siouan drive toward the buffalo range. Linguistically, however, the Kiowas are southern Indians. Their language belongs to the

Tanoan group of Pueblo languages in New Mexico, and some scholars believe that the Kiowas of later history are the same people as the Plains Jumanos of early New Mexico history, whose rancherias were associated during the 1600s and early 1700s with the headwaters of the Colorado and Concho rivers of Texas. How the Kiowas got so far north is not certainly known, but in historical times they were consummate traders, especially of horses, and since the Black Hills region was a major trade citadel they may have begun to frequent the region as traders and teachers of horse lore.

Displaced by the wars for the buffalo ranges in the north, the Kiowas began to drift southward again—or perhaps, since the supply of horses was in the Southwest, simply began to stay longer on the Southern Plains. Between 1790 and 1806, they developed a rapprochement with the Comanches. Thereafter they were so closely associated with the northern Comanches that they were regarded by some as merely a Comanche band, although in many cultural details the two groups were dissimilar. Spanish and American traders and explorers of the 1820s found them camped along the two forks of the Canadian River and on the various headwater streams of the Red River.

The other groups that increasingly began to interact with the Comanches during the 1820s and thereafter had also originated on the Northern Plains. These were the Arapahoes and the Cheyennes, who by 1825 were beginning to establish themselves on the Colorado buffalo plains from the North Platte River all the way down to the Arkansas River.

The Algonkian-speaking Arapahoes and Cheyennes had once been farmers living in earth lodges on the upper Mississippi. By the early 1700s both groups were in present North Dakota, occupying villages along the Red and Cheyenne rivers, where they first began to acquire horses, possibly from the Kiowas. Fur wars instigated by the Europeans drove them farther southwest and more and more into a Plains, bison-hunting culture, one that the women of these farming tribes probably resisted as long as possible. But by the second decade of the nineteenth century the Teton Sioux wedge had made nomads and hunters of the Arapahoes and Cheyennes.

Their search for prime buffalo grounds and for ever-larger horse herds, critical since both tribes had emerged as middlemen traders between the villagers of the Missouri and the horse reservoir to the south, first led the Cheyennes and Arapahoes west of the Black Hills, into Crow lands, and then increasingly southward along the mountain front. By 1815 the Arapahoes were becoming fixed in the minds of American traders as their own analogue on the Southern Plains; the famous trading expedition of August Pierre Chouteau and Jules De Mun that decade was designed to exploit the horse and robe trade of the Arapahoes on the Arkansas. By the 1820s, when Stephen Long's expedition and the trading party including Jacob Fowler penetrated the Southern Plains, the Arapahoes and Cheyennes were camping with the Kiowas and Comanches on the Arkansas. The Hairy Rope band of the Cheyennes, renowned for their ability to catch wild horses, was then known to be mustanging along the Cimarron River.

Three factors seem to have drawn the Arapahoes and Cheyennes so far south. Unquestionably, one factor was the vast horse herds of the Comanches and Kiowas, an unending supply of horses for the trade, which by 1825 the Colorado tribes were seizing in daring raids. Another was the milder winters south of the Arkansas, which made horse pastoralism much easier. The third factor was the abnormally bountiful game of the early nineteenth-century Southern Plains, evidently the direct result of an extraordinary series of years between 1815 and 1846 when, with the exception of a minor drought in the late 1820s, rainfall south of the Arkansas was considerably above average. So lucrative was the hunting and raiding that in 1833 Charles Bent located the first of his adobe trading posts along the Arkansas, expressly to control the winter robe and summer horse trade of the Arapahoes and Cheyennes. Bent's marketing contacts were in St. Louis. Horses that Bent's traders drove to St. Louis commonly started as stock in the New Mexican Spanish settlements (and sometimes those were California horses stolen by Indians who traded them to the New Mexicans) that were stolen by the Comanches, then stolen again by Cheyenne raiders, and finally traded at Bent's or Ceran St. Vrain's posts, whence they were driven to Westport, Missouri, and sold to outfit American emigrants going to the West Coast! Unless you saw it from the wrong end, as the New Mexicans (or the horses) seem to have, it was both a profitable and a culturally stimulating economy.

Thus, around 1825, the Comanches and Kiowas found themselves at war with Cheyennes, Arapahoes, and other tribes on the north. Meanwhile, the Colorado tribes opened another front in a naked effort to seize the rich buffalo range of the upper Kansas and Republican rivers from the Pawnees. These wars produced an interesting type of ecological development that appeared repeatedly across most of the continent. At the boundaries where warring tribes met, they left buffer zones occupied by neither side and only lightly hunted. One such buffer zone on the Southern Plains was along the region's northern perimeter, between the Arkansas and North Canadian rivers. Another was in present-day western Kansas, between the Pawnees and the main range of the Colorado tribes, and a third seems to have stretched from the forks of the Platte to the mountains. The buffer zones were important because game within them was left relatively undisturbed; they allowed the buildup of herds that might later be exploited when tribal boundaries or agreements changed.

The appearance of American traders such as Bent and St. Vrain marked the Southern Plains tribes' growing immersion in a market economy increasingly tied to worldwide trade networks dominated by Euro-Americans. Like all humans, Indians had always altered their environments. But as most modern historians of Plains Indians and the western fur trade have realized, during the nineteenth century not only had the western tribes become technologically capable of pressuring their resources, but year by year they were becoming less "ecosystem people," dependent on the products of their local regions for subsistence, and increasingly tied to biospheric trade networks. Despite some speculation that the Plains tribes were experiencing ecological problems, previous scholars have not ascertained what role market hunting played in this dilemma, what combination of other factors was involved, or what the tribes attempted to do about it.

The crux of the problem in studying Southern Plains Indian ecology and bison is to determine whether the Plains tribes had established a society in ecological equilibrium, one whose population did not exceed the carrying capacity of its habitat and so maintained a healthy, functioning ecology that could be sustained over the long term. Answering that question involves an effort to come to grips with the factors affecting bison populations, the factors affecting Indian populations, and the cultural aspects of Plains Indians' utilization of bison. Each of the three aspects of the question presents puzzles difficult to resolve.

In modern, protected herds on the Plains, bison are a prolific species whose numbers increase by an average of 18 percent a year, assuming a normal sex ratio (51 males to 49 females) with breeding cows amounting to 35 percent of the total. In other words, if the Southern Plains supported 8.2 million bison in years of median rainfall, the herds would have produced about 1.4 million calves a year. To maintain an ecological equilibrium with the grasses, the Plains bison's natural mortality rate also had to approach 18 percent.

Today the several protected bison herds in the western United States have a natural mortality rate, without predation, ranging between 3 and 9 percent. The Wichita Mountains herd, the only large herd left on the Southern Plains, falls midway with a 6 percent mortality rate. Despite a search for it, no inherent naturally regulating mechanism has yet been found in bison populations; thus active culling programs are needed at all the Plains bison refuges. The starvation-induced population crashes that affect ungulates such as deer were seemingly mitigated on the wild, unfenced Plains by the bison's tendency—barring any major impediments—to shift their range great distances to better pasture.

Determining precisely how the remaining annual mortality in the wild herds was affected is not easy, because the wolf/bison relationship on the Plains has never been studied. Judging from dozens of historical documents attesting to wolf predation of bison calves, including accounts by the Indians, wolves apparently played a critical role in Plains bison population dynamics, and not just as culling agents of diseased and old animals.

Human hunters were the other source of mortality. For nine thousand years native Americans had hunted bison without exterminating them, perhaps building into their gene pool an adjustment to human predation (dwarfed size, earlier sexual maturity, and shorter gestation times, all serving to keep populations up). But there is archaeological evidence that beginning about A.D. 1450, with the advent of "mutualistic" trade between Puebloan communities recently forced by drought to relocate on the Rio Grande and a new wave of Plains hunters (probably the Athapaskan-speaking Apacheans), human pressures on the southern bison herd accelerated, evidently dramatically if the archaeological record in New Mexico is an accurate indication. That pressure would have been a function of both the size of the Indian population and the use of bison in Indian cultures. Because Plains Indians traded bison-derived goods for the produce of the horticultural villages fringing the Plains, bison would be affected by changes in human population peripheral to the Great Plains as well as on them.

One attempt to estimate maximum human population size on the Southern Plains, that of Jerold Levy, fixed the upper limit at about 10,500 people. Levy argued that water would have been a more critical resource than bison in fixing a limit for Indian populations. Levy's population figures are demonstrably too low, and he lacked familiarity with the aquifer-derived drought-resistant sources of water on the Southern Plains. But his argument that water was the more critical limiting resource introduces an important element into the Plains equation.

The cultural utilization of bison by horse Indians has been studied by Bill Brown. Adapting a sophisticated formula worked out first for caribou hunters in the Yukon, Brown has estimated Indian subsistence (caloric requirements plus the number of robes and hides required for domestic use) at about 47 animals per lodge per year. At an average of 8 people per lodge, that works out to almost 6 bison per person over a year's time. Brown's article is not only highly useful in getting us closer to a historic Plains equation than ever before; it is also borne out by at least one historic account. In 1821 the trader Jacob Fowler camped for several weeks with 700 lodges of Southern Plains tribes on the Arkansas River. Fowler was no ecologist; in fact, he could hardly spell. But he was a careful observer, and he wrote that the big camp was using up 100 bison a day. In other words, 700 lodges were using bison at a rate of about 52 per lodge per year, or 6.5 animals per person. These are important figures. Not only do they give us some idea of the mortality percentage that can be assigned to human hunters; by extension they help us fix a quadruped predation percentage as well.

Estimates of the number of Indians on the Southern Plains during historic times are not difficult to find, but they tend to vary widely, and for good reason, as will be seen when we look closely at the historical events of the first half of the nineteenth century. Although observers' population estimates for the Comanches go as high as 30,000, six of the seven population figures for the Comanches estimated between 1786 and 1854 fall into a narrow range between 19,200 and 21,600. Taken together, the number of Kiowas, Cheyennes, Arapahoes, Plains Apaches, Kiowa-Apaches, and Wichitas probably did not exceed 12,000 during that same period. Contemporaries estimated the combined number of Cheyennes and Arapahoes, for example, as 4,400 in 1838, 5,000 in 1843, and 5,200 in 1846. If the historic Southern Plains hunting population reached 30,000, then human hunters would have accounted for only 195,000 bison per year if we use the estimate of 6.5 animals per person.

But another factor must have played a significant role. While quadruped predators concentrated on calves and injured or feeble animals, human hunters had different criteria. Historical documents attest to the horse Indians' preference for and success in killing two- to five-year-old bison cows, which were preferred for their meat and for their thinner, more easily processed hides and the luxurious robes made from their pelts. Studies done on other large American ungulates indicate that removal of breeding females at a level that exceeds 7 percent of the total herd will initiate population decline. With 8.2 million bison on the Southern Plains, the critical upper figure for cow selectivity would have been about 574,000 animals. Reduce the total bison number to 6 million and the yearly calf crop to 1.08 million, probably more realistic median figures for the first half of the nineteenth century, and the critical mortality for breeding cows would still have been 420,000 animals. As mentioned, a horse-mounted, bison-hunting population of 30,000 would have harvested bison at a yearly rate of less than 200,000. Hence I would argue that, theoretically, on the Southern Plains the huge biomass of bison left from the Pleistocene extinctions would have supported the subsistence needs of more than 60,000 Plains hunters.

All of this raises some serious questions when we look at the historical evidence from the first half of the nineteenth century. By the end of that period, despite an effort at population growth by many Plains tribes, the population esti-mates for most of the Southern Plains tribes were down. And many of the bands seemed to be starving. Thomas Fitzpatrick, the Cheyennes' and Arapahoes' first agent, reported in 1853 that the tribes in his district spent half the year in a state of starvation. The Comanches were reported to be eating their horses in great numbers by 1850, and their raids into Mexico increased all through the 1840s, as if a resource depletion in their home range was driving them to compensate with stolen stock. In the painted robe calendars of the Kiowas, the notation for "few or no bison" appears for four years in a row between 1849 and 1852. Bison were becoming less reliable, and the evolution toward an economy based on raiding and true horse pastoralism was well under way. Clearly, by 1850 something had altered the situation on the Southern Plains.

The "something" was, in fact, a whole host of ecological alterations that his-torians with a wide range of data at their disposal are only now, more than a century later, beginning to understand.

As early as 1850 the bison herds had been weakened in a number of ways. The effect of the horse on Indian culture has been much studied, but in working out a Southern Plains ecological model, it is important to note that horses also had a direct effect on bison numbers. By the second quarter of the nineteenth century the domesticated horse herds of the Southern Plains tribes must have ranged be-tween .25 and .50 million animals (at an average of 10 to 15 horses per person). In addition, an estimated 2 million wild mustangs overspread the country between south Texas and the Arkansas River. That many animals of a species with an 80 percent dietary overlap with bovines and, perhaps more critically, with similar water requirements, must have had an adverse impact on bison carrying capacity, especially since Indian horse herds concentrated the tribes in the moist canyons and river valleys that bison also used for watering. Judging from the 1910 agricul-tural census, 2 million or more horses would have reduced the median grassland carrying capacity for the southern bison herd to under 6 million animals.

Another factor that may have started to diminish overall bison numbers was the effect of exotic bovine diseases. Anthrax, introduced into the herds from Lou-isiana around 1800, tuberculosis, and brucellosis, the latter brought to the Plains by feral and stolen Texas cattle and by stock on the overland trails, probably had considerable impact on the bison herds. All the bison that were saved in the late nineteenth century had high rates of infection with these diseases. Brucellosis plays havoc with reproduction in domestic cattle, causing cows to abort; it may have done so in wild bison, and butchering them probably infected Indian women with the disease.

Earlier I mentioned modern natural mortality figures for bison of 3 percent to 9 percent of herd totals. On the wilderness Plains, fires, floods, drownings, droughts, and strange die-offs may have upped this percentage considerably. But if we hold to the higher figure, then mortality might have taken an average of 50 percent of the annual bison increase of 18 percent. Thirty thousand subsistence hunters would have killed off only 18 percent of the bison's yearly increase (if the herd was 6 million). The long-wondered-at wolf predation was perhaps the most important of all the factors regulating bison populations, with a predation percent-age of around 32% of the annual bison increase. (Interestingly, this dovetails closely with the Pawnee estimate that wolves got 3 to 4 of every 10 calves born.) Wolves and other canids are able to adjust their litter sizes to factors like mortality and resource abundance. Thus, mountain men and traders who poisoned wolves for their pelts may not have significantly reduced wolf populations. They may have inadvertently killed thousands of bison, however, for poisoned wolves drooled and vomited strychnine over the grass in their convulsions. Many Indians lost horses that ate such poisoned grass.

The climate cycle, strongly correlated with bison populations in the archaeological data for earlier periods, must have interacted with these other factors to produce a decline in bison numbers between 1840 and 1850. Except for a dry period in the mid- to late 1820s, the first four decades of the nineteenth century had been a time of above-normal rainfall on the Southern Plains. With the carrying capacity for bison and horses high, the country south of the Arkansas sucked tribes to it as into a vortex. But beginning in 1846, rainfall plunged as much as 30 percent below the median for nine of the next ten years. On the Central Plains, six years of that decade were dry. The growth of human populations and settlements in Texas, New Mexico, and the Indian Territory blocked the bison herds from migrating to their traditional drought refugia on the periphery of their range. Thus, a normal climate swing combined with unprecedented external pressures to produce an effect unusual in bison history—a core population, significantly reduced by competition with horses and by drought, that was quite susceptible to human hunting pressure.

Finally, alterations in the historical circumstances of the Southern Plains tribes from 1825 to 1850 had serious repercussions for Plains ecology. Some of those circumstances were indirect and beyond the tribes' ability to influence. Traders along the Santa Fe Trail shot into, chased, and disturbed the southern herds. New Mexican *Ciboleros* (bison hunters) continued to take fifteen to twenty-five thousand bison a year from the Llano Estacado. And the United States government's removal of almost fifty thousand eastern Indians into Oklahoma increased the pressure on the bison herds to a level impossible to estimate. The Southern Plains tribes evidently considered it a threat and refused to abide by the Treaty of Fort Holmes (1835) when they discovered it gave the eastern tribes hunting rights on the prairies.

Insofar as the Southern Plains tribes had an environmental policy, then, it was to protect the bison herds from being hunted by outsiders. The Comanches could not afford to emulate their Shoshonean ancestors and limit their own population. Beset by enemies and disease, they had to try to keep their numbers high, even as their resource base diminished. For the historic Plains tribes, warfare and stock raids addressed ecological needs created by diminishing resources as well as the cultural impulse to enhance men's status, and they must have seemed far more logical solutions than consciously reducing their own populations as the bison herds became less reliable.

For those very reasons, after more than a decade of warfare among the buffalo tribes, in 1840 the Comanches and Kiowas adopted a strategy of seeking peace and an alliance with the Cheyennes, Arapahoes, and Kiowa-Apaches. From the Comanches' point of view, it brought them allies against Texans and eastern

Indians who were trespassing on the Plains. The Cheyennes and Arapahoes got what they most wanted: the chance to hunt the grass- and bison-rich Southern Plains, horses and mules for trading, and access to the Spanish settlements via Comanche lands. But the peace meant something else in ecological terms. Now all the tribes could freely exploit the Arkansas Valley bison herds. This new exploitation of a large, prime bison habitat that had been a boundary zone skirted by Indian hunters may have been critical. In the Kiowa Calendar the notation for "many bison" appears in 1841, the year following the peace. The notation appears only once more during the next thirty-five years.

One other advantage the Comanches and Kiowas derived from the peace of 1840 was freedom to trade at Bent's Fort. Although the data to prove it are fragmentary, this conversion of the largest body of Indians on the Southern Plains from subsistence/ecosystem hunters to a people intertwined in the European market system probably added critical stress to a bison herd already being eaten away. How serious the market incentive could be is indicated by John Whitfield, agent at William Bent's second Arkansas River fort in 1855, who wrote that 3,150 Cheyennes were killing 40,000 bison a year. That is about twice the number the Cheyennes would have harvested through subsistence hunting alone. (It also means that on the average every Cheyenne warrior was killing 44 bison a year and every Cheyenne woman was processing robes at the rate of almost one a week.) With the core bison population seriously affected by the drought of the late 1840s, the additional, growing robe trade of the Comanches probably brought the Southern Plains tribes to a critical level in their utilization of bison. Drought, Indian market hunting, and cow selectivity must stand as the critical elements—albeit augmented by minor factors such as white disturbance, new bovine diseases, and increasing grazing competition from horses—that brought on the bison crisis of the midcentury Southern Plains. That explanation may also illuminate the experience of the Canadian Plains, where bison disappeared without the advent of white hide hunting.

Perhaps that would have happened on the American Plains if the tribes had held or continued to augment their populations. But the Comanches and other tribes fought a losing battle against their own attrition. While new institutions such as male polygamy and adoption of captured children worked to build up the Comanches' numbers, the disease epidemics of the nineteenth century repeatedly decimated them. In the 1820s, the Comanches were rebuilding their population after the smallpox epidemic of 1816 had carried away a fourth of them. But smallpox ran like a brush fire through the Plains villages again in 1837–1838, wiping whole peoples off the continent. And the forty-niners brought cholera, which so devastated the Arkansas Valley Indians that William Bent burned his fort and temporarily left the trade that year. John C. Ewers, in fact, has estimated that the nineteenth-century Comanches lost 75 percent of their population to disease.

Did the Southern Plains Indians successfully work out a dynamic, ecological equilibrium with the bison herds? I would argue that the answer remains ultimately elusive because the relationship was never allowed to play itself out. The trends, however, suggest that a satisfactory solution was improbable. One factor that worked against the horse tribes was their short tenure. It may be that two centuries provided too brief a time for them to create a workable system around horses, the swelling demand for bison robes generated by the Euro-American market, and the expansion of their own populations to hold their territories. Some of those forces, such as the tribes' need to expand their numbers and the advantages of participating in the robe trade, worked against their need to conserve the bison herds. Too, many of the forces that shaped their world were beyond the power of the Plains tribes to influence. And it is very clear that the ecology of the Southern Plains had become so complicated by the mid-nineteenth century that neither the Indians nor the Euro-Americans of those years could have grasped how it all worked.

Finally and ironically, it seems that the Indian religions, so effective at calling forth awe and reverence for the natural world, may have inhibited the Plains Indians' understanding of bison ecology and their role in it. True, native leaders such as Yellow Wolf, the Cheyenne whom James W. Abert interviewed and sketched at Bent's Fort in 1845–1846, surmised the implications of market hunting. As he watched the bison disappearing from the Arkansas Valley, Yellow Wolf asked the whites to teach the Cheyenne hunters how to farm, never realizing that he was reprising a Plains Indian/Euro-American conversation that had taken place sixty years earlier in that same country. But Yellow Wolf was marching to his own drummer, for it remained a widespread tenet of faith among most Plains Indians through the 1880s that bison were supernatural in origin. A firsthand observer and close student of the nineteenth-century Plains reported,

> Every Plains Indian firmly believed that the buffalo were produced in countless numbers in a country under the ground, that every spring the surplus swarmed like bees from a hive, out of great cave-like openings to this country, which were situated somewhere in the great 'Llano Estacado' or Staked Plain of Texas.

This religious conception of the infinity of nature's abundance was poetic. On one level it was also empirical: Bison overwintered in large numbers in the protected canyons scored into the eastern escarpment of the Llano Estacado, and Indians had no doubt many times witnessed the herds emerging to overspread the high Plains in springtime. But such a conception did not aid the tribes in their efforts to work out an ecological balance amid the complexities of the nineteenth-century Plains.

In a real sense, then, the more familiar events of the 1870s only delivered the *coup de grâce* to the free Indian life on the Great Plains. The slaughterhouse effects of European diseases and wars with the encroaching whites caused Indian numbers to dwindle after 1850 (no more than fourteen hundred Comanches were enrolled to receive federal benefits at Fort Sill, in present-day Oklahoma, in the 1880s). This combined with bison resiliency to preserve a good core of animals until the arrival of the white hide-hunters, who nonetheless can be documented as taking only about 3.5 million animals from the Southern Plains.

But the great days of the Plains Indians, the primal poetry of humans and horses, bison and grass, sunlight and blue skies, and the sensuous satisfactions of a hunting life on the sweeping grasslands defined a meteoric time indeed. And the meteor was already fading in the sky a quarter century before the Big Fifties began to boom.

◈ *F U R T H E R   R E A D I N G*

Gary C. Anderson, "Early Dakota Migration and Intertribal War: A Revision," *Western Historical Quarterly* 11 (1980), 17–36

——, *Kinsmen of Another Kind: Dakota-White Relations in the Upper Mississippi Valley, 1500–1862* (1984)

Donald J. Berthrong, *The Southern Cheyennes* (1963)

R. David Edmunds, "Indians as Pioneers: Potawatomies on the Frontier," *Chronicles of Oklahoma* 65 (1987–1988), 340–353

John C. Ewers, "Intertribal Warfare as the Precursor of Indian-White Warfare on the Northern Great Plains," *Western Historical Quarterly* 6 (1975), 397–410

——, *Teton Dakota History and Ethnology* (1938)

George Bird Grinnell, *The Cheyenne Indians: Their History and Ways of Life,* 2 vols. (1924)

J. Evetts Haley, "The Comanchero Trade," *Southwestern Historical Quarterly* 38 (1935), 157–177

Harold Hickerson, *The Chippewa and Their Neighbors: A Study in Ethnohistory* (1970)

——, *Mdewakaton Band of Sioux Indians,* Vol. 1 of *Sioux Indians* (1974)

Preston Holder, *The Hoe and the Horse on the Plains: A Study of Cultural Development Among North American Indians* (1970)

George E. Hyde, *Indians of the High Plains* (1961)

——, *Red Cloud's Folk: A History of the Oglala Sioux Indians* (1957)

Mark A. Judy, "Powder Keg on the Upper Missouri: Sources of Blackfeet Hostility, 1730–1810," *American Indian Quarterly* 11 (1987), 127–144

Charles L. Kenner, *A History of New Mexican–Plains Indian Relations* (1969)

Robert H. Lowie, *Indians of the Plains* (1954)

Roy W. Meyer, *History of the Santee Sioux: United States Indian Policy on Trial* (1967)

——, *The Village Indians of the Upper Missouri: The Mandans, Hidatsas, and Arikaras* (1977)

Roger L. Nichols, "Backdrop for Disaster: Causes of the Arikara War of 1823," *South Dakota History* 14 (1984), 93–113

Wilbur S. Nye, *Bad Medicine and Good: Tales of the Kiowas* (1959)

Francis Paul Prucha, "American Indian Policy in the 1840s: Visions of Reform," in John C. Clark, ed., *The Frontier Challenge: Responses to the Trans-Mississippi West* (1971)

——, "Indian Removal and the Great American Desert," *Indiana Magazine of History* 59 (1963), 309–322

Rupert Norval Richardson, *The Comanche Barrier to South Plains Settlement* (1933)

Carl Coke Rister, *Border Captives: The Traffic in Prisoners by Southern Plains Indians, 1835–1875* (1940)

——, *Comanche Bondage* (1955)

Frank R. Secoy, *Changing Military Patterns on the Great Plains: 17th Century Through Early 19th Century* (1953)

John E. Sunder, *The Fur Trade on the Upper Missouri, 1840–1865* (1965)

Robert A. Trennert, Jr., *Alternative to Extinction: Federal Indian Policy and the Beginnings of the Reservation System, 1846–1851* (1975)

William E. Unrau, *The Kansa Indians: A History of the Wind People, 1673–1873* (1971)

Ernest Wallace and E. Adamson Hoebel, *The Comanches, Lords of the South Plains* (1952)

Encounter, Continuity, and Change

The American Indians' adjustment to European people and culture took many forms. Peaceful accommodation and violent warfare marked the extremes of an encounter that has continued to evolve since 1492. From the beginning, some Europeans desired to include Indians in their society by converting them to Christianity and by inculcating other European habits and practices. Missionaries took a leading role in this effort. For their part, Indians were interested in learning new and useful things from Europeans, but they tenaciously held on to the cultural values and beliefs that continued to serve them. Missionaries and secular teachers alike were often baffled by the cultural conservatism that they saw in their Indian parishioners and students.

Europeans believed that formal education—religious and secular—was a means to assert control over Indians and to eradicate their tribal identity. But Indians retained their unique identity and, in the twentieth century, seized education and used it for their own purposes. Once viewed as a potential threat to cultural survival, education is now a tool that Indians wield to preserve their cultures while adjusting to new challenges as the sixth century of their encounter with Europeans begins.

The Jesuit missionaries in this engraving probably meant well, but the Indian Don Luis de Velasco evidently did not think so. Velasco was a Pamunkey Indian from Virginia who lived with Spanish and learned their ways in both Spain and Mexico in the 1560s. After returning to his homeland with the Jesuits, he abandoned Christianity and slew the priests. (Special Collections, Bridwell Library, Southern Methodist University, Dallas, Texas)

Indians of the northern United States used elaborate belts of wampum beads to commemorate important events such as peace agreements. This is the Hiawatha belt, which is said to symbolize the founding of the Iroquois Confederacy. (© New York State Museum)

Although Indians had no formal schools before the arrival of Europeans, they conveyed knowledge and power through rituals. In the buffalo dance shown here, old hunters pass on their skills to young men. [After Karl Bodmer (Swiss 1809–1893). Engraving with aquatint, Joslyn Art Museum, Omaha, Nebraska]

TENS-QUA-TA-WA

or THE ONE THAT OPENS THE DOOR

Shawnese Prophet

Brother of Tecumthe

Painted for Gov. Lewis Cass by J. O. Lewis at Detroit 1823.

Some Indians, among them the Shawnee religious leader Tenskwatawa, continued to rely on dreams and spiritual experiences to acquire knowledge long after contact with Europeans. Tenskwatawa taught his followers to reject European teachings and urged them to fight against the Americans at the time of the War of 1812. (J. O. Lewis, hand-colored lithograph, c. 1835. Courtesy Amon Carter Museum, Fort Worth, Texas)

Indians quickly grasped the advantages of European material culture and learned many European techniques. This is a blacksmith shop at the Zuni pueblo in the 1850s. (Richard H. Kern, in Lorenzo H. Sitgreaves, *Report of an Expedition Down the Zuni and Colorado Rivers,* 1853)

The mission was the central institution for the education of Indians under Spanish aegis. In this California mission, several hundred Indians at a time learned trades and the Spanish language as well as the Catholic religion. (The Bettmann Archive)

Although Pueblo Indians practiced Catholicism and took up some other aspects of European life, they often preserved their own religious practices, too. At Zuni, the Indians had both kivas (subterranean chambers used for Pueblo religious rites) and a Catholic church. (Reproduced from the collection of the Library of Congress).

(right) In the early nineteenth century, the Cherokee Indians incorporated the alphabet and writing into their daily lives. Elias Boudinot edited the *Cherokee Phoenix,* which was published in English and the Cherokee language. This is the front page for February 21, 1828. (American Antiquarian Society)

ᏣᎳᎩ ᏗᎪᏪᎳᏗᏍᏗ

CHEROKEE PHŒNIX,

VOL. I.   NEW ECHOTÁ, THURSDAY FEBRUARY 21, 1828.   NO. 1.

EDITED BY ELIAS BOUDINOTT.

PRINTED WEEKLY BY

ISAAC H. HARRIS,

FOR THE CHEROKEE NATION.

At $2 50 if paid in advance, $3 in six months, or $3 50 if paid at the end of the year.

To subscribers who can read only the Cherokee language the price will be $2,00 in advance, or $2,50 to be paid within the year.

Every subscription will be considered as continued unless subscribers give notice to the contrary before the commencement of a new year.

The Phoenix will be printed on a Super-Royal sheet, with type entirely new procured for the purpose. Any person procuring six subscribers, and becoming responsible for the payment, shall receive a seventh gratis.

Advertisements will be inserted at seventy-five cents per square for the first insertion, and thirty-seven and a half cents for each continuance; longer ones in proportion.

☞ All letters addressed to the Editor, post paid, will receive due attention.

[Cherokee syllabary text]

A GOOD CONSCIENCE.

What is there, in all the pomp of the world, the enjoyments of luxury, the gratification of passion, comparable to the tranquil delight of a good conscience? It is that which diffuses its fragrance over every thing near it without exhausting its store. Unaccompanied with this, the gay pleasures of the world are like brilliants to a diseased eye, music to a deaf ear, wine in an ardent fever, or dainties in the languor of an ague. To lie down on the pillow, after a day spent in temperance in benevolence, and piety, how sweet is it! How different from the state of him, who reclines, at an unnatural hour, with his blood inflamed, his head throbbing with wine and gluttony, his heart aching with rancorous malice, his thoughts totally estranged from Him who has protected him in the day, and will watch over him, ungrateful as he is, in the night season! A good conscience is, indeed, the peace of God; passions belled to sleep, close thoughts, cheerful temper, a disposition to be pleased with every obvious and innocent object around; these are the effects of a good conscience; these are the things which constitute happiness; and these condensed to dwell with the poor man, in his humble cottage in the vale of obscurity. In the magnificent mansion of the proud and vain, glitter the exteriors of the joyous, the gilding, the trapping, the pride and the pomp; but in the decent habitation of piety is oftener found that dew nest of heavenly peace; that solid good, of which the parade of the vain, the frivolous, and voluptuous, is but a shadowy semblance.

Christian Philosophy.

Flattery.—Few things are more universally condemned than flattery yet there are few men, who are seldom its influence, and still fewer, who have courage sufficient to repel it with a faithful rebuke. The following anecdote is recommended, as affording a specimen of just contempt to flatterers. A certain clergyman in New England, eminent both for talents and humility, was one day accosted by a parishioner, who highly commended some of his performances, of which the clergyman himself had a very low opinion. After patiently hearing him a few moments, the clergyman replied: "My Friend, if I had known you gave me no better opinion of myself than I had before, but give a worse opinion of you."

CONSTITUTION OF THE CHEROKEE NATION,

Formed by a Convention of Delegates from the several Districts, at New Echota, July 1827.

WE, THE REPRESENTATIVES of the people of the CHEROKEE NATION in Convention assembled, in order to establish justice, ensure tranquility, promote our common welfare, and secure to ourselves and our posterity the blessings of liberty; acknowledging with humility and gratitude the goodness of the sovereign Ruler of the Universe, in offering us an opportunity so favorable to the design, and imploring his aid and direction in its accomplishment, do ordain and establish this Constitution for the Government of the Cherokee Nation.

ARTICLE I.

Sec. 1. THE BOUNDARIES of this nation, embracing the lands solemnly guarantied and reserved forever to the Cherokee Nation by the Treaties concluded with the United States, are as follows; and shall forever hereafter remain unalterably the same to wit:—Beginning on the North Bank of Tennessee River at the upper part of the Chickasaw old fields; thence along the main channel of said river, including all the islands therein, to the mouth of the Hiwassee river, thence up the main channel of said river, including Islands, to the first hill which closes in on said river, about two miles above Hiwassee old Town; thence along the ridge which divides the waters of the Hiwassee and little Tellico, to the Tennessee river at Tallassee; thence along the main channel, including Islands, to the junction of the Cowee and Nanteyalee; thence along the ridge in the fork of said river, to the top of the blue ridge; thence along the blue ridge to the Unicoy Turnpike road; thence by a straight line to the main source of the Chestatee; thence along its main channel, including Islands, to the Chattahoochy; and thence down the same to the Creek boundary at Buzzard Roost; thence along the boundary line which separates this and the Creek Nation, to a point on the Cocsa river opposite the mouth of Wills Creek; thence down along the South bank of the same to a point opposite to Fort Strother; thence up the river to the mouth of Wills Creek; thence up along the East bank of said creek, to the West branch thereof, and up the same to its source; and thence along the ridge which separates the Tombeckbee and Tennessee waters, to a point on the top of said ridge; thence due North to Camp Coffee on Tennessee river, which is opposite the Chickasaw Island; thence to the place of beginning.

Sec. 2. The Sovereignty and Jurisdiction of this Government shall extend over the Country within the boundaries above described, and the lands therein are, and shall remain, the common property of the Nation; but the improvements made thereon, and in the possession of the citizens of the Nation, are the exclusive and indefeasible property of the citizens respectively who made, or may rightfully be in possession of them; Provided, That the citizens of the Nation, possessing exclusive and indefeasible right to their respective improvements, as expressed in this article, shall possess no right nor power to dispose of their improvements in any manner whatever to the United States, individual States, nor to individual citizens thereof; and that, whenever any such citizen or citizens shall remove with their effects out of the limits of this Nation, and become citizens of any other Government, all his or their improvements as citizens of this Nation shall cease; Provided nevertheless, That the Legislature shall have power to re-admit by law to all the rights of citizenship, any such person or persons, who may at any time desire to return to the Nation on their memorializing the General Council for such

[Cherokee syllabary text]

Sec. 2. The Cherokee Nation, as laid off into eight Districts, shall so remain.

readmission. Moreover, the Legislature shall have power to adopt such laws and regulations, as its wisdom may deem expedient and proper, to prevent the citizens from monopolizing improvements with the view of speculation.

ARTICLE II.

Sec. 1. THE POWER of this Government shall be divided into three distinct departments;—the Legislative, the Executive, and the Judicial.

Sec. 2. No person or persons, belonging to one of these Departments, shall exercise any of the powers properly belonging to either of the others, except in the cases hereinafter expressly directed or permitted.

ARTICLE III.

Sec. 1. THE LEGISLATIVE POWER shall be vested in two distinct branches; a Committee, and a Council; each to have a negative on the other, and both to be styled, the General Council of the Cherokee Nation; and the style of their acts and laws shall be,

"RESOLVED by the Committee and Council in General Council convened."

Sec. 2. The Cherokee Nation, as laid off into eight Districts, shall so remain.

Sec. 3. The Committee shall consist of two members from each District, and the Council shall consist of three members from each District, to be chosen by the qualified electors of their respective Districts for two years; and the elections to be held in every District on the first Monday in August for the year 1828, and every succeeding two years thereafter; and the General Council shall be held once a year, to be convened on the second Monday of October in each year at New Echota.

Sec. 4. No person shall be eligible to a seat in the General Council, but a free Cherokee Male citizen, who shall have attained to the age of twenty-five years. The descendants of Cherokee men by all free women, except the African race, whose parents may be or have been living together as man and wife, according to the customs and laws of this Nation, shall be entitled to all the rights and privileges of this Nation, as well as the posterity of Cherokee women by all free men. No person who is of negro or mulatto parentage, either by the father or mother side, shall be eligible to hold any office of profit, honor or trust, under this Government.

Sec. 5. The Electors, and members of the General Council shall, in all cases except those of treason, felony, or breach of the peace, be privileged from arrest during their attendance at election, and at the General Council, and in going to, and returning from, the same.

Sec. 6. In all elections by the people, the electors shall vote *viva voce*. Electors for members to the General Council for 1828, shall be held at the places of holding the several courts, and at the other two precincts in each District which are established by the law under which the members of this Convention were elected; and the District Judges shall superintend the elections within the precincts of their respective Court Houses, and the Marshals & Sheriffs shall superintend within the precincts which may be assigned them by the Circuit Judges of their respective Districts, together with one other person, who shall be appointed by the Circuit Judges for each precinct within their respective Districts; and the Circuit Judges shall also appoint a clerk to each precinct.—The superintendents and clerks shall, on the Wednesday morning succeeding the election, assemble at their respective Court Houses and proceed to examine and ascertain the true state of the polls, and shall issue to each member, duly elected, a certificate; and also make an official return of the state of the polls of election to the principal Chief, and it shall be the du-

During the late nineteenth and early twentieth centuries, Indian girls and young women attending Bureau of Indian Affairs schools received training in sewing and other domestic skills. Pictured here are students in the Genoa, Nebraska, school in 1910. (National Archives)

Bands and orchestras at off-reservation boarding schools symbolized progress toward assimilation. This Phoenix Indian School band played on tour in the Southwest as well as before local audiences. (Arizona Historical Foundation, Arizona State University)

The arrival of the Indian New Deal in the 1930s encouraged more support of Indian cultures in the government schools. Navajo students at the Albuquerque Indian School thus could learn or improve their weaving. (Center for Southwest Research, General Library, University of New Mexico)

Athletics has been an important avenue for Indian student achievement. In the 1980s and 1990s, Indian school teams such as the Wyoming Indian High School basketball team of 1984 won many state championships. (Photograph by Tom Stromme/Wyoming State Journal)

Elgin Badwound announces the graduates of Oglala Lakota College in June 1984. U.S. senator Jim Abner helps hand out the diplomas. (*Lakota Times/Indian Country Today*)

The first of the modern Indian colleges, Navajo Community College, has provided a wide range of courses. Classes in Navajo history and culture are an important feature of the curriculum. (© 1975 Michael Heron)

In urban centers and reservation communities alike, the powwow has brought old and young together. The powwow has become a major expression of Indian identity and pride in the modern era, as exemplified in this scene at the St. Paul American Indian Center in 1977. (© Randy Croce, 1977)

Indians in the Far West

The Indians of the Far West are not well known to the average American. Yet, the re gion west of the Rocky Mountains was home to scores of tribes and to hundreds of thousands of Indians. In California—the most heavily populated region—the majority of these peoples lived in small communities (sometimes called rancherías) and survived by hunting and collecting plant foods. In the Great Basin (Nevada and parts of Oregon, Utah, and Idaho), the Paiute and Shoshone Indians also dug for roots in their arid homelands. In all of these areas, the Indians practiced a division of labor by gender: men brought in game and fish; women gathered nuts and acorns, and dug for tubers. Whites who saw these women at work with digging sticks called them diggers, a term they used as a racial slur to all Indians in the region, regardless of ethnicity or gender.

Before the Mexican War began in 1846, the Indians of the Great Basin and the California interior were out of the way of Anglo-American expansion. Spanish and Mexican settlement was limited to the Pacific coast south of the San Francisco Bay area. A few explorers and Anglo trappers had crossed the Great Basin, and a trickle of overland immigration had filtered into California. The Anglos who settled in Mexican California clustered around John A. Sutter's fort in the Sacramento valley. The Sierra Nevada, their foothills, and the northern reaches of the province remained in Indian hands. Then, in the late 1840s, Mormons established settlements in Utah, which was still a part of Mexico. Although it was the stated policy of the Mormons' leader, Brigham Young, to maintain peaceful relations with the Shoshone Indians, friction arose as Mormon farmers took up arable lands and squeezed the Indians' hunting and gathering grounds.

The Treaty of Guadalupe-Hidalgo (1848) that ended the Mexican War transferred California and the Great Basin to the United States. More important, in January 1848 Sutter's workers found gold in the Sierra Nevada foothills, and the discovery set off a frenzied, worldwide rush for the precious metal. Tens of thousands of gold seekers stampeded into California. These men—and most of them were young men—had little regard for Indian life or property. As a result, the California Indian population plunged from about 150,000 in 1848 to approximately 32,000 in 1860. At the same time, increasing numbers of overland immigrants passed through the Great Basin and imposed new pressures on Indian life there.

◈ *D O C U M E N T S*

Some historians of California have characterized the 1850s as a romantic and heroic episode that quickly established civilization in the Far West after a brief and boisterous
gold rush. The following documents, however, show that for Indians, the gold rush had
a darker side. The first selection is Charles D. Ferguson's frank rationale for killing Indians along the overland trail—or anywhere else they might be encountered. In the early
years of the gold rush, Indians outnumbered whites and in many areas remained an important part of the California labor force. In 1850 the state's legislature passed a law, reproduced in the second document, that provided for the indenture of Indians. This law
consigned some California Indians to a life of servitude to white masters. The third document is a description of the gold rush by William Joseph, a Nisenan Indian. The fourth
selection gives an Indian agent's bleak report on the living conditions of Indians residing in the California Mother Lode region, the foothills of the Sierra Nevada. The documentary selections close with a Pomo Indian account of the mistreatment of Indian
workers in California.

A White Man's Rationale for Killing Indians
on the Overland Trail, 1849

. . . One evening, after camping, a scout of the Oregon party rode in and reported
a party of Indians camped about five miles ahead, about twenty in number; that
having seen signs of the band, he had followed on unobserved until he found them
camped; that they had evidently been there some time, as they had built huts. All
were up in arms in a few minutes, and ready to start for them. The women were
as much excited as the men. But the captain put a stop to their haste; told them the
better plan would be to wait till night and crawl carefully out and bag the whole
party. His plan was adopted, and guns were cleaned and ammunition looked after.
It was arranged that some should remain with the women and children, and the
rest to start about eleven o'clock, surround their camp, and at a signal rush in and
surprise the ferocious native. Three of our party volunteered—there was no lack
of volunteers, the trouble was, all wanted to go, which would leave the home-
guard too small. But the women were not afraid to remain alone; they wanted the
"red devils rubbed out," as they expressed it. While the preparation was being
made for the raid upon the Indian camp, an amusing little incident occurred. The
captain had a little dumpy stub of a boy, some six or seven years old, about as
thick as he was long, who came stubbing up to his father, saying: "Fader, fader, I
want you to buy me a wyfle." "What do you want a rifle for, my son?" said the
father. "I want to shoot the Ingins," replied the precocious son and heir, emphasizing his answer with one of his father's most profane curses. "That's right, my
son," said his father, "I'll buy you a rifle," and his eye beamed with fatherly pride.
He was proud of his son's speech, and, doubtless, regarded him as a rising young
[hero]. I think if that boy had cut down all the cherry trees in Oregon, and then
lied about it, the old man would have cheerfully gone his bail and carried up the
case. If the biography of that father has ever been written and placed in the librar-
ies of Oregon, it will probably be found that he was not a descendant of a Puritan
family.

  It was midnight when we started, and half-past two when we arrived in sight of the Indian camp. Their fires were burning dimly. The captain ordered a halt, and then he crawled up a little nearer and reconnoitered. There were eighteen of our party. The captain returned, placed the men about equal distance apart around the camp, and ordered each to crawl silently to within about one hundred yards of the camp, and there lie perfectly quiet till a signal from him, when we should come down upon them. It was understood that the raid was to be made just at break of day, or when light enough to see that none escaped. Judging from the systematic manner in which he went about the work, I think it was not the first Indian camp he had surprised. I had lain full three-quarters of an hour when the signal was given by one most unearthly yell from the captain. The prime object thereof was to bring the redskins out of their tents. In an instant every man was on his feet, running and yelling at the top of his voice, and in less time than it takes to tell the story, twenty-seven wild and ferocious Indians were changed into harmless spirits of the air, never more to take the war-path or surprise and slaughter a party of emigrants.

Some may think it was a cruel and unmanly proceeding, but had those who think so been situated as we were—whose companions had been massacred before our eyes; whose dead of a few days before still lay naked and unburied in the cañon, and those we hastily buried exhumed and stripped of their grave clothes; driven to the extreme verge of starvation; saved from death only by the mere chance of having fallen in with another party; standing guard by night, and sending out scouts by day to look out for a ferocious enemy, as the man-eating tiger lurking near villages and isolated homes in Hindustan is watched for and hunted by the natives—I think, if happily they survived to return, it would be with modified views of the emigrants' dealings with the plundering and murderous tribes of the interior of the continent in the year of grace '49.

Still, if anyone thinks otherwise, and believes that a free and roving tribe, uncontrolled by military force, can be humanized and civilized by any process known to civilized or Christianized man, I nevertheless would warn him not to risk his person among them. Powder, not prayer, is their only civilizer. You cannot manage him by reasoning with him and persuading him, as the wag said he controlled his vicious and cantankerous mule. Nothing will convert an Indian like convincing him that you are his superior, and there is but one process by which even that can be done, and that is to shut off his wind. I never knew but one "truly good" Indian, and he was dead. I have heard considerable romance, from persons inexperienced, about the brave and noble red man, but I never yet have met one. All I have ever known have been cowardly and treacherous, never attack like men, but crawl upon you, three or four to one, and shoot you down, as they did sixteen of our party in the cañon. Then why not attack them, not wait to be attacked by them, and then only in self-defense take, perhaps, one of their worthless lives? In all modern civilized warfare, to surprise the enemy and kill, if they do not surrender, is the climax of military renown. The world applauds, congress promotes, parliament does likewise, graciously voting the hero of the hour, at the same time, a little hundred thousand pounds and a dukedom, and even bishops, priests and clergy offer prayers and incense to divine Providence for the delivery of their equally civilized and equally honorable and patriotic enemy into their hands! But if a party of emigrants surprise and annihilate a band of Indians, who, perhaps, only the day before had murdered every man, woman and child of a large train, and spattered the wagon wheels with the brains of babes, why, the Christian world holds up its hands in breathless horror. But what is the difference? The Indian is the emigrant's enemy. If the emigrant gets the advantage, why should he not take it, for most surely the Indian will? I do not believe in wanton cruelty to the Indian, but when you are in a country where you know he is your enemy, and is not only waiting his chance but looking out for his opportunity, why not cut him down, as otherwise he most surely will you?

A California Law for the Government and Protection of the Indians, 1850

The People of the State of California, represented in Senate and Assembly, do enact as follows:

1. Justices of the Peace shall have jurisdiction in all cases of complaints by, for, or against Indians, in their respective Townships in this State.

2. Persons and proprietors of land on which Indians are residing, shall permit such Indians peaceably to reside on such lands, unmolested in the pursuit of their usual avocations for the maintenance of themselves and families: *Provided,* the white person or proprietor in possession of lands may apply to a Justice of the Peace in the Township where the Indians reside, to set off to such Indians a certain amount of land, and, on such application, the Justice shall set off a sufficient amount of land for the necessary wants of such Indians, including the site of their village or residence, if they so prefer it; and in no case shall such selection be made to the prejudice of such Indians, nor shall they be forced to abandon their homes or villages where they have resided for a number of years; and either party feeling themselves aggrieved, can appeal to the County Court from the decision of the Justice: and then divided, a record shall be made of the lands so set off in the Court so dividing them, and the Indians shall be permitted to remain thereon until otherwise provided for.

3. Any person having or hereafter obtaining a minor Indian, male or female, from the parents or relations of such Indian minor, and wishing to keep it, such person shall go before a Justice of the Peace in his Township, with the parents or friends of the child, and if the Justice of the Peace becomes satisfied that no compulsory means have been used to obtain the child from its parents or friends, shall enter on record, in a book kept for that purpose, the sex and probable age of the child, and shall give to such person a certificate, authorizing him or her to have the care, custody, control, and earnings of such minor, until he or she obtains the age of majority. Every male Indian shall be deemed to have attained his majority at eighteen, and the female at fifteen years.

4. Any person having a minor Indian in his care, as described in the foregoing Section of this Act, who shall neglect to clothe and suitably feed such minor Indian, or shall inhumanly treat him or her, on conviction thereof shall be subject to a fine not less than ten dollars, at the discretion of a Court or Jury; and the Justice of the Peace, in his discretion, may place the minor Indian in the care of

some other person, giving him the same rights and liabilities that the former master of said minor was entitled and subject to.

5. Any person wishing to hire an Indian, shall go before a Justice of the Peace with the Indian, and make such contract as the Justice may approve, and the Justice shall file such contract in writing in his office, and all contracts so made shall be binding between the parties; but no contract between a white man and an Indian, for labor, shall otherwise be obligatory on the part of an Indian.

6. Complaints may be made before a Justice of the Peace, by white persons or Indians; but in no case shall a white man be convicted of any offence upon the testimony of an Indian.

7. If any person forcibly conveys any Indian from his home, or compels him to work, or perform any service against his will, in this State, except as provided in this Act, he or they shall, on conviction, be fined in any sum not less than fifty dollars, at the discretion of the Court or jury.

8. It shall be the duty of the Justices of the Peace, once in six months in every year, to make a full and correct statement to the Court of Sessions of their county, of all moneys received for fines imposed on Indians, and all fees allowed for services rendered under the provisions of this Act; and said Justices shall pay over to the County Treasurer of their respective counties, all money they may have received for fines and not appropriated, or fees for services rendered under this Act; and the Treasurer shall keep a correct statement of all money so received, which shall be termed the "Indian Fund" of the county. The Treasurer shall pay out any money of said funds in his hands, on a certificate of a Justice of the Peace of his county, for fees and expenditures incurred in carrying out the provisions of this law.

9. It shall be the duty of Justices of the Peace, in their respective townships, as well as all other peace officers in this State, to instruct the Indians in their neighborhood in the laws which relate to them, giving them such advice as they may deem necessary and proper; and if any tribe or village of Indians refuse or neglect to obey the laws, the Justice of the Peace may punish the guilty chiefs or principal men by reprimand or fine, or otherwise reasonably chastise them.

10. If any person or persons shall set the prairie on fire, or refuse to use proper exertions to extinguish the fire when the prairies are burning, such person or persons shall be subject to fine or punishment, as a Court may adjudge proper.

11. If any Indian shall commit an unlawful offence against a white person, such person shall not inflict punishment for such offence, but may, without process, take the Indian before a Justice of the Peace, and on conviction, the Indian shall be punished according to the provisions of this Act.

12. In all cases of trial between a white man and an Indian, either party may require a jury.

13. Justices may require the chiefs and influential men of any village to apprehend and bring before them or him any Indian charged or suspected of an offence.

14. When an Indian is convicted of an offence before a Justice of the Peace punishable by fine, any white person may, by consent of the Justice, give bond for said Indian, conditioned for the payment of said fine and costs, and in such case

the Indian shall be compelled to work for the person so bailing, until he has discharged or cancelled the fine assessed against him: *Provided,* the person bailing shall treat the Indian humanely, and clothe and feed him properly; the allowance given for such labor shall be fixed by the Court, when the bond is taken.

15. If any person in this State shall sell, give, or furnish to any Indian, male or female, any intoxicating liquors (except when administered in sickness), for good cause shown, he, she, or they so offending shall, on conviction thereof, be fined not less than twenty dollars for each offence, or be imprisoned not less than five days, or fined and imprisoned, as the Court may determine.

16. An Indian convicted of stealing horses, mules, cattle, or any valuable thing, shall be subject to receive any number of lashes not exceeding twenty-five, or shall be subject to a fine not exceeding two hundred dollars, at the discretion of the Court or Jury.

17. When an Indian is sentenced to be whipped, the Justice may appoint a white man, or an Indian at his discretion, to execute the sentence in his presence, and shall not permit unnecessary cruelty in the execution of the sentence.

18. All fines, forfeitures, penalties recovered under or by this Act, shall be paid into the treasury of the county, to the credit of the Indian Fund as provided in Section Eight.

19. All white persons making application to a Justice of the Peace, for confirmation of a contract with or in relation to an Indian, shall pay the fee, which shall not exceed two dollars for each contract determined and filed as provided in this Act, and for all other services, such fees as are allowed for similar services under other laws of this State. *Provided,* the application fee for hiring Indians, or keeping minors, and fees and expenses for setting off lands to Indians, shall be paid by the white person applying.

20. Any Indian able to work and support himself in some honest calling, not having wherewithal to maintain himself, who shall be found loitering and strolling about, or frequenting public places where liquors are sold, begging, or leading an immoral or profligate course of life, shall be liable to be arrested on the complaint of any resident citizen of the county, and brought before any Justice of the Peace of the proper county, Mayor or Recorder of any incorporated town or city, who shall examine said accused Indian, and hear the testimony in relation thereto, and if said Justice, Mayor or Recorder shall be satisfied that he is a vagrant, as above set forth, he shall make out a warrant under his hand and seal, authorizing and requiring the officer having him in charge or custody, to hire out such vagrant within twenty-four hours to the best bidder, by public notice given as he shall direct, for the highest price that can be had, for any term not exceeding four months; and such vagrant shall be subject to and governed by the provisions of this Act, regulating guardians and minors, during the time which he has been so hired. The money received for his hire, shall, after deducting the costs, and the necessary expense for clothing for said Indian, which may have been purchased by his employer, be, if he be without a family, paid into the County Treasury, to the credit of the Indian fund. But if he have a family, the same shall be appropriated for their use and benefit: *Provided,* that any such vagrant, when arrested, and before judgment, may relieve himself by giving to such Justice, Mayor, or Re-

corder, a bond, with good security, conditioned that he will, for the next twelve months, conduct himself with good behavior, and betake to some honest employment for support.

William Joseph (Nisenan)
Describes the Gold Rush, c. 1849

Long ago the Indians had a camp on the north side of the oke·m mountain, the white people call that Mt. Oakum. The bluff by the river at the north side of that, (they) call that pu·lak' Bluff, and the white people call that Buck's Bar, in that river Indians and white men prospected for gold.

On the west side of Mt. Oakum two white men had their home in a small log cabin. From there they used to go to work at the river every day. The door of their house being left open, an Indian boy who was hunting around, felt hungry and went to that house to eat. When he had finished eating he saw two buckskin sacks full of gold, and silver money on that table. He took (it), put (it) in his pocket, and went off with (it).

When the two men came home from work they missed the gold and the money. They followed that Indian's tracks. They tracked (him) to the Indian's camp. They saw (him) playing cards and putting down sackfuls of gold. The white men took him right there. They took back all the money. But they took him all the same to a little valley on the west side of Mt. Oakum.

The white men gathered. From there, afterwards, they summoned all the Indian chiefs. They kept him there all day, waiting for one chief. When it was about three o'clock, they put a rope around (his) neck.

At length, that chief arrived. The Indians said, "(They) are waiting for you, they are going to hang the boy, go and prevent (it)!"

That chief went in the center (of the group of people). He talked, speaking white language, "Captain he says, Lowas he says, Hemas he says, 'Hang him up!'" he said.

(The white people) said to the mule, "Get up!" (The mule) pulled (him) up by the rope and hanged (him). All the Indians hollered and cried. When (he) was dead, (they) let (him) back down. They gave (him) to the Indians. The Indians took the body along and burned (it).

After that the Indians did not burgle or steal anything belonging to white people, "That is the way (they) will treat us if they catch (us)," they said. When the chiefs made speeches they said, "Do not take anything from (them), do not steal from (them), (they) will treat you that way if they catch (you)! Those white men are different men, they are not our relatives," they said, "(They) will hang you without mercy!" they said. All the chiefs preached that. They talked about that at every big time [celebration]. The Indians were very much afraid of the whites in the early days. That is what was done, the whites were bad in the old

From Hans Jorgen Uldall and William Shipley, *Nisenan Texts and Dictionary,* vol. 46 of University of California Publications in Linguistics, pp. 177–181. Copyright © 1966 the Regents of the University of California.

days, those who prospected for gold. Those who have come now brought women along, white women, those ones were good, they gave us all kinds of food when we went to their houses. That was bad whites in the early days, those who prospected for gold. Those who came next were good whites, married people, that was how it was in the old days.

About a year after that hanging (an Indian boy) found gold in a creek while he was hunting a deer, he killed the deer near that. He looked around for a tree to hang it on. He saw this gold. He took the deer along instead of hanging it up. When he brought (it) in to camp he told his relatives, "There is a lot of this gold, let us go tomorrow!" he said.

That morning at dawn they went, only the men, they left the women. They all brought a lot of gold. They took (it) to town to exchange (it), five or six times to that town, the same fellows.

The white men talked about (it), "Those Indians bring in a lot of gold from somewhere," said the storekeeper. Those white men talked about (it), those who worked on that river, "Let us watch those Indians, where is it they are always going?" they said. They saw those fellows go, the white men tracked (them) that way. From the hills they watched them at work. When the sun was in the west the Indians went back from work. (The white men) went past them in the opposite direction and found the gold.

The whites gathered and went there. When the Indians tried to go to work they found the whites there. They sneaked away, "That is those fellows, those who hanged that boy!" they said. That way those white men stole their prospecting place. The whites name that Indian Digging. The white men made a small town there and a ditch, and then they placer-mined with a lot of water and went twenty feet into the mountain.

This is over now, even the town is dead now, only one keeps a store there, a Chinaman. That is still called Indian Digging. That is what they did long ago, those fellows are dead and gone, there is not one of the Indians alive now. That is that.

An Indian Agent Views Conditions in the California Mines, 1854

Navada City. Dec. 16, 1854

In accordance with your request, I have proceeded to obtain from the best information possible the number of Indians in Navada and adjoining Counties, the names & number of their respective tribes, Their present condition and means of living, and herewith have the honor to report to you the result of my examinations. . . .

In order the more satisfactorily to ascertain their numbers & condition, I have been compelled to visit the most of their camps, and the counties of Yuba, Sierra Navada, and Placer, in person and altho' my Estimates may not be strickly correct, yet they may be relied upon to be as near as correct as the nature of the circumstances will permit. The difficulty of ascertaining their exact number arises from the fact that they are frequently changing their camps from one section of their respective domain to another and sub-dividing their camps so as to be more convenient to the towns & ranches of the Whites. The great number of deaths which have in the last few years occured among them have tended to mislead many as to their real numbers at present. It will be seen by reference to this report that death has reduced their numbers in these counties more than half in the last 4 years. The cause of this mortality has been attributed to different causes. Some allege that it is the result of the change of their mode of living, being now compelled to live on entirely different food to what they were formerly accustomed. Again it is said it is caused by adopting the Customs of the Americans in wearing clothes, that habitual use of ardent spirits which some traders have very improperly and illegally sold to them. These are some of the causes which have tended to swell the list of mortality among them, but the greatest number of deaths has been caused by that great Indian Scourge the Small Pox. This disease has in some instances entirely extinguished some of the smaller tribes, there being so few left by the disease that they have abandoned their camp and joined their neighboring tribes.

At this time there is none of this disease among them. Yet I find many of the Indians sick in the camps, I have visited and evidences of Mourning in almost every family. The disease with which they seem to be complaining most of this time, is a kind of slow feever which I think is the result of eating excessive quantities of spoiled meat, offal picked up by them about the various butcher pens which are to be found all over the mining country. With this refuse flesh they fill themselves, and perhaps it will be another week before they will get another meal, this creates diseases. Near the Emigrant road, and in the foothills many of the emigrant Stock die, diseased & the Indians driven by pinching hunger have lived upon these carcasses. In one tribe I visited 7 had died from this cause, (as was supposed) in the two weeks preceeding my visit. . . .

"Their present condition" is worse in my opinion than when the country was first settled by the Whites. They arrange their camps for the Winter more carelessly than formerly. Their manner of building huts now is to set up a few old sticks about ten feet in length & about eight feet apart at the base and fastened at the top by vines or withes. On this conical shaped frame they throw . . . brush and cover that either with old pieces of canvas obtained from deserted tents, or set up the bark of the pine against it making a kind of shelter from the rain of the winter season. An Apurture is left in the hut about two feet wide and three feet high through which the family and dogs crawl into them. They build a fire in the center around which they sit and sleep apparently comfortable. I am informed that prior to the settlement of the country by the Whites, they covered most of their huts with dirt, thus making them a perfect shelter and quite warm and comfortable in the winter.

Ten or twelve of these huts compose one camp they are generally crowded close together leaving the chiefs or sub-chiefs hut in the center.

They subsist chiefly upon Flour & Beef. They purchase it in the towns & at the ranches near which they camp with the gold dust they obtain by panning arround in the gold mines.

Sometimes a Miner will permit them to take a pan of dirt from his claim from which they get some gold. They scrape up the dirt about the end of the sluice boxes which sometimes pays them very well. On the rivers they obtain gold by scraping out the crevasses that has been abandoned by the Whites. The mining is done almost exclusively by the Squaws. I have known a company of four or five Squaws to obtain as much as $8. in one day. With this they purchase flour & beef & most generally of the worst that there is in Market.—Meat that can not be sold to others is sold to them.

The men are very indolent spending their time mostly laying about camp. Formerly they exercised more in search of game. Now there is no game since the settlements of the Whites. The Deer which were in the greatest abundance around their camps are now entirely driven off or killed. The Hares & Quail are mostly destroyed by the White man, and now the country is entirely without game up on which the Indian can at all subsist. They hunt but little therefore, and seldom kill anything but a few squirrels. They have nothing to [do]. When their Squaws fail to bring them enough to eat they will go arround the ranches in the country & kitchens in towns & beg something to eat. In the counties I have visited all the streams are mining streams & the water is constantly muddy which drives all the fish out.

Prior to 1849 in one weeks fishing on the Yuba & its tributaries in the fall season the Warriors would kill enough fish to last them through the Winter. These were dried & packed in their huts to be used when wanted in the Winter. At present there are no fish in the streams. A few Warriors visited the shoals in the Yuba near Col. Brofitts ranch this past fall for the purpose of fishing, but I am informed that they could eat them as fast as they caught them. This source of subsistence is entirely destroyed. Another great source of suffering among the Indians arises from the singular, & to the Indian unaccountable fact that the crop of acorns have failed completely for the last three years. The acorns formerly furnished them an abundant supply of Bread & that without any trouble to them. They think this is very strange & wonder much Why the Oaks bear no more. The present season a few acorns are to be found in the foot hills in Yuba County. Not one has been seen in Navada & Sierra Counties. . . .

Augustine (Pomo) Tells of California, 1849

. . . Salvador Vallejo had a claim on sixteen leagues of land, around the west side of Clear Lake. Stone and Kelsey [white settlers] came and built an adobe house at where Kelseyville now stands. They had nothing but one horse apiece when they came into the valley. They got all the Indians from Sanel, Yokia, Potter Valley and the head of the lake to come to the ranch, and of all those there he chose twenty-six young Indians, all stout and strong young men, and took them to the mines on Feather River, and among them was Augustine. This was in the summer time. In one month the Indians had got for them a bag of gold as large as a man's arm. They gave the Indians each a pair of overalls, a hickory shirt and a red handkerchief for their summer's work. They all got home safely.

They then made up another party of one hundred young men, picked from the tribes as the others had been, and went again to the mines. This was late in the fall of the year or early winter. They did not feed the Indians, and the water was so bad that they could not drink it, and they got sick, and two of them died there. The Indians got dissatisfied and wanted to go home. Finally, they told the Indians to go home. On the road they all died from exposure and starvation, except three men, who eventually got home. Two of these men are still living, and their names are Miguel and Jim. Stone and Kelsey got back before the three Indians did, but could give no satisfactory answer to the inquiries concerning the whereabouts of the Indians who had gone off with them. They were afraid of the Indians and did not go among them very much. At length the three arrived and told their story, but the Indians kept hoping that some more of them would come in the next spring, having spent the winter in the rancherias of some of the Sacramento Valley Indians, but in this they were doomed to disappointment.

Stone and Kelsey took the gold they had got on their first trip and went to Sonoma Valley and bought one thousand head of cattle with it. It took six trips to get them all into Big Valley. There were twelve Indian vaqueros [cowboys], of whom Augustine was the chief, on each trip. They did not give these vaqueros very much to eat, and nothing for their wages. Stone and Kelsey also bought all the cattle that Vallejo had in the valley at this time. The whole valley was full of them, and they would number about two thousand head, any way, if not more.

Stone and Kelsey used to tie up the Indians and whip them if they found them out hunting on the ranch anywhere, and made a habit of abusing them generally. They got a lot of strong withes, which came from the mountain sides and were very tough, and kept them about the house for the purpose of whipping the Indians with all the time. When a friend of any of the vaqueros came on a visit to the ranch, if they caught them, they would whip them (the visitors). The Indians all the time worked well, and did not complain. If the Indians questioned them about the Indians who had died in the mountains, they would whip them.

Stone and Kelsey then tried to get the Indians to go to the Sacramento River, near Sutters Fort, and make there a big rancheria. They would thus get rid of all except the young men, used about the ranch as vaqueros, etc. The Indians worked for two weeks, making ropes with which to bind the young men and the refractory ones, so as to be able to make the move into the Sacramento Valley. The old and feeble ones they could drive, but they were afraid the young men would fight them and kill them. They told the Indians that, if they killed them, they would come back again in four days, and the Indians believed this, and thus they were held in subjection. The Indian women made flour for the ranch, with mortars, and it took them all day to pound up a sufficient quantity for the use of the place. The Indians were mad on account of the fact that the others had died in the mountains, and then, when they wanted to move them off to the Sacramento Valley, they became still more enraged, and the plan was then set out on foot to kill them.

The Indians did all the work in building the adobe house, there being some four or five hundred of them engaged at it all the time for two months. They had to carry the water with which the adobes were mixed a distance of about five hundred yards, in their own grass buckets. Men and women all worked together. For all this number of people they only killed one beef a day, and they had no bread, nor anything else to eat except the meat. The more work the Indians did, the more they wanted them to do, and they got crosser and crosser with them every day.

Augustine was sent to work for Ben. Kelsey in Sonama Valley, and after about a month he came home to visit his friends, and as soon as Andy Kelsey saw him there he tied him up in a sweat-house on his feet and kept him standing there for a week. At the same time he tied up six others for the same period. When he had punished them he sent all but Augustine to Napa County, taking a lot of the other Indians with them, and just before starting off with them whipped four of the number. They were sent down there to build an adobe house for Salvador Vallejo, and they were gone for a long time. He also took Indians down to the lower valleys and sold them like cattle or other stock.

Finally the Indians made up their minds to kill Stone and Kelsey, for, from day to day they got worse and worse in their treatment of them, and the Indians thought that they might as well die one way as another, so they decided to take the final and fatal step. The night before the attack the Indians stole the guns of Stone and Kelsey and hid them. Early in the morning the Indians made the attack on them. Kelsey was shot in the back with an arrow, which was shot at him through a window. He then ran out of the house, across the creek to where there was a rancheria, and an old Indian caught him there and struck him on the head with a stone and killed him dead. Stone, when Kelsey was shot, ran into a small house near the adobe and shut the door. The Indians then cut the fastenings of the door and he then tried to make his way through the crowd to the big house, having in his hand a large knife. He did not attack the Indians with it, but used it as a protection for himself. He had on a long-tailed coat, and as he passed along the crowd was crushed in upon him by the outer circles, and he was caught by the tail of the coat and jerked down, and trampled upon, and his throat cut with his own knife, and left for dead. He jumped up and ran into the house, and the Indians supposed up stairs where the bows and arrows, which they had taken from the Indians, were stored. The Indians heard a rattling noise and thought he was up stairs, but he was not. It was only his death struggles which they heard. They feared to follow and see where he was, for if he had access to the bows and arrows he could use them as well as an Indian, and would thus probably kill some of them. The Indians buried both men, Kelsey near the rancheria where he fell, and Stone near the house. When the soldiers came up these bodies were taken up and they were both buried together.

The Indians then all went to Scotts Valley and Upper Lake, or wherever else they pleased, as they all now felt that they had their liberty once more and were free men. The killing of Stone and Kelsey occurred in the winter. In the spring following the soldiers came to Kelsey's ranch and found that the Indians were on an island in a rancheria. They then sent and got their boats and cannon and went to Lower Lake, where they got some Indian guides to show them the way to the rancheria, at Upper Lake. When the soldiers came up they went over into Scotts Valley, and on the road found one Indian, whom they killed. The rest ran into the brush, and afterwards went to the rancheria at Upper Lake. They killed two Indians in Scotts Valley. A part of the soldiers went from Lower Lake to Upper Lake in four boats, and the balance of them went on horseback around the Lake. They took the cannon by land, and passed through Scotts Valley on the road. They found a rancheria there and the Indians ran into the brush. They fired the cannon twice into the brush, but did not kill any Indians.

The two parties met at the point near Robinson's place, below Upper Lake. In Scotts Valley the Indians had a rifle, the one taken from Kelsey at the time of the killing. This they discharged at the soldiers, which was the cause of their shooting the cannon at them. The entire party camped where the boats landed that night. In the morning early the party with the cannon went around the head of the lake and got on the north side of the island, and those in the boats went into the slough on the south side of the island. Before leaving, however, they killed their two Indian guides, one being shot and the other hung. They then began firing at the Indians with their small arms. Five Indians went out to give them battle; one with a sling and the other four with bows and arrows. *The cannon were not fired at all.* The Indians took to the tule [reeds] and water and swam around and kept out of the way of the soldiers as much as possible, and there were only *sixteen* of them killed there that day. The soldiers then went over to Potter and Yokia Valleys. They did not find the Potter Valley Indians, but they had a fight with the Yokias. The Indians fought well considering their arms, and many of them were killed—over one hundred, at least. The soldiers returned to San Francisco by way of Sonoma. Afterwards about twenty men came up and sent word to the Indians in Scotts Valley to come to Kelsey's ranch and make a treaty. The Indians went down and the treaty was made. Ben, Moore drove the cattle of the Kelsey estate out of the valley. He had ten men with him. . . .

◈ *E S S A Y S*

In the 1850s, the gold rush was so chaotic that sorting out its effects on Indians is a difficult matter. Although Indians died at astonishing rates in this era, some did find ways of adapting to the strikingly new and dangerous conditions. In the opening essay, Albert L. Hurtado, an associate professor of history at Arizona State University and the coeditor of this volume, examines several California regions and argues that Indians had different experiences according to time, place, and historical circumstances. Historian Brigham D. Madsen, professor emeritus at the University of Utah, in the second essay describes the impact of Mormon settlement and overland immigration on the Shoshone Indians of Utah, Nevada, and Idaho. Both essays depict a world where Indians had little room to maneuver and where Anglo-Americans used brutal means to dominate the native population. In Utah the situation was complicated by mistrust and bigotry between Mormons and non-Mormons.

What might the federal government have done to improve the situation in California and Utah? What strategies for survival seemed most effective for Indians?

Indian and White Households on the California Frontier, 1860

ALBERT L. HURTADO

In 1851 Major John Bidwell, a prominent Butte County farmer, commented on Indian affairs in gold rush California. In comparison with conditions in eastern states, he emphasized, California's settlers had not only to contend with Indians on the frontier, but they were "all *among* us, *around* us, *with* us—hardly a farm house—a kitchen without them." According to Bidwell, when a farmer needed laborers he told the Indians to "go into his fields," and in return he fed and clothed them. He thought the Indian farm workers looked up to an employer with "a kind of filial obedience to his commands" and expected from him "a kind of parental protection." The earnest farmer contrasted his description of agrarian paternalism with the activities of "malicious and brutal vagabonds" who roamed the country murdering Indians. Such depredations caused native people to retaliate in kind, "thereby exposing the industrious and well disposed miner to dangers and death." In these desperate times, Bidwell believed, Indians were "sure to cling around and shelter themselves under the protection of him who treats them best."

Bidwell's remarks evoke a strikingly different picture of Indian and white relations than the one conveyed by the usual Anglo-American frontier stereo-types. Instead of resisting the whites, restricting settlement, and impeding devel-opment, California's Indians worked obediently in the whites' fields and houses in return for food and shelter. The relationship that Bidwell described was in part the product of nearly a century of Hispanic colonization, with traditions of Indian and white relations far different from Anglo-American practices. Herbert E. Bol-ton [a prominent historian] compared these different customs and noted that in Anglo-America "the only good Indians were dead Indians," while in Hispanic America Indians were assimilated and exploited. Moreover, Bolton believed that California and other parts of the Spanish Borderlands were "the meeting place and fusing place of two streams of European civilization," each with substantially different histories with regard to the Indian.

The fusing of Anglo and Hispanic traditions was not a smooth process in gold rush California, especially for Indians. Some Anglos adopted Hispanic labor practices as a convenient expedient, while others sought to drive Native Ameri-cans out of the work force where Indians could expect to find little protection. The federal government established a stopgap, temporary reservation system that ministered to only a fraction of the Indian population. Ineffectual federal admin-istration enabled the state government to take a powerful role in Indian affairs. Although the state constitution outlawed slavery, the legislature passed chapter 133, "an act for the government and protection of the Indians," that provided for the indenture of loitering and orphaned Indians, regulated their employment, and defined a special class of crimes and punishment for them. Some students of Cali-fornia history have referred to this law as a form of legalized slavery. Certainly it resembled the "black codes" adopted by slave states as a means to control free blacks and bondsmen alike. Simultaneously, the state government subsidized scores of military campaigns aimed at Indian communities considered threaten-ing to white settlement. In fact, these expeditions often killed Indians indiscrimi-nately.

To describe this situation as chaotic hardly does it justice. The gold rush proved to be a catastrophe for the Indians. By 1860 the native population had fallen from perhaps 300,000 to about 32,000. According to Sherburne F. Cook, the preeminent demographer of California Indians, native numbers continued to fall until about 1900, when they reached a population nadir of between 20,000 and 25,000. Cook postulated that Indian demographic decline was due to starvation, homicide, and a "palpable fall in the birth rate concerning which we have little factual knowledge."

Cook's lack of knowledge about the declining birthrate is not surprising. Like other poor working people, the California Indians left no well-documented record of their daily lives. But using techniques derived from social history and demography, it is possible to find evidence that gives a fuller understanding of the gold rush's effect upon native survival. This evidence shows how Indians were useful to white society in the 1850s and provides insights into the ways that Anglo and Hispanic traditions merged on the Spanish Borderland frontier. At the same time, it furnishes a fresh perspective for Native American history, for the California experience is a case study of the process of Indian integration with white society in the mid-nineteenth century. Amidst the turbulent disorders of a unique age, native Californians became the mudsills of Victorian society in the American West.

The 1860 federal census offers a starting point for this reexamination, since it contains a wealth of information on Indian people at the household level. The Constitution and the census law of 1850 empowered United States marshals to enumerate the population in 1860. Under this authorization federal officers enumerated Indians to determine political apportionment and taxation. The census takers received two cents for each person they counted, thus giving them an incentive to do a thorough job.

In 1860 the census takers enumerated 17,798 Indians in California, by far the highest state Indian population. Excluded were reservation Indians, those in flight or rebellion, and those "retaining their tribal character," who were estimated to number 13,540. The manuscript census includes such demographic data as name, age, sex, and usually occupation for nearly 18,000 Indians. Often marital status is indicated or can be inferred from circumstantial evidence. In addition, all this data was organized on the basis of each dwelling visited by the census officer, thus making possible an analysis of the household. Moreover, since the enumerated Indians frequently lived in close association with whites, the manuscript census provides a close-up view of their relations with one another.

The census indicated several general demographic characteristics of the California population that must be taken into account in any study of Indian people in 1860. The state contained 379,994 persons, 70 percent of whom were males and 60 percent of whom were white males. Overall, the population was young—nearly 60 percent were under thirty. Of the four racial categories identified in the census—white, colored, Indian, and Asian—all showed exceedingly low female-to-male ratios. Such ratios usually mean that a population will not be able to reproduce itself unless new females of child-bearing age can be acquired elsewhere by migration or by intermarriage with other groups.

Like the white population, the enumerated Indians were mostly young males (see Table 1). Theoretically, this Indian population was the soundest reproductive group because it had the highest female-to-male ratio. Statistically, however, Indian women bore fewer live children and raised fewer of them to maturity than their white counterparts. The published census reveals that the Indian population was not distributed uniformly throughout the state. Fresno County had the highest reported population with 3,294, while Sierra and Yolo counties reported no

Table 1   Regional Indian Population by Age and Sex

REGION	0–14			15–39			AGE AND SEX 40–59			60+			TOTALS		
	% M	% F	F/M	% M	% F	F/M	% M	% F	F/M	% M	% F	F/M	N M	N F	TOTAL
1	16.92	14.27	.84	26.58	23.41	.88	7.86	5.23	.67	3.40	2.34	.69	4640	3834	8474
2	19.84	13.94	.70	31.10	17.04	.55	7.42	3.39	.46	4.66	2.61	.56	1690	992	2682
3	13.04	7.42	.57	47.68	25.11	.53	4.72	1.20	.25	0.82			884	450	1334
4	14.01	14.26	1.02	39.58	17.08	.43	8.60	2.37	.28	3.12	0.98	0.31	3059	1625	4684
5	24.36	19.39	.80	22.28	28.37	1.27	3.37	1.92	.57	0.32			314	310	624

Regions 1–5 are the Southern, Central Coast, Sacramento Valley, San Joaquin Valley, and Northern regions respectively.

% M = the percentage of males in the regional population.

% F = the percentage of females in the regional population.

F/M = the ratio of females to males.

[N = the number of Indians in each category.]

Indian residents. Likewise, sex and age ratios varied from county to county. The differing regional population patterns displayed in Table 1 assume a larger significance when viewed through the microscope of household analysis.

For comparative purposes this study subdivides California into five areas with differing settlement histories: the Southern, Central Coast, Sacramento Valley, San Joaquin Valley, and Northern regions. To analyze Indian households I reviewed the unpublished manuscript censuses for precincts that illustrate demographic patterns consistent with those in the published census. I have categorized households in which Indians are found according to five types: No Family, Simple Family, Simple Family Plus Others, Extended Family, and Multiple Family. Household types are compared with data about ethnicity of the household head, as identified by the census takers. For the purposes of this study there are only three kinds of ethnic households: Indian, Non-Indian, and Mixed. Indian households were headed by Indians, although people of other backgrounds may have lived there. Conversely, Non-Indian households were headed by non-Indians and may have included other ethnic representatives. A Mixed household was headed by a conjugal couple, one of whom was an Indian. The correlation of ethnicity and family structure shows wide variations in patterns of Indian household life by their historical origins.

The Southern region was originally the home of Indians whom anthropologists associate with the southern California culture area near the coast and the Great Basin culture area further inland. These people, like other California Indians, divided their labor between the sexes, with men hunting and fishing and women gathering plant foods. Parents often arranged the marriage of their children, a practice that reflected the economic and social utility of the unions. Most couples lived in single family households near the husband's parents. Generally speaking, only chiefs, shamans, or other powerful men had more than one wife.

The Indians in the Southern region were the first California native people to experience Hispanic colonization. Beginning in 1769 Spanish soldiers and missionaries founded a series of twenty-three missions, four military presidios, and three pueblos. With two centuries of frontier experience, Franciscan missionaries sought to convert the native people to Catholicism and place them on the lowest rungs of the Spanish social ladder as farmers and laborers. The neophytes, as the native converts were called, formed the labor pool for the mission system, the primary economic institution of the colony. The mission profoundly affected the neophyte and adjacent Indian populations; they died at a rapid rate, thus requiring the recruitment of new converts from the interior valleys. Still the demographic decline continued, undercutting the missions' source of labor and causing their decay as the economic mainstay for Spanish California. After 1821 the success of the Mexican Revolution led to the secularization of the missions, the distribution of their vast property holdings, and the dispersal of the neophytes. Some of the Franciscan-trained natives returned to their homes in the interior, while others found work in the Mexican settlements or on large land-grant ranchos that replaced the missions as the dominant institution in the province. Under Mexico, Indians remained California's basic labor force. For Indians, eighty years of relations with Hispanic people led to a statewide demographic decline from an estimated 300,000 to about 150,000, due principally to disease.

After the United States acquired California, the native population decline was exacerbated by the gold rush, even outside the mining regions. The discovery of gold led to a great influx of non-Indian people who soon outnumbered the native people. In the Southern region, Los Angeles grew rapidly and became an important, albeit a slow-moving, regional trading center. The new immigrants displaced many of the old Mexican landholders, but Indians remained as house servants and field hands. Their subservient position was institutionalized to a certain extent by the enforcement of chapter 133, which provided for the arrest and indenture of loitering and intoxicated Indians. Local authorities added another legal feature—every week in Los Angeles Indian prisoners were "auctioned off to the highest bidder for private service." At week's end the rancheros paid these coerced Indian workers partly with liquor, helping to assure enough intoxicated Indians for the next auction and a steady supply of labor. Under the threat of arrest and auction, Indians competed fiercely for a limited number of steady jobs as house servants at wages reportedly from fifty cents to one dollar per day.

The sample household analysis of Los Angeles Indians illustrates the results of these local social and economic conditions (see Table 2). More than half of the Indians lived in Non-Indian households, and most of them lived in No-Family quarters on nearby ranchos with other male workers. Nearly 20 percent of the Indians were household servants in Non-Indian homes. About 30 percent of the sample Indian population lived in Indian-headed households, but less than half of them lived in dwellings with identifiable conjugal couples. There were almost as many Indians living in Mixed households as there were in Indian-headed families.

Examples from the manuscript census provide additional insights into the nature of Los Angeles Indians' town and country life. Typically, Indian household servants lived in the homes of people who were at least moderately well to do. Twenty-five-year-old Indian servant Maria, for example, lived in the house of Polish merchant David Solomon, his wife, and their three children. Solomon owned $1,000 in real and $4,000 in personal property. Maria, no doubt, assisted Mrs. Solomon with domestic chores and the many tasks associated with raising three children, all of whom were less than five years old. Indian men as well as women worked as domestics, and occasionally an Indian couple served in a household, but this was rare.

Some of the large landholders on the town's outskirts kept large houses filled with family, friends, and employees. Abel Stearns, a Massachusetts man who became one of the wealthiest southern Californians, lived with his wife and nineteen unrelated people, including Juan and Antonio, Indian laborers. One of Stearns's neighbors, Mexican Californian Julian Chaves, was a person of more modest means, but he kept eight Indian servants, including six males in their twenties. The former American fur trapper William Wolfskill, according to the manuscript census, kept more Indians on his rancho than any of his Los Angeles counterparts. Altogether there were thirty-seven Indians living on Wolfskill's property, including eleven male farm workers, eight washerwomen, a servant, and their children. Wolfskill's rancho was an exception; most ranchos kept only a few workers, except during peak seasons of the year.

Compared with other regions, Los Angeles Indians married non-Indians

Table 2 Los Angeles County Indian and White Sample Households

HOUSEHOLD TYPE	NON-INDIAN			INDIAN			MIXED			TOTAL		
	C	N	%	C	N	%	C	N	%	C	N	%
No family	52	125	26.77	16	75	16.06				68	200	42.83
Simple family				4	15	3.21	6	15	3.21	10	30	6.42
Simple family plus others	51	93	19.91	2	8	1.71	13	42	8.99	66	143	30.62
Extended family	1	7	1.50							1	7	1.50
Multiple family	6	35	7.49	2	45	9.64	3	7	1.50	11	87	18.63
Total	110	260	55.67	24	143	30.62	22	64	13.70	156	467	100.00

C = the number of households with Indian members.
N = the number of Indians in each category.
% = the percentage of the sample Indian population in each category.

fairly often (see Tables 2–6). There were twenty-two households with Mixed couples—about 14 percent of the households sampled. Los Angeles Indian women had spouses from Mexico, Kentucky, and elsewhere. The estates of their non-Indian spouses varied greatly, from moderate wealth to apparent pauperism.

George Harwood Phillips has recently described the history of Los Angeles Indians as a dual process of "economic integration" and "social disintegration." Phillips writes that Indian society disintegrated as a result of a limited and essentially exploitative economic role and that the disintegrative process was indicated by Indian drunkenness, vice, and violence, "which in turn led to a drastic population reduction." A main contributor to the decrease in Indian numbers was disease that, in Phillips's view, took its toll among the weakened natives. Beyond the immediate impact of disease, as the analysis of Los Angeles households shows, comparatively few Indians lived in situations in which reproduction and child rearing were feasible. In short, the Los Angeles social order that integrated most Indians into Non-Indian and No Family households substantially contributed to the overall demographic decline. Social disorder, at least as contemporary whites defined it, may have been an ancillary symptom of Los Angeles' socioeconomic conditions.

The 1860 household patterns of Los Angeles Indians were extreme by comparison with households in other parts of Hispanic California. The divergency of living conditions is illustrated in the Central Coast region. In anthropological terminology, the Central Coast Indians belonged to the Central California culture area. Like their southern neighbors, these people were basically monogamous and patrilocal, although anthropologists have reported occasional polygyny. With Spanish settlement in the eighteenth century, Central Coast Indians entered the Franciscan missions, where they suffered the usual consequences of disease and demographic reduction. During the 1820s and 1830s, mission secularization dispersed the Indians to the surrounding ranchos and urban settlements, where they worked as herdsmen and servants. By the time of the gold rush, the Central Coast Indians were gaining social acceptance in the Mexican community. Increasingly, people of undiluted Indian ancestry were recorded in local records as *vecinos* and *vecinas* (citizens) rather than *indigenas* (Indians).

In 1860 the Indian population of the Central Coast region was only about one-third as large as that in the Southern region (see Table 1). The Central Coast Indians were mostly young males, although the age and sex ratios were not so radically deformed as those in other parts of California. The ratio of females of child-bearing age to males shows there was an important deficit of potentially fertile women in the Indian population.

The town of Monterey and its surrounding ranchos provide a household population sample that sheds additional light on the historical demography of the region. The correlation of household types and ethnicity indicates that a majority of Monterey's Indians lived in Indian households (see Table 3). Most of the remainder lived in Non-Indian households, while a small segment of the sample were residents of Mixed households. By household type, Indians were distributed about equally among No Family, Simple Family, and Simple Family Plus Others households. The largest correlative Indian group was living in Simple Families, while the next largest number of Indians lived in Non-Indian Simple Families

Table 3   Monterey County Indian and White Sample Households

	ETHNICITY											
	NON-INDIAN			INDIAN			MIXED			TOTAL		
HOUSEHOLD TYPE	C	N	%	C	N	%	C	N	%	C	N	%
No family	14	16	11.94	8	27	20.15				22	43	32.09
Simple family				8	37	27.61	3	6	4.48	11	43	32.09
Simple family plus others	18	36	26.87	1	5	3.73	1	4	2.99	20	45	33.58
Extended family	1	3	2.24							1	3	2.24
Multiple family												
Total	33	55	41.04	17	69	51.49	4	10	7.46	54	134	100.00

C = the number of households with Indian members.
N = the number of Indians in each category.
% = the percentage of the sample Indian population in each category.

Plus Others. About 32 percent of the population sample lived in Indian and Non-Indian No Families.

The Monterey census indicates that Indians played economic roles similar to those in southern California. Most of the men were unskilled laborers working on white ranchos, while women labored as domestics in the homes of affluent whites. The Indian women in these homes were usually between the ages of fifteen and forty, although servants as young as eight were recorded. The Indian domestic staff in the David Spence home offers an example. Spence, a wealthy merchant and landowner, lived with his wife, their son and daughter-in-law, and two grandchildren. The Spences kept three female Indians to serve them, aged twenty-five, twelve, and eight. The Spence home was not unlike those of Spence's landed Mexican contemporaries—the Garcias, the Sepulvedas, and the de la Torres. In Monterey's genteel Anglo and Mexican society, for those households classified as Simple Family Plus Others, Indian servants were the others.

Monterey Indian Simple Family and No Family households differed in their social composition, but they were similar in other respects. Both households were composed of working people variously identified as laborers and servants. In some cases the census takers even identified children as servants. For example, in the Indian Simple Family household apparently associated with the rancho of County Treasurer Thomas Day, the Indian parents as well as their children, ages eleven, four, and one, were identified as farm servants. In the mind of the census taker, as this classification implies, Indian occupational status was to some extent hereditary.

The Indian and white household structure in Monterey was the result of several generations of Hispanic colonization and tradition. Like Los Angeles, Monterey's Indians were integrated into the social and economic structure, but they had an additional measure of control over their lives because they headed most of their own households. Still, the deficit of potential Indian mothers and the relative lack of identifiable conjugal couples meant that the Monterey population could not easily sustain itself. Moreover, while Monterey Indians lived in relative peace, they also lived in poverty. None of them reported any real or personal property to the enumerators. As in Los Angeles, Indians in Monterey comprised a part of the working class whose reproductive future was in doubt.

Until the 1840s, permanent settlement in California was confined to a fairly narrow strip of land near the coast. The great interior spaces—the central valleys and the sierras—remained in the hands of native people who were troubled only by the incursions of a few Hispanic exploring expeditions. The natives of this region have also been classified within the Central California culture area, and like their western neighbors, they were principally monogamous and patrilocal, with polygyny reserved for the privileged few.

The first important intrusions in the Sacramento Valley region began in 1827 when American, and subsequently Hudson's Bay Company, fur trappers began to exploit this territory. In 1833 the Hudson's Bay brigade brought a virulent form of malaria to the region, already the habitat of the anopheles mosquito. The insect quickly spread the malaria among the Indians, and it is estimated that twenty thousand native people died in the lowlands of the Great Central Valley in a few summer months. Severely weakened by this epidemic, the valley Indians could not successfully resist the first permanent non-Indian settler, John A. Sutter, who used Indian workers after 1839 to build New Helvetia, a fortified frontier enterprise near the confluence of the American and Sacramento rivers.

By the time of the Mexican War, Sutter and other newcomers controlled most of the Sacramento Valley and the Indians in it. But for native people the worst was yet to come. Sutter's Indian and white workers discovered gold on the American River in January of 1848. During the first season of gold mining, the experienced California settlers maintained the usual white employer–Indian employee relationship, with native workers digging and panning gold for non-Indians. By the end of 1848 there arrived a huge influx of miners who were unfamiliar with the established place of Indian laborers in California. These latecomers drove most Indian people out of the mines, attacking and murdering the native work force, leaving only a remnant population in the mining districts.

In the 1860 census only a handful of Indians were enumerated in the mining counties of the Sierra foothills, but modest populations were recorded in the bordering Sacramento Valley agricultural counties. More than 60 percent of the male Indians were under forty, about twice the number of their female cohorts. Proportionately, there were more Indian women of child-bearing age in the Sacramento Valley than in any other region except the Northern, but they produced fewer children. Indians over forty were downright rare, accounting for less than 7 percent of the population (see Table 1).

Reasons for these disparities are found in the household structure of Indians in Butte County (see Table 4). More than 70 percent of the Butte Indians lived in Indian No Family households, and most of them were male workers. The remaining Indians were about equally divided between Non-Indian No Family and Simple Family Plus Others households as workers and servants. Three Indians lived in Mixed households. Most remarkably, in the 1860 Butte census there were no identifiable Indian conjugal couples.

The Indian living arrangements on Bidwell's Rancho Chico illustrate the kind of household that dominated Indian life in Butte County. Bidwell kept fifty-two Indians on his rancho, and fifty-one of them lived in Indian No Family households. They lived in four dwellings and were segregated by sex. Thirty-nine male herders, gardeners, and farm laborers lived in three households. Eleven women day laborers lived in a separate dwelling headed by a male named Yummarine, who was designated chief. Ten of the women were in their prime child-bearing years, between the ages of sixteen and thirty-one, yet there were no children listed in the census. Given the segregated living conditions, the absence of children was not surprising. In 1860 the Indians at Rancho Chico were there to work, not to raise families or sustain tribal population.

The Butte County ranchos with Indian households like those on Rancho Chico were all large operations. Bidwell owned $52,000 in real estate and $56,640 in personal property. Former Pennsylvanian J. A. Keefer employed twelve young Indian men and four young women. He owned $3,800 worth of land and had personal property valued at $10,000. Similarly, R. W. Durham claimed $8,000 in real estate and personal property worth $2,000 and employed twenty-one male Indians, all except one in their twenties.

As in Monterey, most of the Butte County Indians who lived in Non-Indian

Table 4 Butte County Indian and White Sample Households

| | ETHNICITY | | | | | | | | | | | |
| | NON-INDIAN | | | INDIAN | | | MIXED | | | TOTAL | | |
HOUSEHOLD TYPE	C	N	%	C	N	%	C	N	%	C	N	%
No family	11	15	12.61	6	85	71.43				17	100	84.03
Simple family							2	3	2.52	2	3	2.52
Simple family plus others	10	16	13.45							10	16	13.45
Extended family												
Multiple family												
Total	21	31	26.05	6	85	71.43	2	3	2.52	29	119	100.00

C = the number of households with Indian members.

N = the number of Indians in each category.

% = the percentage of the sample Indian population in each category.

Simple Family Plus Others were servants, but unlike their coastal counterparts, most were young males. On the whole, Butte servants lived in modest homes of white couples with some money, although there were occasional servants in impoverished households.

On the whole, Butte County contrasted sharply with Monterey and Los Angeles in its demographic composition. The Sacramento Valley Indian population seemed precariously based on one generation, with a sharp deficit of women of child-bearing age, although the whole Butte native population may have been more broadly based than the census shows. In the margin of the manuscript census an officer wrote, "16 Indians in Rancheria unemployed," implying that Indians who did not work were not enumerated. If there were other unenumerated Indian communities in the county, they cannot be identified. To have stable family lives, Indian people would have to establish them outside the social and economic realm of 1860 Butte County ranchos, where the sexes were segregated and marriage and child rearing were discouraged.

In 1860 living conditions for Indians in California's Great Central Valley were by no means uniform. At the southern end of the valley, in the San Joaquin region, Indian household structure contrasted sharply with the Butte County sample. The San Joaquin region Indians were also associated with the Central California culture area with mainly monogamous marriage customs, but their historical experience was markedly different. While no permanent non-Indian settlers reached their area until the late 1840s, the Franciscan missionaries had progressively recruited neophytes from the San Joaquin Valley as the coastal population died out. Some of the interior Indian neophytes fled the missions to return to their old homes, and frequently they took mission and rancho horses with them. By 1819 Indians from the valley were raiding the mission herds regularly. It was said that even the San Joaquin women and children rode horseback. One observer claimed that the Indians of that region held regular horse fairs. Periodically, the Spanish and Mexican authorities sent armed expeditions to the San Joaquin Valley to capture runaway neophytes and reclaim stolen horses, but they were never able to quell Indian livestock raiding. While Mexicans and Indians rode east and west, American and Hudson's Bay trappers marched north and south, trapping and trading for furs. Indians continued to hold sway even after the 1833 malaria epidemic swept thousands of them away. Sutter occasionally sent his Indian troops south to suppress livestock raiding, but there were no permanent non-Indian settlements in this region until after the gold rush brought thousands of whites into the area.

The gold rush had an uneven impact upon the San Joaquin region's Indian population. San Joaquin, Mariposa, Merced, and Stanislaus counties were virtually depopulated, but according to the 1860 census, Fresno County had 3,294 Indian people, the largest Indian population in the state, and adjacent Tulare County had 1,340 Indians. In Fresno County the Indians remained a substantial majority, since there were only 999 whites and 312 other non-Indians in the county.

The concentration of Indians in Fresno County was due in some measure to the presence of the Fresno River Farm, an Office of Indian Affairs subagency that operated until 1861. The farm was the home of several Indian groups who tilled the soil under white supervision. To augment the farm's produce, some of the agency Indians worked on local ranchos. Even Indians who lived in the mountains relied to some extent on the Fresno River Farm. For example, the Mono Indians worked for white settlers during planting and harvest times, mined gold in the winter and spring, and gathered "the natural products of the mountains," a federal subagent reported. In addition, the Mono Indians received some food and clothing from the subagency. With all these sources of supply, the federal official believed, the Monos had "been able to provide themselves with a comfortable living for Indians." The Fresno River Farm was also a refuge for Indians who were driven off their land by whites.

The Fresno County household sample reveals another distinctive pattern. Almost 90 percent of the Fresno Indians lived in Indian households; more than 50 percent of the sample population lived in dwellings containing identifiable conjugal couples. Fewer Indians lived in all kinds of Non-Indian homes than in any other region, and less than 1 percent lived in Mixed households (see Table 5).

Not only did Fresno's native people live in Indian households, they lived in their own communities. One of these communities contained 286 Indians in thirty-seven households. The census officer recorded a forty-year-old man named Wuemekana as chief of the community. Wuemekana lived with his wife and three children, a sixty-year-old servant, the servant's wife, and their four children, plus a forty-year-old woman. No other household listed a servant in this entire large community. Except for Wuemekana's servant, the census taker indicated no non-Indian occupations but occasionally noted that a man was a "brave," which apparently indicated a different status, at least in the mind of the white officer. In other communities the census taker found a "Great War Chief," a woman "fortune-teller," and several Indian "doctors."

Native people defined their own household and social relationships within Fresno County's Indian communities, even though they worked periodically for white ranchers. Outside the Indian communities the patterns in Non-Indian No Families were similar to those found in Butte. Young Indian men lived with whites as servants. Most of the Non-Indian household heads appeared to be men of moderate means or better, with sufficient capital to afford a servant.

Although, as previously stated, Fresno County Indians remained the local majority population and many of them retained some control over their community and household lives, they were somewhat reliant on the white economy and federal assistance for survival. Far from being autonomous native societies in Indian country, the Fresno Indians were a dependent and declining refugee population with a deficiency of women of child-bearing age.

The last example of Indian household life comes from the Northern region, formerly the territory of the northwestern, northeastern, and a small part of the central California culture areas. Polygyny seems to have been more frequent in the two northern culture areas than it was in other parts of California, but like the others, most societies were patrilocal. As in other California native societies, marriage served economic and social functions that extended beyond the conjugal family and affected their larger kin groups.

Hispanic colonization had no direct effect on these people; they first encountered whites when the fur trade began in the late 1820s. The Hudson's Bay Com-

Table 5   Fresno County Indian and White Sample Households

					ETHNICITY										
	NON-INDIAN			INDIAN			MIXED			TOTAL		
HOUSEHOLD TYPE	C	N	%	C	N	%	C	N	%	C	N	%
No family	15	43	8.88	28	169	34.92	2	2	0.41	43	212	43.80
Simple family				11	58	11.98				13	60	12.40
Simple family plus others	9	10	2.07	20	147	30.37	1	2	0.41	30	159	32.85
Extended family												
Multiple family				5	53	10.95				5	10	10.95
Total	24	53	10.95	64	427	88.22	3	4	0.82	91	484	100.00

C = the number of households with Indian members.
N = the number of Indians in each category.
% = the percentage of the sample Indian population in each category.

pany established friendly relations with the northern Indians, who insured safe passage from Oregon to California, but the fur trade caused hostility between some tribes. The Modoc Indians, for example, raided neighboring tribes for slaves they traded in Oregon for horses and other goods. These raids continued until the gold rush, when as elsewhere in northern California, the first permanent non-Indian settlers arrived. Only poor mines, located in rugged country, were found in the Northern region, so the area attracted comparatively few miners. Furthermore, some Indian groups strove to keep the whites out of their territory. There was armed conflict in mining districts everywhere in the state, but in the northern mines there was almost uninterrupted warfare between 1850 and 1865. State volunteers and federal troops frequently killed Indians indiscriminately, drove off the survivors, or took them to reservations and indentured them under the provisions of chapter 133. In short, worse conditions for Indians can hardly be imagined than those found in this country in 1860.

As might be anticipated, federal census takers enumerated fewer Indians in the Northern region than in any other area in the state. But the small Indian population in the 1860 census presents a unique demographic picture (see Table 1). There were nearly as many Indian women as men in the total population, and there were more women of child-bearing age than their male cohorts. Children under fourteen formed more than 40 percent of the Indian population; nearly 95 percent of the enumerated native people were under forty.

The Trinity County household sample is likewise unique (see Table 6). Nearly three-quarters of the enumerated people lived in Mixed Simple Family and Multiple Family households. All of the conjugal couples consisted of white males and Indian females. Their racially mixed offspring—sometimes recorded as half-breeds by the census takers—were counted as Indians. Typically, the husbands of these unions were landless farmers and miners with little or no personal property. Most of the males were between twenty and forty years of age, but their spouses were very young, usually between the ages of thirteen and twenty.

The emotional depth of these unions is difficult to judge, and it is not unreasonable to suspect that many of them were alliances of male convenience. Still, the manuscript census indicates that about half of the white partners conferred their last names on their spouses and children. Two families from the manuscript census offer illustrations of this point. David Peters, a landless Pennsylvania blacksmith with $190 worth of personal property, headed a Trinity Mixed household. Peters was thirty, and his Indian wife, Ellen Peters, was eighteen. They had a two-month-old infant son named Samuel Peters. On the other hand, J. Stewart, a propertyless miner from Maine, lived with an Indian woman, Mary Jane, and her two-year-old daughter, Mary Ann. Peters seems to have married Ellen and legitimized—at least for the census taker—his young son. Stewart apparently did not seek to formalize his relationship with Mary Jane or her daughter.

Conjugal coupling did not necessarily indicate conjugal bliss nor a humane attitude on the part of the white men who lived with Indian women. A white army officer remarked upon the casual brutality that erupted in one Mixed household in 1862. A frontiersman had lived in the Northern region with an Indian woman for years when without warning the man beat "his own child's brains out against a tree and kill[ed] the squaw, its mother" because he had no other way of getting rid

Table 6   Trinity County Indian and White Sample Households

HOUSEHOLD TYPE	ETHNICITY											
	NON-INDIAN			INDIAN			MIXED			TOTAL		
	C	N	%	C	N	%	C	N	%	C	N	%
No family	9	12	15.19	1	1	1.27				10	13	16.46
Simple family							18	35	44.30	18	35	44.30
Simple family plus others	8	9	11.39				8	16	20.25	16	25	31.65
Extended family												
Multiple family							2	6	7.59	2	6	7.59
Total	17	21	26.85	1	1	1.27	28	57	72.15	46	79	100.00

C = the number of households with Indian members.
N = the number of Indians in each category.
% = the percentage of the sample Indian population in each category.

of them, and "to keep them from falling into another person's hand." These intimate murders convey the terrible possibilities of a Mixed household in the wartorn and remote Northern region.

The Trinity County Indian and white social arrangements were distinct from those in other regions in the state. There was no place for Indian households within the compass of white society. Indian labor was important specifically in the context of the family, where women performed the wifely duties of housework and child rearing. The Trinity Indians who lived in Non-Indian households had a place in arrangements that resembled those in Butte and Fresno counties. Young Indian men lived in white households as servants, acting, in a sense, as surrogate wives—cooking, cleaning, and serving for white men.

The regional patterns of Indian and white household life found in the 1860 census illustrate the variety of the native experience in the decade following the gold rush. In regions with Hispanic traditions, individual Indians and families were integrated into the larger society as rancho workers and servants in middle- and upper-class homes. Out of the direct path of the gold rush and in areas with substantial Hispanic populations, Anglos in Los Angeles and Monterey counties seemed to conform to the social patterns that were evident among their Hispanic neighbors. In contrast, Butte County ranchers used Indians as workers but rigidly segregated Indian households by sex. In this Anglo-dominated region, white settlers valued Indian labor, but the Indian family had no role to play in Butte society. To the south in Fresno County, Indians were the majority and maintained their own communities with households that they defined. Nevertheless, Indians in Fresno County relied on whites for seasonal work on farms and livestock ranchos. In Trinity County, Indians filled the usual servant's role in Non-Indian households, but more of them lived in Mixed homes as the spouses and children of white men. These different patterns mark the range of household life for Indians who were permitted to live in white society.

Despite the regional variations in households, two trends can be seen throughout California. Except for the Northern region, there were fewer women of child-bearing age than their male cohorts. Even in the north, a significant number of potentially fertile Indian women lived with white men, thus creating a shortage of women available to Indian men. The scarcity of potential mothers was a severe problem for California's Indian population, already under stress and in rapid, prolonged decline. The second trend apparent in the manuscript census was the movement of a large proportion of Indians into living situations that were not conducive to reproduction. This movement explains in part the fall in the birthrate noted by Cook some years ago. To our understanding of Indian death and survival we may now add the limiting effects of household arrangements that discouraged Indian marriage and child rearing. Economic and social integration created conditions that permitted individual Indians to survive but also contributed to an overall decline in native numbers.

A better knowledge of Indian and white household arrangements raises an old and troubling problem that extends beyond California's borders. Given the economic and social possibilities of nineteenth-century America, was integration into white society a better alternative for Indians than segregation or even armed resistance? In Anglo and Hispanic California, the transformation of native Californians from a racial and cultural majority into a working-class minority contributed to their drastic, tragic population decline. Bolton's two streams of European civilization rushed together in California and nearly obliterated native people on the northwestern flank of the Spanish Borderlands frontier. More research is needed to understand the broad range of social and demographic questions implicit in this study. We are fortunate that such questions are only academic for us. California Indians faced them directly. Somehow they quietly persisted, living in a land radically transformed during the course of a single lifetime. For them, the 1860 census charts the landscape of survival and demographic decline.

Mormons, Forty-Niners, and the Invasion of Shoshone Country

BRIGHAM D. MADSEN

As the Shoshone people watched the first emigrant parties hurry through tribal lands on the way to Oregon and California, few realized that these travelers signaled the end to a way of life that had been good for native inhabitants. Within a few years the Mexican War would take place, thousands of Mormon farmers would occupy the fertile and well-watered spots, and thousands more gold-hungry argonauts would begin to exploit Indian food supplies. In the coming years, the first fumbling attempts by the federal government to administer Indian affairs would result in almost hopeless confusion. Mormon leaders, sincere in their initial attempts to appease the Northwestern Shoshone and Ute tribesmen by feeding rather than fighting, would soon reveal that they could be as ruthless as other frontiersmen if native recalcitrance got in the way of saintly objectives. Forty-niners would show less patience and would make no pretense to appease or placate the unfortunate Indians. As elsewhere on the frontier, such incidents would point eventually to major confrontation. However, the decade of the 1840s was a period of experimentation as Shoshone, overlander, settler, and Indian agent alike sought an accommodation between different cultures.

The first pioneers to cross the continent to Oregon and California were so few in number that Indians appear to have shown little apprehension. Early contacts between the two groups were limited. When emigrant William Newby traded with some friendly Shoshone near Soda Springs in 1843, they were the first Indians he had met in two months. The Indians travelers met were often helpful, sometimes cutting and carrying grass for wagon parties, herding and guarding stock, engaging in mutually beneficial barter, or even agreeing to deliver letters for the homesick emigrants. Indian guides were especially appreciated as they mapped out routes, located springs and water holes, and showed the way to river fords or assisted in stream crossings. For example, the trail marked out by the Stevens-Murphy party beyond the Humboldt Sink could not have been accomplished without the help of a Northern Paiute Indian chief who described the route and then led the way. Similarly, Peter Burnett of the Marcus Whitman wagon

From Brigham D. Madsen, *The Shoshoni Frontier and the Bear River Massacre* (Salt Lake City: University of Utah Press, 1985), pp. 25–39. Permission granted by publisher.

train gave credit to a faithful and competent Indian guide who helped steer the party to Oregon. But there were harbingers of hostilities to come. A few early emigrant groups on occasion kidnapped some Indians as unwilling guides to make locating grass and water more certain.

Inevitably, calloused frontiersmen with little regard for Indians accompanied the growing tide of emigrants, and by 1845 relations with Snake River and Humboldt Shoshone bands began to deteriorate. A brutal Texan named Jim Kinney, for example, decided, while traveling west of Fort Hall in 1845, that he wanted a slave to do chores. Capturing a passing Indian, Kinney handcuffed him, tied a rope around his neck, and hitched the unfortunate man to the rear of his wagon. After whipping the Indian until satisfied that his spirit was broken, Kinney pressed him into service as a driver and to help with other menial duties. Kinney boasted that if his captive escaped "he could follow him" with the help of his family dog, and would "kill him to show the other Indians the superiority of the white man. He said he had killed plenty of negroes and an Indian was no better than a negro." But one night the new slave took off with some hams and Kinney's prized Kentucky rifle. As it turned out, the tracking dog was unsuccessful and the Shoshone escaped. Other members of the wagon train were afraid to stand up to Kinney but secretly rejoiced when the Indian got away. In a similar incident, a son of guide Caleb Greenwood shot an Indian who accidentally frightened his horse. The animal had almost thrown his rider, much to the amusement of other members of the party. Young Greenwood then left in a hurry to escape his father's anger, and Caleb was forced to order one of the party to shoot the mortally wounded Indian in the head to relieve his suffering.

In a reflection of mounting tensions, Lansford Hastings cautioned emigrants in his 1846 guidebook against the practice of selling or trading weapons to Indians and others on the road near Green River and Fort Hall. Rifles and other arms, he warned, might well be needed for self-defense as the journey proceeded. The Hastings warning was justified. Chester Ingersoll's party lost six animals stolen by Indians on the Humboldt River in 1847. Ingersoll concluded, "After that we shot at every Indian we saw—this soon cleared the way." Ansel McCall, in 1849, came upon three men from Missouri who intended to shoot the first Indian they saw, believing that Indians had stolen their horses. McCall thought "this inconsiderate retaliation upon a whole race for the acts of one of its members leads to half the conflicts that occur."

By 1847 a pattern of white emigrant attacks and Shoshone and Paiute retaliation was beginning to emerge as a constant in western travel. The encounters would never reach the extremes depicted in western movies or by some fiction writers, where encircled wagons were charged by hundreds of merciless Indian warriors, but would cause enough deaths and suffering on both sides to make western travel and settlement a sanguinary chronicle.

A major intrusion into Indian lands occurred in July of 1847 with the settlement of the Salt Lake Valley by Brigham Young and his followers. Driven from their homes in Nauvoo, Illinois, and seeking a refuge from mob violence, the Latter-day Saints looked forward to a colony in Mexican territory in the desert Great Basin that would be secluded and isolated from the rest of the world. The Mexican cession to the United States placed them once again under American control but left them for a time well beyond the effective bounds of federal influence or protection.

When the Saints entered the valley of the Great Salt Lake, they were fortunate in choosing a spot that was not heavily populated with Indians, although within a week of arrival the pioneers were visited by both Ute and Shoshone interested in trading. In a fight over a stolen horse, four of the Shoshone pursued and killed a Ute warrior and then expressed their anger that the Mormons had traded with the Utes. "The Shoshones claimed that they were the owners of the land and that the Utes had come over the line to interfere with their rights. They signified to the brethren by signs that they wanted to sell them the land for powder and lead." Heber C. Kimball, second in command to Brigham Young, was quick to warn against selling guns and ammunition to the Shoshone, but more important, he expressed strong disapproval of any land purchase. Indeed, he rejected the very "idea of paying the Indians for the lands, for if the Shoshones should be thus considered, the Utes and other tribes would claim pay also." Kimball expressed a special kind of Mormon "manifest destiny," which was not unknown among other frontiersmen, when he continued that the land belonged to "our Father in Heaven and we expect to plow and plant it."

In keeping with this, the Mormons made no pretense of compensating any of the Shoshone of the great Basin for their aboriginal lands, although Brigham Young soon announced his policy that it was "manifestly more economical, and less expensive to feed and clothe, than to fight them." There were some exceptions to this, but mostly Young insisted that his people adhere to it despite the later drain on Mormon food supplies by hungry natives whose best lands had been taken over by aggressive white farmers. In a typical statement to the Utah territorial legislature in his position both as governor and as superintendent of Indian affairs, Young later explained:

> We exhort you to feed and clothe them so far as lies in your power; never turn them away hungry from your door; teach them the art of husbandry; bear with them in all patience and long suffering, and never consider their lives as an equivalent for petty stealing; remember that it is a part of their existence, practiced by them from generation to generation, and success in which paved the way to renown and influence amongst them. Induce them from those ideas and notions by your superior wisdom and genial influence and intercourse with them. . . . Finally brethren, be just and quiet, firm and mild, patient and benevolent, generous and watchful in all your intercourse with them; learn their language so that you can explain matters to them and pay them the full and just reward of their labor, and treat them in all respects as you would like to be treated.

Nevertheless, Young's humanitarian policy differed more in degree than in real substance, as he demonstrated in February 1849 when he dispatched a militia company of about forty men to Utah Valley to "chastize" a band of seventeen Indians under Cone and Blue-Shirt, who had been stealing and killing cattle and running off horses from the settlement at South Willow Creek. In a battle lasting almost four hours, the troops killed four of the Indian men and "then warned and fed" the women and children of the band before sending them off to the care of other "Snake Indians."

Yet another Indian difficulty occurred early in 1849 when mountain man Barney Ward was accused by Louis Vasquez of Fort Bridget of being involved in the murder of a Bannock Indian. Vasquez reported that the tribe now "talked of coming to the valley to war upon the whites." Brigham Young was convinced that Jim Bridger [mountain man and fur trader] was behind the whole affair and "is death on us" because of his jealousy of Mormon trade with the Indians. The Bannock who was supposedly murdered was later discovered alive and well at Fort Hall. This ended the scare, but the incident reinforced the pragmatic Young, who was a pessimist about the prospects of saving the souls of the Indians. "As for the old Indians now alive," he wrote, "entering into the new and everlasting covenant, they will not do it, but they will die and be damned. . . . They will not be converted in many years."

A much more important development in 1849 to Mormon and Indian alike as well as for this study, was the passage of thousands of gold-seekers on their way to California. The Gold Rush emigrants transformed the economy of Salt Lake City as they traded their excess baggage and wagons for pack horses to continue the journey. The argonauts also had a tremendous impact on the Shoshone and Paiute. Only small numbers of emigrants had crossed the continent each year before the California rush, but in 1849 about 25,000 traveled to the coast, and perhaps 45,000 went in 1850. Approximately 10,000 in 1849 and 15,000 in 1850 went through the City of the Saints and followed the Salt Lake Road north around the end of Great Salt Lake and thence to Nevada. From the Salt Lake settlement north across the Bear River and past the Promontory Mountains was Northwestern Shoshone territory, so these Indians tasted the discouragement of having to deal with hordes of whites moving through their homeland.

Grasses along the trails were destroyed, wild game was depleted, and firewood exhausted, creating an immediate and devastating impact on the Northern Paiute and Shoshone people. Two incidental comments by travelers passing through the Northwestern Shoshone area emphasized the effect even small groups could have on game. Charles Glass Gray recorded on successive days while nearing Bear River Crossing that "several of our men . . . brought in 12 fine prairie hens" and "5 of us today shot 50 *large sage hens*. . . ." Three years later, Mariett Cummings wrote that he was able to catch thirty-two fine speckled trout from Weber River in two days of fishing. Such takes were multiplied many times, soon reducing important Indian food sources.

Nearly all the tribes along the Oregon and California trails insisted, as did the Northwestern Shoshone, that the Gold Rush emigrants were trespassers on Indian lands and that travelers should pay a tribute or tax for the privilege of crossing. The Forty-niners responded much the same as had Heber C. Kimball. Isaac Lord angrily wrote, "The whole is a gross imposition. The . . . 'idea' that an old Indian should lay claim to a tract of land as large as all the New England States, and levy black mail on all passers, is sufficiently absurd; but when it is done by the connivance of the U.S. government . . . language becomes useless." Sarah Royce thought that a tribute "demand was unreasonable! that the country we were traveling over belonged to the United States, and that these red men had no right to stop us." Major Osborne Cross of the Mounted Rifle Regiment of 1849 argued,"If these people really deserved compensation for the wood used, which was of itself too absurd to think of for a moment, it was a proper subject to lay before the Indian department." However, a few emigrants like James Hutchings, acknowledged Indian land ownership and recognizing the justice of a crossing fee willingly paid up. The Shoshone and Northern Paiute never acknowledged the right of white men to usurp the land. It was not until the twentieth century that the government agreed to compensate the western tribes for some of their aboriginal lands.

It was the indiscriminate killing of Indians by white travelers that contributed most to retaliatory attacks by the natives. The twenty-five member Colony Guard outfit of New York City was so apprehensive about the Indians that they provided each man of their Forty-niner group with a large knife, a Colt revolver, and a hair-trigger rifle. When the order of rifles came, they were rejected as "being too light in weight," and heavier weapons were requisitioned.

With such fears, it is little wonder that night guards sometimes fired at anything that had the slightest resemblance to a lurking warrior. When "an Indian of doubtful appearance" entered the camp of James A. Pritchard looking for something to eat, Pritchard took his gun, ordered him to stop by the fire, and warned that he would be instantly shot if he moved at all before sunrise. The next morning the Indian was given breakfast and sent on his way. Captain Howard Stansbury took extra precautions for his expedition when he learned that "a mortal offence had been taken by the Shoshones or Snake Indians . . . arising from a gross and wanton outrage which had been a short time before inflicted upon them by a company of unprincipled emigrants, by whom their women had been most brutally treated, and their friends murdered while attempting to defend them." Bands of white robbers, often disguised as Indians, sometimes raided the Gold Rush parties, adding to the numbers of unprovoked attacks by the travelers on innocent Indians. Mormon John D. Lee wrote about a group of ferrymen who left the Platte River ferry ten days early to escape one such band hiding in the Wind River Mountains.

Trail fights in 1849 were inspired by both emigrant parties and Shoshone and Northern Paiute raiders. The Foster Company of California pioneers rallied its fifty men just west of the Malad River north of Great Salt Lake when they observed smoke in the mountains because a group of emigrants under a Captain Walker had murdered Indians for their horses. The Foster party expected an attack any minute. Another emigrant train met a company of eighteen young men between the Goose Creek Mountains and Humboldt River who had been embroiled in "quite a fight with the Indians. Two men were killed and four wounded—one died afterwards from his wounds. . . . " The survivors returned to winter in Salt Lake Valley after their wagons were burned and their provisions were destroyed. In late October 1849, Brigham Young's secretary recorded that some Snake Indians had attacked a party of gold-rushers. Farther west, Elijah Howell came upon a physician who had been camped for a week after he had lost his cattle on the Humboldt to Indian marauders. And Alonzo Delano reported that one wagon train had lost twenty-seven mules on the Lassen trail. Bereft of their draft animals, the men had to leave their wagons and start walking the rest of the way to California.

Indian strategy was often oriented to the trails. Emigrant cattle and mules were killed or disabled by shooting arrows into the animals. After the emigrants passed, the Indians harvested the meat. Elijah Farnham rejoiced that his group was able to put one over on the hungry natives by using "up the flesh of the dead cattle so clean that the diggers did not get a morsel for their pains."

Larger horse- and cattle-stealing raids were mounted by the Indians along the trails in 1850. The *Deseret News* of July 13, 1850, advised its readers to be careful when trading horses with the Indians because an animal might be reclaimed later by the emigrant from whom the horse had been stolen. In the same newspaper dated October 5, 1850, a group of Mormons arriving in Salt Lake City from California reported that a band of Indians was holding a herd of no fewer than 1,000 stolen animals in a secure canyon near the head of the Humboldt River. Emigrants sometimes blamed Mormons. Charles Bush, for example, was sure they had instigated Indian depredations by exciting the natives "against us so they kept us in continued alarme both night and day. . . . Often time the grass was fired by night thereby endangering our lives and property."

Instead of such overt attacks on wagon trains, the Shoshone and Paiute more often visited the emigrant camps to trade for goods and convinced many a would-be gold-digger that Indian skill at swapping was not to be underrated. Finley McDiarmid, on his 1850 trip, was impressed that the Shoshone were "very sharp traders. . . ." A member of W. S. McBride's party sold a good rifle to a Shoshone and received in return eight five-dollar gold pieces that later turned out to be a Cincinnati hardware merchant's tokens.

There can be no doubt that the growing numbers of gold-seekers who thronged through their homeland north of Salt Lake City aroused the Northwestern Shoshone during 1850. The California-bound travelers found it necessary to stand guard every night "against surprise by Indians who are said to be very thievish and treacherous on this route." Calvin Taylor thought that despite their horse-stealing proclivities the Shoshone were friendly "owing no doubt to the proximity of the Mormons of whom they stand in dread." Adam M. Brown described the "Digger Indians they met near Bear River Crossing" as the "most miserable specimens of the red race our eyes ever rested upon. They subsist upon roots, carrion, and a species of cricket, . . . and frequently do immense injury to the crops of grain." It was the Indian propensity to raid farmers' fields that caused the chief difficulties between the Mormon people and the Northwestern bands in 1850.

In a prelude to later Shoshone troubles, settlers at Fort Utah (now Provo) encountered problems in January 1850 when three young Mormons shot and killed Old Bishop, a Ute who refused to give up a shirt he claimed he purchased from one of the Saints. The three men then disemboweled the Indian, filled the body cavity with stones, and sank it in Provo River. Old Bishop's tribesmen soon discovered the corpse and began to kill the settlers' stock and to fire on people outside the fort, taunting them when they forted up by calling the Mormons "old women and cowards . . . [who] were afraid to fight them." Fort Utah Saints asked Brigham Young to allow them to fight the Indians, and the Mormon leader "decided to grant the brethren their request." Anticipating friction, Young had warned the Utah Valley settlers the autumn before to stop mixing with Indians "promiscuously." "If you would have dominion over them, . . . you must not treat them as your equals. You cannot exalt them by this process. If they are your equals, you cannot raise them up to you."

With the concurrence of his council and after assurances of military aid from Captain Howard Stansbury, Young dispatched a force of 150 men from Salt Lake Valley to help the Utah Valley settlers chastise their native adversaries. In a three-day seige, eight Indians were killed. Another nineteen "ceased to breathe" when they were hunted down by horsemen on the ice of Utah Lake. John Hudson, the schoolteacher at Fort Utah, assisted in the battle, explaining, "Hostilities were concluded after the annihilation of the Indians in which we were much assisted by the measles & the severity of the weather. . . . " Only one white man was killed in the engagement. In this instance, as on numerous future occasions, the feeding policy yielded to fighting Indians who made bold to challenge the Mormons because, as Captain John W. Gunnison explained, the white settlements had "encroached on hunting and fishing grounds, and the usual winter camping places, and scared off the game."

Hostilities also developed during 1850 when Shoshone winter camps were usurped by small Mormon settlements along the Weber River, at North Ogden, and at a few scattered sites in Box Elder (present Willard and Brigham City). A band of "Weber Utes" (actually Shoshone) with about sixty-five warriors under their chief, Little Soldier, camped on the south side of the Weber River, while another band of Northwestern Shoshone numbering about eighty-five warriors under an old chief, Terrikee, camped at the big bend of the river. Mormon leaders were uneasy about the number of Indians near their homes and in February 1850 organized a militia company of thirty-five men that included about fifteen Gold Rush emigrants wintering in Ogden. When the latter resumed their journey in the spring, the company was reduced to only twenty members.

Both Shoshone groups also left in the spring, but Terrikee led his people back to Ogden in August. They began acting "very bad," riding "through grain fields and melon patches . . . " and Chief Terrikee soon sent his people away again and intended to leave shortly himself. But on the night of September 17, when he tried to retrieve his ponies out of Urban Stewart's cornfield, he was "killed dead on the spot" by Stewart who thought he was stealing corn. Stewart sought help from his neighbors. When they refused, feeling it too "dangerous to do so," Stewart asked a furiously anti-Mormon emigrant, Reverend J. W. Goodell, for help, but Goodell also turned him down.

The frightened Mormon farmers and their families and Goodell sent for help and crowded into the settlement to wait. While the militia was gathering, word came that Terrikee's band had pursued two settlers and butchered one, an emigrant, who, according to Goodell, had joined the Mormon church only the day before. The new convert, a "Broth Camel" (Brother Campbell), left a wife and family in the States but had also been planning to take a second wife under the Mormon law of polygamy.

About 150 militia set out immediately for Ogden, the news of the killing tending "to hasten this expedition very much." A flurry of orders dispatching troops, ordering a fort built, and commanding that the Northwestern Shoshone be reproved demonstrate how seriously Brigham Young and his military lieutenants took the incident.

Young's military leader, General Daniel H. Wells, then sent old mountain man Barney Ward to bring about peace. Ward was instructed to tell the Shoshone that any white man who said the Mormons were not friends of the Indians was a *"liar."* Wells also agreed to negotiate with the Shoshone about their land claims if "they will stop molesting our people." In Ogden, the militia made a fruitless attempt to catch the guilty Shoshone and only succeeded in mistaking each other for marauding Indians. General Horace Eldredge, in his final report of the incident to Wells, concluded, "We found some of their seeds on the road which they had spilled and would not take time to gather. It is my opinion that they are satisfied. They have had blood for blood, Campbell for Terrikee, and will return to their tribe contented."

Concerned for the safety of unwary emigrants, General Wells sent out parties to warn wagon trains to be on guard and to talk to the Indians. Five troopers were to read a proclamation to emigrants stating:

To the Emigration on the Road

   We have sent Master L. Robinson with a small detachment to inform you that a little difficulty having occurred with the Shoshones or Snake Indians, you should be on your guard, you should travel in companies and keep a good watch, especially at nights. We do not know as there is any danger but "caution is the parent of safety" therefore be wise and harken to the counsels of wisdom.

Yours Respectfully
By orders of Brigham Young
Gov.

The decade of the 1840s had started out on a note of harmony that persisted until 1845 when travelers' irresponsible and ethnocentric actions and the destruction of grasses and game stirred the Indians to retaliate. A major source of Indian anger was white refusal to acknowledge aboriginal ownership of the land, and Shoshone anger increased when Salt Lake and other nearby valleys were settled by the aggressive Mormons in 1847 and after. Indian raiders began to shoot and steal livestock and avenge the deaths of their slain people. The most serious hostilities between the newcomers and the native inhabitants occurred, perhaps naturally enough, in the settled Mormon areas in Utah, such as Fort Utah, where a three-day battle resulted in twenty-seven Indian deaths and one Mormon casualty. More far-reaching in its consequences was the death of the Shoshone chief, Terrikee, and troubles only increased as Mormon farmers continued to press north into Northwestern Shoshone territory.

Mormon Indian policy in Utah was shaped during the first three years of settlement. Despite the constant pleas of Brigham Young to his people to treat the neighboring Indians as brothers in the gospel, native hostility over white encroachment periodically activated enough resentment on the part of the Saints that Young had to accede to requests for the chance to spill Indian blood. It was significant that in the battle at Fort Utah, federal troops from Captain Stansbury's command fought shoulder-to-shoulder with the Mormon militia, foreshadowing the way in which the aid of United States soldiers would be welcomed in later years against recalcitrant Northwestern Shoshone. It was also clear that Young entertained the ethnocentric views of the time that native Americans were not the equal of whites and must be treated as inferior people.

The advent of the Forty-niners introduced a complex new dimension to Indian relations in the Great Basin. The gold-rushers were young and impatient to get to the diggings in California, and, as mere passers-by, had little patience with the Mormons, whose sinister hand they could discern in every Indian problem. Their great numbers made busy thoroughfares out of the western trails, cluttering and denuding the watercourses that were the chief resources of the natives. Inevitably they introduced a new and trying era in Indian relations.

Thousands of newcomers to California also made certain the political organization of that area into a territory. Under the Compromise of 1850, Brigham Young became governor and superintendent of Indian Affairs for Utah, but he wasn't sworn in until February 3, 1851. Although Brigham Young's policies as superintendent were influenced by his religious views of the natives as descendants of the tribes of Israel, he frequently fell back upon frontier beliefs about the supremacy of the white man. Nevertheless, he was more knowledgeable about the Indians in his jurisdiction and quicker to act than the Oregon superintendent who was simply too far removed from the Shoshone in the Boise and Fort Hall regions to be effective and who remained ignorant about these bands for many years.

◈ *F U R T H E R   R E A D I N G*

Lowell J. Bean, "Morongo Indian Reservation: A Century of Adaptive Strategies," in Sam Stanley, ed., *American Indian Economic Development* (1978)

Stephen Dow Beckham, *Requiem for a People: The Rogue Indians and the Frontiersmen* (1971)

Gae Whitney Canfield, *Sarah Winnemucca and the Northern Paiutes* (1983)

Lynwood Carranco and Estle Beard, *Genocide and Vendetta: The Round Valley Wars of Northern California* (1981)

Robert Chandler, "The Failure of Reform: White Attitudes and Indian Response in California During the Civil War Era," *Pacific Historian* 24 (1980), 284–294

C. F. Coan, "Adoption of the Reservation Policy in the Pacific Northwest, 1853–1865," *Oregon Historical Quarterly* 23 (1922), 1–38

Sherburne F. Cook, *The Conflict Between White Civilization and California Indians* (1976)

Vine Deloria, Jr., *Indians of the Pacific Northwest from the Coming of the White Man to the Present Day* (1977)

Clifford M. Drury, "Oregon Indians in the Red River School," *Pacific Historical Review* 7 (1938), 50–60

Ferol Egan, *Sand in a Whirlwind: The Paiute War of 1860* (1972)

Jack D. Forbes, *Native Americans of California and Nevada* (1969)

Van Garner, *The Broken Ring: The Destruction of California Indians* (1982)

Francis Haines, "The Nez Perce Delegation to St. Louis in 1831," *Pacific Historical Review* 6 (1937), 71–78

Robert F. Heizer and Alan F. Almquist, *The Other Californians: Prejudice and Discrimination under Spain, Mexico and the United States to 1920* (1971)

Ake Hultkrantz, *The Shoshones in the Rocky Mountain Area* (1974)

Albert L. Hurtado, "California Indians and the Workaday West: Labor, Assimilation, and Survival," *California History* 69 (Spring 1990), 2–11, 77–79

——, *Indian Survival on the California Frontier* (1988)

Alvin M. Josephy, *The Nez Perce Indians and the Opening of the West* (1965)

Harry Kelsey, "The California Indian Treaty Myth," *Southern California Quarterly* 15 (1973), 225–235

Theodora Kroeber, *Ishi in Two Worlds: A Biography of the Last Wild Indian in North America* (1961)

Clare V. McKanna, "The Treatment of Indian Murderers in San Diego, 1850–1900," *Journal of San Diego History* 36 (1990), 65–77

Lucellus V. McWhorter, *Hear Me My Chiefs! Nez Perce History and Legend* (1952)

Brigham Madsen, *The Bannock of Idaho* (1958)

——, *The Lemhi: Sacajawea's People* (1980)

——, *The Northern Shoshoni* (1980)

Warren Metcalf, "A Precarious Balance: The Northern Utes and the Black Hawk War," *Utah Historical Quarterly* 57 (1989), 24–35

Christopher Miller, *Prophetic Worlds: Indians and Whites on the Columbia Plateau* (1985)

Dale L. Morgan, "The Administration of Indian Affairs in Utah, 1851–1858," *Pacific Historical Review* 17 (1948), 383–409

Jack Norton, "Traversing the Bridge of Our Lives," *American Indian Quarterly* 13 (1989): 347–358

——, *When Our Worlds Cried: Genocide in Northern California* (1979)

George Harwood Phillips, *Chiefs and Challengers: Indian Resistance and Cooperation in Southern California* (1975)

——, *The Enduring Struggle: Indians in California History* (1981)

——, "Indians of Los Angeles, 1781–1875: Economic Integration, Social Disintegration," *Pacific Historical Review* 69 (1980), 427–451

James J. Rawls, "Gold Diggers: Indian Miners in the California Gold Rush," *California Historical Quarterly* 55 (1976), 28–45

——, *Indians of California: The Changing Image* (1984)

Allen P. Slickpoo, *Noon nee-me-poo (We the Nez Perce): Culture and History of the Nez Perces* (1973)

Beverly P. Smaby, "The Mormons and the Indians: Conflicting Ecological Systems in the Great Basin," *American Studies* 16 (1975), 35–48

War and Peace, 1851–1886

Beginning with the Treaty of Fort Laramie, signed in 1851 by the Lakotas, Cheyennes, Arapahos and other groups, and continuing at an accelerated pace over the following decade, federal policymakers sought to bring peace to the West and thereby hasten the United States' westward expansion. Conflict with the Santee Sioux in 1862 and with the Navajos in the early 1860s—the latter conflict culminating in the Navajos "Long Walk" to temporary incarceration in New Mexico in 1864—demonstrated that even the Civil War could not entirely deter the government from its efforts. Once the Civil War had ended, national attention could focus even more undividedly on the West. The completion of the first transcontinental railroad, the destruction of the buffalo, an enthusiastic application of the Homestead Act of 1862, and the interest in land speculation all helped to speed the whites' migration.

Not all Indians resisted militarily, nor were all removed from their homelands. Nevertheless, in the course of several decades, the worlds of most tribes changed dramatically—socially, economically, and politically. Wars and campaigns, as well as repeated negotiations over treaties and agreements, followed in rapid order. There were victories in battle: Chief Joseph, Crazy Horse, and other Indian leaders clearly achieved success at one time or another. However, by the early 1880s, armed resistance by native peoples largely had been crushed. Sitting Bull had returned from Canada, where he had fled to avoid confinement on the reservation, and Crazy Horse was dead.

As early as 1871, Congress declared that no more treaties would be signed; agreements still would be negotiated, but the change in nomenclature signified that times had changed. With Geronimo's final surrender in 1886 at Skeleton Canyon, Arizona, just north of the boundary between Arizona and the state of Sonora in Mexico, an era truly had come to an end. Could the government have made other choices or achieved other results? Why might some Native communities have fought and others chosen different tactics?

◈ DOCUMENTS

These documents primarily present Indian perspectives on a turbulent and often tragic era. However, the first selection is excerpted from the annual report of the Commissioner of Indian Affairs, Dennis N. Cooley, who notes the significance of the conclusion of the Civil War and the potential consequences for the Indian people who had supported the Confederate cause. In the second excerpt, Howard W. Gorman, former vice-chairman of the Navajo (Diné) tribal council and for many years a distinguished elder in the Ganado area of northern Arizona, offers his views on the causes of the Navajos' Long Walk from Fort Defiance in Arizona and Fort Wingate in New Mexico for over 200 miles to Fort Sumner, or Bosque Redondo, in east-central New Mexico. Gorman's account is an example of Indian oral history, so important in preserving tribal perspectives on significant events. How does Gorman interpret the reasons for conflict? The third document, the federal treaty signed with the Sioux at Fort Laramie, Wyoming, in April 1868, is one of the most famous treaties between a native community and the United States. Treaties of the time used standard language, and the excerpt reprinted here gives some flavor of that tone. The treaty reflects the priority given to agriculture, education, and railroad construction. It also reveals that the Sioux, so recently victorious in the war over the Bozeman Trail, anticipated that the document would guarantee them a significant hunting territory and control over their sacred Black Hills in perpetuity. Allen P. Slickpoo, a Nez Perce historian, provides his view of the famous war of 1877 in the fourth document. He notes that other historians have not always given proper attention or credit to his people. In the last selection, three Apaches—Ace Daklugie, Charlie Smith, and Jasper Kanseah—present oral historical testimony about their remarkable counterpart, Geronimo. Their words were recorded by Eve Ball, a longtime non-Indian resident of New Mexico who had gained the confidence and respect of her informants.

Commissioner of Indian Affairs Dennis N. Cooley on the Consequences of the Civil War, 1865

. . . The council assembled at Fort Smith, September 8, and delegates were present in the course of the sittings (though not all in attendance at first) representing the Creeks, Choctaws, Chickasaws, Cherokees, Seminoles, Osages, Senecas, Shawnees, Quapaws, Wyandotts, Wichitas, and Comanches. Immediately upon the opening of proceedings, the tribes were informed generally of the object for which the commission had come to them; that they for the most part, as tribes, had, by violating their treaties—by making treaties with the so-called Confederate States, forfeited all *rights* under them, and must be considered as at the mercy of the government; but that there was every disposition to treat them leniently, and above all a determination to recognize in a signal manner the loyalty of those who had fought upon the side of the government, and endured great sufferings on its behalf. On the next day the delegates were informed that the commissioners were empowered to enter into treaties with the several tribes, upon the basis of the following propositions:

1st. That each tribe must enter into a treaty for permanent peace and amity among themselves, each other as tribes, and with the United States.

2d. The tribes settled in the "Indian country" to bind themselves, at the call of the United States authorities, to assist in compelling the wild tribes of the plains to keep the peace.

3d. Slavery to be abolished, and measures to be taken to incorporate the slaves into the tribes, with their rights guaranteed.

4th. A general stipulation as to final abolition of slavery.

5th. A part of the Indian country to be set apart, to be purchased for the use of such Indians, from Kansas or elsewhere, as the government may desire to colonize therein.

6th. That the policy of the government to unite all the Indian tribes of this region into one consolidated government should be accepted.

7th. That no white persons, except government employees, or officers or employees of internal improvement companies authorized by government, will be permitted to reside in the country, unless incorporated with the several nations.

Printed copies of the address of the commissioners involving the above propositions were placed in the hands of the agents, and of members of the tribes, many of whom were educated men.

On the third day the delegates from the loyal Chickasaws, Choctaws, Senecas, Osages, and Cherokees, principally occupied the time with replies to the address and propositions of the commissioners, the object being partly to express a willingness to accept those propositions, with some modifications, if they had been clothed with sufficient power by their people, but chiefly in explanation of the manner in which their nations became involved with the late confederacy. The address of the Cherokees was especially noteworthy, inasmuch as they attempted to charge the causes of their secession upon the United States, as having violated its treaty obligations, in failing to give the tribe protection, so that it was *compelled* to enter into relations with the confederacy. The next day the loyal Seminoles expressed their willingness to accede to the policy of the government, and to make peace with those of their people who had aided the rebellion. The president of the commission then read a reply to the address of the loyal Cherokees above referred to, showing, from original and official documents, that, *as a tribe*, by the action of their constituted authorities, John Ross being then, as at the time of the council, their head, they had, at the very opening of the rebellion, entered into alliance with it, and raised troops for it, and urged the other tribes to go with them, and that they could not now, under the facts proven, deny their original participation in the rebellion. (The documents establishing the bad faith of John Ross had but recently come into possession of the department. They are very interesting, and taken in connexion with his course at Fort Smith in keeping aloof from the council, but exercising his powerful influence to prevent an amicable settlement with the hitherto disloyal part of the nation, will be found fully to justify the course taken by the commission in refusing to recognize him in any manner as chief of the Cherokees.)

The loyal Creeks on this day presented their address of explanation, setting forth the manner in which their nation, by the unauthorized action of its chief, entered into treaty relations with the confederacy, and the terrible sufferings which the loyal Creeks endured in battle and on the march to Kansas seeking protection from the United States, and asking "to be considered not guilty."

It being certain that no final treaties could be now concluded with the tribes represented, for the reason that, until the differences between the loyal and disloyal portions were healed, there could be no satisfactory representation of most of them, it was determined to prepare for signature by the commission, and by the delegates representing all factions and opinions, a preliminary treaty, pledging anew, on behalf of the Indians, allegiance to the United States, and repudiating all treaties with other parties; and on the part of the United States agreeing to re-establish peace and friendship with them. . . .

Friendly relations were established between the members of the various tribes hitherto at variance, except in the case of the Cherokees. The ancient feuds among this people are remembered still, and the Ross, Ridge, and Boudinot difficulties have never been healed.* This portion of the nation was ably represented in council by Boudinot and others, and having learned from the action of those representing the loyal party that if they came back it must be as beggars and outlaws, asked the protection and good offices of the commission. Efforts were then made on the part of the commission to effect a reconciliation, but all that could be brought about was a promise upon the part of those representing the loyal party to present the question to their council, which is now in session, and I entertain the hope that soon I shall be able to furnish you a report of their proceedings, in which they offer fair and honorable terms of adjustment. If, however, I should be disappointed in this reasonable expectation, I trust the government will take the matter in hand, and, by a just and equitable division of their property, make a final settlement of all their difficulties.

When the majority of this nation returned to their allegiance to the government, in 1863, action was taken by their council, under direction of John Ross, confiscating the property of those who still continued in the service of the confederacy, thus cutting off about five thousand five hundred of the nation, leaving them homeless and houseless. This destitute portion of the tribe are still refugees on the Red river, suffering from the want of every necessary of life, and existing only upon the charity of the humane people of northeastern Texas. The department has, however, sent a special agent to look into the wants of these refugees, and must rely upon Congress for the necessary means to relieve their necessities. . . .

Howard W. Gorman, a Diné Elder, Tells of the Long Walk of the Navajos (1864), recorded 1973

. . . The Long Walk to Fort Sumner—what was the cause of it? It began because of the behavior of a few *Diné*. A handful, here and there, riding horseback, killed white people and others that were traveling overland, and took their belongings. So the soldiers, commanded by Kit Carson, were ordered out. Carson was nick-named *Bi'éé' Łichíí'ii* (Red Clothes).

A man named *Ahsáabinii'í* (Double Face), a very stubborn man, known as a thief and a killer, killed white people, and he and his group took their property. Today, they could be referred to as gangsters. He and his men troubled the camps of the white people who were traveling overland westward seeking gold. They killed the Whites, taking their mules, horses and other belongings. Then, to the

---

*Major Ridge and Elias Boudinot had opposed Ross and had agreed to the treaty that forced most of the Cherokees on the Trail of Tears. Ridge and Boudinot were killed in Indian territory because of their signing of this treaty.

Text by a Diné elder from Ruth Roessel, editor, *Navajo Stories of the Long Walk Period,* Navajo Community College Press, 1973, pp. 23–32. Reprinted by permission of the Navajo Community College Press.

white people, they would say, "We are not harming anyone and don't expect a conflict."

Unexpectedly, *Bi'éé Łichíí'í* (Red Clothes' Soldiers) arrived, destroying water wells—contaminating them, breaking the rocks edging the waterholes or filling up the holes with dirt so that they became useless. They also burned corn-fields and the orchards of peaches. That is what they did to us unexpectedly and unreasonably, because most of us were not harming anybody. In the open fields we planted squash and corn. And we lived peacefully, not expecting a conflict. We naturally were a peaceful people. We were not warlike; but, still, we had those soldier visitors.

During that time women were very skilled in weaving, and the *Diné* always were dressed well. Many men were skilled in silversmithing, and there was a lot of silver for them. They even made bridles; they depended upon no one. They had everything they needed. Then the word was heard about Red Clothes and his sol-diers, over near *Nazlini,* at a place called *T'iisnidiitsooí* (Yellow Cotton Slope), up the ridge near the white rocks where my ancestors lived. They were living there when they heard of the soldiers. Around *Lók'aahnteel* (Ganado) they in-vaded, killing anything, even some of the *Diné's* sheep and horses, and destroy-ing the waterholes. Those who wondered and asked why and what was going on—and refused to take orders—were shot or were killed with other weapons. Then, upon the ridge near *T'iisnidiitsooí,* one evening, with a fire built outdoors, we were warned by the lights of other fires which showed across on the red ridge near a place called *Be'ek'idhatsoh* (Big Lake). The troops were on the move over there. *Diné* living down in the valley also were warned of the lights from a look-out on top of Red Mesa, also called Kit Carson Mesa. It was from this mesa that the soldiers were seen. . . .

Many *Diné* were killed, but one man, *Baa' Haaidiiłééh* (Preparing a Warrior) was a hunch-backed man, and he survived by jumping from the cliff on the can-yon wall onto some bushes below which were covered with deep snow. He ran from there, receiving no injury from the jump. That is how it was told. Most of the rest were killed. One received a wound across the forehead, and blood trickled down. He raised his hand and yelled, "What is happening, and why are you doing this? Wait! Wait!" When he waved and shouted, "*Naakaii Chílii* ordered his men to stop what they were doing. Also, someone supposedly tried to escape with a child, but left it behind. The little girl lay there in her cradle, with her face down. The headboard, arching over the child's head, must have protected it from injury. A soldier walked over to the child and picked her up; and the wounded man was treated with a bandage on the wound across his forehead. The place was a tragic sight. Many of those who had been attacked were my clan relatives.

The wounded man was taken as a captive, and the soldiers moved away on the trail. They already were camped at *Ch'ínílí* (Chinle). A few days later the captive was ordered into *Tséyi'* (Canyon de Chelly); and, to make sure he would return, he was told, "If you don't return, you will be killed just like the rest. Now go into *Tséyi'* and order all those that live in the canyon to move out. From here we'll go to *Tséhootsooi* (Fort Defiance). We'll be leaving soon."

Sixteen Navajos came out from the canyon, even though they didn't want to, but they knew that the *Nóóda'i* (Ute Indians) were on the loose, riding horseback, and that they were dangerously aggressive. When the sixteen were evacuated, the journey began, but a few remained in the canyon. Those that stayed feared the enemies too much to move. It was impossible to go across to *Dziłíjiin* (Black Mountain). Earlier, many had moved towards *Naatsis'aan* (Navajo Mountain) before the enemies started raiding; and many had settled there. It is a really desolate area. It's a torn-up area. To this day people get lost, even Boy Scouts.

Navajos had moved into the Navajo Mountain area for permanent settlement, driving their horses and sheep. This took place before the soldiers arrived. . . .

From Fort Defiance the Navajos started on their journey. That was in 1864. They headed for *Shash Bitoo'* (Fort Wingate) first, and from there they started on their Long Walk. Women and children traveled on foot. That's why we call it the Long Walk. It was inhuman because the Navajos, if they got tired and couldn't continue to walk farther, were just shot down. Some wagons went along, but they were carrying army supplies, like clothes and food. *Jaanééz* (mules) pulled the wagons. So the Navajos were not cared for. They had to keep walking all the time, day after day. They kept that up for about 18 or 19 days from Fort Wingate to Fort Sumner, or *Hwééldi*.

On the journey the Navajos went through all kinds of hardships, like tiredness and having injuries. And, when those things happened, the people would hear gun shots in the rear. But they couldn't do anything about it. They just felt sorry for the ones being shot. Sometimes they would plead with the soldiers to let them go back and do something, but they were refused. This is how the story was told by my ancestors. It was said that those ancestors were on the Long Walk with their daughter, who was pregnant and about to give birth. Somewhere beyond *K'aalogii Dził* (Butterfly Mountain) on this side of *Bilín* (Belen), as it is called, south of Albuquerque, the daughter got tired and weak and couldn't keep up with the others or go any farther because of her condition. So my ancestors asked the Army to hold up for a while and to let the woman give birth. But the soldiers wouldn't do it. They forced my people to move on, saying that they were getting behind the others. The soldiers told the parents that they had to leave their daughter behind. "Your daughter is not going to survive, anyway; sooner or later she is going to die," they said in their own language.

"Go ahead," the daughter said to her parents, "things might come out all right with me." But the poor thing was mistaken, my grandparents used to say. Not long after they had moved on, they heard a gunshot from where they had been a short time ago.

"Maybe we should go back and do something, or at least cover the body with dirt," one of them said.

By that time one of the soldiers came riding up from the direction of the sound. He must have shot her to death. That's the way the story goes.

These Navajos had done nothing wrong. For no reason they had been taken captive and driven to *Hwééldi* (Fort Sumner). While that was going on, they were told nothing—not even what it was all about and for what reasons. The Army just rounded them up and herded them to the prison camp. Large numbers of Navajos made the journey. Some of them tried to escape. Those who did, and were caught, were shot and killed. . . .

The Fort Laramie Treaty with the Sioux (Lakota), 1868

Articles of a treaty made and concluded by and between Lieutenant-General William T. Sherman, General William S. Harney, General Alfred H. Terry, General C. C. Augur, J. B. Henderson, Nathaniel G. Taylor, John B. Sanborn, and Samuel F. Tappan, duly appointed commissioners on the part of the United States, and the different bands of the Sioux Nation of Indians, by their chiefs and head-men, whose names are hereto subscribed, they being duly authorized to act in the premises.

Article 1.   From this day forward all war between the parties to this agreement shall forever cease. The Government of the United States desires peace, and its honor is hereby pledged to keep it. The Indians desire peace, and they now pledge their honor to maintain it.

If bad men among the whites, or among other people subject to the authority of the United States, shall commit any wrong upon the person or property of the Indians, the United States will, upon proof made to the agent and forwarded to the Commissioner of Indian Affairs at Washington City, proceed at once to cause the offender to be arrested and punished according to the laws of the United States, and also re-imburse the injured person for the loss sustained.

If bad men among the Indians shall commit a wrong or depredation upon the person or property of any one, white, black, or Indian, subject to the authority of the United States, and at peace therewith, the Indians herein named solemnly agree that they will, upon proof made to their agent and notice by him, deliver up the wrong-doer to the United States, to be tried and punished according to its laws; and in case they wilfully refuse to do so, the person injured shall be re-imbursed for his loss from the annuities or other moneys due or to become due to them under this or other treaties made with the United States. And the President, on advising with the Commissioner of Indian Affairs, shall prescribe such rules and regulations for ascertaining damages under the provisions of this article as in his judgment may be proper. But no one sustaining loss while violating the provisions of this treaty or the laws of the United States shall be re-imbursed therefor.

Article 2.   The United States agrees that the following district of country, to wit, viz: commencing on the east bank of the Missouri River where the forty-sixth parallel of north latitude crosses the same, thence along low-water mark down said east bank to a point opposite where the northern line of the State of Nebraska strikes the river, thence west across said river, and along the northern line of Nebraska to the one hundred and fourth degree of longitude west from Greenwich, thence north on said meridian to a point where the forty-sixth parallel of north latitude intercepts the same, thence due east along said parallel to the place of beginning; and in addition thereto, all existing reservations on the east bank of said river shall be, and the same is, set apart for the absolute and undisturbed use and occupation of the Indians herein named, and for such other friendly tribes or individual Indians as from time to time they may be willing, with the consent of the United States, to admit amongst them;

and the United States now solemnly agrees that no persons except those herein designated and authorized so to do, and except such officers, agents, and employees of the Government as may be authorized to enter upon Indian reservations in discharge of duties enjoined by law, shall ever be permitted to pass over, settle upon, or reside in the territory described in this article, or in such territory as may be added to this reservation for the use of said Indians, and henceforth they will and do hereby relinquish all claims or right in and to any portion of the United States or Territories, except such as is embraced within the limits aforesaid, and except as hereinafter provided.

Article 3.   If it should appear from actual survey or other satisfactory examination of said tract of land that it contains less than one hundred and sixty acres of tillable land for each person who, at the time, may be authorized to reside on it under the provisions of this treaty, and a very considerable number of such persons shall be disposed to commence cultivating the soil as farmers, the United States agrees to set apart, for the use of said Indians, as herein provided, such additional quantity of arable land, adjoining to said reservation, or as near to the same as it can be obtained, as may be required to provide the necessary amount.

Article 4.   The United States agrees, at its own proper expense, to construct at some place on the Missouri River, near the center of said reservation, where timber and water may be convenient, the following buildings, to wit: a warehouse, a store-room for the use of the agent in storing goods belonging to the Indians, to cost not less than twenty-five hundred dollars; an agency-building for the residence of the agent, to cost not exceeding three thousand dollars; a residence for the physician, to cost not more than three thousand dollars; and five other buildings, for a carpenter, farmer, blacksmith, miller, and engineer, each to cost not exceeding two thousand dollars; also a school-house or mission-building, so soon as a sufficient number of children can be induced by the agent to attend school, which shall not cost exceeding five thousand dollars.

The United States agrees further to cause to be erected on said reservation, near the other buildings herein authorized, a good steam circular-saw mill, with a grist-mill and shingle-machine attached to the same, to cost not exceeding eight thousand dollars.

Article 5.   The United States agrees that the agent for said Indians shall in the future make his home at the agency-building; that he shall reside among them, and keep an office open at all times for the purpose of prompt and diligent inquiry into such matters of complaint by and against the Indians as may be presented for investigation under the provisions of their treaty stipulations, as also for the faithful discharge of other duties enjoined on him by law. In all cases of depredation on person or property he shall cause the evidence to be taken in writing and forwarded, together with his findings, to the Commissioner of Indian Affairs, whose decision, subject to the revision of the Secretary of the Interior, shall be binding on the parties to this treaty.

Article 6.   If any individual belonging to said tribes of Indians, or legally incorporated with them, being the head of a family, shall desire to commence farming, he shall have the privilege to select, in the presence and with the assistance of the agent then in charge, a tract of land within said reservation, not exceeding three hundred and twenty acres in extent, which tract, when so selected, certified, and recorded in the "land-book," as herein directed, shall cease to be held in common, but the same may be occupied and held in the exclusive possession of the person selecting it, and of his family, so long as he or they may continue to cultivate it.

Any person over eighteen years of age, not being the head of a family, may in like manner select and cause to be certified to him or her, for purposes of cultivation, a quantity of land not exceeding eighty acres in extent, and thereupon be entitled to the exclusive possession of the same as above directed.

For each tract of land so selected a certificate, containing a description thereof and the name of the person selecting it, with a certificate endorsed thereon that the same has been recorded, shall be delivered to the party entitled to it, by the agent, after the same shall have been recorded by him in a book to be kept in his office, subject to inspection, which said book shall be known as the "Sioux Land-Book."

The President may, at any time, order a survey of the reservation, and, when so surveyed, Congress shall provide for protecting the rights of said settlers in their improvements, and may fix the character of the title held by each. The United States may pass such laws on the subject of alienation and descent of property between the Indians and their descendants as may be thought proper. And it is further stipulated that any male Indians, over eighteen years of age, of any band or tribe that is or shall hereafter become a party to this treaty, who now is or who shall hereafter become a resident or occupant of any reservation or Territory not included in the tract of country designated and described in this treaty for the permanent home of the Indians, which is not mineral land, nor reserved by the United States for special purposes other than Indian occupation, and who shall have made improvements thereon of the value of two hundred dollars or more, and continuously occupied the same as a homestead for the term of three years, shall be entitled to receive from the United States a patent for one hundred and sixty acres of land including his said improvements, the same to be in the form of the legal subdivisions of the surveys of the public lands. Upon application in writing, sustained by the proof of two disinterested witnesses, made to the register of the local land-office when the land sought to be entered is within a land district, and when the tract sought to be entered is not in any land district, then upon said application and proof being made to the Commissioner of the General Land-Office, the right of such Indian or Indians to enter such tract or tracts of land shall accrue and be perfect from the date of his first improvements thereon, and shall continue as long as he continues his residence and improvements, and no longer. And any Indian or Indians receiving a patent for land under the foregoing provisions, shall thereby and from thenceforth become and be a citizen of the United States, and be entitled to all the privileges and immunities of such citizens, and shall, at the same time, retain all his rights to benefits accruing to Indians under this treaty.

Article 7.   In order to insure the civilization of the Indians entering into this treaty, the necessity of education is admitted, especially of such of them as are or may be settled on said agricultural reservations, and they therefore pledge themselves to compel their children, male and female, between the ages of six and sixteen years, to attend school; and it is hereby made the duty of the agent for said Indians to see that this stipulation is strictly complied with; and the United States agrees that for every thirty children between said ages who can be induced or compelled to attend school, a house shall be provided and a teacher competent to teach the elementary branches of an English education shall be furnished, who will reside among said Indians, and faithfully discharge his or her duties as a teacher. The provisions of this article to continue for not less than twenty years.

Article 8.　When the head of a family or lodge shall have selected lands and received his certificate as above directed, and the agent shall be satisfied that he intends in good faith to commence cultivating the soil for a living, he shall be entitled to receive seeds and agricultural implements for the first year, not exceeding in value one hundred dollars, and for each succeeding year he shall continue to farm, for a period of three years more, he shall be entitled to receive seeds and implements as aforesaid, not exceeding in value twenty-five dollars.

　　And it is further stipulated that such persons as commence farming shall receive instruction from the farmer herein provided for, and whenever more than one hundred persons shall enter upon the cultivation of the soil, a second blacksmith shall be provided, with such iron, steel, and other material as may be needed.

Article 9.　At any time after ten years from the making of this treaty, the United States shall have the privilege of withdrawing the physician, farmer, blacksmith, carpenter, engineer, and miller herein provided for, but in case of such withdrawal, an additional sum thereafter of ten thousand dollars per annum shall be devoted to the education of said Indians, and the Commissioner of Indian Affairs shall, upon careful inquiry into their condition, make such rules and regulations for the expenditure of said sum as will best promote the educational and moral improvement of said tribes.

Article 10.　In lieu of all sums of money or other annuities provided to be paid to the Indians herein named, under any treaty or treaties heretofore made, the United States agrees to deliver at the agency-house on the reservation herein named, on or before the first day of August of each year, for thirty years, the following articles, to wit:

　　For each male person over fourteen years of age, a suit of good substantial woolen clothing, consisting of coat, pantaloons, flannel shirt, hat, and a pair of home-made socks.

　　For each female over twelve years of age, a flannel skirt, or the goods necessary to make it, a pair of woolen hose, twelve yards of calico, and twelve yards of cotton domestics.

　　For the boys and girls under the ages named, such flannel and cotton goods as may be needed to make each a suit as aforesaid, together with a pair of woolen hose for each.

　　And in order that the Commissioner of Indian Affairs may be able to estimate properly for the articles herein named, it shall be the duty of the agent each year to forward to him a full and exact census of the Indians, on which the estimate from year to year can be based.

And in addition to the clothing herein named, the sum of ten dollars for each person entitled to the beneficial effects of this treaty shall be annually appropriated for a period of thirty years, while such persons roam and hunt, and twenty dollars for each person who engages in farming, to be used by the Secretary of the Interior in the purchase of such articles as from time to time the condition and necessities of the Indians may indicate to be proper. And if within the thirty years, at any time, it shall appear that the amount of money needed for clothing under this article can be appropriated to better uses for the Indians named herein, Congress may, by law, change the appropriation to other purposes; but in no event shall the amount of this appropriation be withdrawn or discontinued for the period named. And the President shall annually detail an officer of the Army to be present and attest the delivery of all the goods herein named to the Indians, and he shall inspect and report on the quantity and quality of the goods and the manner of their delivery. And it is hereby expressly stipulated that each Indian over the age of four years, who shall have removed to and settled permanently upon said reservation and complied with the stipulations of this treaty, shall be entitled to receive from the United States, for the period of four years after he shall have settled upon said reservation, one pound of meat and one pound of flour per day, provided the Indians cannot furnish their own subsistence at an earlier date. And it is further stipulated that the United States will furnish and deliver to each lodge of Indians or family of persons legally incorporated with them, who shall remove to the reservation herein described and commence farming, one good American cow, and one good well-broken pair of American oxen within sixty days after such lodge or family shall have so settled upon said reservation.

Article 11.   In consideration of the advantages and benefits conferred by this treaty, and the many pledges of friendship by the United States, the tribes who are parties to this agreement hereby stipulate that they will relinquish all right to occupy permanently the territory outside their reservation as herein defined, but yet reserve the right to hunt on any lands north of North Platte, and on the Republican Fork of the Smoky Hill River, so long as the buffalo may range thereon in such numbers as to justify the chase. And they, the said Indians, further expressly agree:

1st. That they will withdraw all opposition to the construction of the railroads now being built on the plains.

2d. That they will permit the peaceful construction of any railroad not passing over their reservation as herein defined.

3d. That they will not attack any persons at home, or travelling, nor molest or disturb any wagon-trains, coaches, mules, or cattle belonging to the people of the United States, or to persons friendly therewith.

4th. They will never capture, or carry off from the settlements, white women or children.

5th. They will never kill or scalp white men, nor attempt to do them harm.

6th. They withdraw all pretence of opposition to the construction of the railroad now being built along the Platte River and westward to the Pacific Ocean, and they will not in future object to the construction of railroads, wagon-roads, mail-stations, or other works of utility or necessity, which may be ordered or permitted by the laws of the United States. But should such roads or other works be constructed on the lands of their reservation, the Government will pay the tribe whatever amount of damage may be assessed by three disinterested commissioners to be appointed by the President for that purpose, one of said commissioners to be a chief or head-man of the tribe.

7th. They agree to withdraw all opposition to the military posts or roads now established south of the North Platte River, or that may be established, not in violation of treaties heretofore made or hereafter to be made with any of the Indian tribes.

Article 12.   No treaty for the cession of any portion or part of the reservation herein described which may be held in common shall be of any validity or force as against the said Indians, unless executed and signed by at least three-fourths of all the adult male Indians, occupying or interested in the same; and no cession by the tribe shall be understood or construed in such manner as to deprive, without his consent, any individual member of the tribe of his rights to any tract of land selected by him, as provided in article 6 of this treaty.

Article 13.   The United States hereby agrees to furnish annually to the Indians the physician, teachers, carpenter, miller, engineer, farmer, and blacksmiths as herein contemplated, and that such appropriations shall be made from time to time, on the estimates of the Secretary of the Interior, as will be sufficient to employ such persons.

Article 14.   It is agreed that the sum of five hundred dollars annually, for three years from date, shall be expended in presents to the ten persons of said tribe who in the judgment of the agent may grow the most valuable crops for the respective year.

Article 15.   The Indians herein named agree that when the agency-house or other buildings shall be constructed on the reservation named, they will regard said reservation their permanent home, and they will make no permanent settlement elsewhere; but they shall have the right, subject to the conditions and modifications of this treaty, to hunt, as stipulated in Article 11 hereof.

Article 16.   The United States hereby agrees and stipulates that the country north of the North Platte River and east of the summits of the Big Horn Mountains shall be held and considered to be unceded Indian territory, and also stipulates and agrees that no white person or persons shall be permitted to settle upon or occupy any portion of the same; or without the consent of the Indians first had and obtained, to pass through the same; and it is further agreed by the United States that within ninety days after the conclusion of peace with all the bands of the Sioux Nation, the military posts now established in the territory in this article named shall be abandoned, and that the road leading to them and by them to the settlements in the Territory of Montana shall be closed.

Article 17.   It is hereby expressly understood and agreed by and between the respective parties to this treaty that the execution of this treaty and its ratification by the United States Senate shall have the effect, and shall be construed as abrogating and annulling all treaties and agreements heretofore entered into between the respective parties hereto, so far as such treaties and agreements obligate the United States to furnish and provide money, clothing, or other articles of property to such Indians and bands of Indians as become parties to this treaty, but no further.

In testimony of all which, we, the said commissioners, and we, the chiefs and headmen of the Brulé band of the Sioux nation, have hereunto set our hands and seals at Fort Laramie, Dakota Territory, this twenty-ninth day of April, in the year one thousand eight hundred and sixty-eight.

N. G. Taylor,	[SEAL.]
W. T. Sherman,	[SEAL.]
Lieutenant-General.	
Wm. S. Harney,	[SEAL.]
Brevet Major-General U.S. Army.	
John B. Sanborn,	[SEAL.]
S. F. Tappan,	[SEAL.]
C. C. Augur,	[SEAL.]
Brevet Major-General.	
Alfred H. Terry,	[SEAL.]
Brevet Major-General U.S. Army	

Attest:

A. S. H. White, Secretary

Executed on the part of the Brulé band of Sioux by the chiefs and headmen whose names are hereto annexed, they being thereunto duly authorized, at Fort Laramie, D. T., the twenty-ninth day of April, in the year A.D. 1868.

Ma-za-pon-kaska, his x mark, Iron Shell. [SEAL.]

Wah-pat-shah, his x mark, Red Leaf. [SEAL.]

Hah-sah-pah, his x mark, Black Horn. [SEAL.]

Zin-tah-gah-lat-skah, his x mark, Spotted Tail. [SEAL.]

Zin-tah-skah, his x mark, White Tail. [SEAL.]

Me-wah-tah-ne-ho-skah, his x mark, Tall Mandas. [SEAL.]

She-cha-chat-kah, his x mark, Bad Left Hand. [SEAL.]

No-mah-no-pah, his x mark, Two and Two. [SEAL.]

Tah-tonka-skah, his x mark, White Bull. [SEAL.]

Con-ra-washta, his x mark, Pretty Coon. [SEAL]

Ha-cah-cah-she-chah, his x mark, Bad Elk. [SEAL.]

Wa-ha-ka-zah-ish-tah, his x mark, Eye Lance. [SEAL.]

Ma-to-ha-ke-tah, his x mark, Bear that looks behind. [SEAL.]

Bella-tonka-tonka, his x mark, Big Partisan. [SEAL.]

Mah-to-ho-honka, his x mark, Swift Bear. [SEAL.]

To-wis-ne, his x mark, Cold Place. [SEAL.]

Ish-tah-skah, his x mark, White Eyes. [SEAL.]

Ma-ta-loo-zah, his x mark, Fast Bear [SEAL.]

As-hah-kah-nah-zhe, his x mark, Standing Elk. [SEAL.]

Can-te-te-ki-ya, his x mark, The Brave Heart. [SEAL.]

Shunka-shaton, his x mark, Day Hawk. [SEAL.]

Tatanka-wakon, his x mark, Sacred Bull. [SEAL.]

Mapia shaton, his x mark, Hawk Cloud. [SEAL.]

Ma-sha-a-ow, his x mark, Stands and Comes. [SEAL.]

Shon-ka-ton-ka, his x mark, Big Dog. [SEAL.]

Allen P. Slickpoo (Nez Perce) Reviews
the Nez Perce War (1877), recorded 1973

The Nez Perce War of 1877 resulted from many years of frustration, mistreatment, and broken promises. However, the act that made it all explode was the opening of the Wallowa Valley to white settlers, and the subsequent effort to make Chief Joseph and his band move onto the reservation from the Wallowa Country.

After 1875, as more and more settlers came into the Wallowa Valley, there was an increasing amount of trouble between them and the Indians. Each group felt that it had a right to be there and that the other did not. Frequent clashes, including the killing of an Indian in July 1876 led to consultations, councils, and visits by Monteith [Indian federal agent to the Nez Perce], military authorities, and a special commission. The series of councils which began on May 3, 1877, resulted in an agreement whereby the Indians were to gather their stock and move to the reservation. The chiefs selected lands for their new homes and were given thirty days to move.

Monteith and General Howard have been criticized for demanding that our ancestors move onto the reservation in thirty days. Our people felt that they needed at least six months to round up their stock, and that the thirty-day limit was an injustice for which no legitimate excuse has ever been offered. Indeed, now that the chiefs had agreed to move and had selected their lands, such haste does not seem to have been necessary. Consequently, Monteith must share the blame for whatever effect this had on the opening of hostilities. The manner in which the war started, however, suggests that the thirty-day ultimatum was not the principal cause of the war.

In mid-June, the people were ready to cross the boundaries of the reservation. At this time the White Bird Band was performing a tel-lik-leen ceremony, a ceremony in which the warriors, both young and old, ride in a circular fashion about the village. Traditionally, the men would show their battle trophies and relate their experiences in battle.

One elderly warrior named Ha-khauts Il-pilhp (Red Grizzly Bear), who was on the sidelines, told three young men as they passed him, "What are you doing this ceremony for, what bravery have you done, when your 'mother and father' have just been killed on the Wel-kil-khit (Horseshoe Bend of the Salmon River, near Slate Creek)?"

He was referring here to the killing of an elderly man and his wife by some whites. The old couple had come on the whites' homestead and when told to leave because the country was no longer theirs, had misunderstood and instead stood still and smiled to show their friendly intentions. This insulted one of the whites who drew his gun and shot both of them out in the garden. The news of this murder had traveled fast and had already reached the village at Lah-ma-ta (White Bird).

Allen P. Slickpoo, *Noon-Nee-Me-Poo: We, the Nez Perce* (Lapwai, Idaho: Nez Perce Tribe, 1973), pp. 183–194.

Upon hearing this the three young men, named Wah-ly-tits, Sop-sis-il-pilhp, and Wah-tsum-yosc became angry and determined to get revenge. Wah-ly-tits was particularly angry because his father had been killed in 1875 by a white man named Larry Ott who had managed to escape punishment.

The three set out immediately for the settlements located on the Salmon River. The first white to be killed was a man who had treated the Indians badly. Then two more men who had incited the hatred of the Indians were also killed. The three then went back to the village to get reinforcements. In spite of the fact that the chiefs were opposed to war and continued violence, sixteen other young men joined the first three. A few became drunk after capturing some whiskey, and the killings, which had begun as reprisals, became a free-for-all. The settlers became alarmed and the military moved, not to capture the murderers, but to attack Indian villages, and the war was on. . . .

The news of the deaths on the prairie spread instantly. The whites began to talk of war and the Nez Perces in the area began to move away so that they would not be caught in the crossfire or be blamed for the murders. The Nez Perces at Lapwai told General Howard, the commander of the U.S. Army in that part of Idaho, that the raids were ones of revenge and not a declaration of war. However, Howard chose to believe white informants who said that the Indians were beginning an uprising and he began to act as if he were at war with the Nez Perce nation.

Howard first decided to quickly take the Indians at Whitebird village where the whole disturbance had started and sent a force of ninety-nine soldiers under a Captain Perry to accomplish that task. Perry, however, commanding largely raw recruits, chose to fight after a thirty-six hour forced march and lost the battle. Against a force of sixty to sixty-five Indian braves, many of whom were armed only with bows and arrows, he lost thirty-four soldiers with four wounded. He also lost many horses and rifles which the Indians confiscated.

When Howard heard of this defeat, he sent for reinforcements and when these men arrived about a week later, set out in pursuit of the Indian forces with a view to forcing their defeat and subsequent removal to the reservation. Then a long pursuit began which lasted over a three-month period and was marked by battles and skirmishes.

The first of these battles after Whitebird was at Cottonwood where a whole detachment of soldiers was ambushed and killed. The battle of the Clearwater was next. Howard had been following the Nez Perces for two weeks unable to even come close enough to them to know how many there were. They finally came across the main body of the Nez Perces by chance on a ridge near Stites, Idaho, now called Battle Ridge, and began the battle. Howard began on the offensive, but quickly dug in when the Nez Perces began to resist. Lines were held for some thirty hours. After a time our forces decided to retreat and plan their next move. Many of the younger men wanted to travel to the Plains and join forces with other tribes. They believed that once they were out of Howard's area, he would no longer pursue them, and since they also believed that the quarrel was entirely with Howard and not with the United States government, they felt once they were in the Buffalo Country the fighting would be over. Many of the other men, including Joseph, were against this move and wanted to stay and fight in

Idaho. The first group prevailed, however, and it was decided to move to the Buffalo country. . . .

Once the decision to go to the Buffalo country was made, our people left Kamiah, where they had gone after the battle of the Clearwater, and started up the Lolo Trail, a traditional path to the Plains. Howard planned to proceed to Missoula via an easier road, but had to wait in Kamiah for replacements to calm the frightened settlers. The Nez Perces, therefore, got a good start before Howard could begin to move. When our people arrived at "Fort Misery" near Kamiah, they had to cross the river near the First Presbyterian Church. Here refuge was refused for fear of the church's becoming involved. Flags and white clothes were displayed for the soldiers to see.

Once the Nez Perces arrived at Travelers Rest in Lolo Pass they felt they had outdistanced General Howard and so could proceed with more ease toward the Plains. They then held several conferences with the aim of deciding where they were to go and by which route. The Nez Perces at a later date did get through to the Sioux, but they learned that the Sioux were not interested in helping them but only in keeping out of range of the U.S. Army. They were also very short of food and did not think they could support more people. However, after the Battle at Bear Paw, White Bird and his band did manage to find refuge in Canada.

It was finally decided at Lolo Summit that they would proceed in a southerly direction to the Ross Hole Country, on to the headwaters of the Jefferson, then south to Yellowstone National Park. From there they would go to the Shoshone River of Wyoming, which was the home of their good friends, the Crow.

They proceeded on to Big Hole and here were surprised by a Colonel Gibbon who attacked their camp at dawn and in a fierce charge completely overrode one section of the camp. Children, women, young and old, everyone in sight was killed by the charging soldiers. In the other part of the camp those who were not hurt by the main charge attacked and soon had Gibbon and his men on the defensive. While this was going on Joseph was able to move the rest of the camp; the warriors followed soon after and the Nez Perces were able to escape capture again.

General Howard had not given up and doggedly followed the Nez Perces on their flight. After many more weeks of moving northward marred by small skirmishes here and there, the Nez Perces, convinced by now that they had left General Howard behind, stopped to camp and lay in supplies in that region of Montana known as the Bear Paws. Here General Miles caught up with them and after a prolonged battle where the soldiers were at an advantage partly because they had a twelve-pound cannon, the Nez Perces surrendered. In a speech that has become famous, Joseph handed his rifle to General Miles and said:

> Tell General Howard I know what is in his heart. What he told me before, I have in my heart. I am tired of fighting. Our chiefs are killed. Looking Glass is dead. Tulhulhutsut is dead. The old men are all dead. It is the young men who say yes or no. He who led the young men is dead. It is cold and we have no blankets. The little children are freezing to death. My people, some of them, have run away to the hills and have no blankets, no food; no one knows where they are—perhaps freezing to death. I want to have time to look for my children and see how many of them I can find. Maybe I shall find them among the dead. Hear me, my chiefs. I am tired; my heart is sick and sad. From where the sun now stands I will fight no more, forever.

And so another chapter in the history of a proud and brave people came to an end.

It is interesting to note that many blamed Joseph and Looking Glass for letting the people take their time as if they were not at war. Ho-toe-toe, who had been in command, was removed because he was a half-breed and the full-bloods resented his leadership. Evidently neither Joseph nor Looking Glass realized that Gibbon was moving in from the south. Later, in speaking of the flight and battle, Joseph said, "I knew that I had made a mistake by not crossing into the country of the Red Coats [Royal Canadian Mounted Police], also in not keeping the country scouted in my rear." However, Joseph did not speak of the other things which helped to defeat him and which must have made his heart sad and heavy. One was that along the whole line of flight, the whites were helped again and again by other Indians, even the Crow who were friends of the Nez Perces. For instance, the first wave of General Miles' forces were Cheyenne scouts, and a few days prior to the battle at Bear Paw, the Nez Perces had a running battle with Colonel Sturgis and a group of River Crow. It may seem strange that another tribe would aid the whites to defeat their brothers. Perhaps they did this because of the material rewards promised by the U.S. Army. Then too, Nez Perce horses were highly prized throughout the northwest and many other Indians joined in with the hope of getting many horses.

During the Nez Perce War, many of the battles were referred to as skirmishes by the government. This terminology has also been used by many historians and writers who insist on calling important battles skirmishes. Many of these encounters were full-fledged battles, as the troops who fought in them well know. Battles such as the battle of Cottonwood, of the Clearwater, at Fort Misery, near the Kamiah Valley, at the Clearwater River crossing, and on the Lolo Trail, just to mention a few, were certainly more than skirmishes. In many of these battles, the soldiers under their trained commanders did not come off too well. Many times our warriors were able to hold off vastly superior forces, and often demonstrated a knowledge of classical military strategy. General Howard dared not mention these encounters for his own protection and often tried to write them off by calling them skirmishes. We know them for what they were however, full-scale battles.

Ace Daklugie, Charlie Smith, and Jasper Kanseah (Chiricahua Apaches) Remember Geronimo, n. d.

[Ace] Daklugie

Not until after the death of my father, Juh, did Geronimo become very prominent. After that he just took over. He was a Bedonkohe and never was elected to the chieftainship. Naiche was chief, but he was very young—too young for the leadership. It took a man to lead the Chiricahua. Geronimo was of middle age, a well-known fighter and superb leader, and he was also a Medicine Man. No White

From *Indeh: An Apache Odyssey*, by Eve Ball, pp. 101–105. New edition copyright © 1988, by the University of Oklahoma Press.

Eyes seem to understand the importance of that in controlling Apaches. Naiche was not a Medicine Man; so he needed Geronimo as Geronimo needed *him*. It was a good combination. Geronimo saw that Naiche was accorded the respect and recognition due a chief and that he always occupied the seat of honor; but Geronimo planned the strategy, with Naiche's help, and made the decisions. Of course, had Juh or Geronimo been chief, nobody could have usurped their prerogatives. But don't forget that not being a Medicine Man was a great handicap to Naiche.

Several years after our capture, and after I returned from school, I lived in Geronimo's village and was his confidant and interpreter. I accompanied him everywhere he went. When he took pneumonia at Fort Sill and was sent to the hospital, Eugene Chihuahua sat beside him during the day and I at night. And he died with his hand in mine. Even in his delirium, he talked of those seventeen men who had eluded five thousand men of the army of the United States for many years; and eluded not only them, but also twenty-five hundred Mexican soldiers—seventy-five hundred men, well armed, well trained, and well equipped against seventeen whom they regarded as naked savages. The odds were only five hundred to one against Geronimo, but still they could not whip him nor could they capture him.

But I am Geronimo's nephew and there are people who might think that I am biased. Go see Charlie Smith. As a child he and his mother were captured by Geronimo's band. Charlie was with Geronimo and Naiche about a year, I think, before going to Florida.

Charlie Smith

. . . I'll never forget that winter. Geronimo would line the boys up on the bank, have us build a fire and undress by it, and then make us plunge into the stream, breaking the ice as we went. The first time he did this, I thought that the ordeal would be over when he let us get out of the water. But no—time after time we warmed ourselves by the fire and returned to the icy water. There were times when I just hated him. Geronimo would stand there on the bank, with a stick in his hand. What for, I don't know; I never saw him strike anybody. But we knew he might and that was enough. Nobody defied Geronimo.

Was I present during the fighting? Geronimo had the women and children along, and of course they saw what happened. If pursued, he, as did all Apaches, tried to protect them by sending them ahead; but ordinarily, when fighting occurred, it was because he laid an ambush, and every one of the band was there. Some of the women were very good shots—good fighters, too. Lozen, sister of Victorio, was called The Woman Warrior; and though she may not have had as much strength as one of the men she was as good a shot as any of them.

When actually on the warpath the Apaches were under very strict rules. Even words for common things were different. Women would go with their husbands, but they could not live together. No unmarried woman was permitted to go with them. Lozen? No, she was not married; she never married. But to us she was as a Holy Woman and she was regarded and treated as one. White Painted Woman herself was not more respected. And she was brave! Geronimo sent her on missions to the military officers to arrange for meetings with him, or to carry messages.

When Geronimo crossed the border into New Mexico or Arizona, it was usually to get ammunition. I do not think that he wanted to kill, but there were cases when he had no choice. If he were seen by a civilian, it meant that he would be reported to the military and they'd be after us. So there was nothing to do but kill the civilian and his entire family. It was terrible to see little children killed. I do not like to talk of it. I do not like to think of it. But the soldiers killed our women and children, too. Don't forget that. There were times that I hated Geronimo for that, too; but when I got older, I knew that he had no choice.

Stealing horses was fun. I was not quite old enough to get in on that, and how I envied those who were! It was usually the boys, too, who shot the fire-arrows to set houses ablaze. I never saw that done but twice, though. I did see many, many people killed. I wish I could forget it. Even babies were killed; and I love babies.

But Geronimo was fighting not only to avenge his murdered mother, wife, and children, but for his people and his tribe. Later there were Apaches who were bitter against Geronimo, saying that it was his fault that they were sent to Florida and were prisoners of war for twenty-seven years. Well, if they'd had the fighting spirit of Geronimo, they need not have been sent. The big difference was that he had the courage to keep on and they were quitters. Some of them have "gone white" and blame Geronimo for everything. I don't respect them. They were cowards. I won't name them. I am ashamed that they are Apaches.

And don't forget that Geronimo knew that it was hopeless. But that did not stop him. I admire him for that. He was a great leader of men, and it ill becomes the cowardly to find fault with the man who was trying to keep them free. And don't forget that he was fighting against enormous odds, or that nobody ever captured him.

Jasper Kanseah (nephew of Geronimo)

My father died before I was born, and my mother died when they drove us like cattle from Cochise's reservation to San Carlos. I had nobody but my grandmother and she had to walk. I was little, and when I couldn't keep up she carried me. She told me that Geronimo was my uncle, but I didn't remember him till he came to San Carlos. When he came my grandmother had already gone to the Happy Place, and I had nobody. But Indian women were good to me, and even when they were hungry they gave me some of the food their own children needed. We never went hungry till we got to San Carlos; and there we almost died because there was no food.

I think that I was eleven when my uncle, Geronimo, came and took me with him. And he gave me to Yahnosha to be his orderly and learn to be a warrior. I stayed with Yahnosha and cooked his food, and got his horse and fed and watered it; and I never spoke unless somebody asked me a question. And I ate what was left. No matter what happened, I didn't complain. And even when I talked I had to say it differently. (On the warpath we don't talk as we do most of the time, but differently.) I had to think what Yahnosha wanted next and then get it for him before he told me. But I was proud to be taught by a great warrior and I tried to do everything right.

I knew Geronimo and I knew that he was the victim of liars. He was lied about by many of his own people for whom he was fighting. He was betrayed by them. He was betrayed by Miles. I am not sure but that he was betrayed by Crook, though some think not. But I know that he was lied to by Miles. That man did not do what he promised. Geronimo was a really great fighting man, and Miles was a coward. Everything he needed for his troops was provided for him and them, but Geronimo had to obtain food for his men, and for their women and children. When they were hungry, Geronimo got food. When they were cold he provided blankets and clothing. When they were afoot, he stole horses. When they had no bullets, he got ammunition. He was a good man. I think that you have desperados among you White Eyes today that are much worse men and are more cruel than Geronimo.

◈ *E S S A Y S*

Raymond J. DeMallie, a professor of anthropology at Indiana University at Bloomington, and the director of that university's Institute for Indian Studies, is a leading ethnohistorian of Plains Indian life. In the first essay, he demonstrates that one potential source for Indian perspectives and values is the deliberations over treaties. Even with the forced nature of the discussions and the inevitable problems over interpretation, native representatives often negotiated eloquently and fiercely for their people. Robert M. Utley, a retired historian for the National Park Service and the author of the second selection, is the most eminent scholar of the U.S. Army's actions in Indian country during the latter half of the nineteenth century. This excerpt from his widely praised overview of the Indian frontier provides several examples of the dramatic conflicts of the time. Again, it is important to consider what choices were available to different Indian individuals and groups; how leadership is defined; and what resulted from a generation of warfare.

Touching the Pen: Plains Indian Treaty Councils in Ethnohistorical Perspective

RAYMOND J. DeMALLIE

When Europeans met American Indians in the New World, the clash of human populations resulted in epidemics of disease; social, economic, and political pressures; religious conflict; and sometimes war. All such intercultural conflict takes place in two very different contexts, that of each of the cultures involved. Each culture constitutes a separate and distinctive idea system symbolizing the world, everything in it, and the relationship of all the parts. Culture as a symbol system provides the framework in which human behavior is motivated, perceived, and understood. Abstractly, the clash of two peoples may be viewed as the clash of two idea systems.

But culture contact is not abstract; it is in reality acted out through individual human beings. The historical record documents their behavior and motives and

Reprinted from *Ethnicity on the Great Plains,* edited by Fredrick C. Luebke, pp. 38–51, by permission of the University of Nebraska Press. Copyright © 1980 by the University of Nebraska Press.

draws out of the accumulation of many individuals' actions a general understanding of larger events. It is rarely possible to separate human behavior from the motivating ideas of the cultures in which the behavior occurs. The clash of ideas cannot be observed as easily or in the same manner as conflict between individuals. However, an understanding of the fundamental conflicting ideas is essential to illuminate historians' accounts of the past by placing individual action within the ideological context out of which it arose.

The large body of transcripts of formal council proceedings between representatives of the United States government and representatives of American Indian tribes provides a unique opportunity to observe the clash of idea systems. Reduced to rhetoric, physical weapons laid aside, the opponents faced each other as representatives of their own societies and cultures and attempted to win tactical battles by the manipulation of concepts. Both white Americans and Indians alike attempted to use all of their intellectual skills, as well as the oratorical and persuasive devices of their cultures, to sway the council in their own interest. The verbatim records of the proceedings are therefore primary sources for analyzing cultural concepts self-consciously utilized to gain diplomatic advantage. They are primary documents for the ethnohistorian, whose research combines historical methodology with the comparative and theoretical insights of anthropology.

One objection to the use of this material for historical or anthropological study is that it was inadequately or falsely interpreted from the original Indian languages. However, this is a futile objection. The interpreters were almost always named in the documents; most were mixed-bloods or non-Indian men married into an Indian tribe. They were the only interpreters the Indians had and their translations are as accurate as any ever obtained at that time. Significantly, after reading through a good number of the transcripts it is possible to pick out Indian idioms that are difficult to translate and that were therefore expressed in various ways in English, as well as standard words and phrases that were consistently translated in the same way but whose English glosses obviously did not accurately express the original idea in the Indian language. In many of these cases it is possible to postulate with a fair degree of certainty what the actual words were in the Indian original. Such difficulties in translation do not make the task of reconstructing ideological systems impossible; in fact, they make it easier, for it is in these areas where translation was difficult that differences in ideological systems are most clearly pointed up.

Solemn councils between representatives of both sides were the only acceptable means recognized by both Indians and whites for establishing formal relations between two peoples. For the Indians the council was the traditional way of making peace or negotiating with another people. For the white Americans it had been the custom, since the days of Jamestown, to counsel with the Indians. Under United States law, written treaties, signed by representatives of both sides, were the only legal means for dealing with Indian tribes, and councils evolved as the forum where treaties were presented to Indians and they were persuaded to sign them.

But if the council as a diplomatic forum was commonly understood by both whites and Indians, the concept of the treaty was not. For plains Indians, the council was an end in itself. What was important was the coming together in peace, smoking the pipe in common to pledge the truthfulness of all statements made, and the exchange of opinions. Plains Indian political systems did not use voting as the mechanism for settling issues; consensus politics was the rule. Issues had to be discussed from all points of view until a clear consensus was reached. Until that occurred, no decision was made, and once it was reached, no vote was necessary. Thus, from the Indians' point of view, the council *was* the agreement.

For white Americans, the council with its associated feasts and gift giving was only a preliminary to the real agreement, which was embodied in written form. The success of the council depended not on what was said, but on whether or not the necessary leaders, or later, the requisite percentage of the male population, could be induced to sign the document.

"Touching the pen," the action of the Indian in touching the end of the pen while the scribe marked an *X* after his name, was frequently objected to by Indian leaders. They did not understand the process, were suspicious of it, and felt it unnecessary. Whites, on the other hand, considered it to be essential. For individual Indian leaders, touching the pen apparently signified that they were validating all they had said at a council; in many cases the record of the treaty proceedings makes it clear that the Indian leaders did not realize their signatures committed them to *only* those statements written in the treaty. Sometimes, it is equally clear, treaty commissioners played on this to trick Indians into signing documents containing provisions to which they had not agreed.

The predominant historical view of treaty making is that Indians were taken advantage of by whites, who usually presented them with documents prepared in advance which they were persuaded, bribed, or threatened into signing. There is a great deal of truth to this view, but it ignores an important aspect. American Indian leaders were not mere pawns of the U.S. government. They did use political strategies to combat whites on their own ground and sometimes they were able to gain important concessions. They were at other times unsuccessful, and frequently their techniques were too subtle even to be understood by the commissioners. But analysis of some of these means provides important insights into plains Indian diplomacy and opens new dimensions for understanding the fundamental conflicts between Indians and whites on the western frontier.

This paper draws upon examples of treaty making among the Sioux, Kiowas, Comanches, Cheyennes, and Arapahoes from 1851 to 1892. First the 1851 Fort Laramie treaty council is examined as representative of plains treaty councils and as illustrating the symbolic perspective in ethnohistory. Then various examples of Indian diplomacy are presented to illustrate the range of strategies that can be abstracted from the verbatim proceedings and to demonstrate the value of this approach.

The 1851 Treaty Council

The 1851 treaty council held near Fort Laramie may be taken as a model of plains treaty councils. It was on a larger scale than most since an estimated ten thousand Indians were present representing ten bands of Sioux as well as Cheyennes, Assiniboins, Shoshones, Arikaras, Gros Ventres (Hidatsas), Mandans, Arapahoes, and Crows. The encampment lasted nearly three weeks, from September 1 to

September 21. During this period the commissioners met the Indians in council only about eight days. The rest of the time was occupied with the Indians counseling among themselves while the commissioners drew up a map of tribal territories, in Sunday recesses, and in waiting for the wagon train that was bringing the presents to be distributed after the treaty was signed.

Three general features of the council suggest a minimal model for plains treaty councils. The first is the ritual aspects, as practiced by both Indians and whites; the second is the recitation of both sides' demands and requests; and the third is the distribution of presents.

Ritual Aspects. The ritual aspects of this council are fairly well recorded and are extremely significant for reconstructing the event in its fullest context. The Sioux and Cheyennes made the first gesture by erecting a large council lodge composed of several tipis to form a kind of amphitheater. This was the usual form for the council lodge when various bands came together and so was the culturally prescribed stage for serious deliberations. The U.S. commissioners took the next step by erecting a large tripod on which to hoist the American flag.

Preparations for the council were completed on a Saturday, but the commissioners announced that since the next day was "the white man's Medicine Day," no business could be transacted. The council began on Monday. Only headmen were allowed to enter the council lodge, and the order of their seating, by tribe, was arbitrarily decided by the commissioners. The council was called to order each day by the firing of the cannon and raising of the flag. The council began and ended with the smoking of the pipe by all the Indians and the commissioners. Colonel D. D. Mitchell, the chief commissioner, made an opening speech to set the moral tone of the meetings:

> I am sent here to transact business with you. Before commencing that I propose to smoke all around with you. The ceremony of smoking I regard as an important and solemn one, and I believe you all so regard it. When white men meet to transact important business, and they desire to test their truth and sincerity, they lay their hands on the Bible, the Book of the Great Spirit—their Great Medicine—and take an oath. When the red man intends to tell the truth, and faithfully fulfill his promises, he takes an oath by smoking to the Great Spirit. The Great Spirit sees it all and knows it. Now I do not wish any Indian to smoke with me that has any deceit or lies in his heart—or has two hearts—or whose ears are not bored to hear what his Great Father at Washington has to propose, and perform whatever is agreed upon. All such will let the pipe pass. I don't want them to touch it.

At least three important points about this speech should be noted. First, the commissioner attempted to speak to the Indians in terms they would understand. The reporter who covered the council remarked on this aspect as follows: "His [Mitchell's] expressions were short, in simple language, such as they could readily understand, in many cases adopting various forms, and employing their own hyperbolical mode of thought. Between sentences he paused to see that the interpreters understood him correctly, and to allow time for them to communicate it to their respective tribes." Second, the commissioner made it clear that he considered the Indian form of oath by smoking the pipe to be a legitimate one, comparable to the white man's swearing on the Bible. Third, the use of the term *Great*

Father at Washington must be considered to have been at least ambivalent. To some Indians it may have seemed a white man's claim that the Great Spirit lived in Washington, a boast that the whites enjoyed a closer relationship to God than did the Indians.

The smoking of the pipe by the commissioners was a self-conscious bow to Indian custom. In return the commissioners demanded at the end of the council that the Indians defer to the white man's custom of touching the pen to the treaty paper. Since they had already sworn themselves to truth, signing the treaty was redundant for the Indians, but they clearly understood it as an important ritual for the white men.

The other impressive bit of ceremony on the part of the whites was the celebration on the second Sunday of a Roman Catholic mass. In a large tipi in the half-breed camp, Father P. J. De Smet said mass and preached to the assemblage in French. The pomp and ceremony of the event was as impressive to the St Louis newspaper reporter who accompanied the treaty commission as it was to the Indians. Of De Smet the newspaper man wrote: "The Indians regard him as a Great Medicine man, and always regard him with marked respect and kindness."

Throughout the council the Indians reciprocated rituals by holding dog feasts, warrior society dances, and displays of horsemanship.

Demands and Requests.   The second aspect of the council, the exchange of demands and requests, was done in the usual formal manner. On the first day Colonel Mitchell delivered a speech outlining the commission's intentions in visiting the Indians and enumerating the points of the proposed treaty. On ensuing days the Indian chiefs were allowed to give their responses. These were not spontaneous speeches, but were developed out of council meetings in the various tribal camps, and were essentially tribal or band position statements. Toward the end of the meeting the commissioners read the treaty, article by article, and the Indians were asked to sign. The only contribution that the Indians had been allowed to make to the actual content of the document was in terms of tribal boundaries. At this treaty council there was no real negotiation, in part because the Indians were not being asked to give up any land.

The Arapaho and Sioux responses to the 1851 treaty council are representative of two distinct strategies used by plains tribes to attempt to win favor and gain concessions from the United States. The Arapaho attitude may be characterized as conciliatory and the Sioux attitude as defiant. It must be clearly understood that these are descriptive of diplomatic strategies, not of individual emotions.

The Arapaho chiefs decided to go along with the whites in their various demands. They expressed particular gratitude that there would be an end to all warfare. Addressing Mitchell, Cut Nose, an Arapaho chief, stated: "You, Grandfather, are doing well for your children in coming so far and taking so much trouble about them. I think you will do us all much good; I will go home satisfied. I will sleep sound, and not have to watch my horses in the night, or be afraid for my squaws and children."

The oldest of the Arapaho chiefs, Authon-ish-ah, in a speech addressed to the

Arapahoes themselves, seemed to take the tack that the chiefs alone could no longer take full care of the people, and that they would have to rely on the whites. He said: "Fathers and children, we give you all up to our white brethren, and now we shall have peace, the pleasantest thing in the world. The whites are friends to us, and they will be good to us if we don't lie to them. . . . The whites want to be good to us; let us not be fools, and refuse what they ask."

The Arapahoes agreed to appoint Little Owl as head chief of the tribe, and through him to transact all business with the whites. Cut Nose addressed Mitchell as follows:"We have chosen our chief as you requested us to do, Father. Whatever he does, we will support him in it, and we expect, Father, that the whites will support him." The Arapahoes clearly pointed out the reciprocal nature of the agreement as they understood it. Cut Nose requested that the whites pick out a country for themselves to live in, and not trespass into Arapaho hunting grounds. He also suggested that the whites "should give us game for what they drive off."

The Arapaho position, then, established rigid reciprocity between whites and Indians, the Arapahoes symbolically acknowledging the white men's power and binding them through the treaty to support the Indians. From the Arapaho viewpoint, the treaty worked to their advantage.

The Sioux attitude was very different. From the beginning they refused to cooperate in the matter of choosing a head chief. Blue Earth, the old Brulé chief, told Mitchell: "We have decided differently from you, Father, about this chief for the Nation. We want a chief for each band, and if you will make one or two chiefs for each band, it will be much better for you and the whites. Then we will make soldiers of our young men, and we will make them good men to the whites and other Indians. But Father, we can't make one chief."

However, Mitchell was unyielding. He demanded that the Sioux bands all come together and unite as a single nation. Regarding bands he said, "Your Great Father will not recognize any such divisions." In the end Mitchell had to select representatives from each of the ten bands to be chiefs, and then select one of them to be head chief. His candidate, Frightening Bear, was then duly elected to the office by all of the band chiefs. The new head chief was not eager for the position. He said, "Father, I am a young man and have no experience. I do not desire to be chief of the Dahcotahs. . . . If you, Father, and our Great Father, require that I shall be chief, I will take this office." It is very clear that the whites had imposed a new political office on Sioux society, one unlike any they had ever had before. Since it potentially entailed great power, Frightening Bear publicly spoke of his worry that he would be assassinated out of jealousy. Certainly the Sioux did not accept the idea of having a head chief.

The Sioux also objected strenuously to drawing boundaries around tribal territories. Blue Earth said, "We claim half of all the country; but we don't care for that, for we can hunt anywhere." Black Hawk, an Oglala, told the council:

> You have split the country and I don't like it. What we live upon we hunt for, and we hunt from the Platte to the Arkansas, and from here up to the Red But[t]e and the Sweet Water. . . . These lands once belonged to the Kiowas and Crows, but we [the Oglalas, Cheyennes, and Arapahoes] whipped these nations out of them, and in this we do what the white men do when they want the lands of the Indians."

Mitchell explained that the boundaries were not intended to limit the tribes in any way, so long as they remained at peace. Nonetheless, the Sioux never accepted the boundaries.

The Sioux presented the council with a number of demands of their own. Big Yancton asked for horses, cattle, and fowl to make reparation for damages done to the Indians. A chief of the Blackfoot Sioux asked for a hundred wagonloads of goods each year, and asked that they be sent more buffalo as well. The latter request may have represented a challenge to the white men's claim to have been sent to the Sioux by the "Great Father."

Painted Bear, a Yankton Sioux, may well have summarized the dominant Sioux attitude of the time in the following words: "Father, this is the third time I have met the whites. We don't understand their manners, nor their words. We know it is all very good, and for our own good, but we don't understand it all. We suppose the half breeds understand it, and we leave them to speak for us."

Many of the Sioux did not want to have any dealings with the United States. Their chiefs continually expressed their inability to understand the whites as well as their reliance on the mixed-bloods for advice. Unlike the Arapahoes, they refused to put trust in the whites and continued to pressure them for specific demands and concessions.

Distribution of Presents.   The third aspect of the council was the distribution of presents. Token presents were given in advance to the headmen of each tribe to redistribute to their followers. This served to validate their status in the tribe by giving tangible proof of the esteem in which they were held by the whites. At the end of the council, after the treaty was signed, the wagon train came up and the bulk of the presents were distributed. This was the most significant part of the council for most of the Indians present. The event is memorialized in Sioux winter counts as "The winter of the big distribution." The whites at the council clearly understood the importance of the gift-giving aspects of the event. The reporter wrote: "It is a standing rule with all Indians, that whenever they meet, especially upon occasions of this character, they must have presents of some kind or other. . . . Without these no man living—not even the President of the United States—would have any influence with them, nor could he get them into council, or keep them together a day."

Plains Indian Diplomacy

This general model of treaty making—ritual, counseling, and gift giving—holds from the earliest plains treaty councils with the Lewis and Clark expedition down through the various commissions that negotiated with the tribes beginning in the 1880s for the breakup of reservations by agreeing to the allotment of lands in severalty and the sale of "surplus" land for white settlement. The elaborateness of gift giving and ritual decreased, on the whole, through time, and the extent of negotiation somewhat increased, but the treaty council remained a relatively stable institution throughout the period.

Perhaps the single most frustrating aspect of the entire history of treaty making was the inability of the two sides to communicate with one another meaningfully. Both whites and Indians used the councils to deliver speeches composed in advance. Specific objections or questions by Indians were rarely answered when they were raised, but were answered a day or more later in the course of lengthy speeches. Many questions went unanswered, and many objections were simply ignored. Treaty commissioners frequently excused this practice by saying that the Indians' speeches were being recorded to be taken back to Washington. The commissioners told the Sioux in 1865, "We will take back all your words, and the Great Father will read all you have said." But in reality neither the Great Father nor anyone else ever read them. Most remain unpublished or generally unavailable.

Examination of these documents solely from the perspective of reconstructing chronological history is quite disappointing. Usable historical data often seem to be altogether lacking in the speeches, replaced instead by rhetorical devices. Rarely do the speeches, white or Indian, rely on logic. These are not intellectual debates about matters that can easily be discussed. They are the records of more dramatic conflict between mutually exclusive ways of life.

Study of Indian diplomatic techniques provides a wealth of data on tribal cultures. Some trends may be seen over time that are suggestive of deeper changes in Indian cultures. One such trend involves the expressed attitude toward land. At the 1851 treaty council there seems to have been, from the white man's point of view, a rather practical attitude put forward by the Indians. They were capable and eager to discuss boundary issues. In the quote from Black Hawk given earlier, the idea of landownership by right of conquest is clearly articulated. Later, when the whites returned to ask the Sioux for more land for roads, they refused. At an 1865 council Lame Deer, a Miniconjou chief, stripped off his clothes and said to the commissioners: "I stand here naked and this is my condition. Why will you trouble me for my land, my brothers? You told me you would not ask me for anything." Other leaders tried other strategies. Some claimed the land because they were born on it, because the bones of their forefathers lay in it, or because it had been given to them by God. One That Killed the White Buffalo Cow, a Lower Brulé chief, told the commissioners in 1865: "Who does all this country here belong to? It is ours. It belonged to our fathers and our fathers' fathers." Yet at the same time, Iron Nation, another Lower Brulé chief, said of his people, "The older ones came from Minnesota. There we were born."

The council proceedings suggest that Indians thought about land according to its utility; it was not measured or conceived of in the white man's way. When the 1865 commission asked Lone Horn, the Miniconjou chief, if he would like to live on the Missouri River, he answered simply, "When the buffalo comes close to the river, we come close to it. When the buffaloes go off, we go off after them." The same commission asked the Indians where Frog, the Lower Brulé chief, lived. Iron Nation answered, "Everywhere; where he is." The attitude expressed seems to suggest that land was not seen as the constant—people and animals were the constant features. Hence the justification for Indian ownership of land tended to be expressed in terms of people and buffalo.

Later, when the Indians' land base was already severely eroded and tribes became more specifically tied to land in the form of reservations, purely religious reasons tended to be adduced to argue for retaining that land which was left. A typical example is the statement of Iseo, a Kiowa leader, in 1892: "Mother earth is something that we Indians love. . . . We do not know what to do about selling our mother to the government." Another example is this statement by Spotted Horse, a Cheyenne, in 1890: "We look upon this land as a home and as our mother and we don't expect to sell it." Old Crow, another Cheyenne, told the same commission: "The Great Spirit gave the Indians all this country and never tell them that they should sell it. . . . If you have had any such word from the Great Spirit that gave them this land I would like to hear it."

The point here is to suggest that detailed study of the treaty council proceedings may provide more data than might at first glance be expected on such complex and abstract issues as changing attitudes toward land.

Tactics

A survey of Indian diplomatic tactics that repeatedly occur in treaty council records reveals an interesting variety as well as significant differences among tribes. A few examples will be discussed here to illustrate the variety and nature of these tactics, as well as the value of such data to an understanding of Indian cultures.

Sometimes religious and moral justifications were presented by Indian orators to treaty commissioners in order to explain the Indians' perspective on the white man. An excellent example of this type of diplomacy is provided by a council in November 1866, held in Kansas at the Big Bend of the Arkansas River. Commissioners were investigating the Indian situation on the southern plains and preparing for a great council that would be held the following year at Medicine Lodge Creek. The commissioners counseled with Lone Wolf, head chief of the Kiowas, and a delegation of headmen in order to discover information about past hostilities and to impress on the Indians the necessity of peace.

> Colonel J. H. Leavenworth told the Kiowas: "The Great Chief at Washington has heard some bad news about you and he has sent out two of his chiefs to see if they are true. . . . The names of those that have acted badly we have put on a piece of paper, and we shall tell the Great Chief what we know about them and he will decide whether they live or die. If any of your people go to Texas or Old or New Mexico and commit depradations the Great Chief will not forget it, but he will send an army of his men and exterminate you.

These threats were not well received by the Kiowas. They had long heard whites boast of the power of the Great Chief or the Great Father in Washington, but they had never experienced it themselves. They were skeptical and they were angered to be ordered not to raid the whites to the south since it was economically important to them and also provided them with the regular means by which young men gained status to raise themselves in the social hierarchy.

Rather than take a stance blatantly antagonistic to that of the commissioners, Lone Wolf allowed White Bird, an old medicine man, to make the first speech in reply to the whites. The record of the proceedings reads as follows:

The Indians then laid two circular pieces of paper on the floor; one blue and one white. Otank or White-bird, an old Indian then went through a form of prayer and spoke as follows to Lone Wolf in Kiowa, who repeated it to the Interpreter in Comanche.

   Lone Wolf—That piece of paper (pointing to the white) represents the earth. There is a big water all around the earth. The circular blue paper is the sky. The sun goes around the earth. The sun is our father. All the red men in this country, all the Buffalo are all his (old man's). Our Great Father the sun told us that the white man would kill all of them, there is no place for us to hide because the water is all around the earth. When my time comes to die I intend to die and not wait to be killed by the white men. I want you to write to the Great Chief and tell him that I understand my Great Father the sun, that my Great Father the sun sent me a message, that I went around the prairie poor and crying and the Great Father the sun sent me a message that I can read. A long time ago when I was little I began to study medicine and when we make a treaty with the white man I see it and know whether it is good or not. I am the man that makes it rain, I talk to the Great Father. If I have any difficulty with anyone and wish them to perish with thirst I stop the rain and if I wish them well I cause it to rain so that the corn can grow. My Great Father the sun told me that fire and water were alike, that we cannot live without either of them. This is all the old man's talk, he wishes to go to Washington.

   He (Lone Wolf) then said that he wished to talk for himself. I do not know what the Great Chief at Washington will think of the old man's talk.

   Capt. Bogy—We have similar men among us who converse with the Great Spirit.

White Bird's speech is significant in several ways. It lays out an entire cosmology and belief system which is in direct contradiction to that of the whites. It puts the Great Chief in Washington into perspective under the power of the true Great Father, the sun. White Bird claims an especially close relationship to the sun, manifested in his power to control rain. Implied in his speech is his own belief that he is closer to the Great Spirit than is the white man's Great Chief. His desire to go to Washington was very likely motivated by a feeling that if he could but meet this Great Chief face to face he could best him with his power, matching him trick for trick.

   Diplomatically, this speech was a good choice because it led into the refusal by the Kiowas, at least for the moment, to commit themselves to follow the will of the president, and provided moral and ethical grounds on which to do so. Unfortunately, it was probably ineffective. Bogy's comment relegates the speech to mere mysticism. Doubtless the commissioners simply missed the point. But the speech provides a good model of the Kiowa world as they presented it to oppose the view of the world propounded by the whites.

   The use of kinship terms was another diplomatic tactic manipulated by Indians and whites alike. The 1865 treaty commissioners told the Miniconjou Sioux: "Your Great Father, the President, has selected us to come out to this country to visit his red children, the Dahcotahs. . . . The President, your Great Father, has not sent us to make peace because he is weak. . . . On the contrary, he pities his red children."

   Lone Horn, the Miniconjou head chief, seems to have felt the need to maneuver around the father-child relationship established by the commissioners, clearly limiting the father role to the president and excluding the commissioners from it. He therefore addressed the commissioners as follows: "My friends, I will begin my speech with claiming relationship to all of you. I will call you my brothers." This is significant since the relationship between brothers in Lakota society was the closest of all family relationships; one could not refuse anything to a brother without giving mortal offense. The Sioux in particular, reflecting the great emphasis placed in their culture on kinship, were adept at manipulating kinship metaphors in order to attempt to jockey whites into positions where they would be forced to make concessions. Later in his speech Lone Horn chided the commissioners: "It is good that you, my friends, my brothers, make peace with me, but it seems to me you are holding back, and do not like to make peace freely." Unfortunately, the whites probably never understood the kinship strategy. Even in the example discussed here the commissioners failed to pick up on the significance of Lone Horn's statement and did not reciprocate by calling him brother. If they had, they would have placed themselves in the reciprocal brother relationship and would have improved their own bargaining position as well.

Government commissioners frequently used the expression "our red children" to put Indians into a subordinate position. Just as frequently, Indian orators exploited the father-children metaphor to ask for favors. In plains Indian cultures this relationship was a very important one in which the father gave freely to his children. At a Sioux treaty council in 1856, Bear Rib addressed General W. S. Harney as father: "My Father! What is there better to wish for than a father." Much later, in 1892, Lone Wolf, the Kiowa chief, used the metaphor ironically to make his point that Indians should be protected from land allotment. He said to the commissioners: "You will believe me when I say we were like babies not knowing how to get up and take care of ourselves."

Kinship terms used at treaty councils are significant symbols. They functioned as diplomatic devices that must be explored in order to understand the dynamics of the event. They are not merely paternalistic, racist, or subservient designations to be ignored in favor of what was really being said. Especially from the Indians' point of view, the use of kin terms was not a mere token, but embodied the real message of what was being communicated.

Another diplomatic tactic frequently used was to set up an equivalence between Indians and whites to provide a moral basis from which to ask that Indians be treated the same as whites. Eagle Drinking, a Comanche, told a commission in 1865: "I bear in my mind and heart the same feelings as the Great Father in Washington. I speak to my people as the Great Father at Washington does to his." In 1867 the Comanche chief Ten Bears told the commissioners: "My Great Father at Washington has the same heart that I have although I live on the prairies." In the same year the Comanche chief Rising Sun told the commissioners: "The Great Father is warm hearted, so am I."

It would be easy to proliferate examples, but the tactic was the same. By establishing the common humanity of whites and Indians, a moral base was established from which to negotiate for concessions. Many other tactical devices were also frequently manipulated for diplomatic advantage, among them the use of writing, factionalism, dependence on the government, shaming the government for broken promises, and emphasizing tribal differences.

Treaty council proceedings are valuable documents for reconstructing the symbolic expressions of Indian cultures as Indian orators attempted to use their skill to best the white man at diplomacy. These documents are major resources for the study of plains Indians, reflecting cultural changes through time. The publication of treaty council proceedings and thorough studies of them will vastly enrich our understanding of native American cultures on the plains and allow some reconstruction of the Indians' points of view as they were threatened with cultural extinction in the face of white American expansion.

Wars of the Peace Policy, 1869–1886

ROBERT M. UTLEY

... The Peace Policy aimed at placing all Indians on reservations, where they could be kept away from the settlements and travel routes and where ultimately they could be civilized. The Indians often had other ideas—if not at first, then after they had sampled the reality of life on the reservation. Virtually every major war of the two decades after Appomattox was fought to force Indians onto newly created reservations or to make them go back to reservations from which they had fled. From such perspective, it is not surprising that warfare characterized the Peace Policy.

As the years passed, moreover, the Peace Policy ceased to command the wide support it had at first. The army, in particular, grew more openly critical. Except for an occasional Lieutenant [Charles] Drew or Colonel [Benjamin] Grierson [known for their humane approaches to Indians], officers scoffed at the notion of conquest by kindness, and they had little use for the idealistic yet often corrupt people and purposes of the Indian Bureau. As General Sheridan remarked simplistically in 1869, "If a white man commits murder or robs, we hang him or send him to the penitentiary; if an Indian does the same, we have been in the habit of giving him more blankets." And as Lieutenant Schuyler observed at the Camp Verde [Arizona] Reservation, the Indians "can be governed for the present only with a hand of iron, which is a manner of governing totally unknown to the agents of the Indian Bureau, most of whom are afraid of the Indians and are willing to do anything to conciliate them." Western sentiment, always militant, encouraged the army in its view of the Peace Policy. "Let sniveling quakers give place to bluff soldiers," ran a typical editorial comment.

Who is friendly and who is not? military officers not unreasonably asked the civilian authorities. Those on the reservation were friendly and the exclusive responsibility of the Indian Bureau, came the answer; those off the reservation were hostile and the responsibility of the army. Superficially, it seemed a logical solution to a chronic dilemma. It drew a line that no one, including the Indians, could mistake. But as the record of the Fort Sill [Oklahoma] "city of refuge" demonstrated, a reservation could harbor a great many Indians of unfriendly disposition.

From Robert M. Utley, "Wars of the Peace Policy, 1869–1886," from *The Indian Frontier of the American West, 1846–1890* (Albuquerque: The University of New Mexico Press, 1982), pp. 164–201. Reprinted by permission of the University of New Mexico Press.

Unfortunately, except for the rare Satanta [a Kiowa leader] who bragged of his exploits, their individual identities remained unknown or unprovable. Aggravating the army's frustration, garrisons on or near reservations had to watch helplessly while civilian corruption and mismanagement—or so it seemed to them—prodded Indians toward an armed hostility that would have to be suppressed at the risk of army lives. As General Sherman complained to a congressional committee in 1874: "The Indian Bureau keeps feeding and clothing the Indians, till they get fat and saucy, and then we are only notified that the Indians are troublesome, and are going to war, after it is too late to provide a remedy."

Except by government decree, moreover, Indians off the reservation were not necessarily belligerent. They might be out hunting, or headed for a visit with friends in another tribe, or simply wandering about seeing the country. Even a whole band off the reservation did not automatically mean hostility. Indeed, few such could be clearly labeled friendly or hostile; ambiguity more accurately described their temper. Was Black Kettle's village on the Washita [River, in southern Colorado] friendly or hostile? No chief and no band more diligently pursued peace. Yet it was the trail of a party of Black Kettle's young men, their hands stained with the blood of Kansas settlers, that led Custer's cavalry to the luckless chief's winter lodges. The army never learned to discriminate between the guilty and the innocent simply because rarely was a group of Indians unmistakably one or the other.

The army did not pursue its Indian-fighting mission very creatively. Occasionally a General Crook recognized his foes as superb guerrilla fighters who called for techniques quite different than had Robert E. Lee's gray legions. Crook fought Indians like Indians and usually, in fact, with Indians. But the army as an institution never evolved a doctrine of Indian warfare, never taught its aspiring officers at West Point the difference between conventional and unconventional war, and never issued official guidance for troops in the field.

Lacking a formal doctrine of unconventional war, the army waged conventional war. Heavy columns of infantry and cavalry, locked to slow-moving supply trains, crawled about the vast western distances in search of Indians who could scatter and vanish almost instantly. The conventional tactics of the Scott, Casey, and Upton manuals sometimes worked, by routing an adversary that had foolishly decided to stand and fight on the white soldiers' terms, by smashing a village whose inhabitants had grown careless, or by wearing down a quarry through persistent campaigning that made surrender preferable to constant fatigue and insecurity. But most such offensives merely broke down the grain-fed cavalry horses and ended with the troops devoting as much effort to keeping themselves supplied as to chasing Indians.

But when they worked, these offensives worked with a vengeance. They were a forerunner of "total war" against entire populations, as pioneered by Sherman and Sheridan against the Confederacy. Under the guidance and inspiration of these two leaders—the one now General in Chief of the army, the other heading the strategic Division of the Missouri, embracing all the Great Plains—the army set forth to find the enemy in their winter camps, to kill or drive them from their lodges, to destroy their ponies, food, and shelter, and to hound them mercilessly across a frigid landscape until they gave up. If women and children got hurt or killed, it was lamentable, but justified because it resolved the issue quickly and decisively, and thus more humanely. Although prosecuted along conventional lines and often an exercise in logistical futility, this approach yielded an occasional victory, such as the Washita, that saved it from serious challenge.

No better than the army did the Indians adapt to new conditions. The westward surge of the white people after the Civil War confronted them with a crisis of apocalyptic implications, yet they met it, like the army, in the same old ways. Despite the common danger, tribal particularism and intertribal animosities remained as strong as ever. Sometimes tribes came together in alliance against an especially visible threat from the whites, but rarely did such an alliance hang together for very long. Even unity within a tribe proved elusive. Factions differed on how to deal with the white encroachment; some resisted, some accommodated, and some wavered and even oscillated between the two extremes. The highly individual character of tribal society inhibited the rise of leaders who could bring together diverse opinions, and, to make matters worse, the proliferation of "government chiefs" demoralized the traditional political organization. As one astute observer remarked, army officers, Indian superintendents and commissioners, and even agents had created so many chiefs that "Indian chiefs, like brevets in the army, are become so common they are not properly respected."*

Nor did fighting methods change. Indian culture still developed a superb fighting man. Warriors still practiced guerrilla tactics masterfully and made uncanny use of terrain, vegetation, and other natural conditions, all to the anguish of their military antagonists. But Indian culture also continued to emphasize the individual and withhold from any man the power of command, except through personal influence. Thus team discipline tended to collapse when opportunities for personal distinction or differing opinions on strategy or tactics arose. Man for man, the warrior far surpassed his blueclad adversary in virtually every test of military proficiency; but unit for unit—however great the numbers—the Indians could not come close to matching the discipline and organization of the army. When Indians made the mistake of standing and fighting on the army's terms, they usually lost.

In the end, however, the relative fighting qualities of the opponents made little difference. Despite all the wars of the Peace Policy, the Indians did not succumb to military conquest. The army contributed to the final collapse, of course, with "war houses" scattered all through the Indian country and with campaigns that hastened an outcome ordained by more significant forces. More than the army, railroads, settlements, and all the numbers, technology, and other trappings of an aggressive and highly organized society brought defeat to the Indians. Every white advance came at the expense of resources, especially wild game, essential to the Indian way of life. As the open land and its natural bounty shrank, the reservation offered the only alternative to extinction. For the Indians, General Sherman's jest held deadly portent: "I think it would be wise," he said of the

---

*Brevets were soldiers who were temporarily granted higher rank without higher pay.

Sioux insistence on hunting on the Republican River, "to invite all the sportsmen of England and America there this fall for a Grand Buffalo hunt, and make one grand sweep of them all."

Yet the Indians' armed resistance to the westward movement, and the army's armed response, form dramatic and significant chapters in the history of both peoples and of the frontiers across which they faced each other. In the Trans-Mississippi West, the final and most intense phase coincided with the final phase of the westward migration and settlement of the whites and was a direct consequence of the Peace Policy's imperative to confine all Indians to reservations.

Kintpuash had tried the reservation and did not like it. An able, ambitious young man, he and other Modoc leaders had signed a treaty in 1864 ceding their homeland among the lake-dotted, lava-scored plateaus of southern Oregon and northern California and had agreed to live on a reservation with Klamaths and Snakes. Homesick, bullied by the more numerous Klamaths, some sixty to seventy families followed Kintpuash back to their old homes on Lost River, just south of the Oregon-California boundary. As more and more whites took up homesteads on the ceded lands, tensions rose. Officials of the Indian Bureau pressed Kintpuash—with other whites, they knew him as Captain Jack—to go back to the reservation. Persuasion failing, they asked the army to use force. That move provoked the Modoc War of 1872–73.

At dawn on November 29, 1872, cavalry attacked the village of Kintpuash. After an exchange of fire, the Indians fled, later crossing Tule Lake in boats. Another party of Modocs, under a leader the whites called Hooker Jim, rode around the east side of the lake, killing settlers along the way. On the lake's southern shore they united in a wild expanse of black lava that nature had piled into a gigantic fortress. They knew its every fissure, cavern, and passageway. Patches of grass subsisted their cattle. Sagebrush and greasewood yielded fuel. Water came from Tule Lake. As the big army that quickly assembled discovered, it could not be penetrated by assault, reduced by artillery bombardment, or taken by siege. It swiftly drew national attention as "Captain Jack's Stronghold."

Kintpuash conducted the defense with great skill. For four months, with only about sixty fighting men, he held off an army whose numbers ultimately approached a thousand. Again the government decided to try diplomacy. A peace commission arrived and erected a lone tent on the plain outside the lava beds. Negotiations commenced. So did Kintpuash's troubles. Factionalism accomplished what an army could not. Hooker Jim and others challenged Kintpuash's course and taunted him for refusing to kill the peace commissioners in a bold stroke aimed at winning a reservation on Lost River. Ridiculed and humiliated, he finally agreed. On Good Friday, April 11, 1873, the Modoc leaders suddenly interrupted the peace talks, drew hidden weapons, and fell on the white negotiators. One escaped, but three were left on the ground shot, stabbed, and stripped. (Miraculously, one later recovered.)

The deed sealed the fate of the Modocs, for the head of the commission was none other than the commander of the military department, Edward R. S. Canby, who thus gained dubious distinction as the only regular army general slain by Indians in the entire history of the Indian Wars. (Others called general, such as

Custer, held the rank by brevet or volunteer, not regular, commissions.) Foolishly the Modocs had called down upon themselves the wrath of an outraged nation. The army responded with more troops and better leadership at the same time that quarrels among the Modoc leadership intensified. Finally the Indians scattered from the lava beds and were run down, group by small group, by pursuing columns of soldiers. On June 1 a detachment found Kintpuash and his family hiding in a cave. His "legs had given out," he explained.

Against people who had treacherously murdered a popular war hero, the precepts of the Peace Policy could not be expected to govern. Kintpuash and three others involved in Canby's death died on the gallows; their heads were cut off and shipped to the Army Medical Museum in Washington. A furious General Sherman demanded that Kintpuash's followers, who had compiled such an extraordinary record of skill and courage in holding the lava beds, be scattered among other tribes "so that the name of Modoc should cease." In October 1873, 155 in number, they were resettled fifteen hundred miles to the east, in Indian Territory. The name did not cease, but their demand to live in their homeland ceased to be heard.

The Modoc War—more accurately, the slaying of General Canby—badly crippled the Peace Policy. Newspapers everywhere saw it as dramatic evidence that Indians could not be trusted or reasoned with. Whether favoring extermination or civilization, editors judged Canby's death a grievous blow to the Peace Policy. As always, however, events on the Great Plains more profoundly influenced public opinion and shaped policy than those elsewhere in the West. Throughout the 1870s, warfare with the Plains Indians rose to a thunderous finale on the Little Bighorn in 1876 that was almost universally regarded as marking the demise of the Peace Policy. Like the Modoc War, the Plains wars centered chiefly on the issue of whether or not tribes were to live on reservations as demanded by the Peace Policy.

On the southern Plains, the big nomadic tribes had agreed to reservations in the Medicine Lodge treaties. They actually lived there—Kiowas and Comanches at Fort Sill, Cheyennes and Arapahos at Darlington—because General Sheridan's winter operations of 1868–69, especially Custer's persistent and wide-ranging marches, had made fugitive life tiring and insecure. But reservation life proved confining; clothing and ration issues scant, of poor quality, and badly selected for Indian wants; and the encroachments of white cattlemen, whiskey peddlers, horse thieves, and other opportunists unnerving, if not demoralizing. Particularly ominous to the Indians, white hunters slaughtered the buffalo for their hides alone, leaving carcasses by the hundreds of thousands to rot on the prairies. Kiowas and Comanches regularly raided in Texas and Mexico, as they always had, while Cheyennes and Arapahos raided less often in Kansas. Discontent and mutual aggression finally boiled over in the Red River War of 1874–75.

For a time, while Satanta and Big Tree languished in the Texas penitentiary and the government held 124 women and children seized in an attack on a fugitive Comanche village, reservation-based raiders had restrained themselves. But the release of these captives, in exchange for promises of good behavior, had removed the restraint. The spring and summer of 1874 found Indians raiding in Texas and Kansas with new ferocity. In particular, Comanches and Cheyennes attacked a camp of white hide-hunters at Adobe Walls in the Texas Panhandle, where Kit Carson had fought the Kiowas in 1864, and Kiowas under Lone Wolf ambushed a detachment of Texas Rangers near the site of the Salt Creek Massacre of 1871. These aggressions provoked the government to lift the ban against military operations on Indian reservations. Suddenly army officers at the Fort Sill and Darlington agencies were compiling lists of "friendly" Indians. Everyone else, sure to be classed as "hostiles," headed west, beyond the reservation boundaries. Some eighteen hundred Cheyennes, two thousand Comanches, and one thousand Kiowas moved in large encampments among the breaks surrounding the headwaters of the Washita River and the various forks of the Red, in the Texas Panhandle—hence the designation "Red River War."

Suddenly this country, hitherto so remote and secure, swarmed with soldiers. From north, east, south, and west, five columns converged. One routed the Indians at the base of the caprock near the mouth of Palo Duro Canyon. Another fell on a Comanche village nestled deep in the canyon itself. August sun parched the land and dried the water holes. September brought days of rain, bank-full streams, prairies of mud, and an ordeal the Indians remembered as "the wrinkled-hand chase." Winter loosed blizzards and numbing cold. Through it all, the soldiers kept after the Indians. There were few clashes and little bloodshed, but gradually the exhaustion of the chase, the discomforts of weather and hunger, and, above all, the constant gnawing fear of soldiers storming into their camps at dawn wore them down. As early as October, some had tired and drifted back to the reservation. By the spring of 1875, all had returned.

At the agencies the Indians discovered white officials behaving with a sternness uncharacteristic of the Peace Policy. Throughout the winter, as parties straggled in from the west, army officers confined leaders who were somewhat capriciously judged guilty of particular "crimes" or simply of functioning as "ringleaders." Satanta found no disposition toward leniency; back he went to the Texas penitentiary, where three years later, in despair, he threw himself from an upper window to his death. As spring came to Fort Sill, soldiers herded seventy-four Indians, shackled and chained, aboard eight wagons. Among them were such noted chiefs as Gray Bear, Minimic, and Medicine Water of the Cheyennes; Lone Wolf, Woman's Heart, and White Horse of the Kiowas; and Black Horse of the Comanches. With women wailing their grief, the caravan moved out and headed for the railroad. After days of travel the Indians, so recently at large on the Staked Plains, found themselves enclosed by the thick walls and bastions of an ancient Spanish fortress on the Florida coast.

The army had gained a clear victory, not only over the Indians but over the more extreme proponents of the Peace Policy. From his Chicago headquarters General Sheridan had directed the strategy of convergence. Generals John Pope and Christopher C. Augur had overseen its execution. At least two field officers, Colonels Nelson A. Miles and Ranald S. Mackenzie, had won great distinction in carrying it out. Both had gained battlefield victories, Miles in the caprock fight, and Mackenzie in the celebrated charge into Palo Duro Canyon. But in the end it was not combat success but convergence, unremittingly prosecuted, that had won the war. Confinement of the "ringleaders" far from their homes and families helped ensure that another war would not occur. Never again did Kiowas, Comanches, Cheyennes, or Arapahos revolt against their reservation overlords. Never again did Texas and Kansas settlers suffer aggression from these tribes. Nor did Generals Sherman and Sheridan forget the lessons of the Red River War as they turned their attention to the northern Plains.

Here, Sioux, Northern Cheyenne, and Northern Arapaho had yet to be finally brought within the reservation system. Oglalas and Brulés drew rations at the Red Cloud and Spotted Tail agencies in northwestern Nebraska, where these two chiefs maneuvered tortuously between the opposing forces of white officialdom and their own people. Other Sioux formed tenuous connections with agencies along the Missouri River, the eastern border of the Great Sioux Reservation—Hunkpapas and Blackfeet at Grand River, Miniconjous and Sans Arc at Cheyenne River, and still others at Crow Creek and Lower Brulé. Cheyennes and Arapahos mingled with Sioux at Red Cloud. In all, these agencies counted perhaps twenty-five thousand adherents.

But the strength of the adherence wavered with the seasons and the competing influence of rival chiefs, for off to the west roamed a hard core of kinsmen who had no intention of abandoning the free life of the chase for the dubious attractions of the reservation. They looked for leadership to a chief of surpassing influence. Of compelling countenance and commanding demeanor, quick of thought and emphatic of judgment, Sitting Bull held power not only as war and political chief but also as religious functionary. "He had a big brain and a good one," recalled an old warrior, "a strong heart and a generous one." At the agency Indians he hurled a taunt: "You are fools to make yourselves slaves to a piece of fat bacon, some hard-tack, and a little sugar and coffee." And in fact, many did not. Nothing prevented them from sampling the old hunting life in the summer and the hardtack and coffee in winter. Back and forth they shuttled between the agencies and the camps of Sitting Bull and other "nontreaty" chiefs.

These "northern Indians" stirred up constant trouble. While on the reservation, they kept the agencies in turmoil, for they were ungovernable, a danger to white officials, and a bad influence on the agency Indians. While off the reservation, they did not always keep to the unceded hunting grounds guaranteed by the Treaty of 1868, but sometimes raided along the Platte and among the Montana settlements at the head of the Missouri and Yellowstone rivers.

That the whites called them hostiles and accused them of breaking the treaty while also enjoying its bounty did not bother these hunting bands. They could point to some treaty violations by the other side as well. For one thing, in 1873 surveyors laid out a route for the Northern Pacific Railroad along the northern margins of the unceded territory. For another, and most infuriating, in 1874 "Long Hair" Custer led his soldiers into the Black Hills, part of the Great Sioux Reservation itself, and there found gold. Miners swarmed into the Indian country, and the government, making only a token effort to keep them out, hesitatingly broached the subject of buying the part of the reservation that contained the Black Hills. Then, late in 1875, runners arrived in the winter camps of the hunting bands with a stern message from the Great Father: Come to the agencies at once or be considered hostiles against whom the army would make war.

They ignored the summons, and as spring turned to summer in 1876 they discovered blue columns converging on their hunting grounds. In March, one attacked an Oglala camp on Powder River but bungled the follow-up and re-treated under assaults of bitter cold and deep snow. As the snow melted, the fugi-tive camps swelled. Worsening conditions at the agencies, the Black Hills issue, and the attempt to take away the freedom to roam the unceded territory set off an unusually large spring migration of agency Indians to the camps of the hunting bands. June found them coming together in a village that steadily expanded as it moved slowly westward across the streams flowing northward into the Yellow-stone. These Indians were not looking for a fight, but, as never before, they were proud, confident, and at the height of their power. Chiefs of ability fortified the leadership of Sitting Bull—Black Moon, Gall, Hump, Lame Deer, Dirty Mocca-sins, Lame White Man, and the incomparable Crazy Horse. Since his triumph as head of the party that decoyed Captain Fetterman out of Fort Phil Kearny ten years earlier, Crazy Horse had emerged as a splendid war leader and uncompro-mising foe of reservations.

By mid-June the Indians camped on a creek that ran into a river they knew as the Greasy Grass. Earlier, on the Rosebud, they had staged their annual Sun Dance. Sitting Bull had experienced a vision, in which he saw many dead soldiers "falling right into our camp." The people had thrilled to the image and the prom-ise. Now scouts brought word of soldiers marching down the Rosebud. Crazy Horse led a large force to do battle. For six hours they fought, and after the Indi-ans called off the fight the soldiers retreated.

But this was not the triumph foretold by Sitting Bull. Soldiers had not fallen into their camp. Down to the Greasy Grass the village moved, and here the largest number yet of agency Indians joined the alliance. Six separate tribal circles—Hunkpapa, Oglala, Miniconjou, Sans Arc, Blackfoot, Northern Cheyenne—ex-tended for three miles along the banks of the Greasy Grass. The village probably counted twelve hundred lodges and mustered almost two thousand fighting men.

True to Sitting Bull's prophecy, many soldiers were in fact about to fall into this village. As in the Red River War, General Sheridan had plotted a strategy of convergence. Advancing from the south, General Crook had struck the camp on Powder River on March 17 but had been driven back by winter. In May he sallied forth again, only to be stopped and turned back at the Battle of the Rosebud on June 17. Meantime, General Alfred H. Terry approached from the east, and Col-onel John Gibbon from the west. They joined on the Yellowstone at the mouth of the Rosebud. From here Terry launched a striking force of some six hundred cav-alry, under the same Long Hair Custer who had invaded the Black Hills two years earlier. Custer followed the Indian trail up the Rosebud, across the Wolf Moun-tains, and down to the Greasy Grass, which his map labeled the Little Bighorn. The village there, because of the recent arrivals of agency Indians, contained about three times as many warriors as he had expected. On the scorching Sunday of June 25, 1876, his soldiers fell into it.

George Armstrong Custer presided over one of the most complete disasters in American military annals. A century later it still commanded public fascination and fueled heated controversy. More immediately, the Sioux and Cheyennes dis-covered what the Modocs had so painfully learned; the slaying of a big white chief could spell the doom of a people. Custer's Last Stand shocked and outraged Americans, shook the Peace Policy to the verge of collapse, brought a flood of soldiers to the Indian country, and afforded rationalization for forcing the agency chiefs, hitherto held back by the militant opposition of the northern Indians, to sell the Black Hills. An "agreement"—it resembled a treaty in all but name—legitimized the sale. For the Sioux and Cheyennes, final defeat lurked unseen in their soaring victory amid the brown hills overlooking the Greasy Grass.

Once again, winter combined with soldiers who could brave its blasts destroyed Indian resistance. Until the first snows the Sioux and Cheyennes, now fragmented in bands, easily eluded the big armies that ponderously gave chase. But winter, as usual, made them vulnerable. In the frigid, misty dawn of November 25, 1876, eleven hundred cavalrymen under Colonel Ranald S. Mackenzie burst into the Cheyenne village of Dull Knife and Little Wolf in a canyon of the Bighorn Mountains. Forty Cheyennes died, and the rest watched helplessly from the bluffs as the soldiers burned their tipis, clothing, and winter food supply. That night the temperature plunged to thirty below zero. Eleven babies froze to death at their mothers' breasts.

The suffering Cheyennes took refuge with Crazy Horse, but the soldiers tracked down these people too. In January 1877, on Tongue River, Sioux and Cheyenne warriors clashed with "walk-a-heap" bluecoats in a fight that petered out in a blinding blizzard. These soldiers had built a rude fort at the mouth of the Tongue, and they kept to the field all winter. Tired and discouraged, the Indians opened talks with the soldier chief at this fort. He wore a huge overcoat, and they called him "Bear's Coat." He was the same Colonel Nelson A. Mills who had so resolutely pursued the southern Plains tribes in the Red River War.

Bear's Coat's combination of fight and talk, together with peace feelers put out from Red Cloud Agency through the agency chiefs, gradually strengthened the peace elements in the hostile camps. Spring saw the surrender of almost all the fugitives. On May 6, 1877, Crazy Horse led his Oglalas into Red Cloud Agency and threw his weapons on the ground in token of surrender. Four months later, amid circumstances that are still confusing, he died in a guardhouse scuffle, stabbed by either a soldier's bayonet or another Indian's knife. "It is good," said a fellow chief sadly, "he has looked for death and it has come."

The previous October, in a tense meeting between the lines, Sitting Bull told Bear's Coat that the Great Spirit had made him an Indian, and not an agency Indian. Rather than go to the reservation, he had led his people northward to the land of the "Great Mother." He got along well with her redcoats [Royal Canadian Mounted Police], but he and his people could not find enough food. Bear's Coat watched the boundary line like a hawk and prevented them from riding into Montana to hunt buffalo. Year after year, as they grew hungrier and hungrier, families and groups slipped away to surrender and go to the reservation. At last, in July 1881, Sitting Bull and about fifty families presented themselves at Fort Buford, Montana, the last vestige of the mighty alliance that had overwhelmed Long Hair Custer five years earlier. Sitting Bull handed his rifle to his eight-year-old son and told him to give it to the soldier chief. "I wish it to be remembered," he said, "that I was the last man of my tribe to surrender my rifle, and this day have given it to you.". . .

By 1881, when the surrender of Sitting Bull marked the close of the Plains wars, all tribes of the American West save one had been compelled by military force to go to, or return to, their reservations. Of them all, only the Apaches had not yet been made to face the truth that the reservation represented their only possible destiny. At one place or another in the Southwest, Apache warfare had been virtually continuous since Spanish colonial times. In the early 1870s General Crook had seemed to be on the verge of ending it permanently. His masterful Tonto Basin campaign of 1872–73 had brought about the collapse of the most troublesome Apache groups and their confinement on the reservations set up earlier by Vincent Colyer and General Howard. But Crook went north in 1875, to do less than brilliantly against the Sioux, and the iron military regime relaxed. At the same time the Indian Bureau decided to do away with the multiplicity of small reservations and to concentrate all Apaches west of the Rio Grande on a single reservation. A hot, barren, malarial flat along Arizona's Gila River, San Carlos was a terrible place to live. The final phases of Indian warfare in the United States grew out of the refusal of two powerful Apache leaders and their followers to settle permanently on the San Carlos Reservation.

These leaders were Victorio and Geronimo. Victorio, of the Mimbres, had learned his skills from the great Mangas Coloradas, whom he equaled in courage, stamina, cunning, and leadership. He wanted peace with the whites, and for a time, with Loco, he had pursued it. But soon he saw that few whites were as trustworthy as the good Lieutenant Drew, and the command to settle at San Carlos banished all such notions. Geronimo, of the Chiricahuas, emerged as a leader shortly after the death of Cochise in 1874. Short, thick, scowling, and ill-tempered, he exhibited few appealing traits, even to his own people. But of all Apache leaders, his cousin later remembered, "Geronimo seemed to be the most intelligent and resourceful as well as the most vigorous and farsighted. In times of danger he was a man to be relied upon." No less than Victorio did Geronimo find the order to move to San Carlos in 1876 offensive.

For two years, 1877–79, Victorio tried to find a solution to the dilemma that the government's concentration program had thrust upon him. He even attempted to live at San Carlos. "That horrible summer!" recalled one of his followers. "There was nothing but cactus, rattlesnakes, heat, rocks, and insects. No game; no edible plants. Many, many of our people died of starvation." Victorio also tried to live on his old reservation at Ojo Caliente, but the government had decided to close that place down. He tried to settle with the Mescaleros on the Fort Stanton Reservation, east of the Rio Grande, but that did not work. In fact, nothing worked, and on September 4, 1879, he and sixty warriors attacked a contingent of black cavalrymen near Ojo Caliente in the opening clash of the Victorio War.

In Texas, New Mexico, and Chihuahua, Victorio exacted a terrible price for the government's attempt to put him at San Carlos. With fresh numbers from the Mescalero Reservation, he counted between 125 and 150 warriors. Here and there they darted with lightning speed, cutting down isolated sheepherders and waylaying hapless travelers. Time and again they eluded the soldiers, both American and Mexican, who combed the mountains and deserts in an exhausting and mostly vain effort to destroy the marauders. In July 1880, in the hot, barren wastes of western Texas, Victorio found himself, for a change, thwarted by hard-riding units of black troopers who expertly kept him from the few waterholes and ultimately forced him into Mexico. Hungry, destitute, and low on ammunition, the raiders began to tire. Eastward they drifted, into the parched deserts of Chihua-hua, seemingly without plan or purpose. By October 1880 they camped amid three low peaks rising sharply from the vast desert plain. Tres Castillos, the Mex-icans called them.

At dawn on October 15 the Apaches awoke to the crash of gunfire and the shouts of Mexican soldiers and Tarahumara Indian allies. Their horse herd lost, the Indians scrambled up the boulder-strewn slope of one of the hills, and there they fought back. All day and into the night the two sides exchanged fire. In the dark the Indians tried to slip away, but failed. Singing the death chant, they turned to throwing up rock fortifications for a fight to the last. At daybreak they watched as the Mexicans began filtering upward among the boulders. The struggle was desperate and bloody and, in its final stages, hand-to-hand. When the smoke and dust cleared, seventy-eight Apaches lay dead among the rocks and another sixty-eight herded together as captives. Among the dead was Victorio.

At the time of Victorio's death, Geronimo was living, none too contentedly, at San Carlos. Besides its repugnant natural conditions, the reservation festered with intrigue, intertribal rivalries, incompetent and corrupt agents, and conflict between civil and military officials. White settlers pressed in on the reservation boundaries. Almost any spark could touch off an explosion. It came in August 1881. A medicine man had been preaching a new religion that whites regarded as incendiary. In an attempt to arrest him, the army got into a fight with his follow-ers, shot and killed the prophet, and had to quell a mutiny among the Apache scouts. Frightened by the resulting military activity, Geronimo and other leaders, with seventy-four people, broke out and headed for Mexico.

An especially daring raid in the following spring drew attention to the deteri-orating state of affairs in Arizona. Geronimo and others swooped down on San Carlos, killed the police chief, and forced old Loco and several hundred people to return to Mexico with them. That event prodded the government to decisive ac-tion. Early in September 1882 a familiar figure reappeared in Arizona—the "Gray Fox," General Crook. At once he clamped military rule on San Carlos. To keep the peace here and later to go after the "renegades" in Mexico, he recruited five companies of Apache scouts—"the wildest I could get"—and placed them under his brightest, most energetic young officers. Skilled packers organized efficient and sturdy mule trains. No cumbersome wagons would limit mobility.

The Sierra Madre of Mexico had always afforded Apaches an impregnable fortress. Its steep ridges, piled one on another toward towering peaks and perpet-ually shadowing plunging gorges and canyons walled in vertical rock, sheltered and protected these Indians and provided secure bases for raiding in all directions, on both sides of the international border. One Chiricahua group, the Nednhis, had made this wilderness their home for generations. Their chief, Juh, surpassed all others in power. Geronimo, Nachez (son of Cochise), Chato, Chihuahua, Loco, Bonito, battle-scarred old Nana (who had ridden with Victorio but had escaped Tres Castillos), and others deferred to Juh. But one day Juh fell from a cliffside trail to his death, and increasingly the captains of the Apaches in the Sierra Madre looked to Geronimo for guidance. From their mountain lairs they continued to raid. In a foray of special ferocity, in March 1883 Chato and twenty-five warriors slashed across Arizona and New Mexico, and then faded back into Mexico. In response, Crook marched.

A surprise attack by Apache scouts on Chato's camp high in the Sierra Madre gave notice to all the fugitives that their fortress had been breached. Where Mexican troops had never ventured, Americans had penetrated, and at the head of other Apaches. It came as enough of a shock that one by one the band leaders drifted in to talk with the Gray Fox. Geronimo, who had been raiding in Chihuahua, came last. Squatting around smoky campfires, the Indians listened to the harsh words of this general who so uncharacteristically wore a canvas suit and rode a mule. Surrender, he told them in a threat that he and all his listeners knew he could not carry out, or he would kill them all. At night, in long arguments among themselves, the chiefs debated what to do. Crook's success in reaching them in previously inaccessible refuges, combined with his ability to enlist their own people against them, tipped the balance. "We give ourselves up," Geronimo at last announced, "do with us as you please."

The surrender turned out to be only temporary. Back at San Carlos, tensions began building almost at once. A people accustomed to freedom found military rule irksome; the men especially bridled at the ban on beating their wives and on brewing the volatile intoxicant *tiswin*. In May 1885 off they went again, some 134 people, including Geronimo, Nachez, Chihuahua, and Nana. Once again they hid themselves deep in the Sierra Madre. Once again they discovered white officers leading their own people against them. And once again they quickly tired of keeping always on the run, always apprehensive of a sudden surprise attack. They sent word to the officer in charge of one of the scout units, Captain Emmet Crawford, that they wanted to talk. But before a meeting could be arranged, Mexican militia attacked the scouts, and the captain fell with a bullet in his brain. Later Geronimo and others met with Crawford's lieutenant, Marion P. Maus, and told him they wanted to talk with General Crook.

The meeting took place at Canyon de los Embudos, twelve miles south of the border, on March 25, 1886. Seated on the sides of a pleasantly shaded ravine, the general and the Apaches parleyed. As he had done two years earlier, Crook spoke sternly. Now the terms were harsher. The men with their families must go to a place of confinement in the East for two years, and only then could they return to San Carlos. Otherwise, Crook vowed, "I'll keep after you and kill the last one, if it takes fifty years." After two days of argument among themselves, the Apache chiefs accepted Crook's terms. While the general hastened north to telegraph to good news to his superiors, the Indians moved slowly toward the border. Along the way they found a whiskey peddler. In the midst of a drinking bout Geronimo and Nachez had second thoughts. With twenty men and thirteen women, they stampeded back to the Sierra Madre.

This development profoundly discouraged General Crook. Worse, it brought him into conflict with General Sheridan, who had succeeded Sherman as head of the army. Sheridan had never trusted the Apache scouts, and he thought Crook should use regulars instead. Now he issued orders that not only implicitly criticized Crook's methods but required him to break his word to the Indians who had not fled with Geronimo and Nachez. Rather than carry out such orders, Crook asked to be relieved. Sheridan lost no time in dispatching a replacement, Nelson

A. Miles, now a brigadier general. It was a hard blow to the Gray Fox, for he and Miles had long been bitter rivals, personally as well as professionally. Bear's Coat welcomed the chance to succeed where Crook had failed.

Astutely, Miles made a great show of employing regular soldiers against the Apaches, but in the end he quietly adopted Crook's methods. Apache scouts combed the Sierra Madre, keeping the quarry on the run. As a special peace emissary, Miles sent Lieutenant Charles B. Gatewood, whom the Indians knew as a friend, to see if he could find and persuade them to give up. Ironically, Gatewood was a Crook protégé.

As in the past, the little band of fugitives soon tired of running. On August 24, 1886, they admitted Gatewood and two Indian companions to their camp. At considerable peril to his life, Gatewood stated the new terms: The Apaches must go to Florida and wait for the President to decide their ultimate fate. Geronimo said he and Nachez would give up, but only if they could return to San Carlos. Then Gatewood played his high card. At San Carlos Geronimo would find none of his kinsmen, only rival tribes. All the Chiricahuas, even those who had loyally served Crook as scouts, had been herded aboard railway cars and deported to Florida. Stunned, the Indians debated for a long time, but at last they told Gatewood that they would give up to General Miles personally. In Skeleton Canyon, just north of the border, Geronimo faced Miles and handed over his rifle.

A trainload of Apaches rattling across the Arizona desert toward far-off Florida signaled the end of armed resistance to the reservation system. Every important Indian war since 1870 had been essentially a war not of concentration but of rebellion—or Indians rebelling against reservations they had already accepted in theory if not in fact. Geronimo and his tiny band of followers were the last holdouts, and they only because the wilds of Mexico offered them a haven denied to most other tribes. Thus the wars of the Peace Policy, and indeed the Indian Wars of the United States, came to a close in Skeleton Canyon, Arizona, on September 4, 1886.

◈ *F U R T H E R   R E A D I N G*

W. David Baird, ed., *A Creek Warrior for the Confederacy: The Autobiography of Chief G. W. Grayson* (1988)
Keith Basso, ed., *Western Apache Raiding and Warfare* (1971)
Donald Berthrong, *The Southern Cheyennes* (1963)
Tiana Bighorse, *Bighorse the Warrior* (1990)
Martha Royce Blaine, *Pawnee Passage: 1870–1875* (1990)
John Bourke, *On the Border with Crook* (1891)
Edmund J. Danzinger, *Indians and Bureaucrats: Administering the Reservation Policy During the Civil War* (1974)
Angie Debo, *Geronimo: The Man, His Time, His Place* (1976)
Raymond DeMallie, ed., *The Sixth Grandfather* (1984)
Thomas Dunlay, *Wolves for the Blue Soldiers: Indian Scouts and Auxiliary* (1982)
John Ewers, *The Blackfeet: Raiders of the Northwest Plains* (1958)
George Grinnell, *The Cheyenne Indians; Their History and Ways of Life*, 2 vols., 1923
Alvin Josephy, *The Nez Perce Indians and the Opening of the Northwest* (1965)
Frank Linderman, *Plenty Coups, Chief of the Crows* (1930)

————, *Pretty Shield, Medicine Woman of the Crows* (1932)

Roy W. Meyer, *History of the Santee Sioux: United States Policy on Trial* (1967)

————, *The Village Indians of the Upper Missouri: The Mandans, Hidatsas, and Arikaras* (1977)

James Mooney, *Calendar History of the Kiowa Indians* (1898).

Keith A. Murray, *The Modocs and Their War* (1959)

Peter Nabokov, *Two Leggings: The Making of a Crow Warrior with the U. S. Army* (1967)

John Neihardt, *Black Elk Speaks* (1932)

Joseph C. Porter, *Paper Medicine Man: John Gregory Bourke and His American West* (1986)

John Peter Powell, *People of the Sacred Mountain: A History of the Northern Cheyenne Chiefs und Warrior Societies, 1830–1870,* 2 vols., (1981)

————, *Sweet Medicine: The Continuing Role of the Sacred Arrows, the Sun Dance, and the Sacred Buffalo Hat in Northern Cheyenne History,* 2 vols. (1969)

Robert H. Ruby and John A. Brown, *Indians of the Pacific Northwest* (1959)

Mari Sandoz, *Crazy Horse* (1942)

Sherry Smith, *The View from Officers' Row: Army Perceptions of Western Indians* (1990)

Gerald Thompson, *The Army and the Navajo: The Bosque Redondo Reservation Experiment, 1863–1868* (1976)

Dan Thrapp, *The Conquest of Apacheria* (1967)

Robert M. Utley, *Frontier Regulars: The United States Army and the Indian, 1866–1891* (1973)

————, *The Indian Frontier of the American West, 1846–1890* (1984)

Ernest Wallace and E. Adamson Hoebel, *The Comanches: Lords of the Southern Plains* (1952)

Gene Weltfish, *The Lost Universe: Pawnee Life and Culture* (1965)

Robert Wooster, *The Military and United States Indian Policy, 1865–1903* (1990)

CHAPTER
10

Making the Indians
at Home in America,
1870–1920

As the Indians were increasingly confined on reservations, federal officials and re-
formers who saw themselves as "friends of the Indians" sought to assimilate native
peoples into the larger American society. It was time, said one Commissioner of In-
dian Affairs with unconscious irony, to make Indians feel at home in the United
States. But Indian policy during this era must be understood in the context of
the age.

Following the Civil War, the nation began to attract large numbers of immi-
grants. Private property, Christianity, the English language, and the opportunity to
farm or learn a useful trade were considered central to American values and success
in these years. Reformers of federal Indian policy wanted to subject Native Ameri-
cans to the same general efforts to Americanize foreign newcomers, and federal poli-
cies reflected these instincts.

The General Allotment Act of 1887, popularly called the Dawes Act, followed
the model of the Homestead Act of 1862. The Dawes Act broke up communally
owned reservation lands and allotted land to individual families. Any unallotted
land could be sold by the government, with the proceeds made available for educat-
ing the Indians. Catholic and Protestant missionaries consequently brought their
teachings to the reservations. Schools provided instruction in English. In addition,
boarding schools off the reservations allowed federal or mission teachers the opportu-
nity to inculcate white American values without parental intervention at home. On
some reservations, formerly nomadic peoples were confined to encourage their way of
life based on hunting to give way to farming. Of course, the situation varied consider-
ably from one reservation to another. For example, not all lands were allotted; not
all children attended school. Nevertheless, for more than half a century, this assimila-
tionist thrust dominated federal policy, and the effects proved considerable in Indian
country. Under the rapidly changing circumstances of the period, did federal policy-
makers have other choices? Was the course they chose the only pragmatic one?

◈ *D O C U M E N T S*

The General Allotment Act of 1887, also called the Dawes Act after its congressional sponsor, Henry Dawes of Massachusetts, is generally portrayed today as ill advised, although most non-Indians of the nineteenth century thought it a good idea. Not all reservations came under its provisions. But many did, and for those that experienced the impact of allotment and subsequent policies designed to reduce native landholdings, the results were disastrous. Indians in the area that later composed the lower forty-eight states lost two out of every three acres that they had held prior to 1887. A reading of the act, which is excerpted as the first document, gives one a firsthand sense of the federal objectives in the era. The second document, which features closing exercises at the Usage Boarding School, also demonstrates the assimilationist emphasis of the period. Today, nearly all would view such a program as completely ethnocentric or thoroughly racist—labels that would not have occurred to school officials at Pawhuska, Oklahoma, and elsewhere who were dedicated to what they perceived as "the right trail."

Exposure to the cultural transformation that the federal and mission schools sought to achieve ranked high on assimilationists' list of priorities. Students responded in a variety of ways to these schools, some of which were located near their homes, but others of which were hundreds or even thousands of miles away. Richard Henry Pratt's Carlisle Indian Industrial School in Pennsylvania provided a model for many of the early schools, especially up to the first years of the twentieth century. Luther Standing Bear's decision to go east to Carlisle is recorded here in the third selection, an excerpt from his book *Land of the Spotted Eagle*. In the fourth document, Thomas J. Morgan, who served as Commissioner of Indian Affairs, speaks to the need for compulsory education. In these remarks, which were made to reformers gathered for an annual meeting at Lake Mohonk, New York, Morgan argues that Indian parents and children should have little choice in the matter.

The attempt by Ernest Jermark, superintendent of the Fort Berthold reservation in North Dakota, to curtail dances may now provoke chuckles rather than concern. But his circular, which was distributed to local employees and is excerpted in the fifth document, was not at all atypical in the early twentieth century. Jermark and his peers frowned on community celebrations, for, in the exchange of gifts and the display of generosity and reciprocity, tribalism was definitely reinforced. Government employees, of course, wanted to discourage the continuation of the old ways. They puzzled over what to do about Indian tribes who embraced the Fourth of July as an opportunity to cherish old values in the guise of a new, nationally sanctioned holiday.

The General Allotment Act (Dawes Act), 1887

An act to provide for the allotment of lands in severalty to Indians on the various reservations, and to extend the protection of the laws of the United States and the Territories over the Indians, and for other purposes.

Be it enacted by the Senate and House of Representatives of the United States of America in Congress assembled, That in all cases where any tribe or band of Indians has been, or shall hereafter be, located upon any reservation created for their use, either by treaty stipulation or by virtue of an act of Congress or executive order setting apart the same for their use, the President of the Untied States be, and he hereby is, authorized, whenever in his opinion any reservation or any part thereof of such Indians is advantageous for agricultural and grazing purposes, to cause said reservation, or any part thereof, to be surveyed, or resurveyed if necessary, and to allot the lands in said reservation in severalty to any Indian located thereon in quantities as follows:

To each head of a family, one-quarter of a section;

To each single person over eighteen years of age, one-eighth of a section;

To each orphan child under eighteen years of age, one-eighth of a section; and

To each other single person under eighteen years now living, or who may be born prior to the date of the order of the President directing an allotment of the lands embraced in any reservation, one-sixteenth of a section: *Provided,* That in case there is not sufficient land in any of said reservations to allot lands to each individual of the classes above named in quantities as above provided, the lands embraced in such reservation or reservations shall be allotted to each individual of each of said classes pro rata in accordance with the provisions of this act: *And provided further,* That where the treaty or act of Congress setting apart such reservation provides for the allotment of lands in severalty in quantities in excess of those herein provided, the President, in making allotments upon such reservation, shall allot the lands to each individual Indian belonging thereon in quantity as specified in such treaty or act: *And provided further,* That when the lands allotted are only valuable for grazing purposes, an additional allotment of such grazing lands, in quantities as above provided, shall be made to each individual.

Sec. 2.   That all allotments set apart under the provisions of this act shall be selected by the Indians, heads of families selecting for their minor children, and the agents shall select for each orphan child, and in such manner as to embrace the improvements of the Indians making the selection. Where the improvements of two or more Indians have been made on the same legal subdivision of land, unless they shall otherwise agree, a provisional line may be run dividing said lands between them, and the amount to which each is entitled shall be equalized in the assignment of the remainder of the land to which they are entitled under this act: Provided, That if any one entitled to an allotment shall fail to make a selection within four years after the President shall direct that allotments may be made on a particular reservation, the Secretary of the Interior may direct the agent of such tribe or band, if such there be, and if there be no agent, then a special agent appointed for that purpose, to make a selection for such Indian, which election shall be allotted as in cases where selections are made by the Indians, and patents shall issue in like manner.

Sec. 3.   That the allotments provided for in this act shall be made by special agents appointed by the President for such purpose, and the agents in charge of the respective reservations on which the allotments are directed to be made, under such rules and regulations as the Secretary of the Interior may from time to time prescribe, and shall be certified by such agents to the Commissioner of Indian Affairs, in duplicate, one copy to be retained in the Indian Office and the other to be transmitted to the Secretary of the Interior for his action, and to be deposited in the General Land Office. . . .

Sec. 5.   That upon the approval of the allotments provided for in this act by the Secretary of the Interior, he shall cause patents to issue therefor in the name of the allottees, which patents shall be of the legal effect, and declare that the United States does and will hold the land thus allotted, for the period of twenty-five years, in trust for the sole use and benefit of the Indian to whom such allotment shall have been made, or, in case of his decease, of his heirs according to the laws of the State or Territory where such land is located, and that at the expiration of said period the United States will convey the same by patent to said Indian, of his heirs as aforesaid, in fee, discharged of said trust and free of all charge or incumbrance whatsoever. . . .

Sec. 6.   That upon the completion of said allotments and the patenting of the lands to said allottees, each and every member of the respective bands or tribes of Indians to whom allotments have been made shall have the benefit of and be subject to the laws, both civil and criminal, of the State or Territory in which they may reside; and no Territory shall pass or enforce any law denying any such Indian within its jurisdiction the equal protection of the law. And every Indian both within the territorial limits of the United States to whom allotments shall have been made under the provisions of this act, or under any law or treaty, and every Indian born within the territorial limits of the United States who has voluntarily taken up, within said limits, his residence separate and apart from any tribe of Indians therein, and has adopted the habits of civilized life, is hereby declared to be a citizen of the United States, and is entitled to all the rights, privileges, and immunities of such citizens, whether said Indian has been or not, by birth or otherwise, a member of any tribe of Indians within the territorial limits of the United States without in any manner, impairing or otherwise affecting the right of any such Indian to tribal or other property. . . .

Sec. 8.   That the provision of this act shall not extend to the territory occupied by the Cherokees, Creeks, Choctaws, Chickasaws, Seminoles, and Osage, Miamies and Peorias, and Sacs and Foxes, in the Indian Territory, nor to any of the reservations of the Seneca Nation of New York Indians in the State of New York, nor to that strip of territory in the State of Nebraska adjoining the Sioux Nation on the south added by executive order. . . .

Closing Exercises of the Osage Boarding School, 1913

Program
Part 1

1-Opening Chorus---"Sailors Glee"

Sopranos:	Dica Hildebrand,	Fannie Taylor
Altos:	Lola Perrier,	Pearl Quinton
Tenors:	Philip Carson,	Jacob Duran
Basses:	John Taylor,	Joseph Watson

2-Drill of the Dunces

Homer Bigheart	Theodore Pappin
Joseph Daniels	Leroy Tallchief
Harold Littlebear	Louis Tyner
Chester Miller	Charles Wagoshe

3-Maud Muller Pantomime

MAUDS---Nola Childers,   Dica Hilderbrand,   Vernie Hutchinson
    Agnes Taylor,   Elnora Quinton.
JUDGES---Charles A. Bigheart,   Paul Cedar,   Harry Kohpay,
    Walter McKinley,   Joseph Ware.
READER---Agnes Quinton

"Of all sad words of tongue or pen
The saddest are these—"It might have been."

4-Chorus-"Memory Bells."

*Pupils of Sixth
and Seventh Grades.*

"Hear the chiming stealing o'er our hearts today."

5-"The Jolly Waiters."

Jacques, from Fair France .... Paul Cedar
Sambo, from the Sunny South .... Amos Miles
Chin Lee, the Heathen Chinese .... Frank Pappin
Hans, from Deutschland .... Roy Tyner
Paddy, from the Emerald Isle .... Elijah Ware

6-"The Little Turkey Turkees."

A Salaam to Mustapha Ben Adahm, by the Turkees---Mildred Abbott, Mary Elkins, Mary King, Christine Martin, Grace Miller, Ollie Sears, Anna Taylor.

A Salaam to the Turkey Bird and the Turkees, by the Turks-Stanton Bratton, Philip Brokey, Bernard Conville, Howard Miller, Andrew McKinney, Robert Smith, Elijah Ware.

INTERMISSION

Part 2

7-Indian Huntresses.

Nola Childers   Agnes Quinton
Dica Hildebrand   Pearl Quinton
Rose Hunkahoppy   Fannie Taylor
Lola Perrier   Anna Strikeaxe

8-"Choosing a Trail."

Scene 1.

An Indian Camp, portraying the daily activities. Enter Agent from a Government School for the purpose of securing enrollment of the children.

Scene 2.

A few minutes later. Agent asks for Children, Chief objects, and threatens the safety of the whites, but the children are marshaled away to school. War Dance of Warriors and Indian Women.

Scene 3.

Three years later. Government School. The Chief and his Warriors visit the school and show much pleasure and interest in its work and in the progress of their children. They are so fully satisfied as to the advantage and importance of education, that they decide to give the school their hearty support, and thereafter to send their children to school without being asked, keeping them in regular attendance. They join with the children in the singing of a Lullaby.

9-"Mammy's Littl' Honey."

"Now hush ma Pickaninny,
   Yo' must quit yo' wicked way;
An' de lark will come an' wake yo'
   At de dawnin' ob de day."

Luther Standing Bear (Lakota) Recalls His Experiences at the Carlisle Indian Industrial School, 1879

... At the age of eleven years, ancestral life for me and my people was most abruptly ended without regard for our wishes, comforts, or rights in the matter. At once I was thrust into an alien world, into an environment as different from the one into which I had been born as it is possible to imagine, to remake myself, if I could, into the likeness of the invader.

By 1879, my people were no longer free, but were subjects confined on reservations under the rule of agents. One day there came to the agency a party of white people from the East. Their presence aroused considerable excitement when it became known that these people were school teachers who wanted some Indian boys and girls to take away with them to train as were white boys and girls.

Now, father was a "blanket Indian," but he was wise. He listened to the white strangers, their offers and promises that if they took his son they would care well for him, teach him how to read and write, and how to wear white man's clothes. But to father all this was just "sweet talk," and I know that it was with great misgivings that he left the decision to me and asked if I cared to go with these people. I, of course, shared with the rest of my tribe a distrust of the white people, so I know that for all my dear father's anxiety he was proud to hear me say "Yes." That meant that I was brave.

I could think of no reason why white people wanted Indian boys and girls except to kill them, and not having the remotest idea of what a school was, I thought we were going East to die. But so well had courage and bravery been trained into us that it became a part of our unconscious thinking and acting, and personal life was nothing when it came time to do something for the tribe. Even in our play and games we voluntarily put ourselves to various tests in the effort to grow brave and fearless, for it was most discrediting to be called *can'l wanka,* or a coward. Accordingly there were few cowards, most Lakota men preferring to die in the performance of some act of bravery than to die of old age. Thus, in giving myself up to go East I was proving to my father that he was honored with a brave son. In my decision to go, I gave up many things dear to the heart of a little Indian boy, and one of the things over which my child mind grieved was the thought of saying good-bye to my pony. I rode him as far as I could on the journey, which was to the Missouri River, where we took the boat. There we parted from our parents, and it was a heart-breaking scene, women and children weeping. Some of the children changed their minds and were unable to go on the boat, but for many who did go it was a final parting.

On our way to school we saw many white people, more than we ever dreamed existed, and the manner in which they acted when they saw us quite indicated their opinion of us. It was only about three years after the Custer battle, and the general opinion was that the Plains people merely infested the earth as nuisances, and our being there simply evidenced misjudgment on the part of

Wakan Tanka [the Creator in the Lakota religion]. Whenever our train stopped at the railway stations, it was met by great numbers of white people who came to gaze upon the little Indian "savages." The shy little ones sat quietly at the car windows looking at the people who swarmed on the platform. Some of the children wrapped themselves in their blankets, covering all but their eyes. At one place we were taken off the train and marched a distance down the street to a restaurant. We walked down the street between two rows of uniformed men whom we called soldiers, though I suppose they were policemen. This must have been done to protect us, for it was surely known that we boys and girls could do no harm. Back of the rows of uniformed men stood the white people craning their necks, talking, laughing, and making a great noise. They yelled and tried to mimic us by giving what they thought were war-whoops. We did not like this, and some of the children were naturally very much frightened. I remember how I tried to crowd into the protecting midst of the jostling boys and girls. But we were all trying to be brave, yet going to what we thought would end in death at the hands of the white people whom we knew had no love for us. Back on the train the older boys sang brave songs in an effort to keep up their spirits and ours too. In my mind I often recall that scene—eighty-odd blanketed boys and girls marching down the street surrounded by a jeering, unsympathetic people whose only emotions were those of hate and fear; the conquerors looking upon the conquered. And no more understanding us than if we had suddenly been dropped from the moon.

At last at Carlisle the transforming, the "civilizing" process began. It began with clothes. Never, no matter what our philosophy or spiritual quality, could we be civilized while wearing the moccasin and blanket. The task before us was not only that of accepting new ideas and adopting new manners, but actual physical changes and discomfort had to be borne uncomplainingly until the body adjusted itself to new tastes and habits. Our accustomed dress was taken and replaced with clothing that felt cumbersome and awkward. Against trousers and handkerchiefs we had a distinct feeling—they were unsanitary and the trousers kept us from breathing well. High collars, stiff-bosomed shirts, and suspenders fully three inches in width were uncomfortable, while leather boots caused actual suffering. We longed to go barefoot, but were told that the dew on the grass would give us colds. That was a new warning for us, for our mothers had never told us to beware of colds, and I remember as a child coming into the tipi with moccasins full of snow. Unconcernedly I would take them off my feet, pour out the snow, and put them on my feet again without any thought of sickness, for in that time colds, catarrh, bronchitis, and *la grippe* were unknown. But we were soon to know them. Then, red flannel undergarments were given us for winter wear, and for me, at least, discomfort grew into actual torture. I used to endure it as long as possible, then run upstairs and quickly take off the flannel garments and hide them. When inspection time came, I ran and put them on again, for I knew that if I were found disobeying the orders of the school I should be punished. My niece once asked me what it was that I disliked the most during those first bewildering days, and I said, "red flannel." Not knowing what I meant, she laughed, but I still remember those horrid, sticky garments which we had to wear next to the skin, and I still squirm and itch when I think of them. Of course, our hair was cut, and then there was much disapproval. But that was part of the transformation process and in some mysterious way long hair stood in the path of our development. For all the grumbling among the bigger boys, we soon had our heads shaven. How strange I felt! Involuntarily, time and time again, my hands went to my head, and that night it was a long time before I went to sleep. If we did not learn much at first, it will not be wondered at, I think. Everything was queer, and it took a few months to get adjusted to the new surroundings.

Almost immediately our names were changed to those in common use in the English language. Instead of translating our names into English and calling Zinkcaziwin, Yellow Bird, and Wanbli K'leska, Spotted Eagle, which in itself would have been educational, we were just John, Henry, or Maggie, as the case might be. I was told to take a pointer and select a name for myself from the list written on the blackboard. I did, and since one was just as good as another, and as I could not distinguish any difference in them, I placed the pointer on the name Luther. I then learned to call myself by that name and got used to hearing others call me by it, too. By that time we had been forbidden to speak our mother tongue, which is the rule in all boarding-schools. This rule is uncalled for, and today is not only robbing the Indian, but America of a rich heritage. The language of a people is part of their history. Today we should be perpetuating history instead of destroying it, and this can only be effectively done by allowing and encouraging the young to keep it alive. A language unused, embalmed, and reposing only in a book, is a dead language. Only the people themselves, and never the scholars, can nourish it into life.

Of all the changes we were forced to make, that of diet was doubtless the most injurious, for it was immediate and drastic. White bread we had for the first meal and thereafter, as well as coffee and sugar. Had we been allowed our own simple diet of meat, either boiled with soup or dried, and fruit, with perhaps a few vegetables, we should have thrived. But the change in clothing, housing, food, and confinement combined with lonesomeness was too much, and in three years nearly one half of the children from the Plains were dead and through with all earthly schools. In the graveyard at Carlisle most of the graves are those of little ones. . . .

Indian Commissioner Thomas J. Morgan on the Need for Compulsory Education, 1892

We must either fight the Indians, or feed them, or educate them. To fight them is cruel; to feed them is wasteful; to educate them is humane, economic, and Christian. We have forced upon them—I use the term not in any offensive sense—citizenship, and we are limiting severely the period of preparation. Unless they can be educated for the proper discharge of their duties and for the enjoyment of their privileges as citizens, they will fail to be properly benefited by the boon that we are conferring upon them. The government of the United States has at large expense provided accommodations for from twenty to twenty-five thousand of their children in schools maintained wholly or in part by the government. The people will not long continue to expend these two and a quarter million dollars a year for the education of these children if those to whom it is offered are unwilling to accept it. If they refuse to send their children to school, these schools will be closed; and the people who have been made citizens will be thrown upon

themselves, and be left to survive or perish, according to their individual inclination. A large body of them to-day are unwilling to send their children to school.
The schools are open, they offer to them every facility for learning English, they
offer them free board, free tuition, free clothing, free medical care. Everything is
freely offered, they are urged to come, but they refuse; and there is growing up,
under the shadow of these institutions of learning, a new generation of savages.
We are confronted, then, with this simple proposition: Shall we allow the growth
of another generation of barbarians, or shall we compel the children to enter these
schools to be trained to intelligence and industry? . . .

Let me illustrate: At Fort Hall in Idaho, where the Shoshones and the
Bannacks are, there is a school population of about two hundred and fifty. The
people are degraded. They wander about in the mountains. Their women do most
of what little work is done. They live in a beastly way (I use the term thoughtfully,
I have seen it); and they are refusing to send their children to school. We have
spent thousands of dollars in making the school at Fort Hall one of the most attractive reservation schools that is anywhere to be found. We have two thousand
acres under fence. We have a large herd of cattle, and we have a noble body of
employees. We are pleading with these people to put their children in school on
the reservation, almost within sight of their own homes, within twenty or thirty
miles' ride of any part of the reservation; but they say: "No. The medicinemen say
it is bad medicine." Now, shall we compel them?

In Fort Yuma the Indians live in the sand, like lizards, and have till recently
gone almost naked. They send their children to the school till they reach the age
of ten or eleven years. Then they are out, the girls roaming at will in that vicinity,
the boys loafing about the miserable village of Yuma, wearing their hair long and
going back to the ways of the camp. One of the saddest things I ever attended was
an Indian mourning feast on that reservation, within sight of that school. Now, the
question for me is, Shall I compel those children to enter school, to receive a
preparation for citizenship?

At San Carlos are the Apaches, who are regarded as the most vicious of the
Indians with whom we have to deal. They are held practically as prisoners, the
San Carlos Agency being under control of the military. For years there has been
a military officer in command, supported by two or three companies of colored
soldiers. The conditions on that reservation are simply deplorable, and I would
not dare in this audience to more than allude to the conditions existing there.
These people decline to send their children to school; but I have within the last
twelve months taken from that reservation about two hundred of them. They are
to-day well fed and properly clothed, are happy and contented, and making good
progress. Did I do right?

Voices.—Yes! Yes!

Morgan.—I must illustrate by numerous other instances. We have provided
these schools for the benefit of the children, not, primarily, for our own benefit.
We have done it in order that they may be brought into relationship with the
civilization of the nineteenth century. It is an expression of the sentiment that is
generated here on these mountains. It comes, I believe, from God. Now, then, the
question is simply, Shall we say that, after having made this abundant provision
and having offered it to the children, we will allow those who are still savages in
their instincts, barbarians in their habits, rooted to their conservatism—that we

will allow them to keep their children out of these institutions of learning, in order that they may be prevented from becoming like white men and women?

I say, No; and I say it for these reasons: We owe it to these children to see to it that they shall have the advantages of these schools. We owe it to their children that are to come after them that they shall be born of educated parents, and not of savages. We owe it to the old people themselves. The most pitiful things that I have been confronted with on the Indian reservations are the old men and old women, wrinkled, blind, and wretched, living on the ash-heap, having no care, with no protection, turned out to die. The other day, as I stood by the side of that little Santee girl, her father said to me, as he pointed out an old wrinkled woman, "My mamma"; and a most horrible creature she was. We owe it to these people to educate their children, so that they can go back to their homes and take care of the fathers and mothers who are no longer able to take care of themselves. We owe it to ourselves. We have undertaken to do this work: we have laid aside sentiment; we have laid aside everything except regard for the welfare of the children, and simply said, This thing ought to be done. Now, I say the one step remaining is for us to say that it shall be done.

I would first make the schools as attractive as they can be made, and would win these children, so far as possible, by kindness and persuasion. I would put them first into the schools near home, into the day schools, if there are any, or into the reservation boarding-schools, where there are such. Where it is practicable, I would allow them large liberty as to whether they shall go to a government school or a private school. I would bring to bear upon them such influences as would secure their acceptance voluntarily wherever it could be done. I would then use the Indian police if necessary. I would withhold from them rations and supplies where those are furnished, if that were needed; and when every other means was exhausted, when I could not accomplish the work in any other way, I would send a troop of United States soldiers, not to seize them, but simply to be present as an expression of the power of the government. Then I would say to these people, "Put your children in school"; and they would do it. There would be no warfare. At Fort Hall to-day, if there were present a sergeant or a lieutenant, with ten mounted soldiers, simply camped there, and I sent out to those Indians and told them that within ten days every child of school age must be in school, they would be there. Shall it be done? It *will* be done if public sentiment demands it: it will not be done if public sentiment does not. . . .

Ernest Jermark Tries to Curtail Indian Dances, 1922

Fort Berthold Agency
Elbowoods, N. Dak.
January 30, 1922

To whom it may concern:

At a council of the Indians, held on the 22nd inst., at Bird Lying Down's Lodge, it was agreed that dancing, exchanging of presents, traveling from one dance hall to another, and dancing feasts were being carried to excess.

Carolyn Gilman and Mary Jane Schneider, editors, *The Way to Independence* (St. Paul: Minnesota Historical Society, 1987), p. 224. Reprinted by permission of the State Historical Society of North Dakota.

I am extremely pleased to know that the Indians themselves have recognized this condition for the reason that in those excesses, in my opinion, exists the principal harm in Indian dancing. It is realized that Indians, as well as whites, must have recreation and amusement, but it is also realized that such recreation and amusement, in order not to become a nuisance or detrimental to the best interests of the Indians, must not be carried to excess.

With the idea of curtailing and to control these dances, it is deemed adbisable [advisable] to make certain special rules, which, it is my understanding, the Council approves:

1st. Permission for Indian dances must be obtained in writing from the office, such permission to show the date and place.

2nd. Dances are to be limited to legal holidays.

3rd. Citizens attending Indian dances to be required to observe the same rules as non-competent Indians.*

4th. No presents to be exchanged or gifts made at the dances.

5th. Big feasts and donations of food stuffs for dances to be discontinued, except on special occasions under special permission.

6th. No men under 21 or girls under 18 years of age to be permitted to dance, or wear dance costumes at the dances.

7th. Promiscuous running from one dance hall to another must be stopped. Dances are to be conducted during the evening only. No dancing later than 2 A.M. and all Indians to return home not later than the following morning.

In order to carry out the rules, as above set forth, I earnestly request the cooperation of every Indian on this reservation, whether citizen or restricted.

(signed) Ernest Jermark
Superintendent

⟡ *E S S A Y S*

Robert A. Trennert, a professor of history at Arizona State University, has studied the impact of federal policy on different dimensions of Indian life. The first essay, on the education of Indian girls at nonreservation boarding schools during this era, is drawn in part from his book on Phoenix Indian School, one of the major schools in the Southwest. Trennert notes the objectives of such schools and also records some of the pupils' responses to their surroundings. In the late nineteenth and early twentieth centuries, public education generally was not available to young Indian men and women; for those who wanted schooling, places such as Phoenix were usually the only option.

As this essay suggests and as other research has confirmed, the Indian schools, although particularly rigid in their initial form, were not always unwilling to incorporate changes into their policies over time. Nonetheless, their overall goals remained fundamentally the same until the Indian New Deal of the 1930s.

---

*In this context, "non-competent Indians" refers to Indians who were not citizens, and thus were judged unable to make their own decisions about their lands.

Melissa L. Meyer is an associate professor of history at Dartmouth College. Her essay on the White Earth Anishinaabeg, excerpted as the second selection, addresses the impact that federal land policies could have on native communities. Meyer is interested both in the effects of Euro-American political and economic interests on federal policy and in the costs that dispossession inherently inflicted on the people of White Earth. Meyer's essay is important for several reasons. Not only has she focused on a part of the Indian America infrequently studied by historians, but she gives due appreciation to the Anishinaabeg (Ojibwa or Chippewa) as adaptive, incorporative individuals who indeed were making significant strides economically and socially before they felt the full brunt of federal policies. How does this image of a progressive, adaptive society contrast with other portraits drawn of reservation communities of this era?

Educating Indian Girls and Women at Nonreservation Boarding Schools, 1878–1920

ROBERT A. TRENNERT

During the latter part of the nineteenth century the Bureau of Indian Affairs made an intensive effort to assimilate the Indian into American society. One important aspect of the government's acculturation program was Indian education. By means of reservation day schools, reservation boarding schools, and off-reservation industrial schools, the federal government attempted to obliterate the cultural heritage of Indian youths and replace it with the values of Anglo-American society. One of the more notable aspects of this program was the removal of young Indian women from their tribal homes to government schools in an effort to transform them into a government version of the ideal American woman. This program of assimilationist education, despite some accomplishments, generally failed to attain its goals. This study is a review of the education of Indian women at the institutions that best typified the government program—the off-reservation industrial training schools. An understanding of this educational system provides some insight into the impact of the acculturation effort on the native population. Simultaneously, it illustrates some of the prevalent national images regarding both Indians and women.

The concept of educating native women first gained momentum among eighteenth-century New England missionaries who recommended that Indian girls might benefit from formal training in housekeeping. This idea matured to the point that, by the 1840s, the federal government had committed itself to educating Indian girls in the hope that women trained as good housewives would help their mates assimilate. A basic premise of this educational effort rested on the necessary elimination of Indian culture. Although recent scholarship has suggested that the division of labor between the sexes within Indian societies was rather equitable, mid-nineteenth-century Americans accepted a vision of Native American

Copyright by Western History Association. Reprinted by permission. The article first appeared as "Educating Indian Girls at Nonreservation Boarding Schools, 1878–1920" by Robert A. Trennert, *Western Historical Quarterly,* Vol. 13 (July 1982): 271–290.

women as slaves toiling endlessly for their selfish, slovenly husbands and fathers in an atmosphere of immorality, degradation, and lust. Any cursory glance at contemporary literature provides striking evidence of this belief. Joel D. Steele, for example, in his 1876 history of the American nation described Indian society in the following terms: "The Indian was a barbarian. . . . Labor he considered degrading, and fit only for women. His squaw, therefore, built his wigwam, cut his wood, and carried his burdens when he journeyed. While he hunted or fished, she cleared the land . . . and dressed skins."

Government officials and humanitarian reformers shared Steele's opinion. Secretary of the Interior Carl Schurz, a noted reformer, stated in 1881 that "the Indian woman has so far been only a beast of burden. The girl, when arrived at maturity, was disposed of like an article of trade. The Indian wife was treated by her husband alternately with animal fondness, and with the cruel brutality of the slave driver." Neither Steele nor Schurz was unique in his day; both expressed the general opinion of American society. From this perspective, if women were to be incorporated into American society, their sexual role and social standing stood in need of change.

The movement to educate Indian girls reflected new trends in women's education. Radical changes in the economic and social life of late-nineteenth-century America set up a movement away from the traditional academy education of young women. Economic opportunity created by the industrial revolution combined with the decline of the family as a significant economic unit produced a demand for vocational preparation for women. The new school discipline of "domestic science," a modern homemaking technique, developed as a means to bring stability and scientific management to the American family and provide skills to the increasing number of women entering the work force. In the years following the Civil War, increased emphasis was placed on domestic and vocational education as schools incorporated the new discipline into their curriculum. Similar emphasis appeared in government planning for the education of Indian women as a means of their forced acculturation. However, educators skirted the question of whether native women should be trained for industry or homemaking.

During the 1870s, with the tribes being confined to reservations, the government intensified its efforts to provide education for Indian youth of both sexes. The establishment of the industrial training schools at the end of the decade accelerated the commitment to educate Indian women. These schools got their start in 1878 when Captain Richard Henry Pratt, in charge of a group of Indian prisoners at Fort Marion, Florida, persuaded the government to educate eighteen of the younger male inmates at Hampton Normal Institute, an all-black school in Virginia, run by General Samuel C. Armstrong. Within six months Pratt and Armstrong were pleased enough with the results of their experiment to request more students. Both men strongly believed that girls should be added to the program, and Armstrong even went so far as to stipulate that Hampton would take more Indian students only on condition that half be women. At first Indian Commissioner Ezra A. Hayt rejected the proposal, primarily because he questioned the morality of allowing Indian women to mix with black men, but Armstrong's argument that "without educated women there is no civilization" finally prevailed.

Thus, when Pratt journeyed west in the fall of 1878 to recruit more students, he fully expected half to be women.

Pratt was permitted to enlist fifty Indian students on his trip up the Missouri River. Mrs. Pratt went along to aid with the enlistment of girls. Although they found very little problem in recruiting a group of boys, they had numerous difficulties locating girls. At Fort Berthold, for instance, the Indians objected to having their young women taken away from home. Pratt interpreted this objection in terms of his own ethnocentric beliefs, maintaining that Indian tribes made their "squaws" do all the work. "They are too valuable in the capacity of drudge during the years they should be at school to be spared to go," he reported. Ultimately it required the help of local missionaries to secure four female students. Even then there were unexpected problems. As Pratt noted, "One of the girls [age ten] was especially bright and there was a general desire to save her from the degradation of her Indian surroundings. The mother [age twenty-six] said that education and civilization would make her child look upon her as a savage, and that unless she could go with her child and learn too, the child could not come." Pratt included both mother and daughter. Not all the missionaries and government agents, however, shared Pratt's enthusiasm. At Cheyenne River and other agencies a number of officials echoed the sentiments of Commissioner Hayt regarding the morality of admitting girls to a black school, and they succeeded in blocking recruitment. As a result, only nine girls were sent to Hampton.

Although the educational experiences of the first Indian girls to attend Hampton have not been well documented, a few things are evident. The girls were kept under strict supervision and were separated from the boys except during times of classroom instruction. In addition, the girls were kept apart from black pupils. Most of the academic work was focused on learning the English language, and the girls also received instruction in household skills. The small number of girls, of course, made it difficult to implement a general educational plan. Moreover, considerable opposition remained to educating Indian women at Hampton. Many prominent reformers expected confrontations, or even worse, love affairs, between black and red. Others expressed concern that Indian students in an all-black setting would not receive sufficient incentive and demanded they have the benefit of direct contact with white citizens.

Captain Pratt himself wanted to separate the Indians and blacks, and despite the fact that no racial trouble surfaced at Hampton, he pressured the government to create a school solely for Indians. Indian contact with blacks did not fit in with his plans for native education, and he reminded Secretary Schurz that Indians could become useful citizens only "through living among our people." The government consented, and in the summer of 1879 Pratt was authorized to open a school at Carlisle Barracks, Pennsylvania, "provided both boys and girls are educated in said school." Thus, while Hampton continued to develop its own Indian program, it was soon accompanied by Carlisle and other all-Indian schools.

Under the guidance of General Armstrong at Hampton and Captain Pratt at Carlisle, a program for Indian women developed over a period of several years. Although these men differed on the question of racial mixing, they agreed on what Indian girls should be learning. By 1880, with fifty-seven Indian girls at

Carlisle and about twenty at Hampton, the outlines of the program began to emerge. As rapidly as possible the girls were placed in a system that put maximum emphasis on domestic chores. Academic learning clearly played a subordinate role. The girls spent no more than half a day in the classroom and devoted the rest of their time to domestic work. At Carlisle the first arrivals were instructed in "the manufacture and mending of garments, the use of the sewing machine, laundry work, cooking, and the routine of household duties pertaining to their sex."

Discipline went hand in hand with work experience. Both Pratt and Armstrong possessed military backgrounds and insisted that girls be taught strict obedience. General Armstrong believed that obedience was completely foreign to the native mind and that discipline was a corollary to civilization. Girls, he thought, were more unmanageable than boys because of their "inherited spirit of independence." To instill the necessary discipline, the entire school routine was organized in martial fashion, and every facet of student life followed a strict timetable. Students who violated the rules were punished, sometimes by corporal means, but more commonly by ridicule. Although this discipline was perhaps no more severe than that in many non-Indian schools of the day, it contrasted dramatically with tribal educational patterns that often mixed learning with play. Thus, when Armstrong offered assurances that children accepted "the penalty gratefully as part of his [her] education in the good road," it might be viewed with a bit of skepticism.

Another integral part of the program centered on the idea of placing girls among white families to learn by association. The "outing" system, as it was soon called, began almost as quickly as the schools received students. Through this system Pratt expected to take Indian girls directly from their traditional homes and in three years make them acceptable for placement in public schools and private homes. By 1881 both Carlisle and Hampton were placing girls in white homes, most of which were located in rural Pennsylvania or New England. Here the girls were expected to become independent, secure a working knowledge of the English language, and acquire useful domestic skills. Students were usually sent to a family on an individual basis, although in a few cases several young women were placed in the same home. Emily Bowen, an outing program sponsor in Woodstock, Connecticut, reveals something of white motives for participation in the service. Miss Bowen, a former teacher, heard of Pratt's school in 1880 and became convinced that God had called upon her to "lift up the lowly." Hesitating to endure the dangers of the frontier, she volunteered instead to take eight Indian girls into her home to "educate them to return and be a blessing to their people." Bowen proposed to teach the girls "practical things, such as housework, sewing, and all that is necessary to make home comfortable and pleasant." In this manner, she hoped, the girls under her charge would take the "true missionary spirit" with them on their return to their people. . . .

The size of the girls' program increased dramatically during the 1880s. The government was so taken with the apparent success of Carlisle and Hampton that it began to open similar schools in the West. As the industrial schools expanded, however, the women's program became institutionalized, causing a substantial deviation from the original concept. One reason for this change involved economic factors. The Indian schools, which for decades received $167 a year per student, suffered a chronic lack of funds; thus, to remain self-sufficient, they found themselves relying upon student labor whenever possible. Because they already believed in the educational value of manual labor, it was not a large step for school officials to begin relying upon student labor to keep the schools operating. By the mid-1880s, with hundreds of women attending the industrial schools, student labor had assumed a significant role in school operations. Thus, girls, originally expected to receive a useful education, found themselves becoming more important as an economic factor in the survival of the schools.

The girls' work program that developed at Hampton is typical of the increasing reliance on Indian labor. By 1883 the women's training section was divided into such departments as sewing, housekeeping, and laundry, each in the charge of a white matron or a black graduate. The forty-one girls assigned to the sewing department made the school's bedding, wardrobe, and curtains. At Winona Lodge, the dormitory for Indian girls that also supported the housework division, the matron described the work routine as follows: "All of the Indian girls, from eight to twenty-four years old, make their own clothes, wash and iron them, care for their rooms, and a great many of them take care of the teachers' rooms. Besides this they have extra work, such as sweeping, dusting, and scrubbing the corridors, stairs, hall, sewing-room, chapel, and cleaning other parts of the building." In addition, a large group of Indian girls worked in the school laundry doing the institution's wash.

Conditions were even more rigorous at western schools where a lack of labor put additional demands on female students. At Genoa, Nebraska, the superintendent reported that the few girls enrolled in that school were kept busy doing housework. With the exception of the laundry, which was detailed to the boys, girls were responsible for the sewing and repair of garments, including their own clothes, the small boys' wear, underwear for the large boys, and table linen. The kitchen, dining room, and dormitories were also maintained by women students. Similar circumstances prevailed at Albuquerque, where Superintendent P. F. Burke complained of having to use boys for domestic chores. He was much relieved when enough girls enrolled to allow "the making of the beds, sweeping, and cleaning both the boys' and girls' sleeping apartments." Because of inadequate facilities there were no girls enrolled when the Phoenix school opened in 1891; but as soon as a permanent building was constructed, Superintendent Wellington Rich requested twenty girls "to take the places now filled by boys in the several domestic departments of the school." Such uses of student labor were justified as a method of preparing girls for the duties of home life.

Some employees of the Indian Service recognized that assembly line chores alone were not guaranteed to accomplish the goals of the program. Josephine Mayo, the girls' matron at Genoa, reported in 1886 that the work program was too "wholesale" to produce effective housewives. "Making a dozen beds and cleaning a dormitory does not teach them to make a room attractive and homelike," she remarked. Nor did cooking large quantities of a single item "supply a family with a pleasant and healthy variety of food, nicely cooked." The matron believed that Indian girls needed to be taught in circumstances similar to those they were expected to occupy. She therefore suggested that small cottages be utilized in which girls could be instructed in the care of younger students and perform all the duties of a housewife. Although Mayo expressed a perceptive concern for the inherent problems of the system, her remarks had little impact on federal school officials. In the meantime, schools were expected to run effectively, and women continued to perform much of the required labor.

Not all the girls' programs, of course, were as routine or chore oriented as the ones cited above. Several of the larger institutions made sincere efforts to train young Indian women as efficient householders. Girls were taught to care for children, to set tables, prepare meals, and make domestic repairs. After 1896 Haskell Institute in Kansas provided women with basic commercial skills in stenography, typing, and bookkeeping. Nursing, too, received attention at some schools. A number of teachers, though conventional in their views of Indian women's role, succeeded in relaxing the rigid school atmosphere. Teachers at Hampton, for instance, regularly invited small groups of girls to their rooms for informal discussions. Here girls, freed from the restraints of the classroom, could express their feelings and receive some personal encouragement. Many institutions permitted their girls to have a dress "with at least some imitation of prevailing style" and urged them to take pride in their appearance.

The industrial schools reached their peak between 1890 and 1910. During this period as many as twenty-five nonreservation schools were in operation. The number of Indian women enrolled may have reached three thousand per annum during this period and females composed between 40 and 50 percent of the student body of most schools. The large number of young women can be attributed to several factors: girls were easier to recruit, they presented fewer disciplinary problems and could be more readily placed in the "outing system," and after 1892 they could be sent to school without parental consent.

Women's education also became more efficient and standardized during the 1890s. This was due in large part to the activities of Thomas J. Morgan, who served as Indian commissioner from 1889 to 1893. Morgan advocated the education of Indian women as an important part of the acculturation process, believing that properly run schools could remove girls from the "degradation" of camp life and place them on a level with "their more favored white sisters." The commissioner hoped to accomplish this feat by completely systematizing the government's educational program. "So far as possible," he urged, "there should be a uniform course of study, similar methods of instruction, the same textbooks, and a carefully organized and well understood system of industrial training." His suggestions received considerable support, and by 1890, when he issued his "Rules for Indian Schools," the standardization of the Indian schools had begun. Morgan, like Pratt before him, fully expected his concept of education to rapidly produce American citizens. The results were not what the commissioner expected. While standardization proved more efficient, it also exacerbated some of the problems of the women's educational program.

Under the direction of Morgan and his successors, the Indian schools of the era became monuments to regimentation from which there was no escape. This development is obvious in the increasing emphasis on military organization. By the mid-nineties most girls were fully incorporated into the soldierly routine. As one superintendent noted, all students were organized into companies on the first day of school. Like the boys, the girls wore uniforms and were led by student officers who followed army drill regulations. Every aspect of student life was regulated. Anna Moore, a Pima girl attending the Phoenix Indian School, remembered life in the girls' battalion as one of marching "to a military tune" and having to drill at five in the morning. Most school officials were united in their praise of military organization. Regimentation served to develop a work ethic; it broke the students' sense of "Indian time" and ordered their life. The merits of military organization, drill, and routine in connection with discipline were explained by one official who stated that "it teaches patriotism, obedience, courage, courtesy, promptness, and constancy."

Domestic science continued to dominate the women's program. Academic preparation for women never received much emphasis by industrial school administrators despite Morgan's promise that "literary" training would occupy half the students' time. By 1900 the commissioner's office was reminding school officials that "higher education in the sense ordinarily used has no place in the curriculum of Indian schools." With so little emphasis on academics, it is not surprising that few pupils ever completed the eight-year course required for graduation. Most students spent their time learning to read and write English, make simple calculations, and perhaps pick up a bit of history. One reason for the lack of emphasis on academics was that by 1900 many school administrators had come to feel that Indians were incapable of learning more. One school superintendent did not consider his "literary" graduates capable of accomplishing much in white society, while another educator described the natives as a "child race." Little wonder, then, that the schools continued to emphasize domestic work as the most useful kind of training for women.

In 1901 the Bureau of Indian Affairs published a *Course of Study for the Indian Schools.* This document makes obvious the heavy reliance placed on domestic science and the extent to which the work program had become institutionalized. There are several notable features of the course of study. It makes clear that the Indian Bureau had lowered its expectations for Indian women. It also illustrates the scientific emphasis that had been added to domestic training over the years. Considerable attention was given to protection from disease and unsanitary conditions, nutrition, and an orderly approach to household duties. The section on housekeeping, for example, emphasized the necessity of learning by doing. Indian girls were to be assured that because their grandmothers did things in a certain way was no reason for them to do the same. Sound management of financial affairs was also stressed. Notably absent, however, was any commitment to book learning. In its place were slogans like "Learn the dignity of serving, rather than being served." . . .

Another popular program was the "industrial" cottage. These originated in 1883 at Hampton when the school enrolled several married Indian couples to serve as examples for the students. The couples were quartered in small frame houses while learning to maintain attractive and happy homes. Although the married students did not long remain at Hampton, school officials began to use the cottages as model homes where squads of Indian girls might practice living in white-style homes. By 1900 similar cottages were in use at western schools. The industrial cottage at Phoenix, for example, operated a "well-regulated household" run by nine girls under a matron's supervision. The "family" (with no males present) cleaned and decorated the cottage, did the regular routine of cooking, washing, and sewing, and tended to the poultry and livestock in an effort "to train them to the practical and social enjoyment of the higher life of a real home."

The outing system also continued to be an integral part of the girls' program. As time went on, however, and the system was adopted at western locations, the original purposes of the outings faded. Initially designed as a vehicle for accultur- ation, the program at many locations became a means of providing servants to white householders. At Phoenix, for example, female pupils formed a pool of cheap labor available to perform domestic services for local families. From the opening of the school in 1891, demands for student labor always exceeded the pool's capacity. One superintendent estimated that he could easily put two hun- dred girls to work. Moreover, not all employers were interested in the welfare of the student. As the Phoenix superintendent stated in 1894, "The hiring of Indian youth is not looked upon by the people of this valley from a philanthropic stand- point. It is simply a matter of business." In theory, school authorities could return pupils to school at any time it appeared they were not receiving educational bene- fits; but as one newspaper reported, "What a howl would go up from residents of this valley if the superintendent would exercise this authority." . . .

An important factor in understanding the women's program at the industrial schools is the reaction of the girls themselves. This presents some problems, how- ever, since most school girls left no record of their experiences. Moreover, many of the observations that have survived were published in closely controlled school magazines that omitted any unfavorable remarks. Only a few reliable reminis- cences have been produced, and even these are not very informative. Despite such limitations, however, several points are evident. The reaction of Indian girls to their education varied greatly. Some came willingly and with the approval of their parents. Once enrolled in school, many of these individuals took a keen in- terest in their education, accepted discipline as good for them, and worked hard to learn the ways of white society. An undetermined number may have come to school to escape intolerable conditions at home. Some evidence suggests that schools offered safe havens from overbearing parents who threatened to harm their children. For other girls the decision to attend a nonreservation school was made at considerable emotional expense, requiring a break with conservative par- ents, relatives, and tribesmen. In a few cases young women even lost their oppor- tunity to marry men of their own tribe as they became dedicated to an outside lifestyle.

Many girls disliked school and longed to return home. The reasons are not hard to find. The hard work, discipline, and punishment were often oppressive. One Hopi girl recalled having to get down on her knees each Saturday and scrub the floor of the huge dining hall. "A patch of floor was scrubbed, then rinsed and wiped, and another section was attacked. The work was slow and hard on the knees," she remembered. Pima school girl Moore experienced similar conditions working in the dining hall at Phoenix: "My little helpers and I hadn't even reached our teen-aged years yet, and this work seemed so hard! If we were not finished when the 8:00 A.M. whistle sounded, the dining room matron would go around strapping us while we were still on our hands and knees. . . . We just dreaded the sore bottoms." In a number of instances, teachers and matrons added to the trauma by their dictatorial and unsympathetic attitudes. A few girls ran away from school. Those who were caught received humiliating punishment. Runaway girls might be put to work in the school yard cutting grass with scissors or doing some other meaningless drudgery. In a few cases recalcitrant young ladies had their hair cut off. Such experiences left many girls bitter and anxious to return to the old way of life.

The experiences of Indian girls when they returned home after years of schooling illustrate some of the problems in evaluating the success of the government program. For many years school officials reported great success for returned students. Accounts in articles and official documents maintained that numbers of girls had returned home, married, and established good homes. The Indian Bureau itself made occasional surveys purporting to show that returned students were doing well, keeping neat homes, and speaking English. These accounts contained a certain amount of truth. Some graduates adapted their education to the reservation environment and succeeded quite well. Many of these success stories were well publicized. There is considerable evidence to suggest, however, that the reports were overly optimistic and that most returning girls encountered problems.

A disturbingly large number of girls returned to traditional life upon returning home. The reasons are rather obvious. As early as 1882, the principal of Hampton's Indian Division reported that "there is absolutely no position of dignity to which an Indian girl after three years' training can look forward to with any reasonable confidence." Although conditions improved somewhat as time went on, work opportunities remained minimal. Girls were usually trained in only one specialty. As the superintendent of the Albuquerque school reported, girls usually returned home with no relevant skills. Some spent their entire school stay working in a laundry or sewing room, and though they became expert in one field, they had nothing to help them on the reservation. As the Meriam report later noted, some Indian girls spent so much time in school laundries that the institutions were in violation of state child labor laws. In another instance, one teacher noted how girls were taught to cook on gas ranges, while back on the reservation they had only campfires.

Moreover, the girls' educational achievements were not always appreciated at home. Elizabeth White tells the story of returning to her Hopi home an accomplished cook only to find that her family shunned the cakes and pies she made in place of traditional food, called her "as foolish as a white woman," and treated her as an outcast. As she later lamented, her school-taught domestic skills were inappropriate for the Hopis. Girls who refused to wear traditional dress at home were treated in like manner. Under these circumstances, many chose to cast off their learning, to marry, and return to traditional living. Those young women who dedicated themselves to living in the white man's style often found that reservations were intolerable, and unable to live in the manner to which they had become accustomed, they preferred to return to the cities. Once there the former students tended to become maids, although an undetermined number ended up as prostitutes and dance hall girls.

Employment opportunities for educated Indian women also pointed up some of the difficulties with the industrial schools. In fairness, it must be admitted that trained women probably had more opportunities than their male counterparts. Most of those who chose to work could do so; however, all positions were at the most menial level. If a girl elected to live within the white community, her employment choices were severely limited. About the only job available was that of domestic service, a carryover from the outing system. In this regard, the Indian schools did operate as employment agencies, finding jobs for their former students with local families. Despite the fact that some Indian women may have later come to feel that their work, despite its demeaning nature, provided some benefits for use in later life, many of their jobs proved unbearably hard. After being verbally abused, one former student wrote that "I never had any Lady say things like that to me." Another reported on her job, "I had been working so hard ever since I came here cleaning house and lots of ironing. I just got through ironing now I'm very tired my feet get so tired standing all morning." Unfortunately, few respectable jobs beyond domestic labor were available. Occasionally girls were trained as nurses or secretaries only to discover that they could find no work in Anglo society.

The largest employer of Indian girls proved to be the Indian Bureau. Many former students were able to secure positions at Indian agencies and schools; in fact, had it not been for the employment of former students by the paternalistic Indian service, few would have found any use for their training. The nature of the government positions available to Indian girls is revealing. Almost all jobs were menial in nature; only a few Indian girls were able to become teachers, and none worked as administrators. They were, rather, hired as laundresses, cooks, seamstresses, nurses' helpers, and assistant matrons. Often these employees received little more than room, board, and government rations, and even those who managed to be hired as teachers and nurses received less pay than their white counterparts. Summing up the situation in 1905, Indian commissioner Francis E. Leupp noted that whites clearly outnumbered Indian workers in such areas as supervisors, clerks, teachers, matrons, and housekeepers, but the gap narrowed with seamstresses and laundresses. Indian girls could find work, but only in the artificial environment of Indian agencies and schools located at remote western points and protected by a paternalistic government. Here they continued to perform tasks of domestic nature without promise of advancement. Nor were they assimilated into the dominant society as had been the original intent of their education. . . .

The education program for Indian women at the industrial schools from 1878 to 1920 failed to attain its goals. Although there were a few individual success stories, on the whole Indian girls did not assimilate into American society as the result of their education. School authorities, unfortunately, made little attempt to accommodate the native society and tried instead to force Indian girls into the mold of an alien society. As a result, the federal schools did not train Indian women for the conditions they faced upon returning home. Instead, women were trained for an imaginary situation that administrators of Indian education believed must exist under the American system. Taking native girls from their home environment, where learning was informally conducted by parents and relatives, and placing them in a foreign, structured atmosphere accomplished more confusion and hostility than acculturation. . . .

Dispossession and the White Earth Anishinaabeg, 1889–1920

MELISSA L. MEYER

In 1867, U.S. policy makers and Anishinaabe leaders conceived of the White Earth Reservation as a place where the Indians might "conquer poverty by [their] own exertions." Eight hundred thousand acres that included prime farmland in the Red River Valley, valuable stands of pine timber, and lakes and streams supporting seasonal resources on which the Anishinaabeg had relied for generations seemed well suited to meet both subsistence needs and an evolving market orientation. Assimilationists had always thought of Indian reservations as temporary phases in a process whereby American Indians would meld completely into American culture. In this bountiful, isolated area, federal officials hoped that the Anishinaabeg would be able to learn the ways of market farming and successfully "assimilate."

The major focus of U.S. Indian policy in the late nineteenth century was on privatizing reservation resources. Eastern "humanitarians" directed the trend in a belief that inculcating the value of private property and market behavior would hasten Indians' assimilation. Since simply setting a good example for them had failed to achieve desired results, more forceful measures were apparently necessary. They buttressed their faith in the almost magical ability of private property to transform Indians' collective values with a restriction protecting allotted land from sale or alienation for twenty-five years. Western politicians anticipated an economic windfall from "surplus" acres that would be opened after lands had been allotted and lent their support. These sentiments dovetailed to produce the General Allotment Act of 1887. Reservations nationwide were to be divided into privately held parcels of up to 160 acres each, with any remaining acreage opened to "settlement."

Before the act could be fully implemented, however, the direction of national policy shifted in two ways. First, because some Indians at White Earth and elsewhere clearly understood market values, it seemed patently "un-American" to regulate how they managed their allotted property. Policy makers thus sought some mechanism to free "competent" Indians from restrictions. Second, guarded optimism that most Indians could learn to function in a capitalistic economy gave way to pessimistic certainty that their inherent "backwardness" would prevent them from doing so. Social engineers reasoned that Indians had failed to assimilate because they were incapable of it. Policies promoting this end were therefore pointless. With these attitudes in place, the stage was set for local Euro-American

From Melissa L. Meyer, " 'We Can Not Get a Living As We Used To': Dispossession and the White Earth Anishinaabeg, 1889–1920," *American Historical Review,* vol. 96, no. 2 (April 1991), pp. 368–394. Reprinted by permission of the American Historical Association and the author.

businesses and speculators to gain access to recently privatized resources. After the turn of the twentieth century, the vision of reservations populated by Indian landowners swiftly fell victim to the drive for the increasingly efficient incorporation of reservation resources into the rapidly maturing U.S. industrial capitalist economy. Allotment policy has been blamed for the rapid loss of reservation land in the early twentieth century, but, in truth, it never had a chance to succeed.

Before Euro-Americans rushed to acquire White Earth's resources, the Indians had successfully adapted to the reservation. It served as a haven of sorts and allowed immigrants to escape economic limitations of the forest and lake country of north-central Minnesota and to perpetuate their lifeways. Had they retained the land base, the White Earth Anishinaabeg might have continued to adapt. But "assimilation" went awry for the Anishinaabeg, and corporate gain won out. Dispossession undercut a generations-old pattern of Anishinaabe self-support and flexible adaptation that had persisted into the twentieth century. Under the guise of "assimilation," U.S. government policies brought them increased poverty, disease, and diaspora. . . .

The White Earth case illustrates the general processes of incorporation and marginalization in the late nineteenth and early twentieth centuries and the effects of dispossession. This essay will focus on the economic strategies evolved by members of two ethnic groups among the White Earth Anishinaabeg as they adapted to opportunities offered by the environment and the expanding market economy. It will examine how legislation formulated by Euro-American political and economic interests eliminated the Indian-owned land base. Finally, it will explore the impact of dispossession on reservation residents.

The White Earth Reservation lies in a transition area where prairie meets forest. Several glacially created features influenced subsequent environmental developments. The western part of the reservation is on the flat plain of Glacial Lake Agassiz. Streams flow west to the Red River, draining the area rather than producing extensive bogs. The Red River then flows northward to Hudson Bay. The Alexandria Moraine and Wadena drumlin area account for many small lakes and hills in the central and southeastern parts of White Earth.

When White Earth was set aside, short grasses that interspersed with pockets of oak savanna covered the Red River Valley. At the prairie's edge, a narrow band of deciduous forest formed an almost complete barrier between the coniferous forest and the prairie. Oak predominated among diverse tree species in the hardwood forest, while only occasional stands of white birch interrupted the uniformity of coniferous forests. . . .

U.S. policy makers and Anishinaabe leaders had the foresight to make White Earth Reservation straddle the prairie-forest transition area. Forest and lake country to the east supplied marketable timber and subsistence resources, while fertile prairie land to the west in the Red River Valley offered opportunities to engage in agriculture. Clearly, White Earth did not resemble arid western reservations where harsh environments consigned assimilationists' plans to failure from the start. In this sense, White Earth's ecosystem sustained diversity, allowing residents the freedom to choose among a number of options for making a living. In terms of incorporation or world-systems theory, it lay in a "region of refuge" or "marginal-peripheral area." Geographic isolation had retarded extensive market development and Euro-American settlement. More favorable marketing arrangements awaited better transportation links. If the government's assimilation programs had a chance to succeed anywhere, White Earth should have become a showcase.

Anishinaabe immigrants from across northern Minnesota came to the White Earth Reservation. Formerly, bands of between 500 and 1,000 bilaterally related kin had congregated on the shores of Red Lake, Leech Lake, Gull Lake, Mille Lacs, Cass Lake, Lake Winnibagoshish, Nett Lake, White Oak Point, Otter Tail Lake, and at Grand Portage and Fond de Lac on Lake Superior. They still recognized patrilineal totemic clan affiliations, but clans had increased in number since European contact. Political authority was egalitarian and consensual despite the emergence of "hereditary" leaders like Wahbahnahquod (White Cloud) and Bugonaygeshig (Hole-in-the-Day). Although many were satisfied to remain where they were, others turned their eyes to the White Earth Reservation with thoughts of beginning anew.

Members of another social group also found White Earth to be an attractive prospect. When French and English fur traders had married Indian women, they drew on the strength of kin ties to secure trading alliances. Now they and their métis offspring came to form a society of their own, relying on their bilingual, bicultural skills to mediate between conservative Indians and the larger American society. Men of mixed descent such as Clement Beaulieu and John Fairbanks adapted easily to reservation life. They operated the Beaulieu-Fairbanks trading posts as a monopoly and supplied all Anishinaabe reservations from their base of operations in Crow Wing at the confluence of the Crow Wing and Mississippi rivers. Franco- and Anglo-Anishinaabe men were attuned to national legislation and understood the workings of the market. When the Treaty of 1867 provided for removal to White Earth of the Gull Lake Band, situated adjacent to Crow Wing, they knew that they would also have to move in order to perpetuate the symbiotic relationship.

Thousands of people of mixed descent were displaced by the decline of the fur trade in northern Minnesota and Wisconsin. Many who could claim an affiliation with one of the Anishinaabe bands joined the exodus to White Earth. The Pembina band, composed of métis from the Turtle Mountain Reservation in North Dakota, was relocated to White Earth in 1876. These enterprising individuals brought their market orientation with them in search of a renewed economic niche.

Immigrant Anishinaabe bands tended to maintain band ties, social roles, leadership roles, and economic and cultural patterns after removal to White Earth. Bands with a more conservative orientation to adaptation settled to the east, where they could perpetuate the seasonal harvesting round. Those who cared to try their hand at market agriculture settled to the west, where fertile prairie land beckoned. White Earth Village, in the midsection of the reservation, was a focal point for entrepreneurs and cultural brokers of mixed descent. Chain migrations characterized the removals as groups of immigrants joined friends and family at various sites. In this fashion, settlement patterns perpetuated band affiliations. Not all band members settled together, however; a degree of dispersal fostered commingling of those who shared a similar economic and cultural orientation.

In the past, the Anishinaabeg had engaged in a regular round of harvesting activities that amply supplied their needs. Game (especially white-tailed deer), fish, wild rice, maple sugar, berries, and garden produce such as pumpkins, corn, and potatoes formed the basis of the Anishinaabe subsistence economy. Each resource matured at a certain time of year, prompting frequent movement and a division of labor by gender and age. Men and women, young and old, all performed important functions in the seasonal round. At each stage of the annual cycle of provisioning activities, families followed one another to group camps "twenty or perhaps fifty miles and back," no one wishing to be left behind. Participation in the Euro-American trade in furs altered the contours of the cycle but did not destroy it.

Throughout a typical year, division of labor meant that women spent more time cultivating and gathering floral resources, and their provisioning activities kept them near lake environments. More of their gender-specific activities, especially child care and meal preparation, occurred on a daily basis. Women generally preferred working in large groups, although they frequently cooperated in households as well. Except for ricing and sugaring, for which they had primary responsibility, women remained near villages more often than men. Men's gender-specific activities related more to faunal resources and carried them farther away from central camps for longer periods of time. Although men of a household had occasion to work together, they did so less frequently than women and usually in smaller groups. Primary responsibility for trade and diplomacy had rested with men before the establishment of reservations, and this pattern continued at White Earth. Men also provided for community defense, although military dangers posed less of a threat during the reservation era.

Even if most tasks were associated with one specific gender, divisions were not hard and fast. Participation in the fur trade had altered gender roles, intensifying women's responsibility for hide processing and men's involvement in trapping and trade. Reservation life stimulated a further reordering that undermined hunting and diplomacy as central activities. Nonetheless, egalitarian relationships characterized Anishinaabe society, and individuals might deviate from the general pattern without fear of recrimination.

Although movement from one place to another characterized the seasonal pattern, predictable timing and locations gave the annual cycle great stability. The diverse resource base provided a hedge against failure of any single resource. Taken as a whole, this subsistence strategy particularly suited Minnesota's north country. It had endured through generations, and the Anishinaabeg had adapted it to the Euro-American fur trade. Conservative White Earth residents continued in this pattern, integrating new elements they found beneficial. The richness of White Earth's previously uninhabited prairie-forest transition area allowed the seasonal round to persist into the twentieth century. This circuit of provisioning activities gave the Anishinaabeg a degree of control over their situation. As long as they had recourse to the seasonal round, they could sustain themselves when farming failed. It served as the cornerstone of autonomy for the White Earth Anishinaabeg in the late nineteenth and early twentieth centuries. . . .

U.S. policy makers had always viewed agriculture as the key to Indians' assimilation. Social engineers envisioned Indians becoming self-sufficient tillers of the soil who would produce a specialized cash crop to sell on the market. Most of those who took advantage of the land-allotment benefits of the 1889 Nelson Act and created prosperous farming enterprises lived in the western part of the reservation. As early as 1885, the agent at White Earth observed that fully 75 percent of the produce was "raised by mixed blood Indians." By 1901, Agent Simon Michelet found that "the Indians . . . [had] not taken advantage of this fine farming land"; instead, those of mixed descent predominated among Indian farmers.

The amount of land cultivated by Indians steadily increased from 1887 to 1894 with principal cash crops being wheat, oats, potatoes, and later, flax, all of which rose in value. Between 1894 and 1904, the number of acres under cultivation declined and leveled off, even though the number of Indians reported to be living on and cultivating their allotments increased from a mere 52 in 1889 to 730 by 1904. Despite the downward trend, federal authorities pointed to these figures as evidence of the U.S. government's successful assimilation programs. While land was abundant and under Indian control, those who could supply sufficient operating capital might succeed in market agriculture at White Earth. Only a limited sector of the White Earth population made this type of commitment. . . .

Besides agriculture, agency administration also provided opportunities for wage labor and generated a significant cash flow. Ambitious programs undertaken by the government created a limited number of positions for manual laborers. Teamsters hauled agency and school supplies from neighboring towns. Upkeep and maintenance of agency buildings, building and repair of roads and bridges, and sawing lumber and constructing homes for immigrant Indians all involved periodic wage labor. Schools employed women as cooks, seamstresses, and laundresses. When less skilled Indians were hired to work at the agency, they filled these sorts of manual labor positions. The Indian Office usually recruited physicians and most schoolteachers from outside the reservation. However, educated Indians sometimes held skilled positions as interpreters, schoolteachers, police, government farmers, as well as temporary posts generated by the removal and allotment processes. The agent appointed individuals to agency positions, and favoritism played an important role in hiring. Often, Indians of mixed descent who spoke English, understood the agency bureaucracy and institutions of U.S. society, and lived near the agency filled these positions. . . .

White Earth's resource base adequately supported the diverse population only as long as it remained under Indian control. The Treaty of 1867 stipulated that the White Earth "Chippewa" should retain all lands within reservation boundaries. The Nelson Act of 1889 altered this arrangement by mandating allotment of the land base in severalty. It also established a twenty-five-year trust period to protect allotted lands from alienation until Indian owners learned to manage their property. Neither the language of the Treaty of 1867 nor the Nelson Act anticipated the wholesale loss of resources that was to follow in the early twentieth century. . . .

Allotment of the White Earth land base under the Nelson Act did not transform the Anishinaabeg into market farmers as policy makers had hoped. In fact, in the short run, it made very little difference at all. Most Indians continued to pursue familiar strategies for making a living. National policies often fell far short of the rhetorical ideal when implemented at the local level. For instance, federal officials did not achieve an equitable division of White Earth's land base. Forested land was of greater immediate value than prairie or swampland, but all types were ultimately allotted, leaving no surplus land to be sold. The allotting process deviated from Nelson Act specifications in two ways: Congress unilaterally reduced the size of agricultural allotments to 80 instead of 160 acres, and the deadline for removal was postponed several times to allow the U.S. Chippewa Commission more time to persuade reluctant Indians to move to White Earth. Since pine lands located to the east were ineligible for allotment at first, many Indians could not locate their allotments close to their places of residence. Some reported never even having seen their allotments. Under the Steenerson Act (1904), each allottee was to receive an additional 80 acres. If the remaining unallotted land base proved inadequate, it was to be divided *pro rata.* Only if the pine lands were allotted could these provisions be met.

At the same time, a rider attached to the Indian Appropriations Act (1904) authorized the Anishinaabeg to sell timber on their allotments. Together, Minnesota congressmen Moses E. Clapp and Halvor Steenerson succeeded in securing the passage of legislation that would allow lumber companies access to White Earth's timber. Local agent Michelet conspired with lumber companies and assigned the most valuable pine land to individuals who had already agreed to sell the timber; tract books show that many names had been penciled in early and then traced over on allotment day. To complicate matters further, Michelet failed to divide the pine lands *pro rata,* and several hundred Indians received no additional land at all. Those Indians who appreciated land as real estate had surveyed available parcels in advance and camped in line overnight to secure the best of them. Some, like Duane Porter, who arrived at the scheduled allotment time, "got disgusted . . . and . . . went away," realizing that "the Indian was not going to get fair play; the mixed bloods were going to get all the pine." The inequity that occurred that day was never remedied and contributed to smoldering resentment between White Earth residents that subsequent developments were soon to fan into factional flames. That Indian people should learn capitalistic acquisitiveness was deemed more important than equity and accurate implementation of established laws.

Whereas a heady optimism regarding Indian capabilities had fueled national allotment legislation, policy makers pared down their expectations after the turn of the century. Rhetoric about unlimited Indian potential metamorphosed into a pragmatic approach born of a pessimistic appraisal of what Indians had actually achieved—or failed to achieve. In keeping with this shift in attitude, policy makers reasoned that Indians who had embraced capitalistic values should be free to manage their affairs as they saw fit. As a corollary, resources of "noncompetents" were to be utilized by American economic interests and assimilation programs were to be scaled back. The incorporation of allotted resources into the U.S. economy had begun.

To achieve these goals, the Burke Act (1906) proposed to terminate the trust period and issue fee patents whenever the secretary of the interior was convinced of an allottee's "competence." In less than a year, however, rampant abuses forced the commissioner of Indian Affairs to acknowledge that liberal interpretation of the term "competence" increasingly meant that allotted lands were fair game for those interested in gaining access to reservation land.

On June 21, 1906, less than two months after passage of the Burke Act, Minnesota congressmen Clapp and Steenerson again succeeded in passing legislation through Congress that removed restrictions on allotted lands at White Earth even more effectively than the Burke Act, with none of the accompanying humanitarian rationale. The "Clapp Rider" removed all restrictions governing "sale, incumbrance, or taxation" of allotted land within the White Earth Reservation held by *"adult mixed bloods."* State politicians foresaw no delays in implementing the law. Recently privatized resources of the White Earth Anishinaabeg were to be incorporated into the market economy with smooth efficiency, enriching local businesses and speculators and avoiding time-consuming "competency commissions" associated with the Burke Act. The true intent of the push to remove restrictions on allotments was stripped bare in Minnesota.

Owners of land and lumber companies had anticipated passage of the Clapp Rider and hired influential brokers of mixed descent, Gus Beaulieu, Ben Fairbanks, and John Carl most prominently, to arrange mortgages with individual allottees. To skirt the lack of an established mechanism to determine blood status, they had allottees sign affidavits attesting to their blood status well before Congress passed the rider. These affidavits carried no force of law, but they illustrate how business interests stood ready to pounce on allotted lands at White Earth. Typically, $25 sufficed to "reserve" an allotment until the law took effect, when the allottee was to receive the remainder of the mortgage due. Mortgages were to accrue 10 percent interest, to be collected in advance, and run for ten years. Lenders then foreclosed on property in short order. During the first three weeks the Clapp Rider was in effect, Becker County alone recorded over 250 mortgages.

Charges of fraud and corruption followed closely on the heels of the Clapp Rider of 1906. Complaints from mixed bloods and full bloods alike were rife: intermediaries misrepresented contents of documents, understated the value of land parcels, and distributed liquor to cloud allottees' judgment; promises of large amounts of money never materialized; and land offices recorded sales from ineligible minors and deceased allottees. Not only had unsuspecting Indians bound themselves to unfair agreements but land dealers and lumber companies also took advantage of their naïveté by giving them worthless substitutes for cash. Tin tokens and due bills marked "non-negotiable" could be redeemed for goods only at specific stores at substantial discounts. Those with an interest in Indian lands at White Earth conceived of every imaginable scheme to take unfair advantage of the recently "freed" allottees.

Prior to land fraud, political ties at White Earth were based on band affiliations. Inequity in the allotment process, however, combined with key leaders of mixed descent positioned to serve the needs of land and lumber companies, prompted a fundamental political realignment among conservative band leaders. Calling themselves full bloods, conservative band leaders like Mille Lacs leader Wahweyeacumig, Leech Lake leader Ahbowegeshig, and Mississippi leader Mayzhucegeshig united to oppose the ethics of those they called mixed bloods, who favored policies that rescinded the U.S. government's trust responsibility and opened allotted resources to exploitation by business interests. The political "bosses" were not above using wagons to round up eligible voters or manipulating parliamentary rules of procedure to their advantage. Isabel Schneider, an interpreter, complained, "Resolutions . . . were railroaded through . . . and the Indians were bewildered in the council." Gus Beaulieu and Ben Fairbanks were paid by major lumber company owners "to keep prominent Indians who might stir up trouble quiet." And Ben Fairbanks used his influence as a merchant "to coerce Indians . . . to . . . support [the bosses'] designs" by withholding credit if they failed to lend political support. It is no wonder that Ahbowegeshig and other leaders of the "Full Blood Faction" charged, "The half-breeds have been . . . taking pine lands and . . . have prevented the full blood Indians from taking them. . . . They have become wealthy on account of these allotments."

Regional towns and economic interests were big winners in the scramble to acquire White Earth's resources. Reservation railway stations—Callaway, Ogema, Waubun, Mahnomen, and Bejou—as well as nearby off-reservation towns—Detroit Lakes, Park Rapids, Frazee, Bagley, Ada, Fosston, and Crookston—all supported activities of local banks and land companies that speculated in White Earth's resources. Local businessmen had lobbied for the new legislation and welcomed the economic benefit promised by removal of restrictions on allotted resources. A number of powerful local businessmen formed interlocking directorates, serving on the boards of directors of several companies in which all shared an interest. Several, such as Fred Sanders, H. A. Krostue, and M. J. Kolb, were repeatedly implicated in fraudulent land transfers. In the three years following the Clapp Rider of 1906, purchases by three local number companies, Nichols-Chisolm, Park Rapids, and Wild Rice, neatly divided the eastern wooded townships according to watersheds. Each company gained easy access to its mills, and their cooperation stifled competition, reducing prices paid for timber to below market value. Some had argued that Indians would profit from selling their land, but the real beneficiaries proved to be local American business interests.

Reports of fraud and exploitation, however, instantly threw land titles into confusion. And judicial solutions did not come easily. How much white blood made an individual a "mixed blood"? Who among the White Earth Anishinaabeg were of mixed descent and thereby eligible to sell their allotments? Resolving these thorny issues occupied those involved for the next fourteen years. After lower courts considered a number of different fractional delineations, the Supreme Court decided in 1914 on the broadest possible construction of the law. A "mixed blood" was an Indian with any admixture of white blood, no matter how small. Lifeways, cultural affiliation, or "competence" to manage one's affairs would have no bearing whatsoever. When genealogical inquiry failed to produce evidence that would stand up in court, policy makers turned to two anthropologists who claimed to have devised physiological tests that would settle the matter once and for all. Dr. Ales Hrdlicka of the Smithsonian Institution and Dr. Albert E. Jenks of the University of Minnesota journeyed to the White Earth Reservation to pull hair samples and examine teeth structure and skin tone. They did not confine their comments to general physical characteristics but ultimately testified in court on the blood status of specific individuals. Information derived in this fashion directly contributed to formulation of the "1920 Blood Roll," which legally codified individual Indians' blood status and finally allowed clouded land titles to clear. Outright racism received the imprimatur of academia in the course of legalizing the largest number of land transfers.

Although national policy makers emphasized "competence" to justify termination of the trust relationship, this criterion did not prevail at the White Earth Reservation. Federal officials tried to interpret blood status literally at White Earth, with absurd consequences. The vast majority of White Earth Anishinaabeg (92 percent) were declared "mixed bloods" and were free to sell or be victimized.

For those mixed bloods who managed to retain their allotments despite all odds, tax forfeiture proceedings loomed as a threat. Policy makers had interpreted the Clapp Rider of 1906 to mean that White Earth mixed bloods had been declared citizens and were liable to support public services. Newly organized Mahnomen County, with a high proportion of tax-exempt trust land, had to provide many services on a limited tax base. Mahnomen and Becker County officials levied high taxes and increasingly seized remaining allotted lands in tax forfeiture proceedings, which came to be the primary method of obtaining allotted lands as the twentieth century wore on. Some suspected that land speculators were behind this latest means for acquiring allotted lands. By 1920, almost all allotted reservation land lay effectively beyond Indian control.

Long-term consequences of the assault on allotments were not readily apparent as long as titles remained clouded. New owners were unable to use land as collateral to borrow money and feared to "develop" land lest they lose their improvements when titles cleared. Ironically, the land fraud that occurred between 1906 and 1915 helped perpetuate the subsistence-oriented way of life by delaying actual legal conveyance of land parcels. Such uncertainty allowed Indians to continue to reside where they pleased and piece together their livelihoods in their accustomed manner. But the veil of confusion was only temporary; circumstances of life were soon to change for all White Earth Anishinaabeg.

Historians have held allotment policy responsible for the loss of millions of acres of reservation land nationwide. Certainly, the privatization of reservation lands that had previously been held collectively set the stage for their eventual loss. But, at White Earth, allotment policy was never implemented as intended. Barely five years after all allotments had been made, new legislation sidestepped the twenty-five-year protective restrictions and allowed most land to be sold. In the short run, the culprit was not the Nelson Act (the Minnesota equivalent of the Dawes Act), but the Clapp Riders (the Minnesota equivalent of the Burke Act). Events at White Earth occurred within the basic contours of national policy, but special legislation accomplished the same end even faster and more effectively. The failure of politicians and business interests to foresee the difficulties they would encounter because of their use of the term "mixed blood" gave the White Earth Anishinaabeg a bit of breathing space, but not for long.

Just as privatized land at White Earth came under attack, federal administrators denied the Anishinaabeg benefits that revenue might have brought them. The Chippewa in Minnesota Fund, held in trust by the government, served as depository for proceeds from the sale of ceded land and timber, which were slated to underwrite assimilation programs for all reservations in northern Minnesota.

Anishinaabe tribal funds financed schools, hospitals, social welfare programs, agricultural instruction, and rudimentary economic foundations on the reservations. Facile generalizations about Anishinaabe dependence on welfare gratuities mask the fact that they essentially financed their own "assimilation." Despite this, U.S. policy effectively barred them from exercising any control over these funds.

In its role as guardian, the U.S. administration mismanaged the Chippewa in Minnesota Fund almost from its inception. U.S. Chippewa Commissioners illegally spent thousands of dollars traveling through northern Minnesota to persuade Anishinaabe people to move to White Earth. Mismanagement in the care and sale of timber cost the Anishinaabeg millions. Legislation repeatedly commuted homestead fees for settlers on ceded lands, denying revenue to tribal funds. Policy makers ignored objections of tribal leaders and slated money from the Chippewa in Minnesota Fund to cover some costs associated with ditching and draining wetlands on ceded lands north of Red Lake. Compensation for confiscated land—swampland claimed by the State of Minnesota and timberland taken for the Chippewa National Forest—was not forthcoming for twenty to forty years. Under these circumstances, the Chippewa in Minnesota Fund often showed a deficit, and the government was forced to forward money to carry out its assimilation programs. The Anishinaabeg were often in debt to the government because of actions taken by federal officials in their role as guardian of Indians' resources.

Policies governing timber cutting at White Earth denied the Anishinaabeg a chance to capitalize on their timber resources. Most policies mandated that timber simply be sold off in bulk. The Indians were fortunate if they received wages for their labor. Even the Morris Act (1902), which instituted the "bank scale" to correct abuses in the appraisal and auction of timber, made no provision for manufacturing wood products as at La Pointe and Menominee, Wisconsin. Had U.S. administrators managed Anishinaabe timber according to principles of conservation and sustained yield, principles not unheard of at the time, the Indians might have derived greater benefit from this revenue-generating resource. Assimilationists mistakenly intended that the Anishinaabeg should become yeoman farmers, not successful lumbermen.

Long-term observers knew that the assault on White Earth's resources on all fronts portended dire consequences for the Anishinaabeg. With keen foresight, agents predicted that dispossession would "condemn [them] to destitution and beggary." . . .

Increasingly, Euro-American landownership restricted Indians' access to seasonal resources. They soon began to encounter fences and "No Trespassing" signs along lake fronts and in areas where they had once moved freely. Always the backbone of the subsistence economy, the seasonal round lost its capacity to sustain the growing population. Disruption of the seasonal round fostered poverty and disease at White Earth as available resources decreased, causing a related decline in nutrition and the overall health of the population. Under such conditions, diseases took a deadly toll.

White Earth gained national notoriety for its peoples' abysmal diseased condition. Pulmonary infections were a plague, with tuberculosis, the "coughing sickness," being the primary killer. Thousands suffered from trachoma, or "sore eyes," which produced blindness in its advanced stages. Responding to the emergency, federal officials converted boarding schools to hospitals and sanatoriums to house the diseased. Doctors ordered a special diet to bolster the strength of children in eastern schools who had grown weak from hunger and infection. Inspectors conducted house-to-house examinations of Indians to gauge the extent of sickness more accurately and determine what effect home life had on Indians' health. Especially in the eastern forests and cut-over areas, they found deplorable conditions. The loss of land had uprooted people and forced congested living arrangements, which fostered the spread of communicable diseases. In one home, diseased inhabitants just sat and stared. Inspector Warren Moorehead pointed out, "We cannot expect the Indians to be healthy if they continue to live as they do." Land alienation and environmental degradation had worked to sap the life-blood of the people.

Health inspectors were convinced that poor sanitation and ignorance of proper nutrition and methods to combat disease could only be remedied through educational measures. Physicians began a series of evening lectures to acquaint Indians with the nature of diseases that afflicted them, how to treat them, and how to stop their spread. Field matrons began regular rounds in which they instructed Indian women on hygiene, nutrition, child care, and housekeeping. Health officials embarked on a "Save the Babies" campaign in response to the alarmingly high infant mortality rate. By 1920, their efforts had met with some success, but conditions that spawned diseases worsened, and poor health continued to plague Indians at White Earth.

Alienation of land and resources eliminated the Indian-owned land base necessary to their autonomy and future development. By 1915, only 300 Indians were farming, and the acreage cultivated had decreased from a high of 9,125 in 1894 to a mere 2,400. Agriculture no longer seemed to be a worthwhile option for most. Indian Office inspector H. S. Taylor recommended abandoning the White Earth experiment because it was "impossible to have a constructive policy upon this reservation. . . . [T]he land is gone." As available resources and economic opportunities constricted, White Earth residents increasingly opted to leave the reservation in order to make their ways in nearby towns and cities. In 1915, Taylor bemoaned the failure of the White Earth experiment, noting, "Its people . . . are now scattered to the four winds with no interest in it." White Earth enrollees received their annuity checks "in hundreds of post offices—from Canada to the Gulf of Mexico and from the Pacific to the Atlantic." Rather than a gradual process in which population outstripped resources, this change was an abrupt one in which loss of resources made it increasingly difficult for people to adapt and remain on the reservation.

The rhetoric of assimilation and allotment policies emphasized independent, small-scale market agriculture as the salvation of Indian people nationwide. The policies failed to achieve this goal. Government policy also encouraged Indians to adopt American cultural patterns. Some inclined in that direction on their own; others used the means supplied in ways that policy makers had not intended. The

Anishinaabeg adapted to changing circumstances more through their own efforts than through congressional largess or coercion. The expansion of market capitalism was a more powerful agent of change than U.S. assimilation policy.

Minnesota congressmen and business interests did succeed in incorporating White Earth's material resources into the U.S. economy, despite their mistakes in phrasing legislation. In the process, they also made it impossible for the majority of White Earth Indians to remain a land-based people. The policies put in place brought about dispossession of both ethnic groups, whether individuals understood the workings of the market or not. Policy makers' chief accomplishment was the "assimilation" or marginalization of the Anishinaabe people (and many other native groups) at the bottom of the American social and economic hierarchy, where thousands of transoceanic immigrants and southern freed slaves had begun. Only elite entrepreneurs of mixed descent fared better. A few profited directly from the dispossesion process. Others had the knowledge and wherewithal to migrate, adapt, and eventually prosper. But most Indians entered the mainstream of American society from a landless and impoverished position.

Before dispossession, the Anishinaabeg had been able to adapt and do well at White Earth. Its geographic isolation and ecological diversity sustained multiple strategies for making a living. The expanding market economy, which offered opportunities for selling seasonal produce, wage labor, and commercial farming, also eased the adjustment immigrants faced. Cultural brokers mediated between conservative Anishinaabeg and agents of American society, activities characteristic of "regions of refuge." In 1907, the White Earth Anishinaabeg were well on their way toward establishing an economic and social structure that would allow residents with different ways of life to remain on the reservation and prosper.

Dispossession destroyed the White Earth experiment, and a larger view of economic conditions may help explain why dispossession occurred when it did. The rising price of wheat in the late nineteenth and early twentieth centuries served as the initial incentive to develop rich agricultural lands in the Red River Valley. Completion of the Minneapolis, St. Paul, and Sault Ste. Marie Railroad through the western tier of townships at White Earth linked the area to Twin Cities markets, reduced transportation costs, and provided a focus for Euro-American settlement. Lumbermen stood waiting at White Earth's eastern borders, having worked their way through forests from the east. White Earth's "undeveloped" resources looked attractive to these local business interests. Nonetheless, the protective restrictions of the Nelson Act were designed to combat precisely this type of threat.

These conditions arose just as support for the agrarian ideal on reservations was waning. Blaming the failure of programmatic directives to assimilate Indians on the Indians themselves and their inherent "backwardness," policy makers lost interest in social engineering, lifted restrictions from "competent" Indians, and tolerated an accelerated alienation of allotted reservation lands. At White Earth, a powerful clique of state politicians and local business interests accomplished dispossession even more effectively by enabling "mixed bloods" to sell their land and dispensing with any philanthropic justification. Allotment had occurred first on the reservations where resources were most valuable. Removal of protective restrictions probably followed a similar pattern. In the case of White Earth, events did not follow the national pattern, they helped to set it.

If left alone to live out their lives under the Nelson Act, the White Earth Anishinaabeg might have continued to adapt. Instead, Euro-American farmers replaced Indian landowners and White Earth timber went to fuel a burst of settlement further west. Through resource extraction, White Earth passed from being a "region of refuge" to a "dependent" or "full-blown periphery." Its people were marginalized. Most scattered, hoping to find niches elsewhere as day laborers.

The particular constellation of circumstances reviewed above explains the timing of dispossession for the White Earth Anishinaabeg. Their experiences, however, parallel those of other dispossessed Indian groups. In most cases, population growth elsewhere generated demands for resources that had little to do with the needs or desires of indigenous people. The related processes of incorporation of resources and marginalization of people account for similarities in the White Earth experience, dispossession of eastern coastal tribes in the late seventeenth century, removal of southeastern tribes in the 1830s, and the exploitation of Indian coal, oil, natural gas, and uranium after World War II. Potential illustrations are legion. Echoing those who came before her, Lucy Thompson, born at White Earth in 1906, reflected on changes that had occurred during her lifetime. "Now the white people claim everything that the Indians used to use in the olden days. . . . If they could do it, they'd take everything. . . . The only thing they'd leave us is our appetites."

◈ *F U R T H E R   R E A D I N G*

Devon Irene Abbott, "Medicine for the Rosebuds: Health Care at the Cherokee Female Seminary, 1876–1909," *American Indian Culture and Research Journal* 12 (1988), 59–71

Norman Bender, *New Hope for the Indians: The Grant Peace Policy and the Navajos in the 1870s* (1989)

Todd Benson, "The Consequences of Reservation Life: Native Californians on the Round Valley Reservation, 1871–1884," *Pacific Historical Review* 60 (1991), 221–244

Leonard Carlson, *Indians, Bureaucrats and the Land: The Dawes Act and the Decline of Indian Farming* (1981)

Michael C. Coleman, "Problematic Panacea: Presbyterian Missionaries and the Allotment of Indian Lands in the Late 19th Century," *Pacific Historical Review* 54 (August 1985), 143–159

John R. Finger, "Conscription, Citizenship, and Civilization: World War I and the Eastern Band of Cherokee," *North Carolina Historical Review* 63 (July 1986), 283–308

Robin Fisher, *Contact and Conflict: Indian-European Relations in British Columbia, 1774–1890* (1977)

Henry E. Fritz, "The Last Hurrah of Christian Humanitarian Indian Reform: The Board of Indian Commissioners, 1909–1918," *Western Historical Quarterly* 16 (April 1985), 147–162

William T. Hagan, *Indian Police and Judges: Experiments in Acculturation and Control* (1966)

———, *The Indian Rights Association: The Herbert Welsh Years, 1882–1904* (1988)

Alexandra Harmon, "When Is an Indian Not an Indian? 'Friends of the Indian' and the Problems of Indian Identity," *Journal of Ethnic Studies* 18 (1990), 95–123

Markku Henriksson, *The Indian on Capitol Hill: Indian Legislation and the United States Congress, 1862–1907* (1988)

Ted C. Hinckley, "We Are More Truly Heathen Than the Natives: John G. Brady and the Assimilation of Alaska's Tlingit Indians," *Western Historical Quarterly* 11 (1980), 37–55

Herbert T. Hoover, "The Sioux Agreement of 1889 and Its Aftermath," *South Dakota History* 19 (Spring 1989), 56–94

Frederick E. Hoxie, *A Final Promise: The Campaign to Assimilate the Indians, 1880–1920* (1984)

Helen Hunt Jackson, *A Century of Dishonor* (1886)

Robert Keller, *American Protestantism and United States Indian Policy, 1869–82* (1983)

Barbara Leibhardt, "Allotment Policy in an Incongruous Legal System: The Yakima Indian Nation as a Case Study, 1887–1934," *Agricultural History* 65 (Fall 1991), 78–103

Janet A. McDonnell, *Dispossession of the Indian Estate, 1887–1934* (1991)

———, "Land Policy on the Omaha Reservation: Competency Commissions and Fee Patents," *Nebraska History* 63 (1982), 399–412

Valerie Sherer Mathes, *Helen Hunt Jackson and Her Indian Reform Legacy* (1990)

Clyde Milner, *With Good Intentions: Quaker Work Among the Pawnees, Otos, and Omahas in the 1870s* (1982)

——— and Floyd A. O'Neil, eds., *Churchmen and the Western Indians, 1820–1920* (1985)

Craig Miner, *The Corporation and the Indian: Tribal Sovereignty and Industrial Civilization in Indian Territory, 1865–1907* (1976)

L. G. Moses, "Wild West Shows, Reformers, and the Image of the American Indian, 1887–1914," *South Dakota History* 14 (Fall 1984), 193–221

Francis Paul Prucha, ed., *Americanizing the American Indian: Writings by the "Friends of the Indian," 1880–1900* (1973)

———, *American Indian Policy in Crisis: Christian Reformers and the Indian, 1865–1900* (1976)

———, *The Churches and the Indian Schools, 1888–1912* (1991)

Charles Roberts, "The Cushman Indian Trade School and World War I," *American Indian Quarterly* 11 (Summer 1987), 221–240

David D. Smits, "Squaw Men, Half Breeds, and Amalgamators: Late 19th Century Anglo-American Attitudes Toward Indian-White Race-Mixing," *American Indian Culture and Research Journal* 15 (1991), 29–61

Paul Stuart, *Indian Office: Growth and Development of an American Institution, 1865–1900* (1979)

Robert A. Trennert, "Fairs, Expositions, and the Changing Image of Southwestern Indians, 1876–1904," *New Mexico Historical Review* 62 (April 1987), 127–150

———, *The Phoenix Indian School: Forced Assimilation in Arizona, 1891–1935* (1988)

Wilcomb Washburn, *The Assault on Indian Tribalism: The General Allotment Law (Dawes Act) of 1887* (1975)

New Communities,
New Identities,
1890–1920

*In the early twentieth century, the conventional wisdom held that Indians soon
would disappear. Statues such as James Fraser's* The End of the Trail *and photo-
graphs such as Edward Curtis's* The Vanishing Race *spoke to the prevailing belief
that Indians would be assimilated fully into American life.*

*Yet despite all the problems Indian individuals and communities confronted, na-
tive peoples did not disappear.*

*True, the final decades of the nineteenth century and first decades of the twenti-
eth used to be portrayed in bleakest terms, emphasizing exclusively the negative effects of the Dawes Act, of Indian boarding schools, and of other dimensions of federal
policy. But this interpretation arguably presents only part of the picture, so Chapter
11 appropriately explores* other *aspects of a complex era. The chapter emphasizes Indian responses and adaptations to this new age. On the national level, these included
new organizations such as the Native American Church and the Society of American
Indians.*

*On individual reservations, people faced compelling questions and made far-
reaching decisions about the nature of leadership within the community, the kind of
economy that could be developed, and the focus of the education their children
should receive. Land allotment eventually ran its course as criticism swelled in the
1920s about the predominant goals of federal policy. Largely unnoticed, individuals
and groups had weathered the trying period and in many instances had built foundations for further revitalization in the years to come.*

◈ D O C U M E N T S

The ghost-dance movement, inspired by the Paiute Indian prophet Wovoka, may be
seen as either the end of an era or the beginning of a new day. Wovoka's teachings were
interpreted in varying ways by the tribal emissaries who made the pilgrimage to western

Nevada to see him. In Lakota country the practice of the ghost dance, or—perhaps more properly—spirit dance, triggered overreaction by federal agents and ultimately led to the tragic confrontation between the Sioux and the Seventh Cavalry at Wounded Knee, South Dakota, late in 1890. Ethnologist James Mooney interviewed Wovoka and studied the involvement of different native communities in the ghost dance. The first document is taken from Mooney's classic work on this subject and features an opening Arapaho ghost-dance song.

One of the key questions confronting all Westerners in the early twentieth century concerned the allocation of a precious resource: water. Indians won an important legal victory in 1908, when the U.S. Supreme Court, in *Winters* v. *United States,* decided that the Gros Ventres and Assiniboines of the Fort Belknap reservation in northern Montana were entitled to sufficient water to allow them to carve out a living on their land. This decision, excerpted in the second selection, became known as the Winters Doctrine, and it embodied the concept that Indians had particular rights to water, regardless of their record of prior use of it. Another intriguing legal issue of the time revolved around the ritual use of the hallucinogenic drug peyote by Indians who had become members of the Native American Church. At congressional committee hearings in 1918, reprinted in the third document, James Mooney and his associate Francis La Flesche (Omaha) testified in favor of the stimulant's use by church members. To the present day, the consumption of this substance remains controversial, but the Native American Church is now the most important national Indian religious organization of this century. The Society of American Indians was a relatively short-lived association. During its existence from 1911 to the mid-1920s, however, it foreshadowed later organizations, among them the National Congress of American Indians. Then as now, Indians argued about what the federal government's role in Indian life should be, whether the Bureau of Indian Affairs (BIA) should be abolished, and whether individual Indians should seek employment within the bureau. The debate reprinted in the fourth selection occurred during one of the society's annual meetings. Sherman Coolidge, Carlos Montezuma, and other participants figured prominently in the organization.

In the fifth document, Anna Moore Shaw's reminiscences about her years at the Phoenix Indian School and her life during this era show how despite adversity, Indians were doing their best to adjust and to persevere in difficult times. Going to boarding schools could mean loneliness, cultural deprivation, and inadequate vocational training. However, as Shaw points out, the schools also could be places where people fell in love, played sports, and took their first steps toward independent adulthood. When nearly all the old boarding schools such as Phoenix eventually closed in the 1970s and 1980s, many Indian alumni protested.

The Ghost Dance Doctrine and an Opening Arapaho Ghost Dance Song, 1890

You must not fight. Do no harm to anyone. Do right always—Wovoka.

The great underlying principle of the Ghost-dance doctrine is that the time will come when the whole Indian race, living and dead, will be reunited upon a regenerated earth, to live a life of aboriginal happiness, forever free from death, disease, and misery. On this foundation each tribe has built a structure from its own mythology, and each apostle and believer has filled in the details according to his own mental capacity or ideas of happiness, with such additions as come to him from the trance. Some changes, also, have undoubtedly resulted from the transmission of the doctrine through the imperfect medium of the sign language. The differences of interpretation are precisely such as we find in Christianity, with its hundreds of sects and innumerable shades of individual opinion. The white race, being alien and secondary and hardly real, has no part in this scheme of aboriginal regeneration, and will be left behind with the other things of earth that have served their temporary purpose, or else will cease entirely to exist.

All this is to be brought about by an overruling spiritual power that needs no assistance from human creatures; and though certain medicine-men were disposed to anticipate the Indian millennium by preaching resistance to the further encroachments of the whites, such teachings form no part of the true doctrine, and it was only where chronic dissatisfaction was aggravated by recent grievances, as among the Sioux, that the movement assumed a hostile expression. On the contrary, all believers were exhorted to make themselves worthy of the predicted happiness by discarding all things warlike and practicing honesty, peace, and good will, not only among themselves, but also toward the whites, so long as they were together. Some apostles have even thought that all race distinctions are to be obliterated, and that the whites are to participate with the Indians in the coming felicity; but it seems unquestionable that this is equally contrary to the doctrine as originally preached.

Different dates have been assigned at various times for the fulfillment of the prophecy. Whatever the year, it has generally been held, for very natural reasons, that the regeneration of the earth and the renewal of all life would occur in the early spring. In some cases July, and particularly the 4th of July, was the expected time. This, it may be noted, was about the season when the great annual ceremony of the sun dance formerly took place among the prairie tribes. The messiah himself has set several dates from time to time, as one prediction after another failed to materialize, and in his message to the Cheyenne and Arapaho, in August, 1891, he leaves the whole matter an open question. The date universally recognized among all the tribes immediately prior to the Sioux outbreak was the spring of 1891. As springtime came and passed, and summer grew and waned, and autumn faded again into winter without the realization of their hopes and longings, the doctrine gradually assumed its present form—that some time in the unknown future the Indian will be united with his friends who have gone before, to be forever supremely happy, and that this happiness may be anticipated in dreams, if not actually hastened in reality, by earnest and frequent attendance on the sacred dance. . . .

[Mooney visited Indian communities who had embraced the Ghost Dance, including the Southern Arapahos of Oklahoma. One of the Arapaho songs follows:]

Songs of the Arapaho

Opening Song—Eyehe′! Nä′nisa′na

> Eyehe′! nä′nisa′na,
> Eyehe′! nä′nisa′na,
> Hi′nä chä′sä′ äticha′nï′na He′eye′!
> Hi′nä chä′sä′ äticha′nï′na He′eye′!
> Na′häni nä′nithä′tuhŭ′na He′eye′!

Na'hăni nä'nithä'tuhŭ'na He'eye'!
Bi'taa'wu' da'naa'băna'wa He'eye'!
Bi'taa'wu' da'naa'băna'wa He'eye'!

Translation

O, my children! O, my children!
Here is another of your pipes—*He'eye'!*
Here is another of your pipes—*He'eye'!*
Look! thus I shouted—*He'eye'!*
Look! thus I shouted—*He'eye'!*
When I moved the earth—*He'eye'!*
When I moved the earth—*He'eye'!*

This opening song of the Arapaho Ghost dance originated among the northern Arapaho in Wyoming and was brought down to the southern branch of the tribe by the first apostles of the new religion. By "another pipe" is probably meant the newer revelation of the messiah, the pipe being an important feature of all sacred ceremonies, and all their previous religious tradition having centered about the sĕicha or flat pipe, to be described hereafter. The pipe, however, was not commonly carried in the dance, as was the case among the Sioux. In this song, as in many others of the Ghost dance, the father or messiah, *Hesûna'nin,* is supposed to be addressing "my children," nänisa'na. The tune is particularly soft and pleasing, and the song remains a standard favorite. The second reference is to the new earth which is supposed to be already moving rapidly forward to slide over and take the place of this old and worn-out creation. . . .

The U.S. Supreme Court Supports Indian Water Rights: *Winters* v. *United States,* 1908

. . . The case, as we view it, turns on the agreement of May, 1888, resulting in the creation of Fort Belknap Reservation. In the construction of this agreement there are certain elements to be considered that are prominent and significant. The reservation was a part of a very much larger tract which the Indians had the right to occupy and use and which was adequate for the habits and wants of a nomadic and uncivilized people. It was the policy of the Government, it was the desire of the Indians, to change those habits and to become a pastoral and civilized people. If they should become such the original tract was too extensive, but a smaller tract would be inadequate without a change of conditions. The lands were arid and, without irrigation, were practically valueless. And yet, it is contended, the means of irrigation were deliberately given up by the Indians and deliberately accepted by the Government. The lands ceded were, it is true, also arid; and some argument may be urged, and is urged, that with their cession there was the cession of the waters, without which they would be valueless, and "civilized communities could not be established thereon." And this, it is further contended, the Indians knew, and yet made no reservation of the waters. We realize that there is a conflict of implications, but that which makes for the retention of the waters is of greater force than that which makes for their cession. The Indians had command of the lands and the waters—command of all their beneficial use, whether kept for hunting, "and grazing roving herds of stock," or turned to agriculture and the arts of civilization. Did they give up all this? Did they reduce the area of their occupation and give up the waters which made it valuable or adequate? And, even regarding the allegation of the answer as true, that there are springs and streams on the reservation flowing about 2,900 inches of water, the inquiries are pertinent. If it were possible to believe affirmative answers, we might also believe that the Indians were awed by the power of the Government or deceived by its negotiators. Neither view is possible. The Government is asserting the rights of the Indians. But extremes need not be taken into account. By a rule of interpretation of agreements and treaties with the Indians, ambiguities occurring will be resolved from the standpoint of the Indians. And the rule should certainly be applied to determine between two inferences, one of which would support the purpose of the agreement and the other impair or defeat it. On account of their relations to the Government, it cannot be supposed that the Indians were alert to exclude by formal words every inference which might militate against or defeat the declared purpose of themselves and the Government, even if it could be supposed that they had the intelligence to foresee the "double sense" which might some time be urged against them.

Another contention of appellants is that if it be conceded that there was a reservation of the waters of Milk River by the agreement of 1888, yet the reservation was repealed by the admission of Montana into the Union, February 22, 1889, c. 180, 25 Stat. 676, "upon an equal footing with the original States." The language of counsel is that "any reservation in the agreement with the Indians, expressed or implied, whereby the waters of Milk River were not to be subject of appropriation by the citizens and inhabitants of said State, was repealed by the act of admission." But to establish the repeal counsel rely substantially upon the same argument that they advance against the intention of the agreement to reserve the waters. The power of the Government to reserve the waters and exempt them from appropriation under the state laws is not denied, and could not be. *The United States* v. *The Rio Grande Ditch & Irrigation Co.,* 174 U.S. 690, 702; *United States* v. *Winans,* 198 U.S. 371. That the Government did reserve them we have decided, and for a use which would be necessarily continued through years. This was done May 1, 1888, and it would be extreme to believe that within a year Congress destroyed the reservation and took from the Indians the consideration of their grant, leaving them a barren waste—took from them the means of continuing their old habits, yet did not leave them the power to change to new ones.

Appellants' argument upon the incidental repeal of the agreement by the admission of Montana into the Union and the power over the waters of Milk River which the State thereby acquired to dispose of them under its laws, is elaborate and able, but our construction of the agreement and its effect make it unnecessary to answer the argument in detail. For the same reason we have not discussed the doctrine of riparian rights urged by the Government.*

---

*Under the doctrine of riparian rights, the owner of land bordering on a water source such as a river could divert as much water as he or she deemed necessary, regardless of the seniority of property ownership or the needs of others. This system comes from the English tradition and was used in the eastern United States but generally not in the West.

James Mooney and Francis La Flesche (Omaha)
Testify About Peyote, 1918

Statement of James Mooney, Bureau of American Ethnology

. . . I am one of the ethnologists of the Bureau of American Ethnology. In April I shall have filled 30 years' service in the bureau. A large part of my time has been spent with the tribes of the southern plains, who are particularly devoted to the use of peyote and to the religious rite connected with it. For the most part of the first six years I lived as a member of a family among the Kiowa. In connection with a general study of Indian things among the Kiowa, Commanche, Apache, and associated tribes, and the Cheyenne and Arapaho of Oklahoma, and several other tribes in the other parts of the country, I have made peyote a subject of investigation. It is so closely connected with Indian life in southwestern Oklahoma that any ethnologist going there to make investigations soon has it brought to his attention, and I became interested in it.

I have gotten from the Indians their own story of the origin of the religious rite. You must understand that the use of this plant is not an ordinary habit, but that it is confined almost entirely and strictly to the religious ceremony, excepting that it is frequently employed also for medicinal purposes. It is not an ordinary habit in the way that a man takes to drinking whisky. There are certain times, seasons, and reasons for the use of it. I studied the ceremony first as a scientific observer with the Kiowa, and later in pursuance of a special investigation of the subject. I visited a number of other tribes, among them the Mexican tribes of the Sierra Madre, and as far south as the City of Mexico. Besides what I know of the use of peyote among the tribes in western Oklahoma, I know in a less degree of its use among the tribes in Mexico, from whom those to the north have obtained their knowledge of it.

Peyote grows in the arid regions. It is a small cactus, with a root very much the size and shape of an ordinary long radish, and the part used by the Indians is the sliced-off top, dried to about the size of an ordinary silver quarter or half dollar. Here it is [showing a small boxful of samples of peyote]. It has different Indian names in the various tribes. It is sometimes incorrectly called mescal by the whites, but its proper name is peyote, the Spanish derivative from the old Aztec name. This is the dried top, the blossoming top of a small cactus which grows close to the ground. It grows abundantly about Laredo, Tex., where it is gathered and dried by Mexicans and shipped to the dealers in Oklahoma, who supply the Indian trade. Our tribes, in the ceremonial, eat it dry, using only the top, because, on account of the white blossom center surrounded by circles of white points, they regard it as the vegetable representative of the sun. In Mexico, not only do the Indian tribes use it in the ceremonial way, but the common people of Mexico use it also in a medicinal way. Both Indians and Mexicans slice up the whole plant and make a decoction of it in warm or cold water. What I have here I got myself from a trader, who handled it in western Oklahoma, but I have also dug up the growing plant about Laredo. . . .

The Kiowa story of its origin is that some young men went on the warpath to the south and were gone for so long a time that their friends at home became afraid they would never return. There was a young woman, a sister of one of the war party, who went out to a hill beyond the camp every evening to watch for her brother, in accordance with the Indian custom, and pray for his return. Finally one evening she fell asleep, and a spirit came to her in a dream, telling her that there was something growing out of the ground under her head which would bring her to her brother if used according to the instructions which the spirit then gave her. When she awoke she looked and found a number of peyotes growing. These she gathered and took back to camp, and then, calling the old men together, told them how to prepare everything for the ceremony as the spirit had directed. They set up the tepee and performed the rite, and in the peyote vision they saw where the young man was lying alone, wounded and starving, and they sent out a party and brought him home to his sister. There is always a religious myth in connection with the peyote rite. That is the story the Kiowa tell of how the rite came to them. Each tribe has its own story. The Kiowa say the Comanche knew of it before they did. Both tribes say they got it from the Mescalero and Tonkawa, and probably these got it originally from the tribes near the Mexican border, who in turn had it from the tribes in old Mexico. It has come to the more northern tribes only recently.

You have seen the plant as used. As to their method of using it ceremonially, they have a regular time—Saturday night running into Sunday morning. They set up a special tepee and go into it, after preliminary preparation, about 9 o'clock in the evening. I have seen as many as 30 or more sitting in a circle inside the tepee. They have a drum and rattle. After an opening prayer the leader hands out four peyotes to each man. Each man chews up one peyote after another, making a pellet of each, which he swallows. Then the singing begins. There is one regular song at the beginning, one song at midnight, one song at daylight, and one song at the close, with other songs all through the night as each man chooses, two men singing at a time, one accompanying with the drum and the other with the rattle. The singing goes on through the night, the drum and rattle passing around the circle repeatedly. There is a fire in the center of the tepee and a large sacred peyote on a little crescent-shaped mound behind it. While two men keep up the songs the others are praying or remain in a state of contemplation, looking toward the fire and the sacred peyote. The ceremony goes on in this way through the night. At intervals the worshippers eat more peyotes. At midnight there is a sort of baptismal ceremony, when one man brings in a bucket of spring water, over which the leader recites a prayer, after which they sprinkle themselves with it. The leader stands up while making the prayer. They pray for all their friends and for themselves, as we pray. If there are any sick in camp, they may be brought in to be prayed for. If a woman is sick, her husband brings her in, and they pray for her and give her some of the peyote to eat. She does not prepare it herself, but it is prepared for her. With the peyote-using tribes that I know best, the Kiowa and Comanche, the only occasion on which a woman is present is when she is there to be prayed for as a member of the family of the man who accompanies her. . . .

In the morning the daylight song is the signal for the woman to prepare the food. Later on there is the closing song, and with that the ceremony ends. Special food has been prepared for the worshippers and is eaten before they leave the tepee. Then they go out and sit about chatting with their friends until dinner.

Dinner is a family affair. The Indian families come in wagons for miles around as to a church gathering, just as in some parts of the country white families come in wagons to a country church, where they attend a service and afterwards have dinner in the open and sit around until the evening, when they go home. There is nothing at all bad about it, nothing whatever in the nature of an orgy. I can say from experience that there is nothing that the most rigid white man could consider immorality. There is no physical or mental prostration. There is no collapse after it is over. There is only the natural effect of having been up all night with some stimulant that would prevent their feeling fatigue. . . .

Statement of Mr. Francis La Flesche, Bureau of American Ethnology, An Omaha Indian

. . . I have had numerous opportunities to study the use of the peyote among the Poncas, the Osage, and my own people, the Omahas. I had heard extraordinary stories told about its effects, about the immorality that it produced, and about the promiscuity of the people who used the peyote at their meetings. I expected to find evidence of the truth of these stories.

When I went among the Osage people, some of the leaders of the peyote religion were anxious for me to attend their meetings, and wishing to know what effect this "medicine," as they called it, had upon each individual, I accepted the invitation. I attended a meeting at which the gentleman who has just spoken to you, Mr. Arthur Bonnicastle, was present, and sat with him. At about 6 o'clock in the evening the people entered their "meeting house" and sat in a circle around a fire kindled over some symbolic figures marked in the center of a shallow excavation in the middle of the room. The peyote was passed around, some of it in pellets of the consistency of dough, and some prepared in liquid form. The drum was ceremonially circulated and accompanied by singing. From all that I had heard of the intoxicating effects of the peyote I expected to see the people get gloriously drunk and behave as drunken people do. While I sat waiting to see fighting and some excitement the singing went on and on and I noticed that all gazed at the fire or beyond, at a little mound on top of which lay a single peyote. I said to the man sitting next to me, "What do you expect to see?" He said, "We expect to see the face of Jesus and the face of our dead relatives. We are worshiping God and Jesus, the same God that the white people worship." All night long the singing went on and I sat watching the worshipers. It was about 5 o'clock in the morning when suddenly the singing ceased, the drum and the ceremonial staff were put away, and the leader, beginning at the right of the door, asked each person: "What did you see?" Some replied, "I saw nothing." Others said, "I saw the face of Jesus and it made me happy." Some answered, "I saw the faces of my relatives, and they made me glad." And so on, around the entire circle. I noticed that there were only a few who had been able to see faces, the greater number of the men and women saw nothing. It was explained to me by the leader that these revelations come quickly to those whose thoughts and deeds are pure. To those who are irreverent, they come slowly, although they may come in time. This meeting, as well as others that I have been permitted to attend, was as orderly as any religious meeting I have seen in this and other cities. . . .

I do not know about the medicinal qualities of the peyote, whether it can cure consumption or any other disease that the human flesh is subject to, but there is one disease it has cured—the disease of drunkenness.

About 15 years ago, my people passed through an extraordinary experience. White men came among them, generally known as "boot-leggers," to sell whisky and lemon extract. What the whisky was made of I don't know—these "boot-leggers" would sell anything that could produce drunkenness. My people fell into the habit of using this stuff—manufactured by white people—and kept using it until they were in the very depths of degradation. In their drunkenness they attacked men, women, and children. Crimes have been committed that have never been heard of, crimes that have gone unpunished, and white people and Indians alike became afraid to go out at nights on the road for fear of meeting drunken Indians. There came a time when there was a lull in this storm of drunkenness, and after awhile we heard that the peyote religion had been adopted by the Omahas, and there were not as many drunkards as before the introduction of it.

Practically all of those of my people who have adopted the peyote religion do not drink. The peyote plant does much toward destroying the appetite for intoxicants. Moreover, any use of spirituous liquors is forbidden by the teachings of the new religion.

I have a respect for the peyote religion, because it has saved my people from the degradation which was produced by the use of the fiery drinks white people manufacture. . . .

Members of the Society of American Indians Debate Indian Employment in the Bureau of Indian Affairs, 1916

The question was raised by Dr. [Carlos] Montezuma that Indian employees in the service of the Indian Bureau could not be loyal to the Indian race and to their real interests. His argument was that the Indian Bureau did not conserve the best interests of the Indians.

President [Sherman] Coolidge desired to defend the loyalty of the Indian employee, and calling Vice-President Roe-Cloud to the chair, he took the floor.

The President   I do not know how many times I must get up and say that I believe an Indian who is a Government employee can be loyal to his race and at the same time be loyal to his Government. Is the fact that I am a clergyman of an Episcopalian church to keep me at the same time from being loyal to the Government?

Dr. Montezuma   The Indian Bureau, not the Government.

The President   The Government is represented by the Indian Bureau.

Dr. Montezuma   I think not.

The President   I think it is.

Dr. Montezuma   It ought to be, but it is not.

The President   The Government ought sometimes, as a Government, to represent the sense of the American people but it does not always represent them as a whole, the American people as a whole.

Dr. Montezuma   Let us start right out on that. It puts me in a very embarrassing position to place me in a position that I am saying anything against the

Government; I am not. I explained that to you when I started out, that I have nothing against the Government—it is the *system*, it is the system we are after, the Indian Bureau, not the Commissioner of Indian Affairs, or anything of that sort, it is the Bureau, it is the system, my dear brother.

The President   I am not talking about the Indian Commissioner or anybody except you and perhaps myself as we differ in regard to occupying a position as Government employee and being loyal to the race and the Government at the same time. I think it can be done. I don't think I was disloyal to the Government when I was in the Government employ in the Indian service; neither do I believe that I was disloyal to my race.

Dr. Montezuma   A hireling only that is to do service. As a hireling he is not himself, he cannot be. There are Indians in the service, and that is what I am trying to express—they are not supposed to do anything that will embarrass the Indian department, not only the whites but everybody. If I went into the Indian service I would shut my mouth on a good many things.

The President   I think so. You would not dare to say some things. It is about time we are setting you right. You say you cannot mix with the Indian Bureau any more than water with oil. I think you can mix with the Indian Bureau. I mixed with the Indian Bureau a good many times. They have the Indian Bureau there so I could mix with them, to help me to do the work on Indian reservations as a kindness to my people. By giving me work I paid my expenses as a missionary to my people. I have an obligation to them and every Indian in the United States has an obligation to them in that sense. We are facing *conditions* whether they suit us or not and we are to use our manhood in facing those conditions and try to help ourselves out of it and help others if we can; that is what we are here for.

Dr. Montezuma   You help the Bureau that is holding you in that condition.

The President   The Bureau cannot hold me any more than it holds you. I am not hired by the Bureau, it has no hold on me. I am a clergyman, I am a subject of this Government and this country and I am a member of the Church but that does not say that I am a slave. . . .

Rev. [Philip] Gordon   I want to say a few remarks. The question of the Indian Bureau, as far as I see, to state my opinion, I disagree some with President Coolidge who says a member in the employment of the Government is at the same time loyal to this Society. I do not want to cast any personal reflections but speaking generally I do not think that is possible.

Mr. Coolidge   I did not say this Society; I said the Indian race. The race may be helped by this Society. That is not what I am talking about. Before this Society ever existed I was a Government employee. *I assert* a Government Indian employee can be equally loyal to his race and to his Government.

Rev. Gordon   It is not possible for an Indian in the employ of the Government to take a step so he can get rid of the Indian Bureau.

Mrs. [Marie] Baldwin   My friends; I am one of those Government clerks that my brothers have been speaking of today. I do not know where at any time the Government clerk does not dare to say just what he thinks about the Indian Bureau, or if he should or wish, as they put it, that they do not dare come out and say it. I do not know where anyone got that idea. *I am sure that very many times*

I have told Indians that I know that I feel and I want the Indian Bureau to be abolished, but I do not believe that it ought to be abolished on the instant. I think the Indians know that there are many Indians who are not ready now to be put out in the world to take care of themselves. They are not prepared to compete with the people that surround them in a business way, or in any other way. You may not know it, but it is a fact that the Indian Bureau is striving to that end, when some day there will be no need of an Indian Bureau. (Applause).

Mrs. [Gertrude] Bonnin   I just wish to make a very few remarks. It seems if I would sit silent it might indicate to people I was afraid to take a stand or express an opinion. In justice to Indian employees in Indian service I must say one word in their behalf. I cannot sit here and hear it said that just out of consideration of holding a job and getting a very small salary they must keep their mouths shut. I do not think that is true. *I am intimately acquainted with certain Indian employees who are prepared to enter the world at large, to compete with people in the different lines of occupation, to make a livelihood and get better things, who, from a sense of duty to and by all the ties of the heart stay in the wilderness. Why? Because there are human beings there today that need their sympathy, and their kindness, just the kind of help that money could never buy, and that the salary from the Government does not pay for. These are to be found among the Indian employees, working under the Indian Bureau and among their own people on the Indian reservation.* In justice to those Indians who wish to be citizens of our beloved America, to be true to the Government of America, to be civilized men and women, to be loyal to their own who are not so far along as they are, these Indian employees are glad to work under the Indian Bureau, to hold their jobs; but that is the least that is pointed out, that it was only from the commercial point of view, that it was only because of a salary that they would not speak. I want it understood that it is not always so. And I want it understood that I know what I am talking about. (Applause).

Mr. President   Is it right for us to act this way? With the consciousness that we are trying to attain the same end, it seems to me we misunderstand one another. We should try to understand "where we are at," to speak in the language of Texas. Some of us are more radical; some want to take the radical method of solving the Indian problem, and others have a notion that this Indian question is in a state of chaos, jumbled. We told that to the President [of the Society of American Indians] when we brought our memorial before him and he gave us audience. We want to do right in all these things; but I do not like to have our discussion seem to show the employees of the Government as disloyal. That sort of thing as a general accusation has been used in regard to the Government employees many times.

We have tried to get Congress to pass certain bills and to clarify the atmosphere for the Indian because it is in a state of chaos. Let us go right. Eliminate the antiquated rules, regulations and laws, by which the Indian Bureau is run and which might be used by some incompetent agent who has got a grudge against us. Get rid of all these old laws and clear the atmosphere for a new start, get ourselves on our feet as soon as we can and then abolish the Indian Bureau, but take care and do not abolish the Indians. That has been tried many times and it has failed. . . .

Anna Moore Shaw (Pima) Remembers Love, Marriage, and Life in Phoenix, 1912–1920

Although the girls and boys were strictly separated at the Phoenix Indian School, we could not help but notice each other. This was especially true as we became teenagers and young adults. You see, in those days most of us spent two years in each grade in order to master the difficult English language along with the subject matter. Indian students most often would be from eighteen to twenty-two when they graduated from eighth grade, old enough for marriage.

The first and only romance of my life began in 1912 when I was fourteen years old. I no longer wore my hair in pigtails, and the attentions of a handsome Pima named Ross Shaw were flattering. We wrote notes because the matron was very strict and only let us see each other at social functions. But sometimes Ross would sneak over to the girls' side of the campus, where we would play croquet until the matron discovered us and shooed Ross back where he belonged. Soon we were going together. We were truly childhood sweethearts. . . .

Ross was one grade higher than me for most of our years at the school, but in 1915 I received a double promotion, so we were in seventh grade together. Like all young lovers, we made plans. After we graduated from eighth grade, we both hoped to attend Phoenix Union High School. A football coach there had already asked Ross to play on the team. We planned to be married after we received our diplomas.

But who could foretell the future? Fate changed our well-laid plans. In the spring of 1916, just before we were to graduate, Pancho Villa, the Mexican guerrilla leader, raided Agua Prieta on the international boundary near Douglas, Arizona. National guardsmen were called in to stop further depredations, and Ross was one of them.

How well I remember the evening in May when he was called. Sergeant Joshua Morris came into the school dining room and picked out the members who were to go. Ross walked out of the dining room and out of my day-to-day life for three long years.

I had to begin my high school education without my fiancé. Of course I saw him on occasional leaves, but these were few and far between. My brother Bill was also gone, serving on the staff of an Indian school in Zuni, New Mexico. Later he volunteered to serve his country as a member of the 158th Infantry Indian Band.

But even though I was lonely for my men, I managed to keep busy. Bill faithfully sent me part of his paycheck each month, and I also took on the job of assistant seamstress at the Indian School, where I was given a small salary and room and board in exchange for my efforts.

Actually, I remained a student at the Indian School, even though I had graduated from eighth grade. With Ross gone I decided to take advantage of a new

Reprinted from *A Pima Past* by Anna Moore Shaw, by permission of the University of Arizona Press, copyright 1974, pp. 137–150.

program which provided graduates with their first two years of high school. Thus it was not until my junior year that I finally entered Phoenix Union High.

Even after that I continued to work and live at the Phoenix Indian School. Each morning I would wait to board a trolley almost at the entrance of the campus. After a clanging and clacking ride through a Phoenix which looked very different from the modern city of today, I would arrive at high school to begin a day of classes. . . .

When Ross finally returned after nearly two years of skirmishing along the border, he was faced with a difficult decision. The United States had declared war on Germany, but guardsmen of Indian descent were told they need not fight. "You are not citizens," their commander told them, "and therefore you are not eligible for the draft. However, those who want to fight may join the army of their own volition."

Quiet moments followed the announcement. Then Joshua Morris whispered to Ross, *"Tt wo hihim k wo cheggia!* (Let us go fight!)."* As the two brave men stepped up to the desk, the other Indian soldiers who had no families to support also rose to their feet and walked up to volunteer. Patriots all, of their own free wills they decided to risk their lives for their native land, as had their ancestors.

The Indian Company F was in the 158th Infantry that included the famous band of which my brother Bill was a member. They received orders to go to Camp Kearney in San Diego, California, where they were assigned to the Fortieth Division, soon to be nicknamed the Sunshine Division. After Theda Bara, a beautiful vampire actress, visited the camp and announced that she considered herself their "godmother," the division came to be called the Vampire Regiment.

Because of the semi-military training the Indians had received at the BIA schools, they made a good record. Thanks and much credit is due the BIA, for the boys were outstanding in marching, fighting, and trench warfare. They were also known for their hardiness; they could walk for miles without tiring when army trucks were not available. It is told how once on a walk to La Jolla a white soldier grew weary and ready to drop. One of the sturdy Pima boys helped him by carrying his heavy pack.

In August 1918 the Fortieth Division was ordered to board the train for an Eastern port, where camouflaged ships awaited to take them across the Atlantic. They landed in England, where they were welcomed heartily. Little urchins followed them on their march to temporary camp, picking up the coins the soldiers threw to them.

Some of the Company F men, including Ross, were sent on to Le Havre, France. The French were also very friendly, and soon the Indians had acquired a few words of the language in order to buy food. They learned to eat the strange long loaves of white bread and got used to the strong smells of wine and garlic in the restaurants.

My brother Bill was also in France, marching with the band. I kept myself busy sending hand-knit sweaters and socks to my loved ones in that faraway land. I also knitted warm things for the Red Cross to distribute to other fighting boys.

Naturally I spent a lot of time worrying about Ross and Bill. Ross' outfit was called to wait behind the battle-line until they were needed. Just before they were to go to the front, the armistice was signed. My brother Bill also never reached the front line of battle, but the 158th Infantry Indian Band was chosen to play in Paris when Woodrow Wilson met with other world leaders to sign the armistice that brought to a close the War to End All Wars.

Some of our Indian boys were not so lucky as Ross and Bill. But in the midst of the heavy fighting they distinguished themselves by their bravery. Indeed, many of our Indian soldiers paid the supreme sacrifice, including Matthew B. Juan of Gila River and Albert Ray and Wallace Anton of the Salt River Reservation. Their remains lie in foreign soil, and to these brave patriots we owe eternal gratitude.

Wallace, who appears in the photograph of Ross' company, was killed in the great Argonne Forest drive just two days before the armistice was signed. Some of his friends have reported his observation when he saw the front line: *"Pegih neh! Ai att heg t-gahgi!* (Well, we have reached what we have been after!)."

When I received the news of Wallace's death I was deeply grieved, for he had been my good friend and classmate at the Phoenix Indian School. He was a clean-cut chap, full of fun, and a bright student. And he was only one of the many Indians who died in World War I!

How unfair it seemed to me when the brave Indian volunteers returned home, still aliens in their native land. It was not until 1924 that Congress finally bestowed citizenship on us Indians. Oh, the irony of it!

In the spring of 1919, while I was taking exams for my junior year in high school, my dream of three years came true. Ross finally came back to Phoenix, his military service completed with honor. After a seven-year romance, at last we could be married. Of course we considered the possibility of a high school education for Ross, but this no longer seemed realistic. The returned soldier was now twenty-seven and as anxious as me to start a family. His three years of serving his country had brought an end to his educational hopes.

Ross had been trained as a tinner and plumber at the Indian School, and he found employment in these trades in a small shop. We rented a tiny house near his work and my high school and settled there together, legally married in the traditional Indian fashion. As my senior year progressed, however, we decided that we should also be wed in the white man's way. I would soon have a diploma—why not a marriage certificate?

Thus the year 1920 was a big one for Ross and me. First came my graduation, which made Ross so very proud. I have to admit that I also felt a certain pride when one of the commencement speakers pointed out that our class was unique in so far as it included the first full-blood Pima Indian girl graduate. None of my dear ones were there to hear that speech—Ross was working nights, and transportation and money problems prevented my parents from coming. My brother Bill was in Chicago, attending a school of music and scrimping to live at the YMCA. But although I missed my family, it was impossible for me to feel lonely, for I was surrounded by proud friends and employees from the Indian School. The Heflins, the family with whom I had recently lived, were also there, wishing me well and giving me gifts.

Our simple wedding, which followed soon after graduation, was also attended by just a few. The ceremony took place in Dr. Clarence Ellis' manse at

Salt River. Ross' sister Jennie and one of Dr. Ellis' missionary friends were the witnesses. We had very few gifts and no reception: in those hard postwar times we simply could not afford the old Pima custom of *hemapig* (gathering), with all the traditional hospitality and feasting.

It did seem only right though, to try to honor another old Pima tradition—that of living with Ross's parents for a short time at least. After all, I hardly knew my new family, and they had had little chance to become acquainted with me. Ross would have to limit his visiting to the weekends because of his job in Phoenix, but at least I could take this chance to get to know my parents-in-law.

The Shaws lived in an old-fashioned Pima home made of saguaro ribs caulked with mud. Indoors, stout mesquite posts held up the log ceilings. There was no plumbing, gas, or electricity. How difficult this simple way of life seemed to Ross and me after our years of enjoying the white man's conveniences!

Ross' mother labored with such sweet patience. How could I help but do the work she expected of me as a new daughter-in-law? Every morning at 3:00 A.M. I would rise to put on the beans and make a huge stack of tortillas for breakfast. Then at 5:00 Mother Shaw would awaken the boys with her traditional call: "You never rest until you die!"

After breakfast Ross' father and brothers would trudge out to their little forty-acre farm, where they walked behind their horse-drawn plow and sowed seeds of cotton, wheat, corn, and beans. After only a short afternoon break they would return to the fields to labor until sundown.

Despite such hard work, the Shaws were always poor, barely able to buy a few groceries each month. Our hearts ached for them in their difficult existence, but both Ross and I knew that laboring beside his parents in the fields each day was not the best way to help. The educations they had strived so hard to give us had prepared us to bring in money from the white man's world; it would be wrong to waste all those years of schooling on a life of primitive farming.

So after only one month of living with the Shaws we left, filled with mixed emotions. True, we had been educated in the white man's ways, but we were still traditional Pimas with strong feelings of duty to our families and an intense love of our land. Perhaps in our hearts we would always be farmers.

Even with the knowledge that we would return on weekends to help with the work and send money for groceries regularly, we felt pangs of guilt and loss as we packed up our meager belongings and set out to try to make a life of our own in the city of Phoenix.

◈ *E S S A Y S*

These essays illuminate the changing nature of Indian life during the late nineteenth and early twentieth centuries and consider the matter of leadership on the reservation and at the national level. David Rich Lewis, an assistant professor of history at Utah State University, in the opening selection presents a sophisticated analysis of Northern Ute leader William Wash. Wash's life illustrates that the old labels *progressive* and *traditional* are misleading: Indians faced new choices and often turned in new directions. To change did not necessarily men to become acculturated. Historian Peter Iverson of Arizona

State University, in his essay about Carlos Montezuma, depicts a complex man, kid-naped and sold as a young boy, who eventually earned an M.D. and entered private practice in Chicago. At first glance Dr. Montezuma might appear to be a model of as-similation. But through his contact with relatives and other community members at the Fort McDowell reservation in Arizona, the Yavapai man changed his ideas about Indian community Life. Montezuma was an early example of an urban Indian who maintained or cultivated ties with a reservation community. He also demonstrated how knowledge of the larger society and fluency in English could be put to use in the cause of Indian rights, as demonstrated by his active role in the Society of American Indians.

Reservation Leadership and the Progressive-Traditional Dichotomy: William Wash and the Northern Utes, 1865–1928

DAVID RICH LEWIS

In June 1865 leaders from the Tumpanuwac, San Pitch, and Pahvant bands of Ute *(Nu'ciu)* Indians gathered at Spanish Fork to relinquish their lands. In return, O. H. Irish, superintendent of Indian affairs for Utah Territory, promised them a permanent reservation in the isolated Uintah Basin of eastern Utah, where they could hunt and gather until such time as the government saw fit to transform them into settled and self-sufficient agriculturalists. These Ute leaders realized they had few options. They themselves were leaders of recent status—men like Tabby who rallied group consensus away from the Ute war leaders Wakara and Black Hawk. Since the Mormon invasion in 1847, they had watched their people suc-cumb to epidemic disease, starvation, and warfare. In 1865 Ute leaders accepted the Spanish Fork Treaty as a tactical retreat and began moving toward their new homeland.

In that year of change—change in leadership, location, and future—a Uintah Ute child was born. Named Na-am-quitch, he was the eldest son of Zowoff and Nunanumquitch. In later years he became known as Wash's Son and finally as William Wash. Wash was both ordinary and extraordinary. He never became a formal political leader of his people, yet his success as a rancher gained him the recognition and respect of both Utes and whites at the Uintah-Ouray Reservation. Agency officials called him one of the more "progressive" full-blood individuals of the Uintah band, one of three Northern Ute bands to share the four-million-acre reservation. Yet Wash frequently frustrated these same agents by rejecting the progressive and acting in what they considered to be very "traditional" ways. Until his death in April 1928, he moved between two cultural worlds on the reservation. He was what Loretta Fowler calls an "intermediary" or a "middle-man," one of the new or transitional types of leader to arise during the early res-ervation years.

The importance of people like William Wash lies not only in their own unique experiences but in their shared experiences and the larger themes which

David Rich Lewis, "Reservation Leadership and the Progressive-Traditional Dichotomy: William Wash and the Northern Utes, 1865–1928," *Ethnohistory* 38:1, pp. 124–142. Copyright Duke University Press, 1991. Reprinted with permission of the publisher.

emerge from study of their lives. Nearly two decades ago Robert Berkhofer, Jr., told ethnohistorians that they must emphasize Indians in their histories, particularly "the uniqueness of the stories of specific individuals." From works on more famous or infamous individuals, the study of Indian biography has begun to focus on "culturally marginal personages," those less-known "bicultural" individuals who spent their lives on the borders between ethnic groups, mastering the knowledge of two cultures without being immobilized by the process.

Berkhofer also suggests that this individualized focus will aid scholars in untangling the web of inter- and intragroup factionalism. Existing models of tribal factionalism generalize "group" traits without getting "bogged down" in individual motivation and variation. Without paying close attention over time to individual actors (who are difficult to find and trace in most records), scholars tend to perpetuate the static . . . categories of "traditional" and "progressive," an unrealistically neat dichotomy or unilinear continuum created by nineteenth- and twentieth-century observers and frequently used to generalize about the social, economic, and political nature of reservation factionalism. Reliance on these sources, particularly by historians who perhaps have been more susceptible to the generalization, produces a two-dimensional, dichotomous picture of native people, issues, and factionalism.

While anthropologists and ethnohistorians eschew the progressive-traditional dichotomy as ethnocentric and value-laden, the terms and their variants still appear all too frequently. Often qualified with quotation marks, they have become a kind of professional shorthand for describing individuals, factionalism, and the process of acculturation. The unspoken understanding is that we are simplifying a complex, dynamic situation out of necessity, trusting that colleagues will recognize our dilemma and hoping that others will not read overly static meanings into these useful, if somewhat misleading, terms. We deny the dichotomy but we fall back on it, perhaps because in our histories we do not understand or cannot fully untangle the temporal threads of personal motive and behavior which guide individuals and draw them into factions or groups.

The weakness of this progressive-traditional dichotomy becomes most apparent in attempts to categorize complex individuals, particularly the intermediaries, the middlemen, the cultural brokers, the "150% men" who operate on the cultural margins. William Wash became such a figure among the Northern Utes. Not a recognized "headman" yet vocal in councils, Wash represents the substratum of reservation politics, the influential individuals who worked the margins of tribal leadership and white acceptance. His experience mirrors that of perhaps a majority of early twentieth-century Native Americans struggling to come to terms with their own culture and with American society.

William Wash was born into a world of both change and persistence as his people moved toward the Uintah Basin. We know little about his early life other than what we can assume given the history of the Uintah Reservation. There the different Utah Ute bands coalesced into a single band called the Uintah. The federal government encouraged Utes to settle near the agency and begin farming. Most, however, continued their seasonal subsistence pursuits and drew rations in order to avoid starvation on the agency farms. Some, like Zowoff and Wash, tried their hand at farming, braving the ridicule of other Ute males for gathering vegetal material and digging in the earth, the subsistence province of women. Raising cattle or hauling freight for the agency came much more easily for Ute men seeking to reproduce male work and subsistence spheres. Wash and his father received special gratuity payments from the Indian Bureau for their farming efforts. By 1891,Wash owned a number of cattle and worked part-time for the agency as a herder. Agents viewed him as a progressive Indian.

According to Ute agents, the definition of "progressive" revolved around two elements, economic and historical. First, agents identified progressive Utes by their subsistence activities, particularly by their commitment to a settled and self-sufficient agrarian lifestyle. This lifestyle was defined in part by their willingness to dress, act, and speak like whites, live in houses, and send their children to school. Second, this designation devolved to a comparison of Ute bands and their reservation histories, particularly after the 1881 forced removal of White River and Uncompahgre Utes from their Colorado homelands to the Uintah and Ouray reservations. The consolidation of the Uintah, White River, and Uncompahgre bands created a number of problems, including a series of inter- and intraband factional disputes over leadership, past treaty negotiations, and the distribution of natural resources and annuity payments.

Out of these disputes Ute agents identified "progressive" and "traditional" factions. The Uintah Utes, because of their long contact history and exposure to reservation agriculture, were the most progressive of the Northern Ute bands. The Uncompahgre band suffered the most internal divisions between the progressive Indians (led by Shavanaux and Alhandra) who settled on river-bottom farms and those (led by Sowawick) who preferred to maintain a more nomadic, up-country, herding and hunting lifestyle. Finally, there were the White Rivers, whom agents classed as wild and rebellious traditionalists, adamantly opposed to any effort to change their way of life. This growing factionalism, based on what agents perceived as a progressive-traditional dichotomy running along band lines, was in fact individualistic, fluid, and issue- and economics-oriented.

William Wash played some role in these factional divisions by virtue of his Uintah band affiliation and his three marriages, particularly the last, to Lucy Alhandra, daughter of the progressive Uncompahgre leader "Charley" Alhandra. More important factors, however, were his economic activities as a farmer, rancher, and agency herder, as well as his familiar relations with the white agents. As agency herder, Wash came under fire from Tim Johnson, spokesman for the White River traditionalists. Johnson claimed that Wash was in league with agency attempts to lease Ute grazing lands in the Strawberry Valley to white Mormon ranchers. Johnson criticized Wash because "he does all kind of work" and asked that Wash and the agency farmer, men who symbolized progressive agriculture, both be "sent away."

In 1903, the White River and Uintah bands faced a common threat, the prospect of allotment. Despite widespread Ute opposition, 75 Uintah and 7 White River Utes out of 280 eligible males signed the allotment article. These, Special Agent James McLaughlin acknowledged, signed mainly to show their goodwill in the face of what they understood to be an inevitable process. Yet by signing the allotment agreement, these individuals reaffirmed a perceived division between "progressive" Uintah and "conservative" White River Utes and created a further division within the Uintah band. William Wash, aged thirty-eight, was one of these progressive Uintah signatories. Dissenting White River leaders threatened to leave the reservation if allotment proceeded; indeed, they carried out that threat in 1906–8, leading nearly four hundred Utes to South Dakota.

With this "tribal" division into two apparently distinct factions, Wash began to consolidate his social and economic position as a progressive spokesman. In 1903, he sold 25,530 pounds of loose hay to the troops at Fort Duchesne, and in 1905 he received his eighty-acre allotment on the southeastern end of Indian Bench above Fort Duchesne. That year he raised ten bushels of potatoes, fourteen hundred bushels of oats, and one hundred bushels of wheat and harvested three hundred tons of alfalfa. His 640 rods of fencing and his log cabin attest to his industry but probably more so to substantial assistance from agency personnel. At the same time, Wash ran a sizable cattle herd in the Dry Gulch region southwest of Fort Duchesne.

In a 1907 council with Uintah Utes, Agent C. G. Hall tried to quiet rumors that "Mormons" were going to take over both the opened reservation and allotted lands. In this council, with the absence of so many Utes in South Dakota, William Wash emerged as a Uintah spokesman. He told the assembly:

> I hear about the way Secretary of the Interior talk to us. I always take Washington's advice. About farming, about everything. I never say no any time. This land that is allotted to me is mine. That make my heart [feel good]. I can't wait to go work my land. I have been working the way Washington want me to. I have a fence around eighty acres. I am putting in some crops. I got hands to work with like everybody. I lost a good deal of money in some way by white men renting my farm. This leasing of land to the whites is a swindle. If I work it myself I get the money that comes from the farming. The Indians do not know how to make money off their land. They don't know whether the white man is handling it right or not.

Beneath his own espousal of white economic values, Wash was apparently concerned about the vacant allotments of those White River Utes in South Dakota, fearing the land would be leased or sold—lost in either case from Ute control. He continued: "About the White Rivers. Washington never told them to go to another country. They are getting themselves poor. Losing everything. This is their home. . . . I want everything to be right. Don't want little children starving. It makes me feel sorry when people move around and let little children get hurt. They are pretty hard up I think. Maybe they come back now to raise something."

The White River Utes did return to the allotted reservation in 1908, under military guard, physically defeated, and with little means of support. Many had no idea where their allotments were, had nothing to work their land with if they wanted to, and were reluctant to work for wages on the ongoing Uintah Irrigation Project. Many ultimately leased their lands to white settlers, hoping to earn some money and protect their water rights against . . . Utah water laws. Wash's hopes seemed dim.

At this juncture we get a glimpse of another side of William Wash, one that casts a different light on his economic activities and social aspirations. Inspector

Harwood Hall visited the reservation shortly after the White Rivers returned and reported that all the Northern Utes "are quite poor, and were it not for rations issued by the government and assistance given many of them by an Indian by name of Wash, who is fairly well off, it is difficult to see how they would secure sufficient food to subsist." From this and other evidence, it appears not only that Wash was accumulating wealth in a white-approved manner (ranching and farming) but that he was using the proceeds (particularly his cattle) to help feed needy members of all three Ute bands. Instead of observing market economy values, he reproduced in part the individualistic role of local Ute leaders by distributing goods in return for sociopolitical recognition. Wash used his position as a cultural intermediary in order to help his people, to gain traditional respect, and to attempt to fill a growing vacuum in Northern Ute leadership.

Between 1912 and 1914, Wash's visibility in tribal affairs increased. He was not considered a "chief" in general Ute councils with the federal government, but he was actively involved in reservation politics, particularly over issues of ranching and land use. Once we discern some of the cultural values and motives behind his actions, it becomes clear that Wash's activities are more complex than can be explained with a static model of factionalism based on a simple progressive-traditional dichotomy.

In 1912, Uintah-Ouray agency stockmen expressed concern with the number of "wild ponies" roaming the 250,000-acre Ute Grazing Reserve. The issue of Ute horses had been a constant source of conflict between Utes and agency personnel. Agents argued that horses gave the Utes too much mobility, perpetuated racing and gambling customs, and grazed ranges more profitably reserved for cattle and sheep. Utes, on the other hand, valued horses as prestige items, traditional forms of wealth, status, and security. They felt (and still feel) an attachment to the horse out of proportion to its market value. The destruction of horses in 1879 precipitated the White River attack on the Utes' Colorado agency. Agents in Utah came to realize that horses, not cattle, defined the social and economic status of Ute men.

In 1912, Wash was one of these men, wealthy both by Ute standards (he owned about fifty horses) and by white (two hundred cattle and forty sheep). He headed [a] . . . kin-based cattle association which controlled 395 cattle, 115 sheep, and one of the four bands of "wild" horses roaming the grazing reserve. His position gave him a great say in Indian Bureau plans to clear the range. At a gathering of seventeen leading Ute stockmen, Wash initiated a plan to periodically round up unbranded horses and divide them among members of the roundup crew. He offered to supply both mounted men and extra saddle horses for the roundup and agreed to the construction of corrals on his land. Wash may have been interested in rounding up wild horses, but it seems likely that he was interested in doing so not to preserve the range for additional cattle and sheep, as desired by the white officials, but to obtain or retain more horses, thereby adding to his source of traditional wealth and status.

In 1913, Ute livestock owners met in council to oppose leasing the Ute Grazing Reserve to James S. Murdock, a white sheepman. Once again Wash spoke for his people, summarizing Ute opposition to the proposed lease:

When we used to talk about this reservation a long time ago, way back in Washington, we leased some land. That is past now. . . . Now the way it is about this land, it is different than before we were allotted. All these Indians understand what you told them to do and now we have talked about it. Now we have some horses, and we know about how to take care of them now and make use of them on this land. The Indian has always held it, they do not want to lease it at all. As we have horses, cattle, and stock there is no place for Murdock to lease, as all the Indians on the grazing land clear up to Lake Fork have stock and we do not want it leased at all. I have the right to depend on that country, I have some cattle of my own.

Superintendent Jewell D. Martin thanked him: "I am glad to hear what Wash has said because he has more stock than any other Indian on the reservation and knows more about the live stock industry here and I am glad he has expressed his judgment."

Two points of interest emerge from this exchange. First, by his words before his assembled peers, Wash indicated his continuing commitment to horses, even his commitment to horses *over* cattle and sheep. He came to this point of view as Ute agents attempted to reduce the number of Ute horses by emphasizing improved livestock and range management. Even progressive Ute stockmen like Wash resisted agency efforts to castrate their "ponie stallions," preferring a culturally derived balance between quantity and quality. Wash emphasized the continuity of the horse, as both symbol and reality, in Northern Ute culture.

Second, Wash opposed leasing the tribally controlled grazing reserve. In council meetings later that year Wash and other progressive ranchers clashed with a group of White River traditionalists over the creation of a tribal herd. The cattlemen argued that a herd would benefit the tribe economically, provide a market for surplus hay, and keep land-grabbing whites from getting a foothold on the reserve through leasing. The White Rivers also feared the threat of white homesteaders, but they desired cash, not cattle—an equitable distribution of benefits from the grazing reserve in the form of lease monies rather than its use by a select few Ute cattlemen.

Although the council approved the proposed tribal herd when the White Rivers walked out, Superintendent Martin killed the plan, which smacked of "tribal interest rather than individual interest." In his haste to stamp out collectivism, Martin missed the point. These progressive cattlemen intended to partition the herd, "allowing each family to take its share of the cattle and take care of them." In effect, these Utes understood better than Martin that the government would spend tribal funds only for tribal (as opposed to individual) economic development plans, that such communalism clashed with their individualistic subsistence traditions, and that in the past, communalistic policies and agency herds had failed. This proposal by Wash and the progressive cattlemen was both a way to get tribal funds over to individuals and a conservative plan to protect the integrity of the Ute Grazing Reserve. Ultimately, it promised to benefit each Ute household in more ways than the simple lease fees desired by the White Rivers—progressive-sounding means securing an essentially conservative outcome.

In 1914, Wash appeared in the middle of another reservation power struggle, between an overly enthusiastic superintendent and commissioner and the Ute followers of the Sun Dance religion. As early as 1905, Ute agents had complained that the annual Ute Bear Dance and Sun Dance were morally and economically counterproductive, that they destroyed health and morals and took people away from their farms at critical times in the growing season. In 1913, Martin failed to convince Ute leaders to hold the Bear and Sun dances together at midsummer agricultural fairs as a sort of commercial sideshow. Unable to co-opt or halt them, Commissioner Cato Sells officially prohibited both dances, which were "incompatible with industrial development and altogether out of harmony with a higher civilization."

While the Bear Dance was one of the oldest of Ute rituals, the Sun Dance religion was a recent innovation. Introduced in the 1890s by Grant Bullethead, a Uintah Ute who learned the ceremony at the Wind River Shoshone Reservation, the Sun Dance filled a void for people struggling with the unrest and dislocation associated with allotment. The dance echoed the individualistic tenor of Ute beliefs while offering group strength through communal participation. The Ute people seized the model, reinterpreted it in terms of their own cultural categories, and reproduced their own religious system, with its emphasis on curing, within the framework of that single dance. The Sun Dance religion offered the Northern Utes an active option for binding themselves together and dealing with the directed changes of an allotted agrarian lifestyle.

Despite the Indian Bureau ban, a number of White River and Uintah Utes proceeded with the 1914 Sun Dance. Upset and uncertain what to do, William Wash telegraphed Interior Secretary Franklin K. Lane: "Indians will hold annual harvest dance about June twenty fifth to thirtieth / ancient custom / supervisor objects / wire reply." Cloaking the Sun Dance in harvest imagery to make it more palatable to white officials was an old Ute tactic, but the reply shot back that the Sun Dance, "or dance of a similar nature, such as usually held at this season of year," was prohibited. Superintendent Martin assured the commissioner that after informing a "bunch of the influential ones" who had sent the telegram, the "better class" of Indians agreed not to dance. Still, two Sun Dances went on as scheduled that summer. Martin reported that about 150 "retrogressive White River Indians" insisted on the dance, which was attended by over three hundred Utes—what he dismissed as a "minor fraction." Martin asked for additional assistance to suppress the dance, for, as they often did, his Indian policemen protected their own people by selectively enforcing Indian Bureau orders.

Was William Wash, the leader of the "bunch of the influential ones" who sent the telegram, also one of the "better class" who agreed not to hold the dance? Or did this group concede defeat to Martin and then participate in the dance anyway? After investigating the dance, U.S. Marshall Aquilla Nebeker reported that Martin "believes that the best Indians, and a majority over all, are supporters of his and are in harmony with his ideas; but I am forced to the opinion that in this he is mistaken; and I could recite many circumstances and conversations which I think are withheld from the Agent, but such recitals would burden this communication and probably would not be considered competent." Nebeker heard and saw what Martin and the Indian Bureau ignored, and he probably heard some of it from Martin's own progressive Utes.

Nebeker reported that the dance took place on the grazing reserve around

Lake Fork, thirty-five miles northwest of Myton, Utah. Other records indicate that William Wash "controlled" that particular area of the grazing reserve and thus that he probably knew about and approved of the dance location. It is possible that Wash was there, supporting the dancers and participating in the group event by his very presence. He was a prominent sponsor of other Sun Dances during this period of suppression. In describing the dances in his youth, Conner Chapoose noted that Ute individuals would sponsor dancers or contribute to the feast following the dance: "They'd either donate a beef if they had any cattle, like for instance Mr. Wash. He would make a statement at the time that he would furnish a beef for the food, and that was supporting the program as they was putting it on." In this and other instances, Wash actively supported a ceremony deemed retrogressive and traditional by the very white officials who dubbed him the leading progressive Ute stockman.

Superintendent Albert Kneale, who replaced Martin in January 1915, was not particularly concerned about the Sun Dance. He considered it to be a fairly benign, rather commercialized celebration put on to attract tourist dollars. Kneale was more concerned about the appearance of peyote at Uintah-Ouray and the threat it posed to the welfare and advancement of the Ute people.

In 1914, Sam Lone Bear, an Oglala Sioux, introduced the peyote Cross Fire ritual to the Northern Utes. Working out of Dragon, Utah, an isolated narrow-gauge railroad terminal seventy-five miles from Fort Duchesne, Lone Bear held services and spread word of the benefits of peyote, particularly its curative properties. By 1916, half of the nearly twelve hundred Northern Utes participated in the peyote religion. Once again, Utes integrated the individualistic, power-seeking, and therapeutic elements of a new ritual into their own belief system. In later years, the Tipi Way became more popular among Northern Ute peyotists, perhaps because Lone Bear's unsavory business dealings and sexual reputation discredited the Cross Fire ritual.

Ute peyotism came under attack between 1916 and 1918 when both Congress and the state of Utah considered bills to outlaw peyote. Witnesses before a House subcommittee testified that peyote roadmen targeted "prosperous" Ute Indians, those with cattle, in order to addict them and "control their funds." They told of once prosperous Ute farms now "neglected" because of peyote addiction and claimed that Lone Bear counselled Ute stockmen to stay at home and pray to Peyote to look after their cattle. Other experts testified to the deaths and other detrimental physical as well as economic effects of the drug on progressive Indian farmers. Superintendent Kneale informed his superiors that "40 to 50 percent of the Indians on this reservation are, or have been, partakers of this drug." Lone Bear, Kneale reported, deliberately set out to interest "some of our very best men, particularly McCook, Witchits, Monk Shavanaux, Captain Jenks, Grant, Corass, and William Wash. These men were all leaders among their people."

As it turned out, Wash, the progressive Uintah Ute farmer, rancher, and emerging leader, was indeed an active and vocal peyotist. In 1917 Kneale called in U.S. marshals to control the liquor and peyote traffic around Dragon. He advised Utes to abandon peyotism because it would kill them. Once again, Wash took his people's problems to the commissioner of Indian affairs. On 12 May 1917, Wash dictated the following letter, signing it with his thumbprint:

My Dear Commissioner:

We want to know why these United States Marshalls come in here and try to get us to stop church. We like Church. We want to meet every Sunday and have Church and pray and be good. We don't want to steal, nor drink whiskey, nor play cards nor gamble nor lie and we want to rest on Sunday and then on Monday we want to work and farm. . . . Sometimes sick people sometimes die and sometimes we eat Peote and it make us better. Sometimes people die and no eat Peote. They die. Maybe eat Peote, no die. Horses die, cows die, sheep die. They no eat Peote. You can't stop them dieing. Anything die. Long time live maybe so eat Peote. We want to be good and we want you to let us have Church and not send Police from Washington to make us stop. You tell us why you do this. We don't know.

I have been here a long time and all the Indians like me and they ask me to write and ask you what is the matter. Randlett Indians maybe so they eat Peote. Pretty good, I guess. The White Rocks Indians no eat Peote. No like it and they like Whiskey and they play cards and fight, maybe so kill 'em. We don't like that, we want to be good.

Assistant Commissioner E. B. Meritt answered Wash's letter, explaining that he opposed the use of peyote because attending and recovering from peyote meetings took too much time, and because "it is bad medicine making many Indians sick, some crazy and killing others." Meritt noted that Utah state law prohibited the sale and use of peyote. He closed in typically paternal fashion by telling Wash, "If you and your people want to be good you should do what we think is right and best for you and what the laws of the State and the United States require that you should do."

Wash and his friends were not satisfied with this reply or with the suggestion that they talk to Kneale. On 3 July Wash responded to Meritt's objections, stressing the positive aspects of peyote use and pointing out that it was no more disruptive than Christian Sunday services:

You say for me to talk the matter over with my superintendent but he won't talk to me cause I eat peyote. He won't shake hands with me. When I have my Superintendent to write for me I don't get any answer for it. . . . He don't like to write letters for Indians. The Superintendent's Indians at White Rocks play cards. He lets them play cards and he don't stop them.

I don't drink any more and I don't play cards nor swear. I go to meeting and eat peyote and that made me throw away drinking, playing cards and swearing. Church makes us good people. We are good when we go to Church. We farm all week and just have church on Sunday, just one day. We all work hard all week and go to church on Sunday after week's work is done. I raise all my own garden, all the food to eat myself and have good garden and just go to Church on Sunday. The Bible say that we should go to church on Sunday and rest. The Missionaries say to go to Church on Sunday too.

Meritt answered quickly this time, apparently aware that he was dealing with an influential and persistent individual. He assured Wash that he would write Kneale and have him explain the laws. He applauded Wash's "progress" and admonished him to give up peyotism. "If you are anxious to do what is right I hope you will stop using peyote and advise the other Indians to do likewise. Peyote will not make Indians live longer but instead will shorten their lives." Meritt advised

Kneale that "by taking this Indian into your confidence it is possible that he can be induced to give up the peyote habit and use his influence in persuading others to do likewise." Kneale replied that he had held "many conversations with Mr. Wash relative to the peyote situation," and that Wash had discussed it with "many other employees in this jurisdiction," but to no avail.

Wash refused to accept the paternal advice of these two men. His own experiences led him to very different conclusions regarding peyote. He wrote Meritt a final note:

> I received your letter of July 18th and will say that I do not wish to hear from you any more. Do not write to me any more and I will not write to you. Indian no eat peyote, he die anyhow. Sometime he die young and sometime live long time. I will die anyhow. I will die if I eat peyote and I will die if I don't. White people die no eat peyote.
>
>   I have a good home and have a good farm. I stay home all the time and watch cattle and sheep. I herd them in the mountain now. I send my boy to white school to learn and be good. I like to have my boy be good and learn to talk and read and write. They don't learn them to be bad and swear and steal, they teach them to be good all the time. I die sometime and my boy will have my house and farm and cattle and sheep. He stay there and live.

With that, Wash ended his correspondence, but not his involvement with the peyote religion.

Who was Wash defending and why? From the available evidence it appears that Northern Ute peyotists were mostly older full-blood Utes, frequently the people Kneale deemed progressive, the "very best men," the "leaders among their people." Peyote use was centered in the communities of Dragon and Randlett and occurred along the Indian Bench all the way to Myton—areas of predominantly Uintah and Uncompahgre Ute settlement (bands always considered the more progressive and economically self-sufficient among the Utes). Some argue that these progressive full-bloods were seeking a way to maintain particularly "Indian" cultural values in the face of directed culture change, to achieve group solidarity as Utes and as pan-Indians. Contemporaries observed that individuals, particularly young educated Indians, adopted peyotism to gain social prominence and leadership status otherwise denied them under existing tribal structures. Wash's active participation can be seen as an attempt both to revitalize or perpetuate elements he believed valuable in Ute culture and, despite his age, to gain social leadership status in addition to his economic prominence.

While many Northern Utes accepted peyotism, there remained a significant faction adamantly opposed to its use, deeming it dangerous, expensive, or simply an intrusive cultural element. The White River Utes living around Whiterocks, long considered conservative traditionalists, apparently rejected peyotism. Wash exposed them by playing off the "virtues" of peyote against their "vices" of gambling and drinking and thus claimed the moral high ground. Other peyote opponents included mixed-blood and younger boarding school–educated Utes from all three bands. In 1924, forty-six White River Utes petitioned the Interior Department and Congress to "prevent the traffic of peyote and remove it from the Indian reservations of the United States." Indian Bureau suppression and factional opposition within the tribe drove peyotism underground in the 1920s and 1930s. In the

1930s the issue merged with an increasing antagonism between full- and mixed-blood Utes over mixed-blood control of the tribal business committee. The resulting social and political factionalism ultimately contributed to the termination of mixed-blood Utes in 1954.

It is unclear whether William Wash became a peyote leader, yet his open defense of it and his defiance surely increased his influence among segments of the Ute people. Peyote did not physically or financially ruin Wash. Kneale recalled that Wash, "a well-to-do and patriotic Ute," purchased one thousand dollars' worth of coupon bonds during World War I. In 1923, Wash owned six hundred head of sheep, which he leased to the care of white herders, as well as several hundred cattle, which he personally supervised. "He also controls a large acreage of farming land and this is leased to white men," wrote Superintendent Fred A. Gross. "He is one of the most progressive Indians we have and is successful in his various activities." While it is possible that Wash's "lapse" into leasing was a result of his peyote use, it is more probable that, since Wash was getting old and his son was in school, he could not personally manage his considerable estate. Leasing then became a viable short-term option that he could supervise to make sure the land was not lost to white ranchers.

Wash's wealth and political recognition increased dramatically in his later years. He was a leading member of the council which chose R. T. Bonnin as the Ute tribal attorney in 1926, and he represented the Uintah band in council meetings designed to form a tribal business committee in 1927. His age, wealth, peyotism, and outspokenness are probably what kept him off the final business committee, yet they gained him the recognition of both Utes and whites as a spokesman for the full-blood and Uintah Utes.

Wash spoke with particular authority on issues affecting Ute lands and land use. In 1925, Uintah Utes included Wash in a delegation bound for Washington, D.C. While other members focused on "missing" annuity payments, siphoned off to pay for the Uintah Irrigation Project, Wash articulated the fears of his people that whites were scheming to gain control of the grazing reserve. Wash told bureau officials that he ran about 570 cattle, 800 sheep, and 70 horses on the grazing reserve, and that "we do not want any white men to come and take that piece of land away from us again because it is very small." He complained of having trouble with trespassing white ranchers and with forest rangers who restricted his access to former Ute grazing lands within the Uinta National Forest, "so that it makes it pretty hard for me to get along with these fellows." And in particular he complained that white homesteaders and irrigation companies took water properly belonging to Ute allottees.

In the second half of his speech, Wash moved from issues affecting Ute ranchers to the desires of those who were not so economically progressive—those without cattle or allotments. In an apparent ideological flip-flop, he suggested that unused portions of the grazing reserve be leased "so all Indians could get a little benefit of it, those that don't own any stock." He also suggested that arable areas of the grazing reserve be allotted to Ute children. He told the commissioner: "I am making this statement because I am old. I may not live long but I would like to have these children allotted because by and by white men might take it away and the children would be homeless. We would like to have the children allotted so that they will have something when they grow up." Wash, the "progressive" farmer and cattleman, recognized both the needs and rights of those Utes without cattle or land to share in the tribal estate. At the same time he reiterated his desire to preserve the integrity of what was left of the Ute land base, to leave enough land and water to sustain Ute identity and independence against the wave of white homesteaders.

Indian Bureau officials listened to Wash and the other Ute delegates and ultimately acted on Wash's recommendation, but they twisted his intent in the process. In 1927 the bureau levied grazing fees on ranchers running more than one hundred horses or head of cattle or five hundred sheep on the grazing reserve. Ostensibly, the point was to provide a more equitable distribution of tribal assets between those using the range and those without livestock, but in fact the fees promised to open more of the reserve to white stockmen who could afford to pay them. These fees posed a major problem for stock-rich but cash-poor Utes who found few outside markets and low prices for their livestock. The fees and regulations themselves posed a threat to Ute sovereignty. Wash, the premier stockman and cultural middleman, was the one individual most threatened by this fee system.

In January 1928 a number of older full-bloods from all three bands gathered in council to petition the Indian Bureau to lift the fees on livestock. Most owned no stock and had no vested interest in the outcome. Sampannies (Saponeis Cuch), a conservative White River leader, vigorously argued that Wash (and all full-bloods) should be allowed to run his stock on the grazing reserve without paying a fee. "We want his stock to be left alone. They have a right on our grazing land," Sampannies told the council. "We are doing this in order that Mr. Wash can hold our grazing land for us for some day some of us other Indians may have stock and want to run our stock on the grazing land." Sampannies, voicing full-blood Ute resentment toward the growing number and the political and economic influence of mixed-blood Utes, declared that anyone of less than one-half Ute blood had no right to use the tribal grazing reserve. Older full-blood leaders like John Duncan, Cesspooch, and Dick Wash and newer Business Committee leaders like John Yesto agreed. They defended Wash's right to use the grazing reserve, praised him as an example for the younger generation, and denied the mixed-bloods. Yet underpinning their support for Wash was an understanding that the real issue was sovereignty, the ultimate right to control their tribal resources. "Why," asked Cesspooch, "should we pay for our own land?"

Wash spoke at the end of the council, summing up the arguments of sovereignty by recapping his life experiences as a cultural intermediary, as one who tried to play by two sets of changing rules and expectations:

> When the agency was first established I was advised that stock raising was very profitable and I took that advice and I have found that it is so. Later on arrangements were made and the grazing land set aside for our use. It was then said that the grazing land was for the Indians['] own use and that they could increase their herds as much as they wanted as long as they had grazing land and were not to be charged any fee whatever. At the present time why should we be charged for our grazing land? I feel that I should be given a little consideration because I am the leading example of the whole tribe. I feel that I have been capable of holding the grazing land as a whole

because I have more stock on the grazing land than any other Indian and the other Indians appreciate the fact that I have held the grazing land for them. That is why they have made their statements here today.

Wash played on his dual role, first in holding tribal land against outsiders and secondly in providing a progressive example of the benefits of work and self-sufficiency for Ute schoolchildren. In closing, he reiterated his long-standing objections to the alienation of Ute land and his hopes for an independent future for his people: "We have always been peaceable people and we intend to live here that way always. This is our home and we do not want to be disturbed. . . . We do not like for any white persons or anybody else to try to have our grazing land thrown open. We object to that very much. We feel that our younger people are beginning to realize the benefits derived from our grazing lands. We do not want to be discouraged by such hard regulations." Yet in the end the commissioner ignored the council and reaffirmed the new fee regulation. Shortly after word of the decision reached Uintah-Ouray, William Wash fell ill. Following a month-long struggle Wash, aged sixty-three, died on 30 April 1928 at his home on the Indian Bench near Fort Duchesne.

Wash's life illustrates some of the fundamental problems scholars face in defining individual Indians, or entire factions, for that matter, as progressive or traditional on the basis of narrow social or economic issues. Defining factions is difficult enough. What variables (kinship, residence, economics, religion, etc.) defined factional groups? Were they "floating coalitions of interests rather than of persons," and were the ends always disputed, or just the means to those ends? The activities of William Wash indicate that individuals frequently transcend the bounds of static factional categories; that these coalitions were informal, fluid, and issue-oriented as frequently as not; and that the means were perhaps more divisive than the ends. Wash plotted a course different from the traditionalist White Rivers, clashing with them over certain issues. Each undoubtedly suspected the other's methods and motives. Yet Wash and his White River opponents united on a number of other issues. Factionalism at Uintah-Ouray evolved from preexisting kinship and band differences, bloomed with economic and land use disputes from the 1880s through the 1930s, and played itself out under the guise of mixed-blood–full-blood politics in the 1950s.

The problem with dichotomizing factions into progressive and traditional elements is, as Fred Hoxie points out, that "there were usually more than two sides to most questions, and no single side coincided with the cause of resistance for the survival of tribal culture." Indian communities contained "a variety of interest groups which took a variety of positions on public issues," and accounting for community or cultural survivals by praising one group as traditional against all others "flattens history and distorts the complexity of reservation life." Equating *progressive* with change and *traditional* with resistance sacrifices individually complex behavior, diminishing our understanding of Native Americans' rationales and responses.

Defining traditional and progressive elements or actions is equally difficult because what passes for tradition changes over time. When innovations can be and are interpreted as cultural continuities, the category *traditional* becomes little more than a temporal indicator. Institutions today regarded as conservative among the Northern Utes (the Sun Dance and peyotism, for example) were revitalized or innovative features in Wash's time. The most conservative elements of Ute society opposed peyote, while so-called progressives embraced the pan-Indian religion. Today at Uintah-Ouray, that group definition would be reversed. Wash's actions, which appeared progressive to agents and other Utes, in time manifested rather conservative intents or results.

Then there is the jockeying for semantic position or advantage. Different sides in a dispute might claim to be traditional in order to gain the moral high ground and discredit the others. Each side usually has some legitimate claims to tradition, and yet each is equally untraditional. The opposite strategy, claiming progressive attitudes and actions for moral or political advantage, is also possible. As Loretta Fowler points out, "Indians have often . . . tried to influence federal policy by presenting themselves and their constituents as 'progressive,'" to preserve or protect certain cultural elements. But this strategy is double-edged. The real problem begins when modern readers see this dichotomy and unwittingly read in a whole set of values and traits which may not be present, allowing no leeway for individual and qualitative distinctions. Given the modern predisposition towards cultural pluralism and the emergence of "pan-traditionalists," progressives have become politically suspect and are not considered particularly "authentic." The result: simplifying or discrediting through semantics alone.

A final problem with the progressive-traditional dichotomy is that it too frequently implies *either* that one is progressive and committed to change *or* that one is traditional and resists attempts to alter cultural features. It also suggests a zero-sum equation, a "cultural replacement" in which one discards Indian ways in proportion to the assimilation of white goods or ways. There appears to be no middle ground in the dichotomy, no ambiguity in individual thought, action, or value, no notion of differential as opposed to unilinear (or unidirectional) change. And yet we acknowledge the presence and importance of certain individuals who embody these ambiguities as cultural middlemen, intermediaries, bicultural brokers in search of balance. As middlemen, they exemplify the coexistence of oppositions. They frequently work both sides (or multiple sides) and run the danger of alienating both reservation officials and various Indian factions. Ambivalence appears more frequently than a progressive-traditional dichotomy among established and emerging leaders and, I would argue, among the more numerous and less visible individuals like William Wash.

These terms are not inherently problematical; indeed, they have some descriptive merit, even if simply as academic shorthand for issue-specific situations. The problem lies in their misuse, in the simplification, the dichotomization, of complex issues, personalities, and relationships. Creating new sets of terms will not solve it. Dividing the progressive-traditional dichotomy into three or four categories—for example, "native-oriented," "transitionals," "lower- and upper-acculturated"—is perhaps better but still suggests overly static organization and a unilinear progression. Describing a group or faction demands a generalization, a search for the "common." But in that search we should never lose sight of individual complexity and variability over time. We must define and redefine circumstances and try to convey the ambiguity of human motive and action within the common. Nowhere are those complexities and ambiguities greater than in the changing nature of nineteenth- and twentieth-century reservation leadership and in the emergence of the intermediaries, the cultural brokers, the William Washes.

Carlos Montezuma and the Fort McDowell Yavapai Community

PETER IVERSON

His live was a circle. Born the son of Coluyevah and Thilgeyah during the 1860s, his life encompassed a world they would never know. He would leave their world as a boy, live in the Midwest and in the East as a child, graduate from a university and a medical school, and marry an Anglo woman named Mary Keller. He would become one of the most outspoken and famous Indians of his day, emerging as a national figure who was drawn to the local affairs of the people he had been forced to leave behind. In his final years, he would withdraw increasingly from his medical career and the world of the city. Terminally ill with tuberculosis, he returned to the Yavapais of Fort McDowell in Arizona. There he died in January of 1923, and there he is buried.

The world would know him as Carlos Montezuma, but this was not a name he acquired at birth. His parents called him Wassaja, which in English could be translated as "signaling" or "beckoning." As Yavapai, his people lived in the central and southern Arizona country. The Yavapais also were known, and are known, as Mohave-Apaches—a confusing and misleading appellation which caused Montezuma no little difficulty late in life. As a Mohave-Apache, Montezuma inevitably became an Apache in the public eye, and his combative nature earned him such titles as "the fiery Apache." But he was not an Apache at all, for the Yavapais belong to the Yuman family. His people had some association with their eastern neighbors, the Tonto and San Carlos Apache. Those ties led to the Mohave-Apache label, even though the Apaches are of Athabascan heritage.

The Yavapais differed from other Yuman peoples in occupying a very large geographical area, which included a variety of terrain and climatic zones. While never numbering more than a few thousand in total population, they utilized an area of perhaps 20,000 square miles. They may have had cultural bonds with other Yuman peoples, but they fought and raided many of them over the years. The Pima and the Maricopa, their neighbors in the Fort McDowell area, historically had been their enemies. This animosity had not entirely disappeared by the time of Montezuma's birth.

By the 1860s, the Anglo-American world rapidly enclosed the world of the Yavapai and other Indians in Arizona. Resistance continued to this incursion, but competition grew for hunting and gathering resources; tensions increased among Native Americans. For good measure, by decade's end drought had settled over the southern part of the region. Anglos and Mexicans east of the Pimas near Florence were farming and starting to take advantage of the Gila River water that the

Peter Iverson, "Carlos Montezuma and the Fort McDowell Yavapai Community," *Journal of Arizona History* 22 (Winter 1981), 415–426. Reprinted by permission of the Arizona Historical Society.

Pimas once had to themselves. In 1871, in one of many clashes that took place between area tribes, a group of Pimas surprised some of the Yavapais, killing a number of them and capturing others. Wassaja and his two sisters survived, but were among the captives.

According to two Pima reminiscences, such captives could expect fair treatment by their captors and be brought up among the tribe. But these were extraordinary times. If a Pima could not take care of his new charge, the captive had to be sold. Such a future awaited Wassaja, whom the Pimas had dubbed Hejelweiikam ("Left Alone"), as well as his sisters. The three were separated at this time and Wassaja would never again see his sisters. They apparently were sold to a man who took them eventually to Mexico, where they died before Montezuma could rediscover them in adult life. Already separated from the rest of his family, he likewise would not see any of his immediate relatives alive. His mother attempted to recover her lost children and was shot by Army scouts; his father was among the Yavapai moved to the San Carlos reservation in the 1870s, where he died. An aunt and cousins would be his closest relatives, still living years later at the Fort McDowell community.

Three Pima men took young Wassaja to the village of Adamsville, near Florence, where they encountered an Italian immigrant named Carlos Gentile. A photographer and artist, Gentile had been attracted to Arizona by recent gold strikes. Though a bachelor, he grew interested in the welfare of the boy, and purchased him for thirty dollars. In Florence on November 17, 1871, Gentile had Wassaja baptized as Carlos Montezuma in the Church of the Assumption. The first name, of course, came from Wassaja's new benefactor; his last name, represented an attempt to give the boy some vestige of his Native American heritage, with the proximity of Montezuma's Castle and other ancient ruins probably influencing the particular selection of surname.

Carlos Montezuma would not return to his homeland for nearly three decades. Traveling with his guardian to Illinois and later to New York, young Carlos attended school in Chicago, Galesburg (Illinois), and Brooklyn between 1872 and 1878. Gentile suffered financial failure following a disastrous fire and eventually Montezuma was entrusted to the supervision of a Baptist missionary representative, George Ingalls. Ingalls brought Montezuma back to Illinois, where a Baptist minister, William R. Steadman, became his guardian. Following two years of preparatory work, Montezuma enrolled at the University of Illinois. He gained a B.S. degree in chemistry and then at the Chicago Medical College earned his M.D. in 1889.

Montezuma spent his first years after medical school as an Indian Service employee. Before he had finished his studies, he had established a friendship with the head of Carlisle Indian School, Richard H. Pratt. Pratt had contacted Commissioner of Indian Affairs Thomas J. Morgan, who in turn had offered Montezuma a position. The Yavapai physician toiled at Fort Stevenson in North Dakota, the Shoshone Agency in Nevada, and on the Colville reservation in Washington before returning eastward in 1893 to accept a post at Carlisle. In 1896 he resigned from the Bureau to enter private practice in Chicago.

His professional years in the West shaped his general perspective on Indian reservations. Essentially, Montezuma viewed reservations as prisons, in which

Native Americans were denied their rights, where their ambitions were discouraged, and where their isolation denied them contact with the white world, save those Anglos who sought to take advantage of them and their land resources. He saw Bureau personnel maintaining the reservation system in order to maintain themselves. Only when abolition of the Bureau had been achieved, could that system be altered.

Montezuma returned to the West on two occasions near the turn of the century. In January 1900, he visited Phoenix, Albuquerque, and Santa Fe, traveling as team physician for the Carlisle football squad. Phoenix Indian School's physical facilities impressed Montezuma, even though he feared "there is too much prejudice against the Indian, it being too near their homes to accomplish much good without any drawbacks." He must have been less impressed by the Phoenix football team, swamped by Carlisle, 83–6.

Montezuma came back to his home country in the autumn of 1901. This time he visited the area of his boyhood, met people who had known him as a child, and re-established personal contact with Yavapai relatives. He met Mike Burns, with whom he had already corresponded, and brothers Charles and George Dickens, who would become important figures in local affairs when Fort McDowell became a federal reserve. With such people, Montezuma began the process of becoming involved in the concerns of his tribesmen and, in so doing, began to understand more fully contemporary Indian life. In Montezuma, other Yavapais would discover a well-educated man who could serve as intermediary and champion. More immediately, they regarded Montezuma as a man sufficiently wealthy to help out less affluent relatives; Charles Dickens'* letter of November 2, 1901, is but one of many cases in point: "please Cousin Carlos will you please send me accordions only worth $3.25 just look at in Montgomery Ward book No. 516— and I know how to play accordians alright. . . . "

By the time of Montezuma's excursions to the Southwest, events were transpiring to make the Fort McDowell reservation a reality. On February 14, 1891, the Interior Department had been given the old military reserve of about 25,000 acres for disposal. In the autumn of 1900, the Bureau of Indian Affairs reported that eight or ten Yavapai families were living on the abandoned military installation. Despite Anglo opposition, Theodore Roosevelt on September 15, 1903, issued an executive order based upon an investigation and recommendation creating the Fort McDowell reserve for the Yavapais. The federal government had to compensate some non-Indian settlers, but the reservation became a reality.

When one considers the date and the era, the creation of McDowell as an Indian reservation symbolizes an impressive landmark. In a time when Indians all over the American West were losing their land, through cession and through sale of allotted lands, the Yavapais had gained rights to a home. In addition, unlike much of the Native American land remaining, it was land with promise; it straddled the Verde River and already included irrigated acreage. The land was theirs. Now they would have to struggle to keep it.

---

*A cousin of Carlos Montezuma's. Around the turn of the century, Indians were often renamed by school-teachers, missionaries, or government agents, at times with comical results.

Less than twenty years remained in the life of Carlos Montezuma. They would be two decades filled with remarkable activity and consuming energy, dedicated to Native American well-being. In particular, he had rediscovered his people. To bring them justice, to promote their vitality, to insure their future home became his special crusade. At the national level, Montezuma figured centrally in the establishment of the Society of American Indians and as a prominent critic of the Bureau of Indian Affairs. Significantly, he would miss the first annual meeting of the Society in the fall of 1911, despite the protests of other pan-Indian leaders; in part, he absented himself because of his suspicion that the organization had been tainted by association with the Bureau, but he also had another matter in mind. It was a time of crisis at McDowell and Montezuma returned there both in 1910 and in 1911.

Key federal officials believed it would be "in the best interests" of the Yavapais not to develop more extensive irrigation works at McDowell. The supposedly "turbulent" nature of the Verde River and the finite number of irrigable acres made such development an expensive and uncertain proposition. Rather, as the intrepid BIA engineer for irrigation, William H. Code, and others contended, the nearby Salt River reservation offered a better opportunity for irrigated farming. They suggested the Yavapais should accept irrigated allotments on Salt River, a reservation already occupied by Pimas and Maricopas. Code, in addition, argued that Indians should pay for benefits from federal projects and that the important *Winters* v. *U.S.* decision by the U.S. Supreme Court could not be applied to an executive-order reservation such as McDowell. The Winters decision of 1908 concluded that in creating the Fort Belknap reservation in Montana the government reserved sufficient water for the Indians to fulfill the purposes of the reservation. Without irrigation the arid land of Fort Belknap was without value; the same conclusion, of course, could have been applied to Fort McDowell. In any event, Code wished conveniently to disregard prior Yavapai use of the Verde—a yardstick traditionally applied in western water law.

The proposal to remove the Yavapais fit in with the overall expansion of the region. The new Salt River Project and the already growing Phoenix metropolitan area influenced the perspective of a man like Code, who worked hand-in-glove with the chief attorney for the Salt River Valley Water Users Association and with Chief Justice Edward Kent. Kent's decree in 1910 in *Hurley* v. *Abbott* ruled that the Yavapais could maintain their present water usage at McDowell, but assumed that they would soon move to Salt River. A month after Kent issued his decree, Bureau inspector Joe H. Norris visited McDowell and reported that removal should be encouraged. But he also noted widespread resistance. It would take "much skill and tact," he observed, to conclude the transfer successfully.

Most Yavapais did not want to move, both because of ties to McDowell and because of continuing antipathy toward the occupants of the Salt River reserve. Under the leadership of an elected leader, Chief Yuma Frank, they petitioned the government on May 10, 1910, against the relocation. At this time, they also appointed Carlos Montezuma as their official representative. Initially optimistic, Bureau Superintendent Charles Coe grew progressively less sanguine about the chances of convincing the Yavapai to vacate their land. "Mischief makers," he reported, stood in the way.

Montezuma gained the reputation among Indian-service personnel as the leading mischief maker of them all. He firmly opposed removal and advised his people not to agree to it under any circumstances. Montezuma did not believe that the Yavapais could keep their land at McDowell once they accepted allotments at Salt River. Charles Dickens and others assured him they would not go to Salt River. The doctor then launched a nationally publicized campaign in the halls of Congress against the change and by 1912 he had become firmly identified in the minds of various Bureau employees as a major source of their problems. In both Arizona and Washington, D.C., these officials refused to recognize Montezuma as a properly certified representative. Moreover, they resented the harsh criticism leveled at them by Montezuma and his allies. They were embarrassed when inconsistencies in policies were noted; they were angered when incompetence was observed and made public. Once Montezuma publicly questioned the abilities and the motives of Bureau employees, he gained the irrevocable image of an irresponsible meddler. Even with personnel changes in the field, local superintendents and other workers would pass along the word that Montezuma was an agitator, an outsider whose influence was significant and pernicious.

During the final decade of his life, Montezuma continued to wage a battle in Arizona that represented more than a struggle to preserve the homeland of the Yavapais. He transcended the usual boundary of tribe to see the common concerns shared by differing Indian communities. In this, he differed from many Yavapais who still nurtured ill feelings against some of their neighbors. George Dickens, for example, wrote in 1916 to Montezuma: "We always do believe that you are the means of having us remain here at McDowell. And had it not been for your aid; we might have been down on the deserts; with Pimas; who are our dead[ly] enemies." For Montezuma, by contrast, the Pimas now were friends who needed his assistance. The Salt River reservation Pimas, as well as Pimas and Maricopas near the community of Lehi, appointed Montezuma as their representative in 1912. Again, the Bureau denied the legitimacy of such an appointment.

Montezuma worked with his attorney, Joseph W. Latimer of Chicago, to forestall removal. In August 1912, it seemed as though they had succeeded. Secretary for the Interior Walter L. Fisher told Latimer that the department as well as the Indian office considered the allotment on the Salt River reservation a mistake for the Yavapais. Rather, the Yavapais should be allotted on McDowell. The Bureau immediately retreated from this position, but Montezuma and Latimer would not let its top officers forget Fisher's pronouncement. The conclusion reached by Fisher surely strengthened their case and helped to delay removal.

As he emphasized the Yavapai right to remain at McDowell, Montezuma also became embroiled in another dispute. In the minds of Bureau employees such as Superintendent Charles Coe, an essential component in the assimilationist program was the discouragement and ultimate elimination of traditional Indian customs. In 1912, 1913, and 1914, Coe carried on a concerted campaign to disallow tribal dances. Such dances, he asserted, had "immoral tendencies" which produced a "degrading effect" on boys and girls. Montezuma contended the Yavapais should be permitted an occasional celebration. In one instance, he convinced the new Commissioner of Indian Affairs, Cato Sells, to sanction a one-night dance in honor of Montezuma. For his indulgence, Sells earned the wrath not only of Coe but of Scottsdale missionary George H. Gebby as well, both of whom thundered about "animal passions" and "unmoral and half-civilized people." Sells soon changed his mind, telling Coe he could "prohibit any of the old time barbarous dances."

It seems ironic that the Coes of Bureau officialdom could clash so bitterly and frequently with a man such as Montezuma. They did, after all, share many of the same ideals, including education, hard work, and an outlook directed toward future goals. But Montezuma had several strikes against him. He was an outsider, an easterner, and a learned Indian with a forceful, aggressive, confident, persistent personality. Montezuma clearly did not respect them or their policies. Better educated, more worldly, and certainly as articulate, Montezuma threatened not only the self-esteem of the agents, but the work they saw themselves trying to accomplish under, at best, challenging circumstances. Montezuma gave voice and power to the misgivings and unhappinesses of Indian people. He made life more difficult. He was in the way.

The animosity reserved for Montezuma, moreover, is telling not merely about these employees, but about life on McDowell and other reservations of the era. Limitations on civil rights are readily apparent. Also obvious are uncertainties surrounding land ownership, land use, and water rights. The problems threatening Indians in southern Arizona bordered on the overwhelming; some were new and bewildering. In a small community such as the Fort McDowell reservation, few had the education, the facility with English, and the experience to be confident in coping with these dilemmas. Montezuma thus proved more than useful to the Yavapais, as he proved more than a nuisance to some Bureau employees. Chief Yuma Frank once described Coe and local farmer John Shafer as people who "impose laws and rules" rather than "advance us to progress"; he reminded Montezuma that "every Indian, from child to oldest age are looking upon you as our protector of our earthly rights."

For a while, Montezuma thought a visit by Sells in 1915 to McDowell might enable the commissioner to understand why the Yavapais did not want to move to Salt River and why they needed a dam at their present location. Upon arrival, however, Sells immediately informed the Yavapais he wanted them to relocate. A new dam cost too much for too little land to justify the expenditure. George Dickens replied that if a dam could not be built, they would stay anyway. This firmness pleased Montezuma, but the commissioner's stance infuriated him, particularly given the price tag for Roosevelt Dam and other projects.

With the inaugural of his magazine, *Wassaja,* in April 1916, Montezuma possessed a new weapon. Increasingly, the events at McDowell gained publicity in his newsletter. As much as he detested the institution of the reservation, he felt strongly that his people were entitled to land and to justice, using *Wassaja* to showcase the evolving centrality of the Yavapai community. Montezuma subjected Sells and local superintendents to scorn and severe criticism. In turn, they complained about Montezuma being "a source of constant trouble breeding," as Superintendent Byron Sharp once put it. They grumbled, too, about Montezuma's supporters. Given Montezuma's image in some of the historical literature as something of a "white man's Indian," it is worth noting that his strongest allies tended to be the most conservative residents of the reservations. Sharp and others labeled such people "the Montezuma crowd," "his henchmen," "the Montezuma bunch," even "the bolsheviki element."

The Bureau of Indian Affairs did have the satisfaction of denying Montezuma official enrollment on the San Carlos reservation—he had applied since his parents had lived there—but Bureau personnel could not deny Montezuma the satisfaction of helping to save McDowell, nor of completing his life's circle by coming home to die. He had started to complain about his health in the summer of 1922. As a physician, he realized he had tuberculosis, that dread disease which claimed so many Indian lives at this time. Eventually, he decided to leave Chicago and make a final trip to Arizona, where perhaps he could regain his former vitality.

It was not to be. Montezuma died in the land of his forefathers, January 31, 1923. He had refused Anglo medical care, saying he wanted to remain with his people. Montezuma is buried on McDowell; the reserve still belongs to the Yavapais. Perhaps the Yavapais of today have inherited some of that same combative spirit, given their long fight against tremendous odds to deny the construction of Orme Dam. Montezuma, surely, would have applauded that quality. In the final paragraph of the last article he would write in *Wassaja,* Carlos Montezuma spoke about the battle that remained for the Society of American Indians. He was writing, too, about his own remarkable career. The words serve as a proper epitaph:

> . . . if the world be against us, let us not be dismayed, let us not be discouraged, let us look up and go ahead, and fight on for freedom and citizenship of our people. If it means death, let us die on the pathway that leads to the emancipation of our race; keeping in our hearts that our children will pass over our graves to victory.

Within the Yavapai community at Fort McDowell, people do remember Montezuma, and his forthright defense of their land continues as a source for inspiration. Interviews conducted on the reserve confirm his legacy. John Williams says, "He said don't move out, so that's why we didn't move out." John Smith remembers: "People were pretty well attached to him. Everybody I knew liked him well. He seemed to love it here. That's why he came back here to die."

Carlos Montezuma looked to a changing world in which the Yavapais and other Native Americans would adapt, survive, and flourish. As he wrote in one of the first issues of *Wassaja,* he knew his people would endure:

> Who says the Indian race is vanishing?
> The Indians will not vanish.
> The feathers, paint and moccasin will vanish, but the Indians,—never!
> Just as long as there is a drop of human blood in America, the Indians will not vanish.
> His spirit is everywhere; the American Indian will not vanish.
> He has changed externally but he is not vanished.
> He is an industrial and commercial man, competing with the world; he has not
>   vanished.
>
> Whenever you see an Indian upholding the standard of his race, there you see the
>   Indian man—he has not vanished.
> The man part of the Indian is here, there and everywhere.
> The Indian race is vanishing? No, never! The race will live on and prosper forever.

◈ *FURTHER READING*

Donald Berthrong, *The Cheyenne and Arapaho Ordeal: Reservation and Agency Life in the Indian Territory, 1875–1907* (1976)
Grace Coolidge, *Teepee Neighbors* (1917)
Angie Debo, *And Still the Waters Run: The Betrayal of the Five Civilized Tribes* (1940)
———, *The Rise and Fall of the Choctaw Republic*, 2d ed. (1961)
Charles Eastman, *From the Deep Woods of Civilization: Chapters in the Autobiography of an Indian* (1916)
———, *The Indian To-day: The Past and Future of the First Americans* (1915)
———, *The Soul of the Indian: An Interpretation* (1911)
William E. Farr, *The Reservation Blackfeet, 1882–1945: A Photographic History of Cultural Survival* (1984)
Loretta Fowler, "Look at My Hair, It Is Gray: Age Grading, Ritual Authority and Political Change Among the Northern Arapahoes and Gros Ventres," in Douglas H. Ubelaker and Herman J. Viola, eds., *Plains Indian Studies* (1982)
E. Jane Gay, *With the Nez Perces: Alice Fletcher in the Field, 1889–92* (1981)
Jesse Green, ed., *Cushing at Zuni: The Correspondence and Journals of Frank Hamilton Cushing, 1879–1884* (1990)
William T. Hagan, *United States–Comanche Relations: The Reservation Years* (1976)
Hazel Hertzberg, *The Search for an American Indian Identity: Modern Pan-Indian Movements* (1971)
Frederick Hoxie, "From Prison to Homeland: The Cheyenne Indian Reservation Before World War I," *South Dakota History* 10 (1979), 1–24
Peter Iverson, *Carlos Montezuma and the Changing World of American Indians* (1982)
———, "Cowboys, Indians, and the Modern West," *Arizona and the West* 28 (Summer 1986), 107–124
Sergei Kan, "Russian Orthodox Brotherhoods Among the Tlingit: Missionary Goals and Native Response," *Ethnohistory* 32 (1985), 196–223
Sally J. McBeth, "Indian Boarding Schools and Ethnic Identity: An Example from the Southern Plains Tribes of Oklahoma," *Plains Anthropologist* 28 (1983), 119–128
John J. Matthews, *Sundown* (1934)
John H. Moore, "Cheyenne Political History, 1820–1894," *Ethnohistory* 21 (1974), 329–359
L. G. Moses, *The Indian Man: A Biography of James Mooney* (1984)
——— and Raymond Wilson, eds., *American Indian Lives: Essays on 19th and 20th Century Native American Leaders* (1985)
Robert Paschal Nespor, "From War Lance to Plow Share: The Cheyenne Dog Soldiers as Farmers, 1879–1930s," *Chronicles of Oklahoma,* 65 (Spring 1987), 42–75
Leo Simmons, ed., *Sun Chief: The Autobiography of a Hopi Indian* (1942)
Luther Standing Bear, *My People, the Sioux* (1928)
Michael L. Tate, "From Scout to Doughboy: The National Debate over Integrating Indians into the Military, 1891–1918," *Western Historical Quarterly* 17 (October 1986), 417–437
Mary Jane Warde, "Fight for Survival: The Indian Response to the Boomer Movement," *Chronicles of Oklahoma* 67 (Spring 1989), 30–51
Peter Whiteley, *Deliberate Acts: Changing Hopi Culture Through the Oraibi Split* (1988)
Raymond Wilson, *Ohiyesa: Charles Eastman, Santee Sioux* (1983)
Victoria Wyatt, "Alaskan Native Wage Earners in the 19th Century: Economic Choices and Ethnic Identity on Southeast Alaska's Frontier," *Pacific Northwest Quarterly* 78 (1987), 43–49
Zitkala-Sa, *American Indian Stories* (1921)

The Indian New Deal

The 1920s saw the emergence of a new kind of reformer, one who began to understand what Indians across the country had understood for decades: that federal Indian policy had failed, and failed badly. Native communities had lost most of their land. Trachoma, tuberculosis, and other diseases plagued the reservations. Boarding schools separated children from their families. Tribal governments were either nonexistent or given remarkably limited powers. Tribal religions, languages, arts, and crafts continued to be discouraged by the Bureau of Indian Affairs. But a reform movement originating in Pueblo country at the beginning of the 1920s led to a full-scale investigation of Indian affairs.

By the start of the so-called Indian New Deal, the leader of this movement, a newcomer to Indian country, had been named Commissioner of Indian Affairs. John Collier held this position longer than any other person had served or would serve in it. Although Congress and conservative forces in the West blocked some of his initiatives, and Collier—for a variety of reasons—personally received mixed reviews from Indian communities, the Indian New Deal clearly marked a turning-away from the assimilationist period.

Like the New Deal itself, the Indian New Deal emphasized community, the arts, and more careful use of the land. In addition, Collier spoke out for Indian religious freedom, including protection of traditional tribal ceremonies and the Native American Church. He also advocated bilingual, bicultural education, where Indian students would be encouraged to learn to read and write their own languages and to learn more about their own cultures as well as to receive instruction in the English language and about American society. Collier supported the right of Native communities to retain separate land bases, and encouraged additions to and consolidation of Indian reservations.

Like many reformers, Collier thought that he knew best, and he tended to impose his ideas more quickly and forcefully than sometimes was advisable. At the same time, he embraced cultural pluralism more fully than his predecessors had. Largely through Collier's efforts, the 1930s were noteworthy for new respect for native cultures and a cessation of land allotment.

Controversial and dogmatic, Collier and his legacy doubtless will be debated for many years to come.

◈ *D O C U M E N T S*

To publicize problems facing the Pueblo Indians of the Southwest, John Collier turned to popular newspapers and magazines to launch his critique of Indian policy. The first document is a good example of the Collier style, and the article's publication in *Sunset* magazine in 1923 alerted a wide audience to some of the difficulties confronting Indian communities. Collier's crusade, along with Indian peoples' ongoing complaints, eventually prompted the federal government to review existing practices and policies. The government survey, headed by Lewis Meriam, was published in 1928 and became known informally as the Meriam Report. Its criticisms helped to spur reforms during Herbert Hoover's administration and more extensive reforms during Franklin Delano Roosevelt's presidency. The second document is reprinted from the introduction to that report.

The primary piece of legislation passed during the Indian New Deal emerged as a compromise between Collier's aims and a cautious Congress. The third document is taken from that law, known as the Indian Reorganization Act (or the Wheeler-Howard Act, after its congressional sponsors). The remaining four documents speak to some of the initiatives and philosophies of the Collier commissionership. In retrospect, one of the most significant reform efforts was in the area of bilingual instruction. Bureau employees helped to develop written forms of a number of Indian languages and then published anthologies for use in Indian schools. "Today" is from one of those readers, a Navajo-English book authored by Ann Clark and translated into Navajo by Robert Young and William Morgan (Navajo).

Although the Bureau of Indian Affairs supported Indian cultures, it mirrored federal policy in its determination to combat soil erosion and promote soil conservation. Its efforts to pare livestock holdings on Indian lands may have been well intentioned, but they struck at the heart of many Native communities, for whom sheep, cattle, and horses had become central to the workings of their society. Not surprisingly, livestock reduction met with fierce resistance from the Navajos, Tohono O'odham (Papagos), and others.

Peter Blaine (Tohono O'odham), then a young man active in tribal politics, in the document reprinted here recalls reactions on his reservation to livestock reduction and to the Indian New Deal generally. In the final document, two other Indian men, Rupert Costo (Cahuilla) and Ben Reifel (Brulé Lakota), offer contrasting judgments of Collier and the Indian New Deal.

John Collier Tells of the Assault on Pueblo Indian Lives and Lands, 1923

The Pueblo Indians of New Mexico are now facing the crisis of their long history. They are the most interesting Red Indians living. They number about 8000 and live in twenty pueblos, or villages, five, six and seven thousand feet above the sea. New Mexico is a land of ruins—there are hundreds of ancient crumbled cities. These living pueblos were ancient when Cortez came to Mexico. They were the northern outposts of that great cultural system of the Mayans and Aztecs and they are its last survivors.

"Plundering the Pueblos" from *Sunset* (January, 1923), pp. 21–26. Reprinted by permission of Lane Publishing Company.

The Pueblos are fighting desperately against a quick destruction. Their opponents in the struggle are certain land-grabbing interests and, for the time being, the executive branch of the Government of the United States. This article is an appeal to American citizens to use their voice and vote to prevent the crowning infamy of the long black record of America's treatment of its aborigines.

The assault on the Pueblos is known by the name of the Bursum bill. This bill, sponsored by Secretary Fall of the Department of the Interior and called by him an "administration measure," was passed by the Senate in September. It was temporarily blocked in the Indian Committee of the House of Representatives by the General Federation of Women's Clubs, by Representative Swing of California and by other friends of the Indians. The effort to drive the bill through will be resumed when Congress convenes in December. This Bursum (Fall) bill will be "countered" by an opposition bill supported by friends of the Indians and of the square deal, and for reasons that will appear below, the struggle will have a national significance.

In simplest terms stated, the Bursum bill deprives the Pueblos of their land and their water and leaves several thousand Mexican and American claimants to fight each other legally for the possession of these lands and waters, to the perennial enrichment of lawyers who are working to enact the Bursum bill.

A Colorful History

One must know something about the Pueblos before he can understand the meaning of their present peril and struggle. A thousand years ago, these Indians built irrigation ditches and dwelt in their towns which are today as strange and as lovely as any cities of old Europe or Asia. They were warlike, but only in defensive war as against the Comanches, Utes and Apaches. They were artists in weaving, pottery, turquoise jewelry and decorative costumes. They were marvelous dancers and singers. Their religious and social organization was very complex, and they had found out a way to be communists* and individualists at one and the same time. They were kind toward children, and their women held high status in the domestic and community life.

What these Pueblos were when the white man came, they still are. The Pueblos of Zuni, Santo Domingo and Taos live on today, mysterious and colorful and vital from the ancient world. Gold-seekers devastated the Indian civilizations of Mexico. The Pueblos had no gold and were spared. The Franciscan monks came from Spain and slowly gained their way to the heart of the Pueblo Indians. The Indians voluntarily became Catholic Christians, but underneath they kept all their earlier pagan wildness and splendor. The Franciscans had no wish to stamp out the beauties of the archaic life, and it is these missionaries, and they alone, who showed statesmanship toward the Indians in the whole of America and through all the centuries to the present day. The approved method of "Americanizing" the Red Man has been and is to kill his soul and poison his body with white men's diseases, cut his long hair and dress him in overalls. Thanks to the Franciscans,

---

*In this context, "communism" refers to active membership within a community.

and to Spain which accepted their leadership in its Indian policies north of Mexico, the Pueblos exist today in their ancient wildness and sweetness, tempered with Christian creed and Christian morality.

Now to the Bursum bill and the proposed extermination of Pueblo life.

When the Pilgrim Fathers were landing in Massachusetts, Spain already was establishing Indian reservations round the pueblos. . . . Each pueblo received a grant of land, in most cases reaching a league to each point of the compass from the church within the Pueblo village—about 17,000 acres of ground. The Spanish understood the basic fact of Pueblo life, which is that the whole social, religious and moral structure of that life rests on the land and exists in terms of the land. Individual Indians were forbidden by Spain to sell this land. The pueblo as a community was forbidden to sell. White men were forbidden to buy or to seize the land. "Hereafter as heretofore," one reads in an old parchment signed by the Spanish Governor Maynez, which is still kept at the San Juan pueblo, "no one can sell or trade this land and no judge can pass on the title for sale. No Spanish governor has power to alienate these your lands." The Indians could loan or rent their land, but they could not sell it.

Law-Breaking "Squatters"

In Lincoln's first presidency, after the United States had annexed New Mexico, Congress re-affirmed these ancient grants, placing the lands in the keeping of the pueblos in fee simple. Each pueblo cherishes its guarantee of land tenure with Abraham Lincoln's signature at the end.

So much for the basic law governing these Indian lands. The practice has been different from the law. For centuries, non-Indian "squatters" have been encroaching. Since the United States became the Indians' guardian the squatters have multiplied faster and faster and have expanded their original claims. While these non-Indians were taking the land, they took the water as well. The Pueblos, through their councils and governors, have protested unceasingly—a vain despairing protest across two hundred years. The civil authorities, corrupt, inert, fearful of the vengeance upon themselves of the squatters, have refused to eject the trespassers. . . . This Bursum bill, sponsored by the Government Attorney and declared to be an administration measure by Secretary Fall, turns upside-down the whole three-centuries-old policy, burns every ancient guarantee to ashes, and instructs the United States Courts to proceed forthwith, without option, to the confirmation of every land seizure whether committed under Spain or Mexico or the United States. . . .

The bill specifies three types of land-claims against the Indians, these three types including all possible claims. First there are the lands occupied "with color of title" prior to 1848 when New Mexico became American. The Court is ordered to admit and to make competent "secondary evidence"—that is, rumor, oral evidence of alleged ancient documents, and anything else that is handy, in proof of these "colors of title." These holdings or claims pre-dating 1848 are to be awarded forthwith to the non-Indians with no compensation to the Indians. The second class of claims are those without color of title—that is, the simple trespasses planted by force without a vestige of legality, at any date prior to the year

1900. These claims represent hundreds of thousands of dollars of value taken from the Indians. The Court is ordered to accept as *prima facie* [legally adequate unless proven otherwise] evidence the surveys made at divers times by the United States Surveyor General. The last of these surveys marked out the lines of the sundry non-Indian claimants in accord with any claim any Mexican or American at the time chose to make, with a resultant increase of several hundred per cent in the alleged holdings of non-Indians. It is called the "Joy Survey," and the survey plats, hundreds in number, explicitly state that the survey was nothing more than a physical depicting of conditions and claims as they then existed (i.e., six years ago). The Joy Survey was not corruptly made. The object was to give the Government advance information as to the non-Indian claims so that the Government Attorney could prepare to meet these claims in court and *defeat them.* The Bursum bill makes this survey into *prima facie* evidence of the boundaries of the claims, adverse to the Indians, thereby turning it into an instrument against the Government and the Indians instead of a means of defense, which was its original and sole intent.

Empty Promises

Now the Bursum bill proceeds to offer compensation to the Indians. Compensation: from public land, irrigable, adjacent to the pueblos. In most instances no such public land exists. As an alternative, the Secretary of the Interior shall compensate the Indians with money which he will administer for their benefit. No appropriation clause; no definition of a method for evaluating the lands to determine the just compensation save that the court shall fix an *unimproved* value (this is land farmed and cultivated by the Indians for generations); merely an instruction to the Secretary of the Interior to "segregate" and administer for the Indians a phantasmal fund which he does not possess and has no means of acquiring. . . .

As for those who have seized Pueblo land since 1900, and down to the date when the Bursum bill becomes law, they too shall be confirmed in their ownership. For these, the Court shall decree a compensation which they, not the Government, will pay into the Department of Interior to be administered for the benefit, if such it be, of the Indians.

The bill is subtly evil in its clause regarding water-rights. Water is the land's life in New Mexico. Year by year the trespassers have been taking away the water which used to flow through these ancient ditches built by the Indians. Sometimes they have simply taken the water, sometimes they have secured an award from one or another branch of the New Mexico local courts. . . .

The Solution of the Problem

. . . The Indian race never produced better fighters than the Pueblo Indians, but there is in them no hatred on which a fanatical and hopeless ferocity could be based in the year 1922. They know their position, their rights and their needs, but they are helpless and voiceless "dependents" and "wards" of a Government which at present seems disposed to protect them with a feather while it attacks them with a club. The Taos Indians stated as clearly as can be stated the solution of the pueblo problem, which is a matter of common sense and honesty merely. The first element in this problem is water for irrigation. There is plenty of water, and every pueblo from Isleta in the south to Taos in the north could be supplied abundantly through inexpensive storage, pumping or drainage systems which at the same time would put into service thousands of acres of land outside the Indian grants. While the Government has been spending millions on irrigation systems elsewhere, these Indians and their non-Indian neighbors have been left to struggle with the elementary system of ditches, dependent on the stream-flow of the moment, which the Indians had devised before the Spaniards came.

With the increase of arable land the decent adjustment of the disputes over land will become a simple matter; without the increase of arable land it is an impossibility. Congress has "plenary" powers to settle this land question. It can empower a disinterested commission to investigate, adjust, award and compensate. Such a body, with quasi-judicial powers but with a flexible discretion which the permanent courts can not exercise, and with the expanded farming area to use as a basis for adjustments, could clear every non-Indian claim that has a shadow of legitimacy while at the same time giving back to the Pueblos all they need for present life and future growth of population. Will there be a future growth of Pueblo population? There will be, if the Pueblos can get their economic and moral basis of land restored and if the gross insufficiency of the Government's medical and health service can be remedied. This latter subject is involved with the organization of the Bureau of Indian Affairs, which is not the topic of the present article.

A nation-wide organization has enlisted itself for the struggle over Indian welfare. The General Federation of Women's Clubs has two million members. It is fundamentally committed and will see this Indian question through to the end. Its Indian Welfare chairman is Mrs. Stella M. Atwood of Riverside, California, whose knowledge of the Indian field is immense and whose sagacity equals her emotional driving power. But the Women's Federation is not enough by itself, and especially in the emergency created by the Bursum bill every individual and every organization loyal to this country's fair name should become active.

Can the Pueblo Indian communities survive even if they receive justice? The answer lies in history. They already have survived four centuries of contact with the white man's world. Even those Pueblos whose condition is most piteous— Tesuque and San Ildefonso, starving, and riddled with preventable and curable disease—have yet not lost their own souls. Still through the veins of their members runs that fierce joy expressed in a dance and song which have lost none of their splendor. Still, and increasingly, they produce objects of beauty—vases and rings and graceful adobe dwellings. Still the members of the tribe are faithful to the tribe, and the old industry continues in the face of discouragements which would disintegrate most white communities. This is true even of these Pueblos which have been the worst wronged. As for Zuni and Taos, they are living mightily forward; they are developing, while holding fast to that which is good in their old life. They have as much to teach to the white man as they have to learn from him. They belong to the future as much as to the past. They are a national asset; and the Bursum bill, which is a blow at them, is a blow at an innocent, helpless and priceless part of America's cultural life.

Lewis Meriam Summarizes the Problems
Facing American Indians, 1928

An overwhelming majority of the Indians are poor, even extremely poor, and they are not adjusted to the economic and social system of the dominant white civilization.

The poverty of the Indians and their lack of adjustment to the dominant economic and social systems produce the vicious circle ordinarily found among any people under such circumstances. Because of interrelationships, causes cannot be differentiated from effects. The only course is to state briefly the conditions found that are part of this vicious circle of poverty and maladjustment.

Health.   The health of the Indians as compared with that of the general population is bad. Although accurate mortality and morbidity statistics are commonly lacking, the existing evidence warrants the statement that both the general death rate and the infant mortality rate are high. Tuberculosis is extremely prevalent. Trachoma, a communicable disease which produces blindness, is a major problem because of its great prevalence and the danger of its spreading among both the Indians and the whites.

Living Conditions.   The prevailing living conditions among the great majority of the Indians are conducive to the development and spread of disease. With comparatively few exceptions the diet of the Indians is bad. It is generally insufficient in quantity, lacking in variety, and poorly prepared. The two great preventive elements in diet, milk, and fruits and green vegetables, are notably absent. Most tribes use fruits and vegetables in season, but even then the supply is ordinarily insufficient. The use of milk is rare, and it is generally not available even for infants. Babies, when weaned, are ordinarily put on substantially the same diet as older children and adults, a diet consisting mainly of meats and starches.

The housing conditions are likewise conducive to bad health. Both in the primitive dwellings and in the majority of more or less permanent homes which in some cases have replaced them, there is great overcrowding, so that all members of the family are exposed to any disease that develops, and it is virtually impossible in any way even partially to isolate a person suffering from a communicable disease. . . .

Sanitary facilities are generally lacking. Except among the relatively few well-to-do Indians the houses seldom have a private water supply or any toilet facilities whatever. Even privies are exceptional. Water is ordinarily carried considerable distances from natural springs or streams, or occasionally from wells. In many sections the supply is inadequate, although in some jurisdictions, notably in the desert country of the Southwest, the government has materially improved the situation, an activity that is appreciated by the Indians.

Lewis Meriam, "General Summary of Findings and Recommendations" from *The Problem of Indian Administration,* Johns Hopkins, 1928, pp. 3–8. Reprinted by permission of The Johns Hopkins University Press.

Economic Conditions. The income of the typical Indian family is low and the earned income extremely low. From the standpoint of the white man the typical Indian is not industrious, nor is he an effective worker when he does work. Much of his activity is expended in lines which produce a relatively small return either in goods or money. He generally ekes out an existence through unearned income from leases of his land, the sale of land, per capita payments from tribal funds, or in exceptional cases through rations given him by the government. The number of Indians who are supporting themselves through their own efforts, according to what a white man would regard as the minimum standard of health and decency, is extremely small. What little they secure from their own efforts or from other sources is rarely effectively used.

The main occupations of the men are some outdoor work, mostly of an agricultural nature, but the number of real farmers is comparatively small. A considerable proportion engage more or less casually in unskilled labor. By many Indians several different kinds of activity are followed spasmodically, a little agriculture, a little fishing, hunting, trapping, wood cutting, or gathering of native products, occasional labor and hauling, and a great deal of just idling. Very seldom do the Indians work about their homes as the typical white man does. Although the permanent structures in which they live after giving up primitive dwellings are simple and such as they might easily build and develop for themselves, little evidence of such activity was seen. Even where more advanced Indians occupied structures similar to those occupied by neighboring whites it was almost always possible to tell the Indian homes from the white by the fact that the white man did much more than the Indian in keeping his house in condition.

In justice to the Indians it should be said that many of them are living on lands from which a trained and experienced white man could scarcely wrest a reasonable living. In some instances the land originally set apart for the Indians was of little value for agricultural operations other than grazing. In other instances part of the land was excellent but the Indians did not appreciate its value. Often when individual allotments were made, they chose for themselves the poorer parts, because those parts were near a domestic water supply or a source of firewood, or because they furnished some native product important to the Indians in their primitive life. Frequently the better sections of the land originally set apart for the Indians have fallen into the hands of the whites, and the Indians have retreated to the poorer lands remote from markets.

In many places crops can be raised only by the practice of irrigation. Many Indians in the Southwest are successful in a small way with their own primitive systems of irrigation. When modern highly developed irrigation systems have been supplied by governmental activities, the Indians have rarely been ready to make effective use of the land and water. If the modern irrigation enterprise has been successful from an economic standpoint, the tendency has been for whites to gain possession of the land either by purchase or by leases. If the enterprise has not been economically a success, the Indians generally retain possession of the land, but they do not know how to use it effectively, and get much less out of it than a white man would.

The remoteness of their homes often prevents them from easily securing opportunities for wage earning, nor do they have many contacts with persons dwelling in urban communities where they might find employment. Even the boys and girls graduating from government schools have comparatively little vocational guidance or aid in finding profitable employment.

When all these factors are taken into consideration it is not surprising to find low incomes, low standards of living, and poor health.

Suffering and Discontent.   Some people assert that the Indians prefer to live as they do; that they are happier in their idleness and irresponsibility. The question may be raised whether these persons do not mistake for happiness and content an almost oriental fatalism and resignation. The survey staff found altogether too much evidence of real suffering and discontent to subscribe to the belief that the Indians are reasonably satisfied with their condition. The amount of serious illness and poverty is too great to permit of real contentment. The Indian is like the white man in his affection for his children and he feels keenly the sickness and the loss of his offspring.

The Causes of Poverty.   The economic basis of the primitive culture of the Indians has been largely destroyed by the encroachment of white civilization. The Indians can no longer make a living as they did in the past by hunting, fishing, gathering wild products, and the extremely limited practice of primitive agriculture. The social system that evolved from their past economic life is ill suited to the conditions that now confront them, notably in the matter of the division of labor between the men and the women. They are by no means yet adjusted to the new economic and social conditions that confront them.

Several past policies adopted by the government in dealing with the Indians have been of a type which, if long continued, would tend to pauperize any race. Most notable was the practice of issuing rations to able-bodied Indians. Having moved the Indians from their ancestral lands to restricted reservations as a war measure, the government undertook to feed them and to perform certain services for them which a normal people do for themselves. The Indians at the outset had to accept this aid as a matter of necessity, but promptly they came to regard it as a matter of right, as indeed it was at the time and under the conditions of the inauguration of the ration system. They felt, and many of them still feel, that the government owes them a living, having taken their lands from them, and that they are under no obligation to support themselves. They have thus inevitably developed a pauper point of view.

When the government adopted the policy of individual ownership of the land on the reservations, the expectation was that the Indians would become farmers. Part of the plan was to instruct and aid them in agriculture, but this vital part was not pressed with vigor and intelligence. It almost seems as if the government assumed that some magic in individual ownership of property would in itself prove an educational civilizing factor, but unfortunately this policy has for the most part operated in the opposite direction. Individual ownership has in many instances permitted Indians to sell their allotments and to live for a time on the unearned income resulting from the sale. Individual ownership brought promptly all the details of inheritance, and frequently the sale of the property of the deceased Indians to whites so that the estate could be divided among the heirs. To the heirs the sale brought further unearned income, thereby lessening the necessity for self support. Many Indians were not ready to make effective use of their individual allotments. Some of the allotments were of such a character that they could not be effectively used by anyone in small units. The solution was to permit the Indians through the government to lease their lands to the whites. In some instances government officers encouraged leasing, as the whites were anxious for the use of the land and it was far easier to administer property leased to whites than to educate and stimulate Indians to use their own property. The lease money, though generally small in amount, gave the Indians further unearned income to permit the continuance of a life of idleness.

Surplus land remaining after allotments were made was often sold and the proceeds placed in a tribal fund. Natural resources, such as timber and oil, were sold and the money paid either into tribal funds or to individual Indians if the land had been allotted. From time to time per capita payments were made to the individual Indians from tribal funds. These policies all added to the unearned income of the Indian and postponed the day when it would be necessary for him to go to work to support himself.

Since the Indians were ignorant of money and its use, had little or no sense of values, and fell an easy victim to any white man who wanted to take away their property, the government, through its Indian Service employees, often took the easiest course of managing all the Indians' property for them. The government kept the Indians' money for them at the agency. When the Indians wanted something they would go to the government agent, as a child would go to his parents, and ask for it. The government agent would make all the decisions, and in many instances would either buy the thing requested or give the Indians a store order for it. Although money was sometimes given the Indians, the general belief was that the Indians could not be trusted to spend the money for the purpose agreed upon with the agent, and therefore they must not be given opportunity to misapply it. At some agencies this practice still exists, although it gives the Indians no education in the use of money, is irritating to them, and tends to decrease responsibility and increase the pauper attitude.

The typical Indian, however, has not yet advanced to the point where he has the knowledge of money and values, and of business methods that will permit him to control his own property without aid, advice, and some restrictions; nor is he ready to work consistently and regularly at more or less routine labor. . . .

The Indian Reorganization Act (Wheeler-Howard Act), 1934

To conserve and develop Indian lands and resources; to extend to Indians the right to form business and other organizations; to establish a credit system for Indians; to grant certain rights of home rule to Indians; to provide for vocational education for Indians; and for other purposes.

Be it enacted by the Senate and House of Representatives of the United States of America in Congress assembled, That hereafter no land of any Indian reservation, created or set apart by treaty or agreement with the Indians, Act of Congress,

Executive order, purchase, or otherwise, shall be allotted in severalty to any Indian.

Sec. 2.   The existing periods of trust placed upon any Indian lands and any restriction on alienation thereof are hereby extended and continued until otherwise directed by Congress.

Sec. 3.   The Secretary of the Interior, if he shall find it to be in the public interest, is hereby authorized to restore to tribal ownership the remaining surplus lands of any Indian reservation heretofore opened, or authorized to be opened, to sale, or any other form of disposal by Presidential proclamation, or by any of the public-land laws of the United States: *Provided, however,* That valid rights or claims of any persons to any lands so withdrawn existing on the date of the withdrawal shall not be affected by this Act: *Provided further,* That this section shall not apply to lands within any reclamation project heretofore authorized in any Indian reservation. . . .

Sec. 4.   Except as herein provided, no sale, devise, gift, exchange or other transfer of restricted Indian lands or of shares in the assets of any Indian tribe or corporation organized hereunder, shall be made or approved: *Provided, however,* That such lands or interests may, with the approval of the Secretary of the Interior, be sold, devised, or otherwise transferred to the Indian tribe in which the lands or shares are located or from which the shares were derived or to a successor corporation; and in all instances such lands or interests shall descend or be devised, in accordance with the then existing laws of the State, or Federal laws where applicable, in which said lands are located or in which the subject matter of the corporation is located, to any member of such tribe or of such corporation or any heirs of such member: *Provided further,* That the Secretary of the Interior may authorize voluntary exchanges of lands of equal value and the voluntary exchange of shares of equal value whenever such exchange, in his judgment, is expedient and beneficial for or compatible with the proper consolidation of Indian lands and for the benefit of cooperative organizations.

Sec. 5.   The Secretary of the Interior is hereby authorized, in his discretion, to acquire through purchase, relinquishment, gift, exchange, or assignment, any interest in lands, water rights or surface rights to lands, within or without existing reservations, including trust or otherwise restricted allotments whether the allottee be living or deceased, for the purpose of providing land for Indians.

For the acquisition of such lands, interests in lands, water rights, and surface rights, and for expenses incident to such acquisition, there is hereby authorized to be appropriated, out of any funds in the Treasury not otherwise appropriated, a sum not to exceed $2,000,000 in any one fiscal year. . . .

Title to any lands or rights acquired pursuant to this Act shall be taken in the name of the United States in trust for the Indian tribe or individual Indian for which the land is acquired, and such lands or rights shall be exempt from State and local taxation.

Sec. 6.   The Secretary of the Interior is directed to make rules and regulations for the operation and management of Indian forestry units on the principle of sustained-yield management, to restrict the number of livestock grazed on Indian range units to the estimated carrying capacity of such ranges, and to promulgate such other rules and regulations as may be necessary to protect the range from deterioration, to prevent soil erosion, to assure full utilization of the range, and like purposes.

Sec. 7.   The Secretary of the Interior is hereby authorized to proclaim new Indian reservations on lands acquired pursuant to any authority conferred by this Act, or to add such lands to existing reservations: *Provided,* That lands added to existing reservations shall be designated for the exclusive use of Indians entitled by enrollment or by tribal membership to residence at such reservations. . . .

Sec. 9.   There is hereby authorized to be appropriated, out of any funds in the Treasury not otherwise appropriated, such sums as may be necessary, but not to exceed $250,000 in any fiscal year, to be expended at the order of the Secretary of the Interior, in defraying the expenses of organizing Indian chartered corporations or other organizations created under this Act.

Sec. 10.   There is hereby authorized to be appropriated, out of any funds in the Treasury not otherwise appropriated, the sum of $10,000,000 to be established as a revolving fund from which the Secretary of the Interior, under such rules and regulations as he may prescribe, may make loans to Indian chartered corporations for the purpose of promoting the economic development of such tribes and of their members, and may defray the expenses of administering such loans. Repayment of amounts loaned under this authorization shall be credited to the revolving fund and shall be available for the purposes for which the fund is established. A report shall be made annually to Congress of transactions under this authorization.

Sec. 11.   There is hereby authorized to be appropriated, out of any funds in the United States Treasury not otherwise appropriated, a sum not to exceed $250,000 annually, together with any unexpended balances of previous appropriations made pursuant to this section, for loans to Indians for the payment of tuition and other expenses in recognized vocational and trade schools: *Provided,* That not more than $50,000 of such sum shall be available for loans to Indian students in high schools and colleges. Such loans shall be reimbursable under rules established by the Commissioner of Indian Affairs. . . .

Sec. 16.   Any Indian tribe, or tribes, residing on the same reservation, shall have the right to organize for its common welfare, and may adopt an appropriate constitution and bylaws, which shall become effective when ratified by a majority vote of the adult members of the tribe, or of the adult Indians residing on such reservation, as the case may be, at a special election authorized and called by the Secretary of the Interior under such rules and regulations as he may prescribe. Such constitution and bylaws when ratified as aforesaid and approved by the

Secretary of the Interior shall be revocable by an election open to the same voters and conducted in the same manner as hereinabove provided. Amendments to the constitution and bylaws may be ratified and approved by the Secretary in the same manner as the original constitution and bylaws.

In addition to all powers vested in any Indian tribe or tribal council by existing law, the constitution adopted by said tribe shall also vest in such tribe or its tribal council the following rights and powers: To employ legal counsel, the choice of counsel and fixing of fees to be subject to the approval of the Secretary of the Interior; to prevent the sale, disposition, lease, or encumbrance of tribal lands, interests in lands, or other tribal assets without the consent of the tribe; and to negotiate with the Federal, State, and local Governments. The Secretary of the Interior shall advise such tribe or its tribal council of all appropriation estimates or Federal projects for the benefit of the tribe prior to the submission of such estimates to the Bureau of the Budget and the Congress.

Sec. 17.   The Secretary of the Interior may, upon petition by at least one-third of the adult Indians, issue a charter of incorporation to such tribe: *Provided,* That such charter shall not become operative until ratified at a special election by a majority vote of the adult Indians living on the reservation. Such charter may convey to the incorporated tribe the power to purchase, take by gift, or bequest, or otherwise, own, hold, manage, operate, and dispose of property of every description, real and personal, including the power to purchase restricted Indian lands and to issue in exchange therefor interests in corporate property, and such further powers as may be incidental to the conduct of corporate business, not inconsistent with law, but no authority shall be granted to sell, mortgage, or lease for a period exceeding ten years any of the land included in the limits of the reservation. Any charter so issued shall not be revoked or surrended except by Act of Congress.

Sec. 18.   This Act shall not apply to any reservation wherein a majority of the adult Indians, voting at a special election duly called by the Secretary of the Interior, shall vote against its application. It shall be the duty of the Secretary of the Interior, within one year after the passage and approval of this Act, to call such an election, which election shall be held by secret ballot upon thirty days' notice.

Sec. 19.   The term "Indian" as used in this Act shall include all persons of Indian descent who are members of any recognized Indian tribe now under Federal jurisdiction, and all persons who are descendants of such members who were, on June 1, 1934, residing within the present boundaries of any Indian reservation, and shall further include all other persons of one-half or more Indian blood. For the purposes of this Act, Eskimos and other aboriginal peoples of Alaska shall be considered Indians. The term "tribe" wherever used in this Act shall be construed to refer to any Indian tribe, organized band, pueblo, or the Indians residing on one reservation. The words "adult Indians" wherever used in this Act shall be construed to refer to Indians who have attained the age of twenty-one years.

Approved, June 18, 1934.

"Today": An Excerpt from a Bilingual Navajo-English Reader, 1942

Today
   we leave my mother's hogan,
   my mother's winter hogan.
We leave the shelter of its
   rounded walls.
We leave its friendly center fire.
We drive our sheep to the mountains.
For the sheep,
   there is grass and shade
   and water,
   flowing water
   and water standing still,
   in the mountains.
There is no wind.
There is no sand
   up there.

Díí jí
   shimá bighandóó ńdii'náh,
   shimá haigo bighandóó.
Hooghan názbasgo nástł' inéé
   bits'áá' ńdii'náh.
Hooghan 'ałníí'gi ko' yéé
   bits'áá 'ńdii'náh.
Dziłgóó nihidibé dah dadíńíilkaad.
Dibé tł'oh dóó chahash'oh
   dóó tó
   dóó tó dańlínígíí
   dóó tó naazkánígíí bá hóló
dziłtahgi.
'Áadi
   doo níyol da
   dóó séí'ádin.

Peter Blaine (Tohono O'odham) Remembers Livestock Reduction, 1981

. . . Before the white man moved the Papago Agency from San Xavier to Sells [two towns on the Tohono O'odham reservations in southern Arizona], there was plenty of cattle, plenty of grass, and plenty of rain. In 1922, when I came to Sells

From *Papagos and Politics* by Peter Blaine, Tucson: Arizona Historical Society, 1981, pp. 75–77. Reprinted by permission of the Arizona Historical Society.

for my brother's body I went through the valleys. Cattle were all over and the grass was high. There was blue grama and common grama grass. The best grass was below the Baboquivari Mountains. Along the foothills there was a grass we called "cotton grass," because it looked like cotton. It was four or five feet high. It grew as high as Johnson grass, but the drought would hit and the cattle ate it clear down to the roots. During droughts cattle will eat anything. If they're starving they'll eat the pads, fruit, and even dig the roots up of a prickly pear cactus. The white cholla cactus they'll eat, clear down to the ground. Of course, they eat mesquite beans, too. But if a drought hit and lasted a long time, many cattle would die.

The government tried to tell the Papago cattlemen that cattle died on our ranges because of too many mesquite trees and too many rodents. Mesquite clearing had started before I came out to Sells. The CCC [Civilian Conservation Corps] started this around Crowhang village. The government claimed that the pasture grass would be better if mesquite trees were cleared off. But the people didn't like this because the cattle ate the beans of the mesquite trees and, more importantly, the mesquite beans were a native food for the Papagos. The mesquite wood was also used for fire and for fences. Mesquite was weaved together to build corral fences. We didn't use wire. Even when wire was made available we didn't use it. The Indians don't like to use wire because the cattle would get cut up by it. They still use the mesquite to build fences.

The people were not asked about this mesquite clearing program. The Crowhang people came to me and asked why and how the government was clearing this important tree from their land. I asked them if they had approved of this work. They said, "No!" This was another time when our people were not asked about work being done. Somebody just made the plans to pull up mesquite and it just went from there. Who approved it? Nobody knows. Finally, after I had the people listened to, this mesquite clearing was moved to the east.

Then the government came up with some thought that rodents were eating grass and grass seeds. We ran a little experiment in the Forest Service, just to see if rodents were causing the grass to go away. There were little plots of land where grass was planted to see if it could grow. We put a little fence around each plot to keep any rodents out. Soon after the experiment started we had some big rains. I then took Mr. Holst out to the Baboquivari Valley to show him all the grass that had grown after the rains. After all good rains there was grass over all the country. The grass around those little plots had grown so high that we couldn't see the fences marking the protected areas. It wasn't rodents at all that hurt our grass. It was just the drought that killed our grass.

It was one of my duties to check all kinds of plants that grow on the reservation. When I was out I would look for new plants. When I saw something unusual I would tell Mr. Holst. We'd go out and study it. One day after a whole week's rain I noticed a plant that looked like an alfalfa. It was growing all over the foothills. I saw it on a trip I was making down to Menager's Dam. I had never seen this plant before. I stopped and pulled up one of these plants. I took it to the old chief down that way. He looked at it and said, "This plant that you have used to grow out here fifty years ago, when we had lots of rain." This was filaree, a plant that was found up in the Apache country. Cattle really liked it. I brought the plant back to the office and showed it to Mr. Holst. I asked him, "How come the little rodents didn't eat the seeds of this plant?"

Sometimes the winter rains were too late and sometimes too early to help the grass on the range. I say that we never overgrazed! The thing that cut down our cattle was drought. If the drought hits, grass dies. We leave it up to the drought, he'll cut down on cattle. We didn't get rid of our cattle just because someone told us to. The Indians knew that it wasn't rodents or too many mesquite trees that caused the lack of grass. It was the lack of rain. We didn't see any sense in cutting our cattle down; we took our chances with the rain. If it rains, good. If not, then we are hurt. If cattle are going to die, let them die. But they will die right here on their reservation. Right here in their home country. That was the answer that we gave the white man and his Agency. I fought my boss all the way on this cutting down of Papago cattle on the reservation. The white man never understood our way on this. . . .

Rupert Costo (Cahuilla) Condemns the Indian New Deal, 1986

. . . The IRA [Indian Reorganization Act of 1934] was the last great drive to assimilate the American Indian. It was also a program to colonialize the Indian tribes. All else had failed to liberate the Indians from their land: genocide, treaty-making and treaty-breaking, substandard education, disruption of Indian religion and culture, and the last and most oppressive of such measures, the Dawes Allotment Act. Assimilation into the dominant society, if by assimilation we mean the adoption of certain technologies and techniques, had already been underway for some hundred years. After all, the Indians were not and are not fools; we are always ready to improve our condition. But assimilation, meaning fading into the general society with a complete loss of our identity and our culture, was another thing entirely, and we had fought against this from the first coming of the white man.

This type of assimilation would be the foregone conclusion of the Indian Reorganization Act. Colonialization of the tribes was to be accomplished through communal enclaves subject to federal domination through the power of the secretary of the interior. Now this view of the IRA is now held by practically all of the historians who write the history of the IRA era.

The record shows otherwise. All one must do is to read and study the hearings held in the Congress, the testimony of Indian witnesses, the evidence of life itself, the statements of the Indian commissioner, and the practically identical tribal constitutions adopted by, or forced upon, the Indians under the IRA. In these constitutions the authority of the secretary of the interior is more powerful than it was before the so-called New Deal. No wonder the Indians called it the Indian Raw Deal.

The IRA did not allow the Indians their independence, which was guaranteed

Rupert Costo remarks in Kenneth Philp, editor, *Indian Self Rule: First Hand Accounts of Indian-White Relations from Roosevelt to Reagan,* 1986, pp. 48–52. Reprinted by permission of Howe Brothers.

in treaties and agreements and confirmed in court decisions. It did not protect their sovereignty. Collier did not invent self-government: the right of Indians to make their own decisions, to make their own mistakes, to control their own destiny. The IRA had within it, in its wording and in its instruments, such as the tribal constitutions, the destruction of the treaties and of Indian self-government.

There are those who believe that most of the Indians who opposed the IRA were members of allotted tribes who had been economically successful with their allotments. This is a simplistic response, and one that displays a serious lack of understanding of Indian affairs and history. Allotments certainly did not originate with the Dawes Act. They also were established in treaties. The Dawes Act did, however, force Indians into the allotment system, with a guarantee that they would have to sell their land, either through taxation or by sheer physical force. Those who survived created what they had always wanted, an estate for themselves and their children, a type of insurance against being moved again like cattle to other lands and the chance to make a decent living on their own land. . . .

On May 17, 1934, in hearings before the Senate, the great Yakima nation, in a statement signed by their chiefs and councilmen, said, "We feel that the best interests of the Indians can be preserved by the continuance of treaty laws and carried out in conformity with the treaty of 1855 entered into by the fathers of some of the undersigned chiefs and Governor Stevens of the territory of Washington." Now these are only a few examples of some of the testimony given by Indian witnesses and by most of the tribes. Many refused to even consider the IRA and rejected it outright.

But the commissioner of Indian affairs reported to the House of Representatives on May 7, 1934, that, "I do not think that any study of the subject with all of the supporting petitions, reports, and referendums could leave any doubt that the Indian opinion is strongly for the bill." He then proceeded with this outright falsification of the facts, saying, "In Oklahoma I would say quite overwhelmingly they favor the bill." Both Congressmen Roy Ayres of Montana and Theodore Werner of South Dakota disputed those statements. They showed that Collier was falsifying the facts.

During April 1934, the tribes that had bitterly opposed the IRA attended some of the ten meetings held by the commissioner of Indian affairs throughout the country. Here, as evidence shows, they were subjected to Collier's manipulations. In May, they came before the House of Representatives and completely reversed themselves. In fact, they gave a blanket endorsement to the Indian Reorganization Act. The congressmen, in shocked disbelief, prodded them again and again. Finally they asked, "If the proposed legislation is completely changed into an entirely different act would you then also endorse it?" The Indian delegates, according to many of their tribesmen and tribeswomen said, without any authority of their people, "Yes. Even then we would endorse it." In short, at least two of the tribal delegates gave a blanket endorsement of the IRA in advance of the final legislation. How did this happen? I can tell you how it happened. They received promises that were never kept. They received some special considerations and they felt the arm of the enforcer ordering them to accept or be destroyed. That was Collier's way, as I very well know.

In California, at Riverside, forty tribes were assembled. All but three voted against the proposed bill. Collier then reported that most of the California tribes were for the proposed bill. The historical record was falsified, and his falsification was swallowed whole by Kenneth Philp who also stated in his book that "several mission Indians, led by Rupert Costo, agreed with an unsigned three-page circular sent around the reservation which claimed Collier's ideas were 'communistic and socialistic.'" The implication is that this was a sneaky, underhanded job. The truth is that there was a complete cover letter with that circular, signed by me and my tribe. We were outraged at the provisions of the proposed bill.

It is a curious fact that, in all the ten meetings held with Indians over the country, in not one meeting was there a copy of the proposed legislation put before the people. We were asked to vote on so-called explanations. The bill itself was withheld. We were told we need not vote but the meetings were only to discuss the Collier explanations. In the end, however, we were required to vote. And I suppose you would call all this maneuvering self-rule. I call it fraud. The Hupa Indians of northern California had two petitions on this proposed bill. One was to be signed by those supporting it; the other, by those who opposed it. In neither case had anyone seen the actual bill, but they rejected it on a massive scale on the basis of the explanations alone.

The Crow rejected the IRA and stated for the record in a letter to Senator Burton K. Wheeler, one of the sponsors of the bill, "That under the Collier-chartered community plan, which has been compared to a fifth-rate *poor farm* by newspapers in Indian country, the Indian is being led to believe that they, for the first time in history, would have self-government." But according to the bill, any plans the Indians might have for such self-government would have to be first submitted to the interior secretary or commissioner of Indian affairs for supervision and approval. Self-government to this extent was already accomplished through the tribal councils and tribal business committees, which, by the way, were organized and functioning long before Collier manifested his great interest in the Indians in general.

Now at these councils, Indians discuss matters they consider of vital interest and initiate measures for better management of their affairs, but no action may become effective without the approval of the commissioner of Indian affairs, or the secretary of the interior. Where is the advantage of an almost similar system bearing John Collier's name? Can we say that this power of the interior was forced upon the commissioner in the final proposed bill? No, not at all. His original bill contained not less than thirty-three references making it obligatory for the interior secretary to approve vital decisions of the tribes.

It is a matter of record that in California Indians were afraid to come to meetings for fear of losing their jobs if they showed disapproval of the Collier proposed bill. On the second day of the Riverside meeting, the Collier enforcers would not allow us to speak, and according to one report of an Indian organization, "they almost threw Rupert Costo out." Another element of the Collier enforcer policy is found in the warning to civil service employees in the BIA by Interior Secretary Ickes that they would be dismissed if they spoke out against Bureau policies on the proposed bill. . . .

Ben Reifel (Brulé Lakota) Praises
the Legacy of John Collier, 1986

While I was a boy growing up on the Rosebud Indian Reservation, we had the most sickening poverty that one could imagine. Tuberculosis was a killer of Indians. The people on the Pine Ridge Reservation and at Oglala were eating their horses to survive. Impoverishment was everywhere.

I remember going to Oglala in 1933 as a farm agent. The superintendent of the reservation, a gentleman by the name of James H. McGregor, looked to me almost as a son. After I graduated from college with a degree in agriculture, he recommended that the commissioner appoint me to be a farm agent. The reason he wanted me to be a farm agent was because, in this particular district on the Pine Ridge Reservation, all of the 1,300 people, except two or three mixed-blood families, had conducted their business with a farm agent who was a graduate of Carlisle by the name of Jake White Cow Killer. He talked Sioux and Lakota in all of his communications with these people. He was a member of the village in that area. McGregor wanted someone who could speak the language.

I was only twenty-five years of age, and the old timers would come in to have their dances. They could have dances only on Saturday night. Bert Kills Close to Lodge came in and said, "I want to get permission to have a dance tonight for our group in the village." I had just received a copy of a telegram signed by John Collier, Commissioner of Indian Affairs. It said, "If the Indian people want to have dances, dances all night, all week, that is their business." So I read it to him. Bert sat there, stroked his braids, looked off in the distance, and he said in Lakota, "Well, I'll be damned." The interesting part of it was, if they did not have the dance Saturday night, they would have a dance a month later, because they felt they were on their own. The Indian policemen were not going to police anybody, and it was just too much for them to have self-determination about their own dances.

Speaking of the benefits of the Indian Reorganization Act, we now have more young men and women in universities and colleges. Some of them are represented here. When I was in college in 1928, I could count the number of Indian students, at least from our reservation, on the fingers of your hand. Now they are in the hundreds and up to the thousands at universities and colleges around the country. We also have community colleges on five or six of our reservations.

The Flandreaux Santee Sioux Indian Tribe is made up of a group of about a hundred families that came into the Dakotas during the massacre in Minnesota [in 1862]. They homesteaded along with the whites around the Flandreaux Indian School. When the Indian Reorganization Act was finally passed, they got a leader and they went to us for assistance. They accepted the act and drafted a constitution, by-laws, and a charter. They also took advantage of the Indian land purchase provisions, and they bought farms around there. And then housing was made

Ben Reifel remarks in Kenneth Philp, editor, *Indian Self Rule: First Hand Accounts of Indian-White Relations from Roosevelt to Reagan,* 1986, pp. 54–58. Reprinted by permission of Howe Brothers.

available under a rehabilitation program for the people who were needy. They got houses on their forty-acre tracts. Last month, under the Supreme Court decision for the Seminoles, they could have bingo. So they are now making good money playing bingo, and the state cannot touch them. This is because the Indian people have rights under the trust responsibility.

But getting back to the Indian Reorganization Act, there was in 1934 an Indian congress at Rapid City to discuss the Wheeler-Howard bill. Walter V. Woehlke, John Collier, and Henry Roe Cloud, a Winnebago Indian, were there. Henry Roe Cloud was probably one of the few Indians at the time that had a doctor's degree. I was quite impressed with him. Henry Roe Cloud had recently been appointed the first Indian to be the superintendent of the Haskell Institute.

And I remember Rev. Joseph Eagle Hawk, one of the dear friends of mine in the community. He was a fine gentleman and a Presbyterian minister. Speaking of Indians not having a right to express themselves, we held this meeting at Rapid City for three or four days. I took leave to go up there because I wanted to see what it was all about. When Roe Cloud finished explaining part of the bill, Rev. Joe Eagle Hawk got up and said to Roe Cloud:

> You know, when we used to ship cattle to Omaha, Nebraska, they would go down to the slaughter house and they had a goat and they would lead a goat through the slaughter. The cattle would follow the goat in, the goat's life would be saved, and all the cattle would be killed. I think that is what you are, this Judas goat.

And he said that before the commissioner. I was impressed.

One of the things discussed at Rapid City was establishing some kind of official constitutional tribal government. When I grew up as a kid on the reservation, we had general tribal councils. What did they talk about when they came together? They passed a resolution asking the secretary of the interior, or the federal government, to allow them to have an attorney to represent them in their claims. When they had any tribal monies in place, the congressmen, about election time, would come around and say we will get you a per capita payment. They would then get a per capita payment, because at that time our Indian people, since 1921, even before that in South Dakota, were entitled to vote in the general election. If there was some of the tribal land to be leased, the general tribal council would come together and pass a resolution.

When I was a kid, there was also an old fellow called Chief High Bald Eagle. In those days we had an Indian trader store and a post office with counters and cages. Old High Bald Eagle was sitting up there with his legs crossed. He must have been about eighty or ninety years old; he looked like two hundred to me. We were having what we called a Scattergood dam constructed not too far away from our home. They were having a big tribal council meeting, and someone said to High Eagle in our language, "Why are you not up there at that big meeting?" He said, "When I was a young man years ago, when things were really important, then our leaders got together. But now, when a child gets constipated just about August eating chokecherries and it gets so his bowels are all stuck up, they have to have a council meeting on it." That is about as important as I thought the council meetings were on the Rosebud Reservation. That was also true at Pine Ridge.

So I was impressed with Collier's idea that Indians would get together and form some kind of governmental operation where they would democratically elect their own people and select their own leaders.

I was also concerned over the years about the tribal courts. Tribal court judges were appointed by the superintendent or the Indian agent. There was no appeal from them. Before the Indian Reorganization Act came along, I remember my brother was thrown in jail because he lived close to where there was a big fight going on and they thought he was a part of it. My younger brother came in where I was working in a store, and he said, "Hey, our brother George is in jail." So what did I do? I knew the superintendent lived near by because I was a close friend of his son. I went over there, and he said, "What happened, Ben?" Well, I told him what happened, and he wrote out a little note which I gave to Andrew Night Pipe, who was the chief of police. Andrew Night Pipe unlocked the door and let my brother go home. That was the sort of thing that was going on, and I felt we needed a better judicial system.

I was really impressed with the original draft of the so-called Wheeler-Howard bill. In it was a section where there would be a circuit court that would move from one reservation to another. Funds would be provided for this court to operate. Under the federal system, there would be the right of appeal from the local court just like any other court. There would be none of this business that goes on where the judges are appointed by the superintendent or the tribal council. The revised bill was cut from forty or fifty pages to just about eleven pages. The court system and several other things were taken out.

After the Rapid City meeting, I asked the superintendent for permission to talk about the bill with the people; he agreed. But he felt that there was a little red tinge to all of this, because one of the remarks he made to me was "I do not mind the little red schoolhouses as long as they are not red on the inside." Nevertheless, he was very supportive of my going out and explaining this bill. Of course, there were those on the reservation who were very opposed to it. And there were those who were for it. Think of me, only twenty-five years old, getting up there arguing with the old timers such as American Horse. I do not know who all the rest of them were. I felt that this was something we could support.

Conditions have improved. Tribal councils have been organized. They are fighting among themselves, but as Floyd O'Neil said, this is no different than Congress. In South Dakota, some tribal councils cannot even write checks, because they are tied up in fussing over who is going to be in control. That is no different than in California where the governor was not going to make payments to employees. The legislative body would not go along. It took the Supreme Court of the United States or the federal court to order them to make payments to the employees. . . .

◈ *E S S A Y S*

A professor of history at the University of North Texas, Lawrence Kelly has written many articles about the Indian New Deal. His biography of John Collier covers the reformer's life and career to 1928. In the essay that follows, Kelly argues that Collier himself provided the initial interpretation of his own commissionership and that until re-cently, historians and other observers accepted this self-serving perspective too uncriti-cally. While not entirely critical of the commissioner, Kelly contends that the Indian Re-organization Act in particular was a much less sweeping piece of legislation than is commonly understood. Because of conservative opposition and Collier's own inability to get Congress to respond, the reality of the Indian New Deal, in Kelly's judgment, fell far short of what Collier initially had envisioned.

D'Arcy McNickle, who was included on the tribal rolls of the Salish-Kutenai of Montana even though he was not of that tribe by birth, worked as an associate of Collier during the New Deal. The author of several major works, including the acclaimed novel *The Surrounded* (1978), McNickle concluded his distinguished career by serving as the director of the Newberry Library's Center for the History of the American Indian (later renamed in his honor the McNickle Center). From his own vantage point, McNickle, as the second essay reveals, considered the new criticism of Collier wide of the mark. Col-lier not only represented a fundamental shift from the assimilationist period but also, in his support for cultural revitalization, day schools, religious freedom, and other crucial matters, helped to establish an early foundation for the modern Indian movement to-ward self-determination.

The Indian Reorganization Act: The Dream and the Reality

LAWRENCE C. KELLY

The genius of John Collier, commissioner of Indian Affairs from 1933 to 1945, was that he saw the bankruptcy of federal Indian policy more clearly than anyone else in his generation. With its emphasis upon the allotment or division of Indian reservations into individually owned parcels of land and the forcible assimilation of Indians into white society, that policy had brought widespread poverty and demoralization to the majority of Indians by 1922. In that year, Collier, much like David, challenged the Goliath of the federal government in a case involving the lands of the Pueblo Indians of New Mexico. His surprising victory in that encoun-ter resulted in the birth of the modern Indian reform movement.

From 1922 to 1933 Collier mounted a steadily increasing assault upon the twin evils of land allotment and assimilation and upon what he termed the "des-potism" of the Bureau of Indian Affairs. At the heart of his reform campaign was the charge that federal policy had failed because it was based upon the false prem-ise that all Americans should conform to a single, uniform cultural standard. So persuasive was Collier in his defense of Indian rights that, when the old order crumbled in 1932, he was named commissioner of Indian Affairs and encouraged to right old wrongs.

Throughout his administration, the longest in the history of the office, Collier fought to realize a dream in which Indian tribal societies were rebuilt, Indian lands rehabilitated and enlarged, Indian governments reconstituted or created anew, and Indian culture not only preserved but actively promoted. In his annual reports and in the many publications that he authored after he left office, Collier

Lawrence C. Kelly, "The Indian Reorganization Act: The Dream and the Reality," pp. 291–312. © 1975 by Pacific Coast Branch, American Historical Association. Reprinted from *Pacific Historical Review,* Vol. 44, (August), by permission.

succeeded in creating the impression that during the New Deal years his dream had been essentially realized. In his autobiography, published in 1963, he wrote: "Our policies had become firmly established statutorily, and rooted in more than 200 tribes. Our legislative program had been accomplished in all respects but one [the creation of an Indian Claims Commission], and had remained intact against all pressures from within and outside of Congress."

In the relatively sparse literature on the Indian New Deal, Collier's assessment of his administration has prevailed. Most of those who have written about the era were his personal friends or associates. Many of them, like D'Arcy Mc-Nickle whose *Indians and Other Americans* is the best available account of the Collier years, were at one time or another employees of the Bureau of Indian Affairs. They have tended, naturally enough, to view events from Collier's perspective.

As a result of Collier's influence, the historiography of the Indian New Deal has obscured the sometimes considerable gap between his administration's rhetoric and its actual achievements. Nowhere is this more true than in the claims which have been advanced for the Indian Reorganization Act of 1934. Rightly regarded as the most significant legislative accomplishment of the Indian New Deal, this act nevertheless fell short of the revolutionary changes in federal Indian policy which are often attributed to it. The failure of the Indian Reorganization Act to attain Collier's basic goals and the subsequent failure of his administration to extend even the act's limited benefits to the majority of Indians are the subject of this essay.

Designed as the "successor to the greater part of several thousand pages of Indian law," the original draft of the Indian Reorganization Act was a lengthy document, forty-eight typewritten pages long. By describing Indian rights and the obligation of the government to secure and preserve those rights in the most minute detail, it sought not only to sweep away the repressive legislation of the past, but also to restore the powers of political and cultural self-determination which U.S. Supreme Court Chief Justice John Marshall had defined early in the nineteenth century. It also provided for the restoration of Indian economies on a communal and cooperative basis.

The original draft was divided into four parts. Title I granted all Indians the "freedom to organize for purposes of local self-government and economic enterprise, to the end that civil liberty, political responsibility and economic independence shall be achieved. . . ." Indian governments created under this provision were to have all the powers common to municipal corporations: the right to elect officials of government, to adopt ordinances for their reservation, to create courts for the enforcement of ordinances, to regulate the use and distribution of property, to levy taxes, and the power to compel the transfer of federal employees for "inefficiency in office or other cause." The United States, for its part, was gradually to transfer to Indian governments all "those functions of government now exercised over Indian reservations by the Federal Government through the Department of the Interior," as well as all powers of control over Indian funds and assets vested by previous laws in federal officials.

In addition, Title I directed that all expenditures of the Interior Department in behalf of Indians, and all congressional appropriations from tribal funds on deposit in the federal treasury, be submitted to Indian tribal councils for approval before being forwarded to the Bureau of the Budget or the Congress. Congress was authorized to appropriate $500,000 annually for the organization of Indian tribal governments, and it was empowered to create a $5,000,000 credit loan fund to assist organized tribes in the pursuit of "community economic development." In an attempt to include in these benefits persons of Indian descent who were no longer members of a recognized tribe, Title I defined an eligible Indian as any person "of one-fourth Indian blood." To increase Indian participation in the Indian Bureau's decision-making processes, Title I also waived civil service requirements for employment, providing instead that Indians could be employed by the bureau under "separate" civil service regulations to be drafted by the Interior Department.

Title II dealt with Indian education. Its most important provision stated: "it is hereby declared to be the purpose and policy of Congress to promote the study of Indian civilization, including Indian arts, crafts, skills, and traditions." To secure the necessary educational benefits and skills which Indians would need to administer their own affairs with competence, an annual appropriation of $15,000 for vocational and college scholarships was requested. An additional $50,000, one-half of which was to be interest-free, was to be appropriated for educational loans.

Title III was concerned with Indian lands. It abolished the land allotment provisions of the Dawes Severalty Act and provided for the return of previously allotted lands to tribal ownership. Surplus lands which had once been part of an Indian reservation, but which had never been patented to whites, were to be restored to tribal ownership. Allotments which the federal government still held in trust for their owners were to remain in that status indefinitely and the power of the Secretary of the Interior to force fee simple patents upon "competent" Indians was revoked. To consolidate the trust allotments and to bring them under tribal control, a major goal of the reform program, the Secretary of the Interior was empowered to compel their sale or transfer to tribal governments created under the provisions of Title I; their sale to other parties was expressly forbidden. All trust allotments not immediately restored to tribal ownership were to revert to tribal ownership upon the death of the current owner.

Title III further provided that it was henceforth the policy of the United States to "undertake a constructive program of Indian land use and economic development, in order to establish a permanent basis of self-support for Indians living under Federal tutelage." The federal government was pledged to acquire lands for landless Indians and to consolidate "Indian landholdings into suitable economic units." To attain these goals, Congress was authorized to appropriate $2,000,000 annually for land acquisition, and the Secretary of the Interior was "authorized and directed" to issue regulations restricting the number of livestock grazed on Indian lands and the quality of timber cut on Indian forest lands.

Title IV proposed the creation of a Court of Indian Affairs, which would have original jurisdiction in all cases involving Indian tribes organized formally under Title I, all cases involving a member of an organized tribe or band, heirship cases, and appeals from tribal courts. The rules governing evidence and procedure in this court were to be consonant with Indian traditions, "existing statutes regulating procedure in U.S. courts notwithstanding." The purpose of Title IV, of course, was to remove Indians who complied with the Indian Reorganization Act from the jurisdiction of state courts and to provide them with a tribunal more closely attuned to Indian concepts of justice than those of English common law.

This original draft of the Indian Reorganization Act contained the details of Collier's dream. Had it been enacted, Indians who organized under its provisions would have gained administrative control over their own affairs and been freed from dependence upon the federal government, except in the single area of financial assistance. The Bureau of Indian Affairs, which Collier had persistently attacked throughout the 1920s as despotic and arrogant, would have been gradually phased out of existence, except for technical assistance programs and budget services which it might render to the self-governing tribes.

In theory, this draft accurately reflected Collier's vision for an ideal new policy. In fact, however, there were several thorny practical problems that Collier and his advisors had overlooked or ignored. One was the opposition of assimilated and semiassimilated Indians to the reimposition of tribal controls over their property and their lives. Because of his own deep knowledge and appreciation of the culture of the Navajo and Pueblo Indians, whose customs and systems of government remained essentially intact, Collier concluded that Indians everywhere would wish to return to tribal, communal life. Such was not the case. Furthermore, despite the emphasis in the act on Indian self-determination, few Indians were consulted while the bill was being drafted. As a result, many of them were suspicious of its intent and confused by its technicalities. The mandatory nature of the bill's provisions relating to the transfer of trust allotments to tribal control was to prove especially divisive in many Indian communities.

Within a few weeks after hearings began in January 1934, angry opposition to the communal land ownership provisions and the restoration of tribal controls over individuals were voiced by Indians in Oklahoma, the Dakotas, and New York, in particular. In these areas where individual land ownership was the rule, rather than the exception, and where tribal cohesion had been seriously weakened by years of assimilationist pressure, there were many Indians who opposed the Indian Reorganization Act as a back-to-the-blanket experiment. Questions about specific parts of the bill poured in from the Indian country. At the same time, it became increasingly clear that many members of the congressional committees did not share Collier's enthusiasm for the restoration of Indian culture and civilization. The wisdom of creating politically autonomous Indian communities was especially questioned.

Throughout the spring of 1934, House and Senate committees discussed, debated, and amended the original draft of Collier's bill. For a while there was doubt that the measure could even be pried out of the House Indian Affairs Committee, but in April, following an appeal by Collier and Secretary of the Interior Harold Ickes to President Franklin D. Roosevelt, the bill was given the President's strong support and Ickes agreed to amendments which ended the controversy. Shortly thereafter the congressional committees deleted the statement in Title II promoting the preservation and enhancement of Indian culture; Title IV, the Indian court provision, was eliminated completely. The mandatory provisions for the transfer of allotted Indian lands to tribal ownership were made voluntary. At the insistence of Burton K. Wheeler, the Senate sponsor of the bill, the self-governing powers of Indian tribes were severely curtailed and made subject to approval by the Secretary of the Interior. Indians who were not members of an officially recognized band or tribe were excluded from most of the act's benefits, as were the 95,000 Indians of Oklahoma and those of Alaska.

In addition to these major modifications of Collier's original draft, less serious but important changes were made in other sections of the bill. Funds for assisting Indians to organize tribal governments were cut in half, from $500,000 annually to $250,000. The clause which would have made all persons of one-fourth Indian blood eligible for benefits was rewritten; eventually only persons of one-half Indian blood were entitled to benefits under the Indian Reorganization Act. The application of the act to all tribes was amended at the request of Congressman Edgar Howard of Nebraska, the House sponsor of the bill. Instead, a referendum was to be held, thereby giving individual tribes an opportunity to reject the act. Despite these limitations, the House Indian Affairs Committee insisted upon doubling the credit loan fund to $10,000,000 and increasing the educational appropriations from $50,000 to $250,000 annually. It was evident, however, that the committee approved these increases more as a means of integrating Indians into the white economic system than as a means of increasing their autonomy.

The Indian Reorganization Act which emerged from Congress in June 1934 did not, therefore, correspond to the dream which Collier had originally envisioned. While the repeal of the land allotment provision of the Dawes Act was a major victory, representing as it did a clean break with the traditional idea that individual land ownership was an essential part of the assimilation process, the historic goal of Indian assimilation was not completely abandoned. By exempting the Indians of Oklahoma from the bill's most important provisions, by denying the right to organize and to receive credit to Indians who did not belong to a recognized tribe or band, by eliminating the provisions which called for the preservation of Indian culture and the creation of a Court of Indian Affairs, and by severely curtailing the political powers of the tribes and reducing the appropriations for tribal organization, Congress made clear that it had little desire to encourage a revival of Indian tribal identity. Those tribes which had somehow managed to retain their lands and their cultures intact would no longer be forced to accept the white man's ways. But those whose lands had become fragmented or lost and whose tribal ties had been weakened or dissolved were not to be encouraged to regroup. Far from a radical break with past policy, the Indian Reorganization Act sought not so much to reverse the nation's historic attitude toward the Indians as to freeze it where it was in 1934.

John Collier never accepted the limitations upon his dream which the Indian Reorganization Act imposed. Throughout his administration he acted as though the original draft of the act was the one which Congress had approved. To his credit, he achieved many of his goals by administrative action, but, as the termination policy of the 1950s clearly demonstrated, administrative reforms unsupported by congressional legislation could easily be repealed or ignored by later administrations. Between 1933 and 1945 the excessively authoritarian powers of the Indian Bureau and its employees in the field were curbed substantially. Indians were vigorously recruited for Indian Bureau positions with the result that by

1945 Collier could proudly claim that sixty-five percent of the bureau's positions were held by Indians. Noxious "espionage laws" passed in the nineteenth century to limit Indian-white contacts on the reservation were repealed. Constitutional guarantees of religious freedom were extended to native religions, and the civil rights of Indians, frequently ignored in the past, were scrupulously protected. Through cooperation with a host of New Deal alphabet agencies, the Indian Bureau improved the economic conditions of thousands of Indians and launched an impressive program of soil and forest conservation on Indian lands. These very real achievements should not, however, be permitted to conceal the fact that in its attempt to extend the political and economic benefits of the Indian Reorganization Act to a majority of Indians, the Collier administration fell considerably short of its goals.

As a result of Congressman Howard's amendment, the Indian Reorganization Act could not be automatically extended to all Indian tribes. Instead, each tribe or band was required to indicate its acceptance or rejection of the act in a specially called referendum. The tribes which voted to accept the act were then permitted, although not required, to draw up a constitution which would guarantee their powers of limited self-government, thereby freeing them from arbitrary intervention by the Department of the Interior in their internal affairs. If they adopted constitutions they also became eligible to incorporate for tribal business purposes and to qualify for loans from the credit loan fund. Those tribes which rejected the Indian Reorganization Act, and those which accepted it but subsequently failed to adopt constitutions, not only forfeited the opportunity to determine their own form of political organization, they also made themselves ineligible for the act's financial benefits. . . .

The only official figures ever published on the Indian Reorganization Act referendum appeared in a 1940 hearing conducted before the House Indian Affairs Committee. In that document it was revealed that 252 Indian tribes and bands had voted in the referendum: 174 in favor of the act, 78 against it. Thirteen bands listed on the bureau's rolls as eligible to vote in the referendum either refused to participate or were found to have no actual members. Included in the figure of 252 tribes and bands were 99 separate Indian bands in California alone whose total population in 1935 was only 23,800. Similar distortions in the bureau's list of "tribes" were evident in the voting from other states. . . .

Although it is impossible to state exactly how many individual Indians came under the protective umbrella of the Indian Reorganization Act, the figures cited in the Indian commissioner's annual report for 1940 appear to be reasonably close to those contained in the referendum tally. They demonstrate clearly that forty percent of the potentially eligible Indians were excluded at the very beginning from the right to create tribal governments under constitutions free from restrictive Interior Department regulations. Because the adoption of a tribal constitution was a prerequisite to tribal business incorporation, these same Indians were also denied access to the credit loan program. As will be demonstrated later, a considerable number of the almost 130,000 Indians who approved the Indian Reorganization Act subsequently failed to adopt constitutions and even more failed to qualify for the credit funds. Moreover, when the 95,000 Indians of Oklahoma at last became eligible to adopt constitutions, only 13,200 did so; and only

5,700 of these ever qualified for access to the credit fund. What these figures reveal is a considerable gap between the benefits of the Indian Reorganization Act as perceived by the administration and those perceived by the Indian community.

An even more revealing method of gauging the lack of Indian support for the Indian Reorganization Act is to examine the actual voting figures in the referendum. Of approximately 97,000 Indians who were declared eligible to vote, only 38,000 actually voted in favor of the act. Those who voted against it totaled almost 24,000, while those who did not vote at all, approximately 35,000, were nearly equal in number to those who voted in favor. The significance of the large number of Indians who failed to participate in the referendum was to become evident only later when they were called upon to adopt constitutions and charters of incorporation.

In referenda held to adopt tribal constitutions between 1934 and 1945, some 92 of the 174 tribes which accepted the Indian Reorganization Act availed themselves of the opportunity; 72 did not. (As a result of the subsequent consolidation of small bands of Indians represented as separate tribes in the original referendum on the Indian Reorganization Act—primarily Papagos, Pimas, and Chippewa— there were 10 less bands eligible to vote for constitutions than for the Indian Reorganization Act.) Thus, of the 252 tribes and bands which participated in the original referendum, 150 failed to adopt the constitutions which had been designed to make them independent from Interior Department interference. Some, like 17 Pueblos of New Mexico, refused constitutions because they believed the inflexibility of written documents would eventually weaken tribal cohesion and lead to factionalism. Others, like 32 bands of California Indians, simply found self-government anomalous in their partially assimilated status. Whatever the reasons, when the individual figures are totaled, what becomes evident is that approximately 103,000 Indians adopted constitutions under the Indian Reorganization Act, but an even greater number, approximately 113,000, did not. If the Indians of Oklahoma are included, the disparity between the number of Indians who adopted constitutions and those who did not becomes even greater: 116,000 under constitutions, 194,000 who were not.

Because of his assumption that all Indians would welcome the opportunity to organize politically as a tribe and to pursue communal economic goals, Collier had not envisioned the possibility that so many of them would spurn his offer. Congressional amendments to the original draft of the Indian Reorganization Act had already dealt a serious blow to his hope of providing legal authority for the regeneration of Indian societies. Now the Indians had further weakened this possibility. In the subsequent referenda on business incorporation which were required by the amended Indian Reorganization Act, there were even further defections from the goals of the New Deal Indian policy.

Of the 92 bands and tribes which adopted constitutions, some 71, representing about 70,500 Indians, took the necessary steps to incorporate for business purposes and to qualify thereby for access to the credit loan fund. On the opposite side of the ledger were 145,500 individuals in 171 tribes and bands who, for various reasons, were rendered ineligible for credit loans. As a result of the Oklahoma Indian Welfare Act, 13 Oklahoma tribes eventually incorporated for business purposes, but since most of them were relatively small groups, their incorporation added only 5,700 Indians to the meager total of 76,200 who qualified for tribal credit loans. If the Oklahoma Indians who failed to qualify for loans are added to those who failed to qualify under the Indian Reorganization Act, the number of Indians who were denied access to the credit fund becomes 234,800.

Just as the existing literature on the Collier years has tended to concentrate on the successes of the administration and has failed to emphasize adequately the deviations from the goals which Collier set forth in the original draft of the Indian Reorganization Act, so too has it tended to fix the blame for failure on a narrow-minded and penny-pinching Congress rather than on the Bureau of Indian Affairs and the Collier administration. This argument—that Congress's failure to appropriate funds authorized by the Indian Reorganization Act crippled the administration's ability to extend self-government and economic aid—is basically sound, but even here there are important exceptions which should be recognized.

It is true that Congress never appropriated the full amounts authorized in the Indian Reorganization Act for the purchase of new lands, for the political organization of the tribes, or for the credit loan program. And it is true that this failure crippled the effectiveness of the Collier administration. But it is also true that the sums authorized in the act, with the exception of those for political organization which were cut in half, were based upon Collier's estimates of the needs of *all* Indians. As has been demonstrated, many Indians either refused to accept the act or subsequently failed to take the steps that were necessary to qualify for its benefits.

The failure to appropriate funds for land purchases was the most serious blow which the Indians and the administration suffered. Although $2,000,000 annually was authorized for this purpose, Congress never appropriated more than $5,075,000 before World War II brought a curtailment of all such expenditures. The reasons for this are many and complex, but for the purposes of this discussion, it will be sufficient to mention only a few of the most important.

A basic problem was the fact that western congressmen, who had opposed the Indian Reorganization Act, dominated the appropriations subcommittee which reviewed the Interior Department budget. Most of them adamantly opposed the expenditure of federal funds which would enable Indians to buy the land of whites. Their opposition increased considerably when they learned the dimensions of the land purchase program, a topic which had not been discussed at any length during the hearings on the Indian Reorganization Act. In 1934 the National Resources Board, acting on the basis of information supplied by the Bureau of Indian Affairs, announced that an estimated 9,700,000 acres were "urgently needed" to enable Indians to attain a basic subsistence level. The price tag was $60,000,000. In addition, the board recommended the acquisition of another 15,900,000 acres, at an estimated cost of $69,000,000, so that Indians could attain "the modest standard of living of rural white people."

Collier also had to wrestle with difficult problems occasioned by his success in attracting funds from various New Deal agencies and by his failure to secure the passage of the original draft of the Indian Reorganization Act. During his first two years in office, when the total annual appropriations for the Indian Office were approximately $20,000,000, he received almost $45,500,000 in emergency appropriations from a number of New Deal agencies. When it became known that five million dollars of these funds were designated for land purchases by the Resettlement Administration alone, Congress balked at appropriating additional funds under the Indian Reorganization Act. An even more difficult problem was created by some 7,000,000 acres of Indian-owned land which were not being utilized by Indians.

These were the so-called "heirship lands," lands whose original owners had died intestate. Over the years so many heirs to these lands had developed that no one could be said to control them. As a result, most of them were leased by the Indian Bureau, often to whites, in order to generate some income for the heirs. In his original draft of the Indian Reorganization Act, Collier proposed to sever the Gordian knot which bound these unproductive lands by authorizing their transfer to tribal ownership or reassignment to Indians who would use them. That provision was eliminated in the final draft; instead, only the voluntary transfer of these lands was approved. To purchase these lands with Indian Reorganization Act funds, Collier learned, would cost at least $35,000,000 and would take every penny of the land purchase funds for the next seventeen and a half years. Rejecting this approach as too costly and too time consuming, Collier instead appealed to the heirs to surrender their claims and to deed the land to the tribe. "They must learn," he wrote, "that for the sake of their race and of their children they should voluntarily transfer the title of their individual holdings to the tribe or the tribal corporation." Unfortunately, he had little success in convincing the heirs, and as their unwillingness to cooperate became more embarrassingly visible, so too did the congressional opposition to the expenditure of taxpayers' dollars for this purpose.

Lastly, it is simply not true that Collier's problems in obtaining funds authorized by the Indian Reorganization Act were attributable solely to the opposition of the legislative branch of government. Recognizing that it would take time to create the machinery necessary for consummating large-scale land purchases, Collier requested only $1,000,000 for land purchases in each of his first two budgets. Both requests were approved. But when the land program was well underway in 1938, it was the Bureau of the Budget, not the Congress, which first applied the ax, reducing his request that year from $2,000,000 to only $500,000. It was also the Bureau of the Budget which finally cut off all funds for land acquisition in fiscal 1940, even prior to the outbreak of the war. Ironically, it was Congress which authorized the continuance of reduced funds through fiscal 1942, thereby enabling the Indian Bureau to complete transactions which it had previously initiated.

Appropriation cuts for the political organization of Indian tribes, while substantial, were less serious than those for land purchases. Collier had lost the most important battle for tribal organization when the amended Indian Reorganization Act cut his annual request of $500,000 in half. Despite further appropriation reductions in this area, however, it must be kept in mind that forty percent of the Indians were never eligible for any of these funds because of their rejection of the Indian Reorganization Act. How many of the remaining sixty percent chose not to adopt constitutions or how many were denied the opportunity to do so because of a shortage of funds is not known, but the Pueblos of New Mexico and many bands of California Indians would surely belong to the first group. Furthermore, it is known that at least five of the larger tribes—the Cherokee of North Carolina, Menominee, Red Lake Chippewa, Yankton Sioux, and Standing Rock Sioux— preferred to continue with constitutions which they had adopted prior to the Collier years; thus, funds for their organization were not required.

Nor was it just budget cuts which slowed down the tribal organization movement. Members of the bureau's Tribal Organization Division, nearly all of them Indians, had begun to have second thoughts about the necessity of written constitutions and the haste which had characterized the first three years of tribal organization. Others registered similar doubts. In 1937 Charles de Y. Elkus, a San Francisco attorney and one of Collier's oldest supporters in the Indian reform movement, wrote the commissioner to register a complaint. The Indians of California and the Pueblos of New Mexico who had "correctly" refused to adopt written constitutions, he stated, now found themselves cut off from the credit loan fund. Because they had not adopted "your particular brand of self-government," Elkus charged, they were being unfairly discriminated against. He insisted that the administration push for an amendment to the Indian Reorganization Act which would remove this disability.

Collier and Assistant Commissioner William Zimmerman replied to Elkus. Both were in essential agreement with his criticism. The bureau, Collier wrote, was presently considering just such an amendment for the Indians of the Great Plains. This amendment, somewhat along the lines of the Oklahoma Indian Welfare Act, would permit Indian cooperatives and individuals, not just tribes with constitutions, to qualify for loans. Such an arrangement, Collier believed, would be "more realistic than the Indian Reorganization Act," and he agreed that the Indians of California should be included in its provisions. This proposed modification, however, was never submitted to Congress. A month after Collier's favorable reply, Elkus learned from Zimmerman that because of growing congressional hostility to the Indian Reorganization Act, it was "undesirable to introduce basic amendments to the IRA" at this time. Zimmerman continued:

> We are somewhat in the position of a sea captain who finds serious leaks in his ship when he is half way across the ocean, or, perhaps, not even half way across. He may complete the voyage with a defective ship, or he may turn around, put his boat in dry dock, only to be told that his craft is not seaworthy and will not be put back in condition. Please do not pursue this analogy too closely.

Thus, for fear of endangering gains already made, the amendment was shelved. Nevertheless, Elkus's letter, together with other reports from field workers in the Tribal Organization Division, did lead to a decision in 1938, not wholly dictated by appropriation cuts, to curtail the tribal organization movement.

As reports about difficulties which Indians were experiencing in making their new governments work filtered into Washington, the leaders of the Tribal Organization Division urged Collier "very definitely" to shift the emphasis away from tribal organization in fiscal 1938 toward "a program of follow up on those tribes already organized." D'Arcy McNickle wrote Collier that a recent problem at the Fort Belknap reservation "brings into sharp focus the realization we all have had that the Reorganization program hits a period of lag just after the tribe completes organization." The problem was "urgent," he wrote, and "the farther away we get from the initial impulse which brought about tribal organization, the more difficult it will be to rescue the program." Other reports complained of the "incredibly high degree of standardization" in the constitution drafted for different groups of Indians and concluded that "such standardization cannot but discredit the whole policy of Indian self-government and lead to the conclusion that these constitutions are nothing more than new Indian Office regulations."

Heeding these criticisms, Collier approved the shift in emphasis. As a result, the quality of self-government began to improve, but the results were never quite so favorable as Collier claimed. As late as 1942, Archie Phinney, a Nez Percé employed in the Tribal Organization Division, reported that while most tribal councils he had seen were functioning "wisely and efficiently" in the transaction of tribal business affairs, self-government had not yet succeeded in attaining that most important goal, "community or tribal spirit." From his work among the Chippewa in Michigan, Wisconsin, and Minnesota, Phinney concluded that most tribal councils functioned as "instrumentalities of the Indian Service," rather than as representatives of the Indian people, and he denounced what he termed "a growing democratic centralism which has kept community participation in tribal affairs at a minimum."

Similar observations may be made about the bureau's handling of the tribal credit-loan program. While only $5,245,000 of the authorized $10,000,000 was actually appropriated during Collier's administration, it will be recalled that Collier himself had requested only $5,000,000 in the original draft. Furthermore, the money which Congress appropriated was available only to the 76,200 Indians whose tribes had adopted charters of incorporation, a figure far short of the number of people whom Collier had originally hoped to organize into economically autonomous tribes. Lastly, and despite Collier's frequent boasts that Indians had proven themselves among the best credit risks in the country, there was the excessively high cost of administering the loan program which resulted in rising concern as years passed. By 1942, when further appropriations for the credit fund were curtailed because of the war, administrative costs of the loan program were annually consuming more than twenty percent of the funds available for loans.

The Indian New Deal marked a turning point in the nation's attitude toward the American Indian. It resulted in the toleration, if not the active encouragement, of Indian culture and civilization. It ushered in a more humane administration of federal policy than ever before in U.S. history, and it brought new hope to thousands of Indians, who, a generation later, began to realize the potential for Indian self-determination which it preserved. Most of the credit for this change in the national attitude is due to John Collier and his dream. Collier's dream did not, however, become reality, and the time has come for historians to recognize both the shortcomings of his administration, and the masterful, but often misleading, public relations campaign which he conducted in its behalf.

The Indian New Deal as Mirror of the Future

D'ARCY McNICKLE (Salish-Kutenai)

We are moving far enough away from the 1930s and the reform movement commonly termed "the Indian New Deal" to view it dispassionately, without a sense of involvement. Strong lines were drawn up in those partisan days, each side charging its opposite with unworthy motives, each side dressing up its own purposes in seemly rhetoric. Now that the dust of combat has settled, one can begin to see what the true issues were, what the gains and what the losses.

First, a brief description of the social, economic, and political conditions which gave rise to programs of reform. One general set of circumstances prevailed during the period. It was a time of deep, seemingly inescapable depression—a time of long soup lines in the cities, of rioting farmers in the countryside, of bank closings, of unemployed businessmen selling apples at street corners. One does not always see behind the headlines and news broadcasts the reality of economic disaster. I walked to work in midtown Manhattan one morning just after a victim of the times had leaped from a tall apartment building and was spread all over the sidewalk. Even nature contrived to add to human misery, for that was a period of the dreadful duststorms, when the topsoil of the wheat-growing prairie states ascended into the jet streams and swirled out over the Atlantic. I saw that, too, standing in shock in a New York street. It was a time when men began to talk about ecological balance, and a documentary film, "The Plow That Broke the Plains," was viewed by hushed audiences. Men came face to face with themselves in those days and questioned the very society they had created, and which had created them.

A time of doom, but it was also a time of opportunity. Under the lash of the desperate emergency, social reform made giant strides. Banking methods were overhauled; the marketing of securities was regulated; vast holding company cartels were broken up; systems of social insurance and unemployment compensation were created. The management of national forests, grazing lands, wild life, water, and minerals was made responsive to the public interest. Vast public works projects were undertaken to repair some of the damage wrought through generations of heedless resource exploitation and abuse. Some of this concern for the environment, and some of the appropriated funds, managed to trickle down to the Indian community.

It is important to understand the conditions that prevailed in the Indian community. The older Indians of that period still lived with the defeats which many tribes experienced in the closing years of the 19th century. The tragedy of the first Wounded Knee affair was less than fifty years in the rear, a brief lifetime.

When Collier assumed the commissionership in 1933, the General Allotment Law had been operating for better than forty-five years, and in that interval some 90 million acres of land had passed out of Indian ownership; an estate of 138 million acres, all owned in common in 1887, had been reduced to 48 million

D'Arcy McNickle, "The Indian New Deal as Mirror of the Future," in Ernest Schusky, editor, *Political Organization of Native North Americans,* University Press of America, 1980, pp. 107–118. Reprinted by permission.

acres. For the most part, the alienated lands were the best lands: the river bottoms, rich grass lands, prime forests. But land losses tell only part of the story. The allotment process, the individualizing of community-owned assets, created forces which had never before operated in Indian society. Families and individuals competed for choice lands, for water or other advantages. Outsiders intruded as homesteaders on so-called surplus lands, and inevitably meddled in the internal affairs of the tribe. Social structure was disoriented in many ways, as non-Indians married into a group, and kin groups were scattered throughout the reservation area. In each allotted reservation a class of landless, homeless individuals came into existence and, having no resources of their own, doubled up with relatives and intensified the poverty of all.

That, too, tells only part of the story. Tribes had been moved about like livestock until, in some cases, the original homeland was no more than a legend in the minds of old men and women. Children had been forcefully removed from the family and kept in close custody until they lost their mother language and all knowledge of who they were, while the schooling to which they were subjected was conducted as an exercise in animal training. Tribal religious practices, when they were not proscribed outright, were treated as obscenities. The bureaucratic apparatus had penetrated the entire fabric of Indian life, usurping tribal decision-making, obtruding into the family, and demeaning local leadership. It was totally oblivious of its inadequacies and its inhumanity.

Part of John Collier's initial problem, as the incoming commissioner, was to remove some of the tar with which he himself had plastered the Bureau. He had been an outspoken and caustic critic of the Bureau, and suddenly he was in the position of asking Indians to have confidence in the institution. While he occupied the office for twelve years, he never entirely extricated himself from the awkward situation.

One of his first acts, intended to moderate the harsh image of the Bureau, was the issuance of an order (Office of Indian Affairs 1934) declaring: "No interference with Indian religious life will be hereafter tolerated. The cultural history of Indians is in all respects to be considered equal to that of any non-Indian group. And it is desirable that Indians be bilingual—fluent and literate in English, and fluent in their vital, beautiful, and efficient native languages."

In a further early effort to undo the past, he secured the repeal of twelve obsolete laws, some dating from as early as 1790, which collectively placed inordinate power over civil liberties in the hands of Bureau officials. The repeal of these laws, needless to say, was not enough to change the authoritarian nature of the Bureau.

Collier, of course, is associated with the Indian Reorganization Act, which in the context of the Roosevelt administration was known popularly as the Indian New Deal. The legislation had been adopted by a reluctant Congress in 1934, reluctant because the Act by open declaration was a denunciation of the policies followed by Congress and national administrations through the previous half-century. The reluctance moreover went deeper than bruised feelings. Most legislation as it emerges from the Congressional mill bears small resemblance to the bright promise that was fed into the hopper. The Indian Reorganization Act was no exception. Congress wanted the "Indian business" cleaned up, but it was not ready or willing to transfer real power to the Indian tribes. This unwillingness was emphasized by the rejection of four critical features: (1) an orderly procedure for transferring services and functions from the Bureau to an organized Indian community; (2) the creation of tribal corporations for the management of reservation resources, with power "to compel" the removal of any federal employee on grounds of inefficiency or "other causes"; (3) a training program to prepare Indians to take over and administer community services, including courses of study in Indian history and culture; and (4) the establishment of a tribal court system, with right of appeal to the federal appellate court and to the Supreme Court.

It was the first piece of major legislation dealing with Indian affairs ever taken into the Indian country and discussed in open meetings. And here the long history of bureaucratic misrule loomed as a major challenge to Collier's reform program. At every one of the regional meetings called to consider the pending bill, the motives and the purposes of the Bureau were questioned, heatedly at times. The distrust and suspicion voiced at these meetings, and in subsequent meetings in Washington, were reflected in the tribal elections that followed. By its terms, the act was not to apply on any reservation where a majority rejected it. Out of 258 tribes, bands, and rancherias voting in these elections, 77 voted against application. The Navajo was one of the tribes voting in the negative.

The bill as introduced in Congress was a document of some fifty typewritten pages, but what emerged was a scant six pages of print. The reduction in bulk was not critical, but what was stricken in the course of debate practically guaranteed that the nature of the bureaucracy would not be altered. By eliminating the provision giving the Indians a deciding role in the selection and retention of reservation employees, colonial rule was left intact. By deleting the articles creating a federal Indian court system, the control over law and order was left in the hands of the Secretary of the Interior, and it encouraged the states, in later years, to seek to extend state law, and state taxation, to reservation lands. One other deletion deserves passing mention. If the article providing for courses of study in Indian history and culture and in administrative management had been retained, Indian studies programs might have been operating forty years ago.

The Indian Reorganization Act did retain two features central to Collier's reform program. The first of these was the prohibition against any future allotment of tribal lands; the other was a watered-down provision dealing with tribal government and property management. While the range of discretionary tribal action was greatly reduced from the original proposal, what remained was tacit recognition of the tribe as a surviving political entity with definable inherent powers. The Act referred specifically to "All powers vested in an Indian tribe or tribal council by existing law"; and that, of course, included treaty stipulations and court decisions, as well as statute law. In addition it recognized the right of a tribe to embody in a written constitution the power to "prevent the sale, disposition, lease or encumbrance of tribal lands." Within this legal framework it became possible for an Indian tribe to function as a municipal body and to exert the common law rights of a property owner.

The legislation was not the emancipating instrument that had been hoped for, and within less than a decade of its enactment the nation was at war, with the moneys authorized for salvaging the Indian community going elsewhere. But the

Act did mark the way into the future—if there was to be an Indian future. In Collier's day that was not at all a certainty; indeed twenty years after the adoption of the Indian Reorganization Act, the Eisenhower administration almost closed out that possibility forever.

To go back a moment: The misgivings and outright opposition expressed by many Indians during the hearings on the Indian Reorganization Act were symptomatic of more basic trouble. Since the United States in 1871 renounced the policy of negotiating treaties with the tribes, a practice that had endured from colonial times, the Indians had not been consulted in any major decisions affecting their property, their family life, or the training of their children. All such matters came within the reach of a bureaucratic structure, which developed attitudes and formalities impervious to Indian participation. And as the bureaucracy hardened, the Indian community withdrew deeper into itself and set up its own barriers to communication.

But Collier's problem did not come entirely from the fact that for those sixty-odd years since the renunciation of treaty-making the government had barred Indians from assuming responsibility for their own lives. The unseen and, indeed, the larger problem had to do with the ethic of social intervention which, in the 1930s, still functioned as a tradition out of the 19th century—a heritage of colonial administration.

In a major crisis that developed early in his administration the reluctance or the inability of the bureaucracy to respond to human conditions had disastrous consequences. The occasion was the decision to reduce Navajo sheep herds, the principal subsistence base of the tribe, in order to bring the animal population into balance with deteriorating range lands. Studies carried out by professional agronomists demonstrated that top soil was blowing away, perennial grasses were being replaced by annual weeds of low nutrient value, summer rains were eroding deep gullies and carrying mountains of soil into newly constructed power and flood control reservoirs, threatening to fill them with silt.

In designing a control program, Collier directed that reduction would be on a "sliding scale," with the largest reduction on the larger herds and a lesser reduction on smaller herds, while herds of a minimum size would be left intact. The directive was later made specific in providing that herds of up to 100 head of sheep would not be reduced. Herds of that size were considered subsistence herds required to provide family support. . . .

A report prepared soon after the reduction program was initiated in 1933 states that: "The larger owners flatly refused to make all the reduction from their herds. After an all-night session (at Tuba City, in November 1933) it was agreed . . . that every Navajo should sell 10 percent of his sheep. . . . This same agreement became widespread over the entire reservation, since the large owners consistently refused to make the total reduction from their flocks. . . ." In practice, the owners of small herds found themselves under greater economic pressure than the owners of large herds; they sold out their entire holdings and found themselves completely dependent on the emergency work programs financed by the government. When these programs ran out of funds, real hardship followed.

Other complications quickly arose. The government had offered to buy sheep at prices ranging from $1.00 for ewes to $2.25–$3.00 for wethers. Chee Dodge, the respected leader of the tribe, argued that the government should concentrate on the purchase of good breeding ewes, at better prices; otherwise, the Navajo livestock owners would offer only old ewes and other non-productive stock and reduction would not be achieved. These prices, however, had been established in Washington by the emergency relief administration, the source of the funds, and they could not be altered in the field. The disappointing results confirmed what Chee Dodge had predicted.

Perhaps the most serious oversight was the failure to recognize the fact that women were in many instances the principal owners of the family herds. Women were not members of the tribal council, however, and they were not consulted as negotiations went forward between the government and the tribal leaders. When the leaders returned to their families and found the women opposed to plans for reduction, any agreements with the government became meaningless.

What Collier did not discover until it was too late to intervene was that field employees sometimes resorted to coercive action. This interference occurred specifically in the eastern Navajo area, where it was expected that legislation, then pending in Congress, would be enacted and would result in extending the eastern boundary of the reservation to include an additional two million acres. In anticipation of the increased acreage, the Navajos of the area were induced to sell their goats, with the idea of eventually replacing them with sheep. By the fall of 1935 formidable opposition had developed against the legislation, making it unlikely that it would be adopted. Nevertheless the goat reduction program went forward. As Collier reported to the Senate subcommittee in the summer of 1936: "In my judgment, we should not have carried out the goat purchase program within the eastern area . . . because we were no longer assured of the enactment of the boundary bill. . . . Why we did proceed with the goat purchases in this area, frankly, I don't know. . . . At the time we did not, at Washington, have any information, or evidence that duress was being, or was to be, employed anywhere. It was not directed to be employed, but on the contrary, all the sales were to be voluntary. However, before the close of the goat purchase operation, I began to receive . . . information that overpersuasion, and even duress, had in fact been employed in this area."

Elsewhere in his statement to the subcommittee, he commented: "The purchase was an error and I cannot, and do not desire, to evade responsibility for that error. . . . I am the Commissioner." . . .

Such episodes were possible because the bureaucracy was the instrument of an older view of the relationship with the Indian people. In that older view Indians were incompetent to make decisions, especially when questions of a technical nature were involved—and livestock management was considered to be of that nature, even though Navajos had been successful herdsmen for several centuries. Indeed, their very success in increasing their herds was in part responsible for their predicament. In a chain of command situation, such as characterizes bureaucratic structure, responsibility is diffused; one is never accountable for someone else's mistakes.

Collier's hope of restoring to the Indian community some measure of self-government was diminished by the same impersonal, insensate play of bureaucratic forces. Anyone who has worked in government knows that project financing is based on performance. If funds allocated to a field project are not expended within a time limit, usually the fiscal year, it is assumed by those who approve budget requests that the money was not needed. The amount approved for a subsequent operating period will likely be reduced. This leads to various stratagems to keep ahead of the finance wizards, the commonest of which is to pile on expenditures before the end of the fiscal period, thus demonstrating the accuracy of the original estimate and the soundness of the project.

The Indian Reorganization Act authorized federal funds to assist tribes in formulating and voting on written constitutions and charters of incorporation. Collier intended that the organization documents should reflect a tribe's traditional ways of arriving at decisions and selecting leaders. To carry out this purpose he recruited a staff of cultural anthropologists, who were to work with the field employees engaged in the program. This move would appear to be one of the first attempts, if not the first, to use anthropologists as technical assistants by a government agency.

The planning came to grief on two counts. When it was discovered in Congress that the Commissioner was spending money on something called anthropology, the appropriation was promptly disallowed and the unit was abandoned although some anthropologists continued working for the Bureau under other titles. A more serious difficulty grew out of the fiscal year syndrome. To satisfy the budget watchers and the wardens of the Treasury, it was necessary to show progress in bringing the tribes under written constitutions. This involved sitting down in meeting after meeting and conducting a tribal drafting committee through a maze of *Whereas* clauses and *Therefore, be it enacted* resolutions. Leaders, who often were non–English-speaking or who had only a primary grade education, were exposed to the full battery of Anglo-Saxon parliamentary syntax, and they had to act before the end of the fiscal year. The result was the hurried adoption of tribal constitutions prepared in Washington and based on conventional political instruments with no provision for action by consensus or for the role of ritual leaders. The tribes were given tools, such as majority rule, for which they had no accustomed usage, and these became devices for community disruption and for petty demagoguery.

One should not conclude from this analysis of the Navajo that no positive gains were registered during the Collier administration. The long record of diminishing land and other resource holdings was halted. The total land base was actually enlarged by some four million acres, the first time in history that Indians gained instead of losing land. Credit financing was begun on a modest scale and made possible resource development and utilization, where previously Indians had leased out tribal and individual lands for lack of capital. A start was made, again modestly, in providing low cost housing. Day schools were built at a number of reservations as an alternative to the off-reservation boarding schools, and they were designed and operated as community centers, anticipating the movement of recent years to provide centers for recreation, adult education, and cultural activities.

These gains, modest as they were, were cut short by the crisis of war. When the shooting was over and Indian GIs and war industry workers came home, they found their reservations in ruins. Employment opportunities were gone, social services were severely curtailed (schools, hospitals, houses in disrepair or shut down entirely), and credit facilities denied. And presently, a hostile administration came to power committed to the ultimate extinguishment of tribal life.

What has come to the surface in tribal communities in recent years, notably at Wounded Knee and on the Pine Ridge reservation generally, is the anger that remained unuttered, but unappeased, for generations. It was an overwhelming anger growing out of the kinds of experiences suggested here; my account of these experiences has been mild and polite. Older Indians, still conscious of the defeats inflicted on their people in the closing years of the last century, withdrew from open challenge and tried passively to live with the white man's inscrutable ways. That former period seems to have come to a crashing end.

The generation of Indian leaders now emerging lacks that consciousness of defeat which inhibited their elders. More than that, as a consequence of international wars, the collapse of colonial empires, rioting and burning in urban ghettos, an economy that destroys the environment, the white man seems not as invincible as he once seemed.

It was possible at Wounded Knee in 1890 for an army unit—Custer's own 7th Cavalry, indeed—to slaughter a Sioux camp of men, women, and children. At that same site in the winter of 1973, armored vehicles and troop detachments surrounded another Indian camp, but no slaughter occurred. Two reasons suggest themselves. The surrounded Indians had access to the world beyond their lines, and they were able to verbalize their grievances to listeners who were sympathetic even though they might not understand what was going on. This access to public opinion was enough to discourage hasty action by gun-carrying troops. An even more compelling restraint was the changed circumstance behind that surrounding army. Men in power no longer had a mandate to kill Indians trying to protect their right to be themselves. Perhaps that is a measurable gain.

Where, then, have we come? One point certainly seems clear. Because Indians are discovering the uses of power in modern society, it is no longer possible to exclude them from the decision-making process in matters affecting their property, their families, the training of their children, or the nature of the accommodation they choose to make within the dominant society. John Collier helped to make these issues evident, but as a man of good will standing outside the Indian community, he was limited in what he could do. He could not substitute his will and vision for Indian will and vision. Nor can any man stand in the place of another.

That, too, is a discovery Indians have made in these very recent years. The simple demonstration of this discovery is the astonishing growth of news media operated by Indian groups reporting on conditions, and the equally remarkable growth of political and cultural organizations devoted to advancing Indian interests. The non-Indian "Friend of the Indian," that 19th-century image of altruistic involvement, is being told politely but firmly to stand aside.

Collier has been charged with turning the clock back on Indian advancement. The basis of the charge, of course, was his insistence on extending religious and cultural freedom to Indian groups and his commitment to the cause of revitalizing Indian society. A modern critic . . . asserts that Collier mistakenly assumed, from his knowledge of Indians of the Southwest, "that Indians everywhere would wish to return to tribal, communal life, if given the opportunity."

What this writer fails to recognize, even in this late day, is that Indians "everywhere" have always been, and remain, more tribal, communal if you will, or conscious of ethnic boundaries, than observers from the outside generally realize. Already in Collier's day the studies of A. Irving Hallowell and others were offering evidence that culturally-wrought personality persists even in circumstances where the outward forms of behavior have accommodated to the dominant society.

Other critics of Collier's effort to build upon the tribal past were people whose ideas had been formed largely in the 19th century, who saw Native society as incapable of development into modern forms. In this view, the Native American existed in a world devoid of logic, or sentiment, or dynamics. Indian life came from nowhere and went nowhere.

Collier challenged this view in many published statements and in his public career. He saw Indian society as "not fossilized, unadaptive, not sealed in the past, but plastic, adaptive, assimilative, while yet faithful to . . . ancient values." And again he . . . wrote: "Societies are living things, sources of the power and values of their members; to be and to function in a consciously living, aspiring, striving society is to be a personality fulfilled."

Whether or not they are aware of John Collier's insight in this matter, Indians today are discovering the truth that lies in this vision. This discovery accounts, in part, for the Indian studies centers that have come into existence at major institutions across the country. The Navajo Community College springs from this vision. In a harsher mode, it accounts for the incidents at Wounded Knee.

Indians were not held back by Collier's efforts to build upon the tribal past. Instead, they have plunged affirmatively into the twentieth century, asserting their identity, and acquiring the skills that will enable them to survive as Indians and members of an Indian community.

◈ *F U R T H E R   R E A D I N G*

David F. Aberle, *The Peyote Religion Among the Navajo* (1966)

George A. Boyce, *When the Navajos Had Too Many Sheep: The 1940s* (1974)

Roger Bromert, "The Sioux and the Indian CCC," *South Dakota History* 8 (1978), 340–356

Joseph Cash and Herbert T. Hoover, "The Indian New Deal and the Years That Followed: Three Interviews," in Peter Iverson, ed., *The Plains Indians of the 20th Century* (1985), 107–132

John Collier, *From Every Zenith: A Memoir and Some Essays on Life and Thought* (1963)

Steven J. Crum, "Henry Roe Cloud, a Winnebago Indian Reformer: His Quest for American Indian Higher Education," *Kansas History* 11 (1988), 171–184

Vine Deloria, Jr., and Clifford Lytle, *The Nations Within: The Past and Future of American Indian Sovereignty* (1984)

Laurence M. Hauptman, "The American Indian Federation and the Indian New Deal: A Reinterpretation," *Pacific Historical Review* 52 (1983), 378–402

_____, *The Iroquois and the New Deal* (1981)

Thomas James, "Rhetoric and Resistance: Social Science and Community Schools for the Navajos," *History of Education Quarterly* 28 (1988), 599–620

Lawrence C. Kelly, "Anthropology and Anthropologists in the Indian New Deal," *Journal of the Behavioral Sciences* 16 (1980), 6–24

———, *The Assault on Assimilation: John Collier and the Origins of Indian Policy Reform* (1983)

Harry Kersey, Jr., "Florida Seminoles in the Depression and New Deal, 1933–1942: An Indian Perspective," *Florida Historical Quarterly* 65 (1986), 175–195

Clayton Koppes, "From New Deal to Termination: Liberalism and Indian Policy, 1933–1953," *Pacific Historical Review* 46 (1977), 543–566

Stephen J. Kunitz, "The Social Philosophy of John Collier," *Ethnohistory* 18 (1971), 213–239

Oliver La Farge, ed., *The Changing Indian* (1942)

K. Tsianiana Lomawaima, "Oral Histories from Chilocco Indian Agricultural School, 1920–1940," *American Indian Quarterly* 11 (1987), 241–254

D'Arcy McNickle, *The Surrounded* (1978)

Floyd A. O'Neil, "The Indian New Deal: An Overview," in Kenneth R. Philp, ed., *Indian Self-Rule: First-hand Accounts of Indian-White Relations from Roosevelt to Reagan* (1986), 30–46

Donald L. Parman, "Inconstant Advocacy: The Erosion of Indian Fishing Rights in the Pacific Northwest, 1933–1956," *Pacific Historical Review* 53 (May 1984), 163–189

———, "The Indian and the CCC," *Pacific Historical Review* 40 (1971), 39–56.

———, *The Navajos and the New Deal* (1976)

Kenneth R. Philp, *John Collier's Crusade for Indian Reform, 1920–1954* (1977)

———, "The New Deal and Alaskan Natives, 1936–1945," *Pacific Historical Review* 50 (1981), 309–327

Ruth Roessel, ed., *Navajo Livestock Reduction: A National Disgrace* (1974)

Robert F. Schrader, *The Indian Arts and Crafts Board: An Aspect of Indian New Deal Policy* (1983)

Graham D. Taylor, *The New Deal and American Indian Tribalism: The Administration of the Indian Reorganization Act, 1934–1945* (1980)

Peter M. Wright, "John Collier and the Oklahoma Indian Welfare Act of 1936," *Chronicles of Oklahoma* 60 (1972), 347–371

Inclusion and Assimilation: World War II to Relocation

When the Second World War began, the Indian New Deal already had lost its impetus, as had the New Deal itself. The nation's attention turned to the international conflict; Indians were no exception. Thousands of Indian men and women served in the armed forces during the war, and thousands more worked in war-related industries. For many, it was their first extended time away from their home area. The experience deeply altered how they saw their communities and themselves. Indians took collective pride in the achievements of people such as Clarence Tinker (Osage) and Ira Hayes (Pima), as well as the accomplishments of the Navajo codetalkers in the Pacific campaign. The codetalkers based a code on the Navajo language and thus could relay messages with speed and accuracy. Although the Japanese learned that an Indian language was being employed, they were not able to break the code by war's end. The Indians' success in adapting to the exigencies of wartime encouraged others after the war to see them as just like everyone else.

The postwar national mood was one of conservatism, and the federal government again began to push less for cultural pluralism and more for assimilation. The passage in 1946 of the Indian Claims Commission Act seemed to speak for a national desire to make things right once and for all. Through the workings of the Commission, Indian tribes attempted to receive just compensation for lands taken from them. Unfortunately, these deliberations took an extended period of time and thus the Native communities incurred major legal fees. Many claims were denied or were awarded only small amounts. In all, Indian tribes gained less than five percent of the total amount they sought through the process. Officials soon pushed to terminate federal services and the protection of Native communities. Certain reservations were abolished. The government also encouraged some forms of reservation economic development, while at the same time promoting the migration of younger men and women to large cities. This mixed message was cloaked in the words of liberation, but many Indians opposed federal withdrawal as a betrayal of the U.S. government's responsibility to hold the reservation lands in trust for the Indians. The shock waves of this termination period, as it generally became known, also had the ironic consequence of catalyzing Indians' political activism and their development of their own economies on their own terms. As with the 1868–1920 period, the termination period proved to be a complex time, one that historians are only now beginning to comprehend.

◈ D O C U M E N T S

Federal officials took great pride in Indian participation in the war effort. The first document comes from *Indians at Work,* a Bureau of Indian Affairs newsletter devoted to individual and group achievements, and is a chronicle of involvement and a reflection of the degree to which native peoples served the United States.

Near the conclusion of the war, Indians gathered in Denver, Colorado, to form what would become a major national Indian organization, the National Congress of American Indians (NCAI). The second document includes the platforms of this meeting and of the second annual conference. As the existence of the NCAI suggested, different individuals and communities faced common problems and drew strength from acting collectively to resolve them. Almost immediately, the NCAI had to deal with the threat of termination of federal trusteeship and the assumption of jurisdiction by the states.

The final three documents feature different perspectives on termination. Senator Arthur Watkins speaks in favor of it, while Cherokee activist Ruth Muskrat Bronson, an influential participant in the first years of the NCAI, and Felix Cohen, the brilliant legal scholar who had assisted Collier in the 1930s, deplore what they see as an abrogation of federal trusteeship. In many ways, their arguments echo down to the present, for they speak to continuing disagreement about the place of Indians in America's history and future.

The Bureau of Indian Affairs Lauds Indian Participation in World War II, 1942

Indians, the truest Americans, everywhere in the United States are deeply concerned and intensely occupied with the prosecution of the war for freedom. From Alaska to Mississippi and from Arizona to Maine, the Indians are giving their lands, their savings, their skills and their lives in the service of their country. In numbers, it is believed, exceeding the per capita contributions of any racial group, including the white, Indians are enlisting in the Navy, the Marine Corps, the Coast Guard and the Army. Their peculiar, inherited talents make them uniquely valuable.

In civilian war work they are equally zealous, and equally effective. Technical training of recent years has converted many Indian men from laborers to specialists. Natural gifts of precision, endurance, poise and high intelligence add great value to their services. War industries are seeking Indian workmen in greater numbers than they can be supplied.

Indians in Every Branch of Service

Prior to the Japanese assault at Pearl Harbor, Indians in the Army alone numbered 4,481, of whom approximately 60 per cent had enlisted in either the Regular Army or the National Guard. In addition to Indians who are Naval Officers, there are 40 Indians in the Navy in branches exclusive of the Marine Corps and the Coast Guard. Perhaps the outstanding Indian Naval Officer is Commander Francis J. Mee, a Chippewa born in Detroit Lakes, Minnesota. Commander Mee has just been promoted from the rank of Lieutenant Commander and has been shifted from the United States destroyer Ellet to a post on the heavy cruiser Portland, where he commands several hundred men. His colleagues and superiors express a deep respect and regard for Commander Mee, who is familiarly identified as "Chief" Mee.

One reason why the service of Indians in the armed forces is important is because of the special skills which are part of the Indian heritage. As scouts, runners, in signal work and in other fields, the modern Indian has demonstrated special aptitudes which are being rapidly recognized and utilized by their commanders.

Items rewritten from the Nation's newspapers reveal typical instances of Indian military performances:

> The fortitude of Private Charley Ball, a 24-year-old Indian boy from the Fort Belknap Reservation in northern Montana, while fighting with General MacArthur's forces on Bataan Peninsula in the Philippines, has won him the Distinguished Service Cross. In a dispatch from the Bataan fighting front, it is related that Private Ball was wounded in a battle against Japanese forces, but despite his wounds he helped cover the withdrawal of his comrades in the 21st Infantry. Ball has two brothers in the armed forces.

> During the opening weeks of the war, it was reported that about 15 young braves from the Sac and Fox Reservation near Tama, Iowa, enlisted in the Army.

> The great, great grandson of old Chief Winnemucca, young Stanley Winnemucca, of Nixon, Nevada, has been accepted by the Marine Corps. Almost a century ago Chief Winnemucca led his warriors to one of the greatest victories ever won by Indian fighters over whites in the battle of Pyramid Lake. He later was a leader in preserving peace in Nevada.

> Kitus Tecumseh, descendant of famous Chief Tecumseh and a member of the United States Navy in World War I, visited the Cedar Rapids, Iowa, Naval Recruiting Station to ask for enlistment in the present war. He served on a submarine chaser in 1918 and is classed as 33 per cent disabled as a result of wounds received then.

> Indian soldiers at Fort Benning, Georgia, have shown adeptness in the white man's war games. One of the top Sergeants has reported that they're making good soldiers. At the time of this report, which was made before war was declared, there were 16

Indians from Oklahoma in the Fourth Signal Battalion at Fort Benning. "Those Indians are the best morale tonic on the shelf," maintains the First Sergeant. "They take a hard job and make a game of it. We could use more like 'em." . . .

Buy Defense Bonds

. . . Purchase of Treasury Stamps and Bonds by Indian groups and individuals has been considerable. A great many of these transactions do not come officially to the attention of the Indian Service because the purchases are made locally with funds not under Government jurisdiction. On record in Washington are purchases of $1,270,000 in Treasury Bonds from April, 1941 to the present. These are not Defense Bonds but the money is, nevertheless, available to the Government. Applications now pending for the purchase of Treasury and Defense Bonds total $19,000. The money for these purchases came from both tribal and individual funds from the sale of land, timber, oil and gas leases, etc.

Applications have been received from various tribes for the purchase of approximately $750,000 in Defense Bonds, but as the funds involved are already in the United States Treasury, nothing would be gained by the purchases and, therefore, the Interior Department disapproved the requests. The spirit of the Indians in making these requests provides further evidence of their patriotic spirit.

Chee Dodge, last of the Navajo war chiefs, has purchased $20,000 of United States Defense Bonds, and has urged Navajos in New Mexico, Arizona and Utah to buy Bonds "as generously as possible." In response to the establishment of sales committees over the Navajo Reservation, Indians are buying Bonds in mounting numbers, Superintendent Fryer of the Navajo Agency has reported.

The Crow Tribe of Montana offered to the Government all of its resources and all of its man power for the prosecution of the war. The Superintendent, himself a Crow Indian, has reported that approximately 70 men and boys of the Tribe have gone into the Service. This is a very large proportion of the eligible man power on the reservation. His son is among those who have already gone into the Army. Even the girls and women of the Crow Tribe are reportedly desirous of entering active military service. The Superintendent stated that several women have already applied for enlistment and he seeks information as to how such service can be arranged.

In Alaska, the Indians and Eskimos are making many contributions which for military reasons cannot be discussed. However, it is no secret that in a considerable area centering at Nome more than 300 women and children (and one man) are working day and night to fashion mukluks (skin boots), parkas (fur outer garments), fur caps, mittens and fur pants for the soldiers. The Army has just ordered 5,000 additional mukluks. All of the work is being done through the Nome Skin Sewers Association, a cooperative organized by the Indian Service under the provisions of the Alaska Act of 1936, a counterpart of the Indian Reorganization Act of 1934.

Many natives are turning over their boats to the armed forces. In one case the incorporated members of a tribe offered land for an air base, without compensation. The land has been accepted but, in the interests of fairness, some payment was provided. . . .

The Platforms of the First Two Annual Conventions of the National Congress of American Indians, 1944, 1945

The First Annual Convention

Denver, Colorado—November 15–18, 1944

This convention formulated and adopted a platform and program consisting of the following points:

1. *The Aboriginal Races of North America.* This organization shall work toward the promotion of the common welfare of the aboriginal races in North America, including the natives of Alaska, protect the rights, develop and advance the better values in these races.

2. *People of Higher Degree Indian Blood.* It shall be the first order of business of this organization to give thought to the situation of the higher degree Indian blood members of the Indian race—to the end that all possible effort be made to safeguard their property and to make provision for the continuation of appropriate services to such members of the various tribes.

3. *Legal Aid Service.* Realizing that many tribes, and the members thereof, do not have the financial means that are necessary with which to employ attorneys to represent them before the various branches of the Federal Government in Washington, this organization purports to establish a Legal Aid Service through which the cause of such tribes, or members thereof, may be properly presented.

4. *News Letter.* In order that information concerning legislation pending in the Congress of the United States, the activities of the Indian Bureau and information of general interest to the Indians may be regularly available, it is proposed that this organization shall publish and distribute as often as possible a News Letter dealing with such matters.

5. *Indian Claims Commission Bill.* This organization shall advocate and take the necessary steps to prevail upon the Congress of the United States to create an Indian Claims Commission authorized to hear, consider and settle the claims of the various Indian tribes of the United States and Alaska against the Federal Government.

6. *Employment of Indians in the Indian Service.* The Secretary of the Interior and the Commissioner of Indian Affairs shall be called upon to give real and meaningful preference to Indians in filling all positions in the Indian Service under Section 12 of the Indian Reorganization Act—and shall advocate in-service training of Indians for Government Career Service.

7. *Franchise for Indians.* This organization shall use its influence and exert its efforts toward securing the right to vote for Indians in the several States where voting privileges are being denied them—if and when this organization is requested by the Indians affected to assist them in vitalizing this right of American citizens.

8. *Consultation with Indians Relative to Indian Legislation.* The Congress

---

"The Platforms of the First Two Annual Conventions of the National Congress of American Indians, 1944 and 1945" found in the W. G. Stigler Papers, Carl Albert Center, University of Oklahoma. Reprinted by permission.

of the United States shall be called upon to adopt a policy of consulting with Indians, through their daily appointed representatives, before enacting any legislation directed specifically or prescriptively at Indians, their lives or their property.

9. *Adherence to Charters of Indian Organizations.* The Department of the Interior and the Commissioner of Indian Affairs shall be urged to examine fully into the provisions of charters that have been granted to Indian organizations under existing law and to give proper regard, consideration and adherence to the provisions of such charters.

10. *Poll of Indian Opinion.* The Executive Council of this organization shall take such steps as may be necessary to bring about a cooperative arrangement with the National Opinion Research Center of Denver 1, Colorado, in conducting a poll of Indian opinion regarding the policies and actions of the Office of Indian Affairs.

Second Annual Convention

Browning, Montana—October 22–25, 1945

This Convention formulated and adopted a platform and program consisting of the following points:

1. *American Indian Day.* To advocate the enactment of Federal legislation which will establish the Fourth Saturday of September of each year as American Indian Day.

2. *Indian Members of the Armed Services.* The Executive Council is authorized to examine into the status of existing legislation regarding Indians in the Armed Services during World War II and to work toward the end of equalizing the opportunities between such Indians and others.

3. *Indian Claims Commission Bill.* This Convention reaffirms the position taken at the Denver Convention in 1944 relative to the creation of an Indian Claims Commission Bill—and urges a more intensive campaign to enact necessary legislation for that purpose.

4. *Indian Health Program.* This organization shall advocate the continued development and extension of a health program and additional facilities for and on behalf of the Indians—and makes particular reference to the building of tuberculosis hospitals in Montana and other States.

5. *Readjustment of the Indian Bureau.* The executive Council is authorized to survey the situations and conditions among the Indians of the United States and Alaska with the object in mind of submitting to the Congress of the United States and the Department of the Interior a program for the readjustment of the administration of Indian affairs in keeping with current conditions and needs.

6. *Segregation of Indian Children.* The Executive Council is authorized and instructed to make a survey as to where Indian children in the public schools of the several States are segregated from other children—and to take necessary steps that will cause such segregation to be eliminated.

7. *Use of Indian Words.* Taking cognizance of the fact that a number of words derived from Indian nomenclature are used in a way that causes an improper reflection upon Indians, this organization proposes to use its influence to bring about a proper and accurate use of such words.

8. *Lands and Property Sought for Public Works Development.* Whereas, Indian lands and property—with particular reference to the Fort Berthold Reservation—are being sought for public works development, the Congress of the United States, the Department of the Interior and the War Department are urged to give full and careful consideration to the contentions of the Indians affected before lands and property are taken for such purposes.

9. *Mt. Rushmore.* That the proper authorities shall be requested to have the profile of an American Indian sculptured on Mt. Rushmore, Black Hills, South Dakota, in honor of the Indians' contribution to the United States and as a symbol of the better values of Indianhood.

10. *The Missouri Valley Authority and the CVA.* That the Congress of the United States be urged not to approve legislation vitalizing the MVA and the CVA for the reason that such approval and development of these authorities would cause a violation of treaties with the Indians affected and would be inimical to the material interest of such Indians.

11. *Statue in Front of the National Capitol Building.* The Executive Council is authorized and instructed to seek the removal of a statue at the main entrance of the Capitol building in Washington—showing an Indian with a tomahawk in the act of scalping a white woman—and to seek its replacement with a statue that is more appropriate. . . .

Senator Arthur Watkins Advocates the Termination of Federal Supervision, 1957

Virtually since the first decade of our national life the Indian, as tribesman and individual, was accorded a status apart. Now, however, we think constructively and affirmatively of the Indian as a fellow American. We seek to assure that in health, education, and welfare, in social, political, economic, and cultural opportunity, he or she stands as one with us in the enjoyment and responsibilities of our national citizenship. It is particularly gratifying to know that recent years of united effort, mutual planning, and Indian self-appraisal truly have begun to bear increasing fruit.

One facet of this over-all development concerns the freeing of the Indians from special federal restrictions on the property and the person of the tribes and their members. This is not a novel development, but a natural outgrowth of our relationship with the Indians. Congress is fully agreed upon its accomplishment. By unanimous vote in both the Senate and the House of Representatives termination of such special federal supervision has been called for as soon as possible. Of course, as with any such major social concern, methods vary in proposed solutions and emotions sometimes rise as to how the final goal should best be reached. A clear understanding of principles and events is necessary. . . . After all, the matter of freeing the Indian from wardship status is not rightfully a subject to debate in academic fashion, with facts marshalled here and there to be maneuvered and

From *Annals of the American Academy of Political and Social Science* 311 (May 1957), pp. 47–55. Reprinted by permission of Sage Publications Inc.

countermaneuvered in a vast battle of words and ideas. Much more I see this as an ideal or universal truth, to which all men subscribe, and concerning which they differ only in their opinion as to how the ideal may be attained and in what degree and during what period of time. . . .

A little more than two years ago—June 17, 1954—President Dwight D. Eisenhower signed a bill approved by the Eighty-third Congress that signified a landmark in Indian legislative history. By this measure's terms an Indian tribe and its members, the Menominee of Wisconsin, were assured that after a brief transition period they would at last have full control of their own affairs and would possess all of the attributes of complete American citizenship. This was a most worthy moment in our history. We should all dwell upon its deep meaning. Considering the lengthy span of our Indian relationship, the recency of this event is significant. Obviously, such affirmative action for the great majority of Indians has just begun. Moreover, it should be noted that the foundations laid are solid. . . .

Unfortunately, the major and continuing Congressional movement toward full freedom was delayed for a time by the Indian Reorganization Act of 1934, the Wheeler-Howard Act. Amid the deep social concern of the depression years, Congress deviated from its accustomed policy under the concept of promoting the general Indian welfare. In the postdepression years Congress—realizing this change of policy—sought to return to the historic principles of much earlier decades. Indeed, one of the original authors of the Act was desirous of its repeal. We should recall, however, that war years soon followed in which Congress found itself engrossed in problems first of national defense and then of mutual security. As with many other major projects, action was thus delayed. . . .

The Indian freedom program will not be accomplished immediately in the case of more large and complex situations, but for most tribes it can be numbered in a few years. Emotional and practical concerns dictate careful but measurable progress toward the goal of complete freedom. Complicated realty and other property problems, the careful clarification and protection of rights, these at times serve to make the process of decontrol lengthy. Meanwhile the Congress, through increased appropriations, is stressing the education of Indian children. The Bureau of Indian Affairs is expanding its adult education and vocational rehabilitation programs to help Indians earn a livelihood and to assume their responsibilities as citizens without special federal services. By action of the Eighty-third Congress Indian health concerns, previously in the Bureau's care, have been transferred to the Public Health Service. Simultaneously through the Bureau's relocation program, increasing thousands of energetic, healthy, skilled Indians compete successfully in our cities, bring their families into new modern homes, and thus in effect remove many conditions of their earlier wardship. Where financial burdens of transition from guardianship to normal citizenship appear evident for a tribe, consideration is given; thus the Eighty-third Congress in precedent-setting legislation provided assurance of aid for the Menominee. When all factors are considered, numerous chain-reaction situations are evident which tend to stimulate the desire for freedom even more conclusively.

We may admit the it-takes-time view, but we should not allow it to lull us into inaction. Freedom of action for the Indian as a full-fledged citizen—that is the continuing aim. Toward this end Congress and the Administration, state and local governments, Indian tribes and members, interested private agencies, and individual Americans as responsible citizens should all be united and work constantly. The legislatively set target dates for Indian freedom serve as significant spurs to accomplishment. Congress steadily continues to inform itself, to seek out, delimit, and assist those Indians most able to profit immediately by freedom from special supervision, and it acts primarily to speed the day for all Indian tribes and members to be relieved of their wardship status. A basic purpose of Congress in setting up the Indian Claims Commission was to clear the way toward complete freedom of the Indians by assuring a final settlement of all obligations—real or purported—of the federal government to the Indian tribes and other groups. . . .

Secluded reservation life is a deterrent to the Indian, keeping him apart in ways far beyond the purely geographic. By way of preparation for future decontrol programs, the Eighty-fourth Congress also passed the Vocational Rehabilitation Act to assist Indians to adapt themselves more readily to off-reservation life. Self-reliance is basic to the whole Indian-freedom program. Through our national historic development the Indian was forced into a dependent position with the federal government more and more, as America advanced westward, tending to sublimate his natural qualities of self-reliance, courage, discipline, resourcefulness, confidence, and faith in the future. Congress has realized this, and has steadily acted more positively to restore to the Indian these qualities. But self-reliance demands opportunity to grow. The Indian must be given the conditions under which—and only under which—self-reliance can be wholeheartedly regenerated. . . .

Completely within the historic policy of Congress in working toward the elimination of special controls over Indians is its concept of the role of the Indian Claims Commission. The Commission assures legal settlement of long-standing claims for redress against the federal government, which many Indians believe should be a necessary condition precedent to effective decontrol consideration. The Commission, set up in 1946, was then empowered to accept petitions until August 13, 1951 and was directed to conclude judgments on all claims by April 1957. Because of the large number of claims filed it had become necessary to extend the life of the Commission, and Congress—intent on providing judicial determination of all claims—passed legislation in 1956 to continue the Commission until the spring of 1962. However, the fact that all claims are not settled does not forestall present decontrol planning. . . .

The basic principle enunciated so clearly and approved unanimously by the Senate and House in House Concurrent Resolution 108 of the Eighty-third Congress continues to be the over-all guiding policy of Congress in Indian affairs. In view of the historic policy of Congress favoring freedom for the Indians, we may well expect future Congresses to continue to indorse the principle that "as rapidly as possible" we should end the status of Indians as wards of the government and grant them all of the rights and prerogatives pertaining to American citizenship.

With the aim of "equality before the law" in mind our course should rightly be no other. Firm and constant consideration for those of Indian ancestry should lead us all to work diligently and carefully for the full realization of their national citizenship with all other Americans. Following in the footsteps of the Emancipation Proclamation of ninety-four years ago, I see the following words emblazoned in letters of fire above the heads of the Indians—*THESE PEOPLE SHALL BE FREE!*

Ruth Muskrat Bronson (Cherokee) Criticizes the Proposed Termination of Federal Trusteeship, 1955

If the official policies of the Federal Government, as reflected by the current policies of the Bureau of Indian Affairs and the actions of the 83rd Congress, continue to be pursued the American Indian (like that other living creature associated with him in history, the buffalo) is likely, similarly, to continue to exist only on the American nickel.

The tragedy is that this may come about through misunderstanding of the issues involved in the proposed termination of Federal trusteeship over the Indian. These issues have been almost completely obscured in a miasma of confusion caused by conflicting financial interests, conflicting opinions on proper psychological solutions, and of justice itself. And, most important of all, caused by uninformed sentiment.

The average American is noted for his sympathy with the underdog. He is also apt to have romantic sentiment for the American Indian. Add to these two admirable qualities a vague sense of guilt for the actions of his forebears in ousting the original inhabitants of the rich land they adopted and for the long and shameful history of broken treaties with these dispossessed, and you have a tendency toward impulsive action based on a desire to make amends. If this action is founded on superficial or inaccurate knowledge rather than on thoughtful study or familiarity with fact and reality the result can be exceedingly serious, even disastrous, for the Indian. This is true in the case of the termination bills since these jeopardize the Indian's very existence and unquestionably would lead to his eventual—literal—extinction.

There is even widespread misconception as to what is involved in the Federal trusteeship. The casually informed citizen, dedicated to fair play, feels there is something definitely insulting in labeling an adult a ward of the government, as though he were being branded as too incompetent to function without a guardian. Actually, today's Indian enjoys all the major rights and obligations of every American citizen: the right to vote, for instance; to move freely about the country (that is, to live on a reservation or not, as he chooses); the right to sue in court and to make contracts, to hold office; the obligation to pay taxes, and to fight and die for his country in the armed forces.

In addition, he has special privileges, which is what trusteeship boils down to, which he gained by bargaining with his conquerors. In the not so distant past the Indians agreed to end their fighting and cede land to white settlers in exchange for certain defined, inalienable lands and specified services which the Indians could not provide for themselves and which are provided by the States and local communities for non-Indian citizens. It is hard to see how benefits make a "second class" citizen out of an Indian, especially when preferential treatment seems not to jeopardize the status of veterans, farmers, subsidized airlines and steamship companies, manufacturers protected by tariffs, or the businessmen with rapid tax write-offs.

On the contrary, it would seem to be our established political philosophy that the economic well-being of particular groups is a legitimate concern of the Federal government—all this aside from the fact that, in the case of the Indians, it is a matter of solemn treaty.

In addition to the treaties which established reservations as the property and home of the Indian people, the Reorganization Act of 1934 affirmed the partnership of Indian tribes and the Federal Government. Consolidating numerous individual treaties that had been effected with Indian tribes over the years, the Indians were granted by this Act the right to exist as distinct communities, with their own properties, culture, and religion, and the promise of certain services to be furnished by the Federal Government normally furnished [to] other citizens by the states was reaffirmed and enlarged upon.

In the 83rd Congress there was a concerted effort to abrogate this Act, by means of over 100 bills claiming to "free" Indians. Ten of those bills proposed termination of trusteeship over specific tribes. Five of them were passed and signed by the President. All of the bills follow the same pattern. They were introduced by less than a handful of men, but were designed to cut down the Indian on many fronts: the family, the band, the tribe and at State level. They would destroy the tribal organizations, abolish tribal constitutions and corporations formed under the Act of 1934 and void Federal-Indian treaties. Government supervision of the sale of Indian property and expert guidance on the development of natural resources which has been provided up to now would also be cut off, thus exposing the individual Indian, the weak as well as the strong, to exploitation by the unscrupulous and those more knowledgeable in the commercial ways of a highly complex and competitive society. This would take away from him the protection that was preventing further depletion of his last remaining resources. Such a loss would be the country's as well as the Indian's, since conservation along with guided expert development would cease.

In addition, there would be a cessation of education, health and welfare services now supplied by the Federal Government, guaranteed by treaty and sorely needed, without assurance that these would be provided by the States or local communities. . . .

Actually very few voices are raised against eventual termination of trusteeship over the Indians. The Indian people themselves, the friends of the Indians, and the authorities on Indian affairs who are deeply concerned about the trend toward termination are frightened and deeply disturbed, not only because of the inequities contained in the legislation proposed in the 83rd Congress, but at the haste, without proper safeguards or study in relation to the conditions of individual tribes.

And most of all, we are deeply concerned that termination is being decided upon *without the consent,* nay, over the protests, of the Indians concerned. Too often when Indian consent is given it has been obtained by unfair pressures amounting to nothing less than administrative blackmail, as in the case of two tribes which accepted termination bills because they were denied their own funds until they consented. This seems to them a shocking violation of faith.

The informed feel that there should be an attack on the major forces that are keeping the Indian from realizing his potentialities: ill health, lack of educational opportunities, widespread poverty. By attacking these problems at the root, they feel the day will be hastened when the Indian people will no longer need the protection of a special relationship with the Federal Government.

Termination of trusteeship, they believe (if it should be undertaken at all), should be carefully planned-for well ahead of the event, after thorough study, with the agreement of the Indians, the Federal agencies involved, the States and local government units, and the other organizations who would assume responsibility for providing the services now given by the Federal Government. Maintenance of the tribal integrity, if this is what the Indians want, must be assured in any program looking toward their future healthy integration into the American way of life. The consent of the Indians, moreover, should not be obtained by pressure amounting to duress such as was used last year in the cases of Menominee and Klamath when it was made clear to these two tribes that they would be permitted to withdraw their own money in the United States Treasury only if that withdrawal was coupled with "termination."

More than one theorist has stated that "the solution to the Indian problem" is the absorption of the Indian into the culture, race and society of the European-oriented American way. Shouldn't the Indian have something to say about this? Should the Indian be forced to give up his beliefs, his way of conducting his affairs, his method of organized living, his kind of life on the land he is a part of, if he chooses not to? Shouldn't the Indians have the same right to self-determination that our government has stated, often and officially, is the inalienable right of peoples in far parts of the world? Do we apply a different set of principles, of ethics, to the people within our own borders? . . .

Felix Cohen Observes the Erosion of Indian Rights, 1953

. . . In appraising changes that have occurred in the Indian field since May, 1950, when Dillon S. Myer took office as Commissioner of Indian Affairs, three fields call for special attention: (1) restrictions upon freedom which apply only to Indians; (2) restrictions upon Indian control of Indian property; (3) organic changes in the power structure of the Bureau of Indian Affairs which underlie the changes in the boundaries of Indian rights and liberties. . . .

Felix Cohen, "The Erosion of Indian Rights, 1950–1953: A Case Study in Bureaucracy." Reprinted by permission of The Yale Law Journal Company and Fred B. Rothman & Company from *The Yale Law Journal,* Vol. 62, pp. 348–390.

In place of the old Jeffersonian formula of "consent" of the governed, one finds the Indian Bureau now using the formula of "consultation." In practice, "consultation" means trying to persuade the Indians to go along with a Bureau program; if the effort fails, then the Bureau asks Congress to adopt the Bureau program anyway. The Commissioner's Withdrawal Memorandum of August 5, 1952, phrases the new formula in familiar terms:

> ... [A]greement with the affected Indian groups must be attained if possible. In the absence of such agreement, however, I want our differences to be clearly defined and understood by both the Indians and ourselves. We must proceed even though Indian cooperation may be lacking in certain cases.

... Faced with evidence that an administrator's drive for enlarged powers moves in a direction totally opposed to his professed ideals, many observers explain this inconsistency by resort to a theory of bureaucratic stupidity or hypocrisy. Under the influence of this theory and the traditional American penchant for blaming national ills on personal devils, there has arisen the doctrine that the only good Indian Commissioner is a dead one. But the problem of bureaucratic aggrandizement has deeper roots than one will find who looks only to the personality or background of individual administrators. For an entire generation American teachers have been urging upon students and citizens the desirability of increased scope for the wise discretion of administrative experts. Those human beings whose lives are most directly affected by that discretion—Indians, immigrants, and government employees—are now reaping the harvest of that teaching. Changes of personnel may relieve some of the harshness and heartlessness of recent Indian Bureau assaults on Indian liberties and Indian property. But a reversal of this trend is not likely to come until Americans assume either a higher respect for inexpert human beings or a lower respect for expert administrators.

It is a pity that so many Americans today think of the Indian as a romantic or comic figure in American history without contemporary significance. In fact, the Indian plays much the same role in our American society that the Jews played in Germany. Like the miner's canary, the Indian marks the shifts from fresh air to poison gas in our political atmosphere; and our treatment of Indians, even more than our treatment of other minorities, reflects the rise and fall in our democratic faith. Here, as in other parts of the world, the undermining of that faith begins with the glorification of "expert administrators" whose power-drives are always accompanied by soft music about "the withering away of the state" or the ultimate "liquidation" of this or that bureau.

It is not cynicism, but simple realism, to note that people whose freedom is being increasingly restricted want the assurance that some day, somehow, the restrictors of freedom will be liquidated or withered away. And certainly it is easier for administrators to act "efficiently" (in their own eyes) or "ruthlessly" (in others' eyes) if they console themselves with the assurance that they are helping, in the long run, to bring about a society in which coercion will disappear. What they forget, and what we need another [British economist] John Maynard Keynes to remind us of, is that in the long run we are all dead, and that while the means we use may be moulded by the ends we seek, it is the means we use that mould the ends we achieve.

⟨⟩ *E S S A Y S*

Alison R. Bernstein's *American Indians and World War II: Toward a New Era in Indian Affairs* (1991), from which the first selection is taken, is an important study of the subject. Now director of the Education and Culture Program at the Ford Foundation, Bernstein draws a careful portrait of the war's impact within native communities. She describes women's changing roles and opportunities, the new contacts made with the outside world by many previously isolated individuals, and new challenges to reservation land bases.

The postwar termination movement is the subject of the second essay, by Donald L. Fixico (Creek, Seminole, Sac and Fox, and Shawnee), a professor of history at Western Michigan University. In the essay Fixico, the author of the principal study that has been published on termination policy, presents a searching discussion of the relocation of Indians from reservation to city and of urbanization's impact on them. Fixico demonstrates that there could be widely varying responses to the urban environment—and thus vastly different results from such experiences. The racism and overall difficulties that Indians confronted could impel retreat. However, those same negative experiences might also inspire new Indian organizations and new forms of Indian community.

The Indian Home Front During World War II

ALISON R. BERNSTEIN

... The wartime economy created an unparalleled number of new jobs off the reservation, more than making up for the loss of reservation work as government-sponsored relief programs dried up. Indians could find good wages and steady employment if they were willing to leave their homes. Those in a position to cash in on wartime prosperity flocked to cities like Los Angeles, Tulsa, Denver, and Albuquerque, set up shantylike communities near defense plants and airplane industries, and started new lives. By war's end 40,000 persons—one half of the able-bodied men who had not entered the military and one-fifth of the women—had left Indian lands for war-related work.

John Collier supported this out-migration even though he knew that it would undoubtedly accelerate assimilation. Early in the war years he wrote, "In some areas, this assimilation has gone forward so rapidly that the net result has been a destruction of Indian culture." Nonetheless, he viewed it as necessary "if Indians are to live side by side with their white neighbors and become integrated into the general stream of American life." Collier faced a serious dilemma. He believed that Indians should support the war, but he recognized that the more they participated in war-related activities, the more they became like other Americans. Thus

Collier's approach to Indian affairs during the war years undermined his goal of preserving and emphasizing a pluralistic society.

While Collier had wanted the Indian service to take the lead role in the mobilization of Indian resources for the war, Washington frequently wound up taking a back seat to the tribes themselves, who were just as eager to become involved. Most tribal councils did not need prodding from the BIA to place their funds and resources at the War Department's disposal. The Klamath Indians in Oregon passed a resolution to build an airfield on the reservation to train both Indian and non-Indian pilots. The Eastern Cherokees announced "all-out cooperation by the tribe in the war program." The Navajo tribal council proclaimed, "Each and every one should consider the war effort first instead of meddling with things at home that could be settled later." The United Pueblos offered all their automobiles and trucks to the New Mexico Carrier Association for the transport of war-related materials.

Tribes also purchased war bonds or donated sums outright. In a special assembly, Uchee and Creek Indians in Oklahoma voted to buy $400,000 in war bonds. The Quapaws, who owned thousands of acres rich in zinc and lead, donated $1 million to the war effort and had to be persuaded to accept the bonds. The Shoshones of Wyoming authorized the Department of the Interior to purchase a $500 bond for each of the 1,000 members of the tribe, and one Sioux tribal council voted not to demand the $5 million recently awarded to them in a suit they had won against the federal government after eighteen years of litigation. "We will wait patiently for a few more years if it will help our country," the chairman of the council announced. At the other end of the socioeconomic scale, members of the Taos Pueblo, among the poorest of Indian tribes, purchased $2,000 worth of bonds from fees charged to amateur photographers for snapping their pictures, and Navajo women collected $75 worth of scrap metal which they traded in for bonds.

Some tribes engaged in friendly fund-raising rivalries. When dancers from the Jemez Pueblo in New Mexico traveled east to give benefit performances to raise money for war bonds, the other pueblos surrounding Jemez pledged to donate proceeds of their pottery sales to purchase bonds. Not to be outdone by the Blackfeet and Crow, the Shoshones authorized the secretary of the interior to exchange all tribally held funds in the Treasury Department for bonds.

For these and other reasons, the Indian service had difficulty keeping track of the total amount of bond purchases. Many individuals made local transactions with funds that were not under government jurisdiction. Others pledged a flat percentage of their salaries at work. Officials estimated that in the period between April 1, 1941, and June 1, 1942, Indians had purchased at least $3.7 million in defense bonds while the Interior Department had rejected an additional $800,000 in applications for war bonds from various tribes and from persons who wished to buy bonds with restricted funds already on deposit in the Treasury. These statistics prompted one senator to remark that the Indians' contributions were "an inspiration to patriotic Americans everywhere."

The buying spree did not subside. In April 1943, Secretary Ickes proudly announced that Indians had bought $12.6 million in war bonds. "This," he noted, "equaled the per capita contribution of any racial group including the whites." By

1945, Collier estimated that Indians had purchased over $50 million in war bonds and stamps, and claimed that the generosity of these first Americans far exceeded that of any other minority group.

Indians compiled this impressive record largely because for the first time many had abandoned the poverty of the reservation to become wage earners on the outside. Of the more than forty thousand Indians who found off-reservation wartime employment, nearly one-fourth, or ten thousand, were Navajo who journeyed throughout the Southwest to secure jobs working for the government, for private industry, or for local white farmers. Over two thousand Sioux Indians left their reservations in the spring of 1942 to work in the construction of military depots and air training centers. Apaches worked on gangs for the Santa Fe railroad and Hopis for the Denver and Rio Grande railroad in Colorado. By 1943 a total of 46,000 Indians had left the reservation, 24,422 of whom were employed in nonagricultural jobs in airplane factories, ordnance depots, shipyards, railroad gangs, coal and copper mines, sawmills, and canneries. The Indian Bureau estimated that this was six times the number of Indians engaged in similar work in 1941. The remaining 22,000 went to work in agriculturally related enterprises.

An Indian's ability to find employment depended on a variety of factors, including the proximity of the job to the reservation. Many Indians were less wary of venturing forth into the white world if they knew they could return easily to the reservation. For example, the Fort Wingate Munitions Depot, built by the army in 1941 and located in western New Mexico adjacent to the Navajo reservation, attracted over three thousand Indian workers. These Indians, nearly half of whom were unskilled laborers and unable to speak English, nevertheless proved acceptable for construction work. Two large defense construction projects built near the Pine Ridge reservation in South Dakota employed two hundred Sioux, and the location of the Aluminum Company of North America's plant near the St. Regis Mohawk reservation in New York state meant that Indians who worked away in the day could return to the reservation at night. Before the war, few of the Papago Indians who lived near the Phelps-Dodge copper mine at Ajo, Arizona, worked there. However, because of increased production needs and the loss of white miners, the company recruited 300 Papago to work in the mine.

Indian graduates of BIA vocational boarding schools had no trouble finding nearby war industry work once they graduated. Aircraft companies in Tulsa and Oklahoma City sought Indians who had trained at the Chilocco Indian School in Oklahoma and the larger Haskell Institute located in Kansas. In November 1942, Chilocco proudly reported that 95 percent or 300 of its sheet-metal-program graduates were employed, while Haskell boasted equally impressive statistics concerning the placement rate of Indians in high-paying defense jobs. Students at the Sherman Indian School in Riverside, California, often did not even wait to graduate before signing up at local defense plants. "The demands for skilled craftsmen are such that Sherman students in welding and sheet metal work are being snapped up before they complete their period of training," the school superintendent wrote Willard Beatty, the Indian service's director of education. To stem the premature exodus of students, Sherman developed a joint program with the Solar Aircraft Company in San Diego whereby students could work while completing their programs. In April 1943, Commissioner Collier announced that these schools had helped nearly three thousand Indians find work in manufacturing air-craft, tanks, and ships, and other war-related industries.

School officials wanted to increase the number of Indian students enrolled in the programs. In a letter to Washington requesting more funds, G. Warren Spaulding, Haskell's principal, complained that "we cannot supply our demand for welders or machinists." He estimated that the six BIA schools were serving only 20 percent, or one out of five Indians who desired or could benefit from such training. When additional funds proved impossible to secure, the schools moved to a six-day program and a summer session to accommodate greater numbers of Indians.

Less-skilled Indians could also find work off the reservation as long as they were willing and able to travel. The navy hired Pueblo Indians from New Mexico to help manage its supply depot in Clearfield, Utah. Chippewa tribesmen worked on Northern Pacific railroad track gangs and joined construction crews in Minne-apolis and St. Paul. Cheyenne and Blackfeet found jobs throughout the Pacific Northwest as maintenance men for state highway systems. Shortly after Pearl Harbor, sixteen Indians from the Cheyenne River reservation journeyed to Rapid City, South Dakota, and were hired on as construction workers at the local air base. A few got on-the-job training as painters and carpenters, eventually joining unions and receiving the astounding wage of $1.10 an hour. Compared to the subsistence life many had led, this was an economic windfall. Word got back to the reservation and within a few months, Rapid City was inundated with Indians. Most of these latecomers found work, although a few ran out of money before getting a job and had to return to the reservation.

Indian women also joined the ranks of workers who left the reservation to seek better employment. Besides the 800 Indian women who were accepted into the Wacs and Waves, hundreds of others received training in Indian service schools and, like the men, went to work immediately in the aircraft industries on the West Coast. In fact, Sherman openly recruited women students for sheet metal and welding classes. Because of the males' uncertain draft status, program direc-tors preferred to admit women students who would, in all probability, complete the course. Indian women, like their white counterparts, were welcomed into de-fense plant work as riveters, inspectors, and machinists. Pueblo Indian women took auto-mechanic training courses offered at the agency headquarters, and learned to haul freight across vast stretches of desert in the Southwest. Estimates place the number of Indian women working in war industries in 1943 at 12,000, or slightly more than one-fourth of the total population that had left the reserva-tions for war-related work. On the basis of these statistics, observers like Bertha M. Eckert, the secretary for Indian affairs of the National YWCA, optimistically predicted that "the Indian girl's swift emigration from the quiet tribal life of the reservation to the speeded-up living of industrial war centers envisions the end of the American Indian's isolation from normal American community life."

In addition, Indian women began to assume new roles on and off the reserva-tion. When regular government teachers were unavailable, they staffed schools in Indian villages and served as paraprofessionals. These new teachers transmitted both an appreciation of Indian culture and an optimism about possibilities for working outside the confines of traditional Indian life. In addition, the women held odd jobs as truck drivers and clerks. Those who did not formally work off the reservation fed the livestock, a traditionally male chore, and tended vegetable gardens that they planted behind their homes. Indian-service employees taught them how to use modern appliances and cook non-Indian foods in nutrition and home economics classes. Several Navajo women even mastered such traditionally male crafts as silversmithing and showed their jewelry alongside the men.

The Second World War had brought about the first mass migration of Indian workers off the reservation. A survey of New York State Indians reported in 1942 that increased industrial activity resulting from the war had virtually absorbed all employable Indians on the state's reservations. Commissioner Collier noted that there were 15 percent fewer Indian families living on reservations in 1943 than in 1941, and by 1944 the Sisseton Sioux, Potawatomi, Navajo, and Pueblo agencies all reported that over one-fourth of the tribal population had moved away from the reservation to take up residence in urban areas.

Social workers claimed that employment off the reservation was the answer to the subsistence problem for a large majority of Indians. Indian service figures on relief expenditures during the 1942–1943 fiscal year bore out the observation. The number of relief cases among Indians declined 50 percent, compared with a nationwide decline of 37 percent. Indian officials in Washington termed this new trend "heartening," interpreting it to mean that for the most part only the non-employable Indians—the aged, children, and physically handicapped—remained on relief. Unfortunately, this was not entirely the case. . . .

When Indian workers went to other parts of the country, they entered environments far different from the ones they left. In general, Indians found that making a transition to city life, to the neighborhoods in which they lived with white people, created more complex problems than learning their jobs. In some cities, for example, Sioux Indians became part of a disorganized and marginal group. While earning income in the city made more cash available to them then they had had on the reservation, they were frequently unable to afford to live in a better part of town. As one anthropologist observed about the relations of Sioux workers and whites, "Residents view Indians as a transient population with no visible wealth and low standards of living and infer they are content to stay where others refuse."

These Indians seldom complained directly about substandard conditions, but signs of discontent nevertheless emerged. Many children did not regularly attend school, and the rate of delinquency was high. In addition, intoxication in public places became a growing problem. Court officials in one city reported that the ratio of drunken Indians to whites was fifteen to one. When Indians ran into trouble, community agencies followed a policy of returning them to their home reservations. Some Indian workers, cut off from family, culture, and traditions, did not last long on the job.

After hearing of the plight of these displaced Indians, Collier tried to find ways to help ease their transition into the white world. He wrote to the American Friends Service Committee in 1944 urging that it create some kind of community center for young Indian workers. "Perhaps you could start hostels in Seattle, Los Angeles, and Minneapolis," he suggested. The organization had little money for this kind of operation although it shared Collier's concern. Groups like the General Federation of Women's Clubs and the YWCA mounted activities for small numbers of Indian women working in defense plants, but this did not begin to meet the need.

In time, a pattern emerged among the Sioux and other tribes where a majority of Indian workers began to move back and forth from the reservations to urban areas. Some only stayed a few months on the job, returning to the reservation when they got homesick or were in difficulty. These Indians, one contemporary study claimed, exceeded those who managed to survive on the outside for the duration of the war. Unfortunately, there was little recorded about those Indians who successfully adapted to nonreservation life since they did not present problems for government and tribal officials.

But whether Indian workers found permanent employment and integrated into the resident population or were constantly on the move, their absence was still felt on the reservation. Members of the All-Pueblo council worried that the drain of able-bodied men from the reservation into war industry work and the armed forces made it impossible for them to maintain their prewar level of agricultural production, let alone keep up with the BIA's demands that they increase production for wartime consumption. "Few men were left to plow for the women, aged, and children," the council observed. Many of the men who remained could not keep up with the work; as a result, women had to assume the responsibilities of planting and harvesting crops in addition to their other chores. A report from the Mescalero agency described Apache women laboring in the fields for the first time in history. Another precedent was set in May 1943 when Indian women worked the second shift in the lumber mills on the Menominee reservation in Wisconsin. This shift had been discontinued for four months because of the labor shortage. Whites in nearby towns pitched in as well. After noting the problems Indians in the Southwest were having trying to herd their livestock, the *New York Times* complimented a group of white cowmen who volunteered to drive the cattle in for the Indians, "rounding out the old tragic story, giving it a happy ending."

Reservation life also suffered as necessary goods and services dried up under wartime rationing. On reservations in the Southwest and Great Plains, where Indians had to travel long distances, the lack of rubber affected community life. The few Indians who owned cars ran out of tires, and the far-from-reliable schoolbus service was discontinued on some reservations. This situation forced Indians to walk anywhere from five to twenty miles to purchase food and other staples. School attendance on the Navajo reservation dwindled as buses that formerly had picked up children were pressed into service for war-related activities.

To reduce travel, the Education Division of the Indian Bureau began building large eight-sided structures, similar in shape to the traditional Navajo hogans, to house students attending nearby day schools. This was ironic since the same agency had fought the concept of the boarding school ten years earlier, arguing that it uprooted students from their families and traditions. J. C. Morgan, the assimilationist chairman of the Navajo tribal council, opposed the hogans because they "encouraged dirt, filth and sickness." He preferred to house the students in missionary boarding schools which would be an even greater "civilizing" influence upon them. He was overruled by Collier, who did not want to encourage church-related groups.

In addition to schools, the shortage of materials also forced the closing of hospitals, community centers, and Indian agency buildings on some reservations and the jobs that went with them. Hardest hit were communities in the remote parts of the Southwest. In Wisconsin the head medicine man on the Ojibwa reservation, who worked on the side as a bus driver, was fired when the tires gave out.

The war took its toll on the Indians' land base as well. Indians who remained at home, especially on isolated reservations, suddenly had to contend with the military's demands for their land. These areas were attractive sites for bombing and gunnery ranges because of their sparse population and lack of highways, railroads, and other utilities. When Indians understood what was being asked of them, most agreed, but a few opposed what they perceived as a new land grab even though the military was willing to lease or purchase the desired property. In 1942, after the army proposed to buy 400,000 acres of the Papago reservation, the chairman of the tribal council wrote President Roosevelt to "direct the Air Corps from seeking this land until every effort to obtain other land has been explored." Similarly, the elders of the Laguna Pueblo wired Commissioner Collier that they would rather not sell or lease their lands for a bombing site.

The largest of these military land deals involved the hasty purchase of over 400,000 acres on the Pine Ridge reservation in South Dakota. In the spring of 1942 the secretary of the army selected this land on the Sioux reservation for use as an aerial gunnery range. The army arranged to purchase over 300,000 acres from individual Indians—frequently paying only the minimal amount of seventy-five cents per acre—and leased the remaining land from the tribe. Then it notified the 128 families living in the area that they had to evacuate their homes within thirty days. These Indians, who were about to harvest their crops, had no time to make alternative arrangements. As one evacuee bitterly recalled, "The War Department was ordering us out and the superintendent of the reservation said that we would be shot if we didn't leave." The plight of these few Sioux Indians echoed another example of Indian removal nearly a century before in the Southeast. "For weeks bewildered families leaving behind them their only home and their scant crops roamed far and near to find a place for a tent," one local Catholic missionary reported. But unlike the Cherokees, who over one hundred years before had fought removal, these Indians left without protest. No one had told them that they could have filed a suit against the government charging hardship damages.

The Indians eventually fought back. In 1944 they convinced Representative Francis Case to write to the BIA requesting information about the gunnery range sale. The Indians who had been forced out were claiming that the army had only bought the surface rights to the land. They told Case that they had retained the oil and mineral rights below. The Indian Bureau responded by indicating that the individuals who had sold their land lost title to all resources and there was nothing the government could do to help. In 1956, after twelve years of Indian protest, Representative E. Y. Berry, a Republican congressman from South Dakota, eventually succeeded in putting through legislation to compensate the Sioux for their financial losses.

This incident involving Sioux lands, although troubling, did not ultimately prove to be the most controversial example of the use and misuse of Indian-held property for war-related purposes. In March 1942, John Collier suggested that the War Relocation Authority lease lands on Indian reservations and turn them into internment camps for Japanese-Americans. After the War Department ordered internment of these citizens from the West Coast, Collier moved swiftly to involve the Indian service by volunteering Indian lands as sites for the "colonization of the Japanese." As with his earlier arguments regarding tribal resources, Collier believed that if he could get the Japanese placed on uncultivated Indian lands, relocation would work to the Indians' benefit. This position was summed up by one of his longtime assistants, Walter Woehlke. "We have to be a little calculating. Barracks for the Japanese would revert to the Indians after the war . . . four or five semipermanent communities would fit into the needs of the Indian program," Woehlke concluded. But this was not Collier's sole reason for wanting to become involved in WRA efforts. The commissioner believed that the Indian service's history of dealing with one minority group could prove helpful in these delicate circumstances. As he noted in a memo to Secretary of the Interior Ickes: "The Interior Department is better equipped than any other agency to provide for the Japanese aliens the type of treatment and care which will make them more acceptable as members of the American population. Available in this connection is the Indian Service's long experience in handling a minority group."

Collier got his wish. In conversations with Milton Eisenhower, the first director of the WRA, Collier offered eight reservations that he believed would be suitable, and the two men eventually settled on two sites—the Colorado River reservation in Poston, Arizona, and the Pima-held Gila reservation outside Phoenix. The first and largest was the Colorado River site, which had some 10,000 to 25,000 acres immediately available. These lands lay on the boundary between California and Arizona, and with its sparse population of some 1,300 Mohave and Chemehuevi Indians, they seemed capable of accommodating thousands of new residents. Although the Colorado River Indian tribes and the Pimas had been incorporated under the Indian Reorganization Act, Collier seemed willing to lease their lands without first discussing the arrangements with the respective tribal councils. He dispatched a planning specialist to the Colorado reservation to explain the details only after he began negotiations with Eisenhower.

Not everyone within the Indian service shared Collier's eagerness to relocate Japanese-Americans on Indian lands. Charles Gensler, the superintendent of the Colorado River agency, opposed the plan. He had been meeting with other government officials who wanted the reservation to produce the guayule plant, a raw product used in the creation of synthetic rubber. "The reservation cannot be made to take care of ten to forty thousand Japanese and then produce its maximum of guayule. . . . Should the Japanese be located here there would be no room for any plantings other than subsistence foods," Gensler argued. Fred Daiker, the Indian commissioner's assistant for welfare and social work, also fought the relocation of Japanese-Americans onto the reservation lands. In weighing the pros and cons of such a decision, Daiker noted: "There is still enough sentiment left for the Indian so that the public may criticize using Indian reservations for these aliens and causing the Indians to be associated with these people. The logical question will be why place them among the Indians after all the wrong that has been done to these people? It will be construed as just another instance of forcing something on the Indian because he can do nothing about it." Although their reasons for resisting the relocation plan differed, neither Daiker nor Gensler opposed Collier on the grounds that internment restricted the civil rights of a group of American citizens. Daiker was concerned, however, about the tribes' rights. "I feel that morally we should consult each Indian group before any commitments are made for establishing aliens on their lands," he concluded, urging Collier to involve the tribes in the negotiations.

Daiker's position mirrored that of the Indians. The Colorado River Indians expressed open hostility to the notion of Japanese-American intruders. Hopi Indians instructed their superintendent to inform Washington that they opposed having Japanese-Americans on their lands even though they were not even slated to receive evacuees. The Navajo indicated that they would not let camp inmates teach in reservation schools despite the shortage of qualified personnel. Finally, as army bulldozers broke ground for dormitories, the Pima tribal council reluctantly agreed to allow the Japanese-Americans to live on a remote part of the Gila River reservation, while officially expressing its anger at not having been consulted earlier. The tribe had no real alternative after the superintendent of the reservation informed them, "It was not the desire on the part of the WRA nor the Department of the Interior that this should be thrust upon them. . . . But the emergency which this war has forced upon us has required that every American citizen heed whatever Army command may be given."

In the summer of 1942, 20,000 Japanese-Americans arrived at the Colorado River site, and the army shipped another 5,000 to Gila River. Together these two sites housed nearly 25,000 persons, or one-quarter of all relocatees. Originally the Indian Bureau had agreed to administer both facilities, but when Dillon Myer replaced Milton Eisenhower as director of the WRA late in 1942, he shifted control over the Pima Camp to army officials. Moreover, Myer refused to authorize the building of a road on the Pima reservation and other improvements despite the agreements made between his predecessor and the Indian Bureau.

Collier angrily wrote Myer in 1944 charging that the WRA was reneging on its commitments to Indians. "There is involved the matter of the government keeping faith with the Indians of the Gila River reservation." But Myer did not have any responsibility for the Indians and ignored Collier's appeals.

Relations between the Indian Bureau and the WRA deteriorated at the Colorado River Camp as well. Although the BIA continued to administer this site until January 1944, Collier could not get Myer to authorize the cultivation of some 25,000 acres for the production of surplus food. Instead, Myer implemented a subsistence program that provided for the development of only 5,000 acres. Once again, Collier's grand scheme to use relocation as a way to improve the Indians' lot fell far short of its intended goals. Even the barracks which Collier had hoped would revert to the Indians when the Japanese left the Poston camp were torn down.

It is difficult to know what effects these relocation activities had on the Indians themselves. The tribes made some additional money from the land leases, and the Japanese contributed in some measure to the increased agricultural productivity of the reservations. But, by and large, there was little interaction between the Indians and their Japanese tenants. WRA Director Myer deliberately tried to keep the Japanese isolated from the Indians, arguing that the evacuees were transients and should not develop ties to their temporary surroundings. Neither minority group had much opportunity to learn from the other. But the Indians did receive a few lessons about the WRA and the BIA's/power to protect Indian interests. Moreover, this episode suggested that Commissioner Collier was not above acting "on the Indians' behalf" in ways that echoed the paternalism of previous, less enlightened federal administrations.

Although few tribes suffered the kinds of dislocations and financial losses which hit the Pine Ridge Sioux or the disappointment and humiliation encountered by the Pimas and Colorado River tribes in their dealings with the Indian Bureau and the WRA, the wartime takeover of these Indian-held resources had significant consequences. The Indian Bureau's one remaining hope that most of the acreage would be resold back to the Indians immediately after the war did not materialize. During the 1930s the Collier administration had struggled to increase the Indian land base, managing by 1940 to purchase a total of four million new acres from whites. The war had partially eroded that accomplishment, leaving almost a million fewer acres by 1945. However, the war had lured thousands of Indians off the reservation and into the cities. Thus the Indians' need for land temporarily appeared less important.

Whether they remained on the reservations or sought better jobs on the outside, the war left its mark on American Indians. Few could remain totally immune from the demands and opportunities created by the war. In 1940 the number of Indians dwelling in cities was less than five percent of the entire Indian population. By 1950, that figure had quadrupled to nearly twenty percent. Before the war the states of Arizona, Michigan, New Mexico, and Washington did not even list an urban Indian population. Afterwards, the 1950 Census revealed over 40,000 urban Indians in these four states alone. At first, only husbands or single men and women left their homes to find employment but soon families followed. The centers of urban Indian life became those cities in which they could get jobs—Oklahoma City, Tulsa, Gallup, Los Angeles, Seattle, Minneapolis, and Denver.

A shift in Indian occupations also occurred during these war years. Where in 1940 nearly one-half of all employed Indian males were classified as farmers or farm managers, by 1946 that figure had dropped to less than 25 percent. In Oklahoma the change was typical. Out of a total Indian population of 53,000 in 1940, 40,000 Indian males were listed as employed in rural farming; by 1950, that figure had declined to 22,000. In 1940, 21 percent of all employed Indian males in Oklahoma were blue collar workers; that figure nearly doubled to 41 percent in 1950.

The war stimulated new demands for labor and raw materials which loosened traditional work roles for men and women. When the shortage of domestic and exported silver threatened to wipe out the Zuni and Navajo silversmithing industry, these draftsmen found other jobs as mechanics and clerks. Navajo blanket weaving became virtually extinct during the war. As one old Indian cynically observed: "Young Indian go fight. Send money home. Old Indian go work for white man on railroad, in mine, on highway, bring big money home. Indian woman work in eating house for white women or in train house [hotel at a train station] making money. White traders buy wool, pay good price. Navajo have lots of money, no wool."

Looking back over the participation of Indians in war-related work, one is struck by the diversity of wartime experiences and the Indians' capacity to adjust to the non-Indian world or, at the very least, to a rapidly changing Indian world. Even those Indians who had difficulties as transient workers nevertheless superficially adopted the non-Indian way of life. In the pre-war period less acculturated Indians bore little resemblance to non-Indians; in dress, family, home, job, income, and customs, the gaps between Indians and their white counterparts were considerable. The reservation had contained the lives of some 400,000 persons who were cut off from the rest of American society. The war unlocked the reservation and introduced thousands of Indians, voluntarily and involuntarily, to the world beyond. As a result, Indians were forced to reconsider whether they wished to maintain their isolation from the rest of American life. Many more learned English, changed their dress, their hairstyles, even their cultural traditions. Navajo, for example, overcame their ancient fears of the dead sufficiently to build cemeteries for tribesmen who lost their lives abroad. Many also overcame their fear of failure in white society. "Now that they have tried their wings, have lived and worked among white people . . . and found that they have made the grade, they are a different type of people," one social worker observed in 1944.

The war accelerated the detribalization process for many Indians. This had not been one of the Indian New Deal's prewar aims, but as time passed, the BIA nevertheless encouraged Indians to put their country first, and its needs above their own. John Collier had no ambivalence about involving Indians in the wartime economy. Quite the contrary. He wrote confidently, "Should economic conditions after the war continue to offer employment opportunities in industry, many Indians will undoubtedly choose to continue to work away from the reservations." After all, he continued, "never before have Indians been so well prepared to take their place among the general citizenry and become assimilated into the white population."

Given these changes, it was not surprising that many political leaders and policy makers viewed the Indian Bureau as, at best, superfluous and perhaps even an obstacle to the integration of Indians into American life. With Indians in the armed forces and living in unprecedented numbers off the reservation, the traditional hold of the BIA over Indian life loosened during the war years. If the war had unleashed Indians from previous tribal patterns, it also undermined their need for the Indian Bureau as well.

The Relocation and Urbanization of American Indians

DONALD L. FIXICO (Creek, Seminole, Sac and Fox, Shawnee)

The experiences of Native Americans during the war years had a two-fold effect on federal-Indian relations in the postwar period. The courageous performance of Native American men abroad and native women in the war industries at home impressed federal officials, convincing them that Indians possessed an aptitude for working side by side with other Americans. Barton Greenwood, Acting Commissioner of Indian Affairs, estimated that 50 percent of the returning veterans had sufficient experience in working with other Americans away from the reservations to compete with them for jobs.

Unfortunately, returning Indian veterans increased the burden on the reservations' already limited economic resources. High unemployment and widespread poverty pervaded Indian country. In response, the government proposed relocating unemployed Indians or those who returned from the war to urban areas where they could find jobs. Greenwood advised that these people be moved as far as possible from their original communities to prevent them from returning easily to their homelands. Theoretically, this strategy would be conducive to successful Indian adaptation to urban living. Federal officials believed that once the new urban migrants had adjusted to living in the cities there would be no need for reservations. Until then, Indians continued to live on reservations under submarginal conditions.

The severe blizzard of 1947–48 worsened the already poor economy for Indian communities, especially for the populous Navajos in Arizona and New Mexico, who suffered extreme destitution. To help alleviate their suffering, the government supplied emergency aid, but the deplorable conditions on the reservation continued. This impelled the federal government to take one more step in establishing a job placement program, which laid the foundation for the relocation program. The Bureau of Indian Affairs began to resettle employable Indians from the Navajo Reservation in urban areas. The Interior Department soon established additional placement offices in Denver, Salt Lake City, and Los Angeles.

Relocation took its place beside termination as the second goal of federal Indian policy in the 1950s. After the withdrawal of trust restrictions from the lands, Native Americans were encouraged to pursue a livelihood in the cities. Although the program began with the Navajos, the government soon began to extend relocation services to all tribes.

In a conference with area directors in January 1951, Commissioner of Indian Affairs Dillon S. Myer had urged funding for the relocation program to begin the recruitment of Indians for urban placement. He had hoped to be able to expand the program quickly by intensifying and broadening recruitment efforts. Critics alleged that relocation had swept Indians off the reservations, scattered them throughout cities, and then they were abandoned by the Bureau. The commissioner denied that the Bureau of Indian Affairs had forced Native Americans to relocate. Myer insistently advocated relocation as a policy congruent with his philosophy of termination—the view that Native Americans should be encouraged to live without federal supervision like other Americans. Moving Indians to urban areas to work and to live would, he believed, escalate their standard of living. Although Myer enthusiastically supported relocation during his three years at the helm of the Bureau, the program failed to gain momentum during his administration.

Even though the application procedure for relocation was amazingly simple and open to young and old alike, Native Americans initially hesitated to volunteer for the new program. However, curiosity about city life eventually induced many people to apply for relocation. Native Americans of all types would frequently arrive at an agency office to inquire, "What is this relocation that I've been hearing about?" A survey of the Klamaths who were known to relocate to Chiloquin and Klamath Falls, two small urban centers near the reservation in Oregon, revealed that they were attracted to stores, schools, and movie theaters. In addition, veterans, relatives, and friends who were among the first to relocate made people on the reservation envious when they talked about their adventures and good times in the cities.

After an initial request for relocation had been filed with a BIA official at an agency or an area office, the paperwork began. After completing a review of the applicant's job skills and employment records, the official usually contacted the relocation office in the city of the applicant's choice. With clothes and personal items packed, the applicant customarily boarded a bus or train to the designated city, where he or she would be met by a relocation worker. Upon arrival, the newcomer received a check to be spent under the supervision of the relocation officer. Next, the officer usually accompanied the new urbanite to a nearby store to purchase toiletries, cookware, groceries, bedding, clothes, and an alarm clock to insure punctual arrival at work. In the city, the poorest of America's poor began a new day in what they hoped was a promising future.

Living by a strict timetable was a new experience for almost all relocated Indians. Often, instructions had to be given to show how a clock worked and the relocatee taught how to tell time. One young Crow Creek Sioux, who began to take college courses to improve his job qualifications, expressed exasperation in adjusting to an hour-by-hour schedule of classes. His traditional conviction that people should live in harmony with nature during a continuum of time conflicted with the concept of regulating one's life according to the minutes of a clock. "I nearly went crazy during the first two weeks of college," he said. "No matter where I was, I always had to be somewhere else at a certain time. There was no rest."

Relocation officers assisted the new migrants in locating places to shop for groceries, and informed them about nearby churches of their denominations. After the relocatee and his or her family were settled, the relocation worker and neighborhood clergyman visited on a regular basis. Normally, the BIA paid the relocatee's first month's rent, including clothing and groceries, and the expenses incurred while traveling to and from work. After the first month the relocatees were on their own, although Bureau workers remained available for counseling and assistance in job placement; BIA officials would keep tabs on the progress of relocatees for the next nine years.

Young adults, especially men, were the most common applicants for relocation. Frequently, they left families behind until they found jobs and housing, and then sent for their families. The most ambitious relocatees were young Indians who possessed some college education. They chose to move to large cities, far from their homelands, to escape their past poverty, and perhaps to forget their traditional heritage. Undoubtedly, they succeeded much better in the transition from native life to urbanization than less-educated relocatees. They successfully competed for jobs, and found adequate housing.

During midsummer 1951, the Bureau of Indian Affairs assigned workers to extend the relocation services in Oklahoma, New Mexico, California, Arizona, Utah, and Colorado. In November, a field office was opened in Chicago to place Navajos in jobs, but shortly afterwards, the BIA incorporated the office as a part of the relocation program to serve all Native Americans. The first relocatees arrived in Chicago in early February 1952. In all, relocation workers processed 442 Native Americans for employment in Los Angeles, Denver, and Chicago during that year. With the Bureau expanding the Navajo placement offices in Salt Lake City, Denver, and Los Angeles to service all Native Americans, a new generation of urban Indians came into being. . . .

BIA publicity portrayed relocation as a "New Deal" for Native Americans, one that offered them a chance to improve their economic status. Indian Bureau officials encouraged Indians to relocate, although ostensibly on a voluntary basis. Throughout the reservations, BIA workers circulated brochures and pamphlets suggesting that a better life awaited Indians in urban areas. Pictures of executives dressed in white shirts, wearing ties, and sitting behind business desks insinuated that similar occupational positions could be obtained by Indians. Photos of a white frame house with shutters enticed the women. The scene suggested that Indians could provide their families with similar homes in suburban America.

Unfortunately, the hard realities of urban life soon destroyed Indian hopes for a successful livelihood and dashed their many dreams. For those who left the reservation and traveled a long distance for the first time, the relocation experience was a threatening cultural shock. Once off a bus and alone in a strange, large city, relocatees encountered a foreign and threatening new world that often proved to be traumatic. Relocatees knew little about such modern gadgets as stoplights, clocks, elevators, telephones, and other everyday objects that Americans took for granted. To avoid a frightening elevator, they would climb the stairs in apartment buildings. Newly relocated Indians who had not yet mastered the English language experienced even more difficulty, and many were embarrassed to ask for assistance. A magazine article described one incident: "In situations of distress, the Indian often remains proudly silent. One relocatee was 'lost' in his room for 24 hours. He had lost the BIA address. And although he had the phone number he was 'ashamed' to ask how to dial." Perhaps the most important complaints from Indians dealt with the noise, tension, and hectic pace of the city life. Some Native American women found the outside bustle of the city too difficult to face and locked themselves in their apartments, afraid to even go to the supermarket.

Toward the end of 1955, the Muskogee area office in Oklahoma reported a decline in people volunteering for relocation from its area. Fear of big-city life inhibited many Native Americans, making them feel lost, insecure, and inferior to the majority population of urban white Americans. Compared to other, more aggressive urban minorities—blacks, Mexicans, and Puerto Ricans—the uneducated, traditional Indians were isolated and at the bottom of the social order.

Relocation officers attempted to prepare Indians for the drastic changes that lay ahead of them and to ease their adjustment to city life. They informed the relocatees of the conditions they would face in industrial areas—working according to a regular schedule, moving through city traffic, paying high rent, encountering hospital expenses, learning to budget money, purchasing suitable clothing

for themselves and their children, and living in a generally non-Indian neighborhood. Despite these efforts, Indians going on relocation experienced considerable
difficulty in adjusting to urban areas. An article in the *Christian Science Monitor*
described the reality of an Indian couple relocating to a city. The story itself depicts a true picture of what relocation was probably like for a family.

> Tony and Martha Big Bear and their family had just arrived in Los Angeles from the
> reservation. Everything was new to Martha and she never said a word and scarcely
> raised her eyes while holding the children during the bus ride to the relocation office.
> The first thing the relocation officer did was to advise Tony about spending money
> wisely. A $50 check was drawn up for Tony and he was told how to open a bank
> account. The Big Bears were then temporarily lodged in a nearby hotel.
>
> Although Tony wanted to be a commercial artist, he settled for a job in an aircraft
> plant. The Indian Bureau placement officer persuaded Tony to accept this job first
> and then he could check into the art field later after he became familiar with Los
> Angeles and when his family had a more permanent place to live. Everything was
> moving too fast for the Big Bears. The field office helped Tony find an apartment—a
> 'slum,' according to most people, but it was better than anything Martha was accus-
> tomed to.

The experience of the Big Bears could easily have been more difficult. Sometimes factories closed down and welfare agencies had to assist relocated families.
Out of necessity, Indian centers soon sprang up in almost every large city to help
deprived Native American people by temporarily furnishing groceries and
clothes. Nearly all relocatees experienced difficulties of one kind or another. A
writer for the *Atlantic Monthly* published a true account involving Little Light,
her husband Leonard Bear, and their five children, a family originally from a
Creek Indian community in Oklahoma. "Today they are slum dwellers in Los
Angeles, without land or home or culture or peace."

The author described meeting Little Light and her children "in the chairless
kitchen-dining-living room of a small shanty on the outskirts of Los Angeles.
Five children, black eyes round with wonder in their apricot faces, sheltered
against her skirt. The walls were unpainted, the floor a patchwork of linoleum.
Through an archway, another room was visible where three beds crowded together. A two-burner stove stood on a box, and on the only other piece of furniture in the room—a battered table—rested the remains of a dinner; some white,
grease-soaked bags which had contained hamburgers and fried potatoes prepared
by the restaurant a few blocks away."

In response to the interviewer's questions, Little Light spoke of how her husband went out drinking every night, of people in stores laughing at her, and about
the need for a doctor for her sick child. She wanted to return to Oklahoma, but
there was not enough money to go back. The woman stared solemnly, and her
face became distorted as she lamented, "They did not tell us it would be like this."

Similar descriptions of unfortunate incidents were published in current magazines and newspapers, thereby reinforcing the negative public image of the BIA
that the termination program had first created. Federal officials countered with
defensive news releases: "As some of you know—if you have been reading your
magazines lately—that word 'relocation' seems to upset certain people—apparently because it suggests uprooting the Indians from their serene pastoral environ-

ment and plunging them down in some kind of a nerve-wracking asphalt jungle. For at least a generation, and probably longer, Indian families have been moving away from the impoverished environment of reservations and seeking better opportunities."

Despite the radical socioeconomic problems facing them, the number of applicants for relocation began increasing on the whole. In the 1956 fiscal year, BIA workers processed 5,316 relocatees through four offices—Chicago, Denver, Los Angeles, and San Francisco. Of this number, 732 were single men, 373 were single women, and 424 had families. Relocation officers noted a growing interest in relocation among Indians, and a backlog of applications existed at almost all Indian agencies.

Some 12,625 reservation Indians had relocated to urban areas by 12 July 1956, and the Bureau expected another 10,000 to apply before 1 July 1957. The proliferating number of applicants prompted the BIA to enlarge the relocation program. To meet the costs of a growing program, Congress authorized generous appropriations for relocation. Commissioner Emmons announced in 1956 that relocation funding had more than tripled, from a level of 1,016,400 dollars in 1955 to a current sum of 3,472,000 dollars. Increased funding enabled the Bureau to broaden its scope of relocation services. Two new offices were planned, and steps were taken to enlarge relocation guidance staffs. . . .

The initial meeting between a potential employer and a relocatee was a crucial step. The Indian who had recently left the reservation sometimes did not make a good first impression. Tattered and threadbare clothes caused employers to pause and study Indian applicants with apprehension. The area director at Gallup, New Mexico, mentioned this point to the commissioner of Indian affairs in his report on Navajo placement activities. The director reported that the Navajos dressed in worn and torn clothes; some dressed in traditional garb; and men wore their hair long, arousing stares from people who were unaccustomed to Indians. Naturally, unconventional dress and sometimes shabby appearance hindered Indians who were looking for jobs and housing, or provoked derogatory comments while they shopped in stores.

The physical appearance of relocatees was less of a problem at factories located near reservations. To encourage Native Americans to seek vocational training and employment, the Bureau of Indian Affairs negotiated contracts with business firms to build plants near reservations. Bulova Watch Company built a jewel-bearing plant near the Turtle Mountain Reservation at Rolla, North Dakota, the first company to locate near a reservation and to hire exclusively Indian employees. On the last day in December 1956, the company threatened to close the installation, provoking sharp reactions. Native American leaders, as well as public officials and Indian interest organizations, urged congressmen and the BIA to retain the plant. Closing the facility would threaten the progress of the Turtle Mountain Indians and the relocation program. Bureau officials believed if all 150 Indian employees at Bulova lost their jobs other Native Americans would question the practicality and advisability of urban relocation or of receiving employment or vocational training through the relocation program. The BIA was also concerned that other industries would be reluctant to accept government subsidies for locating near reservations.

The Department of the Interior especially encouraged industrial development on and near the Navajo Reservation in the Southwest. In December 1956 the Interior Department announced that 300,000 dollars of the Navajo tribal fund was marked for creating an industrial development program. The program would induce industrial plants to locate near the Navajo Reservation, and provide payrolls and job opportunities for tribal members. Two manufacturing companies, Navajo Furniture, Incorporated, and Lear, Incorporated, constructed factories near the reservation. Navajo Furniture, a subsidiary of Baby Line Furniture of Los Angeles, and Lear, a manufacturer of electronic equipment of Santa Monica, California, were each expected to employ an estimated one hundred Navajos.

The need for on-the-job experience among the Navajos was especially important because of the limited supply of jobs near reservations and the threat of layoffs to those who had jobs. Unskilled Indians had to compete with other workers in urban areas for jobs requiring specific skills. Vocational training would prepare relocating Indians for earning their livelihoods in the cities. The Indian Vocational Training Act of 1957 authorized the establishment of job training centers near reservations and in cities to teach trades to relocating Indians. The variety of training increased for several years; eventually, vocational training centers offered training in 125 occupations, and accredited schools existed in twenty-six states.

Vocational training and employment assistance for Native Americans were two primary objectives of the relocation program. The availability of employment in cities naturally led to relocation in urban areas. Hence, the need for employment became the basis for relocation. Relocation did not merely mean removing Indians from reservations to cities, but involved preparing them for placement through vocational training and moving them to areas with high employment opportunities. Public Law 959 emphasized employment for Indians, which became the main service provided by the relocation program and led to changing the name of the "relocation program" to "employment assistance." More importantly, "relocation" had become associated with the negative image of dragging Indians from reservations and abandoning them in cities. The BIA hoped the name change would improve the program's image.

The vocational training program aroused considerable interest among Indian people. The offer of free training, without necessarily having to move to some city, attracted applications. In addition, Bureau officials visited numerous council meetings to promote the advantages of vocational training opportunities. Their efforts increased Indian interest, which also meant increasing the annual cost of the entire relocation program. Congress appropriated $1,016,400.00 for the 1956 fiscal year. The expense per person amounted to $196.00. In fiscal year 1957, the total budget climbed to $3,472,000.00, at a cost of $347.20 per relocatee.

The Department of the Interior sensed a growing Native American voluntarism for relocating services, and announced on 24 July 1957 that seven hundred positions were available for on-the-job training opportunities. Federal efforts to entice industrial expansion, which would produce jobs, were successful when the BIA negotiated contracts with eight companies, including Whitetree's Workshop, an Indian-owned firm that manufactured souvenirs on the Cherokee Reservation in North Carolina. Saddlecraft, Incorporated, of Knoxville, Tennessee, intended to operate a leather-goods plant at Cherokee, North Carolina; and Lear,

Incorporated, of Santa Monica, California, had already developed an electronics plant at Flagstaff, Arizona. The others included Casa Grande Mills, a garment factory in Arizona; New Moon Homes, Incorporated, of Rapid City, South Dakota, which made trailer homes near the Standing Rock Reservation; Navajo Furniture Industries, Incorporated, with a company at Gallup, New Mexico; and Bably Manufacturing Company, a denim garments factory located near the Yakima Reservation. Unfortunately these companies could hire only a small percentage of the growing number of applicants for vocational training.

Federal funding increased in correlation with the rising number of applicants until the high cost caused disagreement among federal officials. Some congressmen supported the relocation program, while others advocated the development of tribal economic resources, a less expensive route. In a confidential letter to Commissioner Emmons, dated 9 October 1957, Congressman E. Y. Berry of South Dakota complained of federal spending on Indian relocation. "I think the time has come to stop this useless waste of the taxpayers' money in hiring an army of bureaucrats to do something that does not in any way benefit the Indian people," Berry wrote.

Skeptical congressmen questioned the high overhead costs. People, especially those unfamiliar with Indian affairs, wanted clarification of the goals and objectives of the relocation program, fearing that the program was getting out of control. Terminationists who wanted to get the government out of the "Indian business" complained about the expanding and ever-increasing cost of the Bureau of Indian Affairs.

A report entitled "The Program of Relocation Services," dated 28 October 1957, reiterated the purpose of relocation. The prime directive was to assist Native Americans who wanted independence from the federal government and were eager to find their place in the free-enterprise system. The Indian citizenry, the report claimed, would eventually become a component of the urban community scene.

The relocation program reinforced the termination policy in decentralizing the federal authority in Washington. With the dispersal of federal responsibilities according to Public Law 280, the states assumed many services to Native Americans. States supplied relocation assistance that Native Americans needed. Homer B. Jenkins, assistant commissioner of Indian affairs, informed the area directors of Portland, Phoenix, Minneapolis, and Muskogee, as well as field relocation officers at St. Louis, Oakland, and Chicago, that applicants who desired vocational training should be referred to state agencies. Jenkins's order was congruent with the termination directive calling for federal withdrawal of government intervention in Indian affairs.

Indian veterans of World War II and the Korean War had a much better chance of succeeding in relocation than reservation Indians who had never left their rural communities. Previous experience with the outside world, plus the possession of knowledge of white American norms and values, accounted for this advantage. For the majority of relocatees, however, urbanization presented a difficult social and psychological adjustment to an alien environment. In early December 1957, a relocation specialist emphasized such problems in a memo to the area director of the Phoenix area office: "Relocation is not easy. It calls for real stamina and vigor—adaptability and strength of character." He added that the

Papago Indians possessed these characteristics, for since 1952, 566 Papagos had successfully relocated to urban areas. Among the Navajos, Tribal Chairman Paul Jones admitted that the relocating program was helpful in removing the surplus population on the reservation that the land could not support. Frequently, tribes worked to rid their reservations of undesirable members through relocation. Shiftless, unmotivated members burdened families, friends, and reservation resources, and relocation offered them an opportunity to leave.

In summarizing Indian affairs for 1957, the Department of the Interior reported that nearly seven thousand native Americans had received relocation assistance in finding jobs and establishing homes in urban areas. Expenditures for the relocation program in 1957 totaled 3.5 million dollars, more than twice the sum appropriated for the previous year. From the close of World War II to the end of 1957, approximately one hundred thousand Indians had left reservations. Interestingly, three-fourths of this number had relocated without federal assistance. Although reservation revenues and economic development were on the rise, with royalties from oil, gas, and other mineral leases doubling over the previous year to total more than 75 million dollars for 1957, the growing Indian population from the war boom was severely straining tribal efforts to provide for all the people.

Relocation climaxed between 1952 and 1957, when over 17,000 persons received services. About 12,625 people were resettled in cities, many of whom were living there with their families. The average cost per relocatee amounted to $403.00. The Chicago field relocation office reported for February and March 1957 that the average male relocatee earned $1.60 an hour, or about $66.00 for a forty-hour week. To maintain services for Native Americans, a total of twelve relocation offices were in operation across the country.

The rising demand for relocation was temporarily jeopardized during the economic recession of 1956–57, when jobs became scarce and cutbacks in production occurred. Employers usually laid off relocatees first, due to their lack of job experience or seniority. As a result, for fiscal year 1958 the number of relocatees decreased by 1,236, or about 18 percent, from the previous year. To survive their economic ills, many Indians of terminated trust status sold their lands at depressed prices. The drop in applications was brief; interest returned the following year, and on 1 April, the BIA reported a surplus of 3,000 applicants. And so the deluge of Indians moving to the cities continued.

Unfortunately, many potential relocatees did not anticipate the difficulties that they might encounter in the cities. Louis Cioffi, a missionary, wrote to President Eisenhower: "Under this program, as you know, Indians are urged away from their reservations, given jobs, which soon come to an end. As you may not know, many have returned to the reservation, discouraged 'and worse off than before.' Successful relocation achieved by the government has been very small indeed." One Indian in Southern California called relocation an "extermination program," and said that Eisenhower believed "the Indians would be integrated by taking all the youngsters off the reservation, the old would die off, the young would be integrated, and the land would become free for public domain, and all the people could grab it."

Conversely, the government reported optimistically that the majority of Indian relocatees were acclimating to urban conditions successfully, and the number returning to reservations was actually miniscule. The Bureau of Indian Affairs maintained that between 1953 and 1957 only three out of ten relocatees returned to their home communities. The BIA claimed that one-half of those 30 percent who returned home did so within the first three months, and that 71.4 percent remained in their urban environment. Critics charged that the percentage of returnees was 75 percent. Such differences in statistics helped to fuel the controversy over the relocation program. In fact, both sides probably manipulated figures to favor or disfavor the "return rate."

Another problem are arose when vocational training programs encountered a significant dropout rate in various occupational areas. In the nurse's aide program the rate was 21 percent; for sawmill workers 50 percent; for manufacturers of Indian artifacts 54 percent; and for furniture workers about 62 percent. Specialized occupations, such as diamond processing, wig-making, and the production of women's fashion items, had the highest dropout rates, due to the monotony of the work. Most likely, a disinterest in the work and its long-range impracticality accounted for the high dropout rate in wig-making and the production of women's fashion items. Often, the relocatees were persuaded to enroll in a number of widely ranging courses, merely to prove that Indians were being trained in diverse occupations.

Monotony and disinterest were not the only reasons why Indians dropped out of vocational training programs. Frequently, relocatees were placed in seasonal jobs, like agricultural work, and in other jobs that lacked employee security. For these reasons, relocatees became suspicious of government officials who ostensibly would find jobs for them. Unfortunately, low wages accompanied these insecure jobs, forcing Indians to gravitate toward poor housing areas in the cities. In Los Angeles, Indian families were placed in slum dwellings and in rundown motor courts. As more families moved to these areas, Indian ghettos developed. Frustration and discouragement compounded homesickness, prompting many to leave the cities.

Other relocatees chose to return because they missed the "openness" of their reservations. Some left well-paying jobs just to return home. In a few cases, however, if a family member died in an apartment the other members of the family did not want to stay because it was taboo to continue living there. One relocatee had a bad dream and decided to go back to the reservation. Relocation officers thought that these reasons were only excuses to leave. What they failed to understand was that bad omens and taboos were a part of the Indian reality and affected behavior accordingly. Other Indian urbanites found modern institutions too overwhelming; in buying on credit, for example, their inability to make installment payments created indebtedness, possibly even bankruptcy.

Racism was another serious problem confronting relocatees in some areas, although Indian-white relations had improved in general. A 1958 "Report of the Labor Force and the Employment Conditions of the Oneida Indians" revealed that discrimination against the Oneidas in northern Wisconsin had declined. Urban communities surrounding the Oneida Reservation, like Green Bay, Appleton, and Neenah, hired Indians on a regular basis; but employers were now selective in their hiring practices because of the Indians' high rates of absenteeism from previous jobs.

A social services director of the Minneapolis Native American Center depicted the Native American hopes and disillusionment with the relocation experience: "I think everybody who comes to the city has a dream—a dream of making it, a dream about improving their lives. But then prejudice slaps them right in the face and they're worse off. Call it culture shock. When your bubble is burst, there's nothing left but to go back home and start dreaming again."

After failing to adjust to urban life and returning to the reservation, the relocatees at least had some job experience for a potentially better livelihood. Many chose to attempt relocation a second or a third time, selecting a different city for each move. Periodically, such opportunistic Indians took advantage of the relocation program and went to different cities for a couple of months on adventurous vacations. Upon returning, they boasted to friends about their good times in Los Angeles, Chicago, or whatever city they had visited.

Although relocation officers were flexible in accepting applicants, not all were easily approved. Reasons for rejection included records of drunkenness, arrests, marital problems, and poor health. Upon resolving these problems, however, Native Americans could have their applications reconsidered. In some instances, relocation officers were criticized and charged with racism for disqualifying certain applicants. But the prejudice was not always directed against Indians. John Dressler, a wise and elderly Washo, stated: "I think the Indian people also is prejudice against the white people because of the mistreatment that they've had. I don't know who's right, whether the Indian's right or the white man's right." Dressler advised that Native Americans should try to prove themselves to be as "hearty, diligent people as they used to be" in order to eliminate poor opinions of other races. In fact, the Washo elder believed that prejudice was mutually practiced. "But in order to eliminate any kind of prejudice, I think two people have to understand each other to eliminate it," Dressler concluded. Cooperation between the two races was essential, both for improving relations between the two peoples and for the successful placement of Indian Americans in urban areas.

Relocation centers varied in their success in carrying out their difficult tasks. Several factors caused the ineffective administration of the relocation program. Most relocation officers were non-Indians who lacked a sound understanding of Native American cultures, thus preventing them from comprehending traditional behavior patterns. Some had worked previously with the War Relocation Authority, which had displaced Japanese Americans during World War II, and they proved to be insensitive to Indian needs and problems. In addition, some offices lacked staffs sufficient to handle the large number of relocatees. Shortages in adequate housing added to the problems, and efforts to stretch funds forced officials to place Indian families in slums and in downtrodden neighborhoods that were mostly populated by other racial groups. . . .

A remedy for Indian estrangement in the cities was the establishment of Indian centers. For instance, St. Augustine's Indian Center and the American Indian Center, both in Chicago's Uptown neighborhood, continue to provide counseling, temporary shelter, and other assistance to urban Indians. Similar centers in other cities offer the same services as well as opportunities for socialization among traditional Native Americans, who are a communal people. Interestingly, mutual tribal concerns and interaction dissolved many barriers between tribal groups who had never before associated with each other. Increasingly, Indian Americans in urban areas have identified themselves as Indians rather than by tribal designation.

Such socialization saved the relocated Indians. In essence, the communal tradition of Indians on reservations was imitated in urban areas. Powwows, dances, Indian bowling teams, Indian softball teams, and other related activities have intensified the survival of Indians as an identifiable ethnic group in the large cities.

Those people who remained on reservations during the relocation years of the 1950s experienced considerable economic difficulty. Even though their living conditions have improved since 1945, they often paid a high price for staying in their reservation homelands. In particular, relocation perhaps resulted in less efficient leadership among reservation tribes during the 1950s. Unfortunately, those tribal members possessing the best qualifications, and who could probably have provided a more effective leadership, were apt to relocate, and after relocating, they rarely returned to the reservation to help their tribes.

Ironically, at the same time, the majority of Indians who moved to urban areas suffered socially, economically, and psychologically. In many cases, urban Indians have traded rural poverty on reservations for urban slums. Their survival in urban areas, however, yielded hope and a brighter future for their offspring. Indian youths growing up in an urban environment often become teachers, lawyers, doctors, and other professionals. It is an unfortunate fact that success in the white world is costing them the heritage of their native culture. Today, Indians continue to experience difficulties in substituting traditional values for those of a modern world—materialism and competition.

One Indian living in California summarized the Native American reaction to relocation best:

> At the very outset, we thought it would be a good thing. It would give Indians an opportunity to spread their wings and gain education and employment and generally become equal to all other men. But after about a year or two years, at the outside, we discovered that there was an ulterior motive behind the earlier relocation program. It was designed, in fact, to get all Indians off all reservations within X number of years. I think at that time, it said twenty years; since then it has been erased, however. So, then we started digging in our heels to prevent total assimilation; assimilation to the degree that we would lose our identity as Indian people, lose our culture and our [way] of living.

◈ *F U R T H E R   R E A D I N G*

Joan Ablon, "American Indian Relocation: Problems of Dependency and Management in the City," *Phylon* 26 (1965), 362–371.
John Adair and Evon Vogt, "Navajo and Zuni Veterans," *American Anthropologist* 51 (1949), 547–568
Karen Blu, *The Lumbee Problem: The Making of an American Indian People* (1980)
William Brophy and Sophie Aberle, eds., *The Indian: America's Unfinished Business* (1966)
Larry Burt, *Tribalism in Crisis: Federal Indian Policy, 1953–1961* (1982)
Ella Deloria, *Speaking of Indians* (1944)

Richard Drinnon, *Keeper of Concentration Camps: Dillon S. Meyer and American Racism* (1987)

Jack D. Forbes, *Native Americans and Nixon: Presidential Politics and Minority Self-Determination, 1969–1972* (1981)

Jere Franco, "Bringing Them in Alive: Selective Service and Native Americans," *Journal of Ethnic Studies* 18 (1990), 1–27

Carole Goldberg, "Public Law 280: The Limits of State Jurisdiction over Reservation Indians," *UCLA Law Review* 4 (Winter 1976), 535–594

Laurence M. Hauptman, *The Iroquois Struggle for Survival: World War II to Red Power* (1986)

Tom Holm, "Fighting a White Man's War": The Extent and Legacy of American Indian Participation in World War II," *Journal of Ethnic Studies* 9 (1981), 69–81

Susan Hood, "Termination of the Klamath Tribe in Oregon," *Ethnohistory* 19 (1972)

Wesley R. Hurt, Jr., "The Urbanization of Yankton Indians," *Human Organization* 20 (1961–62), 227–245

Peter Iverson, "Building Toward Self-Determination: Plains and Southwestern Indians in the 1940s and 1950s," *Western Historical Quarterly* 16 (1985), 163–173.

Broderick Johnson, ed., *Navajos and World War II* (1977)

William F. Kelly, ed., *Indian Affairs and the Indian Reorganization Act: The Twenty Year Record* (1954)

Kirke Kickingbird and Karen Ducheneaux, *One Hundred Million Acres* (1973)

Oliver La Farge, "Termination of Federal Supervision: Disintegration and the American Indian," *Annals of the American Academy of Political and Social Science* 311 (May 1957), 56–70

Michael L. Lawson, *Dammed Indians: The Pick-Sloan Plan and the Missouri River Sioux, 1944–1980* (1982)

Nancy O. Lurie, "Menominee Termination from Reservation to Colony," *Human Organization* 22 (1972), 257–270.

Paul T. Murray, "Virginia Indians in the World War II Draft," *The Virginia Magazine of History and Biography* 95 (1987), 215–231

Elaine Neils, *Reservation to City: Indian Migration and Federal Relocation* (1971)

Gary Orfield, *A Study of the Termination Policy* (1965)

Nicholas C. Peroff, *Menominee Drums: Tribal Termination and Restoration, 1954–1974* (1982)

Kenneth R. Philp, "Stride Toward Freedom: The Relocation of Indians to Cities, 1952–1960," *Western Historical Quarterly* 16 (1985), 175–190.

Nancy Shoemaker, "Urban Indians and Ethnic Choices: American Indian Organizations in Minneapolis, 1920–1950," *Western Historical Quarterly* 19 (1988), 431–447

Theodore Stern, *The Klamath Tribe: A People and Their Reservation* (1965)

Margaret C. Szasz, *Education and the American Indian: The Road Toward Self-Determination Since 1928* (1977)

Jack O. Waddell and O. Michael Watson, eds. *The American Indian in Urban Society* (1971)

Charles F. Wilkinson and Eric R. Briggs, "The Evolution of the Termination Policy," *American Indian Law Review* 5 (1977), 139–184

Edmund Wilson, *Apologies to the Iroquois* (1960)

CHAPTER
14

Indian Self-Determination
and Sovereignty
in Contemporary America

From the 1960s to the present, the American Indian population has become increasingly urban and more visible to the larger American society. Protest movements, including the occupation of Alcatraz Island in 1969 and of the village of Wounded Knee, South Dakota, in 1973, have given prominence to younger activists. At the same time, reservation communities have sought new ways to revitalize their economies, to maintain their languages, and to safeguard their rights. Although more persons now live off the reservations than on them, there can be no question about the continuing social and cultural significance of these enclaves.

Individually and collectively, today's Indians confront complex and central questions about schooling for their children, health care, employment, housing, and their relationship to other Americans. Mineral and water resources, tourism, legalized gambling, and other concerns create opportunities as well as dilemmas. In some ways, Indian communities have faced challenges comparable to those in other rural American communities; yet in other respects, because of their unique historical and legal standing and experience, they are indeed separate.

Although debate goes on about Indians' place and status in America, there can be no doubt, as the twentieth century draws to a close, that the image of the vanishing Indian has proved a myth. Native art, music, and literature have flourished. An unprecedented number of contemporary Indians have entered medicine, law, engineering, and other professions. Powwows and other forums have evolved to provide people from different tribes the chance to be with and learn from one another. Five hundred years after Columbus, American Indians remain as distinct entities within North American life.

◈ D O C U M E N T S

The Chicago Conference of 1961 signaled a new era. Hundreds of Indians from many different tribes gathered in the city to address common concerns. "A Declaration of Indian Purpose," excerpted in the opening selection, spoke to these issues. For young people the conference proved memorable for its encouragement of commonality. By the decade's end, Indian activism had entered a new phase. The "Proclamation from Indians of All Tribes" on Alcatraz Island in 1969 underscored native peoples' dissatisfaction with federal trusteeship. Occupation of the famous island brought international attention to the Indians' grievances, even if the island could not be held in the long run. In Wisconsin, the Menominees launched a drive in 1961 to restore their lands to reservation status. After a twelve-year battle their success in 1973 in overturning the termination of their reservation marked an important victory for American Indians everywhere. Ada Deer, appointed in 1993 to head the Bureau of Indian Affairs, led the fight for restoration. In the third document, she explains how her triumph was achieved.

In the Northwest, a 1974 decision by Judge George Boldt about Indian fishing rights plunged the region into controversy. In the fourth document, Andy Fernando, former chairman of the Upper Skagit Tribal Community, reveals a native perspective on the nature and extent of Indian tradition and rights. The Indian Child Welfare Act of 1978 (document five) also has sparked disagreement. For Cherokee professor of social work Ron Lewis and others who labored to make the law a reality, the act reflected deep concern over the integrity of native families. Under its terms, Indian communities would be empowered in regard to adoption and other family-related matters. In individual cases, publicized nationally through *Sixty Minutes* and other television programs, the matter of the adoption of Indian children by non-Indian families has stirred debate over the rights of the children, of the would-be adoptive families, and of the children's Indian families and communities.

Place is central to Indian life, and the next two documents attest to that centrality. Tim Giago, publisher of *Indian Country Today,* is a widely read and respected journalist. In the sixth selection, he addresses the importance of the reservation to the Indian, present and future. His remarks emphasize that despite ongoing problems, reservations remain home and the base for many Indians' lives. Leading Indian journalist Mark Trahant (Shoshone-Bannock), an editor for the *Salt Lake City Tribune* and former publisher of newspapers on the Fort Hall and Navajo reservations, provides an overview of the contemporary Alaskan scene in the next document. His article emphasizes that the native Alaskan past is integral to histories of Indian communities in the "lower forty-eight."

In the eighth document, anthropologist Deward E. Walker, Jr., briefly comments on one of the most emotional and significant issues of the present—the return and reburial of Indian skeletal remains. Thanks to the work of many Indian and non-Indian individuals, progress is being made in the return of these remains, and of sacred objects, to tribal communities. And in the final documentary selection, Suzan Harjo (Cheyenne) offers forceful testimony before the U.S. Civil Rights Commission on the enforcement of the Indian Civil Rights Act. She leaves little doubt about her position on several concerns, including the use of the name "Redskins" by a professional football team.

A Declaration of Indian Purpose
from the Chicago Conference, 1961

. . . It is a universal desire among all Indians that their treaties and trust-protected lands remain intact and beyond the reach of predatory men.

This is not special pleading, though Indians have been told often enough by members of Congress and the courts that the United States has the plenary power to wipe out our treaties at will. Governments, when powerful enough, can act in this arbitrary and immoral manner.

Still we insist that we are not pleading for special treatment at the hands of the American people. When we ask that our treaties be respected, we are mindful of the opinion of Chief Justice John Marshall on the nature of the treaty obligations between the United States and the Indian tribes.

Marshall said that a treaty ". . . is a compact between two nations or communities, having the right of self-government. Is it essential that each party shall possess the same attributes of sovereignty to give force to the treaty? This will not be pretended, for on this ground, very few valid treaties could be formed. The only requisite is, that each of the contracting parties shall possess the right of self-government, and the power to perform the stipulations of the treaty."

And he said, "We have made treaties with [the Indians]; and are those treaties to be disregarded on our part, because they were entered into with an uncivilized people? Does this lessen the obligation of such treaties? By entering into them have we not admitted the power of this people to bind themselves, and to impose obligations on us?"

The right of self-government, a right which the Indians possessed before the coming of the white man, has never been extinguished; indeed, it has been repeatedly sustained by the courts of the United States. Our leaders made binding agreements—ceding lands as requested by the United States; keeping the peace; harboring no enemies of the nation. And the people stood with the leaders in accepting these obligations.

A treaty, in the minds of our people, is an eternal word. Events often make it seem expedient to depart from the pledged word, but we are conscious that the first departure creates a logic for the second departure, until there is nothing left of the word.

We recognize that our view of these matters differs at times from the prevailing legal view regarding due process.

When our lands are taken for a declared public purpose, scattering our people and threatening our continued existence, it grieves us to be told that a money payment is the equivalent of all the things we surrender. Our forefathers could be generous when all the continent was theirs. They could cast away whole empires for a handle of trinkets for their children. But in our day, each remaining acre is a promise that we will still be here tomorrow. Were we paid a thousand times the market value of our lost holdings, still the payment would not suffice. Money never mothered the Indian people, as the land has mothered them, nor have any people become more closely attached to the land, religiously and traditionally. . . .

To complete our Declaration, we point out that in the beginning the people of the New World, called Indians by accident of geography, were possessed of a continent and a way of life. In the course of many lifetimes, our people had adjusted to every climate and condition from the Arctic to the torrid zones. In their livelihood and family relationships, their ceremonial observances, they reflected the diversity of the physical world they occupied.

The conditions in which Indians live today reflect a world in which every basic aspect of life has been transformed. Even the physical world is no longer the controlling factor in determining where and under what conditions men may live. In region after region, Indian groups found their means of existence either totally destroyed or materially modified. Newly introduced diseases swept away or reduced regional populations. These changes were followed by major shifts in the internal life of the tribe and family.

The time came when the Indian people were no longer the masters of their situation. Their life ways survived subject to the will of a dominant sovereign power. This is said, not in a spirit of complaint; we understand that in the lives of all nations of people, there are times of plenty and times of famine. But we do speak out in a plea for understanding.

When we go before the American people, as we do in this Declaration, and ask for material assistance in developing our resources and developing our opportunities, we pose a moral problem which cannot be left unanswered. For the problem we raise affects the standing which our nation sustains before world opinion.

Our situation cannot be relieved by appropriated funds alone, though it is equally obvious that without capital investment and funded services, solutions will be delayed. Nor will the passage of time lessen the complexities which beset a people moving toward new meaning and purpose.

The answers we seek are not commodities to be purchased, neither are they evolved automatically through the passing of time.

The effort to place social adjustment on a money-time interval scale which has characterized Indian administration, has resulted in unwanted pressure and frustration.

When Indians speak of the continent they yielded, they are not referring only to the loss of some millions of acres in real estate. They have in mind that the land supported a universe of things they knew, valued, and loved.

With that continent gone, except for the few poor parcels they still retain, the basis of life is precariously held, but they mean to hold the scraps and parcels as earnestly as any small nation or ethnic group was ever determined to hold to identity and survival.

What we ask of America is not charity, not paternalism, even when benevolent. We ask only that the nature of our situation be recognized and made the basis of policy and action.

In short, the Indians ask for assistance, technical and financial, for the time needed, however long that may be, to regain in the America of the space age some measure of the adjustment they enjoyed as the original possessors of their native land.

A Proclamation from the Indians of All Tribes, Alcatraz Island, 1969

To the Great White Father and All His People—

We, the native Americans, re-claim the land known as Alcatraz Island in the name of all American Indians by right of discovery.

We wish to be fair and honorable in our dealings with the Caucasian inhabitants of this land, and hereby offer the following treaty:

We will purchase said Alcatraz Island for twenty-four dollars (24) in glass beads and red cloth, a precedent set by the white man's purchase of a similar island about 300 years ago. We know that $24 in trade goods for these 16 acres is more than was paid when Manhattan Island was sold, but we know that land values have risen over the years. Our offer of $1.24 per acre is greater than the 47 cents per acre the white men are now paying the California Indians for their land.

We will give to the inhabitants of this island a portion of the land for their own to be held in trust by the American Indian Affairs and by the bureau of Caucasian Affairs to hold in perpetuity—for as long as the sun shall rise and the rivers go down to the sea. We will further guide the inhabitants in the proper way of living. We will offer them our religion, our education, our life-ways, in order to help them achieve our level of civilization and thus raise them and all their white brothers up from their savage and unhappy state. We offer this treaty in good faith and wish to be fair and honorable in our dealings with all white men.

We feel that this so-called Alcatraz Island is more than suitable for an Indian reservation, as determined by the white man's own standards. By this we mean that this place resembles most Indian reservations in that:

1. It is isolated from modern facilities, and without adequate means of transportation.
2. It has no fresh running water.
3. It has inadequate sanitation facilities.
4. There are no oil or mineral rights.
5. There is no industry and so unemployment is very great.
6. There are no health care facilities.
7. The soil is rocky and non-productive, and the land does not support game.
8. There are no educational facilities.
9. The population has always exceeded the land base.
10. The population has always been held as prisoners and kept dependent upon others.

Further, it would be fitting and symbolic that ships from all over the world, entering the Golden Gate, would first see Indian land, and thus be reminded of the true history of this nation. This tiny island would be a symbol of the great lands once ruled by free and noble Indians.

What use will we make of this land?

Since the San Francisco Indian Center burned down, there is no place for Indians to assemble and carry on tribal life here in the white man's city. Therefore, we plan to develop on this island several Indian institutions:

1. A Center for Native American Studies which will educate them to the skills and knowledge relevant to improve the lives and spirits of all Indian peoples.
2. An American Indian Spiritual Center which will practice our ancient tribal religious and sacred healing ceremonies. . . .

3. An Indian Center of Ecology which will train and support our young people in scientific research and practice to restore our lands and waters to their pure and natural state. . . .
4. A Great Indian Training School will be developed to teach our people how to make a living in the world, improve our standard of living, and to end hunger and unemployment among all our people. . . .

Some of the present buildings will be taken over to develop an American Indian Museum which will depict our native food & other cultural contributions we have given to the world. Another part of the museum will present some of the things the white man has given to the Indians in return for the land and life he took: disease, alcohol, poverty and cultural decimation (As symbolized by old tin cans, barbed wire, rubber tires, plastic containers, etc.). . . .

In the name of all Indians, therefore, we re-claim this island for our Indian nations. . . .

Signed,
Indians of All Tribes
November 1969
San Francisco, California

Ada Deer (Menominee) Explains
How Her People Overturned Termination, 1974

. . . Termination occurred in 1954, it became finalized in 1961. Our people have had a strong sense of identity as a group, also a strong adherence to the land. We live in one of the most beautiful areas in this entire country, even if I have to admit it myself. But, we have beautiful lakes, streams and forests. Senator Nelson, who is a great environmentalist, became so concerned about the development [building and selling cabins and land to outsiders] that was starting to take place that he introduced and pushed through Congress the Wild Rivers Act, and made the Wolfe River which runs through our area part of this, so the development would stop. In 1961, our tribe, which at that time was composed of 3,270 members, had 10 million dollars in the treasury. We were one of the wealthiest tribes in the country and paid for almost all of our services that were provided by the Bureau of Indian Affairs. We had a lumber mill and our land was intact. This changed. First of all, our land and assets were taken out of trust. Our areas are approximately 234,000 acres. This became a separate county in the state of Wisconsin. We are now the poorest county in the state and the poorest in the nation. Again, to make the story short, it's been an economic, political, a cultural disaster, and instead of taking away federal supervision and giving tribal supervision, as you would think by looking at that resolution, and at the termination law, this did not occur. The trust was taken away; all the protection and services of the Bureau of Indian Affairs were taken away, and a very oppressive and private trust was thrust upon us. First of all, we became a county. Our people had no experience in county government, did not understand how a county functioned, what the responsibilities, the obligations of county government were. Many people had no experience in business enterprise. A separate tribal corporation called MEI, Menominee Enterprises Incorporated, was established. However, this was not controlled by the Menominees because we had another group called the Menominee Common Stock and Voting Trust which was established. This consisted of seven members, four white and three Indians. Now, in most corporations, the individual owners elect the board of directors but this did not occur here. The board of directors was elected by the Menominee Common Stock and Voting Trust. Now, to add insult to injury, there were many people declared incompetent. For example, we had a man who was blind who was declared incompetent without due process of law. Some people ran around and made a big list, shipped it to the Bureau of Indian Affairs and it was authorized, so we have many people who are incompetent, we also have the minors, the children under 18. These votes were controlled by the First Wisconsin Trust Company of Milwaukee. So from1961 to 1970, we were controlled by white banking and financial institutions. The only participation that the Menominees were able to have in the tribal affairs was to elect one trustee per year at the annual meeting. It was very frustrating. The hospital was closed, many of the youngsters were consolidated into attending one school, the dropout rate has been phenomenal, we've had many serious problems as a result of termination. It has accentuated the values of competitiveness, selfishness, greed, and it's had a disastrous effect not only on our people as a group, but on many individuals. Many people have gone off to Milwaukee, Chicago and other areas across the country.

However, that thing that galvanized us into action was the fact that our board of directors got into a partnership with land developers. Land developers are not only a problem to the Indians but to every single person in this country, because we don't have enough land that's beautiful that we can preserve for everyone. I think that every one of us ought to be concerned about this. . . . To increase the tax base, we had some fast-talking developers coming up there. We have an area of over 80 natural lakes; they created an artificial lake. They channeled some of these; it's an ecological disaster. The lakes are continually changing. They're pumping water from one to another. The shoreline trees have been destroyed in many areas. We've got motor boats, snowmobiles, pollution, terrible situations. Two thousand lots were slotted for sale and we started demonstrating. We demonstrated, we marched, we started to use the press, we formed a grass roots group called DRUMS, "Determination of Rights and Unity for Menominee Shareholders." This is a real grass roots group, because there were several of us that got together in 1970 and decided that no matter what we felt, it was important to fight for our land and people. . . .

Restoration has three points: (1) putting our land assets into trust, (2) making us eligible for federal services, such as education and health services, and (3) giving us federal recognition as a tribe. Our bill was introduced last year, but we didn't get through the entire legislative process because of the presidential campaign. It was re-introduced again this year in May. . . .

I especially tell this to Indian people because it's a typical response of bureaucrats and other people that work with you. They say, "You can't do it, it's going to take a lot of work and there's no way you can change the system." This is not really true. We have chosen another path and this is to beat the system. Now it's taken four years, and in a way, I feel like I've been preparing for this all my life, because my background is a social worker, community action person, and in social action every now and then you have to put your money where your mouth is, and I feel that we as Indians have to practice our Indian values, which is concern for your tribe, and be involved when it's of vital importance. Now, this has meant that several of us have had to change our lives around. I was in law school; the people that I was starting with are going to be graduating this year and will be joining the legal profession. My car is falling apart, some of the others' cars are falling apart, but along with this we are about to achieve the most significant victory in all of American Indian history. On Tuesday of this week, the House passed our act, the Menominee Restoration Act, with a vote of 404 to 3; everybody wants to know who the three were that voted against it and how did I let them get away. . . .

We started, first of all, tracking every single Menominee that we could. We called people, we made home visits. First we got two people elected into the Voting Trust. The second year we got four people. Even with four of eleven, they elected me the chairperson of the group. They decided then to proceed with this lobbying effort. Now, the platform we ran on was the stopping of land sales, restoration and Menominee Restoration. Last year, we took over and have been working very hard since that time. We have gone around to all Indian groups, major Indian groups in the country, conducted extensive speaking campaigns—we're learning how to use the media too—and it's been very exciting to be a part of this. It's also very exhausting, but on the other hand, it's worth fighting for. It was such a great pleasure to meet and sit in the House gallery last Tuesday to see the whole United States Congress voting on something that one small Indian tribe brought to their attention. I think it's very significant not only for the Menominee tribe, for all Indian tribes, but for American people as a whole, because I was mentioning to Senator Mondale last evening, we were talking about our legislation that we were about to win, and he said, "Yes, it looks like the good guys are going to win," and we are. Now we've done this in a very interesting way and approach. We decided to approach this on a bi-partisan basis, because we feel that everyone's to blame for Indian problems. We went to the Republican Party platform hearing last year in Miami and we got a statement from the Republican platform stating their recognition of Menominee problems and promising a complete and sympathetic hearing of our plea. We received a good reception at the Democratic Party convention, and in the Democratic platform there was a statement opposing the policy of termination. Then we conducted a drive to get as many people of both parties as we could on our legislation, and it was very interesting to see. We've got about 50 people as sponsors from the House and we have everyone from Bella Abzug to Collins, from Illinois. We did the same thing in the Senate, we have people like Senator Goldwater and Senator Kennedy, and all the Republican members of the Senate Interior and Insular Affairs Committee as sponsors of our legislation. Again, this is an incredible accomplishment which can only be attributed to making the system work. I assume that people are on our side until they prove themselves. I think it's very important to understand that people will take different positions depending on the issue and then of course, you kind of blitz them and you use a little humor in your lobby. I learned a lot. I didn't start out being a lobbyist, but if you care enough—I've told everybody that I would do anything to promote the legislation. So one day it was, I decided, be-kind-to-BIA day. I went out and bought two pounds of candy and I started out with the head-quarters—this was before it was taken over—I said to the guard, "I'm starting out with headquarters here and I'm going to sweeten you up a little," and I gave him some candy. Of course, he'd been letting me park there in the BIA parking lot, and usually you have to get all kinds of permits and permissions, etc. I smiled at him and he smiles at me, and every now and then it does, even though we live in a chauvinist society which we're changing, every now and then it does help to use some of your feminine wiles. Anyway, he was very nice and he allowed me to park there, so then I went to see all the secretaries. By the time I got to the top floor, I only had two or three pieces of candy left. So you have to use kind of a light touch in all of this lobbying, and we do have some bumper stickers which we have been selling and distributing around the country. We have to have visibility, and I feel that there is not enough of us Indians, so we have to make our presence count. We feel that it is important to keep our issue before the public, and I've met many interesting people on airplanes and in airports as a result of this. Now, I've given you kind of the highlights, the problems that has engendered this, what we've done about it and in essence, I would say that any citizen in this country can take action on an issue if you're ready to get involved and ready to move on it. . . .

Andy Fernando (Upper Skagit) on the Importance of Fishing Rights in the Northwest, 1984

In the clear light of morning, a young Indian girl casts a small flat stone from the riverbank. It skips across the smooth water slowly circling in a broad eddy. As the stone dances on the water's surface, the ripples it creates break the mirrored reflection of the girl's mother and father pulling a net across the bow of their fourteen-foot river skiff. Wisps of fog rise from the river surface. Gently pushed by a light late-spring breeze blowing from the far shore, the fog spins and swirls into the tall evergreen trees. The river, called Skagit, is wide here—200 yards across: the sparrows darting and gliding along the opposite bank seem no larger than insects to the small girl. The new day sun, just rising above the mountain tops, has already warmed the air, yet the river is cold. The stream has been chilled by melting ancient glaciers and the previous winter's snow. Only a few miles downstream the Skagit will empty into Puget Sound, the river's clean, fresh waters joining the brine that leads to the Pacific Ocean.

The flat stone skips a final time and sinks to the river bottom, joining a thousand other stones thrown by a thousand other children for a thousand years. As the ripples disappear, the girl resumes watching her parents at work, the work she has watched for as long as she can remember. The task is well rehearsed, practiced by each generation, and, according to tradition, taught to the children by example on the river. . . .

The young girl's parents are pulling the net, their backs straining against its weight. Pulling the net across the bow, they remove branches and leaves as they go, returning the previous length of net to the water as they draw the next length into the boat. The sun breaks over the jagged mountain peaks to the east to bathe the scene in a rich golden glow. The dainty fog wisps dance around the boat and disappear, and steam rises from the dew-speckled wool coats worn by the girl's parents. Their backs warmed by the sun and their own effort, the adults pull the heavily leaded line and webbing. The splashing persists near the far end of the net. They resist the temptation to work too quickly, for the entire length of the net must be checked for branches and the possibility of another fish caught during the night.

At last, the girl's parents reach the focus of the commotion. the struggle of the thrashing prey is intense: it takes both adults' weight and strength to pull the catch into the boat. In its fight against the net, the fish has torn a hole three feet wide; sun-drenched beads of water dangle from the ragged strands of webbing. Normally the parents would take time to repair the tear before returning to shore, but they, too, are excited about their first catch of the season. Carefully, they grasp the fish by the tail and remove it from the net by the same direction it entered, the mother stretching back the webbing over the fish's gills.

As the girl's parents row their boat back to shore, aunts and uncles return by boat from net sites up and down stream. Their nets were empty. The boats land simultaneously, and the girl scampers down the beach to meet them, followed closely by her grandparents. Her parents' catch is held high; everyone beams smiles of approval. It is a king salmon, four feet long and 57 pounds—almost as tall as the girl, and heavier than her slight eight-year-old body. Bright scales flash in the sunlight as the salmon is laid back down in the boat and continues to thrash, refusing to end its struggle, its broad tail slapping the floor of the skiff with a loud thumping sound. The king salmon is a large male, and has begun its physical transformation in the journey from saltwater to freshwater, where it would have spawned and died. Its snout is assuming a hook-shape, where before it was round, and its back has begun to arch slightly. Its silver-colored scales, which would have disappeared by the time the salmon spawned, have just begun to darken and recede. Still, this is a prime salmon, worth $1.50 or more a pound to the girl's parents from the commercial salmon buyers who will arrive at their camp later in the day.

But this salmon will not be sold.

According to a centuries-old, Northwest coastal Indian tradition, carried on by the girl's family, this first salmon will neither be sold nor traded nor even preserved for eating later in the year. The many generations born before the girl's grandparents and great-grandparents had each celebrated the same first catch in the late spring of the year. During the long winter months, Indian families mostly remained indoors in their great cedar loghouses along the banks of the river, subsisting on stores of dried salmon, berries, roots, and game. Fresh food, particularly their staple diet of salmon, was scarce during these months. By the spring months of "pedhweywats"—the time of robins whistling—the stocks of food were depleted or spoiled, well-fed game was scarce, and edible plants and berries were not yet ready to harvest. But in those spring months, king salmon would return to the river, completing their four-year cycle from river-hatched eggs to ocean-dwelling juveniles to mature adults ready to spawn their progeny. The spring salmon were few in number, but they returned earlier than other salmon to seek the colder snow-fed streams, and their larger size and firmer flesh made them a fine prize. The entire village would gather together and appoint fishermen to each catch one salmon—no more.

In fine regalia, accompanied by a fanfare of deerskin drum and special village songs, the first salmon caught would be carried from the riverbank to the gathered villagers. A village leader, or shaman, would carefully clean and save the salmon's entrails, then carve away the meat until a carcass of head, bones, and tail was left, still connected. The entrails would be placed in the skeleton, and the framework of bones from the flashing bright salmon laid on a mat of fresh, spring-green ferns. Meanwhile, the villagers would have raised a fire of alderwood, the smoke thick from the new sap filling the wood. The wood's low blaze would cook the salmon slowly, and leave a mild smoke taste in the meat. The pieces of salmon meat would then be skewered on thin sticks carved from small ironwood trees growing along the riverbank; the end of each stick had been sharpened so it could be staked into the ground near the fire. Nearly an hour would pass before the salmon was fully cooked, but the villagers would gladly wait, perhaps speculating to each other about the upcoming season; or talking of where and how they would set their nets, or build their fish traps, or spear their salmon; or reminiscing over the generations before who had gathered in the same campsite to perform the first salmon ceremony.

When the salmon was cooked, everyone would gather to eat. It mattered not whether there were ten villagers or a hundred: each would share equally in the fruit of the first catch. The meal finished, leaders would recount the village stories of great fishermen and hunters of fact, legend, and myth—or all three combined. The headmen and women would speak of the importance of the first salmon ceremony, of sharing the first catch, harvest, or kill, of the high status bestowed to those villagers who were given the gift and the power to provide food for the village.

In the end, the headmen would lift the fern mat cradling the remains of the salmon, and, followed by villagers, walk to the riverbank. The drums would sound and songs ring around the valley, echoes from the steep slopes above singing praise back to the gathering. Placing the fern mat on the water with the salmon's head pointed downstream, the headman would release the mat to float on the river toward the sea, signifying the completion of the salmon cycle. The villagers and the salmon had fulfilled their duty, prescribed by the great spirit. The salmon had returned to the appointed time and place; the villagers had faithfully honored the salmon in sharing and ceremony. The people thereby assured themselves of a good season, and the harvest could begin. . . .

Only a few changes in technology separate this scene in 1983 from 1883. In different settings, through the eyes of different children, the scene is repeated today along the river valleys throughout western Washington and Oregon. But the truth is, without the benefit of the court decision, . . . there might not have been a traditional first salmon ceremony for the young Indian girl to witness. Instead of fishing for salmon by the light of day, the girl's parents would only be setting their gill net at night, fearing arrest by state fisheries police for violating state laws that long prohibited gillnetting, spearing, and other traditional Indian salmon-harvesting techniques in the rivers and bays off-reservation.

Northwest Indian families have for centuries gathered along the riverbanks and saltwater bays to stake their gill nets, to erect wooden fish traps, or to poise long spears in search of salmon. They cherished this part of their lives so that, even as they signed away their traditional lands in treaties with the United States government in1854–55, the Indian people retained the right to fish at their traditional grounds and waters, regardless of where those places were, on-reservation or off. Since they were written, these treaties have been treated as worthless paper by the Washington and Oregon state governments. As the states prevented the Indians from fishing at their traditional places, a strong and important part of Indian culture began to disappear. If not for the court decision, quite possibly the scene of a young girl at the riverbank would soon vanish, and so also vanish one of the few remnants of traditional Northwest Indian society.

But this has not happened. On February 12, 1974, George H. Boldt, senior federal judge for western Washington, emphatically and comprehensively affirmed the right of most Washington Indian tribes to fish for salmon in accordance with federal treaties they had signed 119 years before. The ruling in *U.S.* v. *Washington,* known throughout the Pacific Northwest as the "Boldt decision," was by no means the first court case to deal with the issue of treaty salmon-fishing rights. It was, in fact, the culmination of eighty-seven years of nearly continuous court battles seeking to either restore or prevent traditional Indian fishing for salmon.

The Boldt decision was a milestone, indeed. To the grandparents of the young Indian girl, the decision reaffirms the sanctity of the contract between people and their governments that the treaties signified. The ruling to restore recognition for Indian treaty-fishing rights has been long in coming, and many grandfathers and grandmothers have waited many years for its arrival. To our elders, the court decision is a tribute to the resiliency and tenacity of their ancestors. It is a vindication of the federal government's promise that "the right to fish in usual and accustomed places"—a term central to the treaties—stands for more than fading words on crumbling paper.

Many Indian grandfathers and grandmothers, such as my own, have reminded us that the treaties of 1854–55, made a pledge. Indian elders placed great stock in promises, and remembered well when promises were broken. I recall listening to my grandfather, who often reminded me, as a twelve-year-old spearfisherman, of a right guaranteed by a piece of paper. My grandfather's words were echoed by another elder, Si James, a great orator of the Tulalip Reservation, who said: "My grandfather once told me, for as long as the sun comes up in the east and sets in the west, the word shall be good. For as long as the water comes down from the mountains and goes out to the sound, the word shall be good. For as long as the tide comes to the shore and goes back out again, the word shall be good."

Then Si observed: "The sun still comes up and goes down. The water still comes out of the mountains and goes into the sound. The tide comes to the shore and goes back out again. . . ."

The old man's voice grew silent. He did not finish the story. The word had not been good, and on his face the disappointment was chiseled as sharply as the furrows in his brow.

Our grandfathers and grandmothers remembered how state laws had made fishing by gill net, trap and spear illegal in many rivers and bays, illegal in those ancestral places the treaties called "usual and accustomed." In defiance, our grandparents set their nets by moonlight and withstood harassment and arrest by state police, only to return to fish the rivers again. More than one hundred years ago, our ancestors of many tribes gave up control of tens of thousands of acres in what is now Washington, Oregon, and Idaho in exchange for keeping a few limited rights, including the right to fish in traditional places. To the elders, a promise made was a promise kept, and those who have lived to see the Boldt decision believe now that both parties to the treaty can keep their part of the bargain.

To the parents of the young girl, the court decree would mean return to a traditional vocation and to new opportunities that vocation supports. The parents would carry out a livelihood and lifestyle, through traditional forms of fishing, that retains the best parts of their Indian culture, and permits them to attain that level of respect in the Indian community bestowed upon good fishermen and women.

Decades of decay in many Indian communities have given succeeding generations fewer reasons to follow the traditions and to remain active in tribal society. The Boldt decision has acted as a catalyst to change that. In years past, most talented Indian people left the reservations. Driven away by lack of jobs or a future, they fled to opportunities in the cities. Their exodus sapped strength from the reservations. The fishing right assured by the Boldt decision has reversed the trend. The elation and positive feeling of pulling a fifty-pound salmon into the boat is being translated into social change and activity in more than two dozen Indian communities. Following the 1974 decision, many young Indian people returned to their tribes at first only to fish. But now they stay on because they see renewed activity in their tribal communities. Those people bringing skills have found welcoming tribal councils and communities eager to tap their knowledge and experience. Those willing to learn have found new opportunities, training, and employment in tribally operated housing, health, and service programs, in the many tribally owned businesses that have emerged in recent years, and in the tribal salmon management programs created under the Boldt decision. No one is suggesting that the Boldt decision has solved all the problems in Indian country, but the opportunities created directly or indirectly from the legally secured right to fish are the difference between staying and leaving for many young Indian families. Today, when young Indians leave the reservation for college or to learn a skill, most intend to return and use their knowledge close to home. And many of those young people will return, to stay and build a future.

Even more important than the legal milestone or vocational opportunity the Boldt decision represents for the grandparents and parents in our scene, the judgment holds its greatest promise and value for the young girl, and her children's children. For young Indian boys and girls, the Boldt decision shapes a new image of self. Many of their parents, as children, had watched the adults having to fish by cover of darkness, concealing their nets and boats, furtive glances alert to the arrival of state police. Those children grew to know fishing as a surreptitious, almost embarrassing activity from a diminishing culture, better forgotten in the pursuit of more conventional occupations in the larger non-Indian society.

Today's Indian children form a different impression from the hours and days of long, hard work to earn a rightful, though modest, income from salmon fishing. They learn that salmon fishing is truly a family activity, with every member taking part. Mothers, fathers, grandparents, aunts, uncles, and cousins gather together in family fishing camps on dozens of rivers and bays to share the work and the enjoyment of fishing. Whether the family is earning its income from fishing or simply stocking a home smokehouse or freezer, the children can see firsthand the benefit of its labor. The child learns that the fisherman or woman is a respected member of the tribal community—a person who carries on an honorable tradition. In small measures and unspoken lessons, the Indian child shapes an identity that many elders were never able to savor. The child is learning that, as Indians, the people form a strong community. As a fisherman or woman, the child will one day find self-respect and be respected. As a future parent, this child will have a heritage to give his or her children.

Having this sense of community, respect, and heritage will be very important to our children as they become adults and assume the reins of leadership in their respective Indian communities. For Indian people, this is the key to the Boldt decision, this is its true value. When Judge Boldt died on March 18, 1984, he left his legacy in the strength of the Northwest Indian communities which are drawing new energy and life from the return of the salmon. . . .

We, as Indian leaders, have a responsibility to preserve our right, now that it has been secured, just as our elders fought to preserve it. We must preserve that right, for more than the value it carries today, for more even than the value of saving the past. Our obligation is to preserve the right to fish for our future, for the many Indian children who will wake to the far-off sound of the first splash of the first salmon of the season.

The Indian Child Welfare Act, 1978

To establish standards for the placement of Indian children in foster or adoptive homes, to prevent the breakup of Indian families, and for other purposes.

Be it enacted by the Senate and House of Representatives of the United States of America in Congress assembled, That this Act may be cited as the "Indian Child Welfare Act of 1978."

Sec. 2   Recognizing the special relationship between the United States and the Indian tribes and their members and the Federal responsibility to Indian people, the Congress finds—

(1) that clause 3, section 8, article I of the United States Constitution provides that "The Congress shall have Power *** To regulate Commerce *** with Indian tribes" and, through this and other constitutional authority, Congress has plenary power over Indian affairs;

(2) that Congress, through statutes, treaties, and the general course of dealing with Indian tribes, has assumed the responsibility for the protection and preservation of Indian tribes and their resources;

(3) that there is no resource that is more vital to the continued existence and integrity of Indian tribes than their children and that the United States has a direct interest, as trustee, in protecting Indian children who are members of or are eligible for membership in an Indian tribe;

(4) that an alarmingly high percentage of Indian families are broken up by the removal, often unwarranted, of their children from them by nontribal public and private agencies and that an alarmingly high percentage of such children are placed in non-Indian foster and adoptive homes and institutions; and

(5) that the States, exercising their recognized jurisdiction over Indian child custody proceedings through administrative and judicial bodies, have often failed to recognize the essential tribal relations of Indian people and the cultural and social standards prevailing in Indian communities and families.

Sec. 3.   The Congress hereby declares that it is the policy of this Nation to protect the best interests of Indian children and to promote the stability and security of Indian tribes and families by the establishment of minimum Federal standards for the removal of Indian children from their families and the placement of such children in foster or adoptive homes which will reflect the unique values of Indian culture, and by providing for assistance to Indian tribes in the operation of child and family service programs. . . .

Title I—Child Custody Proceedings

Sec. 101.   (a) An Indian tribe shall have jurisdiction exclusive as to any State over any child custody proceeding involving an Indian child who resides or is domiciled within the reservation of such tribe, except where such jurisdiction is otherwise vested in the State by existing Federal law. Where an Indian child is a ward of a tribal court, the Indian tribe shall retain exclusive jurisdiction, notwithstanding the residence or domicile of the child.

(b) In any State court proceeding for the foster care placement of, or termination of parental rights to, an Indian child not domiciled or residing within the reservation of the Indian child's tribe, the court, in the absence of good cause to the contrary, shall transfer such proceeding to the jurisdiction of the tribe, absent objection by either parent, upon the petition of either parent or the Indian custodian or the Indian child's tribe: *Provided,* That such transfer shall be subject to declination by the tribal court of such tribe.

(c) In any State court proceeding for the foster care placement of, or termination of parental rights to, an Indian child, the Indian custodian of the child and the Indian child's tribe shall have a right to intervene at any point in the proceeding.

(d) The United States, every State, every territory or possession of the United States, and every Indian tribe shall give full faith and credit to the public acts, records, and judicial proceedings of any Indian tribe applicable to Indian child custody proceedings to the same extent that such entities give full faith and credit to the public acts, records, and judicial proceedings of any other entity.

Sec. 102.   (a) In any involuntary proceeding in a State court, where the court knows or has reason to know that an Indian child is involved, the party seeking the foster care placement of, or termination of parental rights to, an Indian child shall notify the parent or Indian custodian and the Indian child's tribe, by registered mail with return receipt requested, of the pending proceedings and of their right of intervention. If the identity or location of the parent or Indian custodian and the tribe cannot be determined, such notice shall be given to the Secretary in like manner, who shall have fifteen days after receipt to provide the requisite notice to the parent or Indian custodian and the tribe. No foster care placement or termination of parental rights proceeding shall be held until at least ten days after receipt of notice by the parent or Indian custodian and the tribe or the Secretary: *Provided,* That the parent or Indian custodian or the tribe shall, upon request, be granted up to twenty additional days to prepare for such proceeding.

(b) In any case in which the court determines indigency, the parent or Indian custodian shall have the right to court-appointed counsel in any removal, placement, or termination proceeding. The court may, in its discretion, appoint counsel for the child upon a finding that such appointment is in the best interest of the child. Where State law makes no provision for appointment of counsel in such proceedings, the court shall promptly notify the Secretary upon appointment of counsel, and the Secretary, upon certification of the presiding judge, shall pay reasonable fees and expenses out of funds which may be appropriated pursuant to the Act of November 2, 1921.

(c) Each party to a foster care placement or termination of parental rights proceeding under State law involving an Indian child shall have the right to examine all reports or other documents filed with the court upon which any decision with respect to such action may be based.

(d) Any party seeking to effect a foster care placement of, or termination of parental rights to, an Indian child under State law shall satisfy the court that active efforts have been made to provide remedial services and rehabilitative programs designed to prevent the breakup of the Indian family and that these efforts have proved unsuccessful.

(e) No foster care placement may be ordered in such proceeding in the absence of a determination, supported by clear and convincing evidence, including testimony of qualified expert witnesses, that the continued custody of the child by the parent or Indian custodian is likely to result in serious emotional or physical damage to the child.

(f) No termination of parental rights may be ordered in such proceeding in the absence of a determination, supported by evidence beyond a reasonable doubt, including testimony of qualified expert witnesses, that the continued custody of the child by the parent or Indian custodian is likely to result in serious emotional or physical damage to the child.

Sec. 103. (a) Where any parent or Indian custodian voluntarily consents to a foster care placement or to termination of parental rights, such consent shall not be valid unless executed in writing and recorded before a judge of a court of competent jurisdiction and accompanied by the presiding judge's certificate that the terms and consequences of the consent were fully explained in detail and were fully understood by the parent or Indian custodian. The court shall also certify that either the parent or Indian custodian fully understood the explanation in English or that it was interpreted into a language that the parent or Indian custodian understood. Any consent given prior to, or within ten days after, birth of the Indian child shall not be valid. . . .

Sec. 105. (a) In any adoptive placement of an Indian child under State law, a preference shall be given, in the absence of good cause to the contrary, to a placement with (1) a member of the child's extended family; (2) other members of the Indian child's tribe; or (3) other Indian families.

(b) Any child accepted for foster care or preadoptive placement shall be placed in the least restrictive setting which most approximates a family and in which his special needs, if any, may be met. The child shall also be placed within reasonable proximity to his or her home, taking into account any special needs of the child. In any foster care or preadoptive placement, a preference shall be given, in the absence of good cause to the contrary, to a placement with—

(i) a member of the Indian child's extended family;

(ii) a foster home licensed, approved, or specified by the Indian child's tribe;

(iii) an Indian foster home licensed or approved by an authorized non-Indian licensing authority; or

(iv) an institution for children approved by an Indian tribe or operated by an Indian organization which has a program suitable to meet the Indian child's needs. . . .

Tim Giago (Oglala Lakota) Explains
the Significance of the Reservation, 1984

... The Indian reservations are nothing but concentration camps!" The young woman addressing the largely non-Indian audience was raised on the Navajo Reservation, but now resides in Los Angeles, California.

She acknowledged my raised hand. I asked her if she really meant what she had just said. Replying in the affirmative, she said quite sadly, "I still have family and friends living on that reservation."

My mind immediately flashed back to the war movies that saturated the market during World War II. The Gestapo interrogator, rawhide quirt in hand, looms menacingly over his victim and says, "You still have relatives living in Cher-many?"

"Aren't your friends and relatives free to leave any time they wish?" I asked. The non-Indian crowd murmured indignantly.

For the life of me, I can't comprehend why many Indians who have left the reservations and selected the urban way of life would malign their former homes, the lands of their ancestors. Do they do it for sympathy? For drama?

One so-called militant Indian, well-known across the land, uses this tactic unabashedly while seeking donations from the college audiences he frequently addresses. In the midst of his tirade against "neo-colonialism and the multinational corporations," he will usually add, "The reservations are nothing but government-controlled concentration camps!" The shock waves this comment generates through the malleable mind is something to behold.

During the days when the Bureau of Indian Affairs was shipping Indian families to the ghettos of the urban centers under the guise of "Relocation" (now euphemistically called "Employment Assistance"), thousands left the reservations with uncertainty and fear, believing the promises of a better life. Many remained in the cities, but many more, disillusioned by the traumatic change in lifestyles, and lonesome for the "uncis" and "tunkasilas" (grandmothers and grandfathers) they had left behind, returned to the lands of their birth.

Many of those who remained became assimilated into the mainstream, addicted to the easy conveniences of city life. Many who returned to the reservations came home angry at a federal government that would use human beings as guinea pigs in an ill-fated experiment.

The bureaucracy, in its infinite wisdom, has created two classes of Indians—the reservation Indian and the urban Indian. Never able to learn from their mistakes, the federal government attempted to divide the meager funds earmarked for Indian programs between the cities and the reservations. Subsistence on the reservation was already below poverty level, and to further dilute the funding available by allocating portions of it to the urban Indians caused anger and division.

From the sprawling ghettos of the inner cities arose the militant Indian factions. Like a burning prairie fire, militancy spread across the reservations. The anger

Tim Giago, "Indian Reservations: The Only Land We Know," in Giago, *Indian Country* (Pierre, S.D.: 1984), pp. 95–97.

that fed the prairie fire soon burned itself out and the reservation Indian, shaken by the tumultuous wave, backed off to assess the damage and evaluate the rapid change.

During the ensuing years, there has been a terrible "brain drain" of talent snatched from the reservations and planted in urban centers. Many educated Indians found the large salaries and the modern conveniences of city life much more inviting than the poverty and hardships of reservation life.

After it became fashionable to be Indian, feathers and braids became more commonplace in the cities than on the reservations. The urban Indians "out-Indianed" the reservation Indians.

Through it all, many Indians with vocational skills and college educations have returned to the reservations. They have set aside their personal ambitions, and have rejoined "the tribe," working toward the common goal of all the people.

Eager for immediate change, they have learned patience. They have discovered that the reservation people will change in their own way, and in their own time, if they decide to. What is progress to the white man isn't necessarily progress to the Indians.

Reservations have become the Mecca for urban Indians, the land base that bespeaks what lies ahead. Without the reservations, there will be no more Indians.

It is something the traditional, reservation Indian has always known. Our past, present and future is embedded in the lands of our ancestors. How can a Sacred Land ever be called a concentration camp?

There are no walls to contain us, or chains to bind us. We stay on the reservation because it is home, it is the land we love, and it is the only thing that gives purpose to our lives. In short, it is the only land we know! . . .

Mark N. Trahant (Shoshone-Bannock) on the Native Peoples of Alaska and Their Struggle for Sovereignty, 1989

Anchorage, Alaska—Beverly Hugo tells her favorite story about the government's ignorance of her Inupiaq way: Last winter, the federal Indian Health Service hired a "consultant" from North Dakota to travel to the top of the Arctic Circle to teach villagers how to stay warm in a cold climate.

The villagers of Barrow, she said, have many problems, including the tragedy wrought by chronic alcoholism. But staying warm is a skill that people who live on the edge of the continent learned many generations ago.

Hugo said the time has come for Inupiaqs to solve Inupiaq problems.

Strapped to Hugo's back, in a colorful cradle-board, was her two-month-old son, John.

"The more I learn," Hugo told a recent Anchorage hearing of the U.S. Senate Select Committee on Indian affairs, "the more I become concerned about what kind of life John will have."

"Native Alaskans' Ire Stirred by Paternalism" by Mark N. Trahant, *Arizona Republic,* July 23, 1989. Reprinted by permission of Phoenix Newspapers Inc.

Native problems in Alaska are like that.

The state and federal governments try to solve Indian problems as if they were the problems of people living in suburbs. Often, Indian leaders complain, they don't even listen to natives who have their own solutions to the problems.

The obstacle to native-sponsored solutions is the distrust between native villagers and urban residents—in Fairbanks or Anchorage—who have moved to this state in search of a new way of life.

"Alaska is basically a racist state," said Howard Weaver, managing editor of the *Anchorage Daily News.* The newspaper won the Pulitzer Prize for Public Service this year for a series chronicling alcohol abuse and suicide problems among natives.

"It's my sense that there's an enormous amount of stereotyping, a division between native and non-native Alaskans who harbor basically racially defined views.

"We're not talking about burning crosses," he said. "But there's not a general appreciation that everyone brings something to the cultural party."

Weaver, who grew up in Anchorage, said that Alaskan society is "virtually segregated."

Racism against Alaskan natives is rooted in the differences between the two cultures.

Most non-natives came to Alaska to build something; to profit from the state's natural wealth. On the other hand, natives were content with the Alaska that's always been; people living in harmony with the land.

"Don't forget what my father and his generation did when they went to Alaska at the turn of the century," a white mining company executive from Anchorage was quoted as saying in a 1974 book about the land claims, *Etok: A Story of Eskimo Power.*

"It was a wilderness. It was tough. Those pioneers who went over Chilkoot pass in '98 suffered and sacrificed, some of them gave their lives. But they built modern Alaska. They built it. There was nothing here when they came and they built it with their bare hands.

"Sure there were natives here when they came, but the natives had never done a (expletive deleted) thing with the land. Sure they lived off it—if you can call it living—but they didn't own it," he said. "And now you're talking about giving them title to the land in Alaska! They don't deserve it."

Extinguishing Land Claims

In 1971, pressured by the push for oil exploration in Alaska, Congress moved to extinguish native land claims and to create a new legal structure for native governance under the Alaskan Native Claims Settlement Act.

One legal scheme created by the act was to divide the natives into 12 regional for-profit corporations, owned by native shareholders, that would use the natural resource wealth to create cash wealth for natives.

Thus, the theory went, Alaskan natives would become self-sufficient. They wouldn't be forced to live on federal dole like the Indians living on reservations in the lower 48 states.

But the theory didn't quite work. Some companies made huge profits investing in real estate in California, while others teetered near bankruptcy because of poor management and lavish lifestyles by corporate executives.

A decade after the claims act was passed, poverty rates for Alaskan natives were nearly twice those of other Alaskans. Moreover, in some, primarily rural areas, the U.S. Census Bureau reports that Alaskan Native poverty rates hovered near 50 percent of the village population.

Declaring Sovereignty

In recent years, in attempts to solve the massive social problems, more and more native villages have asserted legal claims that Alaska has provisions of "Indian country."

The villages have said that they, like Indian tribes in the lower 48 states, have powers of self-determination or village sovereignty.

Last month, the village elders of Aleknagik, part of the Yupiit tribe, declared sovereignty over their lands, saying it could "no longer tolerate the gross mismanagement and confusion by agents and contractors of the state in their attempt to regulate the fish and game resources."

The elders' resolution called for "national and international commitments to the Yupiit people" to be honored.

Earlier this spring, in the village of Quinhagak, residents halted a state trooper from seizing big-game carcasses as evidence of poaching.

In the village of Akiachak, northeast of Bethel, the borough government's powers were transferred wholesale to a tribal council.

Subsistence Fishing Rights

Another battle involved the Kenaitze tribe, whose members live on Cook Inlet about 100 miles southwest of Anchorage. The tribe sued the state to protect its claim of traditional subsistence fishing rights that are granted under federal law to "rural" residents of Alaska.

The state, however, did not want to recognize the Kenaitze as a rural interest because, it said, the Cook Inlet area is a fast-growing suburban area.

"We end as we began," said the U.S. 9th Circuit Court of Appeals in a decision favoring the tribe.

"This is a case involving a clash of lifestyles and a dispute over who gets to fish. Congress, using clear language, has resolved this dispute in favor of the Kenaitze who choose to pursue the traditional way of life by giving them priority in federal waters. The state has attempted to take away what Congress has given," the decision said.

After the decision, however, the state still did not give up. Attorney General Doug Baily has said that the Alaskan Constitution prohibits a special fishery for any race of people.

The state has appealed the decision to the U.S. Supreme Court.

But last month, while the nation focused on the spill from the super-tanker Exxon Valdez, Rep. Don Young, R-Alaska, pushed a bill through the House

Interior Committee that would have changed the federal definition of rural to match the state's version.

Tribal leaders were upset because Young pushed the measure while their staunchest advocate, Interior Chairman Morris Udall, D-Ariz., was in the hospital with pneumonia.

Young has said that the court has misinterpreted congressional intent, but nonetheless withdrew his measure after a storm of protest by native leaders.

Tribal leaders, including Kenaitze leader Clare Swan, said it was just one more attempt by the state to strip away a court victory.

The state and the tribe reached a temporary pact last month allowing the Kenaitze tribe subsistence fishing this year. Next year, however, both the state and tribe predict complicated negotiations over the issue.

The cultural clash is often misunderstood because it's seen as subsistence fishing versus creating new industry and jobs, said Weaver of the *Daily News.*

But subsistence fishing "is really the essential industry of rural Alaska," he said. "It's the only industry that could take care of people—what they love is life."

"Dancing Around" the Issue

Yet village sovereignty is a larger issue than just subsistence rights, an issue that many Alaskans don't want to face, tribal leaders say.

At the Senate Select Committee on Indian Affairs hearing, native leaders were buoyed by statements from its chairman, Sen. Daniel Inouye, D-Hawaii, who said he supported village sovereignty efforts.

Yet in written testimony, Alaska Gov. Steve Cowper highlighted a number of problems facing Alaskan natives—yet did not mention even the issue of village sovereignty.

The issue is a delicate one for the federal government.

The Bureau of Indian Affairs identifies more than 200 villages in Alaska as groups with some attributes of tribal sovereignty. However, in a recent edition of the *Federal Register,* the BIA reported that more than 500 villages are eligible for services and, therefore, some degree of tribal sovereignty.

One measure of that sovereignty is a village constitution approved by the BIA under the procedure of the 1934 Indian Reorganization Act.

For more than ten years, the BIA avoided approving any village constitutions under that act because of claims that the Alaskan Native Claims Settlement Act extinguished that sovereignty.

Last month, however, the BIA changed direction and approved a constitution for the village of Eagle, near the Canadian border. That village had been seeking a constitution since 1978.

"It's clear that the (native) claims based on aboriginal claims to the land were abolished and that aboriginal hunting and fishing rights were abolished," said Joe Donahue, a BIA official in Washington. "But beyond that it's not clear as to the other elements of what is referred to as Indian sovereignty.

"It's a very difficult and complex issue," he said. "The ultimate decisions on which tribes have what kind of sovereignty will probably be decided by the courts."

The notion that tribal sovereignty was extinguished by the Alaskan Native

Claims Act is absurd, said Tom Abel, a village leader from Craig in southeast Alaska.

"We have always had sovereignty—no one gave it to us," he said. Therefore, "how could anyone take it away?"

After years of observing the tragedies of alcohol and suicide in native villages, *Daily News* editor Weaver said, Alaskans "dance around" the issue.

"Village sovereignty is really part of the answer," he said.

While the notion of villages as separate nations is extreme, Weaver said, "I do think the best solution would be some kind of structure that (includes) sovereignty."

Deward E. Walker, Jr., Argues That Anthropologists Must Allow American Indians to Bury Their Dead, 1990

As an anthropologist who has conducted research with many of our country's Indian tribes, I am troubled over my discipline's apparent reluctance to let American Indians bury their dead.

For years, American Indian tribes have struggled to rebury thousands of their dead, whose remains now are held by museums, universities, and federal agencies. In the past, these remains have been gathered from graves and battlefields by federal officials, museum personnel, private collectors, and anthropologists in ways that would be considered highly illegal and unethical if done to other citizens.

In the 19th century, for example, the U.S. Cavalry and state militia beheaded some Indians slain in battle and sent the heads to the U.S. Army Medical Museum, which eventually transferred them to the Smithsonian Institution. Some universities and museums acquired sacred religious objects that Indians sold illegally to pawnshops and other outlets.

The return of Indian remains to their tribes is an issue that has escalated into a national moral crisis. Until recently, tribes' efforts to obtain the remains of their dead have met with only limited and local success. But now Congress is considering legislation that would resolve the issue on a national scale.

Last year Congress passed a historic law requiring the Smithsonian Institution to return to their tribes some of the 19,000 American Indian skeletons it holds. Now another set of bills, including S1980 sponsored by Sen. Daniel Inouye (Democrat of Hawaii), would extend the requirement to the rest of the federal government and to museums run by units of state and local government, including colleges and universities. The bill would require that remains be returned to their tribes of origin, upon the tribes' request. The measure also would require scientists to obtain tribes' consent to keep any remains for future scientific studies. The remains of more than 100,000 Indian dead would be affected, making government efforts to repatriate American prisoners of war and those missing in action seem puny in comparison.

However, it is not certain whether groups representing professional

From Deward E. Walker, Jr. "Anthropologists Must Allow American Indians to Bury Their Dead," *Chronicle of Higher Education* (September 12, 1990). Reprinted with permission of the author.

anthropologists will agree to support the Inouye bill or similar legislation that gives American Indian tribes firm rights to recover religious objects and the remains of their dead. The Society for American Archaeology and the American Anthropological Association initially opposed Senator Inouye's measure, although they now may be softening their opposition in response to modifications in the bill's language.

The only appropriate role for either organization is to support the Inouye bill or similar legislation and to state clearly that anthropology in the United States does not depend on the exploitation and retention of American Indian dead, their grave goods, or their sacred objects. Opposition from anthropologists to the pending legislation can only worsen already strained relations between American Indians and anthropologists and lead to outright bans on future research projects in Indian areas. I cannot imagine anthropology as a viable research discipline in the United States without the continued cooperation of its native people.

Anthropologists, more than any other group, have benefited from the tolerance and good will shown by American Indians, who have borne the burden of our studies of their cultures, communities, and religions over the past century or more.

Given our country's shabby treatment of American Indians in the past, all citizens should join in supporting the pending legislation. But anthropologists should be the first to support such efforts, since we understand the damage to living communities and cultures that plundering graves and withholding the dead from re-burial can do.

To their credit, some universities already have agreed to return skeletal and other materials for re-burial, including Stanford University and the Universities of Idaho, Minnesota, Nebraska, and Tennessee. Others are currently reviewing their policies and may follow those institutions' lead.

The truth is that return of the remains of Indian dead, along with stolen burial or religious property, will not affect legitimate scholarly work. Science and education have never depended on keeping stolen property or bodies against the wishes of next of kin.

Despite the protestations of certain anthropologists, the skeletal and grave materials held by universities, federal agencies, and museums have received relatively little study in the past. Very early in this century, Franz Boas, a founder of anthropology in the United States, came to regard the study of skeletal material as of little value compared with the study of living populations of American Indians. Certain tribes already permit limited study of skeletal materials recovered by anthropologists, and the Inouye bill would allow for some study before collections are returned for re-burial, providing informed consent from tribes is obtained. (Obtaining such consent will be a novel and healthy exercise for a discipline that has become all too closeted and socially unaccountable to those whom it studies.)

It is true that it will no longer be possible for anthropologists to retain "comparative collections" of American Indian skeletal materials indefinitely. This will certainly obstruct some types of anthropological research in the future, but such research should not remain dependent on material held over the objections of living descendants.

Most citizens deeply respect the sanctity of the dead. This value is reflected in the laws and social policy of all 50 states and is one mark of a civilized nation. Increasingly, Americans are beginning to understand that this respect must be extended to include American Indian dead and not just the dead of the dominant majority. It is time for the federal government and anthropologists to extend this respect as well.

Suzan Harjo (Cheyenne) Testifies Before the U.S. Civil Rights Commission, 1988

... We first saw the "Spear an Indian; save a salmon" bumper stickers in the State of Washington. We have see the spread of an increasingly vigorous anti-Indian organized hate-group network that is in virtually every State in this country where there are Indian people. We know that these hate groups are tied to the Aryan Nation, to the Order, to the Klan. We suspect that these hate groups have the same kind of organized crime underpinnings and financing.

We suggest you look into this. This is a problem for us. This is a problem that is creating more scars for Indian country. Even as we speak, the spearing season is going to begin very soon in Wisconsin, and we are going to have even greater problems.

Some of the people who are organized under the name of PARR, Protect America's Rights and Resources—fine-sounding names these hate groups have—are excluding the Indian children from Little League games and not letting the white kids play ball against the Indian kids because they are Indians, and because their parents are fishing and hunting in their traditional ways as their treaty says they can, as the United States agrees, as the courts have said they can.

We have emotional scarring that is taking place. As we sit here, there have been numerous jokes about the upcoming Super Bowl, and certainly I support the Washington Redskins. I love them. I'm going to root for them. I don't think it would be tolerated if there were in the Nation's capital or in any city in America a team called the Blackskins, if I got out on a football field and dressed up in an Aunt Jemima outfit, and this good gentleman got out in blackface in a Steppin Fetchit outfit for the Blackskins.

There would be a race riot in this city and in this country if we had a team called the Jew Boys, if we had a team called the Black Chicks. If we had anything that was derogatory to women or any other racial or religious minority in this country, it would not be tolerated. It is tolerated.

Why is it tolerated? Because that is the era we are in. Everyone has that same old movie running through their heads, and Indians are identified as an era, not as a people. We are not an era like cowboys. We are a people. We are many people. We are diverse. We have a richness of cultural underpinnings without which we would not be able to survive today's conditions of outrageously high unemployment, staggering alcoholism, the highest rate of teenage suicide of any population in this country, which comes from low self-esteem, which comes from having those kids' elders—myself, this good gentleman, our elders, too—mocked, dehumanized, cartooned, stereotyped. That is what is causing the deaths of many of our children.

We can't be polite about these problems anymore. The only way that this Commission could have made itself look any better would have been to do exactly what you did, to drag the BIA up here, the worst agency in the Federal Government, and say, "Hit on tribal courts," one thing that many people don't understand about Indian country, to raise the specter of a lack of democracy in Indian country, which I daresay is the only place where you will find true living democracy in this day and age.

By saying that we have to have separation of powers, you do arrogantly try to interject yourselves between ourselves and our history, ourselves and our tradition, ourselves and what we are passing on to our children.

We are guaranteed the right to be Indian people in perpetuity. There are certain things that we allow. I allow you to refer to me as Cheyenne. I allow you to refer to me as Indian when my name is Jista, the people, or my father, Widulgee Muskogee, the first people of the Wind clan, so we can communicate with each other.

And as you have heard here, many tribes are willing to adopt foreign influences and to allow themselves to make accommodations to the kinds of models for governance that other peoples have. Sometimes they do that if only to be able to survive. Some of us do not wish to do that, and I think you will see that many of us will not oftentimes in the future.

We take ourselves very seriously, so seriously that we laugh at almost everything. That is our way of reacting to these kinds of situations. And by "these kinds of situations" I mean where the Commission has put together a hearing somewhat on tribal courts, somewhat on separation of powers, somewhat on tribal sovereignty—what is it; what is the nature of it?—somewhat on the power of the councils. And to talk about the power of the haves and the have-nots in a situation where Indian country is in a survival mode is really stretching a point, to talk about power of tribal councils. I think that is a really odd thing to think about. . . .

I think there is a lot for this body to look into that it hasn't, and it is trying to focus, or at least there is the perception in Indian country that you are trying to focus on the problems that we have. We are under a colonialized system. We are not, as Mr. Swimmer said earlier, a conquered people. One of the last battles my relatives were in was the Battle of the Little Big Horn, and as I recall we did not lose. . . .

◇ *E S S A Y S*

Free-lance journalist Marjane Ambler has written extensively about environmental and land-use issues in the American West. This excerpt from her book, *Breaking the Iron Bonds* (1990), on Indians' efforts to control the use of mineral resources on their lands, outlines some major social and economic issues in Indian country today. Ambler echoes the sentiments of Tim Giago and other writers in discussing the significance of the reservation as community, and as home.

In the second essay, Charles Roberts (Choctaw), professor of history at California State University, Sacramento, recounts the life of Lesa Phillip Roberts, his grandmother. Her story mirrors a number of key themes in modern Indian life—migration, urbanization, employment, and family—and attests to a changing, continuing, Indian presence in the United States.

The Importance of Economic Development on the Reservation

MARJANE AMBLER

To many people in the United States the Indian reservation is an embarrassment. To them it represents the American version of apartheid—a prison without walls where the government confined Indians to keep them apart from other Americans, similar to the detention centers where Japanese Americans were kept during World War II. When they drive through reservations, they see only the signs of poverty: brightly colored, dilapidated frame houses; abandoned cars; dusty yards. They look for dancers dressed in feathers and bells to entertain them and vaguely wonder why such an archaic institution—the reservation—still exists.

The Indian people who live on reservations see it differently. To them the reservation is home, a locus for their political, social, economic, and cultural lives. Their families and their culture are tied to that patch of land. Young Indian people say they feel as if they are entering alien territory when they cross the reservation boundary to the outside world. The reservation is where they learned to hunt with their grandfathers or to herd sheep with their aunts. They know where to find the springs when the creeks dry up in August; where to cut the straightest lodgepole pines for powwow teepee poles; and where to pick buffalo berries, mint, and yarrow. Since they were young, they have known which places are sacred and where the powwows are held each summer. Most of their relatives still live there. When they drive back into the reservation, they come home.

Why have Indian people clung to their land and the reservation system despite various attempts by the U.S. government during the past century to assimilate them into the mainstream? The answer is critical to understanding why developing a reservation economy is important. . . .

Indian people have been bound by three iron chains: paternalism, exploitation, and dependency. These chains gained their crippling power through the decades as lawmakers vacillated about whether tribes should continue to exist as separate sovereigns or whether their separate rights should be terminated. Many of those who advocated "freeing the Indian" through each period of history were well-meaning but paternalistic. Others were merely greedy and wanted to exploit Indian resources. Whatever their motives the effects of the vacillating policies were the same: The tribes and individual Indians lost more and more of the land and other resources they needed to make them self-sufficient again. This exploitation left them increasingly dependent upon the federal government yet, ironically, resistant to change, because so often in the past change had brought disaster.

The constant conundrum throughout the history of Indian affairs in this country has been finding the best balance between dependency and independence; trust protection and self-determination; autocratic federal control and tribal con-

From *Breaking the Iron Bonds: Indian Control of Energy Development,* by Marjane Ambler, pp. 1–8, 22–30, 260–262, © 1990, by the University Press of Kansas. Reprinted by permission of the publisher.

Contemporary Indian Lands and Communities in the United States (with modern tribal spellings)

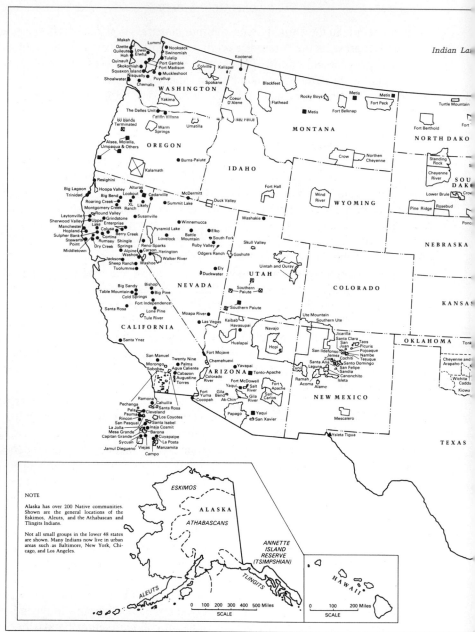

SOURCE: Council of Energy Resource Tribes (1985).

Reprinted from *American Indians: The First of This Land,* by C. Matthew Snipp, © 1989 the Russell Sage Foundation. Used with the permission of the Russell Sage Foundation.

nities

Malecite

Micmac

MAINE ▲ Passamaquoddy
Pleasant Point

Penobscot ▲

Nett Lake Grand Portage
Nett Lake
Deer Creek
Leech Lake Red Cliff Ontonagon
Lake Superior Bay Mills
Du Lac Bad River Lanse
Lac Keweenaw
Court Bay
Oreille Lac Du Ottawa &
Lac Mole Lake Flambeau Chippewa
Prior St. Croix Menominee Potawatomi
Lake Communities Stockbridge
Prairie Munsee
Island Oneida
ESOTA WISCONSIN Botherton
Isabella
Isabella

St. Regis
Mohawk

VER.

N.H.

Lake Ontario

Oneida MASS. Nipmuc
Onondaga CONN. Wampanoag
Seneca Narraganset
Tonawanda Scaticook Pequot
Cattaraugus Mohegan Montauk
Cayuga NEW YORK Paugusett
Alleghany Seneca Shinnecock
Poosepawtuck

R.I.

WA Sac and Fox
Potawatomi

Lake Huron

Lake Michigan

Lake Erie

PENNSYLVANIA N.J.

Miami MARYLAND DEL.
Moor
Nanticoke

OHIO
INDIANA WEST
ILLINOIS VIRGINIA

MISSOURI KENTUCKY Rappananock Mattaponi
Upper Mattaponi Pamunkey
Amherst Chickahominy
County VIRGINIA
Person County
Haliwa

Quapaw
Modoc
Wyandotte
Seneca NORTH CAROLINA Comarie
Cherokee
TENNESSEE Lumbee
Catawba Waccamaw

ARKANSAS SOUTH
CAROLINA
MISS. GEORGIA
Choctaw Summerville
ALABAMA

LOUISIANA
Choctaw
Choctaw Tunica Creek
Coushatta Choctaw
Chitimacha
Houma FLORIDA

☐● Federal Indian Reservation
[⁻⁻⁻] Former Reservations in Oklahoma
▲ State Reservations
■ Indian Groups Without Trust Land
▨ Federally Terminated Tribes and Groups

Brighton

Big
Cypress ▲ Seminole
Miccosukee ▲ Hollywood
Seminole

50 0 50 100 150 200 Miles
SCALE

Indian Population by County, 1980

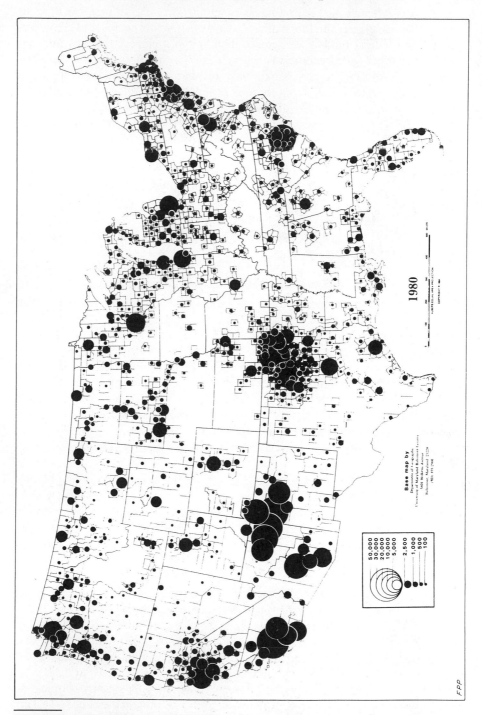

Reprinted from *Atlas of American Indian Affairs,* by Francis Paul Prucha, p. 16, by permission of the University of Nebraska Press. Copyright © 1990 by the University of Nebraska Press.

trol. Today it still underlies all disagreements between tribal and federal officials. For the energy tribes the conflict has been critical. In order to increase their autonomy and self-determination, they know they have to decrease their dependence upon federal funds and increase their self-sufficiency. But this does not mean that a tribe has to become an economic island, consuming only what it produces on the reservation. A tribe will have reached self-sufficiency when it can provide for the needs of community members and determine its own social and economic goals for the future without violating its cultural heritage. . . .

. . . "Energy tribes" refers to tribes that receive a significant portion of their income from energy minerals or that own substantial undeveloped reserves. These include the Fort Peck Assiniboine and Sioux, Blackfeet, Northern Cheyenne, and Crow Tribes in Montana; Fort Berthold Three Affiliated Tribes in North Dakota; Wind River Arapahoe and Shoshone Tribes in Wyoming; Osage Tribe in Oklahoma; Spokane Tribe in Washington; Northern Ute Tribe in Utah; Southern Ute and Ute Mountain Ute Tribes in Colorado; Jicarilla Apache Tribe and Laguna Pueblo in New Mexico; Hopi Tribe in Arizona; and the Navajo Tribe in Arizona, New Mexico, and Utah. . . .

In January 1983 Interior Secretary James Watt for a few days focused the nation's attention on the question of reservation versus assimilation by suggesting that Indians should be "freed" and integrated into the American system. The statement by Watt, a controversial and short-tenured appointee of President Ronald Reagan, infuriated most Indian people, many of whom called for his resignation. Nevertheless, Watt had verbalized sentiments shared by a few Indians and many non-Indians (that is, among those who thought about Indian reservations at all). Watt said, "Every social problem is exaggerated because of socialistic government politics on the Indian reservations. . . . The people have been trained through 100 years of government oppression to look to the government as . . . the provider, and they've not been trained to use the initiative to integrate into the American system."

Apparently mystified by why Indians would stay on reservations, he blamed greedy tribal leaders who somehow coerced their members: "If you're the chief or the chairman, you're interested in keeping this group of people assembled in a desert environment where there are no jobs, no agriculture potential, no water, because if the Indians were allowed to be liberated, they'd go and get a job and that guy wouldn't have his government handout as a government-paid Indian official."

Although President Reagan at that time disavowed Watt's remarks, he later expressed the same misunderstanding about the reservation system. In 1988, responding to Soviet students who asked about American Indians, Reagan said he could not understand what their complaints could be, given that the American people had "humored" the Indians by providing them with reservations where their "primitive life style" was to blame for their poverty.

Indians had heard such rhetoric before. Since the 1880s many people who considered themselves friends of the Indian had championed the cause of assimilation with missionarylike zeal in language similar to Watt's when he said, "We ought to give them freedom, we ought to give them liberty, we ought to give them their rights, but we treat them as incompetent wards." Most of those who had advocated terminating federal protection for tribes in earlier years were probably as bewildered as Watt and Reagan by the negative response.

The 1980 census reported that Indians on reservations had lower incomes and fewer modern conveniences than those who lived off the reservations and had dramatically lower incomes than non-Indians. True, in cultures in which subsistence agriculture and bartering are common, the standard socioeconomic indicators do not necessarily accurately reflect the quality of life. Nevertheless, the extent of the differences between reservation and off-reservation conditions did indicate a serious problem. More than half (58 percent) of the reservation males between 20 and 64 years old were not employed, compared with 26 percent of off-reservation Indian males and 18 percent of all races.

Of reservation Indians, census takers found that 41 percent were living in households with incomes below the poverty level, compared with half as many (22 percent) off-reservation Indians and 12 percent of the U.S. population as a whole. About one-fourth (22 percent) of the reservation households received income from public assistance, compared with 15 percent for off-reservation Indian households and 8 percent for the U.S. population as a whole. Fewer than half (44 percent) of the reservation Indian households had telephones. Poverty and unemployment contribute to extremely high alcoholism and drug use rates as well as other social problems. The social and economic problems on reservations are real, but Watt's analysis of the causes was shallow and his solution—termination—too simple.

So why would anyone stay on the reservations? Watt's theory notwithstanding, tribal leaders do not and cannot coerce members to stay. And, in fact, not everyone does stay. About half of the 1.5 million Indians in the country lived on or near reservations in 1980. Many of the others had left for jobs or schooling, returning on weekends and tribal holidays to renew family and cultural ties. Others may never have lived on reservations and may feel more "Indian" than Crow or Assiniboine or Navajo. They take part in pan-Indian, urban festivities without regard for particular tribal affiliations or traditions. Still others have assimilated most of the values of the dominant culture and rarely think of themselves as Indian at all.

The Indians who choose to live on the reservations do so for many reasons. On some reservations the residents get more medical and economic benefits from the federal and tribal governments than members who live elsewhere, as Watt pointed out. Yet more intangible reasons encourage thousands of Indians to stay on reservations. Despite the "desert environment," many love their land, just as many non-Indians love special places of personal significance. They stay to be with their families and so their children can benefit from time spent with family elders. They participate in tribal religious and traditional activities. Many feel strongly that they want to serve their people.

On the tribal level the reservation land serves three critical, interrelated purposes: cultural, political, and economic. A contemporary reservation Indian does not fit the expectations of the non-Indian who believes the "real" Indian should wear skins and feathers and that his or her reservation should be a living museum depicting the 1700s. For example, one non-Indian visitor decided that he did not like telephone poles because they interrupted the Indians' psychic/spiritual connection to the earth, without asking the Indians whether they appreciated the convenience of finally being able to call friends, government agencies, and doctors. Others seem to think Indians should drop any pretense of being different if they are going to keep changing their life styles. One author ridiculed the contemporary Ute, saying, "What remains of their culture is a mongrelized version of tradition, lore, religion, and a quasi-language that has almost lost its purity." Anthropologist Loretta Fowler says that her colleagues sometimes encourage such misconceptions by focusing upon arbitrary measures of a tribe's traditional life and suggesting that successful adaptation is un-Indian.

On most reservations many traditional cultural values persist. Although tribal members may be wearing three-piece suits with their beads and braids and sporting degrees from Harvard or the University of Oklahoma, they often have retained aspects of their culture that thrive within them, invisible to outsiders. The blue-eyed, outwardly assimilated tribal geologist may go to both a white doctor and a medicine man when she is sick. During his off-hours, a tribal councilman may go on a vision quest as he decides how best to serve his people. The supernatural is often part of everyday life.

Although non-Indians may believe that Indian cultures have not been viable for generations, a University of Chicago study in 1961 affirmed that Indian communities were increasing in population and were, as a whole, "distinct growing communities that still preserve the core of their native style of life." Since then the resurgence of old traditions has continued on many reservations as tribal members learn to tan hides the old way, using the animal's brains; make pemmican and chokecherry delicacies; and perform dances that once were nearly forgotten. On some reservations tribal languages are spoken extensively; children are taught their language by tribal elders, at the insistence of tribal councils. On the Jicarilla Apache Reservation in New Mexico, for example, a 1978 study found that half of the reservation residents spoke their language and one-third of the households used it regularly. A 1987 study on the Navajo Reservation found about 125,000 Indians who spoke Navajo fluently.

Romanticized cultural expectations often cause serious problems. Non-Indians argue against fulfilling the requirements of "old treaties" by saying the people have assimilated and thus are not of the same culture as those who signed the treaties. Members of Congress erect barriers to any kind of economic development that does not fit their expectations. For example, arts and crafts are acceptable, but bingo halls and factories are often restricted. In response, Indian leaders point to the value of adaptation—retaining important aspects of their own cultures while taking from the dominant culture. Adaptation has been key to the Indians' survival on this continent for the past hundred thousand years. Tribes adopted useful tools and trade materials from one another. When the Europeans arrived, tribes adapted to the horse and to the glass trade-beads that today are typically identified with the "traditional" Plains Indian culture. No culture is static; it dies if it does not grow. For the contemporary Indian, the right to change is an important legal right, not just an academic assertion. Since 1908 the U.S. Supreme Court has recognized that the powers of tribal governments, including their water rights, can change to adapt to the twentieth century.

The needs for a cultural, political, and economic base are intertwined. Every ethnic group has faced the challenge of change and its effect on traditional ways, but few in this country have kept their cultures as intact on such a wide scale as the American Indian. The explanation, as many Indians see it, is simple: the land. Reservation lands and the tribes' political authority help distinguish Indians from other religious or ethnic minorities. Although the land and its resources are more than just real estate to be exploited, their economic potential is important to the continued existence of the tribe as a political and cultural entity. Without land, tribal governments would find it difficult to practice self-government or to exercise the limited sovereignty guaranteed to them by the U.S. Constitution. Without economic development to nourish tribal coffers, self-government is meaningless.

A hundred years ago Chief Dull Knife told the Northern Cheyennes of Montana to send their children to school to prepare for the changing times. For that some of his people called him "the wife of a white man," a charge of treason at that time. Yet Dull Knife knew that through education young Cheyennes could help to develop their local economy and tribal government and to preserve Indian rights to land and resources. Just as their adaptation helped them retain their land, so, too, did the land help them retain their culture. In the 1980s the Northern Cheyennes revere Dull Knife and Little Wolf and the land they led them back to after their government-imposed exile to Oklahoma. Every gathering—from pow-wows to school board meetings—opens with a reference to the long journey back to Montana. The official tribal stationery, with pictures of Dull Knife and Little Wolf on the top, says, "Out of defeat and exile they led us back to Montana and won our Cheyenne homeland which we will keep forever."

The invisible culture of the reservation is beside the point to many melting-pot missionaries (such as Watt) who, if they see it at all, see it as an obstacle to economic progress. To them a self-sufficient tribal government just perpetuates an anachronistic system that stands between the Indian and true equality. An example is another Wyomingite, former Governor Lester C. Hunt. In language remarkably similar to Watt's, Hunt argued forty years earlier against the government's continuing to be a "wet nurse" for the Indians. Saying the Indian had "lost his glamor as a showman," Hunt suggested taking away federal services and dividing the land among tribal members so that the "Indian as we know him today would soon lose his identity and would rapidly acquire the American way of living." He professed ignorance of why the Indian had not progressed: "The Indian reservations, probably all of them, are surrounded by the highest types of civilization, and how or why they have been retarded in their advancement as much as they have is a mystery to me." Why have reservations been "retarded" in their economic advancement? Actually, in light of the history of federal Indian policy, the real mystery is how, despite the odds, tribes have been able to retain some of their resources and their culture and to progress economically as far as they have. . . .

*   *   *   *

As a result of growing activism by Indian tribes and intertribal organizations, both major political parties rejected termination in their 1960 party platforms. In the following years the nation's leaders adopted official policies that recognized the continuing importance of reservations and tribal governments. The actual role taken by the federal government did not, however, always reflect those policies. Despite several defeats suffered by tribes in the courts, Congress, and government agencies, the era would be remembered as one of remarkable progress toward tribes' determining their own goals. To benefit from their political progress, however, tribes needed much more on-reservation economic development than had occurred by 1988.

During the administration of John F. Kennedy and during President Lyndon B. Johnson's War on Poverty, money began pouring into the reservations. With unemployment rates as high as 80 percent and health problems worse than anywhere else in the nation, the reservations were logical targets for LBJ's war. The job training and administrative positions created during this period produced many talented and politically astute administrators who later became tribal leaders and reservation entrepreneurs. The antipoverty funds supported a resurgence of tribal governments. College enrollment among Indian students began increasing, and the Red Power movement gained momentum. Educated Indians could hope to find jobs on reservations, and many returned to their own or other reservations. Peter MacDonald, for example, returned to the Navajo Reservation in 1963 to serve as director of the Office of Navajo Economic Opportunity before deciding in 1970 to run for tribal chairman.

The administration of Richard M. Nixon offered a political context for continued efforts to revitalize reservation economies. In a message sent to Congress in 1970, Nixon sought a middle ground that would provide for self-determination without termination:

> This . . . must be the goal of any new national policy toward the Indian People: to strengthen the Indian's sense of autonomy without threatening his sense of community. We must assure the Indian that he can assume control of his own life without being separated involuntarily from the tribal group. And we must make it clear that Indians can become independent of Federal control without being cut off from Federal concern and Federal support.

Nixon recognized the connection between sound reservation economies and self-government. He suggested several initiatives to increase self-determination and self-sufficiency on the reservations. In 1974 Congress acted on one of those suggestions and passed the Indian Financing Act, which established an Indian revolving loan fund to promote economic development of both individual reservation Indians and Indian organizations. Congress also provided for interest subsidies, Indian business grants, and authorized some federal agencies to give special emphasis to Indian economic needs.

In 1975 Congress acted on another of Nixon's suggestions and passed the Indian Self-Determination and Educational Assistance Act. The law signaled a significant reversal of public policy. It directed BIA and the Indian Health Service to contract with tribes that wanted to provide programs and services previously administered by those agencies. The law was critical for both the energy and other tribes because it recognized tribal governments as institutions with long-term viability rather than just transitional structures. It meant they could take over many of the functions that the federal government had performed inadequately, such as monitoring oil fields for thefts, planning land use, and protecting air and water quality and cultural resources.

Stunning court victories accompanied these administrative and legislative recognitions of tribal self-determination. Through the late 1970s and 1980s, however, a backlash plagued Indian tribes, especially concerning their hunting and fishing rights. The public still was not aware of such concepts as "self-determination," "tribal self-government," and "sovereignty"—that is, until they felt their own rights being threatened by these strange, special rights of the Indians. By 1989 the backlash had not won wide favor in Congress as it had during the termination movements of the 1910s and 1950s. Partly as a result of the termination era, tribes and tribal organizations were much more vigilant than they had been in 1953 when House Concurrent Resolution 108 passed unanimously without objection from any member of either house.

The administration of President Jimmy Carter strongly opposed the 1977 backlash legislation, the Native Americans Equal Opportunity Act, which would have abrogated all treaties and terminated federal supervision of Indian people and property. Testifying before a House subcommittee, Interior Secretary Cecil Andrus argued that treaties were legal contracts that were "every bit as legitimate" as, for example, home mortgages. The Indians let go of their property in exchange for the U.S. government's guarantees that it would protect the land, water, and other resources. Just because energy minerals were found under the land or because the government had allowed someone else to use the water did not relieve the United States of its legal obligations, he said.

Instead of adopting the antitreaty legislation Congress in the 1980s adopted laws that recognized greater tribal governmental powers, including several that reinforced energy tribes' powers. In 1982 it passed the Indian Mineral Development Act (IMDA), which allowed tribes to become energy producers instead of just royalty holders, and the Indian Tribal Governmental Tax Status Act, which enabled tribes to issue certain tax-exempt revenue bonds, among other powers. In 1986 Congress amended three environmental laws that recognized tribes' authority to be similar to that of states. At the same time, Congress restricted tribes' efforts to establish gambling casinos and to use tax-exempt bonds to build off-reservation industries.

President Ronald Reagan said in his Indian policy message on January 14, 1983, that he recognized the importance of reservation economic development to tribal governments. He set up the Presidential Advisory Commission on Indian Reservation Economies, with Ross Swimmer (Cherokee) as chairman. Although Indian leaders generally agreed with Reagan that tribes should become self-supporting and reduce their dependence upon federal funds, they were alarmed at Reagan's abrupt and severe budget cuts, which they considered economic termination. In 1981 the Reagan administration had called for a drastic reduction in federal assistance to tribes, including an 82 percent cut in economic development funds. Although Indians represented 0.6 percent of the country's population, they absorbed 2.5 percent of the budget cuts. Unlike other places in the nation, reservations had few businesses to make up the differences. Not only economic development but also health suffered as a result of Reagan's policies.

During Reagan's second term, the National Congress of American Indians (NCAI) also called for the resignation of Reagan's assistant Interior secretary for Indian affairs, Ross Swimmer. A former tribal leader himself (principal chief of the Cherokee Nation), Swimmer understood the role of tribal governments and reservations better than Watt and also took a stronger stance defending tribal natural resources. Nevertheless, when he attempted to reduce the involvement of BIA in tribal affairs, many Indian tribes believed that Swimmer was trying to terminate their relationship with the federal government. Swimmer advocated phasing out BIA, and although some Indians agreed that it should be abolished, most reservation Indians believed the bureau was the only thing standing between them and termination of their reservations' special status.

Despite the political support for Indian self-determination in the 1970s and 1980s and the concomitant recognition for the need for reservation economic development, such development continued to lag. Although some tribes had found that carefully planned programs could bring their members success and productivity, most still were dependent upon federal funds. Reagan acknowledged that "federal policies have . . . inhibited the political and economic development of the tribes . . . and promoted dependency rather than self-sufficiency."

Various studies agreed and pointed to many other ways in which reservation economic development had been inhibited and dependency promoted during the self-determination era. Although they differed radically in political-economic theory and in some of their conclusions, the studies all said that the hurdles were not impossible to overcome. Tribes could become more "self-sufficient," even without the resources that they held prior to the coming of the white man, so long as self-sufficiency did not mean total independence from outside funding, which, after all, neither states nor local governments had yet achieved. Instead tribes could strive to provide for the needs of their people in accordance with their own goals rather than federally imposed goals.

From the 1960s through the early 1980s, federal monies poured into the reservations. As one Indian commentator put it, the government became the Indians' new buffalo. Federal spending for Indian programs rose significantly from $1.08 billion in 1973 to $2.75 billion in 1981 before it began declining again. Yet increasing federal funding alone would not solve the problems, the studies said. Although new social programs created jobs and decreased the suffering of poverty-stricken families, they rarely helped economic development. Thus they increased dependency upon federal government funding.

The studies also agreed that the greatest obstacle was the lack of businesses on reservations. This deficiency caused two serious problems with far-reaching ramifications: First, when money flowed into the reservations (from the government or from mining jobs, welfare, or resource payments), it leaked out again into the coffers of off-reservation banks and grocery, clothing, and liquor stores. A study conducted by Anne Seip and Ahmed Kooros of the Council of Energy Resource Tribes (CERT) staff on such financial leakages showed that money hardly turned over at all on reservations. The second problem created by the lack of businesses on reservations was that because the reservation economy was so underdeveloped, the tribal governments could not support themselves by taxation. Therefore federal funds had to be directed toward basic services—social, educational, and health—instead of economic development.

The studies' conclusions about hurdles and possible solutions help in understanding mineral-based economic development because so many of the concepts relate to both. President Reagan's Commission on Indian Reservation Economies identified several obstacles that tribes erected to economic development, including weak business management, rapid turnover of tribal governments, and an unskilled and unreliable Indian labor force. Although not problems on all reservations, these were serious concerns on many. Tribally owned businesses on many reservations failed to produce profits and had to be continually subsidized by tribal governments. Such enterprises tended to be oriented toward providing jobs and sharing benefits rather than toward profits, and many were hamstrung by tribal politics. The commission said that tribes needed to separate business more from politics, to make their governments more efficient, and to create a more stable work environment for private business.

The commission accused BIA of incompetence and of imposing trust restrictions overzealously and said BIA was incapable of reforming itself to remedy such problems. Consequently, Swimmer and his commission recommended dismantling the agency and privatizing many of its former functions. Not surprisingly, the Department of Interior's task force on economic development did not agree that BIA should be dismantled. In its rebuttal, the task force concluded that the BIA problems could be solved internally.

Nevertheless, the DOI task force agreed with most of the changes the commission recommended in federal labor and economic stimulation laws and regulations. Tribes should be able to issue industrial revenue bonds; regulations for Small Business Administration incentives should be changed to tribes and more Indian-owned businesses could qualify; more federal agencies should be required to give preference under the Buy Indian Act; and national labor and wage laws should be changed so they would not continue to encourage importing non-Indians for reservation jobs.

All of the studies agreed that increased tribal control was key to future success. All said this could be done without forsaking either the trust relationship or tribal cultural values. The CERT study said it most forcefully. Kooros and Seip looked at six reservations where they analyzed the impacts of federal expenditures upon social and economic problems. The study said increasing federal expenditures had "perpetuated tribal dependency" because projects were usually federally managed and delivered, that is, done for the tribes. The study found more success in tribally managed projects, which were funded by the government but administered by the tribes. The projects done by tribes (1) transferred skills and information to the tribe, (2) transferred control to the tribe, (3) enhanced local and tribal employment, and (4) reduced tribal financial leakages. In the success stories, economic, social, and cultural development proceeded together, and tribal infrastructures improved. However, economic efforts that ignored social and cultural factors failed. An earlier government study of light-industrial firms had reached a similar conclusion. Plants that had the lowest failure rate were Indian owned and resource based.

Although some previous studies concluded that in order to succeed, Indian people had to reject their heritage and adopt the dominant culture's values, the CERT study and Swimmer's commission said assimilation was not necessary. Quoting from a World Bank study of tribal issues overseas, the Swimmer commission said cultural and economic self-determination can be combined. Despite its endorsement of traditional values, the commission throughout its report emphasized the need to "modernize" tribal governments and to get away from communal ownership. It said tribal enterprises should be turned over to individual Indian entrepreneurs, either by selling stock or the businesses themselves.

Two commentators writing in a University of New Mexico study had a much different concept of economic solutions for tribes. Roxanne Dunbar Ortiz and Lorraine Turner Ruffing suggested more agricultural cooperatives and more tribal subsidies for small, labor-intensive, traditional occupations. Ortiz said, in fact, that tribal government should intervene—in the form of taxation, service contracts, supervision of outside companies, and internal integration of the economy—to "break the power of monopolistic outside interests." To her, economic development under the power of such outside interests had represented "neocolonialism." Although recognizing that industrialization was not necessarily undesirable for Indian reservations, Ortiz said mineral development under corporate control had deepened the gap between traditional and modern tribal sectors.

In general the studies indicated that without economic development, reservation residents remained completely dependent upon federal funds for jobs and social services and thus subject to the paternalism and exploitation of outsiders. With development, they could become more self-supporting. The tribal governments could provide more services for reservation residents, both Indians and non-Indians. Thus the reservation could become a more viable place to live. . . .

A Choctaw Odyssey: The Life of Lesa Phillip Roberts

CHARLES ROBERTS (Choctaw)

Early last month my grandmother, Lesa Phillip Roberts, who lives in Chowchilla, California, became ninety-eight years old. Since Lesa doesn't know exactly when in February her date of birth is, she has arbitrarily selected the first as a day of celebration. My wife and I, and our two children, ages nine and five, drove down from Sacramento to share in this celebration. I have a need to be near my grandmother in these last years of her life and want my boys to know her in ways that Highway 99 does not permit.

Lesa lives in a duplex with her youngest son, William, in a neighborhood that we have lived in since 1950, moving about from one rental house to another. My aunt Juanita and my cousin Judy, with their families, live across the street, and I have other relatives whose homes are only a few blocks distant. Lesa rarely leaves

From Charles Roberts, "A Choctaw Odyssey: The Life of Lesa Phillip Roberts," *American Indian Quarterly* (Summer 1990), pp. 259–276. Reprinted by permission.

her home, taking only a monthly trip to the local Bank of America to deposit the check she receives from the Veterans Administration. My aunt and cousin take care of the shopping, do most of the cooking and cleaning, and help my grandmother in numerous ways. For over a decade my grandmother has been having problems with her bladder, and for this reason she refuses to travel. She suffers from arthritis, and her eyesight is weakened by cataracts. Lesa moves about now only with the help of a walker, but in my mind she is still a powerful woman, who ministered to my needs and nourished my growth. She has always been the core to which my family has adhered. It may be that, except for us, her life has been insignificant, yet within its course may be felt currents of wider meaning.

Sometime in February, 1890, Lesa was born in a cabin secluded in the backwaters of rural Mississippi. Her home was in Cushtusa, a small Choctaw community some twenty miles southeast of Philadelphia in Neshoba County. Her parents, Buckhorn and Lucie Phillip, were descended from Choctaw who had remained in Mississippi after the tribe had signed a treaty in 1830 that required them to move west to the new Choctaw Nation in Indian Territory. These Mississippi Choctaw, having chosen to remain in their ancestral lands, had struggled for decades to maintain their identity in a society that defined itself in polarities of white and black, the racial categories demanded by slavery and maintained after the Civil War by segregation.

Prior to the 1880s, the Choctaw had little contact with their white and black neighbors. Their villages were built in the areas marginal to swamps, and they eked out a living by hunting and trapping and by raising garden crops. But in that decade, and in the backwash of powerful forces unleashed by the abolition of slavery, they began to lose their isolation and to enter the local economy. By the 1880s railroads had been constructed through central Mississippi, timber companies had begun to clear-cut the yellow pine and broadleaf forests, and more land was opened for cultivation. As the freedmen departed in large numbers for the richer soil of the Yazoo Delta, the Choctaw were recruited as laborers. Most became sharecroppers, working long, hard years for local white farmers, raising only enough corn and cotton to make the barest margin of existence. Others cut and hauled timber for a living or helped in the manufacture of turpentine. Only a few continued to hunt and trap for their livelihoods. The women and young girls wove cane mats and baskets and sewed patchwork quilts and bartered them locally to storekeepers and to the wives of white farmers.

Along with these economic changes, the Choctaw had also entered a period of religious and educational upheaval. Although nearly all of them continued to take part in tribal ceremonies handed down over generations, many were converted to Christianity. In the 1880s Catholic and Baptist missions were established, followed in the next decade by the Methodists. By the 1890s the Baptists had established nine churches, with an aggregate congregation of 392 Choctaw. The Catholic mission, however, had the greatest impact. Under the direction of Father B. J. Bekkers, a priest from Holland who began his service in September, 1882, the Catholics purchased 1,840 acres at Tucker in Neshoba County and invited the Choctaw to live there and work the land. By the first of the century, the Holy Rosary Mission at Tucker had a membership of 690 Choctaw. In 1884 Bekkers opened a school for the Choctaw, the first since the 1830s. Six years later the State of Mississippi established a public school system for the Choctaw, so that by the end of the century most of their children had an opportunity to obtain an elementary education.

At some time early in the 1890s Buckhorn Phillip moved his family to Tucker. Lesa attended the Catholic mission school there for less than a year. When she was nearly seven years of age, her father cut his foot severely in a lumbering accident and bled to death. He was buried at the Holy Rosary Mission cemetery, in a service that was probably conducted by Father Bekkers. The low voices and the candles flickering above his coffin are indelibly fixed in Lesa's memory. After her father's death, Lesa returned to Cushtusa along with her mother and older sister, Fannie.

In 1898 Congress sent representatives of the Special Commission to the Five Civilized Tribes [Choctaw, Creek, Chickasaw, Cherokee, and Seminole], more commonly known as the Dawes Commission, to identify Mississippi Choctaw and advise them of their eligibility for land in the Indian Territory. The Choctaw Nation was to be dissolved, and its land divided among its members, prior to absorption into the new state of Oklahoma. Over the next three years the Dawes Commission worked to establish a roll of eligible Mississippi Choctaw. On May 3, 1901, Lucie Phillip, on behalf of herself and her two daughters, signed an application enrolling them as Mississippi Choctaw.

Late in July, 1903, H. Van V. Smith, a special agent of the Dawes Commission, circulated among the Mississippi Choctaw, offering to take them to the western Choctaw Nation. By terms of the Indian Appropriation Act of March 3, 1903 (32 Stat. 982), Congress had allocated $20,000 for the removal of all Mississippi Choctaw identified as eligible under the 14th article of the 1830 Treaty of Dancing Rabbit Creek, but too impoverished to pay their own removal expenses. On July 21, one of Smith's enrolling agents, J. V. Harris, reached Cushtusa. Lesa's mother applied for removal on behalf of her family. Fannie, who had recently married Putwood Billey, applied separately. Seventeen other Choctaw from Cushtusa also decided to emigrate. Shortly thereafter, as Lesa recalls, her mother sold most of their belongings to a neighbor for $12. On August 10, Harris took them to Meridian, Mississippi, to be interviewed by Special Agent Smith.

After Smith confirmed their eligibility as "identified and indigent" Choctaw, he sent them to the county fairgrounds, where they joined other Choctaw who had accepted the offer of land in the Indian Territory. Smith had scheduled a special train to depart from Meridian on August 12. As they waited, Lesa overhead other Choctaw express their fears and apprehensions. Some were disturbed about having to leave relatives behind, while others worried about debts owed to the farmers whose lands they worked. Local merchants who would lose the Choctaw as customers hovered about the campground, urging them to stay. Land agents and speculators from the Indian Territory pestered them as well, "offering whiskey and money as inducements to sign contracts, alleging that the Government would allot them only low grade lands in the Choctaw and Chickasaw Nations." On the morning of August 12, a speculator from Ardmore, Indian Territory, attempted to organize a stickball game. Apparently he wanted to delay the departure and use the ensuing confusion to induce the Choctaw to doubt Smith's authority. Smith rushed to the fairgrounds, threatened to arrest the speculators, and suspended the game. His actions convinced most of the Choctaw of the government's good faith and persuaded them to pack for departure.

At 5:00 P.M., two hours behind schedule, a special train of the Queen and Crescent Railway pulled out of the station at Meridian. As Lesa boarded the train she realized that her journey would take her hundreds of miles from the sacred soil of Mississippi and from Nanih Waiya, the mound that marked the center of the Choctaw universe. She knew that her ancestors had once taken this route, coming out of the west and carrying the bones of all those who had died on the migration. They had emerged out of the vastness of the continent and settled in Mississippi, charged with the veneration of their dead. For Lesa the movement of the train was a palpable reminder of what the departing Choctaw were losing. On board were 259 full-blood Choctaw whose journeys had begun several days earlier in Leake, Jasper, Newton, Kemper, and Neshoba counties, Mississippi. From Meridian the train made its way to Vicksburg and then crossed the Mississippi River, carrying with the Choctaw their personal belongings and their memories of the past.

At 11:00 P.M. the train halted in Monroe, Louisiana, to pick up five more Choctaw. The next morning it passed through Shreveport and arrived in Texas that afternoon. At Dallas the passengers were transferred to the Missouri, Kansas and Texas line. Their route turned north to Denison, across the Red River, and into the heart of the western Choctaw country. Precisely at midnight, August 13, they arrived at Atoka, where the Choctaw Land Office was located. The Choctaw remained on the train overnight, but Lesa and some of the other youngsters stepped off into the streets of the town, still wet from an early evening shower. The morning air was heavy with their excitement.

Early the next morning the newcomers were taken to Smallwood's Switch, three miles south of Atoka. Vast quantities of food had been prepared for them: barbecued pork, fried potatoes, cornbread, blackeyed peas, *pashofa, banaha,* and other dishes. The Dawes Commission had erected nine-by-nine-foot tents for their shelter, and many of the western Choctaw had gathered to welcome them. Speeches were made, and as Choctaw voices filled the air Lesa's anxiety gradually lessened. Her life stretched before her, a young girl of beauty and promise.

Each of the newly-arrived Choctaw was required to file a proof of settlement with the Choctaw Land Office. On August 15, the day after their arrival, Lesa and her mother reported to William H. Angell, the Commissioner of the Land Office, and indicated their intention to take allotments. From Atoka their applications would be forwarded to the Dawes Commission in Muskogee and then to the Secretary of the Interior in Washington, D.C. For nearly two months, Lesa remained at the camp near Atoka. The Atoka firm of Reynolds and Sample furnished rations to each family on Thursdays, consisting of flour, beef, bacon, cornmeal, dried fruits, coffee, sugar, soda, baking powder, salt, potatoes, and fresh vegetables. Lesa and her mother cooked their own meals, using pots and pans provided by the Commission. When the weather permitted, some of the Mississippi Choctaw hired themselves out to local farmers to pick cotton and to perform other chores. As her mother and sister worked in the fields, Lesa remained in camp to take care of the younger children. On other days she walked in the woods, picked blackberries and wild grapes, and gathered firewood. On one glorious afternoon, as Lesa remembers, she attended a performance of the Sells Brothers Circus in Atoka.

On August 22 Angell reported to the Dawes Commission that the newcomers were in good condition and had little sickness. But, he added ominously, "there had been two deaths, both of which . . . were the result of disease contracted in Mississippi." Doctors T. J. Long and J. S. Fulton of Atoka provided medical attention. Despite their efforts, two more children died. On September 5, Angell reported that "one of these deaths was caused by a congestive chill, and the other by some bowell complaint." By September 9, sickness pervaded the camp. Although Lesa was spared, a large number of the Choctaw had fallen prey to "chills and fever, diarrhea, flux, cold, and in some instances threatened with pneumonia."

The camp was plagued with other problems. Within four days of their arrival, two other children, Eben and Taylor York, ran away, hoping to find their way back to Mississippi. The most serious problem, one with explosive potential, was the harassment of Oklahoma Choctaw and intermarried whites who resented what they perceived as preferential treatment given to the Mississippi Choctaw. Known locally as "Snakes," these Oklahoma Choctaw were influenced by the Creek rebel, Chitto Harjo, and were attempting to thwart implementation of the program of land allotment and dissolution of tribal government. On August 15 the Dawes Commission hired three Choctaw tribal policemen to protect the camp from such harassment and from the avarice of speculators who wanted to lease Choctaw land. Within four more days, they were joined by two additional tribal policemen.

On September 15 the Choctaw Land Office finally acted, sending sixty-six of the Mississippi Choctaw to Bennington in Blue County, where another temporary camp had been erected. Lesa and her mother were not included among this initial group. The Land Office intended to assign the newcomers to an area bounded by the Red River to the south, the line of the Arkansas and Choctaw Railway to the north, the Missouri, Kansas and Texas Railroad to the west, and the St. Louis and San Francisco Railroad to the east. Although this area had been used primarily for pasture and some of it was heavily wooded, Commissioner Angell described it as "a strip of country well adapted for agricultural purposes. . . ." The Land Office expected to place the Mississippi Choctaw on their allotments before the onset of cold weather, and it provided each family with a set of tools: one hammer, one axe, one hatchet, and one frow at a cost of $3 a family. With these tools they were expected to build log cabins and to prepare the land for cultivation in the spring. Angell ordered Thomas Bayless, who was in charge of the camp at Bennington, "to impress upon them the necessity of immediately building log houses and advise them that it will be necessary to build a house within a week or ten days in order that you may secure the tent to loan to other Indians."

Some of the worst fears of the Mississippi Choctaw were soon realized. A portion of them were settled on land without an adequate water supply, and some areas were so overgrown with trees and brush that cultivating the land was virtually impossible. They were also afraid that Oklahoma Choctaw would drive them off their homesteads. Bayless wrote to Angell on September 19 that "there might be some trouble with the Snake Indians in the locality where you are placing the

Mississippi Choctaws in their allotments made by the Commission." A few days later Angell urged Bayless to take the Mississippi Choctaw and simply "place them in their allotments." But, he added, "if they are alarmed over the situation," they should be allowed to return to the camp near Bennington. Even after their settlement, the animosity between Mississippi and Oklahoma Choctaw did not easily abate. For years after their arrival, the Mississippi Choctaw remained a distinct component of the Choctaw nationality, speaking a different dialect and perceived as less adjusted to the modern world.

On September 29 the Choctaw Land office awarded allotments to Lesa and her mother. They had to wait another week, however, before the Dawes Commission approved these selections. On October 6 Lesa, her mother, and fifty-five other Choctaw were taken to the camp at Bennington. By this time the Commission realized that not all of the Mississippi Choctaw could be accommodated in the area near Bennington, so it opened another camp at the Honey Springs Church near Soper. Within fifteen days, the remaining Choctaw were taken to Soper, and the camp at Atoka was abandoned.

Because of the lateness of the season, Lesa remained at the Bennington camp until the following March, when she and her mother were settled upon her mother's homestead. She helped build a cabin, clear the land, and put in a garden. With these labors Lesa began to adjust to the country that would be her home for the next forty-one years. In the next two years she was often hired by local farmers to help with their harvests. She did not attend any of the Choctaw schools, which were now under federal receivership. The sum of her formal education remained the few months of attendance at the Holy Rosary Mission school at Tucker. Her social life was confined mostly to other Mississippi Choctaw and was restricted to the Bennington area.

When Lesa first came to what is now Bryan County, Bennington was a market center for timber, cotton, and other farm products. It contained a cotton gin, two lumber yards, a bank, and several other businesses. There were also four churches, a post office, and a school. Bennington first developed on the site of a Presbyterian mission station established in 1855 by the Reverend Charles C. Copeland. Copeland named the mission after Bennington, Vermont, his native state. When the Choctaw Railroad was constructed in 1902, it bypassed Bennington. With the approval of the Secretary of the Interior, the town was moved two miles to the south at a point where the tracks intersected U.S. Highway 70. After its incorporation in 1903, Bennington grew steadily. Its population in 1907 was 427, and by 1920 it reached 951, despite a number of disasters. The town was ravaged by fires in1906, 1912, and 1913, and it was almost totally demolished by a tornado in May, 1916. After World War I the town was affected greatly by the slump in cotton prices. By 1930 there were only 492 residents, and others would leave during the depression.

In 1907, at the age of seventeen, Lesa was married to Daniel Williams, an Oklahoma Choctaw who worked for a cattle ranch near Bokchito. Daniel's enrollment card shows that he was twenty-four years old at the time of his marriage and was three-fourths Choctaw by blood. Lesa has always been reluctant to discuss her marriages, wishing to keep her memories private. In the few offhand moments that she has talked about her husbands, her feelings were released only with hesitation and tentativeness. In her memory Daniel remains a skillful horseman and possessor of an exuberant personality, yet their marriage was marked by tragedy. A first child lived just for a few weeks after birth. A second son, Morris, was born with a lame foot; he lived to the age of ten, when he died of influenza. Daniel died three years after their marriage, succumbing to pneumonia.

After Daniel's death, Lesa returned to her mother's home. After she observed the appropriate period of mourning, she was married in 1911 to Charles Billey, a Mississippi Choctaw who had emigrated to Oklahoma on the same special train that brought Lesa in 1903. Charles, the son of Rena Billey, was originally from Toles, Mississippi. In 1915, Lesa gave birth to a daughter, Nellie. Her life continued to be shadowed by tragedy. In 1916 she again became a widow when Charles died of tuberculosis. Her mother, Lucie, died in the same year and was buried at the cemetery at Good Springs. Her grief, Lesa recalled, was nearly inconsolable.

In 1916 Lesa was married for a third time. Her marriage to Dawson Billey, Charles's younger brother, also proved short-lived. Two years later Dawson was called to active military duty. Several hundred Choctaw were eventually sent to France, and some were highly decorated, but Dawson Billey never made it to the Western Front. He contracted influenza during the epidemic of 1918, and his life ended at Camp Logan, a training base near Houston, Texas. The most tangible legacy of their marriage was a son, Carl, born July 4, 1917.

On July 14, 1919, Lesa was married to Jesse Roberts, an Oklahoma Choctaw who had recently been discharged from the United States Army. Jesse was born in Blue County, Choctaw Nation, on June 23, 1886. His father was Benjamin Roberts, who was a successful farmer, and his mother was Mulsie Belvin. Jesse's military career was less than glorious. He had enlisted as a private in Company B, 21st Battalion, United States Guards, on May 20, 1918, and was released from active duty seven months later. During this brief period he served at training based in Texas and Louisiana. From May 31 to June 2 he was treated in the infirmary at Camp Nicholls, Louisiana, for [cowpox]. He was also diagnosed as having a case of chronic gonorrheal urethritis.

After so many tragic times Lesa now found in this marriage a measure of security and happiness. Jesse had three brothers and a sister, thus providing Lesa with an extended family. These family ties also introduced her to the Presbyterian church, Chish Oktok, located about six miles southeast of Bennington. Jesse built a three-room frame house on forty acres of land that he and Lesa purchased shortly after their marriage, which became known as the "old Yellow House" after its first coat of paint. Later Jesse added an additional room. This house had neither electricity nor indoor plumbing, and it was lit by kerosene lamps. It was located three miles west of Chish Oktok on RFD #2, and access to it was over a dirt road.

During the first eight years of the marriage Lesa gave birth to four children: Pearl, born in 1920; William, in 1922; Juanita, in 1924, and Gladys, in 1926. Lesa's life settled into a pattern that flowed from the needs of her children and from the cycle of a farming season. She rose early in the mornings to light a wood stove and to prepare breakfasts of bacon, sausage, fried eggs, biscuits and gravy, all washed down with thick coffee. She prepared suppers of fried chicken, pork steak, sweet potatoes, pinto beans, black-eyed peas, corn-on-the-cob, hominy, okra, and peach cobbler. She hauled water from the spring behind the house and gathered firewood. She washed clothes in a large tub, blackened from the fire used to heat the water. She used the same tub to bathe her children. She gathered black walnuts, pecans, and hickory nuts in the woods. She did most of the gardening, raised chickens and guinea fowl, slopped the hogs, and lavished affection on the dogs that gathered beneath the front porch and in the space underneath the house. She told stories to her children, especially in the cold of winter nights, nursed them when they were ill, disciplined them when they misbehaved, and sent them off to school.

Neither Lesa nor Jesse could read or write. Since they lived in one of the poorest counties in Oklahoma, they did not see any compelling reason to require their children to attend school on a regular basis. With the exception of Carl, who spent several years at Jones Academy, the tribal boarding school at Hartshorne, none of their children became proficient in reading. In 1930 an educational survey prepared by C. L. Crutcher for the Bureau of Indian Affairs revealed that five of Lesa's children were of school age. They were expected to attend Manning School, located one-and-a-half miles from the old Yellow House. Nellie, mistakenly identified as age 17, was enrolled in the sixth grade. Carl, listed as age 15, was enrolled in grade four. Pearl, age 10, and William, age 8, were both in the first grade. Juanita, who had just turned 6, was not yet enrolled.

Over the next seven years Lesa's children displayed a pattern of erratic attendance. In the school year 1931–1932, Nellie attended Manning for a total of 16 days; Pearl, 5; William, 18; and Juanita not at all. In the year 1932–1933, Nellie went to school 11 days; Pearl, 33; William, 13; and Juanita, 10. In the year 1933–1934, Nellie attended school 4 days; Pearl, 10; William, 14; and Juanita, 9. In the year 1934–1935, Nellie went to school 56 days, and both Pearl and Juanita, 13. William was not enrolled, nor did he attend the following year. For the year 1935–1936, Nellie was promoted to the ninth grade at the high school in Bennington. She was present for 62 days in the fall, but dropped out of school completely after Christmas. Pearl attended Manning 78 days, and Juanita went on 38 days. At the start of the next school year, they were transferred to the Bennington School. Pearl, who was enrolled in the sixth grade, attended a remarkable 153 days. William, returning to school after a two years' absence, was assigned to the third grade and was present 60 days. Juanita was still enrolled in the first grade and attended 84 days. Gladys was sent to school for the first time and attended 32 days.

It is not surprising that Lesa's children failed to progress beyond the ninth grade nor that public education left them with only a rudimentary knowledge of reading, writing, and computation. Yet it helped them to become bilingual and to acquire an understanding of the world outside Bryan County. Their intelligence was shaped primarily by other forces: the experience of working on and with the land, the culture of a rural community, and the spiritual life that centered on Chish Oktok.

Jesse Roberts was a skillful farmer, and his labor produced numerous bushels of corn and bales of cotton. He also grew oats, sorghum, milo, and peanuts. Once a month he bought supplies at Smith's grocery store in Bennington, driving into town on a wagon pulled by a team of mules named Marty and Joe. Occasionally he went to Durant, the largest town in Bryan County and its seat of government. In 1927 Jesse purchased a black Model-T Ford and drove the family all the way to Oklahoma City, much to the delight of Lesa and the children.

To a great extent the life of the family centered on Chish Oktok, the Presbyterian church where Jesse's father had once been minister. The congregation was mostly Choctaw, and services were conducted in the Choctaw language. Lesa enjoyed listening to hymns sung in both Choctaw and English. Her children also shared this joy. As they grew older the girls, joined by a neighbor, Pauline Nance, formed a quartette and sang at Chish Oktok and at the Pentecostal church nearer their home. William, acquiring the same love for music, learned how to play the guitar. For a time Nellie was superintendent of the Sunday School at Chish Oktok, and Pearl and Juanita gave her assistance. After services the family joined the congregation for a community barbecue and picnic. They played baseball and stickball, lounged about in the shade, and gossiped about their neighbors. In the summers they often went to Cherokee Lake, where the Presbyterians held retreats and Choctaw from many districts attended.

With the onset of the Great Depression, Jesse found working the farm increasingly difficult. He borrowed money on five occasions from the First National Bank of St. Paul, Minnesota, to buy seed and meet expenses. He spent a year in the state prison at McAlester for stabbing a man during an argument over a debt Jesse was trying to collect. When his health began to fail in late 1932, he sought a disability payment from the Veterans Administration. In March, 1933, Jesse was given a thorough physical examination at the V.A. hospital in Dallas, Texas. He was suffering from chronic arthritis and glycosuria, but his claim was dismissed because his illnesses were not related to his military service. The next year his health rapidly deteriorated, despite medical attention from Dr. S. M. Toney of Bennington. At 5:00 P.M., March 7, 1934, Jesse died of "tuberculosis of the lungs." Lesa arranged a funeral through the Peoples Mutual Burial Association of Bennington, and the Veterans Administration provided a coffin valued at $90 and a gray shroud at $10. A few days later his body was interred at Chish Oktok cemetery.

Jesse's death had a shattering effect on the family. Lesa had greater responsibilities on the farm and in the rearing of her children. The two children from her earlier marriages were now assuming lives of their own. In 1935, after returning from Jones Academy, Carl was married to Pauline Nance, who lived over the hill and behind Lesa's property. Although she was not an Indian, Pauline had command of the Choctaw language and was a member of the congregation at Chish Oktok. Her parents were originally from Texas, and her father objected strongly to Carl. Shortly after Carl began courting Pauline, her father fired a load of buckshot into his back. Without informing their parents, they were married in a civil ceremony conducted by Judge Wheeler in Durant. Afterwards Carl built a one-room cabin about a mile from the old Yellow House, on land that he had inherited from his father. Lesa became a grandmother the next year, when Pauline gave birth to their first child, Mamie. Two years later they had a son, Howard. In 1937 Nellie was married to Homer Neal, a white man whom she had met at the Howard Farm where she was working as a cook. They were married in Durant and also chose not to inform Lesa until after the ceremony had taken place. Nellie gave birth to a daughter, Anna Mae, in 1938, and to a son, Jerry, four years later. Pearl, the oldest of Jesse's children, also gave birth to a son, Charles, in August 1941. Since she was not married, her pregnancy caused Lesa a measure of pain.

Throughout the Depression Lesa had a hard time managing the farm. As the family's income fell she sought relief from the regional office of the Bureau of Indian Affairs. On two occasions in 1938 the Bureau issued vouchers to Lesa to pay for groceries, the first for $10 and the second for $9.95. Carl also had difficulty feeding his family. On April 24, 1941, he sent a postcard to Clinton Talley, the Bureau's district agent, asking for assistance. "I have just got able to work," he wrote, "and no work to do, and we have just about ran out of groceries so please send it by mail." Apparently his request was filled, for on July 29 Carl wrote Talley again acknowledging the previous assistance and asking for additional help. "I have got to have some groceries to eat & feed my family," he pleaded, "so if you can help me do it at once because I need help at once."

These hard times eroded the family's confidence, forcing them to think about an alternative to farming. As early as 1936 Homer's sister, Effie, and his brother-in-law, Daniel Collum, had emigrated to California and settled in the San Joaquin Valley. A number of Pauline's relatives also moved to California and found work in the Santa Clara Valley. One of her uncles, Ed Pearson, established a home in Berkeley. Their letters back to Bryan County had a disquieting effect on Carl. When reports about the plethora of jobs created by the war industries in California reached him, Carl decided to act. In July, 1943, he took his family to Durant and boarded the Greyhound bus for California. For a time they stayed with Pauline's uncle in Berkeley. Eventually Carl found work as a welder in one of the four Kaiser shipyards in Richmond and moved his family into a labor camp on Dam Road, located in the hills behind the city. Later that year Nellie and her family also emigrated to California. Homer worked briefly in the Richmond shipyards but, disliking the work and the pressures of living in a large city, soon took his family to the San Joaquin Valley. He found a job with a dairy a few miles outside the town of Madera.

Lesa was perturbed by the splitting of her family, and she decided to join Carl and Nellie in California. Carl began sending her money for transportation. To generate more income Lesa took her family to work in the cotton fields near Bonham, Texas. During the fall of 1943 they picked cotton in fields next to German prisoners of war. Finally, in early June, 1944, Lesa had enough money to travel to California. She bade farewell to her sister, Fannie, and to other relatives and friends. She left most of their belongings and the old Yellow House in the keeping of an uncle, Ed Billey. Thus her family began a journey that would have momentous consequences.

Lesa and her children went first to Durant to board a train heading for Kansas City. She was discomfited by having to abandon her home and the land she had worked so hard and so long. She was saddened at leaving her sister and the graves of her mother and husbands. She knew also that she was losing the security and delights of Chish Oktok. Once again the movement of the train caused Lesa to know that her life was being transformed. After reaching Kansas City the family was separated. Since the trains were overcrowded, William and a cousin, Theodore Billey, were put on the Santa Fe line and sent along the southern route to

California. Lesa and the rest were taken by the Union Pacific directly west into the belly of the continent. As Lesa recalls, the powerful landscape that unfolded before her confirmed her trepidations.

Late in the afternoon of June 4, 1944, they arrived at the station in Richmond. They were greeted by Carl and taken to his apartment at 4301 Cutting Boulevard. Shortly before their arrival, Carl and his family had moved into an apartment complex recently constructed by the federal government and for which they paid a monthly rental of $40. Until the summer of 1945 at least ten persons occupied its four rooms, sharing the two beds and sleeping on the floor. This number was frequently enlarged by friends and relatives from Oklahoma, who also came to Richmond to find work. Other refugees from Bryan County lived in this complex. One of these families was the Watkins, whose son, Wes, became a playmate to Carl's son, Howard. Wes Watkins would later be elected to the United States House of Representatives, representing Southeastern Oklahoma.

The shipyards at Richmond offered jobs to all who came during these war years, and the city itself was in a frenzy of growth and demographic change. Before the war Richmond was a relatively placid industrial city sprawling along a low-lying point on the northeastern shore of San Francisco Bay. Its population of 24,000 was supported mainly by a Standard Oil refinery, a Ford assembly plant, and a dozen smaller industries located on the waterfront. After the United States entered the war, four Kaiser shipyards were constructed in Richmond, and its population mushroomed to over 100,000 persons. The thousands of emigrants who poured into the city created enormous problems in housing and municipal services. The federal government erected huge barracks-style, public-housing projects in the mud flats between the harbor and the town. Schools were so overcrowded that for a time they were run in four shifts. By 1944 they had settled into two shifts. The older residents of Richmond, who were mostly whites, were torn by pride in their city's accomplishments and by resentment of the newcomers, especially the 14,000 blacks and the group they disparagingly identified as Okies.

After their arrival Lesa's children obtained jobs at Kaiser. Pearl was hired as a welder on a segregated night shift, composed exclusively of Indians. William became a trucker's helper, and Juanita worked on a cleanup crew. Gladys, the younger of Lesa's daughters, stayed at the apartment and helped with housework and the grandchildren. Lesa seldom left the apartment, except to buy fruit at Bruno's and to shop at the local Lucky's Market. She could not speak English, and she was always apprehensive around strangers. Her rich interior life could only be released in the soft words of the Choctaw language, in the conversations she had with her children, in the stories she told her grandchildren, and in the songs she sang to them. Often, into the deep of the night, Lesa listened patiently as her children came to her, bringing their discoveries, joys, hopes, and fears.

Coming from the rural isolation of southeastern Oklahoma, Lesa's family did not have the knowledge necessary to accommodate the powerful forces of the urban world. They were overwhelmed by the frenetic pace of the Bay Area, alternately perturbed and exhilarated by the crowded streets of Richmond and its rich mix of nationalities. Nor could they comprehend the money they received each payday. The average worker at Kaiser made $61 a week. Such sums were intoxicating to a family that only a few months before was picking cotton for measly wages in Texas. In moments of respite from work, they took the ferry across the Bay, shopped in San Francisco, had their pictures taken at Fisherman's Wharf, ate at restaurants in North Beach and Chinatown, watched as ships sailed through the Golden Gate into the maelstrom of the war. They became immersed in movies. Several times a week they went to the cinemas in Richmond to be drawn into a world of fantasy and dreams. They went to the USO that was located a few blocks from the apartment, and in the evenings they went to Wade Ray's country and western place where they danced to the music of the Maddox Brothers & Rose and other groups. This music, rooted in the Southwest and adapted to California conditions, appealed strongly to their memories and emotions.

Lesa gave cautious advice to her children, but she could do little to counteract the Bay Area's allurements. Her children began to drink socially at the bars, and for some, alcohol would remain a problem for many years after the war. The girls were courted by sailors and soldiers, finding pleasure in transient relationships. For a time Pearl was attracted to Nick Novak, who worked for the Southern Pacific in Oakland. He often accompanied Pearl, her son, and Carl's children to a playground near the apartment and bought them candy and soft drinks. Gladys became pregnant and, in June, 1945, gave birth in Richmond to a son, Richard. Carl and Pauline also had a third child, Linda, born in Oakland a few hours after Gladys's delivery.

As the war came to an end Lesa had a difficult choice to make. She could return to Oklahoma and to the hard times they remembered too clearly, or she could stay in California and pursue its promise of abundance. Lesa never forced the issue, allowing her children to make the decision. In the summer of 1945 they worked in the orchards near Santa Paula and for Libby's Cannery in Sunnyvale. Then, in September, they packed their belongings into William's 1938 Ford sedan and made their way over the winding course of the Pacheco Pass and onto the expanse of the San Joaquin Valley. They drove to Madera County where a number of Bryan County refuges had settled during the Depression and where Nellie's husband was already employed. They moved into two tar-paper shacks on the north bank of the Berenda Slough, about eight miles west of the small town of Chowchilla. After helping Lesa to relocate, Carl and his family returned to Richmond. They did not move to Madera County until 1947, after their hopes of having a permanent job in the Bay Area dissipated.

Since 1945 Lesa has resided in Madera County. For five years after the war her family followed a migratory lifestyle, but always within the county. They found agricultural jobs: chopping and picking cotton, harvesting grapes, knocking almonds and walnuts. Thus they drifted into a pattern that gave them little security. Winters were especially difficult, for jobs were scarce then. William occasionally found work digging out hardpan or tending smudge pots. The year after their arrival Pearl was married to Daniel Collum, and their union was blessed with a son, Randall, in April, 1947. Sadly, Pearl died on May 9, 1948, of lung cancer and was buried at the Arbor Vitae Cemetery in Madera. She was only 28 years old at the time of her death, and her passing opened a wound in the family that has never healed.

A degree of stability was achieved when Lesa's family moved to Chowchilla in December, 1950, even though they continued to work as farm laborers. Lesa has returned to Oklahoma twice for brief visits, once in the summer of 1948 and again in 1952. But over the years her ties with Oklahoma have been mostly broken. Lesa's sister, Fannie, has died, and she has outlived nearly all the friends and neighbors who shared her activities at Chish Oktok. She has sold all of the property that she inherited from her husbands, and she has sold most of her own allotment with the exception of her inalienable homestead. This land she leased as pasture for many years after the war, but it presently remains unused. Lesa even sold the old Yellow House and its forty acres, when officials in Bryan County brought a foreclosure action against it.

Lesa is now linked to California by powerful bonds of kinship. Her oldest daughter, Nellie, died in 1972, and Nellie's husband, Homer Neal, died a few years later. Their daughter, Anna Mae, committed suicide in the spring of 1971 in Salt Lake City. Pearl's son, Randall, was fatally involved in an automobile accident on the night of November 16,1963, when the car in which he was a passenger rammed into a concrete standpipe. Most recently, in February, 1985, Pauline Billey died of a heart attack. With the exception of Anna Mae, all were buried in the Chowchilla Cemetery. Lesa now has fourteen grandchildren, nine of whom were born in California, thirty-two great-grandchildren, and nine great-great-grandchildren. This extensive family is scattered over the country from Florida to Alaska, but the greater number of them lives in or near Chowchilla.

When Lesa celebrated her most recent birthday, many of her extended family were present. The four rooms of the duplex resonated with their voices. Clearly this woman, born nearly a century ago in Mississippi, has created a substantial legacy, and in her person there is a strength that I would like my sons to understand. As we left for Sacramento at the end of our visit, I was pleased when my older boy, Christopher, went directly to Granny and gave her a kiss on her cheek and talked about his pet frogs. My younger son, Matthew, more hesitant, merely put his hand over hers. Then he smiled and headed for the door.

◈ *F U R T H E R   R E A D I N G*

Akwesasne Notes, *Trail of Broken Treaties: BIA, I'm Not Your Indian Any More* (1974)
———, *Voices from Wounded Knee, 1973, in the Words of the Participants* (1974)
Robert L. Bee, *Crosscurrents Along the Colorado: The Impact of Government Policy on the Quechan Indians* (1981)
Thomas R. Berger, *Village Journey: The Report of the Alaska Native Review Commission* (1985)
Sam and Janet Bingham, *Between Sacred Mountains: Navajo Stories and Lessons from the Land* (1984)
Peter Blue Cloud, *Alcatraz Is Not an Island* (1972)
Robert Burnette and John Koster, *The Road to Wounded Knee* (1974)
Fay G. Cohen, *Treaties on Trial: The Continuing Controversy over Northwest Indian Fishing Rights* (1986)
Stephen E. Cornell, *The Return of the Native: American Indian Political Resurgence* (1988)
Vine Deloria, Jr., *Behind the Trail of Broken Treaties: An Indian Declaration of Independence* (1974)
———, *Custer Died for Your Sins: An Indian Manifesto* (1969)

————, *We Talk, You Listen: New Tribes, New Turf* (1970)

Michael Dorris, *A Yellow Raft in Blue Water* (1987)

————, *The Broken Cord* (1989)

Elizabeth Ebbott, *Indians in Minnesota* (1985)

Louise Erdrich, *Love Medicine* (1984)

————, *Tracks* (1988)

John Finger, *Cherokee Americans: The Eastern Band of Cherokees in the 20th Century* (1991)

John A. Folk-Williams, *What Indian Water Means to the West: A Source Book* (1982)

Loretta Fowler, *Shared Symbols, Contested Meanings: Gros Ventre Culture and History, 1778–1984* (1981)

Charlotte Johnson Frisbie, *Navajo Medicine Bundles or Jish: Acquisition, Transmission, and Disposition in the Past and Present* (1987)

Estelle Fuchs and Robert Havighurst, *To Live on This Earth: American Indian Education* (1972)

Rayna Green, ed., *That's What She Said: Contemporary Poetry and Fiction by Native American Women* (1984)

Laurence M. Hauptman, *Formulation of American Indian Policy in New York State, 1970–1986* (1988)

Bruce W. Hodgins and Jamie Benidickson, *The Temagami Experience* (1989)

Peter Iverson, *The Navajo Nation* (1981)

Joseph G. Jorgensen, *Oil Age Eskimos* (1990)

Alvin Josephy, ed., *Red Power: The American Indians' Fight for Freedom* (1971)

Jerry Kammer, *The Second Long Walk: The Navajo-Hopi Land Dispute* (1980)

Stuart Levine and Nancy O. Lurie, eds., *The American Indian Today* (1966)

Daniel McCool, *Command of the Waters: Iron Triangles, Federal Water Development, and Indian Water* (1987)

N. Scott Momaday, *House Made of Dawn* (1968)

Ernest L. Schusky, *The Right to Be Indian* (1965)

Leslie Marmon Silko, *Ceremony* (1977)

C. Matthew Snipp, *American Indians: The First of This Land* (1989)

Sam Stanley, ed., *American Indian Economic Development* (1978)

Stan Steiner, *The New Indians* (1968)

Omer Stewart, *Peyote Religion: A History* (1987)

Paul Stuart, *Nations Within a Nation: Historical Statistics of American Indians* (1987)

Paul Tennant, *Aboriginal Peoples and Politics: The Indian Land Question in British Columbia, 1849–1989* (1990)

James Welch, *The Death of Jim Loney* (1979)

————, *The Indian Lawyer* (1990)

————, *Winter in the Blood* (1974)

Charles F. Wilkinson, *American Indians, Time, and the Law* (1987)

Geoffrey York, *The Dispossessed: Life and Death in Native Canada* (1989)